THE STRAIGHT PATH

OTHER TITLES ON QUR'ĀNIC COMMENTARY

Ṭabarī: *The Comprehensive Exposition of the Interpretation of the Verses of the Qur'ān* volume I

Ṭabarī: *The Comprehensive Exposition of the Interpretation of the Verses of the Qur'ān* volume II

Rāzī: *The Great Exegesis* volume I

Kāshānī: *A Sufi Commentary on the Qur'ān* volume I

Kāshānī: *A Sufi Commentary on the Qur'ān* volume II

NŪR AL-DĪN AḤMAD AL-KĀZARŪNĪ

THE STRAIGHT PATH
A COMMENTARY ON THE HOLY QUR'ĀN

al-Ṣirāṭ al-mustaqīm fī tibyān al-Qur'ān al-karīm

Volume I

الصراط المستقيم في تبيان القرآن الكريم

Translated by
Khalid Williams

THE ROYAL AAL AL-BAYT INSTITUTE
FOR ISLAMIC THOUGHT
and
THE ISLAMIC TEXTS SOCIETY

This first edition published 2023 by
The Royal Aal al-Bayt Institute for Islamic Thought &
The Islamic Texts Society
Miller's House
Kings Mill Lane
Great Shelford
Cambridge CB22 5EN, UK.

British Library Cataloguing-in-Publication Data.
A catalogue record for this book is
available from the British Library.

ISBN: 978 1911141 48 8 VOL I
ISBN: 978 1911141 49 5 VOL II

CONTENTS

Translator's Introduction vii

THE STRAIGHT PATH
A COMMENTARY ON THE HOLY QUR'ĀN

Volume 1

Prologue	1
Introduction	3
1. The Beginning of the Book, *Sūrat Fātiḥat al-Kitāb*	5
2. The Cow, *Sūrat al-Baqara*	11
3. The Family of ʿImrān, *Sūrat Āl ʿImrān*	90
4. Women, *Sūrat al-Nisāʾ*	127
5. The Table, *Sūrat al-Māʾida*	164
6. Cattle, *Sūrat al-Anʿām*	193
7. The Heights, *Sūrat al-Aʿrāf*	222
8. Spoils of War, *Sūrat al-Anfāl*	252
9. Repentance, *Sūrat al-Tawba*	264
10. Jonah, *Sūrat Yūnus*	287
11. Hūd, *Sūrat Hūd*	303
12. Joseph, *Sūrat Yūsuf*	321
13. The Thunder, *Sūrat al-Raʿd*	337
14. Abraham, *Sūrat Ibrāhīm*	345
15. Ḥijr, *Sūrat al-Ḥijr*	353
16. The Bee, *Sūrat al-Naḥl*	361
17. The Night Journey, *Sūrat al-Isrāʾ*	380
18. The Cave, *Sūrat al-Kahf*	397

Appendix: Persons cited in the text 415
Bibliography 427
Index 429

TRANSLATOR'S INTRODUCTION

The Author of Tafsīr al-Kāzarūnī

Little information has survived about Nūr al-Dīn Aḥmad b. Muḥammad al-Kāzarūnī. No date of birth or death is recorded for him, but only that he was alive in the year 923 AH/1517 CE,[1] at the tail end of the Mamluk Sultanate, during which Islamic scholarship had flourished under the encouragement of the sultans. The name Kāzarūnī speaks to an origin in Kāzarūn, Persia, and in this work the author refers to Jalāl al-Dīn Muḥammad al-Dawānī al-Kāzarūnī (d. 1502)—the renowned theologian and jurist of Safavid Persia—as his teacher, which suggests that at least his early life may have been spent in that region. However, at a certain point he settled in Mecca and apparently rose to some position of authority there, acting as advisor to the chief justice of Ṭā'if.[2] His other titles, al-Shāfiᶜī and al-ᶜUmarī, refer to his legal school and to his descent from the Caliph ᶜUmar respectively.

On Tafsīr al-Kāzarūnī

Al-Ṣirāṭ al-mustaqīm fī tibyān al-Qur'ān al-karīm (The Straight Path: A Commentary on the Holy Qur'ān) is Kāzarūnī's only extant work. The author notes that an alternative title *Ṭawāliᶜ al-anwār* (The Ascending Lights) was suggested by a friend of his, and the work also became known by a third title, *Tafsīr al-akhawayn* (Exegesis of the Two Brothers). In the Arabic edition on which this translation is based, the editor ᶜAbd Allāh al-Shabrāwī notes that one of the five manuscripts he consulted actually bears the title *Tafsīr al-akhawayn*.

There is no known explanation as to how the *tafsīr* acquired the name of *Tafsīr al-akhawayn*; it may be because Kāzarūnī's work was considered a kind of 'brother volume' to the well-known *Tafsīr al-Jalālayn* (Exegesis

1 Brockelmann, *Geschichte*, suppl. II p. 142.

2 Muḥammad al-Makkī, *Tuḥfat al-Laṭā'if*, Beirut: Dār al-Kutub al-ᶜIlmiyya, 1971, p. 290.

of the Two Jalāls) by Jalāl al-Dīn al-Maḥallī (d. 1460) and Jalāl al-Dīn al-Suyūṭī (d. 1505). The two works are somewhat similar inasmuch as they are both short interlinear commentaries on the Qur'ān, and it is likely that Kāzarūnī was familiar with the *Jalālayn*, although his approach differs from it in several regards. The most significant of differences is seen in how Kāzarūnī largely omits reference to the *Isrā'īliyyāt*, the collection of narratives that emerged from the melting pot of religious traditions in the early Islamic period, as converts to Islam from other religions eagerly shared accounts from their traditions that seemed to correspond, however loosely, to passages in the Qur'ān. These accounts were heartily embraced by those exegetes whose approach was to collect whatever information they could possibly find about the text, while others were more circumspect. Kāzarūnī subscribed to the latter approach for the most part, though he was obviously aware of the well-known *Isrā'īliyyāt* accounts and sometimes makes allusions to them, such as in his commentary on verse 38:24, where he seems to introduce the story of David and Bathsheba only to dismiss it in the same breath, employing a degree of brevity that is almost telegraphic.

This 'telegraphic' approach is a frequent feature of the work, especially when the author is referring to passages from other exegeses, or to points of grammar or alternative canonical readings. Often in the course of the translation I found myself stumped by an exceedingly brief turn of phrase, and consulted other major *tafsīr* works only to find essentially the same expression but with twice as many words. This may speak to the rich intellectual environment in which Kāzarūnī lived, where an author could assume a great degree of familiarity with the subject on the part of the reader. Yet this is not to say that Kāzarūnī employs this extremely succinct approach throughout the work. On the contrary, he occasionally takes the opportunity to examine passages in greater detail, particularly with regard to matters of language, theology, and accounts of the historical circumstances behind the revelation of a verse.

One especially notable aspect of Kāzarūnī's work is his attempt to provide explanations for the ordering of the Qur'ānic chapters by finding thematic ties between the concluding verses of one chapter and the opening verses of the next. Kāzarūnī was not the first to attempt this; for instance, between 1456 and 1477, Burhān al-Dīn al-Biqāʿī (d. 1480) had produced his *Naẓm al-durar*,[1] which attempted the same and became

1 See 'Al-Biqāʿī' in David Thomas and Alex Mallett, eds., *Christian-Muslim Relations: A Biographical History*, Boston: Brill, 2013, pp. 537–543.

somewhat controversial because of its frequent quotations from the Bible. However, it is unclear as to whether or not Kāzarūnī was familiar with that work, as he does not make any mention of it and the explanations he gives for the harmonious arrangement of the chapters are often quite different from those that Biqāʿī offers, although naturally at times they overlap when the connection is particularly obvious.

Kāzarūnī begins his exegesis with a brief commentary on the *Fātiḥa*, before pausing to provide an introduction to the work in which he lays out his aims and provides a useful explanation of the distinction between exegesis (*tafsīr*) and interpretation (*ta'wīl*). As he sees it, *tafsīr* is the more rigid of the two, confined to transmission of primary sources from the Islamic tradition, such as *ḥadīth*s in which the circumstances behind a particular revelation are described. *Ta'wīl*, however, is the intellectual pursuit of understanding, and therefore may be—or must be—based on personal opinion. Kāzarūnī's explanations of the thematic links between the chapters of the Qur'ān certainly falls into the latter category, and it is notable that Biqāʿī had faced criticism for his attempt to do the same on the grounds that his approach did not refer to any previous scholarly tradition.[1] Perhaps Kāzarūnī had this in mind when he began his exegesis with a brief but rigorous defence of the use of reason when interpreting the holy text:

> There are many narrations warning of a dire fate for the one who issues *tafsīr* based on personal opinion. Some have cited these as proof that it is altogether forbidden to say anything on the subject without having a primary source for it; but this blanket prohibition is unjustifiable, because the narrations from the Prophet (may God bless him and grant him peace) amount to only a few verses, and the Companions and those who came after them had many contradictory opinions which could not possibly have all come from him...God has made the Qur'ān a source for everything that is needed, but there is not a primary text to explain everything in it; hence, there is no avoiding the use of reason to extract its meanings in light of its fundamentals. And God (Exalted is He) knows best.

Nonetheless, the author displays a conscious effort to rely upon reliable narrations from canonised collections, such as those of Bukhārī, Muslim, Abu Dāwūd, Tirmidhī, and others.

1 Ibid., p. 541.

The author was a staunch adherent to the Ashʿarī school of theology, which was dominant among Sunni Muslims in his time and continues to be so. He was particularly devoted to the great Persian theologian and exegete Fakhr al-Dīn al-Rāzī (d. 1210), to whom he refers simply as 'the Imam' throughout his *tafsīr*. In the course of his exegesis, Kāzarūnī takes the opportunity to defend Ashʿarī orthodoxy whenever it arises, even going so far as to suggest that *God will assuredly bring a people whom He loves* [Q. 5:54] means the Ashʿarī school, and in his commentary on Satan's argument with God in verse 7:12 suggesting that Satan's sin lay in his denial of Ashʿarī doctrine! Nevertheless, he is remarkably impartial at times, such as in his commentary on *Whatever good befalls you, it is from God; and whatever evil befalls you is from yourself* [Q. 4:74] where he is careful to say that although the opponents of the Ashʿarīs can find no support for their position in this verse, neither can the Ashʿarīs cite it in their own defence, as some did.

The author was also clearly a proponent of Sufism, as can be seen by his reference to the Sufi triad of *sharīʿa, ṭarīqa, ḥaqīqa* (the Law, the path, and the reality) in his commentary on verse 3:200, and other similar passages. His work is by no means a 'Sufi exegesis' in the manner of Qushayrī, but these occasional references to mysticism can be numbered among the 'other auxiliary matters which serve to uncover some deeply buried secrets' to which he refers in his introduction.

The same can be said of his occasional forays into language, theology, jurisprudence, history, and other concerns, never with the intention of being exhaustive, but always aiming to provide, as he promises at the outset, 'a refreshing draught to quench the thirst of those who seek exegesis that is brief, especially those who wish to recite the Qur'ān while pondering its meanings'.

Edition Used for the Translation

This translation is based on the Dār al-Risāla edition,[1] which referred to five manuscripts in India, Egypt, Spain and Turkey. The editor ʿAbd Allāh al-Shabrāwī notes that the best preserved of these was the one in the Royal Escorial Library in Madrid, dated 1089 AH/1678 CE, bearing the alternative title *Tafsīr al-akhawayn*.

1 Cairo 2017, ed. ʿAbd Allāh al-Shabrāwī.

NŪR AL-DĪN AḤMAD AL-KĀZARŪNĪ
THE STRAIGHT PATH
A COMMENTARY ON THE HOLY QUR'ĀN

[PROLOGUE]

In the Name of God, the Compassionate, the Merciful

He is my Sufficiency

Mawlā Imām Aḥmad b. Muḥammad al-ʿUmarī al-Shāfiʿī al-Kāzarūnī (may God whelm him in His mercy) said:

I seek refuge with God from Satan the accursed and all his hosts among the jinn and people. In the Name of God, the Compassionate, the Merciful, I shall begin my commentary on the manifest Qur'ān:

The Opening, *al-Fātiḥa*

[1:1] *In the Name of God, the Compassionate, the Merciful.*

[1:2] *Praise be to God, Lord of all Worlds.*

[1:3] *The Compassionate* to all of His creatures, *the Merciful* to the faithful in particular.

[1:4] *Master of the Day of Judgement*: when the worshippers and rebels will be judged. O You Whose exalted Essence is endowed with such Attributes, how could anything but You be worshipped, or sought out for aid?

[1:5] *You [alone] we worship, and You [alone] we ask for help.*

[1:6] *Guide us to the straight path* which leads to the highest stations of those brought near; [1:7] *the path of those whom You have favoured*: the prophets and folk of true faith, especially the master of the first and last, Muḥammad the Trusted Chosen One, aided with the Qur'ān whose prophetic miracle endures across the ages, and also his family and Companions, the rightly guided guides. May the best of Your blessings and peace be upon him and upon them, always and forever! *Not [the path] of those against whom there is wrath*: because of their evil deeds and disobedience; *nor of those who are astray*: because of their errant beliefs. Amen!

To proceed:[1] seeker of the commentary on the Holy Qur'ān (may God keep you firmly on the straight path), I present to you a brief exegesis employing concise language and offering modest explanations and simple benefits, with the aim of unveiling the subtle teachings of the Qur'ān. It contains around twenty thousand useful notes, avoiding excessive prolixity and digressions and sufficing with matters that are the subject of general agreement. It relies on *ḥadīth*s that are sound (*ḥasan*) or authentic (*ṣaḥīḥ*), or on the opinions of the majority of the erudite scholars. It also offers some additional benefits, such as subtle points of connection between certain verses and other auxiliary matters which serve to uncover some deeply buried secrets. It is called *al-Ṣirāṭ al-mustaqīm fī tibyān al-Qur'ān al-karīm* (The Straight Path in the Elucidation of the Distinguished Qur'ān). In addition, one of the righteous also gave it the name *Ṭawāliᶜ al-anwār* (The Ascending Lights).

Upon my word, it is concise and beneficial, a refreshing draught to quench the thirst of those who seek exegesis that is brief, especially those who wish to recite the Qur'ān while pondering its meanings. I do not say this to boast, but merely to offer sincere advice. Yet forgetfulness and error are human nature, and so I ask that if you notice any gaps, then cooperate for the sake of righteousness and close them. Nor number it among the books of the great folk, for there is a great difference between the speaker and the pretender, or between the dark-eyed one and the one with dark-painted eyes. Were it not for the inspirations that came to me in the Sacred House of God, I would not have been able to approach this station, for I had not the means to do so, nor [a way] to procure them; and tending to the essentials of obedience kept me from much study.

I am the needy servant, resident of God's secure city, Aḥmad b. Muḥammad b. Khiḍr, known as Nūr al-Dīn, al-ᶜUmarī al-Shāfiᶜī al-Kāzarūnī—may God drown him in the oceans of His largess along with all who give this prayer an amen! I offer this work to draw nearer to the Master of Sovereignty and Dominion, imploring Him with urgency and dread, asking that He make it a means of benefit for me and for all seekers. May God grant blessings and peace to Muḥammad and his family, Companions and followers!

1 Having begun with some brief notes on *al-Fātiḥa*, the author now pauses to provide an introduction to the *Tafsīr* and an overview of the art of exegesis, before beginning the commentary in earnest.

INTRODUCTION

Let us begin the book with an introduction that might benefit the seekers. When commencing a study of any art, one ought to identify its character and subject, in order to proceed with clarity; its purpose, lest one's efforts be pointless; and its sources and supports, to facilitate its acquisition. Therefore, we say:

The root meaning of *tafsīr* (exegesis) is unveiling and clarifying, and the root meaning of *ta'wīl* (interpretation) is returning and revealing. The science of exegesis is the search for information about the Glorious Qur'ān, in an effort to understand its meaning as well as is humanly possible. Beyond that, it consists of two categories: *tafsīr*, which can only be known through transmission, such as the circumstances of a particular revelation; and *ta'wīl*, which can be ascertained by applying the foundational principles of the Arabic language, and thus is concerned with understanding.

The reason it is permitted to engage in *ta'wīl* based on personal opinion as long as its requirements are met, but not so for *tafsīr*, is that *tafsīr* amounts to a testimony on God's behalf that by this particular expression He meant this particular meaning. Therefore, it is only permitted when there is a primary source for it. This is why al-Ḥākim stated that the *tafsīr* of a Companion should be assumed to have the weight of a prophetic pronouncement behind it. *Ta'wīl*, on the other hand, means to prefer one possible interpretation over another without being definitive about it, and therefore is allowed.

NOTE: There are many narrations warning of a dire fate for the one who issues *tafsīr* based on personal opinion. Some have cited these as proof that it is altogether forbidden to say anything on the subject without having a primary source for it; but this blanket prohibition is unjustifiable, because the narrations from the Prophet (may God bless him and grant him peace) amount to only a few verses, and the Companions and those who came after them had many contradictory opinions which could not possibly have all come from him (may God bless him and grant him peace). Furthermore, narrations and traditions indicate that the text can have many meanings. Thus the prohibition can only mean issuing *tafsīr* without having any knowledge; or interpreting the text in a way that supports a particular false opinion or even a true opinion when the interpreter knows full well that this is not what the text means, such as interpreting *Go to Pharaoh; he has truly transgressed* [Q. 20:24] to signify the struggle against the soul; or rushing directly for the inward meaning without establishing the outward meaning first; or doing *tafsīr* when *ta'wīl* is required. God has made the Qur'ān a source for everything that is needed, but there is not a primary text to explain everything in it; hence, there is no avoiding the use of reason to extract its meanings in light of its fundamentals. And God Almighty knows best.

The Subject of the Art of *Tafsīr*

The subject of the art of *tafsīr* is the Qur'ān from the aforementioned aspect. The Qur'ān is the Arabic discourse that was sent down to Muḥammad (may God bless him and grant him peace) as a miraculous challenge, down to the smallest chapter of it, and then conveyed by mass transmission. The sources of the art are the Book, the Sunna, and the lexicon of the Arabs of antiquity, and its support comes from the two sciences of religious fundamentals and *fiqh*. Its purpose is to identify legal edicts (*al-aḥkām al-sharʿiyya*) pertaining to knowledge and action.

Now since we are commanded to seek refuge with God before reciting the Qur'ān, we shall do the same before commenting on it. What this means is to ask God for safety from harms by the emanation of good things: 'I seek refuge with God from Satan the accursed'—from the evil of the rebellious jinn alone, or from rebellious people too. The name *Shayṭān* is from the verb *shaṭana*, meaning 'to be distant', for he is distant from mercy and righteousness. Or it may be from the verb *shāṭa*, meaning 'to be false'. However, the former is more likely, hence the term *shayṭana* (devilry). The jinn are subtle rational bodies dominated by the element of fire or air, which is either illuminating and felicitous for the righteous among them, or turbid and damning for the devils among them. The traditional expression omits the words 'the evil of', since it is clearly implied by the context that Satan is evil. The definite article either denotes type or familiarity, since all sins occur at his behest. *Rajīm* (cursed) means pelted and rejected, or vilified, or one who pelts people with whispered temptations.

1
The Beginning of the Book
SŪRAT FĀTIḤAT AL-KITĀB

Definition of *Sūra*

The word *sūra* (chapter), as in the *sūra*s of the Qur'ān, means a passage known by a given title. This excludes such things as the *Āyat al-Kursī* [Q. 2:255], because that is only an identifier which does not reach the point of an actual given name. Some stipulated that a *sūra* must contain at least three verses. This is a clarification of the meaning of 'passage' (*ṭā'ifa*) so that such things as the *Āyat al-Kursī* are excluded, rather than a true stipulation, since otherwise it would not be strictly true of any *sūra*.[1] We could avoid this unnecessary quibble by defining *sūra* as a passage of the Qur'ān with a given title that includes three verses. And God knows best.

Definition of *Āya*

The word *āya* (verse) means collections of words in the Qur'ān distinguished by a divider called a *fāṣila*.

Regarding the *Fātiḥat* [*al-Kitāb*],[2] the word *fātiḥa* means 'beginning'. The word is either a gerund with the meaning of the passive participle, or an adjective used as a noun as indicated by the termination *–a*[*t*], which denotes this shift of meaning. *Al-Kitāb* (the Book) denotes the Qur'ān, which is used to mean everything that is found in the written copy and what is shared between it and its parts. 'The Beginning of the Book,' then, means the first of its parts or the first of its individual elements. By common usage, it has become a generic name for this *sūra*, as a personal name,

1 The issue at hand here is the introduction of the term 'at least' into the definition, which some commentators found problematic. Qūnawī discussed the issue at length in his marginal notes on Bayḍāwī's *Tafsīr*.

2 Another name for the *Sūrat al-Fātiḥa*.

because it is one of the accidents which cannot be personified except by the personification of their loci. However, some say that it is the name for what was first written upon the Tablet, and that our recitations of it are like it, but not identical with it.

The Names of *al-Fātiḥa*

The *sūra* has other names, such as *al-Fātiḥa* (The Opening), if we consider this to be another name rather than a truncation of *Fātiḥat al-Kitāb*; *Umm al-Kitāb* (Mother of the Book), because of how it encompasses the foundations of its three aims: praise of God, worship, and promises and warnings; *Sūrat al-Asās* (Chapter of Foundation); *al-Kanz* (Treasure); *al-Nūr* (Light); *al-Wāfiya* (Ample); *al-Shāfiya* (Healer); *al-Wāqiya* (Protector); *al-Kāfī* (Sufficiency); *al-Shifā'* (Cure); *al-Ruqya* (Incantation); *al-Ḥamd* (Praise); *al-Munājāh* (Entreaty); *al-Tafwīḍ* (Reliance); *al-Sab*ᶜ *al-Mathānī* (Oft-Repeated Seven), because of how
Q. 1:1 it is frequently repeated in prayers, except rarely such as in the odd voluntary cycle, or because it was revealed in the Two Sanctuaries; *Sūrat al-Ṣalawāt* (Chapter of Prayers); and simply *al-Ṣalāt* (The Prayer) because of the *ḥadīth*, 'I have divided the prayer…'

[Place of Revelation]

Al-Fātiḥa may be Meccan or Medinan. It may have been revealed once in each city, or half in one and half in the other. The soundest opinion is that Meccan chapters are those which were revealed before the Emigration, while Medinan chapters are those which were revealed after it, even if this took place in Mecca.

[Commentary]

[1:1] *In the Name of God, the Compassionate, the Merciful*: the word *In* (*bi*) here means 'with the help of' or 'with the company of'. Its meaning is thus: 'Seeking the blessing or the aid of the Name of God, I recite or I begin.' The former interpretation is better, since to seek blessing is a more direct expression of reverence than to use it as an instrument for something else rather than itself. It is also better to frame it as *Recite!* [i.e. Q. 96:1, rather than 'I read in the Name of your Lord'], since this acknowledges the reality of the situation and also covers the entire recitation, not only the beginning of it. These words come first to draw attention to them. Furthermore, the fact that *In the Name of* precedes *God* does not undermine the meaning, because it signifies everything that the Name of God entails; and [the use of] *In* is an instrument to achieve this function. This shows why it is *bism Allāh* (In the Name of God) rather than simply *bi-Llāh* (In God), even aside from the fact that *bi-Llāh* is already used to express an oath [i.e. 'by God'], which is not what is intended here. To seek the blessing of words means to pronounce them with the tongue while evoking their meanings in the mind at the same time.

In the Name of God (*Allāh*): *Allāh* means the Essence endowed with all the Attributes of perfection. It is a unique non-derived Name. Zamakhsharī held that it was a generic noun that became a name, from the verb *alaha* meaning 'to be amazed', or from some other root.

The Compassionate, the Merciful: the Compassionate (*al-Raḥmān*) is the One Who wills compassion (*raḥma*) for the faithful. The root meaning of *raḥma* is the tenderness of the heart that engenders kindness. When it is attributed to God, it means the utmost extent of it, as with all other Attributes. The word *Raḥmān* has a more emphatic morphological form Q. 1:1
than *Raḥīm* (Merciful). This refers either to quantity in the sense that the compassion extends to both this life and the next, or to the multitude of its objects; or else it refers to modality in the sense of its majesty and tenderness, and His will for goodness for its own sake as well as evil for the sake of goodness hidden within it. *Raḥmān* comes first, although one might have expected the order to be reversed so as to imply an ascension of degree, because of how the name *Raḥmān* pertains particularly to God alone.

This *basmala* formula[1] is considered a verse of *al-Fātiḥa* by the majority of scholars, though Abū Ḥanīfa and Mālik dissented. There are *ḥadīth*s to support this; and note that *ḥadīth*s with lone narrators are sufficient proof for matters of practical worship. The narration in the two *Ṣaḥīḥ* collections on the authority of Anas that the Prophet (may God bless him and grant him peace), Abū Bakr and ʿUmar would all begin the Qur'ān with *Praise be to God, Lord of all Worlds* [Q. 1:2] does not amount to a refutation of the Shāfiʿī opinion, because it only means that they would begin with this *sūra*, whereby these words are used here to stand as a name for it. In addition, there are three other narrations from Anas which contradict it. Bayhaqī narrated that the Prophet (may God bless him and grant him peace), ʿUmar, Ibn ʿUmar, Ibn ʿAbbās and Ibn al-Zubayr all recited the *basmala* out loud; and there are mass-transmitted

1 The formula *bism Allāh al-Raḥmān al-Raḥīm* (In the Name of God, the Compassionate, the Merciful) is known as the *basmala*.

reports that ʿAlī (may God be pleased with him) did it his whole life. Furthermore, the narrations about reciting it aloud are affirmative, and therefore should take precedence.[1]

[1:2] *Praise be to God, Lord of all Worlds*: that is, every instance of praise, or its quiddity and reality. Lexically, *ḥamd* (praise) means to describe a voluntary virtue, or the effect of it, for the purpose of expressing reverence. Its conventional meaning is an action that expresses reverence to the Giver of blessings for His blessings. Conventional praise and conventional gratitude connote that the servant is to utilise all the favours God has given him for His sake, according to what the Lawgiver has ordained. The terminological meaning of praise is to manifest the attributes of perfection with word, deed or state; this includes God's praise of Himself through the engendering of all things. *Praise be to God*, then, means that praise is His alone: in the first case, this is because no one but He has freedom of volition; and in the latter two cases, it is because all contingent beings rely on Him from the
Q. 1:2 beginning. Blameworthy things are not attributed to Him because it is not blameworthy to emanate, but only to be characterised by a blameworthy thing. He created them for something good hidden within them, as we said.

Lord of all Worlds: the root of the word *rabb* (lord) is from *tarbiya*, which means to guide something towards its perfection bit by bit. It is attributed to Him in the sense of emphasis. The word *ʿālamīn* (worlds) is the plural of *ʿālam*, which means everything through which the Maker can be known,[2] and everything that is not Him. He uses the plural to indicate that it encompasses every type within it, and uses the definite article to indicate that it includes every type as well as every individual. Or it may mean man, since he is a smaller cosmos himself—or indeed a vaster one—for he is an abstract of the divine presence through the Attributes of being, life, knowledge, power, will, hearing, seeing and speech, as well as an abstract of the world through how he exists in nature like the elements, and is composed like the minerals, and grows and reproduces like the plants, and experiences sensation, estimation, imagination, pleasure and pain like the animals, and is bold like the beasts, and schemes like the devils, and is capable of gnosis like the angels, and has rulings collected in him like the Tablet, and has the images of things fixed in his heart with all their universalities like the Supreme Pen. Thus He likened the two of them in a verse, saying, *And in the earth there are signs for those who know*

1 According to the principle in Islamic law that if one primary text affirms something while another negates it, then the affirming text should be given precedence.

2 Related to the verb *ʿalima* (to know).

with certainty, and in your souls. Will you not then perceive? [Q. 51:20–21]. He referred to the intelligent ones collectively by way of emphasising them, or because they were the ones primarily intended. Praise is due to Him for all things manifestly, even the creation of evil, since there is good within it, as was noted before.

[1:3] *The Compassionate, the Merciful*: this emphasises how He is deserving of praise. Or the first mention was to settle the awe instilled by the Name of God, and now the second is to inspire hope in those who are fearful of the Day of Judgement. This applies if the *basmala* is taken to be an integral part of the *sūra*, as was discussed.

[1:4] *Master of the Day of Judgement*: the word *mālik* (master) is from *milk* (ownership), meaning the One Who rules all the entities He owns. It can also be read as *malik* (king), from *mulk* (sovereignty), meaning the One Who rules through issuing commands and prohibitions to all His subjects. The latter is preferred as it brings the opening *sūra* of the Qur'ān in harmony with the closing *sūra*,[1] and also because otherwise there would be repetition since *mālik* and *rabb* mean the same thing, and due to the fact that it has a broader and more encompassing meaning. It is also true that it is the recitation of the people of the Two Sanctuaries, who knew their language best; but this is not the reason for preferring it since all seven modes of recitation are mass-transmitted, and they only recited what they heard. However, one could say that all the narrations reached them, and they chose the narration they recognised to be more venerable. And God knows best. So He is the Master of the Day of Judgement, meaning the time of requital, and always will be. It is not fitting to object that the Day of Judgement is not an ongoing event, because He is the Master of all things beginninglessly and endlessly, and their existence affects nothing but the attachment of His ownership. The attribution of the *Master* to *the Day of Judgement* serves to magnify them both, and affirms that He alone has power over it. Q. 1:3

He chose these five Names[2] because worship evokes divinity, seeking help evokes lordship, seeking guidance evokes compassion, seeking aid evokes mercy, and favour evokes mastery at times of seeking aid, just as the absence of it evokes wrath. Then after distinguishing Himself with these attributes and making Himself almost visible through them, He describes an entreaty to the One Who possesses such attributes:

1 The closing *sūra* features the word *malik*: *Say: I seek refuge in the Lord of people, the King of people* (Q. 114:1–2).

2 God, Lord, Compassionate, Merciful and Master.

[1:5] *You* [*alone*] *we worship, and You* [*alone*] *we ask for help*: to You alone do we dedicate worship, which is the utmost degree of subservience and reverence, and dedicate its means; and You alone do we ask for assistance in performing worship and all other endeavours. The former, or the most important aspect of the latter, is suggested by His Words:

[1:6] *Guide us to the straight path*: the path that does not bend, which is Islam. Keep us firm upon it, or grant us further guidance. Guidance means direction imparted with kindness. The term can be used disparagingly to refer to direction towards evil. There are five types of guidance arranged as follows: the granting of the faculties by which one can be guided, the establishing of proofs, the sending of messengers, unveiling, and grace. The latter is the one that is meant whenever the Qur'ān speaks of the evildoers being denied guidance.

[1:7] *The path of those whom You have favoured*: meaning the prophets
and their ilk. Favouring means the granting of favours to rational beings,
and a favour is something that brings pleasure, whether worldly or oth-
Q. 1:5 er-worldly. Worldly favour can be gifted or acquired: gifted favour is
spiritual and corporeal, while acquired favour is self-purification or bodily grooming. Other-worldly favour is His approval, which is what is meant here, as well as all that leads to it. *Not* [*the path*] *of those against whom there is wrath* to chastise them, such as the Jews or the iniquitous; *nor of those who are astray*: those who stray from the truth, such as the Christians or disbelievers. Straying (*ḍalāl*) means to follow a path that does not lead to the goal. There are many such paths, but only one right path, for the truth of anything is like the target for which an archer aims.

After reciting *al-Fātiḥa*, it is recommended to pause briefly and then say 'amen', which means 'respond or 'so be it'.

2
The Cow
SŪRAT AL-BAQARA

Revealed in Medina

After finishing the *sūra* which is the Mother of the Qur'ān and contains a summary of its purposes, He then begins to elucidate those purposes in detail, stating that this Book, which He has just introduced in general terms, contains no doubt in it whatsoever. So He said,

In the Name of God, the Compassionate, the Merciful

[2:1] *Alif. Lām. Mīm*: these [letters] and their counterparts are a secret between God and His Beloved, or something known only to God. Our responsibility to recite even those words we do not understand is akin to our responsibility to undertake actions whose wisdom we do not ken, and to do so willingly in submission. It is related that Ibn ʿAbbās (may God be pleased with him) said that the letters signify, 'I, God, know best' (*anā Allāhu aʿlam*). Likewise, they say that *Alif Lām Mīm Ṣād* [Q. 7:1] signifies, 'I, God, know best and decide best' (*anā Allāhu aʿlamu wa-afṣal*); and that *Kāf Hā Yā ʿAyn Ṣād* [Q. 19:1] signifies, 'Sufficient, Guide, Merciful, Knowing, Truthful' (*Kāfī, Hādī, Raḥīm, ʿAlīm, Ṣādiq*); and that *Ṭā Hā* [Q. 20:1] signifies 'Pure, Guide' (*Ṭāhir, Hādī*); and that *Ṭā Sīn Mīm* [Q. 26:1 and 28:1] signifies His 'Munificence, Glory and Dominion' (*Ṭawl, Sanā', Mulk*); and that *Ṣād* [Q. 38:1] signifies 'Eternal' (*Ṣamad*); and that *Ḥā Mīm* [Q. 40:1, et al] signifies 'Wise, Sovereign' (*Ḥakīm, Malik*); and that *Ḥā Mīm ʿAyn Sīn Qāf* [Q. 42:1–2] signifies His 'Forbearance, Majesty, Knowledge, Glory and Power' (*Ḥilm, Majd, ʿIlm, Sanā', Qudra*); and that *Qāf* [Q. 50:1] signifies 'Omnipotent' (*Qadīr*); and that *Alif Lām Rā* [Q. 10:1, et al], *Ḥā Mīm* [Q. 40:1, et al], and *Nūn* [Q. 68:1] all signify 'the Compassionate' (*al-Raḥmān*). Perhaps by this they meant that these letters are the sources of all names and the origins of speech itself, and then they gave goodly examples to illustrate them. Other opinions aside from these were also transmitted from them.

One interesting observation that has been made about these letters is that the sum of them amounts to half the total number of letters, and that they cover half the total types of letters. When a number does not have an exact half, its half is rounded to the nearest whole number, sometimes down but usually up, as is explained in the texts of grammar.[1]

Their arrangement into single letters, duals, triplets, quadruplets and quintuplets indicates that the roots of the Book are akin to the roots of the language of the Arabs. The three instances of single letters signify the three types of word.[2] The four dual letter combinations signify the four categories of this: without omission for particles, with omission for verbs, and both with and without for nouns.[3] Their nine-fold occurrence signifies how they can occur in the types of word in three ways, as in *man, in, dhū* [all nouns], and *qul* and *biʿ* [both verbs], and *inna,*
Q. 2:2 *min, mudh* [all particles]. The three triplet combinations signify how they occur among the three categories, and their occurrence in thirteen *sūra*s signifies how the roots of the tripartite morphological forms are thirteen in number: ten for nouns and three for verbs. The two quadruplet and two quintuplet combinations signify how each of them have an original form and a derived form. And God knows best.

[2:2] *That*—this—*Book*: meaning the written Qur'ān, for it is permitted for something to refer to itself with a demonstrative. Another possible meaning was noted earlier, namely that it serves to show the link between the two *sūras*. *In it there is no doubt* that it is from God, if any intelligent person reflects on it. *A guidance*—a tremendous sign towards the truth—*for the God-fearing*: for those who aspire to God-fearing (*taqwā*). The root meaning of *taqwā* is 'to take caution'. In the language of the Law, it means to protect oneself from anything that will harm one in the Hereafter. It has three levels: to protect oneself from eternal damnation, and then from all types of sin, and then from anything that distracts the inner heart from the Real. An example of the first is *He made them abide by the word of God-fearing* [Q. 48:26]; of the

1 The Arabic alphabet contains either twenty-eight or twenty-nine letters depending on whether the *hamza* is counted separately. Of these, fourteen are found in the disconnected letters that open twenty-nine *sūras* of the Qur'ān.

2 *Ism* (noun), *fiʿl* (verb) and *ḥarf* (particle).

3 Two-letter words can be found in all three categories of the Arabic word, but in the case of verbs only when a letter is omitted because of a peculiarity of conjugation.

second, *Yet had the people of the towns believed, and been fearful, We would have indeed opened upon them blessings* [Q. 7:96]; and of the third, *O you who believe, fear God as He should be feared* [Q. 3:102]. He singled out the God-fearing here because they are the ones who benefit from it, while others only go astray despite it, just as nutritious food makes a healthy person healthier but a sick person sicker. Thus He says, *And We reveal of the Qur'ān that which is a cure and a mercy for believers; though it only increases the evildoers in loss* [Q. 17:82].

[2:3] *They who believe in the Unseen*: meaning anything that is beyond the senses. Faith (*īmān*) means to believe in anything that is necessarily known to be part of the Prophet's religion (may God bless him and grant him peace), generally for what is known generally, and specifically for what is known specifically. The scholars of *Ḥadīth* and the early Muslims held that it means conviction in the heart, affirmation with the tongue and action with the limbs. Absence of conviction is hypocrisy; absence of affirmation is disbelief; and absence of action is iniquity. Q. 2:3

Action is not part of the true nature of faith to the extent that the absence of action means the absence of faith, such as was asserted by the Muʿtazila when they spoke of a level between faith and disbelief for those who commit major sins, or by the Khawārij when they attributed disbelief to anyone who sins. Rather, it is a conventional part of it, in the same sense as how a man's fingernails, hair and hand are part of him, or how branches are part of the tree. Faith is the common element between it and belief, and between it and action, which is why it can be used to represent belief or to represent all of them in a literal sense, just as one can use the word 'tree' to refer to the trunk, or to the sum of the trunk, branches, twigs and leaves; but as long as it retains the trunk, one cannot say that it is not a tree. The reality of the meaning of Islam will be discussed in *Sūrat al-Ḥujurāt* [Q. 49]. And God knows best.

[*They who believe in the Unseen,*] *and maintain the prayer*: fulfilling all of its requirements, or being constant in it; *and of what We have provided them expend* on good things. He stresses these three things because of their particular virtue, and says *of what* to exclude excessive spending. Provision (*rizq*) means that which God sends to living beings for their benefit. It is of four types: that which is guaranteed like nourishment, that which is apportioned in the Tablet, that which is owned, and that which is promised on condition of God-fearing. Reliance is obligatory for the first.

[2:4] *And they who believe in what has been revealed to you* in the past, alluding to all of it by reference to the majority of it; *and what was revealed before you* of the [previous] Books. It is an individual obligation (*farḍ ʿayn*) to believe in them in general terms, and to believe in the former with all its details, such that we are required to preserve its details as a communal obligation (*farḍ kifāya*). *Inzāl* (revelation) literally means 'to send down from above', generally by means of an intermediary who bears it. The Qur'ān was sent down through the custody of the angel to him from the Tablet to the lower heaven, and then the scribe-angels were commanded to record it, and then it was revealed gradually according to circumstance. This is the opinion of the majority. Regarding the beginning of the revelation and the question of whether it was transmitted to Gabriel via another angel, along with the command to reveal it, or whether essential knowledge of it was created in Gabriel, there is a difference of opinion.

Know also that they differed concerning its status as created or uncreated. This was due to the contradiction of two analogies, as follows: the Speech of God is an Attribute, and every Attribute is eternal, which means
Q. 2:5 that it must be eternal. Yet the Speech of God is composed of letters which came into existence successively, and anything that is such must be contingent, which means that it must be contingent. The former is correct because of the *ḥadīth*, 'The Qur'ān is God's uncreated Speech,' as well as rationally, because the origin of speech within us is an attribute that allows words to be arranged in a meaningful way, which is the opposite of babble and is something other than knowledge; for we know of speech that belongs to others. Each person's speech is what he arranges in his imagination, and God's Words are what He arranged in His pre-eternal knowledge through His pre-eternal Attribute, which was the origin of its composition and arrangement. This Attribute is eternal, as is the arrangement according to its knowledge-based existence, and so there is no temporal succession in it and hence no contingency. Its temporal succession only applies to its external existence, which itself is outwardly uttered speech. To deny that what exists between the two covers [of the written Qur'ān] is God's Speech is like denying that a poet's poetry is his own speech, for the meaning of it being His Speech is that this speech exists through outwardly uttered existence. Reflect on this, and you will escape from every difficulty. And God knows best.

And of the Hereafter, they are certain: as they ought to be. Certainty means confident knowledge from which all doubts have been banished through reasoning. Thus it cannot be applied to God's own Knowledge.

[2:5] *Those* who are described as such *are upon guidance from their Lord*: firm upon a tremendous gift of guidance from a mighty God; *those are the ones that will prosper*: and attain perfect prosperity, which means the acquisition of one's desires.

[2:6] *As for the disbelievers*: such as Abū Lahab and his ilk. Disbelief means to deny what is necessarily known to be part of the religion of the Prophet (may God bless him and grant him peace), or to do something that indicates this. Disbelief is the absence of faith in that which must be believed in.

If the disbeliever acts as though he has faith, he is a hypocrite (*munāfiq*). If he had faith in the past, he is an apostate (*murtadd*). If he believes in multiple gods, he is an idolater (*mushrik*). If he follows the religion of a divinely-revealed Book, he is a Person of the Book (*kitābī*). If he believes that all events are caused by the passage of time, he is a materialist (*dahrī*). If he believes that there is no Creator, he is an atheist (*mu'aṭṭil*). If he harbours beliefs that happen to be disbelief, he is a heretic (*zindīq*).

Alike it is for them whether you have warned them or have not warned them, they do not believe: this indicates that it is possible for God to hold someone accountable for something they cannot do, since if they came to believe then these Words would not be true. It is rationally possible for Him to hold someone accountable for something that is intrinsically impossible, but He has stated that He will never do so. As for something that is extrinsically impossible—such as something God knows will not occur, or has stated or willed not to occur—it is indeed possible, such as the example in this verse. Thus the wisdom of warning such people is to establish the argument against them, to make the message universal, and to fulfil the Messenger's reward. This is why He did not say 'alike it is for you'. Q. 2:6

[2:7] *God has set a seal on their hearts* so that they do not recognise the truth, *and on* the instruments of *their hearing* so that they do not hear it, *and on their sights is a covering*: a dense veil so that they do not see it. This is a metaphor for the engendering of the impulse that causes them to choose disbelief. He said *hearing* in the singular because the object of hearing is one, namely sound, unlike the objects of the other two. Or it may be functioning as a gerund. *And for them there will be a mighty chastisement*: chastisement (*ʿadhāb*) means a transmission of pain to a living being for the purpose of humiliation.

[2:8] *And some people*, meaning the class of living beings endowed with thought and rationality, *there are who say, 'We believe in God and the Last Day,'* meaning the Resurrection and all that follows it without end; *but they are not believers* in truth. This is proof that the one whose heart contradicts his words is a disbeliever.

[2:9] *They would deceive God and the believers*: by making a display of faith while harbouring disbelief. Deception means to act contrary to the evil one conceals. It is impossible to deceive God, and so what is meant here is that they deceive His creatures. *Yet only themselves they deceive*: the harm of their deception will befall only them; *and they are not aware*: because of their heedlessness.

[2:10] *In their hearts is a sickness*: such as hypocrisy. Sickness means that which befalls the body and upsets its balance. Yet it is used metaphorically to represent psychological maladies which upset the balance of the soul. This verse could bear either interpretation. *And God has increased their sickness*: each time a verse is revealed, their disbelief increases; *and there awaits them a painful chastisement because they used to lie*: on account of their lying, or their belying the messengers. This indicates that all lying is forbidden. Lying means to utter a statement about something that does not reflect the reality of it. The *ḥadīth* about Abraham lying means only
Q. 2:9 that he employed a euphemism, which means to say something that means something other than what it appears to.

[2:11] *When it is said to them, 'Do not corruption in the land,'* with such things as disbelief or betraying the confidences of the Muslims to the disbelievers, *they say, 'We are but reconcilers'*: they claim to be flattering the believers and disbelievers in an attempt to reconcile them. Corruption (*fasād*) means breaking from moderation; reconciliation (*ṣalāḥ*) is the opposite. They can be used in general terms to mean any kind of harm or benefit.

[2:12] *Truly, they are the agents of corruption, but they perceive not.*

[2:13] *When it is said to them, 'Believe as the people believe'*: meaning the Companions. This indicates that the repentance of the heretic, meaning the one who displays Islam but harbours disbelief, should be accepted. *They say, 'Shall we believe as fools believe?'* Foolishness (*safah*) means weakness of judgement; the opposite is mindfulness (*ḥilm*). *Truly, they are the foolish ones, but they know not*: He mentioned knowledge in particular because differentiating truth from falsehood requires additional reflection, unlike recognising the ugliness of hypocrisy, which ought to be obvious.

[2:14] *When they meet those who believe, they say, 'We believe.' But when they go apart*—alone—*to their devils* from among their companions, *they say, 'We are with you* in your religion; *we were only mocking*: playing with the believers.*'* The two sentences each present a different depiction of their hypocrisy, so there is no repetition.

[2:15] *God mocks them*: this means the utmost extent of it, as was said before, or the consequence of it. The use of the present tense implies that it is continually renewed, similar to His Words, *Do they not see that they are tested every year once or twice? Still they do not repent, nor do they remember* [Q. 9:126]. [*God mocks them,*] *extending them*, drawing them on and strengthening them *in their insolence*, their extreme disbelief, *bewildered* with no understanding of how to follow the way. The Muʿtazila, since they deny that anything ugly can be attributed to God, explain away this verse and other similar verses with outlandish figurative interpretations, ignorant as they are of the fact that nothing is ugly for Him and it is unimaginable that He could ever do anything unjust, for He has the power to act in His dominion however He pleases. Ugliness and such attributes apply only to our own deeds with respect to how we acquire them and how they exist through us, as will be discussed later. It is not permitted to interpret a text non-literally unless one has proof that it cannot be read literally, as has been explained in its proper place. And God knows best.

[2:16] *Those are they who have bought error for* innate *guidance*: meaning that they preferred it to it. The root meaning of buying is to give a price so as to attain an item; it then came to be used figuratively to mean forsaking what one has in order to get something else, and more broadly for any kind of exchange. *Yet their commerce has not profited them*: they have not profited from it; *nor are they guided* to its paths, for they have lost their capital. Q. 2:16

[2:17] *Their likeness*: meaning the curious situation of the hypocrites who pretended to be Muslim. The root meaning of *mathal* (likeness, parable) is 'counterpart'; it then came to be used to denote a well-known saying that illustrates a given concept, and thereafter to denote any unusual or notable situation. [*Their likeness*] *is as the likeness of a group who kindled a fire, and when it illumined all about them* and they felt safe, *God took away their light* for the sake of which they lit the fire, so that they remained in darkness and fear. This is akin to how they returned to disbelief after Islam. The reason He used the word *nūr* rather than *ḍaw'* [to mean 'light'] was to make it clear that no light remained whatsoever, not even a little. When the root is absent the branch will necessarily be absent too, and *ḍaw'* is a branch of *nūr* used to denote outspreading rays of light, while *nūr* means the light that exists within a thing, such as the light that exists in the sun. *Ḍaw'*, despite its secondary nature, is more significant because it is what allows sight to occur. *Nūr* alone is not sufficient for this, since the light that exists within a thing only allows that thing to be seen, while to see something else the *ḍaw'* that shines from it is required. And God knows best. [*God took away their light*] *and left them in darknesses*, the darknesses of disbelief, sin and the grave, or the Resurrection, or darkness so dark that it seemed like a multitude of darkness, *unable to see*.

[2:18] They are *deaf* to accepting the truth, *dumb* to speaking it, *blind* to seeing it because of that sudden darkness; *they shall not return* to the guidance they sold. Such is their state.

[2:19] *Or as a cloudburst*, a host of rainclouds, *out of the heaven*, gathering from all around—this represents the Qur'ān; *in which are darknesses* composed of clouds, rain and night, representing the sowers of falsehood; *and thunder*: the voice of the angel of the clouds, representing the warnings of the Qur'ān; *and lightning*: the fire that shoots from his mouth when he is angry, which represents the promises of the Qur'ān. *They put their fingers in their ears against the thunderclaps, cautious of death*: this represents how they are wilfully deaf to the warnings. This is an example of the singular comparison (*tamthīl mufrad*), where individual things are represented by likenesses corresponding to each of them. It could also be considered a compound
Q. 2:18
comparison (*tamthīl mu'allaf*) in the sense that it resembles a modality derived from a collection whose parts fit closely together, so that they become as one, represented with another such modality. An example of this is found in His Words, *The likeness of those who were entrusted with the Torah, then failed to uphold it, is as the likeness of a donkey carrying books* [Q. 62:5]. *And God encompasses the disbelievers*: they cannot escape Him, just as an encompassed thing cannot escape that which encompasses it.

[2:20] *The lightning well-nigh snatches away their sight; whensoever it gives them light, they walk in it*: meaning in its light; this represents their excitement for the bounty that appears to them and stirs their desires; *and when the darkness is over them, they stop*: this represents how they falter whenever tribulation arises. He said *whensoever* for the first and *when* for the second because of their keen desire to walk. *And had God willed, He would have taken away their hearing* with loud enough thunder *and their sight* with bright enough lightning, but He did not will to do so. *Truly, God has power over all things*, whatever they may be, and the actions of His servants are from Him. The *Qadīr* (Powerful) is the One Who does what He will. The name *Muqtadir* means the same when used for Him, but when used for a human it means 'one who seeks to acquire power'. The *Qādir* is the One Who, when He wishes to do something, does it, and otherwise does not. *Qudra* (power) means the ability to make something happen. The root meaning of *shay'* (thing) is the gerund of the verb *shā'a* (to will); here it means 'an object of will', while in the verse *Say: 'What thing is greatest in testimony?'* [Q. 6:19], it means 'a subject of will'. In both, it means something that actually exists. The Muʿtazila define it as something that rationally can exist, or be known or communicated, and so they confine it only to what is possible.

[2:21] *O people*: this covers all who exist in the present and the future, which is not undermined by the narration that the expression 'O people' features only in verses revealed in Mecca, while those revealed in Medina feature 'O you who believe.' *Worship your Lord*: this is addressed to believers, disbelievers and hypocrites alike, because an increase of worship is still worship and so it can apply to them all; *Who created you and those that were before you*: who precede you in state or in time; *so that you may be fearful*: worship Him with the hope that you will join the ranks of the God-fearing who attain perfect triumph. Alternatively, the words *so that* may refer back to *created*, explaining the reason for the creation. The verse indicates that we do not deserve reward for worshipping Him, for He describes it as a way of expressing gratitude for His favours.

[2:22] *He Who assigned to you the earth for a couch*: spreading it out by raising some of it above the water, which does not undermine the fact that the earth is spherical; *and the heaven for an edifice*—a dome—*and sent down water from* the edge of *the sky, wherewith He brought forth fruits for your provision. So set not up compeers to God*—associates whom you worship alongside Him—*while you know* that they are in no way His peers. Q. 2:21

[2:23] *And if you are in doubt concerning what We have revealed*—meaning the Qur'ān—*to Our servant* Muḥammad (may God bless him and grant him peace), *then bring a sūra*—the meaning of *sūra* was discussed earlier—*like it*: akin to what We have revealed in terms of its eloquence and its pronouncements about the Unseen; *and call your witnesses* to help you with your inventions, *besides* (*dūn*) *God*: meaning other than Him—the word *dūn* originally meant 'nearer', and then came to be used metaphorically to denote degree, and then became further broadened to mean simply 'other'; *if you are truthful* in your claim that these are the words of a human being.

[2:24] *And if you do not*: He used the word *if*, which usually denotes doubt, to signify ridicule or to play along with their claim, which is why He then denied it outright by saying [the following]; *and you will not* ever because of its miraculous nature—He said *do not* rather than 'do not bring it' for the sake of brevity—*then fear the Fire whose fuel is humans and stones*, namely your idols which you claim to be intercessors, or sulphur, *prepared for disbelievers*: this indicates that the Fire is already created. He spoke of the location of the punishment rather than the punishment itself in order to emphasise it by leaving it to the imagination, and to inspire fear of the consequence of rebellion and to evoke the chastisement plainly yet concisely. He used the definite article here, but the indefinite in *Sūrat al-Taḥrīm*,[1] because it was revealed later.

[2:25] *And give glad tidings*: [the verb *bashshara*] means 'to give glad tidings', from *bashra* (smile) because of how the recipient of such glad tidings reacts to them; *to those who believe and perform righteous deeds* without any ostentation, on condition that they hold to this until they die, as He says *whoever of you turns from his religion, and dies disbelieving—their deeds have failed in this world and the Hereafter* [Q. 2:217]; *that theirs shall be Gardens*: there are seven Gardens in all: Firdaws (Paradise), ʿAdn (Eden), Naʿīm (Bliss), Dār al-Khuld (the Abode of Eternity), Jannat al-Ma'wā (the Garden of Refuge), Dār al-Salām (the Abode of Peace) and ʿIlliyyūn (the High Dwellings). [...*Gardens*] *from beneath which*—beneath their chambers and trees—*rivers flow* without the need for channels. *Whensoever they are provided with fruits therefrom*—from those Gardens—*they shall say, 'This is* the like of *what we*
Q. 2:25 *were provided with before* in the world.' The reason they will be made to appear like the fruits of the world is so that the soul will incline to them at first sight because of their familiarity. Or it means what they were provided before in the Garden, as a *ḥadīth* suggests, in which case the word *whensoever* is being used in a conventional sense to mean every time except the first one. *They shall be given it in perfect semblance*: in the form which corresponds to the name; *and there for them shall be spouses purified* from all that is detestable or blameworthy in character and appearance. You need not object that this seems pointless because we will not need food, chastity and the like there, because the foods and nuptials of the Garden are not entirely identical to those of this world, but are only called by their names metaphorically. *Therein they will abide* perpetually, because He will resurrect their bodies in forms that are immune to the ravages of time. The [term *khuld* (abiding)] originally meant a long period of stability, whether perpetual or not, which is why it is sometimes clarified by the term *abad* (forever).

And when they objected to the notion that God would give similitudes based on such things as clouds, people kindling fires or spiders, He revealed:

[2:26] *God is not ashamed*: that is, He does not abstain from doing so out of shame, for shame means the contraction of the soul after doing some-

1 *Guard yourselves and your families against a Fire whose fuel is people and stones* (Q. 66:6).

thing wrong, fearing censure, and He is transcendently above such a thing. The basic meaning of the word is 'to feel dread'. He used this word rather than saying 'does not abstain' for the purpose of imparting emphasis, or to echo the words of the disbelievers. [*God is not ashamed*] *to strike a similitude*—to utilise an example—*even of a gnat, or anything above it*: whether larger or smaller. *As for the believers, they know it*—the similitude—*is the truth from their Lord; but as for disbelievers, they say, 'What did God desire by this for a similitude?'* He said this rather than simply 'they do not know' in order to allude to the totality of their ignorance. Desire (*irāda*) means the soul's inclination towards a given action provoking it to doing it, or it means the faculty which is the origin of the inclination. God's desire means the preference of one of the potential objects of His power over another in actualisation, or a meaning which necessitates this preference. *Thereby*, by such similitudes, *He leads many astray and thereby He guides many*: they are *many* in a relative sense, since the guided ones are a minority; *and thereby He leads none astray except the wicked folk* who have gone outside the bounds of faith. Wickedness (*fisq*) in the language of the Law means to stray beyond God's command by committing a major sin. It has three levels: the first is lapsing, which means to commit them occasionally with the knowledge that they are wrong. The second is to become immersed in them without a care. The third is defiance, which means to commit them while declaring that they are not wrong at all, which renders the person a disbeliever outside the bounds of faith. This [latter meaning] is what is meant here. The Muʿtazila say that the one who commits a major sin is neither a disbeliever nor a believer, because they hold that faith means adherence to the three things discussed above,[1] while disbelief means to deny the truth. Yet the primary texts refute their view. Q. 2:27

[2:27] *Those such as break*—the verb *naqaṣa* originally meant 'to sever the cords of a rope'—*the covenant of God*, meaning His Words, *Am I not your Lord?* [Q. 7:172], *after its solemn binding*: its affirmation by means of the sending of messengers with the aforementioned Books; *and such as cut what God has commanded should be joined*: meaning the ties of the womb and the like, which are means of connection between us and God; *and such as do corruption in the land* through sin—*they are the losers*. The loser is the one who loses one of three: property, body or intellect. Here it means the third.

[2:28] *How can you disbelieve in God, when you were dead*—lifeless soil or drops of fluid—*and He gave you life* without anything in-between; *then*

1 Belief, affirmation and action.

He shall make you dead when your times come, that you may pass on to the eternal life; *then He shall give you life* when the Trumpet is blown—as for the life of the grave, it is not stable; *then to Him you shall be returned* after the Resurrection—for their knowledge of the Resurrection ought to be as plain as their knowledge of the rest. The reality of life in us is the faculty of sense or what necessitates it, which is the faculty which conforms to the temperament of species. In God, it means the validity of His being endowed with knowledge and power, which for us requires the presence of this faculty.[1]

[2:29] *He it is Who created for you*—for your benefit in your worldly lives both directly and indirectly, and in your religious lives because of how it points to Him—*all that is in the earth*: this includes the sky and the like, for the original state of all of it is lawful. The expression *all that is in* would not include the earth itself unless it was being used to denote everything in the lower direction in general. *Then He turned*—directed His will—*to heaven and levelled them seven heavens*: He created the heaven
Q. 2:29 after the earth and what it contains, and then spread out the earth afterwards, as Ibn ʿAbbās and others said. This avoids the issue raised by many exegetes that this verse and the verse *And He set therein firm mountains* [*rising*] *above it* [Q. 41:10] contradict the verse *And after that He spread out the earth* [Q. 79:30]. Some of them explained this by taking the word *then* here to denote succession of level, not time, while others argued that the word *after* does not refer to 'spread out', and that *the earth* is the object of another verb suggested by the Words, *Are you harder to create or the heaven which He has built?* [Q. 79:27]. This is unnecessary because the creation of all that is in the earth, such as the mountains, rivers and so on, is not an act of spreading out, nor would it require one, and so they could have been created before being spread out and before the heavens were created, and then spread out after the heavens. This accords with the exegesis of the major Companions. And God Almighty knows best. *And He has knowledge of all things*.

[2:30] *And* remember *when your Lord said*—by way of teaching them and drawing attention to Adam and his importance, for wisdom dictated the creation of a being whose good did not outweigh its evil—*to the angels*: either all of them or the angels of earth alone. The word *malak* (angel) is most likely derived from *mulk* (sovereignty), not from *mulūka* meaning

1 Since one cannot have knowledge or power without life, God must be alive; this is a standard Ashʿarī definition for the life of God.

'message'. Angels are subtle bodies able to take on different forms. The sages say that they are incorporeal substances that differ in reality from rational souls. It is said that they include the ones-brought-near, who are immersed in gnosis of the Real, and then the heavenly angels who direct the affairs between heaven and earth, and then the earthly angels who direct the affairs of earth. *'I am appointing on earth a vicegerent'*: on behalf of God, to discharge His rulings as a test and a challenge for them, not because He needed to. A vicegerent (*khalīfa*) is someone who is left in the place of another to represent them, just as a *khālifa* is someone a chief leaves in charge of his people. Or it may mean the jinn or Adam and his progeny who would succeed one another successively. *They said*—seeking to learn—*'Will You appoint therein one who will do corruption therein and shed blood*: they could only have known of this if God had informed them, or they saw it on the Tablet, or they drew an analogy between one of the Two Weighty Beings[1] and the other; *while we*, not guilty of either of these two traits, *glorify You*—declare Your transcendence beyond all flaws—*with praise*: they said this to show that they were aware that their glorifications were not of their own making; *and sanctify You?'* In other words, 'We keep ourselves pure from sin for Your sake, or we sanctify You beyond all flaws, and so we are more deserving.' *He said, 'Truly, I know what you know not* about what is good.' Then He created Adam from the face (*adīm*) of the earth.

Q. 2:31

[2:31] *And He taught Adam*: by creating intrinsic knowledge in Him, or casting it into his heart; teaching is an action on which knowledge is usually dependent. [*He taught Adam*] *the names* in word, meaning and reality, individually and collectively, like the sources of knowledge—a name is a sign of something and the means by which it is called into the mind; *all of them*: of all things great and small, in all languages, so that he knew them all. Then when his progeny dispersed, each group of people spoke with the language they preferred and forgot the others. You need not object that we know that in each successive age they came up with new names to describe things, because it could be that Adam knew of them and then they appeared through his progeny in later times. The verse suggests that learning language is superior to isolating oneself for worship, and that languages were transmitted directly by God, and that it is possible for the knowledge and perfection of the angels to grow, and that Adam was superior to them in at least one aspect. *Then He presented*

1 Humankind and jinn.

them—meaning the named things—*to the angels and said*, in order to silence their objections, *'Now tell Me*—the word *naba'* (tale) means a report of great significance that is attained as knowledge or strong suspicion—*the names of these if you speak truly* about how you are more deserving of the vicegerency, as you implied.*'* Thus there is no need to object that a question is neither true nor false.

[2:32] *They said* contritely, *'Glory be to You!* Far be it that anything could be hidden from You!' This will be explained further in *Sūrat al-Isrā'* [Q. 17]. '*We know not except what You have taught us*.' This implies, 'You taught him, but not us.' '*Truly, You are the Knower* Whom nothing can escape, *the Wise* Who ordains His creations with wisdom.*'*

[2:33] *He said*, after silencing them, *'Adam, tell them their names'*: so he said, 'You are Gabriel, and you are Michael,' until he reached the crow and stated the wisdom for which it was created. *And when he had told them their names He said*, for rebuke or affirmation, *'Did I not tell you that I know the Unseen*—all that is hidden from creation—*in the heavens and the earth?*
Q. 2:32 *And I know what you reveal*—what you stated with your tongues, such as your aforementioned objection—*and what you were hiding* about how you deemed yourselves more worthy of the vicegerency.*'*

[2:34] *And* remember *when We said to the angels, 'Prostrate yourselves to Adam'*: the meaning of *sajda* (prostration) is to willingly humble oneself. In the Law, it means to place the forehead on the ground in worship, which is what is meant here. They were commanded to prostrate to Adam as their *qibla* (prayer direction), in veneration of him and obedience to God. *So they prostrated themselves, except Iblīs*: Iblīs is a non-Arabic name, or it may be Arabic, derived from *iblās* (despair). Ibn ʿAbbās (may God be pleased with him) is reported to have said that he was from one of the angels who procreate and are called the jinn. Al-Ḥasan is reported to have said that he was the father of the jinn. It is said that God's Words *He was of the jinn* [Q. 18:50] mean that he really was one of them, as well as a kind of angel. *He refused and was proud*: to be proud means to hold yourself superior to someone else; He mentioned it second because it was the last of the two to be manifested. *And so he was*: he was in God's knowledge; or he became *one of the disbelievers*. The verse shows the ugliness of pride and of seeking to delve into God's secrets, and that a command implies obligation.

[2:35] *And We said*, after their prostration, *'Adam, dwell with your wife in the Garden* which was by the Pedestal; you need not object that there is no moral responsibility there, nor any way out of there, for that is only for those who are admitted into it as a reward; *and eat thereof easefully* without discomfort *where you desire* in the Garden; *but do not come near this tree* to eat from it, *lest you be evildoers*: people who put things in the wrong places.' He forbade even going near it to stress its unlawfulness. Most of the Companions held it to be a grape vine, while the Jews said that it was barley.

[2:36] *Then Satan caused them to slip therefrom*—from the tree or the Garden—by saying, *'Shall I guide you...'* [Q. 20:120], whether openly or by whispering it secretly. It is said that after he was expelled [from the Garden], a snake came and grabbed him in its jaws, and he went into it and spoke to them from inside its mouth; and this is why we are commanded to kill snakes. *And he brought them out of what they were in; and We said, 'Go down* to earth—He addressed this to the two of them as well as their children, or to Satan as well[1]—*each of you an enemy to the other*: this means the enmity among their progeny, or between them and Satan; *and in the earth a dwelling shall be yours, and enjoyment for a while*: until death or the Resurrection.' It should not be believed that Adam actually followed Iblīs in this regard; rather, he erred in his interpretation after hearing his insinuation, perhaps by taking the prohibition to be only a discouragement, or taking it to refer to one specific tree rather than any tree of its type. Or it could be that this was before his prophethood (*nubuwwa*), and he did it forgetfully.[2] Know also that Adam was created for the earth, and even if he had not sinned he would have left the Garden by some other means. Q. 2:36

[2:37] *Thereafter Adam received certain words from his Lord*, namely *'Our Lord, we have wronged ourselves,'* and so on [Q. 7:23], and called them out, *and He relented to him* and turned to him with mercy. *Truly, He is the Relenting*: the One Who eagerly accepts repentance, or Who turns to His servants with mercy; *the Merciful* of infinite mercy. The root meaning of *tawba* (repentance, relenting) is 'to return'. For the servant it means to return from sin, while for God it means to return from chastisement to forgiveness.

[2:38] *We said, 'Go down from it altogether'*: this is repeated for emphasis, or the second refers to the station of moral responsibility, since a fall can denote a physical movement or a lowering of status. This is supported by what follows: *'Yet should there come to you from Me guidance* through a

1 The author is explaining why the verb *ihbiṭū* (go down) is addressed to the plural rather than the dual.

2 Ashʿarī doctrine holds that it is impossible for a prophet to commit sin, hence this interpretation.

prophet, *then whoever follows My guidance*, meaning the teachings he brings, *no fear shall befall them* at the moment of the Great Calamity, *neither shall they grieve* for what they have left behind in the world. Fear means sorrow for something that is expected to occur, while grief means sorrow for something that has actually occurred. The only fear that they shall feel is in the world.

[2:39] *'As for*—in contrast to those who follow the guidance—*the disbelievers who deny Our* revealed *signs, those shall be the inhabitants of the Fire, therein they will abide.'*

[2:40] *O Children of Israel*: the name *Isrā'īl* (Israel) is composed of *isrā* meaning 'servant' or 'chosen one' and *īl* meaning 'God'. They are the children of Jacob, and He roused them by invoking their forefather's name. *Remember*, and do not forget, *My favour wherewith I favoured you*: such as the cleaving of the sea and others, for the favours granted to ancestors are also
for their descendants; *and fulfil My covenant*: by obeying, or by following
Muḥammad (may God bless him and grant him peace); *and I shall fulfil your*
Q. 2:39 *covenant*: with reward and pardon. The word *wafā'* (fulfilment) means to
hold to an agreement while *ghadar* (treachery) means to break it, such as by keeping or failing to keep a promise. *And have awe of Me* and no other: it is worded as *wa-iyyāya farhabūn* [literally 'and of Me, then have awe of Me'], with the object of the verb repeated and the word 'then' imparting additional emphasis. The word *rahb* (awe) means fear accompanied by caution.

[2:41] *And believe in what I have revealed*, the Qur'ān, *confirming that which is with you*, the Torah and Gospel, *and be not the first* people *to disbelieve in it* from the People of the Book. *And do not sell* faith in *My signs for a small price*: the world; *and fear Me*: not the loss of leadership.

[2:42] *And do not obscure*—do not mix—*the truth with falsehood*: by adding whatever you please to the Torah; *and do not conceal the truth*—the description of Muḥammad therein—*while you know* that it is true.

[2:43] *And observe the prayer*, the prayer of the Muslims, *and pay zakāt*, their *zakāt*, *and bow with those that bow*: the Muslim faithful. There is no bowing in the Jewish prayer. This verse was meant to forbid them from their practices, and should not be cited as proof that congregational prayer is obligatory.

[2:44] *Will you bid others to piety*, such as following the Torah which affirms the obligation of following Muḥammad, *and forget yourselves* to adhere to piety, *while you recite*—the verb *tatlūna* here can mean 'recite' or 'follow'—*the Book*, the Torah, which forbids this*? Do you not understand* how vile this is? The root meaning of *ʿaql* (understanding, intellect) is 'to restrain'; it became the name for human perception because of how it restrains person from what is ugly, and then the name for the faculty by which the soul perceives. The verse is meant to encourage the admonisher to take admonition himself, not to bar the sinner from admonishing.

[2:45] *Seek help* in times of difficulty *with patience and prayer*: patience means to restrain the soul within the bounds of the dictates of the intellect and the Law. At times of difficulty it is called patience; at times of desire, abstinence; at times of war, courage; at times of tribulation, forbearance. Refraining from speech is called suppression. In this verse, it refers to fasting. The *prayer* meant here is the prayer that *prevents against lewdness and indecency* [Q. 29:45]. *For it*, meaning seeking help in these two, *is grievous*, challenging, *except to the humble* who gladly obey.

[2:46] *Those who reckon* with certainty *that they shall meet* the reward of *their Lord* for bearing His responsibilities patiently, *and that to Him they will return* at the Resurrection.

[2:47] *O Children of Israel, remember My favour wherewith I favoured you,*
and that I preferred you, before you corrupted them, *above all the worlds*: Q. 2:45
this means the worlds of their time, and does not contradict *You are the best community*...[Q. 3:110]. It also implies that humankind is superior to the angels.

[2:48] *And fear* the horrors of *a day when no* righteous *soul for another* sinful soul *shall give satisfaction, and no intercession shall be accepted from it*, from the righteous for the sinful, *nor any compensation*, any ransom or recompense, *be taken* from the sinful one, *neither shall they be helped* or defended from the chastisement—contrary to their claim that because they are the descendants of the prophets, they will intercede for them. The Muʿtazila cite this as proof that there will be no intercession for those who commit major sins, but this is refuted by the mass-transmitted *ḥadīths* about such intercession and by the fact that this verse was revealed specifically to counter a claim of the Jews.

[2:49] *And* remember *when We delivered you from the people of Pharaoh*: Pharaoh was the title of the kings of the Amalekites, the scions of ʿAmalīq b. Lāwadh b. Sām, similar to the titles Khosrau and Caesar for the rulers of Persia and Rome, [respectively]. The Pharaoh of Moses was Muṣʿab b. Rayyān, a descendant of the remnants of ʿĀd. The Pharaoh of Joseph was also named Rayyān, and ruled four hundred years later. This will be discussed further in *Sūrat al-Mu'min* [Q. 40]. [*We delivered you from the people of Pharaoh,*] *who were visiting you with evil chastisement*: passing you around among various heinous forms of torment; the verb *sāma* (to visit upon) comes from *sā'ima*, meaning 'to wander to and fro in the wilderness'; *slaughtering your sons, and sparing your women*: Pharaoh did this because he had heard the portent that the ruin of his kingdom would come at the hands of one of them. *And for you therein*, in your salvation or in their persecution, *was a tremendous trial*, a favour or a test, *from your Lord*.

[2:50] *And when We divided for you the sea, and We delivered you, and drowned the people of Pharaoh*, including Pharaoh himself, fulfilling that prophecy, *while you were beholding* their drowning.

[2:51] *And when We appointed for Moses forty nights*: the verb *wāʿada* (to make an accord with another), which has a reflexive meaning, is used here because on his part Moses promised to attend, and on His part God promised to give him the Torah when the tryst was concluded. The forty nights comprised the month of Dhū al-Qaʿda and the first ten nights of Dhū al-Ḥijja, for the transmission of the Torah. He mentioned nights rather than days because the beginning of the month is counted from the
Q. 2:50 night, and the Arabs usually date events by referring to nights. The night is also the origin, and it was their custom to fast during the night. *Then you took to yourselves the calf* as a god *after him*—after he had left—*and you were evildoers*.

[2:52] *Then We pardoned you*—erasing the sin—*after that so that you might be thankful*.

[2:53] *And when We gave to Moses the Book*, the Torah, *and the Criterion*, the parting of the sea or the added gift of exegesis, meaning the differentiation between truth and falsehood, *so that you might be guided* by them.

[2:54] *And when Moses said to his people* who had worshipped the calf, *'My people, you have done wrong against yourselves by your taking the [golden] calf* as a god. *Now repent to your Maker*—your Creator—from the worship of an object of your own creating. The word *bāriʿ* (maker) comes from *bara'a*, which means to free something from something else, whether as an act of completion or creation. *And slay one another* as you find one another, to prove your repentance. Then a black cloud came over them, so that they would not identify one another and hold back, and seventy thousand were slain, and then the slayers and the slain alike were forgiven. *That will be better for you in your Creator's sight* than sinning, for it is purification from idolatry. *He relented to you* even before you repented; *for truly He is the Relenting* Who eagerly accepts repentance, as we saw, *the Merciful* to those who repent.'

[2:55] *And when you said*—when Moses chose seventy to receive the Torah; they did not say this by way of justifying the worship of the calf, as is often claimed—*'O Moses, we will not believe you* that these Words are truly from God, *till we see God openly* with our own eyes'; *and the thunderbolt*—the fire, the cry or death—*took you, while you were beholding* what had befallen you.

[2:56] *Then We raised you up after you were dead*—having lain insensate for a day and night—*so that you might be thankful* for the favour of this raising.

[2:57] *And We made the cloud overshadow you* in the wilderness to protect you from the sun; *and We sent down upon you manna*, which is *taranjabīn*,[1] from dawn until sunrise like frost, *and quails*, a kind of bird: *'Eat of the good* delicious *things We have provided for you*: and do not save it up.' But they saved it up anyway, and so it was denied them. *And they did not wrong Us* by their ingratitude, *but themselves they wronged* by failing to give thanks for it and for the other favours, such as the sending down of pillars from heaven at night to light their way, and the miraculous preservation of their clothes, and the like.

[2:58] *And when We said* after the wandering, *'Enter this city*, meaning Q. 2:56
Jericho or Jerusalem, which they did not enter until the time of Joshua, *and eat freely therein wherever you will, and enter it at the gate*, the town gate or a temple where they would pray, *prostrating* with your heads bowed in humility, or prostrating to give thanks, *and say, "Exoneration"* do we ask for our sins, *and We shall forgive you your transgressions*: this was directed at the sinners among them; *and We shall give more* reward *to those who are virtuous.'*

[2:59] *Then the evildoers substituted a saying* instead of asking for forgiveness, *other than that which had been said to them*, and asked for their desires, or said *ḥinṭa* (wheat) instead of *ḥiṭṭa* (exoneration) in mockery, and went in dragging themselves on their buttocks with their heads raised in obstinate pride. *So We sent down upon the evildoers wrath*: a chastisement of plague—the word *rijz* (wrath) originally meant a disease that affects camels; *from the heaven for their wickedness*: and before long it had claimed the lives of seventy thousand.

[2:60] *And when Moses sought water*: He mentioned the entrance to the city before this, though it occurred after it, because this is a list of their deeds rather than a single story; *for his people, We* answered his prayer for them and *said, 'Strike with your staff the rock'*: it was a small square-shaped rock from Sinai which they carried with them, or which had remained in

1 A Persian name for honeydew.

his pack. *And there flowed from it*, because of the blow he struck it, after the first gushing forth,[1] *twelve fountains*, each fountain for one of the tribes; there were six hundred thousand of them, and the camp covered twelve miles. *Each people*—each tribe—*came to know their drinking-place. 'Eat and drink of that which God has provided, and do not be degenerate*—do not persist in corruption—*in the earth,* in a state of *seeking corruption'*: the prohibition was of persistence in corruption; or it was akin to, *Do not exact usury, doubled and redoubled* [Q. 3:130]; or it meant to exclude those things which seem to be corrupt but are actually sound, such as how Khiḍr scuttled the ship [see Q. 18:71 and 18:79].

[2:61] *And when you said, 'Moses, we will not endure one sort of food*: meaning manna and quails, which were one food in the sense that this was their constant diet, or in the sense that they ate them mixed together. *Pray to your Lord for us, that He may bring forth for us of what the earth produces: green herbs* (*baql*): meaning any vegetable without a stem; *cucumbers*; *garlic* (*fūm*): meaning wheat, garlic or any grain that can be used to make bread; *lentils*
Q. 2:61
and onions': they were farmers, accustomed to eating such things. *He said, 'Would you exchange what is better* (*khayr*) with respect to taste and benefit *with what is lowlier?* Know that good (*khayr*) in absolute terms means what is beneficial, pleasant and enjoyable; its opposite in absolute terms is evil (*sharr*). Relative good is something that possesses only one of these qualities, meaning that it could also be described as relatively evil. *Go down to a city* (*miṣr*): the word *miṣr* here can be understood as 'a city' or as 'Egypt', the land of Pharaoh, since *miṣr* means a large settlement, from the word *mamṣūr* meaning a place demarked with borders. *You shall have what you demanded.' And abasement and wretchedness were cast upon them* like a dome covering them, despite their wealth, *and they incurred God's wrath*: meaning that they attained it, or earned it. *That was because they used to disbelieve the* revealed *signs of God, and slay prophets*, such as John, *without right*, even by their own standards; or He said this to stress the monstrousness of the act, or to allude to the possibility that such an act could be rightful, such as in the story of Ishmael. *That* disbelief and slaying *was because they disobeyed, and they were transgressors*: disobedience and transgression took them outside God's boundaries. Or it could be read as, 'That was in addition to how they disobeyed,' etc.

[2:62] *Truly, those who believe* in truth or in word, *and those of Jewry, and the Christians, and the Sabaeans*: the verb *yahūd* means 'to be among the

1 *And there gushed forth from it twelve fountains*... (Q. 7:160).

Jews', either from *hāda* meaning 'to repent' or from their forebear Yahūdā (Judah). The word *naṣārā* is the plural of *naṣrānī*; they are the community of Jesus, named after him because of how they gave support (*nuṣra*) to Christ, or because of how they lived with him in Naṣrān or Nāṣira (Nazareth). *Ṣābi'ūn* means 'those outside the religion', and refers to those who live among the Jews, Christians and Magians without any religion, and who venerate the stars. He spoke of these four groups in particular because of their renown; *whoever* among them *believes* with heart and word *in God and the Last Day, and performs righteous deeds* without ostentation, *their wage is with their Lord, and no fear shall befall them, neither shall they grieve*: this was discussed earlier.

[2:63] *And when We made a covenant with you* that you follow the Torah, *and We raised above you the Mount*: Gabriel raised it above them when they refused and held it there until they accepted. Thus it appears that it was coerced, but they earn reward by adhering to it, or some say by acting according to it. *'Take forcefully*—seriously—*what We have given you, and remember*—and do not forget—*what is in it, so that you might preserve yourselves*: so that you remain God-fearing.' Q. 2:63

[2:64] *Then you turned away thereafter* by violating the covenant, *and but for God's bounty and His mercy towards you* through the grace of the Torah, *you would have been among the losers*: the duped ones.

[2:65] *And indeed you know that there were those among you who transgressed the Sabbath*: they were forbidden from hunting on that day, to honour it; *and We said to them, 'Be apes, despised!'* This was a command of creation; when it was issued to them, they were transformed. It is said that the young were transformed into apes and the elderly into swine.

[2:66] *And We made it*, this transformation, *an exemplary punishment for all the former times*, for their contemporaries, *and for the latter, and an admonition to such as who fear.*

[2:67] *And* remember *when Moses said to his people* when he found a man had been murdered for his money by his brother's sons, and then they came to him demanding indemnity for his blood, *'God commands you to sacrifice a cow*: and strike his body with part of it so that he would be brought back to life to speak the name of his killer.' *They said, 'Do you take us in mockery?' He said*, replying to them by way of argument, *'I take refuge with God lest I should be one of the ignorant'*: meaning, 'Your mockery is an accusation of ignorance, of which I am innocent.'

[2:68] *They said, 'Pray to your Lord for us, that He may make clear to us what she may be'*: that is, what attributes she should have. The word *mā* (what) in this sense being used figuratively to mean *ayy shay'* (which), or literally according to the definition of Sakkākī.[1] *He said, 'He says she is a cow neither old, nor virgin, middling between the two*: neither decrepit, nor young and not yet bred, but in-between. He stipulated that it not be young so that they did not choose a newborn or unborn calf. *So do what you have been commanded.'*

[2:69] *They said, 'Pray to your Lord for us, that He make clear to us what her colour may be.' He said, 'He says she shall be a golden cow, bright in colour*: of the most pure yellow—this is a figure of speech; *gladdening to beholders'*: the root meaning of *surūr* (gladness) is delight in the heart upon the attainment of benefit, or the expectation of it. It is similar to *ḥubūr* (joy) and *faraḥ* (exultation), except that the first two are praiseworthy while the third is condemned as it engenders hubris.

[2:70] *They said, 'Pray to your Lord for us, that He make clear to us what she may be*: a gazing cow or a working cow. *Cows are all alike to us; and if*
Q. 2:69 *God wills, we shall then be guided* to it.' This indicates that the divine command is something other than the divine will, since here it was stipulated after the command. The Muᶜtazila and Karrāmiyya cite it as evidence that the [divine] will is contingent, since it means, 'If He creates a will.' The rebuttal of this is that the conditional stipulation refers to the attachment [of the will].

[2:71] *He said, 'He says she shall be a cow not broken to plough the earth, or to water the tillage; one kept secure* from work or flaws, *with no blemish on her*: no mark of any other colour.' *They said, 'Now you have brought the truth* of her true description.' *And so they* procured her, and *sacrificed her, though they very nearly did not*: because of their incessant questioning, or their fear of change, or because it took them forty years to find her.

[2:72] *And when you killed a living soul*: He delayed the first part of the story in order to give precedence to the account of their sins, or to enumerate them, or because they were commanded to perform the sacrifice before the murder occurred; *and you disputed thereon*: arguing or blaming one another; *and God disclosed what you were hiding* about the murderer.

[2:73] *So We said, 'Smite him*—the victim—*with part of it'*: part of the cow, so that he would come back to life. So they struck him with its tongue and he came back to life, revealed his killer's identity, and immediately returned to death. *Even so*, like this revival, *God brings to life the*

1 Sakkākī (d. 1160) argued that *mā* can denote type, as in *mā ᶜindak* ('what do you have?'), or attribute as in *mā Zayd* ('what is Zayd like?').

dead, and He shows you His signs, the signs of His power, *so that you might understand* that the One Who can do this can bring the Resurrection to pass. The reason God did not simply bring the man to life to begin with, without any stipulation, was to charge them with an act of worship and an obligation to fulfil, and to benefit the orphan, and to show the blessing of reliance, and out of compassion for the children, and to show how it is recommended for a seeker to offer something to God, and to allow them to profit from the cow's proceeds, and other such wisdoms.

[2:74] *Then your hearts became hardened*—became coarse and devoid of reflection—*thereafter, becoming as* hard as *stones, or even yet harder*: the word *or* here denotes choice or uncertainty, meaning that the one who knew their state would liken them to stones or something harder. This will be explained further when we come to His Words *the matter of the Hour is but as the twinkling of an eye, or it is even nearer* [Q. 16:77]. He then explained their greater hardness: *for there are stones from which rivers come gushing, and others split so that water issues from them*: they do not mean the same thing, since Q. 2:74
'gushing' (*tafajjur*) means 'a large outpouring', and so there is no repetition here. *And others still fall down* from mountaintops *in fear of God*: in surrender to Him; this describes all of those acts. *And God is not heedless of what you do.*

[2:75] *Are you then so eager*, O believers, *that they*, the Jews, *should believe you* and heed your preaching *when there was a party of them*, from their forebears, *that heard God's Word*—namely the seventy chosen for the tryst—*and then tampered with it* after they returned, *after they had comprehended it knowingly*, knowing what the consequence would be? How could it be with them?

[2:76] *And when they*, the Hypocrites among them, *meet those who believe, they say, 'We believe* that you are in the right'; *but when they go in private one to another, they*, the disbelievers and Hypocrites among them, *say, 'Do you speak to them of what God has disclosed to you* in the Torah, meaning the description of their prophet, *so that they may thereby dispute with you before your Lord?'* So that they say, 'Do you still disbelieve when you know that he is truthful?' *Have you no understanding?* This is meant as a rebuke, and refers back to *Are you then so eager* [Q. 2:75], which was said first to give it precedence. Some said it refers to an elided verb and can be understood as, 'Do you say this, having no understanding?'

[2:77] *Know they not that God knows what they keep secret and what they proclaim?* In both cases, the proof stands against them.

[2:78] *And there are some of them*, the Jews, *that are illiterate*, unable to read or write, *not knowing the Book, but only* knowing *fancies*: lies they heard from their elders. The root meaning of *umniya* (fancy) is something a person thinks to himself. *They do naught but conjecture*: they are people who believe without knowledge.

[2:79] *So woe*: the word *wayl* (woe) means 'perdition', and is the name of a valley in Hell; *to those who write the Book with their hands*: their clerics who write down false interpretations for the portents of Muḥammad (may God bless him and grant him peace) in the Torah. He mentioned their hands in order to emphasise how they personally engage in this; *then say, 'This is from God,' that they may sell it for a small price*: the price is their leadership and the benefit they obtain from their subordinates. *So woe to them for what their hands have written, and woe to them for what they earn* from their subordinates, or from their sins.

[2:80] *And they*, the Jews, *say, 'The Fire shall not touch us*: the word *mass* (touch) means for something to connect to the skin so that it can be felt, while *lams* means 'to deliberately touch'; *save a number of days'*: seven or
forty. *Say*, O Muḥammad, *'Have you taken with God a covenant* about this*?*
Q. 2:79 *Then God will not fail in His covenant. Or do you say*—invent—*against God*
what you do not know?'

[2:81] *Not so; whoever acquires evil*: *kasb* (to acquire) means to attain something beneficial, but here refers to something evil, to impart scorn; *and is encompassed by his error* so that he retains no good deeds at all, meaning the disbeliever, because if his heart believed the words his tongue spoke he would not be encompassed by transgression. The difference between *sayyi'a* (evil) and *khaṭī'a* (error) is that *sayyi'a* can refer to something that is done deliberately for its own sake, while *khaṭī'a* usually means something that is done accidentally.[1] *Those are the inhabitants of the Fire, therein they will abide.*

[2:82] *And those who believe and perform righteous deeds—those are the inhabitants of the Garden, therein they will abide.*

[2:83] *And* remember *when We made a covenant with the Children of Israel* in the Torah, saying to them, *'You shall not worship any other than God; and to be good to parents, and the near of kin; and to orphans, and to the needy*: meaning those who do not have what they need. The word *miskīn* (needy) is from *askana*, meaning 'to be overcome with want'. *And speak well to humans*: such as by enjoining what is right; *and observe the prayer and pay zakāt* as ordained by your religion.*' Then you turned away*—abandoning

1 Qūnawī illustrates *khaṭī'a* by citing the example of someone who kills a man while hunting an animal, or who consumes alcohol and then drunkenly commits a crime. See Isma'īl b. Muḥammad al-Qūnawī, *Ḥāshiyat al-Qūnawī 'alā Tafsīr al-Bayḍāwī*, Beirut: Dār al-Kutub al-'Ilmiyya, 2001, vol. III, p. 457.

the covenant—*all but a few of you, rejecting*: for it was your wont to reject your pacts.

[2:84] *And when We made a covenant with you* in the Torah: *'You shall not shed your own blood*: you shall not fight one another, for they were as if one person because of their connection of religion and kin; *neither expel your own from your habitations*: by banishing one another.*' Then you confirmed it, and you bore witness* over yourselves regarding it.

[2:85] *Then, there you are*—renegades—*killing one another, and expelling a party of you from their habitations, conspiring against them in sin and enmity; and if they come to you as captives, you ransom them; yet their expulsion was forbidden you. What, do you believe in part of the Book* by holding to it, *and disbelieve in part* by engaging in killing, conspiring and expulsion*? What shall be the requital of those of you who do that, but degradation*—humiliation and torment—*in the life of this world*, like the degradation of Qurayẓa by capture and slaying, or the Banū al-Naḍīr by expulsion and taxation, *and on the Day of Resurrection to be returned to the most terrible of chastisement? And God is* Q. 2:84 *not heedless of what you do.*

[2:86] *Those are the ones who have purchased the life of this world at the price of the Hereafter—for them the punishment shall not be lightened*, decreased, *neither shall they be helped*, protected from God's chastisement.

[2:87] *And We gave Moses the Book, and after him We sent successive messengers, and We gave Jesus son of Mary the clear proofs*, prophetic miracles (*muʿjizāt*), *and We confirmed him*, strengthened him, *with the Holy Spirit* (*rūḥ al-qudus*): a sanctified spirit, which was a name with which he would raise the dead, or Gabriel who would accompany him wherever he went; or *qudus* and *Quddūs* (Holy, a Name of God) may be one and the same, in which case it means the Spirit of God; *and whenever there came to you a messenger with what your souls did not desire, you became arrogant*: and disbelieved; *and some you called liars*: such as Jesus and Muḥammad; *and some you slay*: such as Zachariah and John. [In the latter,] the verb is in the present sense because it is evoking the freshness of the past, or because of their attempts to slay Muḥammad (may God bless him and grant him peace).

[2:88] *And they say, 'Our hearts are encased'*: covered with a natural casing to prevent them from understanding what you have brought. *Nay, but God has cursed them for their disbelief*, and so their hearts are cursed because of it, *and little will they believe*: this refers to how they believe in only part of the Book, or it means that they have no faith at all.

[2:89] *When there came to them a Book from God*, the Qur'ān, *confirming what was with them*, the Torah, *and before they had prayed for victory over the disbelievers* by saying, 'Lord God, aid us with the prophet of the end times described in the Torah'; *but when there came to them what they recognised, they disbelieved in it* out of envy; *and the curse of God is on the disbelievers.*

[2:90] *Evil is that for which they sell their souls*: for they sold their reward for disbelief, or truly sold their souls as they claimed; *that they disbelieve in that which God has revealed, grudging*, envying, *that God should reveal of His bounty*, the Book and prophethood, *to whomever He will of His servants; and they were laden with anger upon anger*: because of how they disbelieved in Muḥammad (may God bless him and grant him peace), after having disbelieved in Jesus (may God bless him and grant him peace). *And for the disbelievers there shall be a humiliating chastisement*, while the chastisement of the sinners is meant to purify them.

[2:91] *And when it was said to them*, to the Jews, *'Believe in what God has revealed*: the Qur'ān,*' they said, 'We believe in what was revealed to us*: the Torah,*' and they disbelieve in what is beyond that; yet it is the truth, confirming what is with them*: what is beyond that is the truth, and confirms the truth of the Torah, Q. 2:90 and so to disbelieve in it is to disbelieve in the Torah. *Say: 'Why then*, if you are truthful, *were you slaying the prophets of God before*: the verb is *taqtulūn* (slaying) in the present tense, because the attribute remained with them; and the word *before* refers back to the content of *Why then*, as though it were said, 'Tell me, first of all'; *if you were believers* in the Torah, which forbids this*?'* The deeds of their forefathers were essentially their own deeds, since they approved of them.

[2:92] *And Moses came to you with clear proofs*: manifest prophetic miracles; *then you took to yourselves the calf* as a god *after him*—after he had departed—*and you were evildoers*: accustomed to evil.

[2:93] *And when We made a covenant with you, and raised over you the Mount: 'Take forcefully*—seriously—*what We have given you, and listen*: obey,*' they said, 'We hear* with our ears *and disobey* with our hearts.*'* They professed to have accepted when really they had not. *And they were made to drink the calf in their hearts*: love of the calf entered into their bodies all the way to their hearts, just as dye enters fabric, *on account of their* hidden *disbelief. Say: 'Evil is that which your belief* in the Torah *enjoins on you*, such as worshipping the calf and denying Muḥammad (may God bless him and grant him peace), *if you are believers'*: evil indeed are the things this faith of yours commands you to do.

[2:94] *Say: 'If the Abode of the Hereafter with God*—in His knowledge—*is purely yours and not for other people, then long for death*: pray for death for whomever of us is lying, and challenge him to this ritual; *if you speak truly'*:

had they done so, none of them would have remained.

[2:95] *But they will never long for it, because of that which their own hands have sent before them*: meaning their sins. Their hands symbolise their souls, since the hands are the implements of most deeds. *God knows the evildoers.*

[2:96] *And you shall find them the people most covetous of life, and the idolaters* because of how they deny the Resurrection; *any one of them would love that he might be given life for a thousand years; yet he would not evade the chastisement even if he were given such a life. God sees what they do.*

[2:97] *Say*: *'Whoever is an enemy to Gabriel (Jibrīl)*: the name *Jibrīl* means 'servant (*jibr*) of God (*īl*)'. Anyone who is an enemy to him cannot be sincere, for *he it was that brought it*, the Qur'ān, *down upon your heart by the leave*, the command, *of God, confirming what was before it*, the Books, *a guidance and glad tiding for the believers*: and a chastisement and calamity for the disbelievers.

[2:98] *'Whoever is an enemy to God and His angels and His messengers, and Gabriel and Michael—then truly God is an enemy to the disbelievers'*: that is, to such a person. The noun is favoured over the pronoun to affirm their disbelief. The same applies to similar passages. Q. 2:95

[2:99] *And We have revealed to you clear proofs; and none disbelieves in them except the wicked folk*: when the term 'wickedness' is used to refer to a kind of sin, it means the most heinous form of it.

[2:100] *Why*, in addition to how they disbelieve in Our signs, *whenever they make a covenant, does a party of them reject it* and cast it aside to be forgotten*? Nay, but most of them are disbelievers*: this discounts the possibility that the aforementioned party of them might be the minority.

[2:101] *When there came to them a messenger from God, confirming what was with them, a party of them who were given the Book have cast away the Book of God*, the Torah, *behind their backs* by denying the descriptions of Muḥammad (may God bless him and grant him peace) found therein, *as though they did not know* what it contained.

[2:102] *And they follow what the devils used to relate about Solomon's kingdom*: referring to the book of sorcery which the devils wrote and buried beneath his Pedestal (*kursī*) and then unearthed after his death, saying, 'He was made king by the power of this sorcery, not prophethood, so learn it and disregard his prophethood.' *Solomon disbelieved not*: that is, he did not engage in sorcery, which is tantamount to disbelief; *but the devils disbelieved, teaching the people sorcery* through what they buried and what they said. Sorcery (*siḥr*) means for an evil soul to perform a supernatural act in the pursuit of something forbidden. If it involves words or acts of

disbelief, then it is disbelief; if not, it is a major sin according to Shāfiʿī, and disbelief according to others. The majority say that it is forbidden to learn it except for the purpose of defence against sorcerers if it becomes rampant. The Imam[1] said that there are eight types of sorcery. The first is the sorcery of the Chaldean worshippers of celestial bodies. The second is the sorcery of people of sagacity and powerful souls. The third is seeking help from terrestrial spirits. The fourth is illusion and deception. The fifth is wondrous acts done by means of complex mechanisms, such as a model of a horseman holding a drum which strikes every hour without anyone touching it. The sixth is the utilisation of certain concoctions. The seventh is captivating people's hearts, such as by threatening them by saying, 'I shall do such-and-such to you with the Supreme Name,' so that the person becomes captivated and his senses are dulled, after which the sorcerer may compel him to do as he pleases. The eighth is creating discord among people by means of gossip. The Muʿtazila deny all of this except for illusions and gossip. The truth is that wondrous acts done by means
Q. 2:102 of devices or concoctions, such as the performances of the illusionists and masters of sleight of hand, are not blameworthy, and indeed it is an exaggeration to call such things sorcery. You will be aware that, with this in mind, several of the categories the Imam mentioned can be discounted. One example of this is misdirection, which means to feign an action to distract the minds and eyes of the audience while at the same time doing something else swiftly, so that they are not sure what they have seen.

Know also that a prophetic miracle (*muʿjiza*) is a supernatural act performed by a virtuous soul that calls to virtue, accompanied by a challenge that conforms to it, which cannot be countered. The requirement that it be performed by a virtuous soul that calls to virtue means that the supernatural acts of illusionists and sorcerers are excluded. The requirement that it be accompanied by a challenge excludes the saintly miracle (*karāma*) and the portent (*irhāṣ*).[2] The requirement that the prophetic miracle conform to the challenge excludes a supernatural act that attests to the opposite of the claim, such as if a man said, 'The sign of my prophethood is that this wall will speak,' and then the wall did indeed speak, but declared him to be a liar. The requirement that it cannot be countered excludes the actions

1 Identified by Abū al-Ḥasan ʿAbd Allāh al-Shabrāwī as Fakhr al-Dīn al-Rāzī (d. 1210), the great theologian of Khorasan. See *Tafsīr al-Kāzarūnī*, p. 95 n3 (editor).

2 *Muʿjiza* denotes a miracle granted to a prophet to prove his legitimacy. *Karāma* denotes a miracle granted to a saint. *Irhāṣ* denotes a miracle granted to a prophet before his prophetic mission begins, in order to lay the ground for it.

that can be performed using certain things because of the properties that are innate to them.

The *karāma* of a saint—which means a person who is always directed towards God—is a supernatural act performed by someone who follows a prophet and makes no prophetic claim of his own. This requirement excludes acts of drawing-on (*istidrāj*),[1] or acts which confirm the liar's dishonesty, such as if he prays for a sick person's health and they become even sicker, which is called 'humiliation'. Then there are the supernatural events that occur to save the believers from peril, which are called 'divine aid' (*maʿūna*). And God knows best.

And they taught the people *that which was revealed to the two angels*, the inspired knowledge of sorcery and its corruption, *in Babylon*, a place in Kufa; *Hārūt and Mārūt*: these were the names of those two angels. They had been among the most devoted of angels, but then God created passion in them after the angels spoke ill of us, in order to show our excuse. So they became disobedient, and He gave them to choose between the chastisement of this world or the next. They chose this world, so He chastised them until the Day of Resurrection and made them a tribulation for His servants. The fact that He revealed it to them does not contradict its unlawfulness, because they were taught it in order to avoid it. If someone asked you what adultery was, you would be obliged to explain it to them so that they could recognise it and avoid it. *They*, the two angels, *taught not any person without them saying, 'We are but a temptation*: a test for you; *do not disbelieve*: by learning it.*'* This suggests that this type of sorcery involved disbelief. *From them they learned how*—by means of sorcery—*they might cause division between a man and his wife*: He singled this out for mention because it is the worst form of sorcery. *Yet they did not hurt any person thereby*—with that sorcery—*save by the leave of God*: by His command; *and they learned what hurt them, and did not profit them*, because they learned it in order to engage in it. *And surely they knew well that whoever buys it*, exchanges God's religion for sorcery by choosing it ahead of it; *he shall have no share*—no portion of goodness—*in the Hereafter. Evil, then, would have been that they sold themselves for, if they had but known*: this means that their knowledge was as good as ignorance because they failed to act on it, or that they had instinctive knowledge but not acquired knowledge.

Q. 2:103

[2:103] *Yet if only they had believed* in Muḥammad (may God bless him and grant him peace), *and been fearful* by abstaining from sin; if only they

1 These are supernatural acts granted to a false prophet or saint to increase his delusion.

had done so, they would have been rewarded, for He says: *a reward from God would have been better, if they had but known*. This is akin to His Words, *Those who will be the inhabitants of the Garden on that day will be in a better abode* [Q. 25:24], or is addressed to them according to their own perspective.[1]

[2:104] *O you who believe, do not say* to Muḥammad (may God bless him and grant him peace), *'Observe us*: watch us and be patient with us so that we might understand.*'* This was because the Arabic *rāʿinā* had another vulgar meaning in the language of the Jews with which they would mock him secretly to amuse one another, or because the verb is reflexive which implies a joint participation. *But say: 'Regard us,' and give ear*: be receptive to counsel; *and for disbelievers* who insult their messengers *there awaits a painful chastisement*.

[2:105] *Those disbelievers of the People of the Book and the idolaters do not wish that any good should be revealed to you from your Lord*: out of envy; *but God singles out for His mercy whom He will; God is of bounty abounding*: and He has good reasons for depriving others.

[2:106] *And whatever verse We abrogate*: declaring it no longer in effect,
Q. 2:104 or that it no longer be recited, or both. The root meaning of *naskh* (abrogation) is to remove an image from one thing and transfer it to another. *Or cast into oblivion*: erasing it from hearts, whether it is a command, prohibition or statement, without consideration of the annulment of the ruling or the meaning of the words. This is why it is related that they used to forget a *sūra* that was as long as *Sūrat al-Tawba* [Q. 9] and contained the verse, 'Were the son of Adam to own two valleys or riches, he would desire a third.' *We bring [in place] a better*, more beneficial for people, *or the like of it*, equally beneficial. The verse does not imply that there could not be abrogation without replacement, or with a heftier replacement, nor does it imply that the Qur'ān could not be abrogated by the Sunna, for the former two could be more beneficial, and the Sunna is also from God. Nor does it imply that the Qur'ān is contingent, because they are accidental affairs connected to the meaning upheld by the Eternal Essence. This verse can also be read as *whatever verse We command be abrogated, or postpone*.[2] *Do you not know that God has power over all things*, including the power to abrogate or cast into oblivion?

[2:107] *Do you not know*: this is addressed to the singular pronoun, denoting the Prophet in particular, because of his great knowledge; *that*

1 The issue here is the use of the word 'better', which could be taken to imply that both possible outcomes were good but one was better, though naturally this cannot apply to a comparison between salvation and damnation.

2 With *nunassikh* and *nansa'* rather than *nansakh* and *nunsi* respectively.

to God belongs the kingdom of the heavens and the earth, such that He may do as He wills therein, *and that you have none, besides God, neither guardian* to watch over your affairs, *nor helper?* The difference between them is that a helper (*nāṣir*) could be distant, and a guardian (*walī*) could be incapable.

[2:108] *Or do you desire to question your Messenger*, Muḥammad (may God bless him and grant him peace), *as Moses was questioned, aforetime*, when the Jews said, 'Bring us a Book to read, and we shall believe in you'*? Whoever exchanges belief for disbelief has surely strayed from the even way*: the straight path.

[2:109] *Many of the People of the Book long that they might make you disbelievers, after you have believed, from the envy of their own souls*—not for any pious motive—*after the truth has become clear to them* in the Torah. *Yet pardon* their transgressions *and be forgiving*, leave them be, *till God brings His command* that they may be fought. *Truly, God has power over all things.*

[2:110] *And observe the prayer and pay zakāt. Whatever good you shall offer for your own souls, you shall find it*—its reward—*with God. Truly, God sees what you do*: and will not let your deeds go to waste. Q. 2:108

[2:111] *And they*, the People of the Book, meaning the Jews and Christians respectively, *say, 'None shall enter the Garden except those who are Jews*, as the Jews say, *or Christians*, as the Christians say.*' Such are their desires. Say: 'Produce your proof* that the Garden is for you alone, *if you speak truly.'*

[2:112] *Nay, but whoever submits his purpose*—his being and religion—*to God, being virtuous* by following God's command, *his reward is with his Lord, and no fear shall befall them, neither shall they grieve*, as was explained before.

[2:113] *The Jews say, 'The Christians stand on nothing'; and the Christians say, 'The Jews stand on nothing* that has any basis*'; yet they recite the Book* that confirms the truth of what they disbelieve. *Thus did the ignorant*—like their forefathers—*say the like of what these say. God shall decide between them on the Day of Resurrection regarding their differences* and their transgressions.

[2:114] *And who does greater evil than he who bars God's places of worship, so that His Name be not invoked in them, and strives to ruin them* by demolishing them as the Christians did in Jerusalem, or by rendering them defunct such as how the idolaters barred the believers from Mecca. This applies to every place of worship (*masjid*). The negation of the greater evil here, like other such instances in the Qur'ān, is a common rhetorical device for imparting emphasis, such as the phrase, 'There is no hero but ʿAlī.' It does not mean that no equally evil things exist, nor does it negate the existence of even more evil things, such as idolatry. Even if it were not a rhetorical device, the most that could be said about it would be that it is a general rule for which there are exceptions. *Such people* who bar the way to them *might never enter them, save in fear*: that is, do not allow them to enter them unless there is a treaty. This was an implicit glad tiding that we would be victorious. Abū Ḥanīfa said that they are permitted to enter them in absolute terms, while Mālik did not allow this for the Sacred Precinct because of the verse *the idolaters are indeed unclean* [Q. 9:28]. The Shāfiʿīs made a distinction between the Sacred Mosque and other mosques. *For them in this world is degradation*: slaying and capture; *and in the Hereafter a mighty chastisement*.

[2:115] *To God belong the East and the West*; and so if you are barred from the Sacred Mosque or the Aqṣā Mosque, then *whithersoever you turn* towards the *qibla*, *there is the Face of God*: the prayer direction which He has enjoined. *Truly, God is Embracing*: surrounding creation with mercy; *Knowing* of their deeds. Ibn ʿUmar (may God be pleased with him) related that this was revealed about the traveller's prayer.[1]

Q. 2:115 [2:116] *And they say*—the Jews about Ezra, the Christians about Christ, and the idolaters about angels—*'God has taken to*, made for, *Himself a son.' Glory be to Him!* Transcendent be He above such a thing! *Nay, to Him belongs all that is in the heavens and the earth* by creation and dominion, including those three; *all obey His will*.

[2:117] *Originator of the heavens and the earth*: their maker without the need for material or time. The word *badīʿ* (originator) is not derived from the morphological form denoting the active participle of the verb, but rather denotes an attribute of the Divine pronoun which is broader than a mere participle, since the Attribute is His even outside the moment of the act, in the sense that He always has the power to create. *And when He decrees*—wills—*a thing, He but says to it 'Be!'*—'Occur!'—*and it is*: it occurs. This does not mean a literal utterance, but rather is a representation of how the object of His will is actualised instantaneously without delay. The root meaning of *qaḍā'* (decree) is 'to complete something', whether a word or deed. It is used in a general sense to denote the attachment of His will to the existence of something, which necessitates it.

[2:118] *And they who do not know*—the idolaters or the Jews—*say, 'Why does God not speak to us* directly; *why does a sign not come to us*: such as the springing forth of rivers*?'* It should not be asked why He did not answer them so that they would believe, because the All-Wise does not go against

1 Where the traveller may pray while riding, facing whichever direction the animal is headed.

the dictate of His wisdom at the request or suggestion of an ignorant person; and He had already given them ample signs. *So spoke those before them*, the disbelievers, *the like of what they say*: such as asking to be shown God; *their hearts are much alike* in their obstinacy. *Yet We have made clear the signs to a people who are certain*: who seek certitude.

[2:119] *We have sent you* adorned *with the truth, a bearer of glad tidings* of forgiveness, *and a warner* of chastisement. *You shall not be asked about the inhabitants of Hell-fire*: about why they did not believe. He was forbidden to ask about their state because of the horror of it.

[2:120] *Never will the Jews be pleased with you, neither the Christians, not until you follow their creed*: a creed (*milla*) is the means God established for His servants to reach His presence. It is used here to refer to falsehood, to highlight the opposition between them. *Say: 'God's guidance* with which He has sent me *is the true guidance.' And if you were to follow their* false *whims, after the knowledge that has come to you, you would have against God neither friend, nor helper* to repel His chastisement from you.

[2:121] *Those to whom We have given the Book*, the believers among Q. 2:119
them, *and who recite it with true recitation* free from distortion or omission, *they believe in it*: in their Book or in the Qur'ān; *and whoever disbelieves in it, they shall be the losers.*

[2:122] *O Children of Israel, remember My favour wherewith I favoured you, and that I have preferred you over all the worlds*: all the people of your time.

[2:123] *And beware of a day when no soul shall for another be requited, and no compensation shall be accepted from it, nor any intercession shall benefit it*—the second soul—*neither shall they be helped.*

[2:124] *And* remember *when his Lord tested Abraham*: commandments for one such as him[1] were essentially tests, and so He addressed us here in a way we could understand. The root meaning of *ibtilā'* (test) is to charge with a difficult task; *with certain words*: this means laws (*sharā'iʿ*), since 'words' can signify 'concepts'. Or it refers to ten virtuous habits; five regarding the head: cutting the moustache, washing out the mouth and nose, cleaning the teeth and combing the hair; and five regarding the rest of the body: trimming the nails, plucking armpit hair, shaving pubic hair, circumcision, and washing with water after answering the call of nature. Or it refers to the rites of the *ḥajj*, or to thirty virtuous traits: ten in *Those who repent*...and so on [Q. 9:112]; ten in *Truly, the*

1 Reading *mithlihi* rather than *mas'ala*, as in Maḥmūd b. Abī al-Ḥasan al-Naysābūrī, *Ījāz al-bayān ʿan maʿānī al-Qur'ān*, Riyadh: Maktabat al-Tawba, 1997, vol. 1, p. 117.

people who have submitted...and so on [Q. 33:35], which includes humility in a general sense; and ten in *Truly, prosperous are the believers*...and so on [Q. 23:1–11], which includes humility in prayer. In this case, the word *sā'iḥūn* [in Q. 9:112] would be taken to mean 'those who seek knowledge' rather than 'those who fast', to avoid repetition. *And he fulfilled them*: carried them out in full. *He said*—his Lord said to him—*'I shall make you a leader for the people* until the Day of Resurrection.*' Said he, 'And of my seed?'* Will You make some of them leaders, too? The word *dhurriyya* (seed) is from *dharr*, meaning 'differentiation', or *dhar'*, meaning 'creation'. *He*—God—*said, 'My covenant shall not reach the evildoers'*: implying that some of them would not be fit for it. This is evidence that the prophets are divinely protected from major sins even before their missions begin, and that iniquitous people are not fit for leadership.

Q. 2:125

[2:125] *And when We appointed the House*, the Kaʿba, *to be a place of visitation* (*mathāba*)—a place that is returned to time and again, or a place of reward (*thawāb*)—*for the people, and a sanctuary* for the fearful, or from the chastisement of the Hereafter. Abū Ḥanīfa said that it means a place where criminals who seek refuge there may not be arrested until they leave. So flock to it, and *'Take to yourselves Abraham's station*—the well-known stone there—*for a place of prayer'*: it is said that this means the Sacred Mosque, since all of the Sacred Precinct is a place of prayer, and so it is from the Sunna to pray behind it to seek blessing and emulation. The verb 'take' here can also be read in the past tense: the people took to themselves the Kaʿba as a *qibla*. *And We made a covenant with Abraham and Ishmael* commanding them: *'Purify My House* of all that does not befit it *for those that shall go round it*, those who shall circle it or visit it from afar, *and those that cleave to it*, sit in it, *and those who bow and prostrate themselves*: meaning those who pray in it.*'*

[2:126] *And when Abraham said, 'My Lord, make this* place *a land secure*: He used the indefinite article here and the definite in *Sūrat Ibrāhīm*,[1] although that *sūra* was revealed in Mecca and this in Medina, because here it refers to the time when it was a barren place, while there it refers to when it was a settled place. *And provide its people with fruits* for their comfort; *such of them as believe in God and the Last Day.' He*—God—*said, 'And* I shall also provide for *whoever disbelieves,* but *to him I shall give enjoyment, a little* in his paltry worldly life; *then I shall compel him to the chastisement of the Fire—how evil a journey's end!'*

1 *And when Abraham said, 'My Lord, make this land secure...'* (Q. 14:35).

[2:127] *And when Abraham raised up the foundations of the House, and Ishmael with him*: as he passed the stones to him, he said, *'Our Lord, receive this*—our act of construction—*from us. Truly, You are the Hearing* of our prayers, *the Knowing* of our intentions.

[2:128] *'Our Lord, and make us submissive to You*: make us ever more subservient to You; *and* make *of our seed a community submissive to You; and show us*—teach us—*our holy rites* for the *ḥajj*, *and relent to us* for our shortcomings; or refer to the forthcoming commentary on *God has truly relented...* [Q. 9:117]. *Truly, You are the Relenting, the Merciful*: this was discussed earlier.

[2:129] *'Our Lord, and send among them*—among that community—*a messenger, one of them*: the only messenger sent from their progeny was our Prophet (may God bless him and grant him peace); *who shall recite to them Your signs, and teach them the Book*, the Qur'ān, *and wisdom*, knowledge and action according to it; *and purify them* from iniquity. *You are the Mighty*: the Dominant; *the Wise* Who puts things in their proper places.'

Q. 2:127

[2:130] *Who*—that is, no one—*therefore shrinks from the creed of Abraham*: the word *milla* (creed) has already been explained; it is the source of the Law with respect to how the prophet dictates it to his community. *Dīn* (religion) is synonymous to it with respect to the acceptance of the people to whom it is issued. *Sharīʿa* (Law) means the particular edicts which rectify the earthly lives and other-worldly lives of those people, whether directly issued by the Lawgiver or inferred from those which are directly issued. [*Who therefore shrinks from the creed of Abraham*] *except he who fools*—humiliates, ignores or ruins—*himself?* It could also be read as 'except he who is himself a fool'. *Truly, We chose him in this world, and in the Hereafter he shall be among the righteous*: those of perfect righteousness.

[2:131] And remember *When his Lord said to him, 'Submit*: surrender your affairs to God*'*; *he said, 'I have submitted*—surrendered my affairs—*to the Lord of the Worlds.'*

[2:132] *And Abraham enjoined upon his sons*—Ishmael, Isaac, Midian and Medan—*this* creed; *tawṣiyya* (enjoining) means to present something to someone else which he can utilise for his benefit; *and* [*so did*] *Jacob* to his twelve sons, saying, *'My sons, God has chosen for you the* [*true*] *religion, so see that you die not save in submission'*: hold true to submission until you die.

[2:133] *Or* indeed *were you witnesses when death came to Jacob?* This rebuts the claim of the Jews that Jacob enjoined Judaism upon his children when he died. *When he said to his sons, 'What will you worship after me?' They said, 'We will worship your God and the God of your fathers Abraham and Ishmael*—he mentioned him because of the close association—*and Isaac: One God*—that is, the God of all these people was One and the Same—*to Him we submit.'*

[2:134] *That*—Abraham, Jacob and their progeny—*is a community that has passed away; theirs is what they have earned, and yours*, O Jews, *is what you have earned* and your claim of kinship to them will not avail you. A *ḥadīth* says, 'O scions of Hāshim, do not let the people come to Me offering their deeds, while you come to Me offering naught but your lineage!' *You shall not be asked about what they did*: you shall neither incur their sins nor share the reward of their good deeds.

[2:135] *And they*, the People of the Book, *say* to the Muslims, *'Be Jews or Christians, and you shall be guided'*: this either means that each group says each part respectively, or that the Jews say it all. *Say: 'Nay, rather* we shall follow *the creed of Abraham, a ḥanīf*: one who inclines away from falsehood; *and he was not of the idolaters*: despite what you say.*'*

[2:136] *Say*, O believers, *'We believe in God, and in that which has been revealed to us*, the Qur'ān, *and* the revelation that was *revealed to Abraham,*
Q. 2:134 *Ishmael, Isaac, Jacob, and the Tribes*, the sons of Jacob, among whom were prophets, *and that which was given to Moses, and Jesus, and the prophets*, all of them, *from their Lord. We make no division between any of them* regarding their prophethood, unlike the Jews, *and to Him*—to God—*we submit'* and surrender.

[2:137] *And if they*, the People of the Book, *believe in the like of what you believe in*: this is an implicit denial, similar to *then bring a sūra like it* [Q. 2:23], or it means 'if they believe in the same way as you do'; *then they are truly guided; but if they turn away, then they are clearly in schism*: dispute. *God will suffice you against them*: the future tense imparted certainty, even if it would not be immediate; *He is the Hearer, the Knower.*

[2:138] Hold to *the dye of God*: the disposition upon which He created people, which means common sense or the recognition of justice and the pursuit of truth. Some said it means purification, and that this is a figure of speech where something is referred to by a different word because of its association with it. The Christians immerse their children in saffron-dyed water, claiming that it initiates them into Christianity. *And who*, no one, *has a better dye*, disposition, *than God? And* [say]: *'Him do we worship.'*

[2:139] *Say* to the People of the Book*: 'Would you then dispute with us concerning* the religion of *God, though He is our Lord and your Lord? Our deeds belong to us, and your deeds belong to you*, and each will be rewarded for their deeds; *and to Him we are sincerely devoted* in faith, while you are not.*'*

[2:140] Or indeed *do you say that Abraham, Ishmael, Isaac and Jacob, and the Tribes—they were Jews* in the eyes of the Jews, *or Christians* in the eyes of the Christians? *Say: 'Have you then greater knowledge, or has God?* For He has said, *Abraham in truth was not a Jew, neither a Christian* [Q. 3:67]. *And who*—no one—*does greater injustice than he who conceals a testimony received from God?* They concealed God's testimony regarding those people [the aforementioned prophets and the Tribes], as the Torah affirmed that they were neither Jews nor Christians. *And God is not heedless of what you do.'*

[2:141] *That is a community that has passed away; theirs is what they have earned, and yours is what you have earned; you shall not be asked about what they did*: He repeated this for emphasis and to rebuke the many people who claim righteousness through their forebears.

[2:142] *The fools among the people*—the ignorant people, whether among the Jews or the idolaters of Mecca—*will say*, that is, they have said and will continue to say, *'What has turned them from the qibla they were facing in their prayers formerly?'* This means the Rock [in Jerusalem]. The root meaning of *qibla* is 'to be receptive towards', but it came to mean a place that is faced during prayer. Q. 2:141 *Say: 'To God belong the East and the West*: the requirement of a *qibla* does not mean that one particular place is His and no other, but is only a command to be followed. *He guides whomever He will to a straight path*: dictated by His wisdom.'

[2:143] *Thus*, just as We guided you to it, *We appointed you a midmost community*: meaning a just one. The root meaning of *wasaṭ* (middle) is the point of a thing that is equally distant from its sides. The word then came to be used to denote praiseworthy traits, and then to denote a person endowed with such traits. The verse indicates that consensus is a valid legal proof. *That you might be witnesses to the people* in conveying the message of all the messengers, *and that the Messenger might be a witness over you* and thereby cause you to grow in purity. He said *over* in order to convey a sense of both protection and observation. *And We did not appoint the qibla you were facing* at first in Mecca, since before the Emigration that was the prayer direction, while afterwards it was the Rock; or your heart inclined towards it, namely the Kaʿba, which is why he would place himself so that the Kaʿba was between him and the Rock before the Emigration, as Ibn ʿAbbās related; *except that We might know*—that Our knowledge might be manifested when the prayer direction was changed—*who followed the Messenger* distinctly *from him who turned on his heels* and apostatised, as many did. *For it*, the change of prayer direction, *was a grave thing*, difficult to bear, *save for those whom God guided. But God would never cause your faith to be wasted*: your faith in the first *qibla* or your prayers towards it. *Truly, God is Gentle*—full of mercy—*with people, Merciful*: He delayed the latter Name to close the verse with it.

[2:144] *Indeed, We have seen you turning your face about in* the direction of *the heaven* awaiting revelation decreeing that the *qibla* be changed to the Kaʿba, not out of vain desire but in expectation of the fulfilment of a promise already made. *Now We will surely turn you to a qibla that shall satisfy you*, so that you will assent with natural love and not mere subservience. *Turn your face towards the Sacred Mosque* (*al-masjid al-ḥarām*) wherein fighting and such matters are forbidden (*muḥarram*). The reason He mentioned the Mosque rather than the Kaʿba itself was that this verse was revealed in Medina, and the distant person must face a direction that encompasses the object he is facing. In other words, the Kaʿba is to sit between two imaginary lines stretching out from his eyes, like the two sides of a triangle.

NOTE: Know that there is consensus that when the Kaʿba is in view, it is obligatory to face exactly towards it. As for when it is out of view so that one must employ reasoning, there is a difference of opinion. Abū Ḥanīfa and Aḥmad (may God be pleased with them) said that one must employ reasoning to find the general direction (*jiha*). Mālik said that the people in
Q. 2:144 the Sacred Mosque must face the Kaʿba itself, while the people in Mecca must face the Mosque, the people in the Sacred Precinct must face Mecca, and the people of all the rest of the world must face the Sacred Precinct. The companions of Shāfiʿī (may God be pleased with him) differed in their understanding of his statements about whether the exact or the general direction must be sought. The apparent meaning of the imam's words, and what we have been taught, is that turning one's face towards something means directing it towards its exact location if it is visible, or towards the direction one believes it to be if it is not visible. This means that when reasoning is employed, its object is the general direction, just as the other imams said, except that he said that the way to face it when it is not visible is to turn towards the direction of its exact location. And God knows best. *And wherever you are, turn your faces towards it* when you pray.

NOTE: This verse has been cited by those who hold that it is not permitted to pray obligatory prayers inside the Kaʿba, and also by those who say the opposite. The former argument is that someone who prays an obligatory prayer inside the Kaʿba is facing part of it but facing away from another part of it, which means that he is not entirely facing it, and therefore his prayer is not valid. The latter argument is that if the word *ḥaythumā* (wherever) is universal, it must include anyone who is inside the Kaʿba, who would be commanded to face it while inside it; and if such a person were to do this as well as he was able to, he would fulfil the requirement. And if the word is not universal, then it must not cover such a situation, which means it cannot be cited as proof regarding it. A rebuttal of the former argument is that it is valid to pray directly in front of the Kaʿba outside it. A rebuttal of the second argument is that one could argue that such a person is commanded to exit the Kaʿba first, because anything that is required for the completion of an obligation is itself obligatory. And God knows best.

NOTE: The Kaʿba is the collection of bodies—roof, walls and floor—while the *qibla* is the space which those bodies occupy. If the building were demolished, it would still be valid to pray towards their site from outside it. As for praying inside that space in such a situation, there is a difference of opinion. And God knows best.

Truly, those who have been given the Book, the Torah, *know that it*, this change of prayer direction, *is the truth from their Lord*, because it is stated in their Books that he would pray towards two *qiblas*. *God is not heedless of what you do* by concealing this.

[2:145] *Yet if you should bring to those who have been given the Book every sign*
proving that the Kaʿba is a *qibla*, *they will not follow your qibla* out of envy; Q. 2:145
and you are not a follower of their qibla: the Rock for the Jews and the East
for the Christians—He referred to them as a single direction because they
are equally false; *neither are they followers of one another's qibla*. *If you were to*
follow their whims in their prayer directions *after the knowledge that has come to*
you through revelation, *then you would surely be among the evildoers* like them;
this is meant to instil fear in us.

[2:146] *Those to whom We have given the Book recognise him*, Muḥammad (may God bless him and grant him peace), *as they recognise their sons*: without any doubt. *There is a party of them that conceal the truth* of his description, *while they know* that it is present in their Books.

[2:147] *The truth comes from your Lord; then be not*—you and your community—*among the doubters* in what We have told you.

[2:148] *Every person* from the People of the Book *has his direction*—*qibla*—*to which he turns* his face, and each has worldly deeds which will lead him to God if he fulfils their requirements. *So vie with one another in good deeds* by following the commandments of God Almighty. *Wherever you may be*—People of the Book—*God will bring you altogether* by seizing your spirits or gathering you. *Truly, God has power over all things*.

[2:149] *From whatever place you issue* to travel, *turn your face towards the Sacred Mosque* when you pray. *It*, this command, *is the truth from your Lord*. *God is not heedless of what you do*.

[2:150] *From whatever place you issue, turn your face towards the Sacred*

Mosque; and wherever you may be, turn your faces towards it: He repeated this to dispel the suspicion that it might have been abrogated, and because each instance has its own purpose: the first was to please the Messenger; second, every founder of a Law should have his own *qibla*; and the third was *so that there be not any argument from the people against you*: since the *qibla* of the promised prophet was the Kaᶜba; *excepting the evildoers among them*: such as the idolaters of Mecca, who said, 'He will return to our religion, just as he has returned to our *qibla*.' The intent was to dispel that argument. *So do not fear them*—those evildoers—*but fear Me; and* another purpose of it is *that I may perfect My grace upon you*: meaning the fulfilment of the Law, or as a *ḥadīth* says, 'The perfection of grace is the entrance into the Garden'; *and that you may be guided* to what is right.

[2:151] *As*—this refers back to *that I may perfect*... [Q. 2:150]—*We have sent among you, of yourselves, a messenger to recite Our verses to you and to purify you* from blameworthy attributes, *and to teach you the Book*, the Qur'ān, *and
Q. 2:151 wisdom*, the Sunna, *and to teach you what you knew not*: what you could not know by mere thought.

[2:152] *So remember Me* with obedience, or at times of ease; *I will remember you* with forgiveness, or at times of difficulty. The word *dhikr* (to remember) describes a configuration of the soul that allows it to retain what it recognises, as well as the act of evoking something in the heart or on the tongue. The former is akin to *ḥifẓ* (memorisation), except that one has the sense of recollection, the other of preservation. *And be thankful to Me* by obeying Me, *and be not ungrateful towards Me* by disobeying Me; this explains why they both needed mentioning. Or the latter is a command to be constant in gratitude. Note that He commanded us to remember Him, but commanded the Children of Israel to remember His favours, because of the greater gnosis of this community. Note also that He said *be thankful to Me* rather than 'thank Me', because we cannot but fall short of reaching Him.

[2:153] *O you who believe, seek help* in the pursuit of the Hereafter *through patience* in obeying God and resisting the desires of the soul, which is the Greater Struggle (*al-jihād al-akbar*), *and prayer. Truly, God is with the patient*: providing them aid; this implies *a priori* that He must also be with those who pray.

[2:154] *And say not that those slain in God's way*—such as the martyrs of Badr—*are dead; rather, they are alive* with their Lord, *but you are not aware* of their state, because their life is not of the sort that can be sensed in animate beings, but can only be perceived by the intellect or by revelation. The truth is that after death or slaying, God provides the animate body with subtle sustenance and places it where He wills, whether in ʿIllyyīn or Sijjīn. This will be further explained in *Sūrat Āl ʿImrān* [Q. 3].

[2:155] *Surely We will try you*, afflict you for the purpose of testing, *with something* little *of fear* of the enemy, which was small compared to that from which He protected them, *and hunger*, such as famine, *and diminution of goods and lives* by death, sickness and old age, *and fruits* by blights; *yet give glad tidings*, O Muḥammad, *to the patient* among them.

[2:156] *Those who, when they are struck by an affliction*—a *ḥadīth* says, 'Everything that hurts the believer is an affliction for him'—*say*, whether with their tongues or their hearts, *'Truly, we belong to God* as slaves or property, *and to Him we will return*: to be requited.*'*

[2:157] *Upon those rest blessings* of ample forgiveness *and mercy*—kindness—*from their Lord, and those—they are the truly guided* to what is right.

[2:158] *Truly, Ṣafā and Marwa*—two mountains in Mecca upon which sat two idols, Isāf and Nāʾila, which made the Muslims hesitant to perform Q. 2:155
the rite of rushing between them because of their association with customs of the age of ignorance—*are among the waymarks of God*, the signs of His rites, *so whoever makes the ḥajj to the House, or the ʿumra*: the root meaning of *ḥajj* (pilgrimage) is 'to intend', and *iʿtimār* (visitation) means 'to add'. In the Law, they came to signify the special pilgrimage and visit to the Sacred House. *He would not be at fault if he circumambulated them*: this is proof of lawfulness, which is part of the meaning of obligation, for it means that it is not forbidden or reprehensible. The obligation of the act is affirmed by the Sunna. *And whoever volunteers good* by performing an act of obedience or going beyond his obligation, *God is Grateful* and will reward his good deed, *Knowing* of his states.

[2:159] *Those who conceal*, meaning the Jews, *the clear proofs and the guidance that We have revealed after We have shown them clearly in the Book*, the Torah, *they shall be cursed by God, and cursed by those who curse*: that is, by all those who issue curses, even the disbelievers, for on the Day of Resurrection they will curse one another. The word *laʿn* (curse) means 'to reject angrily'. When it comes from God, it is chastisement in the Hereafter and severance from the reception of His grace in this world. When it comes from anyone other than God, it means a prayer directed against another person.

[2:160] *Except those that repent* of this concealment, *and make amends* by rectifying what they have corrupted, *and show clearly* what they have concealed; *to them I shall turn relenting*: I shall accept their repentance. *I am the Relenting, the Merciful*, as was discussed earlier.

[2:161] *But those who disbelieve, and die disbelieving—upon them shall be the curse of God and the angels, and of people altogether*: even the adherents of their own religion, as was explained.

[2:162] *Abiding therein*: in that curse. *The chastisement shall not be lightened for them, and no respite shall be given them.*

When the Quraysh said, 'Muḥammad, describe your Lord to us,' the following verse was revealed:

[2:163] *Your God is One God*: He repeated the word *God* to affirm the Oneness of divinity, and then further dispelled the notion that there could be any other God than Him by saying *there is no god except Him, the Compassionate, the Merciful.* Then they said, 'If you are truthful, show us a sign.' So He revealed:

[2:164] *Truly, in the creation of the heavens*, which are plural with respect to their levels, *and the earth, and the contrast of the night and day* between light and dark and the like, or their alternation, *and the ships that run in the sea*
Q. 2:161 *with what profits people* in their commerce and the like. He mentioned ships before wind and clouds because the purpose is to evoke the profit of the sea, which comes principally from ships. *And the water God sends down from the heaven with which He revives the earth* with plants *after it is dead, and He scatters abroad in it all manner of crawling thing; and the disposition of the winds*: how they blow in different directions and with differing strengths; *and the clouds compelled*: bent to God's command—the word *saḥāb* (clouds) comes from *saḥb* (to drag) because of how they pull one another around; *between heaven and the earth—surely there are signs* of His Oneness and Omnipotence *for a folk who comprehend*: who use the intellect for its intended purpose.

[2:165] *Yet there be people who take to themselves compeers besides God*: such as idols or priests. A *nadd* (compeer) means something that is similar to something else in its substance. *Loving them* and revering them *as God is loved* and revered; that is, loving them as much as they love God, for the idolater recognises Him but associates other things with Him; or loving them as much as the believer loves God, or as much as they ought to love Him. *But those who believe love God more ardently*, because in times of tribulation the disbelievers forsake their false gods. *Maḥabba* (love) comes from *ḥabb* (seed), used figuratively to mean the seed of the heart because of how firmly it is planted therein. Conventionally, it means your desire for what you deem to be good, whether for enjoyment (*And they give food, despite [their] love of it* [Q. 76:8]) or for benefit (*And another which you love: help from God* [Q. 61:13]) or for virtue (as is the case here). God's love for the servant means His desire to honour him and give him the grace to obey Him. *If those who did evil could but see*, if they could but know, *as they shall when they behold the chastisement* at the Resurrection, *that power altogether belongs to God, and that God is terrible in chastisement*, they would see an awful sight.

[2:166] *When those who were followed disown their followers, and they have seen the chastisement, and* because of the disbelief *the cords are cut away before them*: the cords of connection that existed between them and their followers and all others. The root meaning of *sabab* (cord) is the rope used to guide a tree's growth.

[2:167] *And those who followed say*—expressing a vainglorious wish, as was discussed before—*'Oh, if only we might return again* to the world *and disown them*—the followers—*as they have disowned us* in the Hereafter.*'* *Thus*, by this awful sight, *shall God show them their deeds, anguish*, regret, *for them!* They shall see nothing but regrets in place of deeds. *Never shall they exit from the Fire*: it is worded this way, rather than 'they shall not exit', to stress the impossibility of their exit.

Q. 2:166

[2:168] *O people, eat of what is in the earth, lawful and wholesome*: lawful is what the Law declares good, and wholesome is what upright nature deems good, unlike, for example, eating when one is already full. *And follow not the steps*—the paths—*of Satan*: do not rely on him to determine what is lawful and forbidden, nor declare pleasant food or clothing to be unlawful for yourselves. *He is a manifest foe to you*: an obvious enemy to those who possess insight.

[2:169] *He only commands you to evil and indecency*: his command is figurative in the sense that he tempts you to do evil; the choice of expression serves as a mockery of their perspective. Evil (*sū'*) is what the intellect disdains, or a sin for which there is no prescribed punishment in the Law; and indecency (*faḥshā'*) is what the Law disdains, or a sin for which there is a prescribed punishment. *And that you should speak against God what you do not know*: such as associating partners with Him, or forbidding that which is lawful or vice versa.

[2:170] *And when it is said to them, 'Follow what God has revealed,' they say, 'No! But we follow what we found our fathers doing.' What?* Will they follow them, *even if their fathers did not understand anything* by the attainment of acquired knowledge, *nor were they guided* by following those who did understand*?* This indicates that the one who is qualified to engage in independent reasoning is not permitted to blindly follow the opinion of another.

[2:171] *The likeness of* you and *those who disbelieve is as the likeness of one who shouts to that* animal *which hears*—understands—*nothing, save a call and a cry* from the caller without understanding its meaning. *Deaf* to hearing the truth, *dumb* to speaking it, *blind* to seeing its ways; *they do not comprehend*: He likened them to animals, and then to madmen.

[2:172] *O you who believe, eat of the good things*—the delicious or the lawful things—*wherewith We have provided you*: this is a command of permissibility, or it could denote obligation, such as eating in times of dire hunger, or recommendation, such as joining a guest in a meal. *And give thanks to God* for making them lawful, *if it be Him that you worship*.

He then makes clear what is forbidden by saying:

[2:173] *He has only forbidden you: carrion*, meaning an animal that dies without being slaughtered lawfully; *blood* spilled from the veins; *the flesh of swine* as well as every other part—He mentioned flesh, in particular, because that is the major part of it; *what has been hallowed*—called over with a raised voice when being slaughtered—*to other than God*: such as to an idol. *Yet whoever is compelled* to eat any of these, *neither rebelling*, whether
Q. 2:172 rebelling against the ruler, seizing it from another needy person, or eating it out of greed or desire, *nor transgressing* by having been led into this situation by a sinful motive such as a forbidden journey, or eating more of it than he needs to in order to stay alive, *no sin shall be on him* if he consumes it. So the justification for the permission is dire need along with obedience. The intent here was to confine the forbidden to those things mentioned out of all the things they had permitted themselves; it was not supposed to be exhaustive. *God is Forgiving, Merciful.*

[2:174] *Those who conceal what God has revealed of the Book*, such as the leaders of the Jews, *and sell it for a little price*, the profits they obtain from their subordinates, *they shall consume nothing in their bellies but the Fire*: the bribes they take will become fire inside their bellies, but they will not sense this before they die. *God shall not speak to them on the Day of Resurrection* with any words that will please them, *neither purify them*: cleanse them of pollutants; *and theirs is a painful chastisement*.

[2:175] *Those are they that have bought error at the price of guidance* in this world, *and chastisement at the price of forgiveness* in the Hereafter; *what makes them so patient for the Fire?* This expresses incredulity at their boldness to engage in action that will only send them to Hell.

[2:176] *That* chastisement *is because God has revealed the Book with the truth; and those that are at variance regarding the Book*, by believing in some parts of it but not others, and such things, *are in schism*, conflict, *far removed* from the truth. So when the People of the Book continued to argue at length about the matter of the *qibla*, He revealed:

[2:177] *Piety is not* merely *that you turn your faces* during prayer *to the East*, for the Christians, *and to the West*, for the Jews, based on the location of Mecca. *Piety is [that of] the one who believes in God and the Last Day*, and so does not invent lies about Him: what this means is that prayer comes after faith; *and the angels*, and so does not oppose any of them; *and the Book*, and so does not corrupt it; *and the prophets*, and so does not differentiate between them; *and who gives of his substance, however cherished*—this could also be understood as 'and gives of his substance, out of love for God'—*to kinsmen, and orphans, and the needy*: this was explained earlier; *and the wayfarer*: the traveller who does not have the means to get back home, or the guest, since he is also a wayfarer of a kind; *and beggars*: those who have to resort to begging; *and for* the freeing of *slaves*: such as manumission contracts and ransoms for captives—there is consensus that if a Muslim is in need, then once *zakāt* has been paid it is obligatory to devote funds to that need; *and who observes the prayer and pays the* obligatory *zakāt*: the things mentioned before this were meant either to clarify where it should be distributed, or to describe recommended forms of charity; *and those* Q. 2:177
who fulfil their covenant when they have engaged in a covenant: the style changes here because the former items were things that can only be known from the Law, while the latter items can be deduced by the intellect; *and those who endure with fortitude*: the noun *ṣābirīn* here is in the *naṣb* state[1] to impart praise because of the special virtue of fortitude; *misfortune*, meaning poverty, *hardship*, meaning tribulations and illness, *and peril*, meaning war with the disbelievers, *are the ones who are truthful* in their faith, *and they are the ones who are fearful*.

The verse is a summary of the essential human perfections, which are: sound beliefs, good social relationships and self-refinement. Know that Abū Dharr (may God be pleased with him) asked the Prophet (may God bless him and grant him peace) about piety, and in reply he recited this verse to him. On another occasion, when Wābiṣa asked him about it, he replied, 'It is what puts the heart at ease, and the soul at ease.' This was because the first was asking about the nature of piety, the second about the pursuit of it.

Once in the time of the age of ignorance, conflict broke out between two tribes. One tribe vowed that they would kill a free man in retaliation for any slave of theirs who was killed, and a man for a woman, and two free men for one free man. Then later when they took the matter to the Prophet (may God bless him and grant him peace), God revealed:

1 As though it were the object of an unspoken verb.

[2:178] *O you who believe, prescribed*—obligatory—*for you is retaliation* like-for-like *regarding the slain*, that is, We have obliged that the guilty party be made subject to it: *a free man* is to be killed *for a free man, and a slave for a slave, and a female for a female*. This does not mean that a free man should not be killed for killing a slave, nor a man for killing a woman, nor the opposite, for a text should only be taken to have exclusive import when there does not seem to be any reason for the specific things it mentions to be singled out other than that the ruling applies to them exclusively. The reason Mālik and Shāfiʿī (may God be pleased with them) ruled that a free man should not be killed for killing a slave was the *ḥadīth* of ʿAlī and the action of Abū Bakr and ʿUmar (may God be pleased with them), based on an analogy with the ruling for external body parts. As for the opinion that a Muslim should not be killed for killing a non-Muslim citizen, it is also based on a *ḥadīth* of ʿAlī. This is not abrogated by the verse *a life for a life*… [Q. 5:45], because that is only a description of the ruling in the Torah.
Q. 2:178
But if anyone is pardoned by his brother: that is, if a murderer is pardoned for the blood of his victim, such as if the retribution is foregone or one of the heirs pardons him—what this means is pardoning in return for blood money. The soundest position in the Shāfiʿī school is that retaliation is obligatory, but blood money can be accepted in place of it. *Let the pursuing be honourable, and let the payment to him be with excellence*: let the one who pardons pursue the blood money honourably, and let the pardoned one pay the blood money without delay. *That* allowance for accepting blood money *is an alleviation given by your Lord, and a mercy; and for him who commits aggression* by killing again *after that* pardon, *his is a painful chastisement* in both worlds.

[2:179] *In retaliation there is life for you, O people of pith, so that you might fear*: the law of relation is a crucial means of saving life, because it is a deterrent against murder, and so it is necessary for the sake of saving the lives of both parties. This placement of a thing in the position of its opposite is the height of eloquence and rhetorical brilliance. It is said that the Arabs would refuse to hand over murderers to the authorities because they feared to lose one of their tribe, but this verse implied that handing them over would cause their numbers to increase; and indeed this can be seen in the low numbers of the Abbasids compared to the high numbers of the Alids. This is why it is said that the sword gives life.

[2:180] *Prescribed*—obligated—*for you, when any of you is approached by death*, meaning the things which lead to it, *and leaves behind some good*, meaning wealth or much wealth—it is called *good* to indicate that testaments are recommended for goodly property—*is to make a testament*, a bequest, *in favour of his parents and kinsmen*: they do not overlap, since a kinsman is a second-level relative or beyond; *honourably*: with justice and without giving preference to the wealthy, or going beyond a third of total wealth. Such is *an obligation on those that fear.* This was in the early period of Islam, but it was abrogated by the verse about heirs, as is shown by the *ḥadīth*, 'God has given each person his right. Let there be no bequest to any heir.'

[2:181] *Then if anyone changes it*—the bequest—*after hearing it* from the deceased person, *the sin* of changing it *shall rest upon those who change it. Truly, God is Hearing, Knowing* of your testaments and their alterations.

[2:182] *But if anyone fears*—knows of—*injustice or sin from one making a testament*, such as if they err from justice by preferring a rich person or the like, *and so makes things right between them*—between the heirs and the recipient of the bequest—*then no sin shall be upon him* for doing so. *Truly, God is Forgiving, Merciful.*

[2:183] *O you who believe, prescribed*—obligated—*for you is the fast*: the
fast of Ramaḍān, or fasting three days of every month, or ʿĀshūrā', which Q. 2:181
were subsequently abrogated by the fast of Ramaḍān; *just as it was prescribed for those that were before you* from the time of Noah: this refers to the essence of fasting, not its particular mode; *so that you might guard yourselves* from sin, for it straitens the passages of Satan.

[2:184] *For days numbered:* fast for a few days, or for days whose number is ordained; *and if any of you be sick, or be on a journey*—in contrast to those who begin their journey during it—*then a number of other days*: fast the same number of days you missed; *and for those who are able to do it* because they are in good health and not travelling, *a redemption* if they do not fast: *the feeding of a poor person* with a *mudd* of food, or according to the jurists of Iraq a half *ṣāʿ* of wheat or a *ṣāʿ* of another foodstuff. So at first they were given the choice between fasting and feeding, but then this was abrogated and only fasting was allowed. *For him who volunteers good* by feeding even more people, *that is good for him; but that you should fast* if you are able *is better for you, if you but knew* of its virtues.

[2:185] *The month of Ramaḍān*: this is the subject of the sentence, a proper noun composed of several words. It can also be called 'Ramaḍān' alone without *the month of*, as for the two months of Rabīʿ. It is called Ramaḍān because of how the people were consumed (*irtimāḍ*) by hunger and thirst during it. The month of Shawwāl got its name from *shawl* (to work, to carry), because of how the camel-breeders would do their work at that time of year. Dhū al-Qaʿda is named after *quʿūd* (to sit), because

they would refrain from war at that time. Dhū al-Ḥijja is named after the *ḥajj*, which takes place during it. Muḥarram is named for the banning (*taḥrīm*) of fighting during it. Ṣafar is named after *ṣifr* (naught), because of how Mecca would be emptied of its men during the month as they went out to fight. The two months of Rabīʿ are named after *irtibāʿ* (to reside), because of how the people would stay at home during them. The two months of Jumādā are named after *jumūd* (to freeze), because of how the water would freeze during them. Rajab is named after *tarjib* (veneration), because of how they would venerate the month. Shaʿbān is named after *tashaʿʿub* (to disperse), because of how the tribes would disperse during it. The word *shahr* (month) is named after *shuhūr* (renown), because of how they would look for the new moon and then spread the news of its arrival. The predicate of the sentence is: *is that wherein the Qur'ān was revealed*: that is, revealed about it, or revealed on the Night of Ordainment (*laylat al-qadr*) or the twenty-fourth of it, all at once to the lowest heaven, after which it was revealed piecemeal. The scriptures (*ṣuḥuf*) of Abraham were
Q. 2:185 also revealed on the first of it, and the Torah on the sixth, and the Gospel on the thirteenth. *A guidance for the people* by its miraculous nature, *and as clear proofs*—signs—*of the* sum of *Guidance* to the true edicts (so this is not a case of an indefinite noun being repeated as definite,[1] such as 'he is a scholar, and one of the erudite scholars'); *and the Criterion* between truth and falsehood. *So let those of you who are present at the month*—that is, during it—*fast it*: He did not say 'fast during it' to indicate that the entire day must be fasted. *And if any of you be sick* so that it would be difficult to fast, *or on a journey, then a number of other days*: this abrogates the earlier verse, because it excludes the permission for the person who is not travelling. *God desires ease for you, and desires not hardship for you*, and so He has excused you from fasting in those two instances; *and* He has ordained these edicts *that you fulfil the number*: the number of days in the month by making up for what you miss; *and magnify God for having guided you and that you might be thankful*: this is the reason for the allowance, while what preceded it is the reason for the obligatory make-up, and what preceded that is for the command to observe the full number.

When the Prophet was asked, 'Is our Lord near that we might engage in intimate discourse with Him, or is He distant?' the [following] verse was revealed:

1 In other words, the first instance of *guidance* in the verse does not refer to the exact same thing as the second.

[2:186] *And when My servants question you concerning Me,* tell them: *I am near*: watching over you. *I answer the call of the caller when he calls to Me. So let them respond to Me* when I call them to obey Me with their bodies; *and let them believe in Me*: let them remain constant in their faith in Me in their hearts; *that they might go aright* and be guided. When someone responds to Him in His commands, He will respond to them in their prayers, either by answering their request immediately, or storing it until the Hereafter, or protecting them from an equal evil, as a *ḥadīth* says. He said this rather than 'let them answer Me', though it would mean the same, in order to allude to how He will be pleased with them as long as they do their best to answer Him.

[2:187] *Permitted to you, upon the night of the fast, is to go in to your wives*: that is, to have sexual intercourse with them. Here He uses the word *rafath*, a somewhat vulgar term for sexual intercourse, unlike other places in the Qur'ān where other words are used, in order to allude to the vileness of how they would engage in this before it had been made permitted for them. *They are a vestment for you*, like a bed, *and you are a vestment for them*, Q. 2:186
like a blanket. This symbolises the difficulty of keeping away from them and how close the relationship between them is, or how each of them clothe the other from iniquity. *God knows that you have been betraying yourselves*: ʿUmar (may God be pleased with him) did it and then confessed to it, and so God made it lawful; *and so He has turned to you [relenting], and He has pardoned you* for that treachery. *So now* that it has been permitted you, *lie with them*: the term used here is *bāshara*, the root meaning of which is 'to put skin against skin'; *and seek what God has prescribed for you*: this could mean children, or the Night of Ordainment; *and eat and drink* throughout the night *until the white thread is distinct to you from the black thread at daybreak*: that is, until the white of true dawn is distinct from the black of night. This is proof that the person who is still in major ritual impurity when dawn arrives may still fast validly. *Then complete the fast to the night*: the exclusion of the night serves to negate the practice of continuous fasting. As for the unlawfulness of refraining from breaking the fast between two days, it is established by the Sunna. *And do not lie with them while you cleave to the mosques in devotion*: they used to enter the *iʿtikāf* vigil in the mosque and then go out to have sexual intercourse with their wives before returning to the mosque, but then this was forbidden. *Those* edicts *are God's bounds* between truth and falsehood; *do not approach them*: this is a figure of speech meaning that they should not be transgressed: that is, 'do not transgress from truth to falsehood'. Thus there is no need to object that most of

them are permissions, which cannot strictly be 'transgressed'. *Thus*, by this elucidation, *does God make clear His signs to people so that they might fear.*

[2:188] *Consume not your goods between you in deception*, by unlawful means, *and* do not *proffer them*—present them for judgement—*to the judges*: do not use them to influence them; *that you may consume a portion of other people's goods*, engaged *in sin*, such as false oaths, *while you are aware* that you are in the wrong.

When they asked about the wisdom of the cycle of the moon and how it waxes and wanes, and about the purpose of consecrated pilgrims entering their houses from the rear, the [following] verse was revealed:

[2:189] *They will ask you about the* purpose of *new moons*, and why they first appear slender and then grow. *Say* the purpose of them is that *'They are appointed times for the people and the ḥajj'*: the word *mawāqīt* (appointed times) is the plural of *mīqāt*, meaning a determined amount of time for a particular matter. The word *zamān* (time) means a divided period. The word *mudda* (period) means a duration determined by the movements of
Q. 2:188 the celestial bodies. *It is not piety to come to houses* in the consecrated state *from their rears*: for it was their custom to make passages at the back through which to enter and exit; *but piety is to fear* forbidden things. *Come to houses by their doors* even when in consecration, for it is not an act of piety to refrain from this; *and fear God, that you may prosper*: in hope of prosperity.

[2:190] *And fight in the way of God with those who fight against you*: who are barring you from the *ḥajj* this year, which was the year after Ḥudaybiya; *but aggress not* by beginning the fighting. *God loves not the aggressors* who transgress His bounds. This was abrogated by the verse about fighting.

[2:191] *And slay them wherever you come upon them*: wherever you find them, even in the Sacred Precinct. The verb *thaqifa* (to come upon) originally meant 'to carefully perceive something'. *And expel them from where they expelled you*: meaning Mecca—he expelled them on the day of the Conquest; *sedition*—such as leaving them in the Sacred Precinct, or their expulsion of you from it—*is more grievous than slaying*: than slaying them in the Sacred Precinct. *But fight them not by the Sacred Mosque*—the Sacred Precinct—*until they should fight you there; then if they fight you*, if they begin it, *slay them—such is the requital of disbelievers*: the majority hold that this verse is still in effect, and that it is not permitted to begin fighting in the Sacred Precinct.

[2:192] *But if they desist* from disbelief, *then truly God is Forgiving, Merciful* to them.

[2:193] *Fight them till there is no sedition*—idolatry—*and the religion is for*

God alone; *and if they desist* from idolatry, *there shall be no enmity*—no evil, meaning no requital for it—*save against evildoers*: He called it evil in order to evoke a parallelism.

[2:194] *The sacred month* during which you shall enter Mecca by force *for the sacred month* in which they prevented you from entering it in the year of Ḥudaybiya: that is, one ill turn to repay another. *Holy things*—all things which must be protected—*demand retaliation. Whoever commits aggression against you* by barring you, *then commit aggression against him in the manner that he committed against you*: and enter the city by force. *And fear God* regarding those things which He has not allowed you, *and know that God is with the God-fearing* to protect them.

[2:195] *And spend in the way of God*: such as for the *ḥajj* or *jihād*; *and cast not* yourselves with *your own hands into destruction*: by not spending in His way, or 'your hands' symbolises 'yourselves'. *And be kind* to the needy; *God loves the kind.*

[2:196] *Fulfil the ḥajj and the ʿumra*—fulfil all their rites—*to God*: this implies that both are obligatory, because it is an unqualified command to Q. 2:194 fulfil them without any stipulation that this only applies once they have been commenced, which implies obligation, as anything that is required to fulfil an obligation is itself obligatory. There also exists a canonical reading for the verse with *Perform the ḥajj...*[1] *But if you are prevented* by an enemy: this applies solely to prevention by an enemy according to Shāfiʿī and Mālik; and Ibn ʿAbbās also explained the verse this way (may God be pleased with them), meaning that it is not merely a detail of [Shāfiʿī's] school which his followers blindly accept. It is supported by how the verse goes on to say, *When you are secure...*, as well as the fact that it was revealed about Ḥudaybiya. The Ḥanafīs deem that it also includes sickness and other impediments, based on the *ḥadīth*, 'If someone breaks a bone or is injured, his consecration is ended and he must perform the *ḥajj* the next year.' Tirmidhī did narrate this *ḥadīth*, but other masters deemed it a weak narration; and it is contradicted by a *ḥadīth* of Ḍubāʿa narrated in the two *Ṣaḥīḥ* collections and elsewhere. [*But if you are prevented,*] *then* [*give*] *such offerings as may be feasible*: the word *hady* (offerings) is the plural of *hadiyya*, meaning a sacrificial sheep; *and do not shave your heads*—do not come out of consecration—*until the offerings reach their place*: the place where it is lawful to sacrifice them, which is the halting place according to Shāfiʿī, or the Sacred Precinct according to Abū Ḥanīfa. In any case, it means 'until you

1 With *aqīmū* in place of *atimmū*.

sacrifice them'. *If any of you is sick* such that he must shave his head, *or has an ailment of the head* such as an injury or lice, *then* if he shaves his head early, he must make *a redemption by fast* of three days, *or a voluntary charity* of a *farq*, which is three *ṣāʿ* divided among six needy people, *or a ritual sacrifice* of a sheep or something better. The same applies to any other violation of the consecrated state, even when there is no justification for it. *When you are secure* from fear, and able to enter Mecca, *then whoever offers the ʿumra* during the months of *ḥajj* voluntarily in order to draw nearer to God, *until* he arrives for *the ḥajj*, and then performs the *ḥajj* after finishing the *ʿumra, let his offering be such as is feasible*: Shāfiʿī considers this an expiation sacrifice, which means he may not eat from it, while Abū Ḥanīfa considers it a regular sacrifice like all the others in the *ḥajj*. *Or if he finds none*—no offering to give—*then a fast of three days in the ḥajj* before coming out of consecration; and it is recommended to enter consecration for the other seven; *and of seven when you return* home afterwards, or according to Abū Ḥanīfa as soon as the *ḥajj* is finished; *that is a full ten*: this is a summary to
Q. 2:197 discount the possibility that the word *and* might be taken to mean 'or', or that it is a mere permission rather than a command, or that the *seven* simply designates 'many', or that it is akin to His Words *in four days* [Q. 41:10]. The word *full* is to affirm the importance of this, or to make it clear that the previous three may not be subtracted from it, or simply to indicate that this is the first complete number,[1] as described in the books of the mathematicians. *That* ruling *is for him whose family are not present at the Sacred Mosque*, meaning that he resides far enough away from the Sacred Precinct that he would be allowed to shorten his prayer when travelling there. If he lives any closer, he is deemed to be a resident, or effectively a resident. The strongest opinion in the Shāfiʿī school is that it makes no difference whether this is a temporary or permanent residence. The ruling for the one who wishes to combine the *ḥajj* and *ʿumra* is the same as for the one who wishes to perform them separately, in this regard. *And fear God*: lest you disobey Him; *and know that God is severe in retribution* to those who disobey Him.

[2:197] *The ḥajj is in months well known*: Shawwāl, Dhū al-Qaʿda and ten nights from Dhū al-Ḥijja according to Shāfiʿī, and the Day of Sacrifice too according to Abū Ḥanīfa, and the rest of Dhū al-Ḥijja too according to Mālik. The root of the disagreement is whether it means the time for its consecration, actions and rites, or the rites which ought not be done in

1 In other words, the first number after which the cycle of decimal digits begins to repeat.

any other times. Mālik disliked that the *ʿumra* be performed in the other months. Referring to part of a month as a month is a figure of speech. *Whoever undertakes*—obliges upon himself—*the duty of ḥajj during them* by entering consecration, *then no lewdness* (*rafath*), meaning sex and its precursors, *nor wickedness*, meaning sin, *nor disputing*, arguing, *in* the days of *the ḥajj. Whatever good you do, God knows it*, and He will not let it go to waste. *And take provision* for your Hereafter, or for the *ḥajj*, contrary to the practice of some Yemenis who would go on the *ḥajj* without any provisions, making a display of reliance on God, and then resort to begging people shamelessly. *But the best provision is piety*, which includes refraining from begging. The word *zād* (provision) means extra food that one does not need at the present moment. *And fear Me* alone, *O people of pith*—people of sound minds—for that is what a sound mind would dictate.

[2:198] *You would not be at fault*, guilty of sin, *if you should seek bounty*, provision, *from your Lord* by engaging in commerce or hiring during the *ḥajj*; *but when you press on from ʿArafāt*—ʿArafāt is a plural noun which became Q. 2:198
the name of the well-known mountain, because of how people recognise (*taʿāraf*) one another there, or because Adam and Eve recognised each other there. The expression *Yawm ʿArafa* (the Day of ʿArafa) is not pure Arabic but a later coinage of mixed heritage. It is said that the verse is proof that it is obligatory to stand there—*then remember God at the Sacred Waymark* with supplication and chanting. The Sacred Waymark (*al-mashʿar al-ḥarām*) is a well-known mountain so called because it is a sign of worship and a sacred place. This implies that remembrance there is better than other activities. *And remember Him as He has guided you* to this: the repetition of the command serves as an exhortation to engage in much remembrance; *though previously,* before He guided you, *you were astray*, ignorant.

[2:199] *Then*—because of the distinction between the two acts of pressing on; or some say that they are arranged in inverse order—*press on*, depart, *from where the people press on*: meaning ʿArafa, because Quraysh would never go beyond the limits of the Sacred Precinct and would say, 'We are God's people, and we shall not leave His Sacred Precinct,' and would perform the pressing on from within it [rather than from ʿArafa]. *And seek God's forgiveness; God is Forgiving, Merciful.*

[2:200] *And when you have performed your holy rites*—when you have finished the acts of worship for your *ḥajj*. The root meaning of the word *manāsik* (holy rites) is 'to grasp', in the sense of taking hold of the soul and moving it towards the farthest aim of worship—*remember God as you remember your fathers, or yet more intensely*: in the time of the age of ignorance, they would recount the glories of their forefathers at Minā. *There are some people who say, 'Our Lord, give to us in this world' yet in the Hereafter they will have no part*: no goodly share or pursuit.

[2:201] *And there are others who say, 'Our Lord, give to us in this world good* of all kinds, *and in the Hereafter good* likewise, *and guard us from the chastisement of the Fire* with forgiveness.*'* Some interpreted these three things to denote a righteous wife, the maidens of Paradise, and an evil wife respectively, and other such things, but those are only examples.

[2:202] *Those*—the latter—*shall have a portion from what they have earned*: or both groups shall have a portion due to their prayers, whether in this world or in both; *and God is swift at reckoning*, and will reckon you all in the blink of an eye despite your vast numbers.

[2:203] *And remember*—magnify—*God* after your prayers, and when sacrificing, and at the designated pillars, *during certain days numbered*: these are the days of *tashrīq*,[1] which are called *numbered* here because they are
Q. 2:201 fewer in number than the ten well-known days. *If any man hastens on* by departing *in two days* after stoning the designated pillars, *that is no sin for him; and if he delays* until the third day, *it is not a sin for him*. In the age of ignorance, some would deem it sinful to go earlier, while others deemed it sinful to go later, and so He refuted them both by affirming that the one who departs early incurs no sin by taking advantage of the dispensation, for [as the *ḥadīth* says,] 'God loves that His dispensations be followed just as His strict rulings are.' So such a person incurs no sin, *if he fears* during his *ḥajj*. *And fear God, and know that to Him you shall be gathered* for the requital.

[2:204] *And among people there is he whose speech about* the matters of *the life of this world pleases you*: makes a striking impression on your soul. The meaning of *taʿajjub* (to be pleased or amazed) is a bafflement that overcomes a man when he beholds something due to his ignorance of the cause of the thing he beholds; it is a relative matter. *He calls on God to witness what is in his heart*—swearing that his heart conforms to his tongue—*yet he is most stubborn in dispute*: this refers to Akhnas b. Shurayq, the silver-tongued hypocrite.

[2:205] *And when he turns his back* and goes away from you, *he hastens about the earth to do corruption there* in whatever way he can, *and to destroy the tillage and the stock*: he burned the crops of the Muslims and hobbled their livestock. *And God loves not*—approves not—*corruption*. If you object, 'How could He not approve of it, when He Himself makes some things

1 The three days of ʿĪd at the conclusion of the *ḥajj*.

fall into corruption?' the answer is that corruption means to remove something from a praiseworthy state for no good reason, which He would never do, and He does not approve of it. Something might appear to us as corruption, but only in a relative sense.

[2:206] *And when it is said to him, 'Fear God!' he is seized by vainglory in his sin*: pride drives him to sin. *So Hell shall be enough for him—how evil a cradling!*

[2:207] *But there are other men who sell themselves* through *jihād, desiring God's pleasure*: such as Ṣuhayb, who was tortured in an attempt to force him to renounce the faith, but he gave away all of his possessions and went to Medina; *and God is Gentle with His servants.*

[2:208] *O you who believe, come into submission*, surrender to God, *completely*, in all His laws, or with all your being; the word *kāffa* (completely) is from the verb *kaffa*, meaning 'to gather'. *And follow not the steps*—the tracks—*of Satan; he is a manifest foe to you.*

[2:209] *But if you slip*—if you decline to come into submission—*after the clear proofs*—that it is the truth—*have come to you, know then that God is Mighty*, Omnipotent, *Wise*, and does not take vengeance unjustly; and to know these two is to avoid this fate. Q. 2:206

[2:210] *What do they*—those who slip—*wait for, save that God should come to them* in a manner known only to Him, or that His punishment shall come to them, *in the shadows of clouds* from which mercy is usually expected, so that any punishment that came from them would be severe indeed, *and the angels, and that the matter* of their reckoning and requital *be determined? To God all matters are returned*: so that all can be requited.

[2:211] *Ask*, O Muḥammad, by way of rebuke, *the Children of Israel how many a clear proof did We give them* in their Books regarding the truth of Muḥammad (may God bless him and grant him peace); *whoever changes God's grace* by altering it *after it has come to him*—after he attained knowledge of it or had the ability of attaining it—*God is severe in retribution* upon him.

[2:212] *Decked out fair to the disbelievers is the life of this world*: such that they have turned away from the Hereafter. *Tazyīn* (to deck out) means to make something appealing visually, not intellectually. *And they deride the believers*: the poor among them such as Bilāl and ʿAmmār because of how they renounced the world. *But those who fear*—meaning such believers—*shall be above them on the Day of Resurrection; and God sustains whomever He will without reckoning*: without their necessarily deserving it; abundant provision is not proof of nearness to God.

[2:213] *People*—between Adam and Noah, for twenty generations—

were one community who agreed on the truth; *then God sent forth the prophets* after they began to differ, *as bearers of glad tidings* for the obedient *and warners* to the sinners; *and He revealed with them*—meaning with their class, since most of them followed the [respective] Book of those who preceded them—*the Book with the truth that He might decide between people regarding their differences; and only those who had been given it*—the Book—*differed about it after the clear proofs had come to them out of insolence*, envy and injustice, *one to another*, so that some disbelieved in the Books of others. *Then God guided those who believed to the truth regarding which they were at variance, by His leave*: by His will; *and God guides whomever He will to a straight path.*

He then encouraged the believers who had left behind their possessions and children by saying:

[2:214] *Or did you suppose*—that is, you ought not to have supposed—*that you should enter the Garden without there having come upon you the like of* the remarkable condition of *those who passed away before you? They were afflicted by misery and hardship and were so convulsed*—so persecuted on account of their message—*that the Messenger and those who believed with him said, 'When will God's help come?'* They felt as if it would never come, but then they were told: *Ah, but truly God's help is nigh!* So have fortitude as they did, and you will triumph in the end.

Q. 2:214

[2:215] *They ask you*—the questioner was ʿAmr b. al-Jamūḥ al-Anṣārī—*about what they should expend* voluntarily. They asked about what they should spend, but His answer concerned something more important, namely whom they should spend upon. A question that is asked for the purpose of seeking instruction does not have to be answered directly, unlike a question posed in a debate. So He said: *Say: 'Whatever you expend of good* wealth, *it is for parents and kinsmen, orphans, the needy, and the traveller. And whatever good you may do, God has knowledge of it*: and will reward you.'

[2:216] *Prescribed for you is fighting, though it be hateful*—detestable and difficult—*to you. Yet it may happen that you hate a thing which is good for you*: namely anything you are commanded to do; *and it may happen that you love a thing which is bad for you*: namely anything you are prohibited from doing. *God knows* what is best, *and you know not.*

[2:217] *They ask you about the sacred month, and fighting in it*: this occurred when the Muslim army fought the idolaters during Rajab, thinking that it was still Jumādā. The question was asked by the believers, as is the case for the rest of the five questions. The question is described here in such a way as makes it clear they were asking because of the sanctity of the month. *Say: 'Fighting in it is a grave thing*: a sin. The soundest position on the matter is that this ruling was abrogated, and that the verse does not mean that fighting during the month is absolutely prohibited. This is supported by how the word *qitāl* (fighting) is repeated in the indefinite form both times. The majority say that it was abrogated by His Words *slay the idolaters wherever you find them* [Q. 9:5]. *But to bar from God's way, and disbelief in Him, and* to bar from *the Sacred Mosque, and to expel its* believing *people from it—that is graver in God's sight* than the fighting was; *and sedition*—idolatry—*is graver than slaying.' They*, the idolaters, *will not cease to fight against you until they turn you from your religion, if they are able*: He said *if* to imply a hypothetical and something that is unlikely; *and whoever of you turns from his religion* to theirs, *and dies disbelieving—their* beneficial *deeds have failed*, come to naught, *in this world* regarding the edicts of Islam, *and the Hereafter* regarding the loss of reward. Shāfiʿī cited the qualification *and dies disbelieving* as evidence that this only applies if the person dies in a state of disbelief. *Those are the inhabitants of the Fire, therein they will abide.*

[2:218] *Truly, the believers, and those who emigrate, and struggle in God's* Q. 2:218
way—those have hope of, they may rightly hope for, *God's compassion; and God is Forgiving, Merciful.*

[2:219] *They ask you*—the questioner was ʿUmar, along with others—*about* drinking *wine*: the juice of grapes and dates when it ferments; *and* playing with *divinatory arrows* for the purpose of gambling. *Say: 'In both is great sin*, such as boisterousness and deceit, *and profit for people*, such as strength and the acquisition of wealth; *but the sin in them*—the corrupting influence—*is greater than the usefulness.' And they ask you*—again the questioner was ʿUmar—*what they should expend*: what amount they should spend on the aforementioned people. *Say: 'Comfortably'*: that is, what remains after your needs are met. The word *ʿafw* (comfort) is the opposite of *jahd* (struggle). *Thus*—by this elucidation—*God makes clear* all of *His signs to you that you might reflect* [2:220] *on* the matters of *this world and the Hereafter*, and choose what is best for yourselves. *And they ask you about orphans*: after they had become reticent towards them after the revelation of *Those who consume the property of orphans*…[Q. 4:10]. *Say: 'To set their affairs* in their incomes *is better* than to avoid them. *And if you intermix with them*, mixing your food with theirs, *they are your brothers*, and there is no harm. *God knows well him who works corruption from him who sets aright*: and will requite them both; *and had He willed He would have overburdened you*: He would have burdened you with the struggle of avoiding them altogether. The word *ʿanat* (burden) means 'difficulty'. *Truly, God is Mighty*, Omnipotent, *Wise* in all He does.'

[2:221] *Do not marry idolatresses*—worshippers of idols—*until they believe*: this includes women from the People of the Book, and was further qualified by His Words, *And wedded women*..., and so on [Q. 4:24]. *A believing slave girl is better than an idolatress* who is free, *though you may admire her* for her wealth and beauty. *And do not marry idolaters* to believing women, *until they believe. A believing slave is better than an idolater* who is free, *though you may admire him. Those* idolaters *call to the Fire* and all that leads to it, *while God calls to the Garden* and all that leads to it, *and pardon, by His leave*: by His facilitation; *and He makes clear His signs to the people so that they might remember* the vileness of what He forbids, and the beauty of what He enjoins.

[2:222] *And they ask you*—the questioner was Abū al-Daḥdāḥ, along with some others—*about* the rulings of *the monthly period*: it was their custom to shun menstruating women and refrain from eating with them and keeping their company. The first three questions described in this passage
Q. 2:221 are not preceded with the word 'and' because they asked about them at different times. The others are preceded with 'and' because they asked them over a duration that is conventionally viewed as a single unit of time, such as a month. *Say: 'It is an ailment*: this is an allusion to something unpleasant; *so part with women in the monthly period*: avoid sexual intercourse with them; *and do not approach them* for sexual intercourse *until they are pure*: whether by bathing or dry ablution. Abū Ḥanīfa (may God have mercy on him) said that neither are required as long as the longest duration possible for menstruation has passed. The variant canonical recitation with *until they have been made pure*[1] supports this. *When they have cleansed themselves, then come to them* for sexual intercourse, *as God has commanded you*: meaning vaginal intercourse.*' Truly, God loves those who repent, and He loves those who cleanse themselves* from impurities.

[2:223] *Your women are a tillage*—a site of tillage—*for you; so come to your tillage*—have sexual intercourse with them—*as you wish*: from any direction you wish, as long as it be the place of tillage. The claim of the Jews that vaginal intercourse from behind is detestable to God and results in a cross-eyed child is not true. *And send ahead for your souls* the reward of obedience to God's command; *and fear God* lest you disobey Him; *and know that you shall meet Him* on the Day of Resurrection; *and give glad tidings to the believers* who fear Him.

[2:224] *Do not make God a hindrance*—a barrier—*in your oaths to be pious*

1 With *yuṭṭahharna* rather than *yaṭhurna*.

and God-fearing, and to put things right between people: such as when Abū Bakr al-Ṣiddīq swore that he would not support Misṭaḥ financially because of how he had lied about ʿĀ'isha (may God be pleased with her), which was the direct subject of this verse. *Surely God is All-Hearing* of your oaths, *Knowing* of your intentions.

[2:225] *God will not take you to task* by ordaining a punishment or an expiation *for a slip in your oaths*: this means something that is uttered unthinkingly, such as saying, 'No, by God!' The Ḥanafīs say it means when a man swears on something he believes to be true but is actually false. *But He will take you to task for what your hearts have earned*: meaning what you lie about intentionally. *And God is Forgiving, Forbearing*, and will not punish you immediately for lying.

[2:226] *For those who forswear their women*—swearing that they will not have sexual intercourse with them—*a wait of four months* wherein they may seek neither sexual intercourse nor divorce. *If they revert*—break their oath—*God is Forgiving* to them of the sin of breaking the oath, *Merciful*.

Q. 2:225

[2:227] *But if they resolve upon divorce* and go ahead with it, then there must be an expiation. *Truly, God is Hearing* of their divorce pronouncement, *Knowing* of their deed.

[2:228] *Divorced women*—meaning free women whose marriages have been consummated and who are still menstruating—*shall wait by themselves for three periods*: three instances of purity after bleeding. Divorced slave women must wait for two periods, as the Sunna affirms. The word *qurū'* (periods) is a major plural (*jamʿ kathra*),[1] but is used here because it describes the ruling for all divorced women. Or it could be parsed as *thalātha min al-qurū'* (three of the periods), in which case it would suggest a minor plural referring to 'themselves', by way of implying that divorce ought to be an infrequent occurrence. Our school holds that *qurū'* means the periods of purity, while Abū Ḥanīfa said it meant the period of bleeding.

NOTE: Know that the *ḥadīth*, 'A slave woman is divorced by two pronouncements, and her waiting period (*ʿidda*) is two menstruations,'[2] and the *ḥadīth*, 'Cease praying during the days of your periods,'[3] [they] are not authentic; and even if they were they would not be enough to undermine God's Words in *divorce them by their prescribed waiting period* [Q. 65:1], and the *ḥadīth* cited in the two *Ṣaḥīḥ* collections, the *Muwaṭṭa'* and the *Sunans*

1 Usually denoting a plural of more than ten.
2 Using the term *ḥayḍa* (menstruation).
3 Using the term *aqrā'*, which like *qurū'* is the plural of *qara'*.

of Abū Dā'ūd, Tirmidhī, Nasā'ī, Dārimī and Ibn Māja about the story of Ibn ᶜUmar (may God be pleased with him), which includes, 'Tell him to take her back and keep her until she becomes pure, and then menstruates, and then becomes pure; and then if he wishes he may retain her after that, or divorce her before he touches her. That is the waiting period God commanded for the divorcing of women.' In addition, the narration of Mālik on the authority of ᶜĀ'isha (may God be pleased with her), which includes, 'Do you know what *aqrā'* are? They are the periods of purity.' The most that those other two *ḥadīth*s prove is that the word *qara'* can also be used to mean menstruation, which is not a matter of dispute. And God knows best.[1]

And it is not lawful for them to hide what God has created in their wombs: whether pregnancy or menstruation, for the sake of hurrying the process. This implies that a woman should be taken at her word in this regard. If they believe in God and the Last Day: this is not meant to establish a legal stipulation, but rather as a warning. Their mates, meaning
Q. 2:229
their husbands—the word *baᶜl* (mate) was originally the name of a date palm tree that takes in water through its roots, and the feminine form *baᶜla* can also be used to mean 'wife'—have a better right to restore them to marriage in such time: meaning the waiting period. This was before the revelation of Divorce is twice [Q. 2:229]. If they desire to set things right by retaining them, not if they intend harm. Again, this is a religious warning, not a legal stipulation. Women shall have rights over men similar to those due from them: regarding the obligation, not the nature of them; with justice according to the Law, such as kind company; but their men have a degree above them in merit because of how they gave them their dowries and paid for their upkeep. The root meaning of *daraja* (degree) is 'higher level', just as *daraka* means 'lower level.' God is Mighty, Wise.

[2:229] Divorce that can be recanted is twice: two pronouncements, or some say one pronouncement after another, and it is also said that it is forbidden to pronounce them together; then after that retained with honour or released with kindness: honourable in that it involves nothing that the Law condemns. When asked about the third pronouncement, the Prophet (may God bless him and grant him peace) replied that it is found in the Words setting free, which refer to the third divorce pronouncement. This contrasted with the custom of the age of ignorance,

1 The author is arguing for the position of his school that the term *qurū'* used in this verse means the time of purity after menstruation, rather than the period of menstruation itself.

when there was no limit to the number of divorce pronouncements. With kindness (*bi-iḥsān*) is broader than with honour (*bi-maʿrūf*), since something could be honourable inasmuch as the Law does not condemn it, yet still not be considered kind. It is not lawful for you—this is addressed to the authorities, since they are the ones who arbitrate when such issues arise—to take of what you have given them, meaning the dowry, unless the couple, the husband and wife, fear that they may not maintain God's bounds regarding the marital duties. If you authorities fear they may not maintain God's bounds, neither of them would be at fault if she were to ransom herself: that is, there would be no harm if it were to be taken and granted to her, which indicates a priori that annulment (*khulʿ*) is permitted when both parties agree. Those edicts are God's bounds; do not transgress them. Whoever transgresses God's bounds—those are the evildoers.

[2:230] If he divorces her after the first two, which explains the meaning of released with kindness—the issue of annulment was brought up between them to show that divorce is either free or compensated, and that retention is only possible before the third pronouncement—she shall not be lawful to him after that, after the third, until she marries another husband with a proper consummated marriage. The wisdom of this is to deter the third pronouncement of divorce. As for the reason why the man who engages in a false marriage to free a woman to remarry her former husband is accursed, as is the man for whom this false marriage is done, it is that he got married on condition that his marriage would last no longer than the consummation, or some similar arrangement. If he—the second husband—divorces her, then neither of them would be at fault to return to each other with a brand new valid marriage contract, if they think that they will maintain God's bounds regarding marital commitments. Those edicts are God's bounds, which He makes clear to a folk who have knowledge: who understand. Q. 2:230

[2:231] *When you divorce women, and they have reached their term*—the end of their waiting period—*then retain them with honour*: without any harm; *or set them free with honour*: let them finish their waiting period without lengthening it. He said *with honour* here [rather than 'with kindness'] to indicate that if you cannot be kind, then at least be honourable. *Do not retain them in harm to transgress*: in order to wrong them by stretching out the process, or forcing them to resort to ransoming themselves. *Whoever does that has wronged his soul. Take not God's verses in mockery* by divorcing, freeing, marrying or retaining and then saying, 'We were only joking.'

And remember God's grace upon you, in the form of Islam, *and the Book*, the Qur'ān, *and the wisdom*, the Sunna, *He has revealed to you to exhort you therewith*, and give thanks for them by acting in accordance with them. *And fear God, and know that God has knowledge of all things.*

[2:232] *When you divorce women, and they have reached their term*—when their waiting period is over—*do not debar them*: do not make it difficult for them, O guardians. This is proof that they are not permitted to give themselves away in marriage, for otherwise there would be no way for the guardian to debar them. Nevertheless, the act of marriage is attributed to them since it depends on their consent. [*Do not debar them*] *from marrying their* prospective *husbands when they have agreed together*—the suitors and the women—*with honour*: according to the Law, chivalry and love. This indicates that it is permitted to debar a marriage if the suitor is not a fitting match. *That is an admonition for whoever of you believe in God and the Last Day. That*, meaning refraining from debarring the marriage—this is addressed to the suitors, which is why the plural form is used[1]—*is purer*,
Q. 2:232 more beneficial, *for you, and cleaner* from the impurity of sin. *God knows* this, *and you know not* because of the shortcomings of your knowledge.

[2:233] *Mothers*, even if divorced, may *suckle their children for two full years* at most. He emphasised that they be full years to make clear that they may not be counted laxly. This command denotes a recommendation or obligation if the child will not suckle any but his mother, or if there is no wet-nurse for him or his father is unable to afford one. [*Mothers suckle their children for two full years*] *for such as desire to fulfil the suckling*: in which case two years is the upper limit, though it is permitted to make it shorter. *It is for the father*—the term used here is *mawlūd lah* (the one to whom the child is born), which alludes to the wisdom behind the ruling as well as affirming that the child belongs to the father—*to provide for them* by financially supporting the nursing mother during the period of suckling, *and clothe them honourably* as well as he is able to. Shāfiʿī permitted for the mother to be hired [to nurse the child], while Abū Ḥanīfa forbade this as long as she is still married to him or in her waiting period. *No soul is charged save to its capacity. A mother shall not cause her child harm*: by giving it up. He mentioned the mother first because of her greater compassion. *Neither a father his child*: by wresting it from its mother, thereby harming her. This can also be read in the passive voice[2] as 'a mother shall not be harmed on

1 The word *dhālikum* means 'that' when addressed to a plurality, as opposed to *dhālika*, which is addressed to a single person, nominally the Prophet.

2 This is how most exegetes read it, and how it is almost always translated.

account of her child, neither a father on account of his child'. The child is attributed to the mother and then the father here in order to rouse their compassion towards it. *The heir*—the father's heir if he dies, meaning his child—*has a similar duty*: and so the payment for its suckling should be taken from its inheritance if it has one; or if not, then the mother must suckle it free of charge. *But if the two* parents *desire by mutual consent and consultation* between them—meaning engagement in discussion until an opinion is agreed—*to wean* before the two years are passed, *then they would not be at fault* on either side. *And if you desire to seek nursing for your children* by means of wet-nurses, *you would not be at fault*: this indicates that it is permitted for the husband, as well as preventing the wife from suckling; *provided you hand over what you have given honourably*: lawfully, meaning their payment. The stipulation that no fault is incurred if payment is made is meant as guidance to what is best, not a prerequisite for lawfulness. *And fear God* in His bounds, *and know that God sees what you do*.

[2:234] *And those of you who pass away, leaving wives, they shall*—they must—*wait by themselves for four months and ten*: the reason for this is that a foetus usually begins to stir in three months if it is male, or four if it is female, and so He took the longer term into account, and added ten days for the sake of caution. As for the pregnant woman and the slave, their waiting period is birth and half the term for a free woman respectively. *When they have reached their term, then you* guardians *would not be at fault regarding* allowing them to do *what they may do with themselves*: such as beautifying themselves in a way which was forbidden during their waiting period; *with honour*: avoiding what the Law condemns. *God is aware of what you do*: and will require you for it. Q. 2:234

[2:235] *You would not be at fault regarding the proposal you suggest to women* who are able to accept it, *or hide in your hearts* without presenting it. The term *taʿrīḍ* (suggestion) means to state one's intent using words that are literal, figurative or euphemistic, so that something else is implied but left unsaid. *Kināya* (allusion) means to state one's intent with words that literally denote it but have another primary meaning, such that they are usually only used for one's intent in a secondary sense where the mind makes a leap of logic. The two terms have some overlap. The word *khiṭba* (proposal) conventionally means 'request', while *khuṭba* means 'counsel'. The root meaning is 'the purpose of the speaker's words'. An example of suggestion would be, 'You are beautiful, and I am looking to get married.' *God knows that you will be mindful of them* and unable to be apart from them, and so He permitted such suggestions. So speak to them, *but do not make arrangements* for marriage or sexual intercourse *with them secretly, unless you speak honourable words*: in essence this means: do not make advances towards them unless they are honourable, which means suggestions, not direct proposals. *And do not resolve on the knot of marriage*, which means the things that are required for it to be valid, *until that which is written has reached its term*, meaning the ordained waiting period, for marriage during its bounds is invalid by consensus. He spoke of resolve in order to stress the prohibition of tying such a knot. Know also that there are six stages of impulse that lead us to a deed: the notion, then the thought, then contemplation of it, then desire, then aspiration, and then resolve. Resolving on a matter means taking the decision to do it. *And know that God knows what is in your souls; so be fearful of Him* and do not resolve on such. *And know that God is Forgiving* of those who resolve on it but do not go ahead with it, *Forbearing* such that He does not hasten the chastisement for it.

Q. 2:236

[2:236] *You would not be at fault*—that is, you would not owe any dowry, given how He speaks of *one half of what you have appointed* in the next verse—*if you divorce women while you have not touched them*, had sexual intercourse with them, *nor appointed any obligation for them*, meaning a dowry; but if they are touched or a dowry is appointed, then half or all must be handed over. The term *farḍ* (obligation) here is a name for the dowry (*mahr*). *Yet make provision of comforts for them with honour*: according to the Law, if there was neither touching nor appointment, to make amends for the alienation of divorce. The amount of the provision is decided by the judge according to what he feels is appropriate. *The one of ample means*, the rich man, *according to his means, and the needy man*, the poor man, *according to his means—an obligation on the virtuous*: that is, on you all. He referred to them as virtuous in order to encourage them to be so. Shāfiʿī, in one of the two opinions attributed to him, said that the woman who has been touched and for whom an obligation has been appointed shares in this ruling by analogy, which takes precedence over textual inference.

[2:237] *And if you divorce them before you have touched them, and you have already appointed for them an obligation, then one-half of what you have appointed* must be given to them, in which case no further provision is required; *unless it be that they*, the divorcees, *make remission, or the one in whose hand is the knot of marriage makes remission*: that is, if the husband gives her the entire dowry, which is described as a remission here because of the resemblance, or because of how the verb *ʿafā* can mean both 'to remit' and 'to give amply'. *Yet that you*—you men—*should remit is nearer to piety.*

Forget not kindness between you: that is, be kind to one another. *Truly, God sees what you do* and will not let your kindness go to waste.

[2:238] *Maintain*—be constant in—*the* five *prayers and the middle prayer* between them, or the most virtuous one. The soundest position is that this means the afternoon (*ʿaṣr*) prayer because of the *ḥadīth* to that effect. *And stand* in prayer *submissive to God*: subservient or tranquil. The root meaning of the word *qunūt* (to stand) is 'to stand humbly'. Ibn al-Musayyab is reported to have said, 'This means the *qunūt* [special supplication] of the dawn prayer (*ṣubḥ*).'

[2:239] *And if you are in fear* of an enemy or the like, *then* pray *standing*: this proves the obligation of prayer even when in combat, as Shāfiʿī said; *or mounted*, even if it is not possible to stop and face the *qibla*. *But when you are secure* and no longer in fear, *then remember God*—pray—*as He taught you*, meaning the usual prayer of safety, *that which you knew not*.

[2:240] *And those of you who pass away leaving wives*, they must *bequeath for their wives provision for a year without expulsion*: that is, he must bequeath provision for his wife for a full year and support her so that she is not expelled from her home. This period was then abrogated and replaced with four months and ten days, and the provision replaced with inheritance according to the majority of scholars. Shāfiʿī said that the law about residence is still in effect, while Abū Ḥanīfa disagreed. *But if they go forth* from the home before the year is over, *you would not be at fault*, O heirs of the deceased, *regarding what they may do with themselves* by forgoing the mourning period *honourably* according to the Law and custom. So they have the choice between remaining and taking the provision, or leaving and forgoing it if they do not wish to stay in mourning. *God is Mighty* and exacts vengeance on those who disobey Him, *Wise* in what He commands. Q. 2:238

When the law of provision was revealed with the Words *an obligation on the virtuous* [Q. 2:236], a man said, 'If I wish I shall be virtuous, and if not then I shall not.' Therefore, the verse was revealed:

[2:241] *There shall be provision for divorced women, with honour—an obligation on those who fear* idolatry.

[2:242] *Thus*, by this elucidation, *God makes clear His signs for you, so that you might understand*.

[2:243] *Have you not seen*—the rhetorical question is a demand for assent and affirmation, necessitating that what follows it be affirmed—*those thousands who went forth from their habitations fearful of death?* This means the people of Dāwardān,[1] seventy thousand strong, who left their homes fleeing the plague. Or *ulūf* (thousands) could mean 'gathered together' (*muta'allifūn*). *God said to them* on the road, *'Die!'* In other words, He caused them all to die at once. *Then He gave them life* after they had died, when Ezekiel passed by them and said, 'By God's command, arise!' And they rose and said, 'Glory be to You, Lord God, and praise be to You! There is no god but You.' *Truly, God is bounteous to people, but most people are not thankful*: distracted as they are from the purpose of their creation.

[2:244] *So fight in God's way, and know that God is Hearing* of what the deserters say, *Knowing* of what is in their minds.

[2:245] *Who is he that will lend God a loan that is good*—by offering his life and his property—*and He will multiply it for him manifold?* This is a metaphor for the presenting of a good deed in hope of its reward. *God straitens*, withholds provision from some, *and enlarges* it for others; *and to Him you shall be returned* for His requital.

[2:246] *Have you not seen the council*—the word *malā'* (council) means
Q. 2:244 an important gathering or an assembly for consultation—*of the Children of Israel after* the death of *Moses, when they said to a prophet of theirs*, namely Joshua, *'Send for us a king* for fighting, *and we will fight in God's way.' He*, their prophet, *said*, *'Might it be*: that is, 'Do you imagine?' When the word *ʿasā* (might) is used in the Qur'ān conjugated as a singular verb, it denotes a statement of fact, while when it is conjugated as a plural verb [as here], it denotes a question. *That if fighting is prescribed for you, you will not fight* because of your cowardice*?' They said, 'Why should we not fight in God's way, when we have been expelled from our habitations and our children?'* The people of Goliath had taken their land and captured their children. *Yet when fighting was prescribed for them, they turned their backs* from war, *except a few of them:* 313 men, the same as the number who fought at Badr. *And God has knowledge of the evildoers*: and will requite them.

[2:247] *Then their prophet said to them, 'Truly, God has raised up Saul for you as king*: a commander.*' They said* in their obstinacy, *'How can he be king over us when we have better right than he to kingship* because he is not a scion of the royal house of Judah, while we are. He was a poor water-carrier or tanner. *And he has not been given*, as kings are, *amplitude of wealth?' He*, their prophet, *said*, answering them with four replies, *'God has chosen him over you* was the first, and then came the second: *and He has increased him broadly in knowledge and* strength of *body*, which are the pillars of kingship. Then

1 Near Wasit, Iraq.

the third reply: *God gives kingship*—authority—*to whom He will* and is not asked about what He does; and the fourth: *and God is Embracing, Knowing.'*

[2:248] *And their prophet said to them, 'The sign of his kingship is that there will come to you the Ark*: a box made of gilded boxwood measuring three by two cubits, containing the images of the prophets, which the Amalekites had taken from them. *Therein*, in the Ark, *is a Spirit of Peace*, tranquillity, *from your Lord*: it contained things which served as a source of good cheer in times of strife and war, though there is a difference of opinion about what exactly they were. *And a remnant of what the folk of Moses and the folk of Aaron left behind*: meaning the staff of Moses, fragments of the tablets of the Torah, and the garments of Aaron. The word *folk* is idiomatic rather than literal. *The angels bearing it* in the air, so that the people looked on as they set it down before Saul. *Truly, in that*—the return of the Ark—*shall be a sign for you* that he is God's chosen one, *if you are believers.'*

[2:249] *And when Saul went forth with the hosts* from his land to fight the Amalekites, who numbered eighty thousand, during a time of great heat, *he said* to them because he was not sure he could trust them, *'God will try you with a river* between Jordan and Palestine; *whoever drinks of it, he is not of me* and so should not accompany me to face the enemy; *and whoever tastes it not, he is of me, except for him who scoops up with his hand'*: that is, 'whoever drinks of it is not of me, except for him who drinks a handful and no more'. *But they drank of it* directly with their mouths like animals, *except a few of them*: those who scooped it with their hands were quenched thoroughly by miraculous means, while those who drank with their mouths were not quenched and only became thirstier, and their lips were blackened. Those who scooped numbered a little over 310. *And when he crossed it*—the river—*with those* few *who believed, they* who had scooped the water to drink *said, 'We have no power today against Goliath and his troops'* because of their great numbers. *Those who thought*—who knew—*they would meet God* upon death, who were the minority, *said, 'How often a little company has overcome a numerous one, by God's leave*: by His command; *and God is with the patient'* to aid them.

Q. 2:248

[2:250] *So when they went forth against Goliath and his troops*, who numbered ninety thousand or more, *they said, 'Our Lord, pour out upon us patience, and make firm our feet* by strengthening our hearts, *and grant us victory over the disbelieving folk!'*

[2:251] *And they routed them by the leave of God* and with His help, *and David slew Goliath* with three stones from his pack which had spoken to him on the road, saying, 'You shall slay Goliath with us.' Saul had promised that if he killed Goliath, he would marry him to his daughter and share his kingdom with him; and he kept his promise. *And God gave him the kingship* of the Children of Israel *and wisdom*—prophethood—*and He taught him such as He willed*: such as the speech of the birds and beasts, and metalwork. *Had God not repelled some people by means of others*—such as He did here—*the earth would have surely been corrupted* by the disbelievers; *but God is bounteous to all worlds*.

[2:252] *These* events *are the verses of God We recite to you in truth*: according to reality; *and assuredly you*, O Muḥammad, *are one of the Messengers*: in how you described them without any prior knowledge or learning.

[2:253] *Those messengers*: those who are known to you, or all of them; *some We have preferred above others* in terms of virtuous feats, not the essence of messengerhood (*risāla*). *Some there are to whom God spoke*: Moses on Sinai, and Muḥammad at the Ascension when he was the distance of two bows' length or nearer; *and some He raised in rank*: such as Muḥammad, who was sent to all people. May peace and blessings be upon them all! *And We gave*
Q. 2:252
Jesus son of Mary the clear proofs—prophetic miracles—*and confirmed him with the Holy Spirit*, as was explained earlier. *And had God willed, those who came after them*—after the Messengers—*would not have fought against one another after the clear proofs had come to them; but they fell into variance, and some of them believed, and some disbelieved*: such as the sects of the Christians who fell into fighting. *And had God willed, they would not have fought against one another*: He repeated this for emphasis; *but God does whatever He desires*: granting grace to some and forsaking others.

[2:254] *O you who believe, expend of what We have provided you with* on the obligatory *zakāt before there comes a day in which there shall be neither commerce*, that you might earn your ransoms, *nor friendship* or love, for dear friends on that day will be enemies to one another, *nor intercession* except for those whom the Compassionate permits. *And the disbelievers*—those who refuse to give *zakāt*, who are tantamount to disbelievers—*they are the evildoers* themselves. The restrictive expression is an allusion to the great extent of their evildoing, as though they were the only evildoers in existence.

[2:255] *God, there is no god except Him*: that is, there is no god worthy of worship but Him. If it were read as 'there is no god possible but Him' or 'there is no god in existence but Him', then neither expression would convey the full meaning. *The Living* through Himself, so that He will never die; He alone can truly possess knowledge and power, for they are necessary for Him, and He is transcendently above strength and possibility, since they imply neediness; *the Eternal Sustainer* Who manages creation and through

Whom all things are preserved. *Slumber does not seize Him, neither sleep*: He listed them in the order of their occurrence, since slumber is the drowsiness that precedes sleep. Sleep is a state that occurs regularly to relieve the matter of the brain from the moistures of rising vapours, preventing the external senses from sensing anything. *To Him belongs all that is in the heavens and the earth*: both what is in them and what is of them, which necessarily means that they also belong to Him, and implies this more clearly than simply stating it would. *Who is there that shall intercede with Him save by His leave*: never mind oppose Him in their obstinacy? *He knows what lies before them*: meaning what they perceive or what was before them; *and what is behind them*: meaning what they do not perceive or what will come after them—the pronoun refers to the rational beings in the heavens and the earth; *and they encompass nothing of His knowledge*, the objects of His knowledge, *save such as He wills* for them to know. *His Pedestal*—His knowledge, or His well-known Pedestal, or His authority (the root meaning of *kursī* is a seat large enough to accommodate a single person)—*subsumes the heavens and the earth, and the preserving* Q. 2:256
of them wearies Him not. And He is the Sublime: the One without peer; *the Tremendous* besides Whom all things are miniscule.

[2:256] *There is no compulsion in religion. Rectitude*—faith—*has become clear from error*: disbelief in the manifest signs. The rational person would not choose damnation over salvation after they had been made clear. The root meaning of *ghayy* (error) is *jahl* (ignorance), except that *jahl* refers to doctrine while *ghayy* refers to action. *So whoever disbelieves in the false deity*—meaning everything that leads away from worship of God, or Satan; the word *ṭāghūt* (false deity) comes from *ṭughyān* (injustice)—*and believes in God has laid hold of the most firm handle, unbreaking*: the fixed rope that will never break. *God is Hearing* of words, *Knowing* of intentions.

[2:257] *God is the Protector*—the Trustee of the affairs—*of the believers; He* continuously *brings them forth from the shadows* of ignorance *into the light* of guidance. *And the disbelievers—their protectors are false deities that bring them forth from the light* of innate disposition and their faith in Muḥammad (may God bless him and grant him peace) before his mission began *into the shadows* of corrupted preparedness, or their disbelief in him after his mission began. *Those are the inhabitants of the Fire, therein they will abide.*

[2:258] *Have you not seen*—the question expresses incredulity—*him who disputed with Abraham concerning his Lord, that God had given him kingship?* He extended his kingship for four hundred years. The people then would refer to their kings as lords and gods. *When Abraham said*, when he asked him for proof of his Lord's existence, *'My Lord is He Who gives life, and makes to die,' he*—the one who disputed—*said, 'I give life and make to die'*: by pardoning executions, and by carrying them out. So when it became clear that he understood but was attempting to deceive his people with verbal trickery, *Abraham said*, moving to a concept that anyone could understand: if you are truthful about your power, *'God brings the sun from the East; so bring it from the West'*: since that is its natural destination and so it ought to be easier to do. Thus it may not be argued that Abraham ought to have dispelled the disputant's argument first in order to make clear that he was not stumped by it. Some say that he said to him, 'God restores life by returning the spirit,' to which Nimrod said, 'And have you ever seen this?' So he moved to this line of argument instead, because they were astrologists. *Then the disbeliever was dumbfounded*: stricken silent; *and God guides not the evildoing folk* to sound arguments.

[2:259] *Or* have you seen *such as he*—He singled him out for comparison because of how so many people deny the Resurrection; or it
Q. 2:259 means simply, 'Have you seen him?'—*who passed by a city*: it was Ezra or Khiḍr when passing by Jerusalem after Nebuchadnezzar had laid waste to it; *that was fallen down upon its turrets*: whose roofs had collapsed, or which stood empty though its roofs were still intact. *He said*, marvelling at the thought that it could be restored, *'How shall God give life to this now that it is dead?'* How shall He restore the inhabitants of this place, though they are dead and destroyed? *So God caused him to die* and he remained dead *for a hundred years, and then raised him up* to life. *He*, God, *said* to him, *'How long have you tarried?' He said*, uncertain, *'I have tarried* in death *a day, or part of a day.' He said, 'Nay, you have tarried a hundred years. Look at your food*: the figs or grapes; *and drink*: the juice or grapes he had with him when he died. *It has not spoiled*: changed; the root meaning of *tasannah* (to spoil) is 'to grow mould' as bread and other foodstuffs do as time passes. *And look at your donkey* and its decaying bones, that your insight might increase; *so that We would make you a sign for the people*: he still had black hair and was forty years of age, while his children's hair had turned white. The city had been resettled seventy years after his death. *And look at the bones* of the donkey, or his own bones, for He had brought him back to life in his original body; *how We set them up*: give them life or lift them and arrange them; *and then clothe them with flesh.' So, when it was made clear to him* after having been vague, so that his unseen knowledge became manifest, *he said, 'I know that God has power over all things'*: so he went riding up to the city on his donkey and said, 'I am Ezra,' but they did not believe him until

he recited the Torah from memory, whereupon they recognised him and said, 'He is the son of God!'

[2:260] *And* remember *when Abraham said*, when he saw a wind-battered corpse and wanted to see it restored to life, that his certainty might be strengthened by direct witnessing, or because of what occurred in the aforementioned story of Nimrod, *'My Lord, show me how You give life to the dead'*: the fact that he asked about the *how* of it implies that he was already certain about the life-giving. *He said*, rhetorically, *'Why* do you ask? *Do you not believe?'* The *ḥadīth* 'I would have been more apt to doubt than he' was said out of humility; that is, 'I am lesser than him and I do not doubt, so how could he have doubted?' *'Yes,' he said*, 'I believe *but* I asked *so that my heart may be reassured* by eye-witnessing, just as it is already assured by reason.*' Said He, 'Take four birds*: they were a peacock, an eagle or crow, a rooster and a dove—He chose birds because they are familiar to people, and a plurality of them because of the special properties of every animal—*and tame them to you*: become familiar with them so that you do not confuse them for other birds after they are resurrected; or it means, 'Cut them up.' The words *to you* refer back to *Take*. *Then set a part of them*, after you have cut them up and mixed their flesh, blood and feathers, *on every hill* that is currently visible to you. *Then summon them*—call them to you—*and they will come to you in haste. And know that God is Mighty* such that nothing is beyond Him, *Wise* in His direction.*'* So he did all of that and held their heads in his hand, and then called to them, and the divided parts reassembled, except for the heads. Then he called them again, and the heads reattached. Know also that Abraham's request to witness the revival, and Jesus' frequent raising of the dead to affirm his message, and God's creation and revival of the birds, all indicate that He would sometimes withhold a sign from a particular messenger, even if he was of greater merit, while granting that sign to another messenger, even if he was of lesser merit. Q. 2:260

[2:261] *The likeness of* the spending of *those who expend their wealth in the way of God is as the likeness of a grain of corn that sprouts seven ears* on one stalk, *in every ear a hundred grains; so God multiplies* even more than this *for whom He will*: according to their sincerity and toil; *God is Embracing* with His bounty, *Knowing* of your deeds and intentions.

[2:262] *Those who expend their wealth in the way of God*: meaning all that leads one towards God, such as how ʿUthmān [b. ʿAffān] (may God be pleased with him) supplied the Army of Hardship[1] with a thousand

1 At the Expedition of Tabūk.

camels and their saddles and gear; *then do not follow up their expenditure with reminders of their generosity* (*mann*) *or injury*: the word *mann* means to remind the recipient of a favour of the kindness one has done them; it is a major sin. As for God's Name *al-Mannān*, it means 'the Giver', and He attributed it to Himself when He said, *Rather, it is God Who has done you a favour* [Q. 49:17], regarding the grace of faith. The blameworthy kind of *mann* is to remind another of a material favour one has done them. Many of God's attributes are praiseworthy for Him, but blameworthy for us, such as [His Name] the Proud. *Adhā* (injury) means to act haughtily towards someone because of the favour one has done them. *Their wage is with their Lord* without any debt, *and no fear shall befall them, neither shall they grieve*: this was discussed earlier.

[2:263] *Honourable words*—goodly replies—*and forgiveness* of the beggar's incessant pleas *are better than a voluntary charity followed by injury; and God is Independent*: free of need for your expenditure; *Forbearing* in not hastening your chastisement.

Q. 2:263

[2:264] *O you who believe, annul not* the reward of *your voluntary charity with reproach and injury, as* the nullifying of *one who expends of his substance to show off to people* in desire of praise and renown, *and believes not in God and the Last Day. The likeness of him*—the one who shows off—*is as the likeness of a smooth rock on which is soil* so that it appears to be good soil for farming, just like his deeds, *and a torrent*—a heavy rainfall—*smites it*: this represents the wealth; *and leaves it barren*: smooth and devoid of soil. *They*—people such as this—*have no power over anything that they have earned*: they do not benefit from it. *God guides not the disbelieving folk*: this indicates that ostentation is their attribute, so beware of it.

[2:265] *But the likeness of those who expend their wealth seeking God's good pleasure and to confirm themselves* with the firm belief that God will reward them for it—this implies that the wisdom of expending for the giver is to purify his soul from stinginess and love for wealth—*is as the likeness of a garden*, an orchard, *upon a hill; a torrent smites it and it yields its produce twofold*: as much as two orchards, or simply a large amount, like the phrase *labbayk*;[1] *and if no torrent smites it, then a shower*: their orchard will benefit whether it receives a little water or a large amount. *And God sees what you do*: so do not show off.

[2:266] *Would any of you wish to have a garden of date palms and vines*—He

1 The chant of the *ḥajj* pilgrims, literally meaning 'At Your service twice over,' but implying 'At Your service time and again.'

singled these two out before speaking more generally because of their particular merit—*with rivers flowing from beneath it, and all manner of fruit therein for him; and then old age smites him*, wherein poverty is more difficult to bear, *and he has seed, but they are weak*: infants and females; *then a whirlwind with fire smites it*—the garden—*and it is consumed*. This symbolises the one who does a good deed to show off, for after death he will need it but its fruits will not be there for him. *Thus God makes clear the signs to you, that you might reflect.*

[2:267] *O you who believe, expend* in charity *of the good things you have earned, and* the good things *of what We have produced for you from the earth*: plants and minerals. The words *for you* could be taken as evidence that *zakāt* is not owed on that which is used for livestock and minerals. *And seek not the corrupt of it for your expending*: meaning base things such as dried-out dates; *for you would never take it yourselves without closing your eyes to it*: accepting the poor quality wares begrudgingly. *And know that God is Independent*: free of need for your expenditure, and has enjoined it upon you for your own good; *Laudable* in all that He enjoins. Q. 2:267

[2:268] *Satan promises you poverty* if you expend. A promise can be for an evil thing if it is stated as such, although otherwise it denotes a good thing, while a warning is always for a bad thing. *And [he] enjoins you to indecency*: stinginess. *But God promises you His pardon and His bounty* if you expend; *and God is Embracing* with His bounty, *Knowing* of your deeds.

[2:269] *He gives wisdom*—knowledge and action according to it—*to whomever He will; and he who is given wisdom has been given much good*: for it contains the goodness of this life and the next, and allows one to distinguish the whispers of Satan from the inspirations of the Compassionate. *Yet none remembers*—takes heed—*but the people of pith*: sound intellects.

[2:270] *And whatever expenditure you expend*, of any kind, *and whatever vow you make*, likewise, *surely God knows it* and will reward you. *For the evildoers* who neglect to spend or fulfil their vows, *they have no helpers* to protect them from His chastisement.

[2:271] *If you proclaim*—make public—*your voluntary charity, it is a fine thing* to proclaim them; *but if you conceal them, and give them to the poor, that is even better for you*: this refers to voluntary charity for those who are not known for their wealth. Ibn ʿAbbās (may God be pleased with him) is reported to have said, 'Giving voluntary charity secretly is seventy-something times better, and giving obligatory charity publicly is twenty-five times better.' *And it will absolve you of* some of *your evil deeds. God is aware of what you do.*

[2:272] *You are not responsible for guiding them*: for making them guided; your obligation is only to show them the way. *But God guides whomever He will. And whatever good you expend is for yourselves*: meaning its reward; *for then you are expending, desiring only God's face*: the approval of His Essence; that is, whatever you spend in such a state is ultimately for yourselves. *And whatever good you expend*, even to a disbeliever, *shall be repaid to you in full, and you will not be wronged* by any loss of reward for it. After this was revealed, they began to give charity to disbelievers too; but this applies only to voluntary charity, not the obligatory *zakāt*.

[2:273] *For the poor, who are constrained in the way of God*—devoting themselves to *jihād*, obedience or study—*and who are unable to journey in the land* to earn a living because they are busy with that, *the ignorant person supposes them rich because of their abstinence* from begging, *but you shall know them by their mark* of weakness or signs of exertion. These words are directed to the Messenger, or to everyone. *They do not beg of people importunately* despite their need. This negation of begging importunately seems to be akin to
Q. 2:272 the verse *a cow not broken to plough the earth* [Q. 2:71], meaning that it is only the importunateness that is negated.[1] *And whatever good you expend, surely God has knowledge of it*.

[2:274] *Those who expend their wealth night and day, secretly and openly*: such as [Abū Bakr] al-Ṣiddīq, who gave forty dinars in charity ten by ten in such a manner, or ʿAlī (may God be pleased with him), who gave four dirhams one by one in such a manner, though they were all he possessed. The exact modality in which they gave them is debatable, but the wording of the verse suggests that it was twenty at night in both ways [secretly and openly], and then twenty by day in both ways. And God knows best. The point is that they fill all their differing situations with virtue; *their wage awaits them with their Lord, and no fear shall befall them, neither shall they grieve* at the Resurrection.

[2:275] *Those who consume*—take—*usury*: meaning an unequal exchange of currency or foodstuffs, whether by simultaneous measure or delay. He spoke of all manner of benefit in terms of consumption, since that is the primary mode of it. [*They*] *shall not rise again* from their graves *except as one whom Satan has made prostrate*—beaten or wrestled into submission—*from touch*: meaning possession; so they will only be able to stand like one who is bent-over because of the weight of the usury in their bellies. The verb *khabaṭ* (to make prostrate) literally means 'to beat

1 That is, such people might engage in begging, as long as it is not importune.

wildly'. *That* chastisement *is because they say, 'Trade is like usury'* in its lawfulness. What they meant is that usury is like trade, but it is reversed to add emphasis. *Yet God has permitted trade, and forbidden usury*: so their equivalency is false. *Whoever receives an admonition from his Lord and desists*—takes admonition—*he shall have his past gains* of usury which he made in the age of ignorance, and it shall not be seized from him, *and his affair is committed to God*: to judge among them. *But whoever reverts* to permitting it, *those are the inhabitants of the Fire, therein they will abide* because of their disbelief in Him. Or it refers to the one who returns to consuming it, in which case the *abiding* means a lengthy [but not eternal] stay.

[2:276] *God effaces* the blessing of *usury, but He augments*—gives growth to—*voluntary charity. God loves not any disbelieving sinner*: disbelieving in that he insists that what is forbidden is lawful, and sinful in that he indulges in it.

[2:277] *Those who believe and perform righteous deeds, and observe the prayer, and pay zakāt—their wage awaits them with their Lord, and no fear shall befall them, neither shall they grieve.* Q. 2:276

[2:278] *O you who believe, fear God, and give up the usury that is outstanding* with those who owe it, and do not collect it, *if you are believers.*

[2:279] *But if you do not* leave it, *then be warned* and warn the people *of a* terrible *war from God and His Messenger*: the ruler must fight them after they have been invited to repent, until they desist. *Yet if you repent* of permitting it and taking it, *you shall have your principal sums, neither wronging* by taking more, *nor being wronged* by losing out. This implies that if they do not repent of permitting it, their principal sums will not be returned to them, but rather seized.

[2:280] *And if any man*—any debtor—*should be in difficulties, then* you should give him *respite till things are easier*: do not chase him up to repay or charge him usury. *But that you should give a voluntary charity* by forgiving all or part of his debt *is better for you* than taking it, *did you but know* that the virtue of charity, even though it is voluntary, is greater than that of giving respite, even though it is obligatory, because it is a voluntary act that achieves the purpose of the obligation, and more besides.

[2:281] *And fear a day wherein you shall be returned to God* for the Resurrection, *and every soul shall be paid in full* the reward of *what it has earned; and they shall not be wronged* by losing out on any reward. This was the last verse of the Qur'ān to be revealed. The Prophet (may God bless him and grant him peace) lived for another twenty-one days after its revelation.

[2:282] *O you who believe, when you contract a debt*, such as a loan—in the expression *tadāyantum bi-dayn* (contract a debt), the reason for adding *bi-dayn* is to exclude the other meaning of *tadāyantum*, namely 'to repay' (the distinction between them is that *dayn* means 'debt', while *dīn* means 'repayment')—*for a stated term*, such as a number of days, not for something vague like 'until harvest', which is not a proper stated term; *write it down*: this is a command of guidance [rather than obligation]; *and let a writer write it down between you justly* without adding or subtracting anything; therefore, he must be a pious jurist. *And let not any writer refuse to write it down, as God has taught him*, such as writing agreements. *So let him write, and let the debtor dictate* to serve as a testimony in the presence of the scribe; *and let him fear God his Lord, and not diminish anything of it*: let him not exclude anything from his side of the debt. *And if the debtor be a fool*, legally restricted because of his profligacy or the like, *or weak* of intellect such as a child, *or unable to dictate himself* because he is dumb or ignorant of
Q. 2:282 the language, *then let his guardian*, such as an agent, caretaker or translator, *dictate justly*, truthfully. This is proof of the lawfulness of testimony by proxy when undertaken by a caretaker or agent. *And summon to bear witness* over the debt *two witnesses, men* who are Muslim and free—Abū Ḥanīfa deemed it permitted for disbelievers to bear witness for one another—*or if the two be not men, then one man and two women* for financial matters, as the Sunna established. Abū Ḥanīfa extended this to all testimonies except those relating to legally prescribed punishments and retribution. *Such witnesses as you approve of* based on your knowledge of them, *so that if one of the two women errs*—forgets her testimony—*the other will remind her*: the reason is the reminder, but the error is its cause, so He put the latter in the former's place. *And let the witnesses not refuse when they are summoned* to bear witness. *And be not disdainful* because of the frequency of loaning *to write it down*, whether it be *small or great, with its term*: the time of its due date as agreed by the debtor. *That* writing *is more equitable* (*aqsaṭ*): more just; *qasṭ* means 'injustice', while *qisṭ* means 'equity'; *in God's sight, more upright for* the establishment of *testimony, and nearer, that you will not be in doubt* about the nature and description of the debt, and if any doubts arise you can consult the document; *unless it be trade carried out there and then*, in the immediate moment, *that you give and take between you,* hand to hand; *for then you will not be at fault if you do not write it down*: since it is unlikely to be disputed or forgotten. *And* you are recommended to *take witnesses when you are trading with one another*: even in the present moment. *And let not either writer or witness be harmed*: the verb can be read in the active voice, in which

case it means that the writer should not cause harm by failing to acquiesce or by falsifying, and the witness should not cause harm likewise; or in the passive voice, in which case it means that neither should be harmed by withholding their pay or the like. The majority consider most of the commands in this passage to be meant as recommendations only. *And if you do* cause harm, *that is sinfulness in you. And fear God* lest you disobey Him. *God teaches you* His edicts; *and God knows all things.*

[2:283] *And if you are upon a journey, and you do not find a writer, then a deposit in hand*: trust in that in place of writing. The Sunna made it clear that this is permitted when not travelling as well, even if a writer is available. The term *in hand* indicates that it must be handed over, though Mālik disagreed. *But if one of you trusts another* and does not take a deposit, *let him who is trusted deliver his trust*: the debt is called 'a trust' because he has been trusted to repay it by the forgoing of a deposit, such as by handing him the full sum; *and let him fear God his Lord* lest he renege. *And do not conceal the testimony; whoever conceals it, his heart is sinful*: the sin is attributed to the heart because concealment is a sin of the heart, and it is more rhetorically effective to attribute the sin to the body part that performs it. *And God knows what you do.* Q. 2:283

[2:284] *To God belongs all that is in the heavens and the earth* by ownership and creation. *Whether you disclose what is in your hearts* by speech or action, such as giving testimonies, *or hide it*, such as concealing testimony, *God shall take you to account for it. Then He will forgive whom He wishes, and chastise whom He wishes*: this is an explicit declaration that chastisement is not inevitable. *And God has power over all things*: including concealment and reckoning. The revelation of this verse caused disquiet among the Companions, who said, 'Our hearts are not in our hands!' The Prophet (may God bless him and grant him peace) told them simply to say, 'We hear and obey.' Then God revealed:

[2:285] *The Messenger believes in what was revealed to him from his Lord*: He praised him for his faith, and singled faith out for mention because of its great nobility; *and the believers; each one*—the Messenger and the believers—*believes in God and His angels, and in* the general truth of *His Books, and His messengers.* They say, *'We make no distinction between any of His messengers* regarding belief in them.*' And they say, 'We hear and obey* the Word of God, and we ask *Your forgiveness, our Lord*, for our shortcomings; *to You is the homecoming*: we affirm our belief in the Resurrection.*'* So when they did this, He then revealed:

[2:286] *God charges no soul save to its capacity*: what it is able to bear, and not such things as the thoughts of the soul. This indicates that He does not hold people accountable for doing what is impossible, though it does not mean that He would not be able to do so if He chose. *For it is what it is has acquired* (*kasabat*) of good, meaning what it has found, *and against it is what it has earned* (*iktasabat*) of evil, meaning what it has actively attained; for the soul inclines towards evil and strives harder to attain it. Or at least that is what some say, although it does not accord with His Words, *And whoever commits* (*yaksib*)[1] *a mistake*... [Q. 4:112], and the like, or *whoever acquires* (*yaqtarif*) *a good deed*... [Q. 42:23], which means the same as *yaktasib*. Some said that the distinction [between good and evil] is implied by the use of *for* (*la*) and *against* (*ʿalā*), but this does not accord with *theirs* (*lahum*) *will be the curse* [Q. 40:52] and *upon those* (*ʿalayhim*) *rest blessings* [Q. 2:157].[2] However, one could argue that they denote this only when they are used in an unqualified context without specific mention of good and evil.

Q. 2:286 In any case, this verse abrogated the aforementioned reckoning [of unspoken thoughts] according to the narration of the majority, while ʿĀ'isha (may God be pleased with her) related that the Prophet (may God bless him and grant him peace) explained the reckoning here to mean how God chastises the servant by trying him with tribulations in this world, such as fever and the like, as expiations for sin, in which case the reckoning can be taken to mean rebuke in the world, or the like. Know also that worldly rebuke for the thoughts of the soul would not contradict our belief that they are not punished unless they become firm resolutions, because the meaning here is punishment in the Hereafter.

'Our Lord, take us not to task if we forget, or err: if we slip into error. The verb *akhṭa'* (to err) means 'to make a mistake', while *khaṭa'* means 'to sin deliberately'. It is established by tradition that indeed we will not be taken to task for these and that this prayer has been answered; and therefore when we recite this prayer now, our intent is to ask Him not to expel us from the community of His Beloved (may God bless him and grant him peace). The meaning of 'error' is to do something that ought not to be willed or done, or to do something unlawful without meaning to, or the opposite; the second of these is what is meant here. *Our Lord, burden us not with a load*—a heavy weight of difficult responsibilities, even if we are able to bear them—*such as You did lay upon those before us*, such as the children of Israel. *Our Lord, do not burden us beyond what we have the power to*

1 The same verbal form as *kasabat*. The issue at hand is the precise distinction between the forms *kasab/yaksib* and *iktasab/yaktasib*, which are morphological forms from the same root.

2 Where *la* is used to denote evil, and *ʿalā* means good.

bear: whether tribulations or responsibilities. *And pardon us* by remitting our sins, *and forgive us* by covering them and manifesting kindness, *and have mercy on us* by showering us with kindness: the second is broader than the first, and the third broader than the second. *You are our Patron*—our Master—*so grant us assistance against the disbelieving folk'*: Muslim and others narrated that God Almighty says at the end of each of these prayers, 'I shall' and 'Let it be so.' Praise be to God, the Patron of Favour!

Q. 2:286

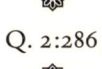

3
The Family of ʿImrān
SŪRAT ĀL ʿIMRĀN

Two Hundred Verses. Revealed in Medina

After praising the Messenger and the believers for their faith in what was revealed to him, and praising them for their various supplications, the text then repeats an affirmation of the truth of what was revealed to him to strengthen them further and dispel any doubt, and to correspond to the opening of the previous *sūra* by dispelling any doubt about the Book. Therefore, He said:

In the Name of God, the Compassionate, the Merciful

[3:1] *Alif. Lām. Mīm*: this was explained before. When recited without a pause before the next verse, the *Mīm* is terminated with a *fatḥa* vowel[1] because the *hamza* [of *Allāh*] is dropped when the words are connected, and so the *Mīm* takes on the *fatḥa* vowel because of how it is followed by the heavy long vowel [of *Allāh*]. Some say that it is given a *fatḥa* to stand in for the *hamza*, which is dropped for the sake of easier pronunciation, just as when counting one says, '*Wāḥid, ithnān*,' and so on.[2]

[3:2] *God! There is no god except Him, the Living, the Eternal*: the Name *al-Qayyūm* (the Eternal) is the emphatic *fayʿūl* form of *qām* (to stand); these Names are both from the Supreme Name.

[3:3] *He has revealed to you* piece by piece *the Book*: the Qur'ān, the one Book whose authority will remain forever, unlike the others; adorned *with the truth, confirming what was before it*: confirming what the Books before it said about it coming from God, or confirming that they too

1 In other words, it is pronounced *Alif-Lām-Mīma'Llāh*...

2 Without joining the numbers together with their case endings, following the usual rules of Classical Arabic.

were from Him; *and He revealed the Torah and the Gospel* in their totality all at once, before they were revealed piece by piece.

[3:4] *Before* its revelation, *as guidance*, as two guides *for people*, for humanity, such that we worship Him by following the Law of those who preceded us, or those who followed those two guides. *And He revealed the Criterion*: the heavenly Books that discriminate between truth and falsehood, or prophetic miracles. *As for those who disbelieve in God's signs, for them awaits a terrible chastisement; God is Mighty*, Omnipotent, *Lord of Retribution* against those who oppose Him. Retribution means the punishment for criminals.

[3:5] *Nothing whatsoever is hidden in heaven and earth from God*: He mentioned *heaven and earth* because our senses do not go beyond them, and put *earth* second because it is lower. The verse is an affirmation of His life.

[3:6] *He it is Who forms you in the wombs as He will*: in whatever configuration, even without a father, like Jesus; and the Former is not the father of what He forms. This verse is an affirmation of His eternality and all-sustaining power. *There is no god except Him, the Mighty* in His dominion, *the Wise* in His creation. Q. 3:4

[3:7] *He it is Who revealed to you the Book*, the Qur'ān, *wherein are verses [that are] clear*, of obvious import, each one of them *forming the Mother of the Book*, the foundation of it to which all else refers; *and others*—other verses—which are *ambiguous*: bearing multiple possible meanings so that their import only becomes clear upon examination and contemplation. The wisdom of encouraging contemplation is to prevent the neglect of the intellect, and to ensure that the reward for it is attained. It is also to combine both categories of Arabic speech; that is, the kind that is understood immediately and bears no alternative interpretation, and the kind that is the inverse of this, like writing and gesturing, so that both types of speech were covered.

NOTE: The common designation of speech into the categories of 'clear' (*muḥkam*) and 'ambiguous' (*mutashābih*) is somewhat unclear, and requires some elucidation. Therefore, it should be noted that ambiguous speech is either intrinsically or extrinsically ambiguous. For the former, it can be found in a simple expression because of its rareness, such as *abb*,[1] or because of its anthropomorphic implication, such as 'the hand of God'. It can also be found in compound expressions, whether because they are ambiguous in their brevity, such as *Ask the city in which we were* [Q. 12:82],

1 In Q. 80:31, a rare word meaning 'pastures'.

or their prolixity, such as *There is nothing like unto Him* [Q. 42:11], or their non-specificity, such as in the verse *But if it be discovered*...[Q. 5:107]. It can also be found in the meaning of the expression, such as the Attributes of God, or the Resurrection, or because the words are not arranged in the order one would expect, such as the verse, *And were it not for some believing men*...[Q. 48:25]. It can also be found in both the expression and the meaning, with the same categories as those just described. As for the extrinsically ambiguous, the ambiguity might be found in the aspect of quantity, such as the question of universality or particularity; or modality, such as the question of obligation or recommendation; or chronology, such as the question of abrogation; or locality, such as the question of the place of revelation; or relativity. All of these [quantity, modality, chronology, locality and relativity] are conditions which could determine the validity or invalidity of a contract.

Q. 3:7

According to the terminology of the scholars of jurisprudence (*uṣūl*), if an expression only has one meaning and cannot bear another, it is called 'explicit' (*naṣṣ*). If it could bear another meaning and both are equally valid, it is called 'ambivalent' (*mujmal*). If one meaning is more obvious than the other, then the more obvious meaning is called 'literal' (*ẓāhir*), and the less obvious is [regarded as] 'allegorical' (*mu'awwal*). The common factor between the explicit and the literal—namely obviousness of meaning—is what is meant by 'clear'. The common factor between the ambivalent and the allegorical—namely lack of obviousness of meaning—is what is meant by 'ambiguous'. So the designations of clear and ambiguous comprise all the categories of expressions. Now this does not contradict the verse *God has revealed the best of discourses, a Book consimilar* (*mutashābih*) [Q. 39:23], nor the verse *A Book whose verses have been set clear* [Q. 11:1], because the former means that the Book's parts resemble one another in terms of authority and rhetoric, while the latter means that the Book's verses are protected from corruption of both expression and meaning.

As for those in whose hearts is deviation from the truth, such as the heretics, *they follow*, attach to, *the allegorical part*, to interpret it in line with their corrupt desires, ignoring the clear part, *desiring sedition* such as leading people astray, *and desiring its interpretation* according to their desires. Once the Prophet (may God bless him and grant him peace) recited this verse and then said to ʿĀ'isha (may God be pleased with her), 'If you see those who follow the allegorical part, they are the ones of whom God spoke, so avoid them.' Another *ḥadīth* states, 'I do not fear for my community, except because of three traits.' One of the traits he named was, 'That the Book is opened for them, but the believer seizes it desiring its interpretation.' *Yet none knows its interpretation*—its reality—*save God. And those firmly rooted in knowledge*—Ibn ʿAbbās (may God be pleased with him) said, 'I am one of them'; most of the early Muslims would pause after the words *save God*[1]—*say, 'We believe in it*: the ambiguous part; *all is from our Lord.' Yet none remembers*—takes admonition from the Qur'ān—*but people of pith*: the folk of sound intellects among those firmly rooted in faith. They also say:

[3:8] *'Our Lord, do not cause our hearts to deviate*—do not allow our hearts to swerve from truth towards interpretations which You do not approve—*after You have guided us* to the truth; *and give us mercy from You*: make us firm. *You are the Bestower* to all who ask.

[3:9] *'Our Lord, You shall gather people for a day*—on a day—*of which there is no doubt* regarding its occurrence. *Truly, God will not fail the tryst'*: the way this is worded in the third person implies that God's nature dictates that He will not fail it. The Waʿīdiyya sects[2] cite this as evidence for their position; but the rebuttal is that the warning issued to the iniquitous will only be carried out on condition that they are not pardoned, and on condition that they fail to repent.

Q. 3:8

[3:10] *As for the disbelievers, neither their riches nor their children will avail them against God*: to save them from His chastisement. The verb *tughnī* (avail) is from *aghnā*, meaning 'to stand in for' or 'to make distant from'. *Those—they shall be fuel for the Fire*: their abode.

[3:11] *As the way of the people of Pharaoh, and the people before them*, which was that *they denied Our signs, and so God seized them for their sins; God is severe in retribution*.

[3:12] *Say*, O Muḥammad, *to the disbelievers* among the Jews, *'You shall be vanquished* in this world *and mustered to Hell—an evil cradling!*

[3:13] *'There has already been a sign*—a proof of the victory of the believers—*for you* disbelievers, *in two hosts that met* on the day of Badr; *one company fighting in the way of God, and another disbelieving; they saw them twice the like of them, as the eye sees*: the disbelievers saw the Muslims as twice their number, though there were around a thousand of them while the Muslims numbered only 310 and a handful more, so that they would be encouraged. Or the Muslims saw their own numbers as twice that of the

1 Rather than reciting it as, *Yet none knows its interpretation save God and those firmly rooted in knowledge; they say...*

2 Meaning those sects who believe that God is inevitably bound to punish sinners and carry out His warnings towards them, and cannot pardon them or remit their punishment, since this would constitute a broken promise, which is impossible for the Divine.

disbelievers, or twice their own number, so that they would be encouraged although in reality they were outnumbered more than three to one. This was at the end of the fighting; as for at the onset, each side underestimated the numbers of their enemy, and so advanced, as He describes: *And when God made you see them, when you met, in your eyes as few; and He made you seem as few in their eyes*...[Q. 8:44]. *God confirms with His help whom He will. Truly, in that* magnifying and minimising *is a lesson for people of vision*: [people of] insight.'

[3:14] *Beautified for people is* the tribulation of *love of lusts*: meaning objects of lust. *Shahwa* (lust) means the soul's agitation towards what it desires. It can be false, such as *they followed their lusts* [Q. 19:59]; or true, such as *therein will be whatever souls desire* [Q. 43:71]; or it could mean either, such as in the present verse: *of women; children; stored-up heaps of gold and silver; horses of mark*: horses that are marked, herding horses, or high breeds; *cattle*: camels, cows and sheep; *and tillage. That is the comfort of the life of this*
Q. 3:14 ephemeral *world; but God—with Him is the more excellent abode*: this is an encouragement to direct one's lust towards that abode instead of those other things.

[3:15] *Say: 'Shall I tell you of something better than that? For those that are fearful* of sin *with their Lord are Gardens beneath* the trees of *which rivers flow, abiding therein, and spouses purified* from all that is tainted, *and beatitude from God* so that He is never wrath with them again. So He described how the lowest level of bliss is the enjoyment of this world, and the middle level is the Garden, and the highest level is His beatitude. *And God is Seer of His servants*, and will reward them according to their deeds. They are:

[3:16] *'Those who say, "O, Our Lord, we believe; so forgive us our sins, and guard us from the chastisement of the Fire!"*

[3:17] *'The patient* in steadfastly resisting caprice (*hawā*) and adhering to the Law; *truthful* in speech; *obedient*: humble and dutiful; *expenders* on righteousness; *imploring God's pardon in the watches of the night'*: meaning the final third of the night, which is a time when prayers are answered.

[3:18] *God bears witness that there is no god* worthy of worship *except Him*: by revealing that which speaks for Him, and upholding its proofs; *as do the angels* by confirming this, *and those of knowledge* by confirming it and arguing for it. He likens His unveiling here to the testimony of a witness. Note that affirming and confirming are both elements of a single metaphorical concept, namely the unveiling, which here is symbolised by bearing witness, and therefore this is not a double metaphor. In this, God is *upholding justice* through His testimony and rule, or assuring justice in them. *There is no god except Him*: a reaffirmation, or the first was to describe while the second is to teach; *the Mighty* in His power, *the Wise* in His acts.

[3:19] *Truly, the* approved *religion with God is submission* (*islām*): following [the religion of] Muḥammad (may God bless him and grant him peace), and no other [religion] is accepted. It can also be read as *that the religion*, referring back to *God bears witness* [Q. 3:18]. *Those who were given the Book differed* about the truth of this submission *only after knowledge* of its truth *came to them, through transgression*—envy—*among themselves*: not because of any valid doubt. *And whoever disbelieves in God's signs, God is swift at reckoning* for their requital.

[3:20] *So if they dispute with you*—if they continue to argue after the proof is established—*say* by way of parting ways with them: *'I have surrendered my countenance*, my being; the face represents the being because it is the noblest of the external body parts, being the locus of the faculties and senses; *to God, as has whoever follows me'; and say to those who have been given the Book, and to the unlettered*, the idol-worshipping Arabs: *'Have you submitted* now that the proof has been made plain, or not*?'* This is a rhetorical question to rebuke their obstinacy and idiocy. *And so if they have submitted, they have been guided, but if they turn their backs, your duty is only to deliver*, and not to ensure that they are guided. *And God sees His servants*: and will requite them. Q. 3:19

[3:21] *Those who disbelieve in the signs of God*, such as the Jews, *and slay the prophets without right* by their own reckoning, such as how the Jews slew forty prophets in an hour, *and slay those who enjoin to equity*, for they slew 170 scholars when they tried to prevent them from slaying their prophets. They were the forebears of those folk, who were proud of them and so were the same as them. *So give them tidings of a painful chastisement.*

[3:22] *Those are the ones whose deeds have failed*, become annulled, *in this world* so that their blood and property is not sacred, *and the Hereafter; and they have no helpers* to repel their chastisement.

[3:23] *Have you not seen those who were given a portion of the Book*, the Torah, *being called to the Book of God*, again the Torah, *that it might decide between them* concerning the matter of stoning the adulterous man when the Prophet (may God bless him and grant him peace) ruled in accordance with it, but they covered up the verse about stoning until Ibn Salām (may God be pleased with him) uncovered it, which enraged them; *and then a party of them turned away, opposed?* It was their wont to turn away from the truth.

[3:24] *That* opposition *was because they said, 'The Fire shall not touch us, except for a number of days'*: meaning a few days, as was discussed earlier; they belittled the prospect of God's chastisement. *The lies they used to invent*—such as the one about how the Fire will not touch them—*have deluded them in their religion*.

[3:25] *But how will it be when We gather them for a day*—on a day—*of which there is no doubt, and every soul shall be paid in full* the requital of *what is has earned*: this indicates that worship will not fail and that the believer will not remain in Hell perpetually, because his faith could not be paid in full there, nor before it, and so it must be after; *and they shall not be wronged* by any loss of reward.

[3:26] *Say: 'O God*: the expression *Allāhumma* means 'O God', or 'O God, turn to us with favour'; *Master of the kingdom* Who has control over all that can be controlled, *You give the kingdom to whom You will*, such as Muḥammad and his Companions, *and seize the kingdom from whom You will*,
Q. 3:24 such as the Jews and Persians; or *kingdom* here means prophethood, and the seizure of it means its transference. *You exalt whom You will, and You abase whom You will; in Your hand is good*: He singled out good alone [and not evil] because it is more respectful, or because of how He ordains all things Himself, or because the context is that of gratitude. He then made clear that both good and evil are under His power by saying: *You are Able to do all things*.

[3:27] *'You make the night to pass into the day and You make the day to pass into the night*: by making one of them grow and the other shrink, or by making them succeed each other. *You bring forth the living from the dead* as a drop, *and You bring forth the dead from the living* as a drop, or the Muslim from the disbeliever and vice versa; *and You provide whom You will without reckoning'*: without straitening, for reckoning is only for small amounts.

[3:28] *Let not the believers take the disbelievers as patrons* whatsoever, lest their love be for anything but the sake of God, *rather than the believers*, who are more worthy of love; *for whoever does that, [they] do not belong to* the patronage of *God in any way*, because there can never be love between enemies; *unless you protect yourselves against them, as a safeguard* against something you fear from them, in which case it is permitted to be open allies with them. *God warns you of His Self* and His chastisement; *and to God is the journey's end*: so beware of Him.

[3:29] *Say: 'Whether you hide what is in your breasts*—your love—*or disclose it, God knows it*: and will requite you for it; *and knows what is in the heavens and what is in the earth; and God is Able to do all things'*: including your chastisement.

[3:30] Remember *the day every soul shall find* the requital for *what it has done of good present before it, and* the requital of *what it has done of evil, it will wish that between it and that* day *there were a great distance. God warns you of His Self*: He repeated this for emphasis; *and God is Kind to His servants*: which is why He warns them for their own good.

[3:31] *Say: 'If you love God*: love is the soul's inclination towards something because of a perfection it perceives in it that motivates it to be nearer to it. When the servant realises that true perfection is God's alone, he will not love anything but Him, and so he will obey His commands. [*If you love God,*] *follow me, and God will love you* by approving of you; and what a difference there is between loving and being loved; *and forgive you your sins; God is Forgiving, Merciful.'*

[3:32] *Say: 'Obey God, and the Messenger.' But if they turn their backs* to obedience, *God loves not the disbelievers* and so He does not love them.

[3:33] *Truly, God preferred* with messengerhood *Adam and Noah*: the
first to be sent to the idol-worshippers; *and the Family of Abraham*: the
last of whom was the Beloved of God (may God bless him and grant him Q. 3:30
peace); *and the Family of ʿImrān*: meaning the father of Mary or Moses,
who lived eighteen hundred years apart; *above the worlds*: kingship was also
among them, when the two families were:

[3:34] A branching *progeny, one of the other*: the word *dhurriyya* (progeny) means 'son', from *dharr* (seed), but can be used as a singular or a plural. *God is Hearer* of your words, *Knower* of your deeds, and He prefers those words and deeds that are upright. And remember:

[3:35] *When the wife of ʿImrān*—Hannah the mother of Mary—*said, 'Lord, I have vowed to You what is within my womb*—and so I shall not put him to work—*as a consecration*: a devotion to Your worship. *Accept this* vow *from me. Truly, You are the Hearer* of my prayer, *the Knower* of my intention.*'* This vow was permitted for them for male children only.

[3:36] *And when she gave birth to her*—to a female child—*she said* in woe and disappointment, *'Lord, I have given birth to a female'*—*and God knew very well what she had given birth to*: this can also be read as 'and God knows very well what I have given birth to' in the first person, in which case it means 'perhaps there is a secret wisdom behind it'. *And the male is not as the female* regarding her vow that the child would serve Jerusalem. The words are put out of order by way of imparting emphasis, such as saying, 'The moon is like his face'; or it is an honour from God to Mary, meaning 'the male you sought would not be like this female, for she and her son will be a sign for the world'. *'And I have named her Mary*: a hopeful name, since it means 'devout'; *and I commend her to You,* to Your care, *with her seed, to protect them from the accursed*, rejected, *Satan'*: and so Satan did not touch her, nor her son.

[3:37] *Her Lord accepted the child with gracious acceptance*: so that she was allowed to stay in His chamber, while only males were usually allowed; *and made her grow excellently*: so that she grew up with virtue and knowledge of God, and grew as much as a year in a single day; *and Zachariah*—her aunt's husband—*took charge of her. Whenever Zachariah went to her in the sanctuary*—the room built for her in the temple, which was called a *miḥrāb* (high chamber) because of its elevation, or because it was a place for resisting (*muḥāraba*) Satan—*he found her with provisions*: summer fruits in winter, and vice versa, or the like. *'O Mary,' he said, 'Whence comes this to you?' She said, 'From God*: she spoke in her infancy, like Jesus. She never suckled, but received provision which descended to her from the Garden. The verse is proof of the existence of saintly miracles (*karāmāt*), since if it was a prophetic miracle (*muʿjiza*) of Zachariah he would not have been confused
Q. 3:37 about it. *Truly, God provides for whomever He will without reckoning*: without straitening them.'

[3:38] *Then Zachariah prayed to his Lord, saying, 'Lord, bestow upon me from You a goodly offspring*: just as you did for Hannah, who was old and barren. *Truly, You are the Hearer* and Answerer *of supplication.'*

[3:39] *And the angels*—that is, one of them, for it was Gabriel—*called to him as he stood praying in the sanctuary, that 'God gives you glad tidings of John*, from your loins, *who shall confirm a Word from God*, meaning Jesus, who was called this because of how he was brought into existence with a single word, 'Be!' like the principal entities (*badʿiyyāt*) in the realm of divine command (*ʿālam al-amr*). He would prostrate to God while still in his mother's womb, and professed his faith in Him at the age of three. *A master*: one followed by his people, for the word *sayyid* (master) comes from *mutawallī al-sawād* meaning 'leader of the group', or it means that he would be a master of his own soul, restraining it from lusts or sins; *and one chaste*: one who keeps himself away from women; *and a prophet of the righteous* prophets who do not commit any sins, major or minor.' It is related that his cousin Jesus never made an error or even thought about doing so.

[3:40] *He said*, expressing his surprise, or asking how they could be returned to youth and fertility, *'My Lord, how shall I have a boy when old age has overtaken me, and my wife is barren?'* He was one hundred and twenty years old, and she was ninety-eight. *He*, the angel, *said, 'So it will be*: meaning the command that a boy be created for you. *God does what He will*: and nothing is beyond His power.' It was in order to manifest this tremendous power that he was inspired to ask this question, so that the answer could be given.

[3:41] *He said,* because his soul was accustomed to the usual human way of things, *'My Lord, appoint for me a sign'* that my wife is with child. *He*, God, *said, 'Your sign is that you shall not speak to people*, that you will be unable to speak to them, except with remembrance of God, *save by tokens*, gestures, *for three days. And remember your Lord*—pray—*much*: this primarily denotes emphasis and not necessarily repetition; *and glorify [Him] at evening and dawn*: at the end and the beginning of the day.'

[3:42] *And* remember *when the angels*, meaning Gabriel, *said, 'O Mary, God has preferred you*—chosen you—*and made you pure* from the touch of men; *He has preferred you above all women of the worlds* with saintly miracles to pave the way for the prophethood of Jesus, that is, from the people of your time.

[3:43] *'O Mary, be obedient to your Lord, prostrating and bowing*—according to the arrangement of the mode of prayer they had in that time—*with those who bow*: that is, prayer with the congregation.' Q. 3:41

[3:44] *That*—the story of Zachariah and Mary—*is of the tidings of the Unseen*: the accounts of things that were not visible to you. *We reveal it to you*, O Muḥammad, *for you were not with them when they were casting quills*—the brass quills with which they used to write the Torah in the river Jordan, or which they would cast into the water to invoke a sign—*for which of them should have charge of Mary* to raise her as their ward; and it was Zachariah's quill that floated, so he took charge of her. Your knowledge of this is only by means of the revelation which We reveal to you. *Nor were you with them when they were disputing* about her raising, such that you could know of this and speak about it; you only know it by means of revelation.

[3:45] *And* remember *when the angels*—meaning Gabriel—*said, 'O Mary, God gives you tidings of* a boy whose existence is by means of *a Word from Him*, not like other children, *whose name is the Messiah (al-Masīḥ)*: *Masīḥ* is the Arabicised form of *Mashīḥā*, meaning 'blessed' or 'anointed with blessing', or 'one unaffected by any blemish that touches him'; *Jesus* (*ʿĪsā*)—[*ʿĪsā* is] the Arabicised form of *Ayshūʿ*—*son of Mary*: He placed the title before the name so as to honour him; and attributed him to Mary, even though she already knew she was to be his mother, in order to make clear that he should not be attributed to any other, and to show that he would be born without a father, for the usual custom of men is to name children after their fathers. *Honoured*—of tremendous status and rank—

shall he be in this world by prophethood, *and the Hereafter* by intercession and the loftiest ranks, *and of those brought close* to God.

[3:46] *'He shall speak to people in the cradle*: meaning when he is still in his infant's bed, before the usual age of speech; *and in his manhood* after he descends, for he was raised up when still in his youth. This was also a glad tiding to her that he would live to an old age, though he was born a month premature and was not expected to live. Moreover, his speech will be clear in his infancy as well as in his manhood; *and one of the righteous*: the folk of perfect righteousness.'

[3:47] *She said*, expressing surprise, or as was explained previously, *'Lord, how shall I have a child when no mortal has touched me?'* She was devoted to the temple, and such people never married or had any other relations. *He said, 'It is such*: a child will be created in you without a father. *God creates what He will*: He said *creates* here, rather than 'does', as before, because of the particular unusualness of the situation, which was an act of engendering without matter. *When He decrees a thing* that He wishes to create, *He says to it only "Be!" and it is.'*

Q. 3:46

[3:48] *And We will teach him*—this can also be read as *He will teach him*—*the Book*, meaning literacy in general or writing, *and wisdom* in general, or knowledge and action according to it, *and the Torah, and the Gospel*, which he knew by heart.

[3:49] *And* We shall make him *a messenger to the Children of Israel*: in his childhood or after he reaches adulthood. Then Gabriel blew into the sleeve of her garment, and she became pregnant, and her story continued as described in *Sūrat Maryam* [Q. 19]. And when God sent him to the Children of Israel, he said to them, 'I am God's messenger to you': *'I have come to you with a sign from your Lord*, which is that *I will create*—shape—*for you out of clay like the shape of a bird, and then I will breathe into it, and it will be a bird*: an alternative recitation has *and it will fly*; *by the leave of God*: by His will. Then he created a bat for them, because it is the most complete of all the flying creatures, and it flew around before them as they looked on. Subsequently, as soon as it was out of their sight, it fell down dead. *And I will heal the blind* (*akmah*): *akmah* means one who is blind from birth; *and the leper*: he singled these two out because they are incurable conditions even in the time of medical advancements in which he was sent. In one day he cured fifty thousand people by supplicating for them on condition that they had faith. *And I will bring to life the dead, by the leave of God*: he repeated this to dispel any suggestion of his own divinity. He raised to life Lazarus who was a friend of his, and the son of an old widow, and the daughter of al-ᶜĀshir, all of whom lived on and had children, and also Shem the son of Noah, who died again immediately afterwards. *I will inform you too of what things you will eat* now, *and what you treasure up*—store—*in your houses* which I have not seen. He would tell a person what he had eaten, and what he would go on to eat. *Truly, in that is a sign for you, if you are believers*: if you have been given the grace of faith.

[3:50] '*Likewise,* I have come to you *confirming that which was before me of the Torah, and* I have come to you *to make lawful for you some of that which was forbidden to you* therein. For example, he permitted them certain fish and birds that have no claws. Some say he permitted them all, and that *some* here means 'all'. *I have come to you* now, as I told you before—the first was to pave the way for the message—*with a sign from your Lord* of my truthfulness; *so fear God, and obey me* in what He has commanded you, namely to uphold God's Oneness and obey Him.

[3:51] '*Truly, God is my Lord and your Lord* by command. He repeated this for emphasis and so that he could elaborate on it by saying: *so worship Him. This*—that which He has commanded you—*is a straight path.'* But they belied him and did not believe in him: Q. 3:50

[3:52] *And when Jesus sensed their disbelief* and how they wanted to slay him, *he said, 'Who will be my helpers unto God?' The disciples*—those who aided his religion, the chosen ones of Jesus and the first to believe in him, who were twelve in number; they were called *Ḥawariyyūn* from *ḥawar*, which means 'pure white'; it is said that they had been cloth-dyers who bleached fabric to make it white—*said, 'We will be helpers of God*, aiding His religion; *we believe in God. Witness*, O Jesus, *that we have submitted.*

[3:53] '*Lord, we believe in what You have revealed* in the Gospel, *and we follow the Messenger* Jesus; *inscribe us therefore with those who bear witness'*: to Your Oneness; or it means the community of Muḥammad (may God bless him and grant him peace), for they bear witness before the people to Your Oneness and the truthfulness of Your Messenger.

[3:54] *And they*, the disbelievers of the Children of Israel, *schemed* against Jesus by hiring someone to assassinate him; *and God schemed* against them by casting his appearance onto the one who wanted to kill him, so that they killed him while Jesus was raised up. *And God is the best of schemers*: the most knowledgeable of them. *Makr* (scheming) means the employment of trickery to lead someone into a bad situation. It is attributed to God here as a rhetorical parallelism or contrast. And remember:

[3:55] *When God said, 'O Jesus, I will gather you*: cause you to sleep; for He raised him up when he was sleeping. God sent for him on the Night of Ordainment in Jerusalem when he was thirty-three years old. Mary lived for another six years after him. Muslim narrated that he will descend and live for another seven years, while Ṭayālisī narrated that it will be forty years; however, they can be reconciled by positing that the forty years refers to the sum of his life before being raised and after descending. *Mutawaffīk* (gather you) could also mean 'take you in pristine physical condition'; *and raise you to Me*: to the place of My grace—the direct use of the pronoun evokes majesty, similar to, *Truly, I shall depart to my Lord* [Q. 37:99]. This interpretation means there is no need to argue that He raised him before gathering him, since the word 'and' does not necessarily denote chronological order. *And cleanse you of those who disbelieve* in your prophethood because of envy, namely the Jews; *and set those who follow you above those who disbelieve until the Day of Resurrection. Then to Me shall be your return*: this is addressed to both groups; *and I will decide between you, as to what you were at variance about* concerning the religion.

Q. 3:56 [3:56] *'As for the disbelievers, I will chastise them with a terrible chastisement in this world*, namely being captured, slain and banished, *and the Hereafter; and they shall have no helpers.'*

[3:57] *But as for the believers, who do deeds of righteousness, He will pay them in full their wages* without reducing it. *God loves not the evildoers*, so how could He reduce it?

[3:58] *This* account *We recite to you of verses and wise remembrance*: containing much wisdom.

[3:59] *Truly, the likeness of Jesus*—his unusual situation—*in God's sight is as the likeness of Adam* in how he was created without a father; *He created him*—moulded him—*of dust, then said He to him, 'Be!' and he was*: that is, He brought him to life. This rebuts the potential objection that 'Be!' is a command of creation and so should have been mentioned before the creation. This means that the pronoun refers to Adam with regard to the end result. The other interpretation means that He formed him in a complete creation, and then He declared, 'I created Him by saying to him "Be!"'—not in the sense that one event followed the other gradually, since the word 'then' generally denotes gradual succession. So He compared an unusual thing with something even more unusual, since the absence of both father and mother is more unusual than the absence of the father alone.

[3:60] *The truth is from your Lord; so be not*—O Muḥammad and your community—*of those who waver* and doubt.

[3:61] *And whoever disputes with you concerning him*, Jesus, *after the knowledge that has come to you* about how He is God's servant and messenger, *say: 'Come! Let us call our children and your children, our wives and your wives, ourselves and your selves*: He included mention of the children and wives, though 'selves' would have covered them all, in order to emphasise that the challenge prayer (*mubāhala*) would cover them all; and He mentioned them first because they are the dearest members of the family, and a man would be willing to give his life in warfare to save them. *Then let us humbly pray* (*nabtahil*): let us supplicate, or curse one another, from *bahla* meaning 'curse'; *and invoke God's curse upon those who lie*: whether us or you.*'* He then gathered ʿAlī, Fāṭima, al-Ḥasan and al-Ḥusayn (may God bless them and grant them peace), and called upon the delegation of Najrān[1] to engage in this challenge prayer, but they declined out of fear and agreed to pay the land tax (*kharāj*).

NOTE: Our master Shaykh Dawānī (may God sanctify his soul) looked into the matter of the permissibility of engaging in the challenge prayer after the time of the Prophet (may God bless him and grant him peace),
and he wrote a treatise about its requirements drawn from the Qur'ān, the Q. 3:62
Sunna, the traditions (*āthār*) and the statements of the imams. The upshot of his argument was that it is only permitted in the case of something very important in the eyes of the Law, when there has been such obstinacy and obfuscation that nothing can settle the matter but a challenge prayer. Therefore, it is only permitted on condition that all arguments and attempts to dispel the confusion have been exhausted, and advice and warnings have been offered but to no avail, and there is a dire and present need for it. And God knows best.

[3:62] *Truly, this is the true story* about Jesus and his mother, regardless of what they claim. *There is no god but God*, and their Trinity is false; *and assuredly God is Mighty, Wise* and there is no god but Him.

[3:63] *And if they turn their backs* from what We have revealed, *God knows the agents of corruption*, which is what they are.

[3:64] *Say: 'O People of the Book, come now to a word agreed upon between us and you* about which no Book or messenger differs: *that we worship none but God, and that we do not associate anything with Him* regarding the deserving of worship; *and do not take each other for lords, beside God'*: such as how the Jews took Ezra or the Christians took Jesus, or how they obeyed the false permissions and prohibitions of their rabbis and priests. The meaning of the term *dūn* (beside) will be discussed in *Sūrat al-Mā'ida*.[2] *And if they turn*

1 The South Arabian Christian chiefs who came to Medina to make a treaty.
2 See Q. 5:116.

their backs from responding to this, *say: 'Bear witness that we have submitted*: and that we believe in His Oneness, unlike you.'

[3:65] *O People of the Book, why do you argue about Abraham*—claiming that he is a Jew or a Christian—*when the Torah was not revealed, neither the Gospel, but after him* for another one thousand and two thousand years respectively, and they are the origins of those religions? *What, do you not comprehend*, and so claim something impossible?

[3:66] *Lo! You are those* fools *who dispute*—argue obstinately—*about that of which you have knowledge*: about what you have read in your Book about the prophethood of Muḥammad (may God bless him and grant him peace); *why do you then dispute concerning that of which you have no knowledge,* about the religion of Abraham, since it is not mentioned in your Book? The one who is ignorant of something only looks into it because he wishes to understand. A man might argue about something of which he has no knowledge, out of obstinacy, but he only looks into that which
Q. 3:65 he does not know because he wishes to understand and learn the truth. *And God knows* about it, *and you know not*.

[3:67] *No! Abraham in truth was neither a Jew, nor a Christian, but he was a Muslim and a* ḥanīf: one who inclines towards the truth; *and he was never of the idolaters*: while you idolise Ezra, the Messiah and false gods.

[3:68] *Truly, the people with the best claim to Abraham are those who followed him* from his own community, *and this Prophet and those who believe*. A *ḥadīth* says, 'Every prophet has allies among the other prophets, and my ally among them is my father and the Friend of my Lord.' It is related that the fundamentals of their religions were one and the same, and the differences in their branches were only minor. *And God is the Protector*—the Helper—*of the believers*.

[3:69] *There is a party of the People of the Book who yearn to make you go astray*: such as how they invited Ḥudhayfa, ʿAmmār and Muʿādh to convert to Judaism. *Yet they cause none to stray except themselves*: by incurring sin; *but they are not aware* of how they alone are astray.

[3:70] *O People of the Book, why do you disbelieve in God's verses* in the Torah and Gospel regarding the prophethood of Muḥammad (may God bless him and grant him peace) *when you yourselves bear witness* to their truth?

[3:71] *O People of the Book, why do you confound*—conflate—*truth with falsehood* by falsifying scripture (*taḥrīf*), *and conceal the truth* about the description of Muḥammad (may God bless him and grant him peace), *while you know* the truth about it?

[3:72] *A party of the People of the Book say* to the others, *'Believe in what has been revealed to those who believe*, meaning the Qur'ān, *at the beginning of the day*, and pray the dawn prayer with them, *and disbelieve at the end of it*, or pray towards the Kaʿba in the morning and Jerusalem in the evening, *so that they*, the believers, *might then turn back* from Islam, thinking that you have turned back because of misgivings that have arisen within you.

[3:73] *'And do not believe except in one who follows your religion*: Judaism.' *Say*, O Muḥammad, *'True guidance is God's guidance*: so your plot will be to no avail; and what you fear is *that anyone should be given the like of what you have been given*, meaning knowledge, *or that they should dispute with you before your Lord* about how you have come to disbelieve in what you were taught; that is, it was envy that drove them to this.' *Say: 'Surely bounty is in God's hand; He gives it to whomever He will; God is Embracing* with His bounty, *Knowing* of all things.

[3:74] *'He singles out for His mercy whom He will* by His own judgement; *and God is of bounty abounding.'*

Q. 3:72

[3:75] *And of the People of the Book is he who, if you trust him with a hundredweight (qinṭār)*—a *qinṭār* was equal to twelve hundred *ūqiya* of gold, and one *ūqiya* was equal to forty dirhams, although nowadays it is equal to ten and five sevenths dirhams, or one and a third *istār*—*he will return it to you*, such as Ibn Salām; *and of them is he who, if you trust him with one dinar, will not return it to you*, such as Finḥāṣ b. ʿĀzūrā', *unless you*, the creditor, *keep standing over him* to nag him to repay it. *That* treachery *is because they say, 'We have no duty towards the* Arab *Gentiles* regarding their property, since God has made it all lawful for us to claim.' *They speak falsehood against God* by claiming such, *while they are aware* of their calumny.

[3:76] *Nay*, they do have a duty towards them; *for whoever fulfils his covenant*—God's covenant in the Torah, by believing in Muḥammad (may God bless him and grant him peace)—*and has fear* of sin, *then truly God loves the God-fearing*.

[3:77] *Those that sell*—trade—*God's covenant* of faith in the Messenger *and their own oaths*, their pledges to God that they would believe in him and support him, *for a small price* such as taking bribes for tampering with the Torah, *there shall be no share for them in the Hereafter; and God shall not speak to them* with anything that pleases them, a euphemism for His wrath, *nor look upon them* with mercy *on the Day of Resurrection, nor will He purify them*: praise them; *and theirs will be a painful chastisement*.

[3:78] *And there is a group of them*, the People of the Book, *who twist their tongues with the Book*, changing it from a revealed text to a falsified one, *so that you* believers *may suppose it as part of the Book*, the Torah, *yet it is not part of the Book; and they say, 'It is from God,' yet it is not* revealed *from God*: this does not mean that our actions are not ultimately God's actions, as the Muʿtazila claim, because the negation of its specific status as a Book revealed by God does not negate the broader sense of its being an act of God. *And they speak falsehood against God, while they know* that they are lying. This was revealed when the Jews said, 'Muḥammad, do you wish for us to worship you as the Christians worship Jesus?' May God bless him and grant him peace!

[3:79] *It belongs not to any mortal that God should give him the Book, the Judgement*—wisdom—*and prophethood* like Jesus, *then that he should say to people, 'Be servants to me instead of God'*: such a gift and such a claim could not possibly coincide. *Rather, 'Be lordly ones (rabbāniyyūn)*—named after the Lord (*rabb*), meaning people of perfection in knowledge and action—*by virtue of what you know of the Book and in what you have studied.'*

Q. 3:79

[3:80] *He would never order you to take the angels and the prophets as lords. Would he order you to disbelieve, after you have submitted?*

[3:81] *And* remember *when God made a covenant with the prophets: 'I have given you the Book and wisdom. Then there shall come to you a messenger*—meaning any messenger in general, or specifically Muḥammad (may God bless him and grant him peace)—*confirming what is with you; and you shall believe in him, and you shall help him'*: and so the communities all had a bond with him. *He said to them, 'Do you affirm* that you will believe and help, *and do you accept My bond*—My firm covenant—*on that condition?' They said, 'We affirm* and we accept it.*' He*, God, *said, 'Then bear witness* against one another, *and I shall be with you among the witnesses* to your affirmation and your witnessing.*'*

[3:82] *Then whoever turns his back after that* pledge, *they are the wicked folk*: those who have gone outside the bounds of faith.

[3:83] *What! Do they desire other than God's religion, when to Him has submitted whosoever is in the heavens and the earth, willingly* such as the Muslims, *or unwillingly* such as the disbelievers by compulsion, or at times of distress, *and to Him they shall be returned?* How, then, could you desire any religion but His?

[3:84] *Say: 'We believe in God, and that which has been revealed to us*: this was a permission for the Prophet (may God bless him and grant him peace) to speak highly of himself in this particular situation; or it was addressed to his community as well, through him; *and that which has been revealed to Abraham and Ishmael, and Isaac and Jacob, and the Tribes*—the branching peoples of the Children of Israel—*and in that which was given to Moses and Jesus, and the prophets, from their Lord; we make no division between any of them* in terms of belief in them; *and to Him we submit.'*

[3:85] *Whoever desires a religion* (*dīn*), a Law (*sharīʿa*), *other than Islam*, obedience (*inqiyād*) to God, *it shall not be accepted from him*: this does not mean that faith (*īmān*) and submission (*islām*) are the same thing, since faith is not a religion. The truth is that submission means the totality of actions, including belief. In *ḥadīth*s the two terms are used interchangeably, while in the Qur'ān they have patently different meanings. And God knows best. So He negated every religion that differs from submission, not the acceptance of what differs from it; for faith is not a religion. *And in the Hereafter he shall be among the losers* because of the annulment of innate guidance.

[3:86] *How*—this expresses incredulity—*shall God guide a people who*
have disbelieved after their belief, if they ever believed at all, *and bore witness*
that the Messenger is true, thereby removing affirmation with speech from
the reality of faith, *and after the clear signs had come to them*, proof of the Q. 3:85
truthfulness of Muḥammad (may God bless him and grant him peace)?
God guides not the evildoing folk who place disbelief in the position of faith.

[3:87] *Those—their requital is that there shall rest on them the curse of God and of the angels and of people altogether*: this implies that it is not permitted to invoke curses on anyone but them.

[3:88] *Abiding therein*: in that curse or in the implied punishment. *The chastisement shall not be lightened for them and they shall not be reprieved.*

[3:89] *But those who repent thereafter*—after that doubt, such as Ḥārith b. Suwayd when he regretted his apostasy—*and make amends, then truly God is Forgiving* of them, *Merciful* to them.

[3:90] *Truly, those who disbelieve after they have believed, and then increase in disbelief, their repentance shall not be accepted* in the moment of death. *Those are the ones who are astray* from mercy.

[3:91] *Truly, those who disbelieve, and die disbelieving, the whole earth full of gold shall not be accepted from any one of them*, if they spent it in charity, *if he would ransom himself thereby* from the torment of the Hereafter. Even if they offered it solely to ransom themselves, and not to lord it over others, it would still not be accepted from them; or it would not be accepted from them even if they offered the same amount again as ransom. *For them awaits a painful chastisement, and they shall have no helpers* to save them from it.

[3:92] *You will not attain piety*—true piety, or God's piety, which is His mercy—*until you expend of* some of *what you love; and whatever thing you expend*, whether it is beloved to you or not, *God knows of it*: and will requite you for it.

[3:93] *All food* that was lawful for Abraham, which did not include pork, *was lawful to the Children of Israel save what Israel*, Jacob, *forbade for himself before the Torah was revealed*, which was after Abraham. He forbade it for himself when he vowed that if his back pain was healed he would forswear camel meat and milk. This is a rebuttal of the Jews' claim that they were unlawful for Abraham, so why would they make them lawful? It is related that he suffered from sciatica, and vowed that if God healed him he would forswear the food and drink he loved the most. *Say: 'Bring the Torah now, and recite it, if you are truthful* about the unlawfulness of camel meat and milk for all the prophets.'

[3:94] *Whoever invents falsehood against God* by claiming that they are forbidden for the prophets, *after that* knowledge—*those are the evildoers*.

Q. 3:93 [3:95] *Say: 'God has spoken the truth*, contrary to their falsehoods, *therefore follow the creed of Abraham, a ḥanīf* who inclined away from falsehood, which is our creed; *and he was not an idolater*: contrary to the idolatry of the Jews.'

[3:96] *The first house established*—founded for the worship of God on the face of the water, two thousand years before the creation of the earth, or after it but before Adam—*for the people was that at Bakka*: a variant name for Mecca, so called because it breaks the neck of tyrants;[1] *a blessed place* of abundant goodness, *and a guidance to all worlds*: because it is their temple and their direction of prayer.

[3:97] *Therein are clear signs*: such as how predators and prey intermingled in the Sacred Precinct, or how every tyrant who sought to attack it was beset with an evil end; or how when rain fell on one of its corners, the crops in the land corresponding to the corner[2] would spring into verdure; or how the pillars [at Minā] still remain there; another is *the station of Abraham*: the stone upon which he stood to build the Kaʿba, and into which his feet sank; *and* another is that *whoever enters it* with respect for it *shall be secure*: whoever enters it will be safe from being slain, or from the chastisement of the Day of Resurrection, as in the *ḥadīth*, 'Whoever dies in one of the Sacred Precincts will be raised in safety on the Day of Resurrection.' Then after mentioning two worldly signs and two otherworldly signs, He left the rest unsaid and moved to something even more

1 From the verb *bakka* (to break the neck).

2 Yemen for the southern corner, Syria for the northern corner, etc.

important, similar to the *ḥadīth*, '[Beloved to me, of your world, are women and perfume;] and the delight of my eyes has been placed in prayer.' *It is the duty of people towards God to make the ḥajj to the House*, meaning to go there to visit it in a specific manner, *if he is able to make his way there*, to the House or the Sacred Precinct. The Prophet (may God bless him and grant him peace) explained that *able* here means having provisions for the journey and an animal to ride. This supports Shāfiʿī's opinion that it means money, which is why a bedridden person who has the funds may pay for another person to go in his stead. Mālik is reported to have said that it means able-bodied, while the Ḥanafīs say it means both. *As for the one who disbelieves* in its obligation, such as the Jews—He said this to refer to those who refuse to go on the *ḥajj*, in order to emphasise how heinous this is. Truly, it is related that a person who is able to go, but refuses, is guilty of disbelief. *God is Independent of all worlds*, and of such people.

[3:98] *Say: 'O People of the Book, why do you disbelieve in God's verses* which show the truthfulness of Muḥammad, the obligation of the *ḥajj* and other matters *when God is Witness of what you do*: and your falsifications*?'* Q. 3:98

[3:99] *Say: 'O People of the Book, why do you bar believers from God's way*—His religion—*desiring to make it crooked*, by means of your deceptions and falsifications, *while you yourselves are witnesses* to the fact that it is God's way*?* The word *ʿiwaj* (crooked) applies to speech, action and the ground, while *ʿawaj* applies to things like walls and pillars. *God is not heedless of what you do.'*

[3:100] *O you who believe, if you obey a party of those who have been given the Book, they will turn you, after you have believed, into disbelievers.*

[3:101] *How can you disbelieve while you have God's verses*—the Qur'ān and others—*recited to you, and His Messenger*, Muḥammad (may God bless him and grant him peace) *is in your midst? Whoever holds fast to God*—to His religion—*he is guided to a straight path* with no crookedness.

[3:102] *O you who believe, fear God as He should be feared*: a *ḥadīth* states that this means obedience without defiance, gratitude without ungratefulness, and remembrance without forgetfulness. This was abrogated by the verse *fear God as far as you can* [Q. 64:16], although some of the early Muslims disagreed about this. *And do not die except as Muslims*: hold to Islam until you die.

[3:103] *And hold fast to God's rope*: the Qur'ān, symbolising how adherence to it saves one from perdition just as holding on to a rope saves one from falling; *together*—united upon it—*and do not scatter* as the People of the Book. *Remember God's grace upon you*—including Islam—*when you were enemies*: this refers to the enmity between the Aws and Khazraj[1] during the age of ignorance, which lasted 120 years; *and He brought your hearts together* with Islam *so that by His grace you became brothers*: bonded by love; *and you were* in the age of ignorance *upon the brink of a pit of fire*—close to falling into Hell—*but He delivered you from it*: saved you from that brink with Islam. A *ḥadīth* says, 'Do not look to a man's fasting or prayer, but look to his piety when he is on the brink of sin.' *God makes clear to you His signs, that you might be guided*: that you might remain constant in guidance.

[3:104] *Let there be*, O believers, *a community*—group (*jamāʿa*)—*among you calling* people *to good*: both worldly and other-worldly. The term *among you* either means that this is a communal obligation, or that it is obligatory for all, even those who engage in wrongdoing; *and enjoining what is right*, which is obligatory or recommended according to what exactly is enjoined, *and forbidding what is wrong* (*munkar*), which is always obligatory since everything that the Law condemns is forbidden. The term *makrūh* (disliked) is not the same as *munkar* (wrong). So He was specific after being
Q. 3:104 general, clarifying the matter in His grace. *Those are the successful*: the ones who attain complete salvation.

[3:105] *Be not as those who scattered and disputed after the clear proofs came to them*: among the communities of old; *those await a mighty chastisement*.

[3:106] *The day when some faces are whitened*, those of the people of truth, *and some faces blackened*, such as those of the heretics like the Khawārij. The people of truth will be marked with white faces and luminous records, bright skin, and light that passes before them and on their right sides, while the sowers of falsehood will be marked with the converse. Each are euphemisms for the manifestation of glory and disaster, and the like. *As for those whose faces are blackened,* they will be rebuked with the words, *'Did you disbelieve after you had believed? Then taste the chastisement for what you disbelieved!'* *Ḥadīth*s indicate that this refers to the heretics such as the Khawārij and the apostates.

[3:107] *But as for those whose faces are whitened, they shall be in God's mercy*: His Garden. The contrasting wording here and the mention of mercy indicates that admission into the Garden is solely down to His mercy; *therein they will abide*.

[3:108] *Those are the verses of God which We recite to you*, adorned *in truth; and God desires not any injustice for the worlds*, because that is impossible, since nothing is obligatory for Him or forbidden to Him, such that He could commit injustice by refraining from it or doing it.

1 The two major tribes of Medina.

[3:109] *To God belongs all that is in the heavens and in the earth, and to Him all matters shall return* for requital.

[3:110] *You are* in God's knowledge, or you were made, *the best community brought forth*—manifested—*to people, enjoining what is right and forbidding what is wrong*: this indicates that consensus (*ijmāʿ*) is a valid legal proof due to the use of the definite articles,[1] because if they could reach consensus on something false they would contradict this; *and believing in God*: that is, you do all this through faith in God. Thus there is no reason to object that faith ought to have been mentioned first, as it is in other verses. *Had the People of the Book believed* in Muḥammad, *it would have been better for them* than believing in only Moses and Jesus. *Some of them are believers*, such as Ibn Salām, *but most of them are wicked folk*: insistent on their disbelief.

[3:111] *They will not harm you except a little hurt; and if they fight against you, they will turn their backs to you* and flee; *then they will not be helped*.

[3:112] *Abasement shall be cast upon them wherever they are found, save* if they hold onto *a rope* of protection *from God, and a rope* of a peace treaty *from the people*: the Muslims. In other words, they will always be abased, except in that instance. *They have incurred wrath from God, and poverty shall be cast upon them*: meaning the poll-tax (*jizya*) and penury. *That* abasement and wrath *is because they disbelieved in God's signs, and slew the prophets without right* even by their own standards. *That* disbelief and slaying *was because they disobeyed and used to transgress*. So after having said, *Some of them are believers*, He then said: Q. 3:109

[3:113] *Yet they*, the People of the Book, *are not all alike; some of the People of the Book are a community upright*: honest and just, meaning the Muslims among them; *they recite God's verses*—the Qur'ān—*in the watches of the night, prostrating themselves*: praying the evening and night prayers, which the People of the Book do not pray.

[3:114] *They believe in God and in the Last Day* without denying any of their characteristics, *enjoining what is right and forbidding what is wrong, vying with one another in good deeds*: unlike the Jews in all of these matters. *Those are of the righteous*: whose states are righteous in God's sight.

[3:115] *And whatever good you do, you shall not be denied it* by the loss of reward; *and God knows the God-fearing*.

[3:116] *As for the disbelievers, their riches shall not avail them, neither their children, against God* in any way. *Those are the inhabitants of the Fire, therein they will abide*.

1 For *al-maʿrūf* (the right) and *al-munkar* (the wrong).

[3:117] *The likeness of what they*, the disbelievers, *expend*, whether on virtuous things or otherwise, *in the life of this world is as the likeness of a wind wherein is a chill*, a devastating icy wind, *that smote the tillage of a people who have wronged themselves* with sins *and destroyed it*: the wind destroyed the tillage so that they did not benefit from their spending, just as the spending of the disbelievers will not benefit them at the Resurrection. *God did not wrong them*: He did not do anything to them that they did not deserve; *but they wronged themselves*: by committing things that deserved punishment.

He then warns us against their evil, saying:

[3:118] *O you who believe, do not take as intimates*—meaning a man's close confidants to whom he tells his secrets—*anyone apart from yourselves*: anyone but Muslims. *Such people spare nothing to ruin you; they would love for you to suffer*: for you to be sorely harmed. *Hatred*—intense enmity—*is revealed by their mouths* when they speak; *and what their breasts conceal is yet greater* than what is revealed. *Now We have made clear to you the signs* that show the neces-
Q. 3:117 sity of sincerity, *if you would understand* what has been made clear to you.

[3:119] *Lo, there you are*: you who mingle and ally with them; *you love them, but they love you not. You believe in the Book, all of it*: while they do not believe in your Book, adhering more firmly to their falsehood than you do to your truth. *And when they meet you they say, 'We believe',* though they say this hypocritically; *but when they are alone* with one another, *they bite their fingertips at you in rage*: for they have no way of defeating you. *Say*, O Muḥammad, *'Perish in your rage!'* This is a prayer that their rage be multiplied until it led to their deaths, even as the strength of Islam was multiplied. *God knows what is in the breasts*: whether rage or otherwise, and He will requite it.

[3:120] *If good fortune befalls you* even slightly, *it is evil for them* and saddens them; *but if evil befalls you, they rejoice thereat. Yet if you endure* their persecution, *and fear* sin, *their guile*—their efforts to do you harm—*will not hurt you at all; God encompasses what they do*: He knows of it, and will requite them for it.

[3:121] *And* remember *when you went forth at dawn from* the chamber of *your family*—meaning ʿĀ'isha (may God be pleased with her)—*to assign the believers their places for battle* at Uḥud; *and God hears* what you say, *knows* your intentions, and will requite you for them.

[3:122] *When two parties of you*—the Banū Ḥāritha and the Banū Asad clans—*were about to lose heart*: lose courage and flee; *and God was their Protector*: their Helper. So how could they lose heart? *And let the believers rely on God*: not on numbers.

[3:123] *God already gave you victory at Badr*—the waterhole between Mecca and Medina, named after a man called Badr who owned it—*when you were abject* in numbers and gear. He used the minor plural form *adhilla*[1] rather than *dhalāʾil* to stress how few their numbers were. *So fear God, that you might be thankful*: that you might be given favour. He referred to thankfulness rather than favour because favour is its cause, or to suggest 'that you might hope to become among those who are thankful'.

[3:124] *When*—when He gave you victory—*you were saying to the believers, 'Is it not sufficient for you that your Lord should reinforce you with three thousand angels sent down?'*

[3:125] *Yea,* indeed that was sufficient. He then promised more by saying, *If you are patient* in the face of the enemy, *and fear* disobeying Me, *and they*, the disbelievers, *come against you instantly, your Lord will reinforce you* at once without delay, *with five thousand angels accoutred*: sent forth, or wrapped up in white turbans and white woollen garments, or riding upon horses with green blazes. Know that God aided them at Badr first with one thousand to fight, equal to the number of the disbelievers, saying, Q. 3:123 *I shall reinforce you with a thousand angels* [Q. 8:9]. He then sent another two thousand, and then another two to reinforce them, as is implied by the Words *rank upon rank* [Q. 8:9]. So there is no contradiction here, nor does this contradict *I shall reinforce you with a thousand angels*. Or it could be that it refers back to *you went forth at dawn* [Q. 3:121], meaning at the Battle of Uḥud, but those angels halted and did not join the fighting because the people did not have the required patience and God-fearing. This interpretation was narrated from Mujāhid.

[3:126] *What God ordained*—meaning that reinforcement—*was only as a glad tiding to you* of victory and how you were in the right, *and that your hearts might be at peace. Victory comes only from God, the Mighty*—the Dominant—*the Wise* in His deeds.

[3:127] *And* your victory was *that He might cut off a party of the disbelievers* by means of slaying, capture or fleeing, *or suppress them*, disquiet them, or both, *so that they fall back,* retreat, *frustrated* and hopeless.

[3:128] *It is no concern at all of yours* to rectify them or punish them; *or He might relent to them*: this refers back to *that He might cut off* [Q. 3:127], and what comes between them is parenthetical; or it means 'unless He relents to them'; *or chastise them; for they are truly evildoers*: and deserving of chastisement.

1 Usually denoting a number fewer than ten.

[3:129] *To God belongs all that is in the heavens and the earth*, and so He may do as He wills; *He forgives whom He wills and chastises whom He wills. And God is Forgiving, Merciful*: so do not pray against them.

[3:130] *O you who believe, do not exact usury, doubled and redoubled*: this is a rebuke, not a stipulation,[1] or it is a description of reality. *And fear God, so that you may prosper.*

[3:131] *And fear the Fire that has been prepared for the disbelievers* intrinsically, and also for the sinners extrinsically, contrary to the what the Muʿtazila say. Abū Ḥanīfa (may God be pleased with him) said that this is the most fearsome verse in the Qurʾān for those who consume usury, since it refers to them as though they are disbelievers, so stern is its condemnation.

[3:132] *And obey God and the Messenger, that you may find mercy.*

[3:133] *And vie with one another hastening*: it is related that hastiness is from Satan, except for five things: repentance from sin, repaying debts that are due, giving a virgin in marriage when she reaches adulthood, burying
Q. 3:129 the dead, and showing hospitality to a guest when he arrives; *to* those things that lead to *forgiveness from your Lord, and to a garden as wide as the heavens and the earth*: as the seven heavens and earths if they were connected together so that they became one single surface, never mind its unimaginable length, as Ibn ʿAbbās said. The intent is to emphasise its vastness. You might object that the Garden is in the heavens, so how could it be as vast as them? The response is that it is in the Pedestal, which is to the heavens as a necklace is to a single link, and its roof is the Throne (*ʿarsh*) of the Compassionate. The Prophet (may God bless him and grant him peace) was asked, 'Then where is the Fire?' He replied, 'Glory be to God! When day comes, where is night?' He then acquainted the elite with it by describing how it contains 'what no eye has seen, nor ear heard'. Ibn ʿAbbās is related to have said, 'God has many worlds, and this is one of them.' *It has been prepared for those who fear* intrinsically, and for others by association, just as one might say that a palace was prepared for the king. This indicates that it has already been created.

[3:134] *Those who expend in prosperity and adversity, and restrain their rage*: from *kaẓama*, meaning to cover the top of a bottle when it is full. A *ḥadīth* says, 'When someone restrains his rage when he is able to discharge it, God fills his heart with peace and faith.' So it means those who refrain from acting on their rage though they are able to do so, *and pardon their fellow people*: refraining from punishing those who deserve it; *and God loves those who are virtuous*, like such people.

1 That is, usury of all kinds is forbidden, whether twofold or otherwise.

[3:135] *And who when they commit an indecency*, a sorely heinous act, *or wrong themselves* with something lesser, *remember God* and His warning, *and pray forgiveness for their sins—and who*, no one, *shall forgive sins but God?—and who do not persist in what they did, knowing* that it is sinful. A *ḥadīth* says, 'The one who prays for forgiveness is not guilty of persistent sin, even if he commits the deed seventy times in one day.'

[3:136] *Those—their requital is forgiveness from their Lord, and Gardens with rivers flowing from beneath them, abiding therein; excellent is the wage of those workers*: namely forgiveness and Gardens. The indefinite noun *Gardens* implies that what they will receive is less than what the God-fearing will, which is also implied by describing the God-fearing as *virtuous* [Q. 3:134], while these as *workers*.

[3:137] *Ways of life*—things that God made occur among the communities of old—*have passed away before you; so travel in the land*—literally to reflect on the traces of their destruction, or metaphorically by journeying with one's thoughts—*and behold*, with your eyes or your insights, *how was the end of those who denied* and reflect on it. Q. 3:135

[3:138] *This* passing away *is an exposition for people, and a guidance, and an admonition for such as are God-fearing.*

[3:139] *Faint not*—do not shrink weakly from war—*neither grieve* for your defeat at Uḥud, *for you shall prevail* in this life and the next *if you are believers*: for faith produces courage through trust in God.

[3:140] *If a wound touched you* on the day of Uḥud—*qarḥ* (wound) can also be read as *qurḥ* (pain)—*a like wound already has touched the others*: the idolaters at Badr; and they did not become cowardly, so neither should you. *Such days*, the days of this world, *We deal out in turn*, sending them to affirm and bolster the proofs [of faith]—not because He does not wish to help, but because things cannot always go the way of the believers as then the world would have no point—*among people*: sometimes for these, and sometimes for those, for countless good reasons; *and that God may know*—that His knowledge may be manifested or established as proof—*those who believe; and that He may take witnesses from among you*: people who attain martyrdom in His cause; *and God loves not the evildoers*: so their victory is not due to His love for them, but rather His desire to test them.

[3:141] *And that God may prove*—purify and cleanse—*the believers* from sins by their defeat, *and efface the disbelievers* by their victory, for if they win they will go to excess, which will be their undoing. *Maḥq* (effacement) means to erase little by little.

[3:142] *Or did you suppose you should enter the Garden without God knowing*—without His knowledge being manifested—*who among you have struggled* and who have not, *and knowing who are patient* in fighting? Surely you will not enter it under those terms; and in fact you did not struggle, and you were not patient.

[3:143] *You were longing for death*—martyrdom—*before you met it. Now you have seen it, looking on* when your brethren were slain. By hoping for martyrdom, you were hoping for the victory of the disbelievers. And on the day of Uḥud, when word went around that Muḥammad had been slain and the Hypocrites encouraged the believers to return to their old religion, the [following] verse was revealed:

[3:144] *Muḥammad is only a messenger; messengers have passed away before him*: whether by being slain or dying natural deaths. *Why, if he should die or be slain, will you turn back on your heels* and go back to the religion of your forebears? Note that slaying means the severing of the spirit from the body, just like death, except that when the active cause is considered one says, 'He was slain,' while when the end of life itself is considered one says, 'He died.' *If*
Q. 3:143 *any man should turn back on his heels, he will not harm God in any way*: but only harm himself; *and God will requite the thankful* for the favour of Islam.

[3:145] *It is not for any soul to die, save by the leave of God* and so cowardice and courage play no part in it, since it is written in *a prescribed term. And whoever desires the reward of this world* by his deeds, *We will give him of it* if We wish—this is an allusion to the ones who rushed to plunder the spoils on the day of Uḥud; *and whoever desires the reward of the Hereafter*—such as those who stayed in their positions and continued to fight—*We will give him of it*: of its reward; *and We will requite the thankful* for God's favours.

[3:146] *How many a prophet has been killed and with him many lordly ones* (*ribbiyyūn*)*!* This [latter word] means the same as *rabbāniyyūn*, as explained above,[1] or groups of people who worshipped their Lord (*rabb*); *but they fainted not*—they did not become weak through fear—*in the face of what afflicted them in God's way*: when they or their prophets were slain; *they neither weakened* before the enemy, *nor did they humble themselves* to them: *istikāna* (to humble oneself) means to be humiliated into disgrace. *And God loves the patient.*

[3:147] *All that they said was*, as they remained steadfast, *'Our Lord, forgive us our sins and our excesses in our affairs and make firm our feet* in warfare, *and help us against the disbelieving folk.'*

[3:148] *And God gave them the reward of this world* with victory and

1 See Q. 3:79.

spoils, *and the fairest reward of the Hereafter; and God loves the virtuous.*

[3:149] *O you who believe, if you obey the disbelievers* when they said at Uḥud, 'Return to the religion of your forebears,' *they will make you turn back on your heels* to idolatry, *and you will revert as losers* in this life and the next.

[3:150] *Nay, but God is your Protector*—your Helper—*and He is the best of helpers*: so do not seek help from any but Him.

[3:151] *We will cast terror into the hearts of the disbelievers* when, on the way back from Uḥud to Mecca, they had the notion of going back to finish off the Muslims completely. This verse was actually revealed even after that, so the use of the future tense is a rhetorical device for the sake of emphasis; *for*, on account of how, *they have associated with God that for which He has revealed no warrant*: no proof. What this means is that it does not exist, as in the poem, 'Rabbits are not roused by its horrors...'[1] *Their abode shall be the Fire; evil is the abode of the evildoers*, such as them.

[3:152] *God was true to His promise* of victory, on condition of patience
and God-fearing, *when you were slaying them*: they slew twenty-two disbe- Q. 3:149
lievers in the early part of the battle; *by His leave*—His command—*until you lost heart* and became cowardly, *and quarrelled over the command* when the archers disagreed about whether to leave their posts to plunder the spoils after they had routed the disbelievers; *and you disobeyed* the Messenger by leaving your posts *after He*, God, *had shown you what you longed for*: meaning the spoils. In other words, when this occurred, He denied you His help. *Some of you desired this world*, such as those who abandoned their posts, *and some of you desired the Hereafter*, such as those who remained firm and continued to fight. *Then He turned you away from them* by defeat, *so that He might try you* and test your firmness; *yet now He has pardoned you* for disobeying the Messenger by leaving your posts, *and God is Bounteous to the believers.* And remember:

[3:153] *When you were ascending*—fleeing—*not turning around for anyone* among you, *and the Messenger was calling you from your rear*: [he was calling] from the back of your group, saying, 'To me, servants of God! I am the Messenger of God, and those who remain will have the Garden!' *So He rewarded you*—God requited you for your decision—*with grief for grief*: with your losses compounded with the report that Muḥammad (may God

1 From a poem by the seventh-century poet Ibn Aḥmar al-Bāhilī. The continuation of the line, '...nor do you see the lizard nesting there', is the one more usually cited as an example of this rhetorical device. The poem describes a place utterly devoid of life; the lizard is not seen there because it does not exist.

bless him and grant him peace) had been slain, or because of the grief you caused the Prophet by disobeying him, so that you would become accustomed to being patient in times of trial. It was to this that He alluded when He said *so that you might not grieve for what escaped you*, such as the spoils, *nor for what befell you*, such as the killing. In sum, this is an exhortation for patience. *And God is aware of what you do.*

[3:154] *Then He sent down upon you, after grief*, after the disbelievers had departed, *security—a slumber*: the Prophet and the believers went to sleep then. It is related that Ibn Masʿūd said that drowsiness during prayer is from Satan, while drowsiness during warfare is a gift of security from God. *Overcoming a party of you*, the believers, *and a party whose own souls distressed them*, the Hypocrites, *thinking wrongly of God, thoughts of* the folk of *the age of ignorance, saying* in doubt, *'Have we any part whatever in the affair?* regarding what God commanded and the help He promised. *Say*, O Muḥammad, *'The affair*—the real help—*belongs entirely to God.' They conceal within their hearts what they do not disclose to you*—their
Q. 3:154 hypocrisy—*saying* when they are alone, *'Had we had any part in the affair* as Muḥammad says, claiming that God helps His allies, *we would not have been slain*—our fellows would not have been slain—*here.' Say: 'Even if you had been in your houses, those for whom it had been appointed*—destined—*that they be slain would have sallied forth to the places where they were to lie*: involuntarily'—they would have gone out so that God's decree could be fulfilled. [It was so] *that God might try*—test—*what was in your breasts*, your secret thoughts, *and that He might prove*, unveil and distinguish, *what was in your hearts; and God knows what is in the breasts* and only tests it to show it to the people.

[3:155] *Truly, those of you who turned away the day the two hosts encountered each other* at Uḥud—*truly, Satan made them slip through* the ill omen of *some of what they had earned*: their sins, such as leaving their posts; *but God pardoned them* for this; *God is Forgiving, Forbearing* and does not dole out punishment immediately.

[3:156] *O you who believe, be not as the disbelievers, who say of their brothers*, their companions, *when they travel in the land* for some purpose and then die abroad, *or are on raiding campaigns* and are slain, *'Had they been with us, they would not have died and would not have been slain'*: do not say such things. The difference between dying and being slain was discussed earlier. *So that God may make that* statement *anguish in their hearts* alone, and not in your hearts. *For God gives life and gives death*: whether you are at home or abroad; *and God sees what you do*: [that is,] if you adopt their ways.

[3:157] *And if you are slain in God's way, or die* in His way, *forgiveness from God and mercy are better than what they amass* of the treasures of this world.

[3:158] *And if you die or are slain, it is to God you shall be mustered*: not to any other, and He will requite you.

[3:159] *It was by the mercy of God that you were lenient*—kindly—*with them; had you been harsh*—cruel—*and fierce of heart, they would have dispersed from about you. So pardon them* for those things that you can pardon, *and ask forgiveness for them* for those things that only God can pardon, *and consult them in the matter* for which no revelation is sent, and which is a suitable subject of consultation, so that it becomes part of the Sunna, and in order that their hearts are set at ease. *And when you are resolved* on a course of action after consultation, *rely on God* for it; *for God loves those who rely*: and will help them.

[3:160] *If God helps you, then none can overcome you; but if He forsakes you* as at Uḥud, *then who is there who can help you after Him*, after He forsakes you? *Therefore, on God let the believers rely.*

Q. 3:157

[3:161] *It is not* right *for a prophet to be fraudulent*: to betray his trust; it can also be read in the passive voice, meaning 'to be accused of falsehood or betrayal'; *whoever defrauds shall bring what he has defrauded*—carrying it upon his neck—*on the Day of Resurrection; then every soul shall be paid in full* the reward for *what it has earned, and they shall not be wronged* in that repayment.

[3:162] *Is he who follows God's pleasure* by obeying Him *like him who is laden with God's anger* by disobeying Him, *whose abode is Hell? An evil journey's end!* The difference between them is that their journeys will end in very different ways.

[3:163] *They*—those who follow—*are of degrees before God; and God sees what they do*: and will requite them for it.

[3:164] *Truly God was gracious to the believers when He sent to them a messenger from among their own*, from their own species, not an angel, *to recite to them His verses*, the Qurʾān, *and to purify them* from the dross of idolatry, *and to teach them the Book*, the Qurʾān, wisdom, the Sunna, *though before* his prophethood *they were in clear error.*

[3:165] *And why, when distress befell you* on the day of Uḥud when seventy men were slain, *and you had afflicted twice the like of it* on the day of Badr, when seventy were slain and another seventy captured, *did you say, 'How is this?'* That is, 'How have we been afflicted so, when we were promised help?' *Say: 'It is from yourselves* because of how you abandoned your posts and took the ransoms. *Truly, God has power over everything'*: including victory and defeat.

[3:166] *And what afflicted you on the day the two hosts encountered*—[referring to the battle between] the Muslims and the idolaters at Uḥud—*was by God's leave* and so destined by Him; *and that He might know the believers.*

[3:167] *And that He might also know the Hypocrites*, that His knowledge of them might be manifested, *when it was said to them*—it was Ibn Ubayy and his companions when they left on the way to Uḥud—*'Come now, fight in the way of God or defend* against the enemy by adding to our numbers,*' they said* in mockery, *'If we knew how to fight, we would follow you* into ruin.*' They that day were nearer to disbelief than to belief, saying with their mouths that which was not in their hearts*: meaning the testimony of faith and their aforementioned statement. The Words *with their mouths* are either meant for emphasis or to clarify that they spoke out loud and not merely to themselves. *And God knows best what they hide.*

[3:168] *Those who said of their brothers*, their companions who were slain at Uḥud, *whilst they themselves stayed put* instead of fighting, *'Had*
Q. 3:166 *they obeyed us* and left with us, *they would not have been slain.' Say: 'Then avert death from yourselves, if you speak the truth'*: about how you had the power to avoid those destined deaths. This indicates that slaying and death are two different things.

[3:169] *Count not those who were slain in God's way* at Badr and Uḥud *as dead, but rather* they are *alive*: this means a spiritual life according to the majority, and a bodily life as well according to some; the Muʿtazila say that it means the life of the Resurrection and the present tense is meant to emphasis its reality; *with their Lord*: close to Him, as was explained in *Sūrat al-Baqara;*[1] *provided for* in the abode of divine generosity. When Muʿāwiya wanted to dig up the spring by the graves of the martyrs of Uḥud, he brought the bodies out of their graves and found that they were still fresh. The spade nicked one of their fingers, and it bled fresh blood.

[3:170] *Rejoicing in what God has given them of His bounty*: this indicates that the human being is not this physical form, but rather an essence that perceives, feels and contemplates innately. A *ḥadīth* says, 'The spirits of the martyrs are in the bodies of green birds flitting around the rivers of the Garden and eating from its fruits, nesting in lamps hanging beneath the shade of the Throne.' In other words, their spirits, retaining their souls by which they perceive and distinguish, inhabit the bodies of those birds enjoying the bliss of the Garden; or they take the form of green birds. What this means is that they attain the fullness of perfection, which corresponds to

1 See Q. 2:154.

those lamps. Martyrs are called *shuhadā'* (witnesses) because their spirits are present now in the abode of peace, while the spirits of others will only arrive at the Resurrection. Or it is because God bore witness to their presence in the Garden. This was discussed before in *Sūrat al-Baqara*. Suddī said that it was related that the martyr will be presented with a book in which is written, 'So-and-so will come to you on such-and-such day, and So-and-so on such-and-such day,' and he will delight in it. *And rejoicing for the sake of* the martyrdom of *those who have not joined them but are left behind* in time or in rank, *that no fear shall befall them, neither shall they grieve*: that is, they rejoice in how those who are behind them will neither fear nor grieve.

[3:171] *Joyful in grace*, reward, *and bounty*, increase, *from God, and that God does not let the wage of believers go to waste.*

[3:172] *For those who responded to God and the Messenger* by going out to Ḥamrā' al-Asad, when they heard of how the disbelievers had decided to go back to annihilate them after having set off home from Uḥud, *after the wounds had afflicted them* at Uḥud, *and feared* disobeying God, *there shall be a great wage.* Q. 3:171

[3:173] *Those to whom people*—meaning the envoy of the idolaters, Nuʿaym b. Masʿūd, and his followers among the Hypocrites—*said, 'The people*—the idolaters—*have gathered against you* by heading out from Mecca towards you, *therefore fear them'; but that* claim *increased them in faith* by affirming their repentance, *and they said, 'God is sufficient for us, an excellent Guardian is He.'*

[3:174] *So they returned with grace*, reward and bodily safety, *and bounty*, profit from commerce such as the Badr market, *from God, and no evil touched them*, such as injury, *and they followed the beatitude of God* by obeying His Messenger; *and God is of bounty abounding* to those who obey Him.

[3:175] *That* speaker, Nuʿaym, *is only Satan rousing fear* in you *of his friends*: those who refused to fight alongside the Messenger, or his allies Abū Sufyān and his companions; *therefore, do not fear them, but fear Me, if you are believers.*

[3:176] *Let them not grieve you, those*, the Hypocrites, *who vie with one another in* aiding *disbelief; they will not hurt God*—His religion—*at all. God desires not to assign them any portion* of reward *in the Hereafter, and theirs is a mighty chastisement.*

[3:177] *Those who purchase disbelief at the price of faith, they will not hurt God at all, and there awaits them a painful chastisement*: this applies generally to the disbelievers, after the previous statement about the Hypocrites in particular.

[3:178] *And let not the disbelievers suppose that what We indulge them in is better for their souls*: *Imlā'* (indulgence) in this context means to give them time and long lives. *We grant them indulgence only that they may increase in sinfulness; and theirs is a humbling chastisement.*

[3:179] *It is not God's purpose to leave the believers in the state in which you are*, O believers and hypocrites, meaning this state of confusion and duplicity, *till He shall distinguish the evil one*, the hypocrite, *from the good*, the true believer, whether by revelation or commandments. *Nor is it God's purpose to apprise you of the Unseen* that you may recognise the two factions, which would undermine the test; *but God chooses of His messengers whom He will* and informs them of some of it. *So believe in God and His messengers* sincerely; *and if you believe and fear* sin, *then yours shall be a great wage.*

[3:180] *Let them not suppose, those who are miserly with what God has given them of His bounty, that it is better for them* to be miserly; *nay, it is worse for them; they shall have hung around their necks what they withheld*—that for which they did not render the *zakāt*—*on the Day of Resurrection*: their wealth will be
Q. 3:178 transformed into serpents hanging around their necks and biting them from head to toe. *And to God belongs the inheritance of the heavens and the earth* when all possessions are annihilated. *And God is aware of what you do*: and will requite you for it.

[3:181] *God has certainly heard the saying of those who said* to Abū Bakr, when they heard the Messenger's command to lend unto God a goodly loan, *'Truly, God is poor, and we are rich*: such that He would need to borrow'—it was Finḥāṣ b. ʿĀzūrā' and his people who said this. *We shall write down what they have said* in the books of record, or metaphorically in the sense that it will not be forgotten; *and their slaying the prophets without right*: even by their own standards. The deeds of their forefathers were essentially their own deeds, since they approved of them, as was said earlier. *And We shall say* to them, *'Taste the chastisement of the Burning*: *ḥarīq* (burning) is the emphatic form of *muḥarriq*, similar to *alīm* (painful). 'Taste' means the perception of flavour, but it can also be used more broadly to mean the perception of all tangible things and states.

[3:182] *'That* chastisement *is for what your hands*—a metaphor for souls because most deeds are done with them—*have sent ahead, and for that God is never unjust towards His servants'*: the emphatic form *ẓallām* (unjust) is used here because He says *servants* in the plural, and so the emphasis pertains to quantity. This is why He calls Himself *ʿĀlim al-Ghayb* (Knower of the

Unseen) and *ʿAllām al-Ghuyūb* (the One Who best knows the Unseen)[1] at various times in the Qur'ān, as well being the One Who informs the oppressed Muslims that they will enter the Sacred Precincts with *their heads shaved* [Q. 48:27]. Or it is because even the slightest amount of injustice from the Almighty would be tremendous, in which case the emphasis pertains to the modality. Or it is because His Attributes are of the highest level. The use of the word *and* here indicates that its status as a cause of the chastisement is qualified by this context, since otherwise it would be possible that He could chastise them for no sin at all. This does not discount that He might not chastise them despite their sins, for refraining from punishing a sinner cannot be called unjust by the standards of revelation, nor those of reason, such that it could be called a cause of the chastisement. The Qur'ān does not state that kindness to a sinner at the Resurrection would be unjust on God's part, as some claim. Nor does the fact that justice implies that the virtuous are rewarded while sinners are punished entail this, since kindness to a sinner is grace, which is above justice. The fact that a certain thing is mentioned does not mean that everything else besides it is negated. Q. 3:183

[3:183] *Those same who said, 'God has already made a covenant with us that we should not believe in any messenger until he brings us an offering to be devoured by fire'*: meaning that when someone from his community offers charity, fire will descend upon it from above and consume it, rendering it to ash. *Say*, O Muḥammad, in response to them, *'Messengers have come to you before me with clear proofs*—patent prophetic miracles—*and with that which you said* regarding the fire. *Why did you slay them, then, if you are truthful* about following the one who brings such signs*?'*

[3:184] *But if they deny you*, then it is nothing new, for *so were denied messengers before you who came bearing clear proofs*— prophetic miracles—*and the Scriptures* (*zubur*): the plural of *zabūr*, which means the revelations that came to them bearing warnings, since *zubur* means the same as *zujur* (warnings); *and the Illuminating Book*: meaning the revelations that came to be compiled for the purpose of imparting laws and edicts.

[3:185] *Every soul shall taste death; you shall surely be paid in full your wages on the Day of Resurrection. Whoever is moved away from the Fire and admitted to the Garden will have triumphed*: attained his goal. This implies that it is possible to enter another place besides those two, as is described in *Sūrat al-Aʿrāf* [Q. 7]. *The life of this world is but the chattel of delusion*: the word

1 With the emphatic form *ʿAllām*.

ghurūr (delusion) can be treated as singular or plural; it means an item sold fraudulently at an auction to trick someone into buying it. This applies to all but the people of the Hereafter, for whom the life of this world is a bargain.

[3:186] *You shall surely be tried*—tested—*in your property* by the responsibility to spend it, *and in your selves* by sickness and obligations; *and you shall hear from those who were given the Book before you, and from those who are idolaters, much hurt*: whether mockery or otherwise; *but if you are patient* in bearing it, *and fear* God—*surely that*, both of them, *is true resolve*: that is, necessary and fundamental; the root meaning of *ʿazm* (resolve) is a firm decision to do something.

[3:187] *And* remember *when God made a covenant with those who had been given the Book*, meaning the scholars, through the mouth of their prophet: '*You shall expound it*—the whole of the Book, in the present—*to the people, and not conceal it'* in the future. *But they rejected it*—the covenant—*behind*
Q. 3:186 *their backs* and disregarded it, *and bought with it a small price* of the trinkets of this world; *how evil is what they have bought*: what they have chosen for themselves!

[3:188] *Do not reckon that those who rejoice in what they have brought*, what they have done, such as how the Jews falsified the rulings of the Torah, *and who love to be praised for what they have not done*, such as by making a show of rectitude, *do not reckon them*—the repetition is for emphasis—*secure from the chastisement; there shall be a painful chastisement for them*: it is related that Ibn ʿAbbās said that this verse means specifically the Jews, regarding this act of theirs.

[3:189] *To God belongs the kingdom of the heavens and of the earth, and God has power over all things.*

[3:190] *Truly, in the creation of the heavens and the earth* and their wonders, as was discussed earlier, *and in the alternation of night and day* in length and shortness: this represents all the different types of change, whether essentially like night and day, or partially like the forms of the elements, or externally like the positions of the celestial bodies, which is the external part and the base of contemplation; *there are signs*—proofs—*for people of pith*: signs of His existence, Oneness, knowledge and power. A *ḥadīth* states, 'Woe betide the one who recites this verse, but does not reflect on it!'

[3:191] *Those who remember God standing* in prayer, *and sitting* if they are unable to stand, *and on their sides* if they are unable to sit: what it means is that they remember Him at all times; *and reflect upon the creation of the heavens and the earth*, contemplating them and saying, *'Our Lord, You have not created this in vain*, without purpose. *Glory be to You!* Far be it that You would do anything in vain. *So guard us against the chastisement of the Fire*: the Word *So* here implies that our knowledge of Him is what prompted us to seek refuge in Him.

[3:192] *'Our Lord, whomever You admit into the Fire* for perpetuity, *You will have abased*: humiliated to the utmost extent; as for the believers who enter it, it will only be to purify them. This implies that spiritual chastisement is more heinous than any other. *Khizy* (abasement) means to be humiliated, whether in your own eyes because of intense shame, or in the eyes of another because of something you have done to deserve it. The verse bears both meanings. This does not mean, nor does the verse *on the day when God will not let down (yukhzī) the Prophet and those who believe with him* [Q. 66:8], that no believer will enter Hell, because the verb there is from *khizāya*, which means disgrace and dishonour, although everyone who enters Hell will be humiliated. It is also possible to read *and those who believe* as the beginning of a new sentence, separate from *the Prophet*. *And the evildoers shall have no helpers* to save them. Nor does this mean there will be no intercession, as the Q. 3:192
Muʿtazila claim, because intercession means to ask for salvation humbly, while the verse means demanding salvation by force.

[3:193] *'Our Lord, we have heard a caller*—Muḥammad or the Qur'ān—*calling to belief, saying, "Believe in your Lord!" And we believed. So, our Lord, forgive us our sins* by Your pure grace, *and absolve us of our evil deeds* by replacing them with good deeds; or the first refers to major sins, the latter to minor sins; *and gather us* at the Resurrection *with the pious*.

[3:194] *'Our Lord, grant us what You have promised us*—Your grace—*through* the words of *Your messengers*: supplicating for something that is already guaranteed is an expression of humility, as well as a plea for the hastening of the promised help, for which no time was set; *and abase us not*—disgrace us not—*on the Day of Resurrection. You will not fail the tryst* of reward for the believers.'

[3:195] *And their Lord answers them: 'I do not let the labour of any labourer among you go to waste, be you male or female—the one of you is as the other*: males to females and vice versa, since they are united in religion and so the promise applies to them both. He then explains the meaning of this labour by saying, *Those who emigrated, and were expelled from their habitations; those who suffered hurt in My way, and fought, and were slain* in war; *them I shall surely absolve of their evil deeds, and I shall admit them to Gardens underneath which river flow.' A reward* granted to them *from God! And God—with Him is the fairest reward* for obedience.

[3:196] *Let it not delude you*, O listener, *that the disbelievers go to and fro in the land*: travelling around to engage in commerce. Pay no regard to their wealth, Muḥammad, lest you be deluded; for their wealth is nothing but:

[3:197] *A little enjoyment* for how short-lived it is; *then their abode is Hell—an evil cradling!* An evil abode it is!

[3:198] *But those who fear their Lord—for them shall be Gardens with rivers flowing from beneath them, abiding therein; a hospitality from God Himself*: the word *nuzul* (hospitality) means what is prepared for the guest before he arrives; and what about after he arrives! *That which is with God is better for the pious* than what the disbelievers enjoy.

[3:199] *And truly there are some among the People of the Book who believe in God, and what has been revealed to you*—the Qur'ān—*and what has been revealed to them*: this refers to Ibn Salām and his companions, or the Negus and his companions; *humble before God, not purchasing with the verses of God a small price*, as those who falsify them do. *Those—their wage is with their Lord. God is swift at reckoning* and will be swift to deliver the promised requital.

Q. 3:196

[3:200] *O you who believe, be patient* in obedience and the bearing of hardship, *and vie in patience*: be more patient than His enemies in bearing the difficulty of war; *and be steadfast*: keep yourselves in obedience and constant remembrance, or station yourselves and your horses to be at the ready. *And fear God* by renouncing all but Him, *that you may prosper* by attaining the noble stations:[1] the Law (*sharīʿa*), which means patience in bearing the difficulties of obedience; the Path (*ṭarīqa*), which means keeping the soul in check by renouncing idle customs; and the Reality (*ḥaqīqa*), which means steadfastness in journeying alongside the Real to open oneself up to inspirations (*wāridāt*).

1 The traditional Sufi triad of *sharīʿa, ṭarīqa* and *ḥaqīqa*, often linked with the (probably apocryphal) *ḥadīth* of the Prophet, 'The *sharīʿa* is my words, the *ṭarīqa* is my deeds, and the *ḥaqīqa* is my inner state.'

4
Women
SŪRAT AL-NISĀ'

Revealed in Medina

After commanding us to be God-fearing, so that we might follow the path of the prosperous, He then repeats the command in the most emphatic way possible, saying:

In the Name of God, the Compassionate, the Merciful

[4:1] *O people, fear your Lord*: that is, His chastisement; *Who created you of a single soul*, Adam, *and from it*, from one of its ribs, *created its mate*, Eve, *and from the pair of them scattered many men and women*: this implies that they were destined to be many, for a wise purpose; *and fear God by Whom you claim [your rights] from one another*: asking one another for your needs by invoking Him, that is, saying, 'I ask you by God'; *and kinship ties*: do not sever them; or it could be read as *and by kinship ties*, meaning that you also ask one another by the right of kinship, saying, 'I ask you by God and by our family tie.' *Truly, God is ever watchful over you*: protecting and observing.

[4:2] *Give the orphans their property* when they reach adulthood, *and do not exchange the evil for the good*: do not take the good part of their wealth for yourselves and render the bad part of it to them; *and absorb not their property into your property* without differentiating them—the extra stipulation here is meant to highlight the heinousness of such a deed. *Truly, that* absorption *would be a great crime*: a sin.

[4:3] *If you fear that you will not act justly towards the orphans*: the children of the widows you marry—it was commonplace to marry such women because of their wealth and beauty; *marry such women as seem good to you*: meaning other women; or *good* here means 'having reached adulthood', in the sense of fruit becoming 'good' when it ripens; so it means 'marry mature women and women other than those widows'. The phrase *as seem* here alludes to their lesser intellect. So marry goodly women, *in twos and threes and fours*: whichever of these numbers you please, whether you stick to one number or change to another. Had He said 'two and three and four', one might take this to mean a total of nine, but such a thing cannot occur in the Qur'ān, because when a number is broken down from its total into parts, it can only be because the ruling differs, as in *a fast of three days in the ḥajj, and of seven when you return; that is a full ten* [Q. 2:196], or because the speaker remembers after having forgotten, which is impossible [for God]. Had He said 'two or three or four', this would have implied that it is not permitted to change from one number to another. *But if you fear you will not be equitable* with all four wives, *then* choose *only one, or what your right hands own*: meaning captives; this implies that the strict equity between wives is not required between captive women, since the two options are presented here as equivalent. *Thus*, by these options, *it is likelier that you will not be unjust.*

Q. 4:4 NOTE: Imam Shāfiʿī (may God be pleased with him) explained this as meaning 'that you will not amass too many dependents', and some fools accused him of mistaking the verb *taʿūlū* (to be unjust) with *tuʿīlū* (to have dependents). The rebuttal of this is that He was alluding to the greater expense caused by having a large family, from the verb *yaʿūlu*, meaning 'to support one's family'. Furthermore, this interpretation is narrated from Zayd b. Aslam the Follower. The use of the verb *ʿāla/yaʿūlu* to mean 'to have many dependents' is related from al-Kisāʾī, Aṣmaʿī and Ibn al-Aʿrābī.

[4:4] *And give women*, O husbands or guardians, *their dowries as a free gift*: given willingly; *but if they are pleased to offer*, if they willingly offer, *you any of it*, any of the dowry, *of their own accord*—the phrase *any of it* encourages them to offer a small amount—*consume it with wholesome appetite*: eat it easily without choking on it, a metaphor for accepting it lawfully without pestering them to offer any more, and implying that it is delicious 'food' that has a goodly outcome.

[4:5] *But do not give to the foolish*—those who do not know how to discharge it properly, whether women or children—*your property which God has assigned to you as maintenance*: for you to administer and live from, so that you do not look to what is in their possession. *Provide for them thereof, and clothe them, and speak to them decent words*: by giving them goodly provision. This means the orphans. The property is called 'yours' by reference to the ones who administer it, and their provision from it is attained by means of commerce, and *decent words* means the act of surrendering it to them when they reach adulthood.

[4:6] *Try*—test—*well the orphans* before adulthood *until they reach the age of marrying; then* when they reach adulthood, *if you perceive in them maturity*—the least bit of rectitude both religiously and worldly—*deliver their property to them. Consume*—spend—*it not wastefully and in haste,* fearing *lest they should grow up* and seize it from you. *If any man* of their guardians *is rich, let him be abstinent* and not take any of their property; *and if he is poor, let him consume honourably*: taking a fair wage for his work. *And when you deliver to them their property*—when they reach adulthood—*take witnesses over them* that they have received it. This is a command of guidance [not obligation], and it implies that the guardian's word should not be trusted unless he has proof. *God suffices as a reckoner*: so be just.

[4:7] *To the men belongs a share of what parents and kinsmen leave*: meaning those to whom they are legal heirs; *and to the women belongs a share of what parents and kinsmen leave*: the repetition is for emphasis; *whether it be little or much—an obligatory share* ordained for them, which cannot be forgone Q. 4:6
even if they were to forgo it. This reason for this will be explained in the verse *God charges you*...[Q. 4:11].

[4:8] *And when the division* of the inheritance *is attended by kinsmen* who are not heirs, *and orphans, and the poor, grant them out of it* before the division—this is a command of recommendation for the adult heir; *and speak to them honourable words*: by being kind to them and praying for them.

[4:9] *And let them fear those* heirs *who if they left behind them weak offspring would be afraid for them; let them fear God* with regards to orphans, *and speak pertinent words*: words that are righteous and compassionate.

[4:10] *Those who consume the property of orphans unjustly are only consuming fire in their bellies*: for it will drag them to the fire of Hell at the Resurrection; *and they shall be exposed to a blaze*: a tremendous fire.

[4:11] *God charges you*—commands you—*concerning* the inheritance of *your children: to the male the equivalent of the portion of two females; and if they*, the daughters, *be women* only *more than two, then for them two-thirds of what he leaves*: the same applies when there are two daughters, contrary to Ibn ʿAbbās who said that they are treated as one daughter because the male is treated as two daughters even if he has one sister, namely two thirds, and because they are closer in kinship than the two sisters, who receive two thirds; or the word *fawq* (more than) could be read as a redundant conjunction. *But if she be one* daughter, *then to her a half*: this implies that a lone son would receive the entire sum because the male receives the equivalent of the portion of two females. *And to his*, the deceased's, *parents, to each one of the two a sixth of what he leaves, if he has*

a child: there is no need to object that he would receive a third if there was a daughter, because she is covered by the inheritance of the closer kin; the father takes what remains after the closer heirs have been given their shares. *But if he has no child, and his heirs are his parents* alone, *then to his mother a third* and the rest to the father by residuary inheritance (*taʿṣīb*), because of how He said *and his heirs are his parents*. *Or, if he has siblings*: meaning two or more; al-Zajjāj related that several grammarians said that the plural [rather than the dual] can be used for two, and the same was attributed to Sībawayh. The word *ikhwa* (literally 'brothers') covers two or more sisters as well, by analogy and consensus; or the one word stands for both because brothers are more prominent. [*Or, if he has siblings,*] *then to his mother a sixth* and the rest to the father. Ibn ʿAbbās would say that the siblings receive the sixth that otherwise would have gone to the mother, because it would have gone to the parents if not for them; but since they exist, God blocked the mother with them. This implies that they are true heirs, because the one who is not an heir cannot block
Q. 4:12 another. In any case, all of these shares can only be apportioned *after any bequest that he may bequeath, or any debt*: the bequest is mentioned first, even though the debt must be paid first, because of its rareness or to draw attention to its importance. The word *or* here indicates that they share the quality of taking precedence over the division. *Your parents and children—you know not which of them is nearer in benefit to you*: so follow My instructions regarding them, for I know better. *A prescription from God. Truly, God is ever Knowing* of what is best, *Wise* in what He decrees.

[4:12] *And for you a half of what your wives leave, if they have no children; but if they have children* or grandchildren through their sons, and so on down the line, *then for you a fourth of what they leave, after any bequest they may bequeath, or any debt, and for them*—the wives—*a fourth of what you leave, if you have no children*, as was discussed; *but if you have children, then for them an eighth of what you leave, after any bequest you may bequeath, or any debt*: there is no difference between one or multiple wives in this regard. *If it be a man leaving an inheritance and he does not have a direct heir*, meaning a man who has no living children or parents, *or it be a woman, but it be that such*—the man or the woman—*has a brother or a sister* from the same mother, by consensus—one variant reading of the verse even adds those words—*then to each of the two a sixth; but if they*, the brothers and sisters, *be more than that, then they share a third* equally between the males and females, because the connection is solely through the female, *after any bequest to be bequeathed or any debt*, as well, *without injury* to the heirs or recipients of the bequest by withholding all or part of their share—this stipulation applies to all the foregoing; *a charge from God*: 'charge' can be considered the object of 'injury'. *God is Knowing* of any injury, *Forbearing* such that He will not hasten the punishment for it.

[4:13] *Those* edicts *are God's bounds*: His laws. *Whoever obeys God and His Messenger, He will admit him to Gardens with rivers flowing from beneath them, abiding therein; that is the great triumph.*

[4:14] *But whoever disobeys God and His Messenger, and transgresses His bounds, He will admit him to a Fire, abiding therein*: He uses the singular *khālidan* (abiding) here, after using the plural *khālidīn* before, in order to allude to the paucity of the transgressors in terms of value and worth. The meaning of 'abiding' is a long stay, as was discussed before. The meaning of 'disobedience' in this context is to deny God's edicts regarding this matter. *And for him there shall be a humbling chastisement*: authentic *ḥadīths* state that being unjust with inheritance causes one to die an evil death.

[4:15] *As for those of your women who commit lewdness*: meaning adultery;
Mujāhid is related to have said that it means lesbianism; *call four* Muslim Q. 4:13
men *of you to witness against them* about what they have done; *and if they witness, then detain them in their houses until death takes them*: until the angels of death come for them; *or God appoints for them a way*: a specific punishment. The majority consider this verse abrogated by His Words, *As for the fornicatress and the fornicator*...[Q. 24:2].

[4:16] *And when two of you commit it*—engage in lewdness—*punish them both* with rebuke, reviling and beating with shoes. This was abrogated when the specific punishment was ordained. Mujāhid is related to have said that this refers to homosexuals; Shāfiʿī's ruling on the matter was that the passive partner who is a *muḥṣan* is not stoned, but rather flogged and banished. *But if they repent* from it *and make amends*: rectify their deeds; *then leave them be* and cease to harm or revile them. *God is ever Relenting, Merciful.*

[4:17] *The repentance that God accepts*—according to His promise—*is only of those who do evil in ignorance*: this includes both deliberate and accidental sin, by the consensus of the Companions; 'ignorant' in this context means that they do not possess perfect knowledge about the evil outcome of their actions because they are overcome by caprice and Satan; *then repent shortly thereafter*: after a short time, not until they are in the throes of death; *God will relent to those. And God is ever Knowing* of your intentions, *Wise* in His acts.

[4:18] *Repentance* that is accepted *is not for those who do evil deeds*—meaning the iniquitous or some say the hypocrites—*until, when death approaches one of them, he says, 'Truly, now I repent'; neither for those who die disbelieving* and then repent in the Hereafter. *Those—We have prepared for them a painful chastisement*.

[4:19] *O you who believe, it is not lawful for you to inherit women* as though they were possessions, as was done in the age of ignorance, *against their will*: this is not a stipulation, but a description of the usual situation; *neither debar them*: do not confine them or restrain them with dominance and beatings if you detest their company; *so that you may go off with part of what you have given them*: whether the dowry or otherwise, in the attempt to make them ransom themselves by giving up some of what is rightfully theirs; *except when they commit flagrant*—the word *mubayyina* (flagrant) can also be read as *mubīna* (obvious), in the sense that it obviously justifies the return of the dowry—*lewdness*: meaning adultery, in which case you may restrain them so that they return the dowry for an annulment. Ibn ʿAbbās and most of the early Muslims said that in such a situation the husband
Q. 4:19 has the right to demand a return of the dowry. *Consort with them in kindness*: with beautiful words and actions; *for if you hate them*, then be patient; *it may happen that you hate a thing wherein God has set much good*: such as a righteous child.

[4:20] *And if you desire to exchange a wife in place of another*, whether by divorce or taking a second wife, *and you have given* or promised *to one a hundredweight*, a large sum, but then you decide to divorce her, *take of it nothing*: no part of the hundredweight. *Would you take it by way of calumny*, falsely accusing her of adultery to make her surrender it, *and manifest sin?* The word *buhtān* (calumny) means a lie so vile that it renders the other party speechless; it can also be used to refer to unjust actions.

[4:21] *How shall you take it*, or any part of it, *when you have gone into each other*, meaning sexual intercourse, *and they have taken from you a solemn covenant*: the marriage contract and its rules*?*

[4:22] *And do not marry women whom your fathers married*, as you did in the age of ignorance, *unless it be a thing of the past*: that is, unless it happened in that time, in which case it is excused; some say it means 'after what was in the past'. *Truly, that*, marrying them, *was*, referring to the past, *obscene and abominable*, sorely detestable to God, *and an evil way*.

[4:23] *Forbidden to you* in marriage *are your mothers*: those who gave birth to you, and those who gave birth to them, and so on; *and daughters*: those whom you begat, and those whom they begat, and so on; *your sisters*: whether full-blooded or half on either side; *your paternal aunts*: every female whose parent is a parent of the male who begot you, or who begot him, and so on; *and maternal aunts*: every female whose parent is a parent of the female who begot her, or who begot them, and so on; *your brother's daughters, your sister's daughters*, and granddaughters and so on; *your foster mothers who gave you milk* on at least five occasions before you reached the age of two; *your foster sisters; the mothers of your wives; your stepdaughters*—the daughters of your wives—*who are in your care*: living in your homes and under your parentage—this is a description of the usual situation and a depiction of the unseemliness of such a bond, not a stipulation according to the majority, although ʿAlī (may God be pleased with him) did consider it a stipulation; *being* [*born*] *of your wives whom you have been in to* in seclusion: a euphemism for sexual intercourse. The second demonstrative pronoun here cannot refer to both instances of *wives* since they are governed by different grammatical operators, namely *your* and *of your*. Nor can *of* refer to *mothers* since then it would have to be interpreted as a new independent clause and an explanatory clause at the same time. Nor can it be taken as a simple conjunction, because this contradicts the *ḥadīth*[1] and the opinion of the majority, excluding ʿAlī who considered the consummation of the marriage a stipulation for the prohibition [in both situations]. *But if you have not yet been in to them you are not at fault* for marrying them; *and the spouses of your sons who are of your loins*: this excludes adopted sons but not sons by nursing, since the ruling for them is the same as for blood sons because of the *ḥadīth*, 'Nursing makes inviolate all that blood lineage makes inviolate'; *and that you should take to you two sisters together*—whether by marriage or ownership of slaves—*unless it be a thing of the past*: conducted in the age of ignorance, in which case it is excused. *God is ever Forgiving* to you, *Merciful* with you.

Q. 4:24

[4:24] *And* forbidden to you also are *wedded women, save what your right hands own* by captivity, in which case they become lawful once enough time has passed to ascertain that they are not pregnant. This applies even if her husband is captured along with her, contrary to the opinion of Abū Ḥanīfa (may God be pleased with him), because of the general import of the traditions and *ḥadīth*s on the matter. Some of the early Muslims said that the same applies to selling slaves as does to capturing, but there are no *ḥadīth*s to support this. *This is what God has prescribed*—made obligatory—

1 Meaning the *ḥadīth* in which the Prophet stated that if a man divorces his wife before consummation, he is permitted to marry her daughter, but not her mother. See Muḥyī al-Dīn Shaykh Zādah, *al-Ḥāshiya ʿalā Tafsīr al-Bayḍāwī*, Istanbul: Maktabat al-Ḥaqīqa, n.d., vol. II, p. 133.

for you. Lawful for you is *beyond all that*, save for what the Sunna exempted, *that you might seek with your wealth* whether to marry or to part, *in wedlock*, honourable, *and not in debauchery*, adultery. *And such wives as you enjoy thereby* through sexual intercourse, even if only a single time, *give them their wages*, deliver to them their dowries, *as an obligation*. It is said that this verse was revealed about temporary marriage (*mutʿa*), but was then permanently abrogated on the day of Khaybar. *You are not at fault in agreeing together, after the obligation*: on any increase or decrease to the dowry, whether an increased sum for an additional period, or a parting with no further payment. *God is ever Knowing* of what is beneficial, *Wise* in His rule.

[4:25] *And whoever has not the means*—the wealth—*wherewith to be able to marry believing freewomen in wedlock*: the majority consider *believing* here to refer to what is best, and Abū Ḥanīfa considered *means* to refer to the ability to provide the wife with lodgings; *let him take* in marriage *believing maids*—slave women—*whom your right hands own*: who belong to others among you. *God knows very well your faith*: so their outward faith is suf-
Q. 4:25 ficient for you; *the one of you is as the other*: you and your slaves are equal in birth and religion, so do not be too proud to marry them. *So marry them, with the permission of their folk*: their owners. This does not necessarily mean that the slave woman can initiate the contract herself,[1] because there is nothing to say that the one who gives permission cannot also initiate the contract. *And give them their wages*: their dowries with the permission of their owners; or it might mean 'give their owners', although Mālik said that the dowry should go to the slave woman herself; *honourably*: without due delay or the like; *they being honest*, chaste, *not debauched*, open adulterers, *or takers of lovers* with whom they engage in adultery in secret. *But when they are given in wedlock, if they commit lewdness*, adultery, *they shall be liable to half the chastisement*, the prescribed legal punishment, *of freewomen*, free virgin women, namely fifty lashes and half a year's banishment, not stoning since it cannot be halved. *That*—marriage to slaves—*is for those of you who fear distress*: namely falling into adultery; al-Ḥasan said that it means iniquity; the root meaning of *ʿanat* (distress) is for a bone to break again after healing from a previous break. *Yet to be patient* and keep chaste *would be better for you*: a *ḥadīth* states, 'Freewomen keep a household righteous, while slave women ruin it.' Another states, 'The one who wishes to meet God pure and purified should marry freewomen.' *God is Forgiving* of the one who is patient, *Merciful* to him.

1 As the Ḥanafīs argue.

[4:26] *God desires to make clear to you* those laws which are unclear, *and to guide you in the ways of those before you*—the prophets—*and to relent to you* and accept your repentance. *God is Knowing* of what is good for you, *Wise* in what He decrees.

[4:27] *And God desires to relent to you*: the repetition is for emphasis; *but those who follow their passions*—the iniquitous ones—*desire that you deviate* from the truth *with a terrible deviation* towards those passions, in conformity to them.

[4:28] *God desires to lighten things for you* in His laws; *for humanity was created weak*: barely able to resist his passions and bear the hardships of obedience, and so it behoves him to treat him lightly.

[4:29] *O you who believe, consume not your goods between you wrongly* by unlawful means, such as stealing or spending on adultery, *except*—but instead—let *it be trading through mutual agreement* that is not illicit. The reason He singled this out for mention is that most transactions take this form. *And kill not yourselves* by engaging in forbidden things. *Truly, God is ever Merciful to you*, and has forbidden harmful things to you out of mercy. Q. 4:26

[4:30] *And whoever does that*, engages in those forbidden things, *through aggression* against others *and injustice* against his own soul, not unknowingly, forgetfully or foolishly—thus it should not be objected that He placed the specific ahead of the general, for going beyond the bounds of justice is deviation (*jawr*), then wantonness (*ṭughyān*), and then transgression (*taʿaddī*), all of which are injustice (*ẓulm*)—*We shall certainly expose*, admit, *him to a* tremendous *fire; and that for God is an easy matter.*

[4:31] *If you avoid the grave sins that are forbidden you*—the best explanation for this is that the grave sins (*kabāʾir*) are those sins for which a prescribed legal punishment (*ḥadd*) or stern warning (*waʿīd*), such as incurring [God's] curse, has been revealed—*We will absolve you of your* minor *evil deeds* by erasing them, *and admit you by an honourable gate* into the Garden. As for the erasure of grave sins, it is decided by the divine will alone.

[4:32] *Do not covet that in which God has preferred some of you above others*: in terms of worldly fortunes; or such as men saying that they wish to be given a greater share of God's reward than women, just as they inherit more than them; or such as women saying the same about sins, or saying, 'We are more in need of our good deeds being multiplied, since we are weaker.' *To men a share from what they have earned* through *jihād* or the like, *and to women a share from what they have earned* through obedience to their husbands or the like. Seek God's bounty through [virtuous] deeds, not mere wishful thinking. *And ask God of His bounty* of the desirable things of this life and the next, not what other people possess. *God is ever Knower of all things*, and will give only to those who deserve.

[4:33] *To each*—to every person who dies—*We have appointed heirs of that which parents and kinsmen leave*: children are not included here; *and to those to whom your right hands were pledged* for their covenants, meaning the contractually-declared dependent (*mawlā al-muwālāt*), which is the ally. *So give them their share*: a sixth. This was abrogated by the verse *And those related by blood are more entitled*... [Q. 33:6]. Abū Ḥanīfa (may God be pleased with him) is reported to have said that if a disbeliever converts to Islam at the guidance of a Muslim and they make an agreement to inherit from each other, they become each other's lawful heirs. *God is ever Witness over everything*: so fear Him.

[4:34] *Men are in charge of women*, responsible for their care, *because of that with which God has preferred the one over the other*, because of the greater perfection of intellect, religiosity and other matters, *and because of what*
Q. 4:33 *they expend of their property* for maintenance and other things. *Therefore, righteous women are obedient*, fulfilling the rights of their husbands, *guarding the unseen* by guarding his property and themselves in his absence, *because of what God has guarded* for them, meaning the dowry and other things. *And those you fear may be rebellious* by haughtily disdaining to heed you, *admonish them* first; *and share not beds with them*: refuse to sleep, talk or have sexual intercourse with them secondly; *and strike them* in a way that does no serious harm (*ghayr shadīd*) thirdly. It is said that this does not incur legal retaliation (*qiṣāṣ*) unless it causes death. *If they then obey you, do not seek a way against them* to harm them. *God is ever High, Great*, and He has more power over you all than you have over your charges, so fear Him.

[4:35] *And if you fear a breach between the two*—a conflict between them which you cannot resolve, O judges—*send forth* with their consent *an arbiter from his folk and an arbiter from her folk* to arbitrate between them for what is best, whether reconciliation or parting; it is best that they be close relatives of each. *If they*, the arbiters, *desire to set things right, God will make them*, the spouses, *of one mind*: for when someone has a sound intention, God will rectify his situation. *Truly, God is ever Knower, Aware* of external and internal realities.

[4:36] *And worship God, and associate nothing with Him*: whether obviously or subtly. *Be kind to parents, and near kindred, and to orphans, and to the needy*: meaning those who do not have enough to support themselves and their families; *and to the neighbour who is near*: meaning the one who lives near to one and is also close to one whether by family or religion; *and to the neighbour who is a stranger*: the outsider whether by family or religion; *and to the friend at your side*: such as the spouse or close friend; *and to the wayfarer*: the traveller or guest; *and to what your right hands own*: whether slaves or livestock. *Truly, God loves not the conceited*: the one who thinks that his wealth makes him noble; *and the boastful*: the one who holds himself above his fellow Muslims because of his lineage or kinship.

[4:37] *Those who are miserly*—a *ḥadīth* states, 'Miserliness and faith cannot coexist in one heart'—*and bid other people to be miserly* by stirring up fear of poverty in them, *and conceal what God has bestowed upon them of His bounty* such as wealth or knowledge, out of greed. *And We have prepared for the disbelievers* and those who show ingratitude to Our favours,[1] meaning such people, *a humbling chastisement*: it is said that most miserly people will have their faith seized from them before they die.

[4:38] *And those who expend of their substance to show off to people*—rather than for God's sake—*and believe not in God and the Last Day. Whoever has Satan for a comrade*—such as them—*then an evil comrade has he.*

[4:39] *And what burden would be upon them*—how would it harm them—*if they were to believe in God and the Last Day, and expend of what God has provided them?* He put faith second in the previous verse because it was the ultimate cause, but put it first here because it is the ultimate end, for when He commanded expending, He made clear that it is only of any use if it is preceded by faith. *God is ever Aware of them.* Q. 4:37

[4:40] *Truly, God shall not wrong* anyone *so much as the weight of an atom*: a single grain of dust, by decreasing their reward, or increasing their punishment; *and if it*—that atom's weight—*be a good deed, He will double it* in reward, *and give* its doer *from Himself*—from His bounty—*a great wage*: such as the Garden.

[4:41] *So how shall it*, the state of those disbelievers, *be when We bring forward from every community a witness*, namely their prophet to bear witness to their state, *and We bring you*, O Muḥammad, *as witness against these*: the witnesses, the believers and the communities?

[4:42] *Upon that day* when We bring them forth, *those who disbelieved and disobeyed the Messenger will wish that the earth might be levelled with them*: burying them like the dead, so that they are rendered nothing more than dust. *And* the fact is that *they will not hide from God any talk*: for their limbs will testify against them after they say, *'By God, our Lord, we were never idolaters'* [Q. 6:23].

1 The term *kufr* means both 'disbelief' and 'ingratitude'.

[4:43] *O you who believe, draw not near to prayer*—keep away from it, or
from the place where it is performed—*whilst you are inebriated* by sleep or
wine. The word *sukārā* (inebriated) comes from *sakr*, meaning 'to block',
because fumes from the stomach block the faculties of the intellect. The
purpose of this is not to prohibit the drunken person from praying, such
that it could be considered a prohibition for people who are mentally
impaired; rather, it is a prohibition of becoming drunk so that one is
prevented from praying, akin to His Words *and do not die except as Muslims*
[Q. 3:102]. It also alerts the one who wishes to pray that he should rid
himself of anything that might distract him. [*Draw not near to prayer
whilst you are inebriated*] *until you know what you are saying, nor whilst you are
ritually impure, unless you are traversing a way*: travelling while no water is
available; that is, after performing dry ablutions; or *traversing a way* can
be taken to mean 'passing through places of prayer', meaning mosques,
which was the position of Shāfiʿī (may God be pleased with him); *until
you have washed yourselves* of your major ritual impurity (*janāba*); this
Q. 4:43 indicates that the dry ablution does not actually bring an end to the state
of impurity (*ḥadath*).[1] *But if you are* ritually impure when you are *sick*
such that using water would harm you; *or on a journey* whether long or
short; *or if any of you comes from the privy*: this is an allusion to the incurring of minor ritual impurity; *or you have touched women*: this could mean
literally touching or a metaphor for sexual intercourse: Shāfiʿī took it
literally, and the same was related from the Mālikīs and Ḥanbalīs, but
only for a passionate touch, while the Ḥanafīs took it to be a metaphor;
and you can find no water: whether there is no water available at all, or
not enough for ablutions: this stipulation refers to all situations, and the
reference to being sick or on a journey while in major ritual impurity[2]
did not need to be repeated for the state of minor ritual impurity,[3] since
it is implicit; *then seek out wholesome soil*—pure earth—*and wipe your faces
and your hands* to the elbows, as that is the literal meaning of the word,[4]
and because there is a *ḥadīth* to that effect, and also due to the analogy
with the wet ablution. The soil must actually come into contact with
the hands, because the verse in *Sūrat al-Mā'ida* says *wipe your faces and your
hands with it* [Q. 5:6]. *God is ever Pardoning, Forgiving*, and so He makes
things easy and issues dispensations.

1 But is only a temporary measure.
2 For which a full bath (*ghusl*) is required.
3 For which a lesser ablution (*wuḍū*) is required.
4 The word *yad* can mean 'hand' or 'arm'.

[4:44] *Have you not seen those who were given a* modest *share of the Book*—the Torah—*purchasing error* with guidance *and desiring that you should err*, O believers, *from the* true *way?*

[4:45] *God has better knowledge of your enemies* than you do, and He has informed you, so be cautious of them. *God suffices as a Protector* to look after your affairs; *and God suffices as a Helper* for you.

[4:46] *Some from among the Jews distort the words from their contexts* by removing some and adding others, or by interpreting it according to their whims, as was discussed before; *and they say* with their words, *'We have heard* what you say, *and* yet with their state they say *we disobey* your commands'; *and 'Hear as one who does not hear'*: meaning 'May you be struck deaf'; *and 'Mind us'* (*rāʿinā*): intending to mock him in their own language, as was discussed before;[1] *twisting with their tongues*: changing words so that they sound like insults; *and slandering religion* by mocking him (may God bless him and grant him peace). *If they had said, 'We have heard and obey'* instead of disobey, *and 'Hear'* without *as one who does not hear, and 'Consider us'* instead of *rāʿinā, it would have been better for them and more upright*: more just, in the manner of the Q. 4:44
folk of the Garden; *but God has cursed them for their disbelief, so they believe not except a little*: meaning a small amount of faith in some parts of their Book, or a small number of them such as Ibn Salām and his ilk.

[4:47] *O you who have been given the Book, believe in what We have revealed*, the Qur'ān, *confirming what is with you before We obliterate faces*, erasing their eyes and noses, *and turn them inside out*: so that they have eyes in the backs of their heads and walk backwards—it is said that this will befall them when Jesus descends; *or curse them*: this refers back to *you who have...*, with the context switched to the third person; *as We cursed those of the Sabbath* by transforming them into apes and swine; *and God's command*—what He wills to occur—*is done* and cannot be stopped.

[4:48] *Truly, God forgives not that anything should be associated with Him. But He forgives other than that to whomever He wills* to forgive, even if they do not repent. The claim of the Muʿtazila that this applies in both places only to repentance or the lack of it is a baseless claim, for the evocation of His will indicates that He is not obligated to punish or to forgive. Their reading of the verse as 'God forgives not that anything should be associated with him, nor does He forgive other than that' is a corrupt interpretation. *Whoever associates anything with God, then he has truly invented*—committed—*a tremendous sin*.

1 See Q. 2:104.

[4:49] *Have you not seen those who praise themselves for purity*: by saying, 'We are God's children' or the like*?* They are akin to the one who praises himself for no lawful reason. Indeed, a *ḥadīth* says, 'If someone feels that he has to praise his fellow, he should say, "I think this of him, but I would not presume to praise someone about whom only God knows the truth."' *Nay, God purifies whom He will*: for He knows the truth about all things; *and they shall not be wronged a single date-thread*: a fibre from inside the core of a date, or a bit of dust you rub between your fingers.

[4:50] *Consider how they invent falsehood against God* by praising themselves; *and that* falsehood *suffices for a clear sin.*

[4:51] *Have you not seen those who were given a* small *share of the Book*, the Torah, *how they believe in al-Jibt and al-Ṭāghūt*, two idols of Quraysh to whom they used to prostrate in order to win their trust, *and say to the disbelievers*—when they asked them, 'Is our religion better, or Muḥammad's religion?'—*'These are more rightly guided than the believers'?*

Q. 4:49

[4:52] *Those are the ones whom God has cursed; and he whom God has cursed, you will never find for him any helper* to repel His chastisement.

[4:53] *Or have they*—they do not have—*a share in the kingdom?* For they claimed that the kingdom would go to the Jews in the end. But if they did have it, *then they would not give the people a single date-spot*: a single hole in the pit of a date, because of their stinginess. So what about if they were in a state of poverty?

[4:54] *Or are they*—indeed, they are—*jealous of people*, Muḥammad and his Companions, *for the bounty that God has bestowed upon them*, meaning prophethood and victory*?* In fact, envy is even worse than miserliness. *For We gave the House of Abraham*, such as David and Solomon, *the Book and wisdom*—prophethood—*and We gave them a mighty kingdom*: and so it is not far-fetched that Muḥammad would be given the like of them.

[4:55] *And there are some of them*, some of the House of Abraham, *who believe in him*, in Abraham, *and some of them who bar from him*: turn from him though he is one of them. *Hell suffices for a blaze*: a fire kindled for their chastisement.

[4:56] *Truly, those who disbelieve in Our signs—We shall expose them*, admit them, *to a Fire; as often as their skins are consumed, We shall replace them with other skins* from their material—the form replaced 120 times every hour; thus there is no need to ask why He should punish a skin that has never sinned; *that they may taste the chastisement. Truly, God is ever Mighty*—Omnipotent—*Wise* in His chastisement.

[4:57] *And those that believe, and perform righteous deeds, We shall admit them to Gardens with rivers flowing from beneath them, abiding therein forever: they shall have therein spouses purified* from all that is base; *and We shall admit them to plenteous shade*: a perpetual shade. This is a metaphor for a goodly resting place, since there will be no sun there.

[4:58] *Truly, God commands you to restore trusts to their owners*, in general. Ibn ʿAbbās said that this refers to everyone who is given anything in trust, though it was revealed specifically about returning the key of the Kaʿba to ʿUthmān b. Ṭalḥa, the nephew of Shayba whose descendants are still the custodians of the Kaʿba, not to be confused with ʿUthmān b. Abī Ṭalḥa. So the trust in this case was the custodianship of the Kaʿba. *And when you judge between people, that you judge with justice. Excellent is the admonition God gives you. God is ever Hearer* of your words, *Seer* of your deeds.

[4:59] *O you who believe, obey God, and obey the Messenger and those in authority among you*: the rulers when they command something lawful, or the scholars. *And if you should quarrel about anything* with those in authority, *refer it to God*, His Book, *and the Messenger* during his lifetime or his Sunna after him—this does not discount analogy, for it means to refer to Q. 4:58
them by examples and to build on their foundations—*if you believe in God and the Last Day. That* referral *is better and more excellent in interpretation* and outcome.

[4:60] *Have you not seen those who claim that they believe in what has been revealed to you, and what was revealed before you?* This refers to a Hypocrite who had a disagreement with a Jew. *They desire to take their disputes to a false deity*: here this means someone other than God and His Messenger, for the Jew called the Hypocrite to the Prophet for arbitration (may God bless him and grant him peace), while the Hypocrite called the Jew to Kaʿb b. al-Ashraf. Then when the Prophet gave them his verdict, the Hypocrite was displeased with it and said, 'Let us go to ʿUmar for arbitration instead.' So they went to ʿUmar and told him what had happened, and when ʿUmar heard their account he struck the Hypocrite down dead, and thereafter became known as the Distinguisher of Truth (*al-Fārūq*); *when they have been commanded to renounce it*: that false god. *But Satan desires to mislead them, far astray*: so far that they cannot find their way back to the truth.

[4:61] *And when it is said to them, 'Come to what God has revealed and the Messenger,' you see the Hypocrites turn away from you vehemently*: entirely.

[4:62] *How will it be*—what will their condition be—*when an affliction befalls them*, such as how ʿUmar slew that Hypocrite, *for what their own hands have sent before them* by turning away from you? *They then come to you*, the Hypocrite's kin, seeking forgiveness or demanding retribution for his blood, *swearing by God that 'We sought only*, by going to ʿUmar for arbitration, *virtue*, the best resolution, *and harmony'* between the two rival parties, and not to disobey you.

[4:63] *Those—God knows what is in their hearts*, the hypocrisy in them, *so turn away from them*, desist from punishing them, *and admonish them*, counsel them, *and say to them among themselves*, meaning privately, *penetrating words* that will have an impact, for private counsel is more likely to be beneficial. Penetrating words (*qawl balīgh*) means words whose meaning exactly corresponds to the intention behind them.

[4:64] *We never sent any messenger, but that he should be obeyed* in what he rules, *by the leave*, the command, *of God* that he be obeyed. *If, when they had wronged themselves* such as by going to anyone but you for arbitration, *they had come to you* in repentance *and asked forgiveness from God, and the Messenger had asked forgiveness for them*—He singled him out for mention here to honour him—*they would have found God Relenting, Merciful.*

[4:65] *But no, by your Lord! They will not believe until they make you judge*
Q. 4:63 *over what has broken out* in dispute *between them, and then find in themselves no inhibition*, discomfort, *regarding what you decide, but submit*, yield to your command, *in full submission*.

[4:66] *And had We prescribed for them 'Slay yourselves' or 'Leave your habitations'*—as the Children of Israel were commanded—*they would not have done it, save a few of them*: the truly virtuous ones; *yet if they had done what they were admonished to do* by obeying Muḥammad (may God bless him and grant him peace), *it would have been better for them, and stronger in establishing* their faith.

[4:67] *And then*, by God, *We would have surely given them from Us a great wage*.

[4:68] *And We would have guided them to a straight path*: leading them to success.

[4:69] *Whoever obeys God and the Messenger, they are with those whom God has blessed of the prophets, and the truthful* (*ṣiddīqūn*)—the most virtuous companions of the prophets—*and the martyrs* in God's cause, *and the righteous* besides them. *What fine companions they are*: all of them.

[4:70] *That* company *is bounty from God. God suffices as Knower* of those who obey Him.

[4:71] O *you who believe, take your precautions*, the instruments for it such as weapons, and be cautious of your enemies, *then move forward*—to *jihād*—*in companies, or move forward altogether*: that is, go forth in whatever way is possible.

[4:72] *Truly, there are some of you who tarry*: who try to avoid going to war, or to hold back others from going—this means the hypocrites; *then, if an affliction befalls you*, such as slaughter, *he says, 'God has been gracious to me, for I was not a witness with them.'*

[4:73] *But if a bounty from God befalls you,* such as spoils, *he will surely cry as if there had never been any affection between you and him*: and as if you had only loved wealth—this is a parenthetical clause. *'Oh, would that I had been with them, that I might have won a great triumph!'*—meaning an ample share of the spoils if they had stayed back.

[4:74] *So let them fight in the way of God, those who sell the life of this world for the Hereafter*: meaning the sincere ones; *and whoever fights in the way of God and is slain or conquers, We shall give him a great wage*: this is a rebuttal to those who said, 'God has been gracious to me,' and so on.

[4:75] *What is wrong with you, that you do not fight in the way of God, and for the oppressed men, women, and children* whom the disbelievers prevented from emigrating—they brought the children to participate in their prayer Q. 4:72
so that by their blessing it would be answered; *who say, 'Our Lord, bring us forth from this town*, Mecca, *whose people are evildoers*, idolaters, *and appoint for us a protector from You* to look after our affairs, *and appoint for us from You a helper'*: this prayer was answered when some of them emigrated and then Mecca was conquered, and ʿAttāb b. Asīd was made their governor and protected them.

[4:76] *Those who believe fight in the way of God, and those who disbelieve fight in the way of the false deity*: Satan. *Fight therefore against the friends of Satan. Truly, the plotting of Satan is ever feeble*: compared to God's plotting. As for the plotting of women,[1] it is only great for us compared to our own plotting; however, in any case, those words were only uttered by the ruler of Egypt, and not God.

[4:77] *Have you not seen those to whom it was said, 'Restrain your hands* from fighting the idolaters of Mecca when they resolved to fight them though they were weak, *and observe the prayer and pay zakāt'? Then, as soon as fighting was prescribed for them* in Medina, when they had grown strong, *lo, a party of them fear people*—the idolaters—*as they would fear God*: that is, as much as they feared God; *or with more fear*: or feared them even more than they feared Him; *and they said, 'Our Lord, why have You prescribed fighting for us? Why not defer us to a near term?'* meaning death. *Say: 'The enjoyment*

1 Reference to Q. 12:28: *So when he saw that his shirt was torn from behind, he said, 'Truly, this is of the guile of you women. Truly, your guile is great.'*

of this world is trifling in every aspect, *and the Hereafter is better for him who fears; and you shall not be wronged a single date-thread'*: as was explained earlier.

[4:78] *Wherever you may be, death will overtake you, though you should be in raised-up towers*: even if you were secure in fortified strongholds, death would overtake you, regardless of what the Hypocrites said about those who were slain at Uḥud, *Had they been with us, they would not have died…* [Q. 3:156], and so on. *And if a good thing*, a blessing, *befalls them*, the hypocrites, *they say, 'This is from God'; but if an evil thing*, a tribulation, *befalls them, they say, 'This is from you'*: O Muḥammad, blaming you for their ill fortune. *Say: 'Everything*—both good and evil—*is from God'*: by His will and engendering. *What is wrong with these people, that they do not understand any tiding*, like beasts? The *tiding* is the Qur'ān, for if they were to reflect on it they would realise that everything is from God.

[4:79] *Whatever good*, blessing, *befalls you*, O human being, *it is from God* by His grace; for all of your obedience combined would not amount to
Q. 4:78 payment for the blessing of existence. It is said that He used the expression *min Allāh* (from God) here, while before He said *min ʿind Allāh* (literally 'from where God is'), because the latter referred to both good and evil, while this refers only to what is good. *And whatever evil*—tribulation—*befalls you is from yourself*: from the ill omen of your own sin, which God directs to you for the purpose of requital. In sum, if you consider the true Doer, then everything is from Him; but if you consider the means, then evil is only from the ill omen of yourself, not from Muḥammad.

Note that this verse was revealed about some people who had amassed wealth, but then when misfortune befell them they blamed their bad luck on Muḥammad (may God bless him and grant him peace), while when fortune befell them they credited it to God. So the *good* and *evil* here does not refer to obedience and sin, which is why He said *whatever good befalls you* rather than 'whatever good you do'. This interpretation shows the falsehood of the position of the Jabriyya sect[1] regarding the first verse, as well as the position of the Qadariyya sect[2] regarding the second, as well as dispelling the suggestion of any contradiction between the two. It also rebuts the suspicion raised by those who said that the verse did not rebut the statement of those people because they made the Prophet the medium of evil, not the origin, while the verse only affirms that God is the origin of everything; but the second verse dispels this suspicion. Thus it is clear that the verse is

1 They believed that all human actions are absolutely compelled by God.

2 They believed in absolute human free will.

not proof for the position of the Sunnis on the matter,[1] nor those of the Jabriyya or Qadariyya sects. *We have sent you*, O Muḥammad, *to people*—all people—*as a messenger; and God suffices as Witness* to your message.

[4:80] *Whoever obeys the Messenger has obeyed God; and whoever turns his back* from obedience to him, *We have not sent you as a watcher over them* to prevent them from sin.

[4:81] *They say, 'Obedience'*: the hypocrites claim that they will obey you when you issue commands to them; *but when they sally forth from you, a party of them harbour*—plan—*other than what they say*: they say aloud that they mean to obey, but they harbour secret plans to do otherwise. *God writes down* in their records *what they harbour*: what they plan. *So turn away from them, and rely on God* the Avenger. *And God suffices as a Guardian* against their evil. It is said that this was abrogated by the verse about fighting.

[4:82] *What, do they not ponder the Qur'ān? If it had been from other than God*, as they claim, *surely they would have found therein much inconsistency* which would have come to light upon examination: it would not all have been equally eloquent, or accurate in its pronouncements about the Unseen. Yet, in fact, there is not even the slightest inconsistency in it. Q. 4:80

[4:83] *And when there comes to them an issue, be it of security* such as a victory, *or of fear* such as a defeat, *they broadcast it*: spreading news of it around, as some of the weak Muslims did before the Prophet and the sagacious members of his Companions had spoken about it, despite the attendant harms of this. *If they had referred it*, that tiding, *to the Messenger and to those in authority*, the people of sagacity, *among them* such as the elder Companions, and had they been silent about it until they were informed of it, *those among them who are able to think it out*, to glean knowledge about it on the side of the Prophet and those in authority, *would have known it from them*: and would have been able to reach an informed judgement about it. *And but for the bounty of God to you and His mercy* of guidance by means of the Messenger, *you would surely have followed Satan* and gone astray, *except a few* of you who would have been guided by their sound intellects, such as Quss b. Sāʿida, who lived before the Prophet (may God bless him and grant him peace). It need not be objected that the verse seems to suggest that most people will not follow Satan, though reality suggests the opposite, as does the *ḥadīth*, 'Islam in disbelief is like a white hair on a black bull,' because these words are addressed specifically to the believers.

1 The author's position was that these two verses do not pertain to the issue of human free will at all, and so do not constitute supporting proof for any of the divergent opinions on the matter, even the orthodox position to which he himself adhered.

[4:84] *So fight in the way of God*: even if you must do it alone; *you are charged only with yourself*: with your own deeds; so struggle even if no one else helps you. This does not contradict the fact that he was sent to charge people with responsibilities, because that is not what is meant here; rather, this verse is akin to His Words, *O you who believe, you are responsible for your own souls*... [Q. 5:105]. This is supported by how the verse continues: *And urge on the believers* to fight; *perhaps God will restrain the might*—the harm—*of the disbelievers*: this was fulfilled at the Battle of Badr, when terror was cast into their hearts; for when the Benevolent says *perhaps*, He means 'without doubt'. *God is mightier and more severe in castigation*: chastisement.

[4:85] *Whoever intercedes with a good intercession*—such as to attain something good for a Muslim, or to repel something harmful from him, or to
pray for goodness for him—*shall receive a share of it*: which is the reward
for intercession. As a *ḥadīth* says, 'When someone prays for his brother
Muslim in secret, his prayer is answered and the angel says to him, "You
Q. 4:84 shall have the same."' *And whoever intercedes with an evil intercession*—that
the Law does not allow—*shall receive a portion from it*: from its burden of
sin. He said *naṣīb* (share) for the good because it can be used to mean any amount small or large, and *kifl* (portion) for the evil because it is usually used to denote an equal amount or a base thing. As for *He will give you a twofold portion* (*kiflayn*) *of His mercy* [Q. 57:28], it means 'two portions of His mercy that will secure you (*yakfil*) from His chastisement'. *God conserves*—measures and apportions—*all things*.

[4:86] *And when you are greeted with a greeting*—when peace is wished upon you—*greet with better than it*: such as by adding 'and the mercy and blessings of God', although tradition states that no more should be added to this greeting, since it already covers everything that is desirable, both security from harm and the attainment and preservation of benefit; *or return it* without adding anything to it, which is a communal obligation whenever a greeting of peace is uttered. This has also been interpreted to refer to the giving and reciprocation of gifts. *Truly, God keeps count of all things*: and will reckon and requite for them.

[4:87] *God—there is no god except Him! He will surely gather you to the Day of Resurrection whereof there is no doubt*: whether regarding the day or the gathering. *And who*—no one—*is truer in statement than God?* For it is rationally possible for everything but Him to lie.

[4:88] *What is wrong with you that you have become* divided into *two parties regarding the Hypocrites* such as Ibn Ubayy—one party declaring them to be disbelievers, the other declaring them to be Muslims—*when God has overthrown them*, returned them to disbelief, *for what they earned*: on account of their sins? *What, do you desire*, O believers, *to guide him whom God has sent astray? And he whom God sends astray, you will never find for him a way* back to guidance.

[4:89] *They*, those people, *long that you should disbelieve as they disbelieve, so then you* and they *would be equal* in disbelief; *therefore do not take friends from among them until they emigrate* by fighting *in the way of God. And if they turn away* from emigrating, and manifest their disbelief, *take them and slay them wherever you find them; and do not take any of them as a patron, or as a helper.*

[4:90] *Except those who attach themselves* and flee from them *to a people between whom and you there is a covenant*: meaning people who have made peace with you, for in that case they are counted among them; *or come to you with their breasts constricted about the prospect of fighting you, or fighting their people*: such as the Banū Hāshim, who came out with the idolaters on the day of Badr. *Had God willed, He would have given them sway over you so that assuredly they would have fought you*: but instead, by His grace, He constricted their breasts from doing that, and held them back. Q. 4:89 *And so if they stay away from you and do not fight you, and offer you peace*—acquiescence—*then God does not allow you any way against them*: to capture them or slay them.

[4:91] *You will find others* among the hypocrites *desiring to have security from you*—desiring you not to slay them or seize their property—*and security from their own people; yet whenever they are returned*, summoned by their people, *to sedition*, idolatry, *they are overwhelmed by it*: and indulge in it; they are overwhelmed by their own souls and by Satan, so there is no repetition here. *So if they do not stay away from you and* if they do not *offer you peace*, acquiescence, *and restrain their hands* from fighting you, *then take them and slay them wherever you come upon them; against them We have given you clear warrant*: a plain justification for fighting them because of their open enmity.

[4:92] *It is not* right *for a believer to slay a believer, except by mistake*: the word *illā* (except) here bears its usual meaning, although some say it means 'not even', as is also said about *unless a person has been wronged* [Q. 4:148], and *excepting the evildoers among them* [Q. 2:150]. In that case, *mistake* would mean more than just pure accident, such as an unintentional act, or doing it to the wrong person; but also instances that are more intentional, such as slaying him by doing something that usually is not done with the intention of killing. *He who slays a believer by mistake, then let him set free a believing slave*: as for deliberate slaying, the rule is affirmed by the Sunna; *and blood-money is to be submitted to his family*—his heirs, in all cases—*unless they remit it as a charity*: in which case there is no blood-money. The Sunna established what the amount of the blood-money should be. *If he*—the slain person—*belongs to a people at enmity with you* who are disbelievers, *and is a believer, then the setting free of a believing slave* without any blood-money, since there is no inheritance between Muslims and disbelievers. *If he belongs to a people between whom and you there is a covenant*—such as a non-Muslim citizen or the citizen of a people with whom there is a peace treaty—*then the blood-money must be paid to his family, and the setting free of a believing slave*: perhaps this refers to instances where the victim is covered by a peace treaty, or is a Muslim and has a Muslim heir. *But if he has not the wherewithal* to free a slave or pay the blood-money, *then the fasting of two successive months;* this has been ordained as *a relenting from God* to him. *And God is ever Knowing* of you, *Wise* in what He ordains for you.

[4:93] *And whoever slays a believer deliberately, his requital is Hell, abiding therein, and God is wroth with him and has cursed him, and has prepared for him a mighty chastisement*: by *abiding* He meant 'staying for a long time'; or the
Q. 4:93 verse may refer to those who never repent, given His Words, *And truly I am Forgiving toward him who repents*…[Q. 20:82], and *But He forgives other than that to whomever He wills*…[Q. 4:48]. This is supported by the consideration that the verse was revealed about Miqyas b. Ṣubāba, who found his brother slain among the Banū al-Najjār, and so the Prophet (may God bless him and grant him peace) ruled that blood-money be given for him; but after he had taken it, he murdered a Muslim and then returned to Mecca an apostate. Or it may mean that this is his requital, but he may be able to evade it by means of a good deed which will earn his pardon. This was related from Abū Hurayra (may God be pleased with him), both with an attribution to the Prophet and without one. Furthermore, several verses and *ḥadīth*s indicate that such a person's repentance will be accepted.

[4:94] *O you who believe, when you are going forth*, travelling, *in the way of God* for *jihād*, *be discriminating*, strive to clarify orders instead of rushing ahead with them, *and do not say to him who offers you peace*, the one who offers a truce or gives you greetings of peace, *'You are not a believer'* but are only pretending to be so out of fear, *desiring the transient goods of the life of this world* by slaying him and plundering his possessions. *With God are plenteous spoils* that will free you of the need for such. *So you were formerly*—when your Islam was only identifiable by a sign—*but God has been gracious to you*: by causing it to spread. *So be discriminating*: the repetition is for emphasis. *Truly, God is ever Aware of what you do*: and He knows your intentions, so beware.

[4:95] *The believers who sit at home* instead of going out to war, *other than those who have an injury, are not the equals of those who struggle in the way of God with their possessions and their lives. God has preferred those who struggle with their possessions and their lives over the ones who sit at home* with an excuse *by a degree*: a tremendous degree. *Yet to each* of them *God has promised good*: the Garden and reward; *and God has preferred those who struggle over the ones who sit at home* without an excuse *with a great reward.*

[4:96] *Degrees from Him*: the difference is in the degree, because they have no excuse, unlike the others; *and forgiveness and mercy. Surely God is ever Forgiving* of their sin, *Merciful* to them.

[4:97] *And those whom the angels take*: meaning the angel of death and his helpers—this was revealed about those whom the angels slew on the day of Badr, who claimed to be Muslims but then joined with the idolaters because of their greater numbers—*while they are wronging their souls*: by refusing to emigrate; *the angels will say* in rebuke, *'What was your predicament?'* What was your position regarding the religion, since you refused to emigrate? *They will say* to excuse themselves, *'We were oppressed in the land'*: '[We were] unable to emigrate or profess our Islam publicly.' *The angels will say* in rebuke, *'But was not God's earth spacious that you might have emigrated therein* to another place where you were able to profess your faith*?' As for such, their abode shall be Hell* because of how they aided the disbelievers; *an evil journey's end* is Hell. Q. 4:95

[4:98] *Except*, however, *the oppressed among the men, women and children*: this indicates that their guardians were obligated to emigrate with them; *who are unable to devise a plan* to allow them travel, *and are not guided to*—aware of—*a way* to the land of Islam.

[4:99] *As for such, perhaps God will pardon them*: this alludes to the importance of the emigration, since even those who had a valid excuse for not doing it needed to be pardoned. *For God is ever Pardoning, Forgiving.*

[4:100] *Whoever emigrates in the way of God will find in the earth many refuges*: places to evade the enemy, or stages of the journey; *and abundance* of provision. *Whoever goes forth from his house as an emigrant to God and His Messenger, and then death overtakes him* on the road, *his wage is then incumbent upon God* as He promised. *God is ever Forgiving* to him, *Merciful* with him based solely on his intention.

[4:101] *And when you are going forth in the land*—travelling a distance of four *barīd*,[1] as established by the Sunna, or six *barīd* according to the

1 A *barīd* is equal to four *farsakh*, usually defined as forty-eight Hashemite miles.

Ḥanafīs—*you would not be at fault if you shorten the prayer*: by halving the cycles of the four-cycle prayer. The apparent meaning of this is that it is permitted to do so, contrary to the Ḥanafīs. It is authentically reported that the Prophet (may God bless him and grant him peace) prayed them in full even when travelling, and approved of ʿĀʾisha (may God be pleased with her) doing the same. As for the statement of ʿUmar (may God be pleased with him), 'The prayer of travel is two cycles, which is complete and not shortened, according to the words of your Prophet', he meant that the shortened prayer is rewarded the same as the complete one. The statement of ʿĀʾisha, 'Prayer was first established as two cycles for every prayer, and then this was retained for travelling, while more were added for residence,' does not preclude the permissibility of adding more [when travelling]. *If you fear that you may be afflicted by those who do not believe*: this is a description of the most usual situation, not a required stipulation, as with similar expressions in the Qurʾān. Several *ḥadīths* make this plain. Or *if you fear* could be taken as a new sentence whose main clause is left unsaid, but can be understood as 'then beware,' or the like. This is suggested by how the verse continues: *The disbelievers are a manifest foe to you*.

Q. 4:102

[4:102] *When you are among them* at home—this follows the Qurʾān's usual mode of address and is not supposed to be exclusive;[1] *and you stand to lead them in prayer*: divide them into two parties, and *let a party of them stand with you* and pray with you while the others face the enemy, *and let them*—those who pray, or those who stand guard—*take their weapons* as a precaution. *Then when they have performed their prostrations*, meaning when they have finished praying, *let them*, those who have prayed, *be behind you* standing guard, *and let another party who have not prayed come and pray with you,* both of them *taking their precautions and their weapons*: *precautions* is an allusion to the implements of caution, imparting emphasis, so there is no need to object that this is a mixture of metaphor and literalism governed by a single verb. The apparent meaning of this scenario is that the imam prays twice, just as the Prophet (may God bless him and grant him peace) did at Baṭn al-Nakhl.[2] Or it might mean that he should pray one cycle out of the two-cycle prayer with each group, so that he leads the first

1 In other words, although it is addressed to the second person singular, it does not apply exclusively to the Prophet.

2 During the expedition of Dhāt al-Riqāʿ, when it came time to pray and the Muslims feared they would be ambushed by the men of Ghaṭafān, who were hiding in the mountains, they performed the 'prayer of peril' (*ṣalāt al-khawf*) as described here.

group in one cycle and then stands waiting for them to finish the second on their own and withdraw to the enemy; and then completes the second cycle with the other group and then sits waiting for them to finish, so that he can say the concluding *salām* with them, as the Prophet did as Dhāt al-Riqāʿ. Six or seven possible modes for the prayer have been related, as the jurists have discussed. *The disbelievers wish that you should be heedless of your weapons and your baggage, that they may descend upon you* as you pray, and attack you *all at once* together. *You are not at fault, if rain bothers you, or if you are sick, to lay aside your weapons* because of their weight—this supports the opinion that it is otherwise obligatory to carry them. *But take your precautions*: be alert at all times. *God has prepared for the disbelievers a humiliating chastisement*: whether they are victorious or defeated.

[4:103] *And when you have performed the prayer*, when you wish to perform it in times of great peril, *remember God*, pray, *standing* with your swords drawn, *and sitting* with your bows ready, *and on your sides* if you are wounded. Or, once you have finished praying, remember Him in every situation to make up for how the prayer was lightened in those ways. Q. 4:103
Then, when you are reassured—when your fear is passed—*observe the prayer* with all its proper actions. *Truly, prayer is*, perpetually, *for believers a prescription* obliged *at specific times*.

[4:104] *Be not faint*—do not weaken—*in seeking the enemy*: fighting the disbelievers. *If you are suffering* from injuries, *they are also suffering as you are suffering; and you hope from God that for which they cannot hope*: namely reward and victory, for they do not believe in the Resurrection and what has been revealed to you; and since you have this advantage over them, you ought to be more patient. *God is ever Knower* of your inner thoughts, *Wise* in what He ordains.

[4:105] *Truly, We have revealed to you the Book*—the Qurʾān—adorned *with the truth so that you may judge between people by that which God has shown you*: taught you by means of revelation. *And do not be a disputant for traitors*: such as Ṭuʿma b. Ubayriq, who stole his neighbour's armour and left it with a Jew for safekeeping, and then accused him of the crime.

[4:106] *And pray for forgiveness from God* for how you almost ruled against an innocent man. *Truly, God is ever Forgiving, Merciful* to those who ask His forgiveness.

[4:107] *And do not dispute on behalf of those who betray themselves* by sinning, and who make their souls treacherous, such as Ṭuʿma and his kin. *Truly, God loves not one who is treacherous*, much given to treachery, *and sinful*, engrossed in sin, such as Ṭuʿma.

[4:108] *They hide themselves* and their sins *from people, but they do not hide themselves from God*: for the only way to hide sin from God is to give it up. *For He is with them while they plot at night with discourse displeasing to Him*: such as accusing an innocent man of a crime. *God is ever Encompassing of what they do*: with knowledge, and will requite them for it.

[4:109] *Ah! There you are*: you fools, the folk of Ṭuʿma; *you have contested on their behalf*—on the behalf of Ṭuʿma and his family—*in the life of this world; but who will contest against God on their behalf on the Day of Resurrection* when He takes them to task, *or who will be a guardian for them?*

[4:110] *Whoever does evil* to another person, *or wrongs himself* alone, *and then prays for God's forgiveness* by repenting, *he shall find God is Forgiving, Merciful*: Ibn Masʿūd is reported to have said that this is one of the most hope-inspiring verses in the Qur'ān. However, Ṭuʿma did not repent, but renounced the faith. Then as he was climbing through a hole in a wall to steal something, the wall collapsed on him, killing him.

Q. 4:108 [4:111] *And whoever commits a sin commits it against himself only*: and so harms none but himself; *and God is ever Knower* of his deed, *Wise* in his requital.

[4:112] *And whoever commits a mistake or a sin*, a major or minor sin, *and then casts it*, either of them, *upon the innocent*, as Ṭuʿma did, *he has thereby burdened himself with calumny and a manifest sin.*

[4:113] *Were it not for God's bounty to you and His mercy, a party of them*—Ṭuʿma's people—*would have intended to lead you astray*: from ruling on the matter justly; *but they lead only themselves astray*: for you are protected from error, and they were the guilty party. *They will not hurt you at all*: for God protects you. *God has revealed to you the Book*, the Qur'ān, *and wisdom*, the Sunna, *and He has taught you what you did not know; and God's bounty to you is ever great*: and one aspect of it is the gift of prophethood.

[4:114] *There is no good in much of their secret conversations*: meaning a private discourse between two people; *except for* the secret conversation of *he who enjoins voluntary charity, or kindness*: meaning that which the Law approves and the intellect does not reject, such as giving help, charity and loans, *or setting things right between people. And whoever does that*—whoever enjoins those things—*desiring God's good pleasure, We shall surely give him a great wage*: so what of the one who actually does them?

[4:115] *But whoever makes a breach with the Messenger*—whoever conflicts with him—*after guidance has become clear to him* through his prophetic miracles, *and follows other than the way of the believers*, such as Ṭuʿma, who fled in apostasy after it was ruled that his hand be amputated, *We shall turn him over to what he has turned to*: We shall leave him to the misguidance he has chosen for himself; *and We shall expose him*, admit him, *into Hell—an evil journey's end*: this is evidence for the unlawfulness of contravening a consensus, if *the way of the believers* is taken to mean those matters of religion upon which they agree. This has been elucidated in the books of jurisprudence.

[4:116] *Truly, God does not forgive that anything should be associated with Him*: He does not forgive the one who meets him as an idolater; *but He forgives all except that, to whomever He will*: even someone who has wronged another, by inspiring the heart of his victim to pardon him, as is stated in an authentic *ḥadīth*. *Whoever associates anything with God has truly strayed far away* from the truth.

[4:117] *What they pray to instead of Him are but females* by their own claim, for they would decorate their idols and call them the daughters of such-and-such tribe; or *ināth* (female) here means 'weak and incapable', just as a sword can be called *anīth* (blunt). *And they pray only to a rebellious Satan*: one who is entirely outside the confines of obedience, though they obey him by worshipping him. Q. 4:116

[4:118] *God has cursed him*: banished him far from His mercy. *And he said*: Satan said this, whether with his tongue or with his deed, as in the poem, 'The basin filled up and said, "That is enough for me!"'[1] So he swore, *'Assuredly I will take to myself an appointed portion of Your servants* by leading them astray. It is said that by *an appointed portion* he meant 999 out of every thousand.

[4:119] *'And I will surely lead them astray* from what is right, *and surely I will fill them with desires* and all manner of delusions; *and surely I will command them* to mutilate, *and they will cut up the cattle's ears* to render them unlawful for *zakāt*—they would call such cattle *baḥā'ir*. *And surely I will command them* to change God's creation, *and they will change God's creation'*: [to change] its form by such things as castration, tattooing or filing the teeth, or its nature such as changing natural disposition. Know that when God made something perfect by its natural disposition, and then humans made it imperfect by his poor management, this amounted to changing His creation. The same applies to all that which He created for a virtuous purpose, but then humans used it for a foul purpose, such as directing the sexual desire towards homosexuality, shaving the beard, and the like. The same is true of declaring forbidden things to be lawful, or lawful things

1 A fragment of an anonymous pre-Islamic poem. The author cites it here as an example of the rhetorical device of the 'tongue of the state' (*lisān al-ḥāl*), where words are attributed to something, sentient or otherwise, to describe its state.

to be forbidden. *And whoever takes Satan for a patron instead of God*—by obeying him—*has surely suffered a manifest loss*: by squandering his capital of natural disposition.

[4:120] *He promises them* but does not keep his promises, *and fills them with desires* for things they will not attain; *but what Satan promises them is only delusion*: fooling them into thinking that there is benefit in something that harbours only harm.

[4:121] *For such—their abode shall be Hell, and they shall find no refuge from it.*

[4:122] *But those who believe and perform righteous deeds, We shall admit them to Gardens with rivers flowing from beneath them, abiding therein forever; God's promise in truth; and who is truer in utterance than God?*

[4:123] *It is not your desires nor the desires of the People of the Book. Whoever does evil* without repenting of it *shall be requited for it*: even if only by worldly tribulations, as a *ḥadīth* states; *and he will not find besides God any friend or helper* to defend him.

Q. 4:120 [4:124] *And whoever does* some *righteous deeds, whether male or female, and is a believer—such shall be admitted into the Garden, and shall not be wronged the dint in a date-stone*: their reward shall not be lessened by even as much as a hole in the stone of a date.

[4:125] *And who*, no one, *is fairer in religion than he who submits his purpose*, surrenders, *to God and is virtuous* by performing virtuous deeds (*ḥasanāt*), *and who follows the creed of Abraham* regarding the fundamentals of the faith, *as a ḥanīf*: one who inclines towards the truth. *And God took Abraham for a close friend*: a chosen one honoured as a friend honours his friend. The word *khulla* (close friendship) means love that penetrates (*yatakhallal*) and mixes with the soul.

[4:126] *To God belongs all that is in the heavens and in the earth; and God is ever the Encompasser of all things* with knowledge and power, so that He will requite them all.

[4:127] *They ask you for a pronouncement concerning* the inheritance of *women. Say: 'God pronounces to you concerning them*: the verb *iftāʾ* (to pronounce) means 'to clarify what is uncertain'; *and what is recited to you in the Book* will also clarify it for you, meaning the verses of inheritance, regarding what is recited *concerning the orphan women to whom you do not give what is prescribed for them*, of their inheritances or dowries, *for you desire to marry them* for their wealth and beauty, yet you do not give them their dowries; *and the oppressed*—the young—*children*: for they would not allow them to inherit, just like women; *and that you deal justly with orphans. Whatever good you do, God is ever Knower of it.'*

[4:128] *And if a woman fears from her husband ill treatment*, meaning that he disdains to keep her company out of hatred, *or rejection*, meaning that he withholds intimacy from her, *they*, the couple, *are not at fault if they are reconciled through some agreement*: such as remitting some of the dowry, the allotment of time [between wives] or the maintenance. *Reconciliation is better* than parting or antipathy, not in the sense that they are all good, but in the sense that reconciliation is a good thing, just as antipathy is a bad thing. *But greed*—strong avarice or antipathy—*has been made present in the souls*: that is, it is their nature and they are never entirely free of it. This lays the ground for the justification for the husband either retaining her, or not staying with her if he prefers someone else. *If you are virtuous* in your marital bond, *and fear* that you should fall short of the truth, *surely God is ever aware of what you do*: and will reward you.

[4:129] *You will never be able to be just to your wives*: for justice means that there should be no inclination at all, yet there will always be a disparity of love, desire and sexual relations between them; *even if you are eager* to be just. *Yet do not turn altogether away* towards one of them alone, *so that you leave her*—the other one—*like one suspended*: as though she is neither married nor divorced. *If you set things right* with justice, *and fear* injustice, *surely God is ever Forgiving* of any imbalanced inclination between them, *Merciful* so that He will not constrict you. Given the latter, it should not be argued that this is a description of forgiveness for something that is impossible to avoid, because it is possible to avoid it by not marrying more than one woman. Thus it is akin to a crime committed by a drunken person. Q. 4:128

[4:130] *But if they separate* by divorce, *God will enrich each of them* on behalf of the other, *out of His plenty*: His vast bounty. It is notable that this enrichment is promised for two opposing situations: parting here, and marriage in *Sūrat al-Nūr*.[1] *God is ever Embracing* with His bounty, *Wise* in what He decrees.

[4:131] *To God belongs all that is in the heavens and in the earth*: and the fullness of plenty is His. *We have charged those who were given the Book before you, and* We have charged *you, 'Fear God,'* saying: *'If you disbelieve, then to God belongs all that is in the heavens and in the earth'*: and your disbelief does not harm Him any more than your gratitude would help Him; He only counsels you for your own good. *God is ever Independent* of His creation; *Praised*: deserving of praise, even if you disbelieve.

1 *And marry off the spouseless among you and the righteous ones among your male slaves and your female slaves. If they are poor, God will enrich them out of His bounty...* (Q. 24:32).

[4:132] *To God belongs all that is in the heavens and in the earth*: and to Him belong all riches and praise. *God suffices as a Guardian*: so rely on Him.

[4:133] *If He will, He can remove you, O people, and bring others*: other people in your stead. *Surely God is ever able to do that.*

[4:134] *Whoever desires the reward of this world, then* he should not confine himself to them alone, for *God has the reward of this world and of the Hereafter. God is ever Hearer* of words, *Seer* of deeds, and will requite you for them.

[4:135] *O you who believe, be upright*—constant—*in justice; witnesses for God* alone, *even though it be against yourselves*: this means to acknowledge, for bearing witness means testifying to the truth; *or parents and kinsmen, whether the person*—the one witnessed against—*be rich or poor*: witness should be borne against him without fear or mercy. *God is closer to the two*: His Law is more deserving of your fear and mercy than either wealth or poverty. *So do not follow any whim*, fearing *lest you swerve; for if you twist* your tongues by bearing false testimony, *or refrain* from bearing it, *surely God is ever aware of what you do*: and will requite you for it.

Q. 4:132 [4:136] *O you who believe, believe*—maintain your faith—*in God and His Messenger and the Book which has been revealed to His Messenger*, the Qur'ān, *and the Book which was revealed before*, all of the revealed scripture. *And whoever disbelieves in God, and His angels, and His Books, and His messengers, and the Last Day*—in any one of those—*has truly strayed far away* from the truth.

[4:137] *Truly, those who believed*, such as the Jews in Moses, *and then disbelieved*, such as how they worshipped the calf, *and then believed* again afterwards, *and then disbelieved*, such as how they disbelieved in Jesus, *and then increased in disbelief*, such as how they disbelieved in Muḥammad (may God bless him and grant him peace), *it was not for God to forgive them, nor to guide them to a way* to the truth, because it was so unlikely that they would repent, not because it would not have been accepted from them if they had. Or it means that if someone keeps going back and forth between disbelief and faith, he will not be forgiven. It is related that ʿAlī said that such a person should be executed and his repentance not accepted.

[4:138] *Give tidings to the hypocrites that for them there is a painful chastisement.*

[4:139] *Those who take disbelievers for friends instead of believers—do they desire power with them*, with which to dominate the believers? *Truly, power belongs altogether to God*: and none have power but those to whom He grants it.

[4:140] *It has been revealed to you in the Book*—in *Sūrat al-Anʿām* in the verse, *When you see those who engage in discourse about Our signs, turn away from them*... [Q. 6:68]—*that when you hear God's signs being disbelieved in and mocked, do not sit with them*, with those who disbelieve and mock, *until they engage in some other talk*: other than talk of disbelief and mocking; *for otherwise you would surely be like them*: for you are well able to turn away. *God will gather the hypocrites and disbelievers, altogether, into Hell*: just as they gathered to mock here.

[4:141] *Those who wait in watch for you*: waiting for something to befall you; *and, if a victory comes to you from God, say, 'Were we not with you?'*: 'So give us the spoils.' *But if the disbelievers have some luck* and win a victory over you—He altered the expression in order to express disdain for them—*they say* to the disbelievers, *'Did we not gain mastery over you* however we could by means of slaying and capturing, *and did we not defend you against the believers*: by slowing them down and refusing to aid them*?' God will judge between you on the Day of Resurrection* according to what is inside you; *and God will never grant the disbelievers a way over the believers*: by a decisive argument, or a total victory in this world. This is evidence that the sale of a Muslim slave to a non-Muslim owner is invalid. The Ḥanafīs cite it as proof that the apostasy of a Muslim woman's husband constitutes an Q. 4:141
irrevocable severing of the marriage; but the rebuttal of this is that it is still possible for the marriage to be salvaged, if he returns to Islam before the waiting period is over.

[4:142] *The Hypocrites seek to trick God* by their own claim, *but He is tricking them*: requiting them for their trickery. *When they stand up to pray, they stand up lazily*—reluctantly—*and to be seen by people*: to make them think that they are sincere; *and they do not remember God* at all, or they do not pray, *save a little* when people are around; and if they were sincere even in this little, it would amount to a substantial amount.

[4:143] *Wavering all the time*: going back and forth between disbelief and faith; *not to these, neither to those*: not belonging to the believers, nor to the disbelievers. *And he whom God sends astray, you will never find for him a way* back to guidance.

[4:144] *O you who believe, take not the disbelievers as friends instead of the believers* as the hypocrites do. *Do you desire to give God over you a clear warrant*: a plain proof of your hypocrisy*?*

[4:145] *Truly, the hypocrites will be in the lowest level of the Fire*: the seventh pit which consists of sealed iron coffers in the Fire, or rooms closed around them set ablaze from above. This is because of how in addition to their disbelief they were also guilty of mockery or treachery. The meaning of *daraja* and *daraka* was discussed above.[1] Note also that *ḥadīth*s such

1 See Q. 2:228.

as 'There are three traits which, if a man possesses them, make him a hypocrite' and the like are meant as severe warnings about such traits, and are not meant to be taken literally. *And you will never find a helper for them*: to bring them out of it.

[4:146] *Save those who repent* of hypocrisy, *and make amends* by rectifying their deeds, *and hold fast to God and make their religion purely God's* without ostentation. *Those are with the believers* at the Resurrection; *and God will certainly give the believers a great wage*: and they will share in it.

[4:147] *Why would God chastise you if you are thankful* for His favours *and believe?* For He is the Absolute Rich. As for the disbeliever's punishment, it is because his insistence on disbelief is like an imbalance of temperament that leads to sickness; and if it is brought to an end by faith, he becomes safe from its ill consequences. He mentioned the specific before the general[1] in order to draw attention to it. *God is ever Thankful* for your deeds, even if they are few, *Knowing* of your states.

Q. 4:146 [4:148] *God does not like the utterance of evil words out loud, unless a person has been wronged*: and so prays out loud against the one who wronged him. Some say that uttering evil out loud is always wrong, and that *illā* (unless) here means 'not even', as was discussed earlier in regards to *except by mistake* [Q. 4:92]. *God is ever Hearer* of his prayer, *Knower* of the deed of the one who wronged him.

[4:149] *If you show good*—piety—*or conceal it, or pardon evil* from your brother, *then surely God is ever Pardoning, Powerful*: Able to exact vengeance.

[4:150] *Those who disbelieve in God and His messengers and seek to divide between God and His messengers* by believing in Him but disbelieving in them, *and say, 'We believe in some* of them, *and disbelieve in some,' and seek to adopt a* middle *way between them*: between disbelief and faith, though there is no middle way between them.

[4:151] *Those are the disbelievers truly*: whose disbelief is total and firm, without doubt; *and We have prepared for the disbelievers a humiliating chastisement*.

[4:152] *And those who believe in God and His messengers and do not seek to divide between any of them* regarding faith in them, *those—We shall surely give them their wages. God is ever Forgiving* of them, *Merciful* with them.

[4:153] *The People of the Book ask of you*—stubbornly—*to cause a Book to be revealed to them from the heaven*: all at once, written with heavenly ink, like the Torah. *They asked Moses for something greater than that*: and so it is

1 In other words, thankfulness before faith.

no surprise that they should ask this; *for they said, 'Show us God openly*: visibly*'*; *so the thunderbolt*—a fire from the heavens—*seized them for their evildoing*: their stubborn questioning. *Then they took to themselves the calf* as a god *after clear proofs*— prophetic miracles—*had come to them; yet We pardoned that*: by accepting their repentance; *and We bestowed upon Moses clear authority* over them despite their unbridled obstinacy. This was a tiding of the coming victory of His Beloved (may God bless him and grant him peace).

[4:154] *And We raised above them the Mount* when they refused to accept the edicts of the Torah, *at the covenant with them*, because of how they had agreed to accept it, *and We said to them* to begin, *'Enter the gate, bowing* in humility,*'* as was discussed earlier;[1] *and We said to them, 'Transgress not the Sabbath*: and do not violate it by fishing*'*; *and We took from them a firm covenant* regarding this.

[4:155] *So* We did what we did to them *for their breaking their covenant and disbelieving in the signs of God*—His prophetic miracles—*and slaying the prophets wrongfully* even by their own reckoning, *and for their saying, 'Our hearts are covered up* vessels for knowledge*'*; for all of this did We do with them what We did. *Nay, but God sealed them for their disbelief*: this rebuts their claim; *so they do not believe, except for a few* of them, those named before. Q. 4:154

[4:156] *And for their disbelief* in Jesus, in addition to how they broke their covenant, *and their uttering against Mary a tremendous calumny*: namely the accusation of adultery.

[4:157] *And for their saying, 'We slew the Messiah, Jesus son of Mary, the Messenger of God'*: that is, as he claimed to be; or they described him thus by way of mockery; or this is how God Himself described him. *And yet they did not slay him nor did they crucify him, but he was given the resemblance to them*: they mixed up Jesus and a young follower of his, or Ṭīṭānūs the Jew who tried to kill him. God condemned them for this act because of how they boasted of doing it, not merely on account of how they said this based on their own reckoning. *And those who disagree concerning him*, Jesus, *are surely in doubt regarding him*: some of them claim to have killed him, while others claim that his face was moved onto another body, while others claim that he was the son of God, who raised him to Him, while others claim that the human aspect (*nāsūt*) was crucified while the divine aspect (*lāhūt*) was raised up, and so on. *They do not have any knowledge of him, only the pursuit of conjecture*: which here means doubt and so does not contradict how before He said they were 'in doubt'; in other words, but

1 See Q. 2:58.

they only pursue conjecture. *And they did not slay him for certain* as they claim, or they certainly did not slay him.

[4:158] *Nay, God raised him up to Him*: for the heavens are the locus for the manifestation of His authority. *God is ever Mighty, Wise* in what He plans.

[4:159] *And there is not one of the People of the Book but will assuredly believe in him*, in Jesus, *before his death*: before the death of that person of the Book, when he sees the angel of death and realises that he was God's servant and messenger, though it will do him no good at that point; or it means the People of the Book at the time of the descent of Jesus when the Antichrist emerges, for he will destroy him and all the religions will be united under the religion of Islam, after which he will remain for forty years and then die, and the Muslims will perform his funeral prayer. It is related that he will be buried beside ʿUmar (may God be pleased with him). *And on the Day of Resurrection he will be a witness against them* to their disbelief in him, or their belief in him according to the second interpretation.

Q. 4:158

[4:160] *And because of the* wanton *evildoing of some of those of Jewry, We forbade them certain good things that were lawful for them*: this alludes to His Words, *And to those of Jewry, We forbade every beast with hoof*...[Q. 6:146]. Note that things are made forbidden for one of three reasons: the first is that they are inherently criminal, and such things are forbidden by both the Law and the intellect. The second is that their harm outweighs their benefit, even if the intellect might think otherwise. The third is to serve as a way of breaking the passion of certain people, even if the forbidden thing is very beneficial, in which case the Law forbids it to those who deserve this, as in the subject of the present discussion. *And because of their barring from God's way many*: that is, many people, or much barring.

[4:161] *And because of their taking usury when they had been forbidden it* in the Torah, *and their consuming people's wealth through falsehood*, such as bribery; *and We have prepared for the disbelievers among them*, and not those of them who believe, *a painful chastisement*.

[4:162] *But those of them who are firmly rooted in knowledge, and the believers*, all of them, *believing in what is revealed to you*, the Qur'ān, *and what was revealed before you, and those who observe* (*muqīmīn*) *the prayer*—the word *muqīmīn* is in the *naṣb* state here to impart praise;[1] it is not, as was reportedly stated by ʿĀ'isha, a mistake on the part of the scribes—*and pay zakāt*,

1 Rather than *muqīmūn* in the *rafʿ* state, as all the other nouns in the list are, as subjects of the nominal sentence. The Arabs would change the grammatical state of nouns to draw attention to them or to impart praise, as though saying 'and consider also these'.

and those who believe in God and the Last Day—to them We shall surely give a great wage.

[4:163] *We have revealed to you as We revealed to Noah, and the prophets after him, and We revealed to Abraham and Ishmael and Isaac, and Jacob, and the Tribes*—the sons of Jacob—*and Jesus, and Job, and Jonah, and Aaron, and Solomon; and We gave to David the Psalms* (*zabūr*): meaning his Book; or it can be read as *zubūr*, the plural of *zubur,* meaning 'Inscribed Books'. He singled out these prophets for mention because of their great nobility.

[4:164] *And* We sent *messengers We have told you of before* in the Meccan chapters, *and messengers We have not told you of; and God spoke directly to Moses*: this is the highest level of revelation. In other words, your situation regarding revelation is the same as theirs, for you have been given all that they were given, and the one who opposes you is like the one who opposes them.

[4:165] We sent *messengers bearing glad tidings* to the obedient, *and warnings* to the sinners, *so that people might have no argument against God after the messengers*: that they would say, 'No one was sent to us to warn us.' *God is ever Mighty* in what He wills, *Wise* in what He plans. When these verses beginning *We have revealed to you…* were revealed, they said, 'We do not bear witness to you, nor do these rebellious ones.' So God revealed: Q. 4:163

[4:166] *But God bears witness with what He has revealed to you*: the Qurʾān which proves your prophethood; *He has revealed it through His knowledge*: adorned with the object of His knowledge which people require for their worldly and other-worldly lives, or by His knowledge that you are most deserving of receiving His revelation; *and the angels also bear witness* to your prophethood. *And God suffices as a Witness* to it, for He has manifested plain proofs of it.

[4:167] *Truly, those who disbelieve and bar from the way of God have gone far astray* from what is right.

[4:168] *Truly, those who disbelieve and who have done wrong*: in a general sense, or by concealing your prophethood and dying in that state; the Words *done wrong* are proof that the substantive legal rulings (*furūʿ*) are addressed to the disbelievers as well as the believers;[1] *it is not for God to forgive them, neither to guide them to any path.*

1 This is a matter of dispute among the scholars of jurisprudence. Some hold that the only command that is issued to disbelievers is the command to embrace faith, while others hold that all the other edicts of the religion are issued to them also, and hence they 'do wrong' by not heeding them.

[4:169] *Except for the path of Hell*—which is the only direction He guides such folk—*abiding therein forever; and for God that is an easy matter.*

[4:170] *O people, the Messenger* Muḥammad (may God bless him and grant him peace) *has now come to you with the truth from your Lord; so believe, for it is better for you* to believe. *And if you disbelieve, then surely to God belongs all that is in the heavens and in the earth*: and so He is free of need for you. *And God is ever Knowing* of your states, *Wise* in His actions.

[4:171] O *People of the Book*, the Christians or the Jews as well, *do not go to extremes*—do not transgress the limit—*in your religion* concerning Jesus, whether going too far or not far enough, as was discussed before; *and do not say about God except the truth*: by declaring His transcendence beyond such things as begetting sons. *The Messiah, Jesus son of Mary, was only the Messenger of God and His Word*—for He brought him into being with the word 'Be!' or His argument—*which He cast to Mary* when Gabriel breathed His Word into the sleeve of her garment, so that it reached her womb in the way in which the father impregnates the mother; or it means how
Q. 4:169 Gabriel breathed the spirit that gives life to the body; *and a spirit* that was issued *from Him* without any matter. *So believe in God and His messengers, and do not say, 'Three* are our gods': God, the Messiah and Mary, or the three hypostases, as will be explained later. *Refrain* from this Trinitarianism, for *it would better for you* to do so. *God is but One God. Glory be to Him*—transcendent be He—*that He should have a son! To Him belongs all that is in the heavens and in the earth*: through sovereignty and creation. *God suffices as a Guardian*: and is free of need for a son to be His agent.

[4:172] *The Messiah would never disdain*—would never be too proud—*to be a servant of God, neither would the angels who are nigh*: though they do not have fathers or mothers, and their power is beyond that of humanity; so what of a weak human being who did have a mother? This does not mean that they are superior to the prophets, for their mention here after the conjunction *neither* is meant as a way of imparting emphasis by alluding to their greater power and their lack of mothers, not to their general superiority. It is also a rebuttal to those who worship both the Messiah and the angels too. Even if we allowed that interpretation for the sake of argument, it would still not be proof that either class [of angels or humans] is superior to the other in an absolute sense. *Whoever disdains to worship Him, and waxes proud*: disdain is above pride because it means pride accompanied by revulsion; thus the verse implies an unfolding by degree: 'whoever disdains, and whoever is proud, and whoever does not disdain'; *He will assuredly muster them to Him, all of them*: for requital.

[4:173] *As for those who believed and did righteous deeds*—that is, those who did not disdain—*He will pay them in full their wages, and He will give them more of His bounty; and as for them who disdain* to worship Him *and are too proud* to assent, *He will chastise them with a painful chastisement, and they shall not find for themselves, besides God, any friend or helper.*

[4:174] *O people, a proof*, Muḥammad (may God bless him and grant him peace), *has now come to you from your Lord, and We have revealed to you a manifest light*: the Qur'ān.

[4:175] *As for those who believe in God, and hold fast to Him*—grasping onto the Qur'ān and trusting in God—*He will surely admit them to mercy from Him* which ensures salvation, *and bounty* which surpasses their deeds; *and He will guide them to Him by a straight path* to knowledge, action and the Garden.

[4:176] *They will ask you for a pronouncement* about indirect heirs. *Say: 'God pronounces to you concerning indirect heirs* (*kalāla*): family ties that are not direct.[1] *If a man perishes*—dies—*having no children* or living parents, *but he has a sister* (whether full-blooded or half to the same father; the ruling Q. 4:173
for the half-sister to the same mother was discussed earlier), *hers is half of what he leaves, and he*, the man, *is her heir*, the sister's heir in the same way, *if she has no children* or living parents. *If there be two sisters* or more, *theirs are two-thirds of what he*, the brother, *leaves; if there be siblings, men and women, then the male shall receive the equivalent of the portion of two females. God makes clear to you* the truth, *lest you go astray; and God has knowledge of all things*: including what is best for you in your lives and your deaths.' And God knows best what is correct.

1 In other words, neither directly ascendant nor descendant.

5
The Table
SŪRAT AL-MĀ'IDA

Revealed in Medina

After clarifying for us what is true and what is false lest we go astray, He then commands us to fulfil His covenant, which means to follow what He has clarified for us, now and forever. So He says:

In the Name of God, the Compassionate, the Merciful

[5:1] *O you who believe, fulfil your bonds*: meaning every pact you have made with yourselves, and between you and God, and between God and you,[1] whether the Law made it obligatory by means of the Book, the Sunna or the intellect. These refer to that for which God has instilled[2] knowledge in us so that we can attain understanding of it through instinct or the least bit of contemplation, as is indicated by the verse, *And when your Lord took from the Children of Adam, from their loins their seed and made them testify*... [Q. 7:172]. This makes six[3] in total. Every bond is either inherently binding, or made binding by our agreement to commit to it. The latter may be either obligatory or recommended to fulfil, or obligatory or recommended to abstain from fulfilling.[4] This makes twenty-four categories of bonds. Fulfilment means to adhere to the terms of the covenant.

He then expands on these bonds by saying, *Lawful to you is the beast*—meaning any dumb animal—*of the cattle*: the construction is meant to

1 The exegesis of al-Rāghib al-Aṣfahānī, from which the author seems to have drawn this passage, presents these three types of bond as 'a bond between God and the servant; a bond between the servant and himself; and a bond between the servant and another human being'. Al-Rāghib al-Aṣfahānī, *al-Tafsīr*, Medina: Umm al-Qurā University Press, 1422 AH, vol. 1, p. 247.

2 Reading *rakkaza* rather than *dhakara*; ibid.

3 Reading *sitta* for *sunna*; ibid.

4 Such as a promise to commit a sin or impious act.

explain the type, like 'a garment of silk'. 'Cattle' (*anʿām*) means camels, cows and sheep, and also by extension deer and wild cows; *except that which will presently be recited to you*: meaning that which is forbidden in the verse, *Forbidden to you is carrion*...[Q. 5:3]; *game not being lawful to you when you are on pilgrimage* (ḥurum): meaning when you are in the state of consecration. *Truly, God decrees whatever He desires*: whether permitting or forbidding.

[5:2] *O you who believe, do not profane God's sacraments*: the rites of the *ḥajj*, such as by hunting while in the state of consecration, or it means His religion; *nor the sacred month*: by beginning fighting during it—most consider this to be abrogated; *nor the offering*: meaning the sacrificial animals dedicated to the Kaʿba—that is, do not interfere with them, even if they are not garlanded; *nor the garlands*: the sacrificial offerings that are decorated with garlands of palm fibres or leaves; *nor profane those repairing, heading, to the Sacred House, seeking bounty, provision, from their Lord* by means of commerce, and beatitude by their own claim—this included disbelievers, but it was then abrogated by the verse the idolaters are indeed unclean...[Q. 9:28]. *But when you are discharged, then hunt for game if you wish to. And let not hatred of a people that barred you from the Sacred Mosque* in the year of Ḥudaybiya *cause you to commit aggression* by barring them from the *ʿumra* as revenge for this. *Help one another to righteousness in that which you have been commanded to do, and piety in avoiding that which has been forbidden; do not help one another to sin, disobedience*, and enmity, injustice. *And fear God. Truly, God is severe in retribution.* Q. 5:2

[5:3] *Forbidden to you is carrion*: meaning that whose spirit departed without a proper slaughter; *and blood* that has spilled from the veins; *and the flesh of swine; and what has been hallowed with a raised voice to other than God*: as was discussed earlier;[1] *and the beast strangled to death; and the beast beaten down*: killed by a heavy blow; *and the beast fallen*: meaning the animal that dies by falling from a high place; *and the beast gored to death* by another animal; *and what beasts of prey have devoured*: what they have eaten from so that it died, even if they be hunting animals; *except for what you have slaughtered duly* from those latter five before it died by those means, while it still had some life in it. Slaughter means to cut the windpipe and gullet with a sharp object. He listed these latter five things, even though they are all types of carrion, because of how the disbelievers considered them to be methods of proper slaughter. And forbidden also is what has been

1 See Q. 2:173.

sacrificed for idols (*nuṣub*): the *nuṣub* were idols around the Kaʿba which they used to venerate with sacrifices, and so they were forbidden even if the Name of God was invoked during their slaughter. *And forbidden also is that you apportion*—that you seek to determine how to apportion your affairs—*through the divining of arrows*: they would use arrows on which were written 'my Lord commands me', 'my Lord forbids me', or nothing at all, and follow the instruction of whichever arrow they drew, or draw again if they got the blank one. Or this refers to how they would divide the meat from the sacrifices made to those aforementioned idols, in which case it was mentioned here with the other things because of how they would do all of them at the Kaʿba. *That apportioning is wickedness*: because although it resembles drawing lots, it also involves laying claim to knowledge of the Unseen and inventing lies about God, if 'my Lord' is taken to mean God, or idolatry if it is taken to mean one of the idols. Or, in the case of the second interpretation, it is because it means ignoring the proper price and value of the commodity. *Today*, in the
Q. 5:4 present moment, *the disbelievers have despaired of ever destroying your religion; therefore do not fear them* that they might come to dominate you, *but fear Me alone*. *Today*, the Day of ʿArafa at the Farewell Pilgrimage, *I have perfected your religion for you*: and no further rulings about the lawful and the forbidden would be revealed thereafter; *and I have completed My favour upon you*: by completing the religion; and *I have approved Islam for you as religion* among all religions. This sentence is parenthetical, after which the topic at hand continues: *But whoever is constrained and forced to consume one of these forbidden things by emptiness*—hunger—*not inclining purposely to sin*, such as by eating more of it than he needs, *then God is Forgiving* of him, *Merciful* to him and will not take him to task for it.

[5:4] *They ask you about what is made lawful for them. Say: 'The good things are made lawful for you'*: meaning that which sound natural disposition does not deem foul, as long as there is not a primary text or analogy to establish that it is forbidden. *And the hunting creatures you have taught*: meaning the game caught by the carnivores and birds of prey which you use for hunting; *training* [*them*] *as hounds*: teaching them how to hunt for you. The word *mukallib* (one who trains hounds) means the one who teaches an animal to hunt, because every carnivore can be called a *kalb* (hound); a *ḥadīth* says, 'Lord God, set one of Your hounds upon him!' *Teaching them of what God has taught you*: meaning the strategies of hunting. *So eat what they have caught for you* as long as they have not eaten from it, even if they killed it, *and mention God's Name over it* when you retrieve it, or when you eat it; this is a recommendation. *And fear God* regarding what He has forbidden. *Truly, God is swift at reckoning*, and will take you to task for what is hidden as well as what is open.

[5:5] *Today the good things are permitted to you, and the food*, the slaughtered meat, *of those who were given the Book*, the Jews and Christians, *is permitted to you, and permitted to them is your food*: that is, you may feed them your own slaughtered meat. *Likewise, the believing virtuous* free *women, and the virtuous* free *women of those who were given the Book before you, if you give them their wages*: their dowries. The stipulation of this for the lawfulness of marrying them is meant to stress its obligatory status, while the stipulation of virtue is meant as an encouragement to do what is best. *In wedlock* honourably, *and not illicitly* by open adultery; *or taking them as lovers*: consorts to engage in fornication with them. *Whoever disbelieves in faith*—that is, whoever disbelieves in the Law by rejecting it, or whoever abandons the faith—*his work has failed*, been squandered, *and in the Hereafter he shall be among the losers*.

Q. 5:5

[5:6] *O you who believe, when you stand up to pray*: that is, when you wish to pray but you are in a state of minor ritual impurity (*muḥdith*), given the contrast with how later in the verse he says, *If you are defiled* (*junub*),[1] or how He says *or if any of you comes from the privy*...and so on.[2] Some say it is a command of obligation for the one in minor ritual impurity, and a command of recommendation for the one who is already pure, as well as a way of informing the Prophet (may God bless him and grant him peace) that he did not have to refrain from all actions if he incurred minor impurity, since before this he used to desist from all action in such a situation. *Wash your faces, and your hands*: that is, run water over them; there is no need to rub them, contrary to Mālik who required this; *up to the elbows* and including them, as a *ḥadīth* confirms; *and wipe your heads*: the word *ruʾūsikum* (your heads) is preceded by the particle *bi*, which implies 'some' or 'part'—*masaḥtu al-mandīl* means 'I touched the cloth', implying all of it, while *masaḥtu bi'l-mandīl* means 'I touched part of the cloth.' Ibn Mālik related that Abū ʿAlī said in *al-Tadhkira* that *bi* can take the meaning of *min* (from) in the sense of 'part'. This is what Abū Ḥanīfa followed (may God be pleased with him), though he did not accept that it can mean even the smallest amount of the head, since this would already be covered by washing the face. The

1 Meaning major ritual impurity, which is incurred by sexual activity.
2 Describing minor ritual impurity.

rebuttal of this is that it is also obligatory to observe the proper order of body parts when washing. *And your feet up to the ankles*: *arjul* (feet) can be read *arjula* as the object of the verb *wash*, or *arjuli* as the object of *wipe*, in which case it is said to denote permission, though the use of the word *and* seems to preclude this. Abū Zayd said that the Arabs used the word *masḥ* (wipe) to mean washing and wiping together, and so the most that could be said here is that it is ambiguous. Yet a great number of authentic *ḥadīth*s—so many that they reach the level of mass-transmission—state that it is obligatory to wash the feet.[1] Thus there is no room to argue that the word *feet* is governed by the verb *wipe* in the *arjula* reading as a second direct object of the verb. The reason the feet are mentioned after wiping the head in this way is to allude to how one should be careful not to waste water when washing them, since this would otherwise be likely to occur. Thus it is akin to the words of the poem: *mutaqallidan sayfan wa-rumḥan* (unsheathing a sword and a spear).[2]
Q. 5:6 This is because washing and wiping are similar in meaning. The nature of the figure of speech here is that wiping does not have a limit, while washing does, and so the intended meaning is 'wash lightly'. Some said that, in fact, it does mean 'wipe your feet' just as the head is wiped over, but then this was abrogated by the Sunna. The mention of the head in between the hands and feet is proof that the order must be followed, just as it is described here. The use of the particle *fa*[3] before the verb *wash*—as well as [its use in] the Sunna—proves that forming the right intention before beginning is also obligatory.

If you are defiled, purify yourselves: by bathing; *but if you are sick, or on a journey, or if any of you comes from the privy*: this was explained earlier;[4] *or you have touched women, and you cannot find water, then seek out wholesome soil, and wipe your faces* all over, *and your hands* up to and including the elbows, striking the earth twice, according to the Sunna—the commentary for this was given earlier; *with it* (*minhu*, literally 'from it')—that is, with some of it, which means that a smooth rock cannot be used for dry ablutions. Arguing that *minhu* means 'from it' in the sense of 'beginning with it' is

1 Rather than merely wiping them with damp hands, which is the root of the debate here.

2 Where 'spear' is governed by the verb 'unsheathing', though one does not usually speak of unsheathing a spear; the reader is invited to imagine the presence of a second verb such as 'carrying' to apply to the spear, just as in the verse we can imagine a second instance of the verb 'wash' preceding 'your feet'.

3 Meaning 'then' or simply introducing a main clause, but also evoking a sense of purpose and deliberation.

4 See Q. 4:43.

wildly far-fetched, as was explained in *Kashshāf*[1] and elsewhere. The argument that it means 'from it' in the sense of 'from the impurity' contradicts the apparent meaning; and in any case, this is already implied by the word *then*. Perhaps the reason this verse was repeated was to reaffirm it in the context of the other laws about purity.

God does not desire all this *to make any hardship for you; but He desires* it *to purify you* outwardly and inwardly; *and that He may perfect His grace upon you*: by elucidating how it may be manifested; *so that you might give thanks* for His grace, that He might increase it.

[5:7] *And remember God's grace upon you*—both religiously and worldly—*and His covenant which He made with you* at the Pledge of Riḍwān, *when you said, 'We hear and we obey'* no matter what. *And fear God* lest you break His covenant. *Truly, God knows what is in the breasts* and the secrets they harbour.

[5:8] *O you who believe, be upright* with the truth *before God*: not ostentatiously; *witnesses in equity*: justice. *Let not hatred of a people cause you not to be just; be just* even with the enemy, for that is true justice; *that is nearer to God-fearing*: this is akin to the verse, *The inhabitants of the Garden on that* Q. 5:7
day will be in a better abode...[Q. 25:24]. *And fear God. Truly, God is aware of what you do*: and will requite you.

[5:9] *God has promised those who believe and perform righteous deeds*; and He then elucidates what this promise is by saying: *they shall have forgiveness* if they have sinned, *and a great wage*.

[5:10] *And they who disbelieve and deny Our signs—they shall be the inhabitants of Hell-fire*.

[5:11] *O you who believe, remember God's favour upon you, when a people*—namely Quraysh—*purposed to extend their hands against you*: to slay you when you were busy praying the afternoon prayer, and so Gabriel came bearing instructions for the prayer of peril[2] and informed you of their plot; *but He restrained their hands from you. And fear God; and in God let the believers put their trust*.

[5:12] *God had made a covenant with the Children of Israel, and We raised up from among them twelve leaders* from the twelve tribes, charged to honour the command that had been issued to them to enter the Levant and fight the tyrants. *And God said, 'I am with you* with aid. By God, *surely if you observe the prayer and pay zakāt, and believe in My messengers and succour them*: aid them; the root meaning of *taʿzīr* (succour) is 'to repel', and so it

1 The exegesis of Zamakhsharī (d. 1144).
2 See Q. 4:102.

is used to mean defence against evil or the repelling of enemies, which is aid; and it is also used to mean 'rebuke', in the sense of the *ḥadīth*, 'Help your brother, whether he is the transgressor or the transgressed against'; *and lend to God a goodly loan*: by expending on good causes; *I will absolve you of your evil deeds, and I will admit you to Gardens with rivers flowing from beneath them. So whoever of you disbelieves after that* covenant, *surely he has strayed from the right way*: the way of truth.' The reason He said *after*, even though it was still true before the covenant, was because it was even more evil to do it afterwards.

[5:13] *So because of their breaking their covenant, We cursed them*—sent them far from Our mercy—*and made their hearts hard*: solid and enveloped in a firm casing to make them even harder. *They pervert words*—the Words of God—*from their contexts*: this was discussed earlier; *and they have forgotten a portion of what they were reminded of* from the Torah, for they did not act according to it; *and you will never cease*, O Muḥammad, *to discover some*
Q. 5:13 *treachery on their part, except for a few of them*: such as Ibn Salām and his ilk. *Yet pardon them, and forgive*: turn away—this was abrogated by the verses about fighting. *Truly, God loves the virtuous.*

[5:14] *And with those who say, 'We are Christians'* (*Naṣārā*)—meaning those who claimed to give support (*nuṣra*) to God's faith, or those who hailed from Nazareth (Nāṣira) in the Levant—*We made a covenant, and they have forgotten a portion*, an ample share, *of what they were reminded of* in the Gospel about following Muḥammad (may God bless him and grant him peace). *So We have stirred up*, destined, *among them*, among their factions—the Nestorians, Jacobites and Melkites—*enmity and hatred*, total enmity, *until the Day of Resurrection; and God will assuredly tell them of what they wrought*, and the requital which it earned.

[5:15] *O People of the Book*—the two Books—*now there has come to you Our Messenger*, Muḥammad (may God bless him and grant him peace), *making clear to you much of what you used to conceal of the Book*: such as the verse about stoning, and the glad tidings Jesus gave about Aḥmad; *and pardoning much* of your perversions and treachery, which He commanded be pardoned; thus it need not be objected that he was not obliged to reveal the truth which they concealed. *There has come to you from God a light*, the Qur'ān, *and a lucid Book,* [5:16] *whereby God guides whoever follows*—meaning whoever He knew would follow—*His good pleasure* through faith *to the ways of peace*, salvation, *and brings them forth from the shadows* of disbelief *into the light* of faith *by His leave*: by His will. *And He guides them to a straight path* which leads to God.

[5:17] *They indeed are disbelievers*—the Jacobite Christians who believe in the total identity (*ittiḥād*) of Jesus and God—*who say, 'God is the Messiah, son of Mary.'* Or it means all the Christians, who cite his attributes such as raising the dead and knowledge of the Unseen as proof of his divinity, in which case the sentence is reversed, as when one says, 'A generous man is Zayd.' *Say: 'Who, then, can do anything against God*—literally 'who owns anything from God', a figure of speech such as when one says, 'I do not own even the horse's head,' meaning that you are powerless—*if He desires to destroy the Messiah, son of Mary, and his mother, and all those who are on earth?'* For they are all equal beneath His power, and this dispels any divinity in them. *And to God belongs the kingdom of the heavens and the earth, and all that is between them. He creates what He will* without any origin. *God has power over everything* that is possible.

[5:18] *The Jews and Christians say, 'We are the sons of God*: hence they say, 'We are akin to His sons in His affection for us,' or they claim that they are His chosen people, like 'the sons of the world'; or it means Ezra and Jesus, Q. 5:17
as when the king's retinue says, 'We are the kings'; *and His beloved ones.' Say: 'Why, then, does He chastise you for your sins* in this world by such things as transformation, and in the Hereafter with something that is worse, even if it only be for a few days, by your own claim? The loving father would not punish in that way. *Nay, you are mortals from among those He created*: and the Eternal One would not beget a mortal. *He forgives whom He wills*, such as the believer, *and He chastises whom He wills,* such as the Jews, and you have no distinction above anyone else.*' For to God belongs the kingdom of the heavens and of the earth, and all that is between them; to Him is the journey's end*: where He will requite all.

[5:19] *O People of the Book, there has come to you Our Messenger,* Muḥammad (may God bless him and grant him peace), *making clear to you* the religion, *after an interval*: the word *fatra* (interval) is from the verb *fatara*, meaning 'to become blunt and lesser than it was'; *between the messengers*: for there were 600 years between him and Jesus, during which time there were three prophets among the Israelites and the one Arab prophet, Khālid b. Sinān; *lest you should say, 'There has not come to us any bearer of glad tidings nor any warner.' Truly, there has come to you a bearer of glad tidings and a warner*: so there is no excuse. *God has power over all things*: including the power to send messengers successively, or with intervals.

[5:20] *And* remember *when Moses said to his people, 'O my people, remember God's favour to you, when He established among you prophets* from the time of Abraham to Jesus, numbering 4,000 prophets, *and established you as kings* possessing servants, after you had been slaves in the past, *and gave you such* graces *as He had not given to any in all the worlds* before you, for the religion of each prophet was more complete than that of the one who preceded him.

[5:21] *'O my people, enter the Holy Land*—meaning Jerusalem or the Levant—*which God has ordained for you* in the Preserved Tablet, as long as you are faithful and obedient. So this does not contradict the verse which includes *it shall be forbidden them for forty years* [Q. 5:26]; or it means 'apportioned' or 'gifted', if *forty* refers to the duration of the forbidding.[1] *And do not turn back in flight*: in fear of the tyrants there; *or you will end up as losers* of the rewards of this life and the next.'

[5:22] *They said, 'O Moses, there are tyrants in it* whom we cannot defeat—a tyrant (*jabbār*) is one who forces the people to bend to his will; *we will never enter it until they depart from it; and if they depart from it, then we will enter.'*

[5:23] *Then there said two men*, Joshua the nephew of Moses and Caleb the brother-in-law of Miriam, *of those who feared* God, *and to whom God had been gracious* by giving them strength and protection—they were
Q. 5:21 from the aforementioned leaders—*'Enter against them by the gate*: through the gate of their city. *For if you enter by it, you will be victorious*: by the fulfilment of God's promise and the weakness of their hearts. *Put your trust in God, if you are believers* in Him.'

[5:24] *They said, 'O Moses, we will never enter it so long as they are in it. So go forth, you and your Lord, and fight* the tyrants. *We will be sitting here.'*

[5:25] *He*, Moses, *said* then, *'My Lord, I control none but myself and my brother*: because the one who was obedient to him was, in a sense, under his control. He did not add mention of those two men because he had seen how his people had changed; or they were included in his statement as his brothers in religion. *So separate us*—judge between us, or distance us—*from the wicked folk.'*

[5:26] *He*, God, *said, 'Then it*, the Holy Land, *shall be forbidden them* to enter ever; *for forty years they shall wander*: the words *forty years* refer to the duration of the wandering; *lost in the land*. The people in the wilderness all died, including Moses and Aaron, except for Joshua and Caleb; and then Joshua went with their children, who were not yet twenty years of age, and conquered it two months after Moses died. It is also said that *forty years* refers to the duration of the forbidding. *So do not grieve for the wicked folk* out of sympathy for Moses.'

1 The verse can be read as *it shall be forbidden them for forty years; they shall wander lost in the land*, or *it shall be forbidden them; for forty years they shall wander...*, depending on whether *forty* refers to the forbidding or the wandering.

[5:27] *And recite to them*, O Muḥammad, *the story of the two sons of Adam*: Cain and Abel; and let this recitation be adorned *with the truth. They each offered a sacrifice (qurbān)*—meaning anything that is done to draw closer to God—*and it was accepted from one of them*: Abel, who offered a sheep that the fire consumed, which was the same as the sacrifice with which Ishmael was spared; or some say it was a fattened camel; *and not accepted from the other*: from Cain, who offered crops, specifically some poor-quality wheat. The reason for the offering was a disagreement about the marriage of Abel's twin sister. Ibn ʿAbbās (may God be pleased with him) is reported to have said that the cause of it was that there were no poor people to accept charity, and so the fire accepted it instead. This inspired envy in his brother, and so *He said* to him, *'I will surely slay you.' The other*, Abel, *said, 'God accepts only from the God-fearing*, and so why would you slay me because my offering was accepted?

[5:28] *'Yet*, by God, *if you extend your hand against me to slay me, I will not extend my hand against you to slay you; I fear God, the Lord of the Worlds*: Abel was stronger than him, but his piety stayed his hand. Q. 5:27

[5:29] *'I desire that you should end up with my sin*: all of it, or '[I want you to have] the sin of murdering me'; *and your own sin* because of which your offering was not accepted, *and so become an inhabitant of the Fire. That is the requital of the evildoers'*: what he meant was, 'If that is to be our fate, then I desire that it be for you, not for me.' It was not that he wanted this for him because he hated him. Some say that it actually means 'that you should not end up with my sin'.

[5:30] *Then his soul prompted him*—made it seem easy to him—*to slay his brother, so he slew him*: he was twenty years old at the time; *and became one of the losers*. Subsequently, after he had killed him, he did not know what to do with the body:

[5:31] *Then God sent forth a raven* to another dead raven, *scratching*—pecking with its beak—*into the earth to show him*: the subject of the verb 'show' could be God or the raven; *how he might hide the shame*—the corpse—*of his brother*: for his death had been a shameful thing. *He said, 'Woe to me!* An expression of despair meaning, 'O my ruin, come forth!' *Am I not able to be as this raven, and so hide my brother's shame?' And he became one of the remorseful*: for the loss of his brother, but not for his act of murdering him. It was not a true repentance; and in any case, repentance does not absolve a man from the rights he owes to other people. Then his body turned black, and his parents renounced him.

[5:32] *On account of that*—his murder of his brother—*We decreed for the*

Children of Israel that whoever slays a soul for other than slaying *a soul, or for corruption in the land* such as idolatry or highway robbery, *it shall be as if he had slain humankind altogether*: because he established the act of murder, which the people then followed. A *ḥadīth* says, 'The first son of Adam to commit murder is jointly responsible for the sin of every other murderer.' Or it means that all humankind will act as the murdered person's family if he had no family of his own. *And whoever saves the life of one* by acting as the cause of its continued life, *it shall be as if he had saved the life of all humankind*, because he established that act, and because humankind are like a single body, and the one who injures part of it is like the one who injures all of it, and just so for the one who protects it. Exegeses of this verse often note that the believers all act as the family of the one who is killed unlawfully. As for slaying the disbelievers, it is like amputating a gangrenous limb to save the rest of the body. *Our messengers have already come to them*, to the Children of Israel, *with clear proofs*, prophetic miracles, *but after that many of them still commit excesses in the land*: by engaging in slaying and such things.

Q. 5:33

[5:33] *Truly the only requital of those who fight against God and His Messenger*, meaning those who fight their allies, or those who disobey their commands by engaging in highway robbery or the like, *and hasten about the earth to do corruption there, is that they shall be slain* without crucifixion if they engage in murder alone, *or crucified* after being slain for three days if they engage in both murder and robbery, according to Shāfiʿī, *or have their hands and feet cut off on opposite sides* if they engage in robbery without murder, the right hand and left foot, as he explained, *or be banished from the land* if they only stir up fear. Banishment means that they be captured and expelled, or that they flee from the Islamic lands. The Ḥanafīs say that it means imprisonment. So the word *or* in the verse implies detail, not choice. This is how Ibn ʿAbbās and others explained it. *That is a degradation*—a disgrace—*for them in this world; and in the Hereafter theirs will be a great chastisement* if they are idolaters, for otherwise the punishment of this world is an expiation for the sin.

[5:34] *Except for such as repent before you overpower them*: if they are idolaters, then all of it is excused, while if they are Muslims only God's right is excused, as is implied by: *for know that God is Forgiving, Merciful.* In the case of murder, the obligation of the punishment is waived, but it remains permitted [for the family of the victim] to demand lawful retribution.

[5:35] *O you who believe, fear God, and seek the means to Him*: draw near to Him by obeying Him; *and struggle in His way so that you might prosper.*

[5:36] *Truly, as for the disbelievers, if they possessed all that is in the earth, and the like of it with it, by which to ransom themselves*, to offer it in payment to spare themselves *from the chastisement of the Day of Resurrection, it would not be accepted from them; theirs shall be a painful chastisement*.

[5:37] *They will desire to exit from the Fire, but they will not exit from it; theirs shall be a lasting chastisement*: this refutes those who say that they will become accustomed to the torment of Hell after a time.

[5:38] *And the thieving male and the thieving female* who steal the value of a quarter dinar or more—thieving (*sariqa*) means to take the property of another person surreptitiously from a place where it has been adequately stowed for safekeeping, for which there are certain specific stipulations—*cut off their hands*: their right hands from the wrist; and if they repeat the offence, then their left feet from the ankle joint, and then the left hand, and then the right foot, all of which was established by the Sunna; *as a requital for what they have earned, and an exemplary punishment from God; God is Mighty* in His retribution, *Wise* in His decree.

[5:39] *But whoever repents after his evildoing*—his thievery—*and makes* Q. 5:37
amends by rectifying his deeds, *God will truly relent to him* and accept his repentance. This means he will be excused from the punishment of the Resurrection, but not the amputation of the hand, according to the majority. *Truly, God is Forgiving, Merciful*.

[5:40] *Do you not know*, O you who ought to know, *that to God belongs the kingdom of the heavens and the earth? He chastises whom He wills and forgives whom He wills, and God has power over all things*.

[5:41] *O Messenger, let them not grieve you, those who vie with one another in disbelief*: do not be saddened by their gleeful indulgence in disbelief; *such as those* Hypocrites *who say with their mouths, 'We believe* in you,*' but their hearts do not believe; and from among those of Jewry who listen to calumny* and accept their false tales, *listening to other folk* instead of you, *who have not come to you* because of their pride, such as Qurayẓa, who asked about the ruling of stoning on behalf of the people of Khaybar. *They pervert*—transfer—*words from their contexts* in which God placed them, such as how they changed the ruling about stoning the adulterer to a sentence of lashing and the blackening of the face. *They say, 'If you are given this* perverted ruling, *then take it*: accept it; *but if you are not given it*—but he rules differently, such as by affirming the sentence of stoning—*then beware* of accepting it.*' Whomever God desires to try*—to punish or to send astray—*you cannot avail him anything against God* by repelling it, as was discussed before. *Those are they whose hearts God did not desire to purify* from idolatry; this refutes the position of the Muᶜtazila. *Theirs shall be degradation in this world*: such as the exposing of the hypocrites and the poll-tax on the Jews; *and in the Hereafter theirs shall be a great chastisement*.

[5:42] *Listeners to calumny* with full knowledge of its falsehood; *and consumers of unlawful gain*: forbidden food devoid of blessing. He singled out consumption because that is where the majority of the profit is expended. *If they come to you, then judge between them or turn away from them*: as you wish. It is said this was abrogated by His Words, *Judge between them, according to what God has revealed* [Q. 5:48]. *If you turn away from them, they cannot harm you at all*: this was abrogated by His Words, *And judge between them according to what God has revealed* [Q. 5:49]. *And if you judge, then judge justly between them; God loves the just*.

[5:43] *But how is it that they make you their judge when they have the Torah, wherein is God's judgement* concerning the sentence of stoning; for they did not ask for your judgement out of desire for the judgement of God. *And then they turn away* from your verdict of stoning *after that*: after asking for your judgement? *Such are not believers*: neither in you nor in their own Book.

Q. 5:42

[5:44] *Truly, We revealed the Torah, wherein is guidance* to the truth, *and light* that unveils things that are obscure, *by which the prophets, who had submitted*—unlike the Jews who did not submit—*judged*; and We revealed *for those of Jewry; as did the rabbis* judge by it, *and the priests, according to that which they were bidden to observe of God's Book*: that is, by means of God's command to those three to preserve His Book from alteration. As for the Qur'ān, no alteration occurred within it because He did not entrust its preservation to anyone but Himself, and said, *Truly, it is We Who have revealed the Remembrance, and assuredly We will preserve it* [Q. 15:9]. *And they were witnesses to it*: watching over it to prevent it being substituted. *So do not fear people*, O Jews, in the matter of revealing God's judgement, such as the description of Muḥammad or the verse about stoning; *but fear Me, and do not sell*—exchange—*My signs for a small price*: the riches of this world. *Whoever does not judge according to what God has revealed*—wilfully and obstinately—*such are the disbelievers*.

[5:45] *And therein We prescribed for them*—for the Jews—*that a life for a life* that is slain, *and an eye for an eye* that is plucked out, *and a nose for a nose* that is cut off, *and an ear for an ear* that is torn off, *and a tooth for a tooth* that is pulled out; *and for wounds retaliation* wherever retaliation is possible. *But whoever forgoes it*—forgoes the retaliation by pardoning—*out of charity, then that shall be an expiation for him*: all of the blood-money for all of his sins, or half of it for half of them, and so on, as is described in an authentic *ḥadīth*. *Whoever does not judge according to what God has revealed, those are the evildoers*.

[5:46] *And We caused Jesus son of Mary to follow in their footsteps*—the footsteps of the prophets—*confirming the Torah before him; and We gave to him the Gospel, wherein is guidance and light* like the Torah, *confirming the Torah before it* and not differing with it except rarely, *and as a guidance and an admonition to the God-fearing*.

[5:47] *So* We gave it to them, or We said to them: *let the People of the Gospel*—before its abrogation—*judge according to what God has revealed* to you *regarding it. Whoever does not judge according to what God has revealed—those are the wicked folk*: the ones who have strayed beyond the bounds of obedience to Him. He described them as *disbelievers* because of how they belied it, and then as *evildoers* because of how they did not judge according to it, and then as *wicked folk* because of how they strayed beyond its bounds.

[5:48] *And We have revealed to you the Book*, the Qurʾān, adorned *with the*
truth, confirming the general truth of the *Book that was before it, and watching*
over it (*muhaymin*): from *haymana* meaning 'to witness and protect'—that Q. 5:46
is, watching over the general class of scripture in regards to everything that
accords with it, for all the rest has been corrupted. *So judge between them*—
between any two disputing parties—*according to what God has revealed* to
you, *and do not follow their whims* by straying *away from the truth that has come*
to you. To every one of you, to every community of people, *We have appointed*
a Law, a path, *and a way*: a way of life—that is, with regards to practical
laws, for there is no disagreement about fundamental principles. Hence
this does not contradict His Words, *He has prescribed for you as a religion that*
which He enjoined upon Noah... [Q. 42:13], nor His Words, *They are the ones*
whom God has guided; so follow their guidance... [Q. 6:90], because there He
was referring to fundamental principles. That said, it is permitted for us
to worship Him by following the laws of those who came before it by
adding certain specific matters to our religion. *If God had willed, He would*
have made you one community: one group following one Law; *but* He did
not will this, *that He may try you*—test you—*in what* laws *He has given to*
you: that the obedient might be distinguished from the disobedient. *So vie*
with one another in good deeds: by racing towards them. *To God you shall all*
return, and He will then inform you of that in which you differed: by rewarding
the faithful and punishing the wicked.

[5:49] *And* We revealed to you to *judge between them*—between the People of the Book when they said, 'Judge our rival for us, that we might believe in you, and the others will follow us'—*according to what God has revealed* to you, *and do not follow their whims; and beware of them lest they seduce you*—send you astray—*from part of what God has revealed to you. But if they turn away* from your verdict, *then know that God desires to smite them* with a punishment in this world, such as the banishment of the Banū al-Naḍīr or the fighting of Qurayẓa, *for some of their sins*: including how they turned away from your verdict. *Truly, many people are wicked folk*: outside the bounds of obedience to God.

[5:50] *Do they desire the judgement*—the religion—*of the age of ignorance*, which is the pursuit of caprice? *Yet who is better in judgement than God for folk of certainty?* It is *for* them in the sense that they are the ones who will benefit from it.

[5:51] *O you who believe, do not take Jews and Christians as patrons*: do not live among them as dear friends. *They are patrons of each other*: and they all view you with enmity. *Whoever amongst you affiliates with them, he is one of them*: and will be resurrected and punished with them, even if he was not a disbeliever in this world. *God does not guide* to the path of salvation *the folk who do wrong* against themselves by allying with them.

Q. 5:50

[5:52] *And you see*, O Muḥammad, *those in whose hearts is sickness*, doubt, *vying with one another for them*, for love of them, *saying, 'We fear lest we suffer a turn of fortune*: such that power ends up in the hands of the disbelievers.' *But it may be that God will bring victory* for the Muslims, *or some commandment from Him*: such as that some of them be banished and their property seized; *and then they will end up, for what they kept secret within themselves*—namely their hypocrisy—*remorseful*.

[5:53] *And they say, those who believe*, to one another, incredulous at their deceit, *'Are these the ones who swore by God their most earnest oaths that they were surely with you?'* And then He says: *Their deeds have failed*: their good deeds have come to naught; *and they have become losers*.

[5:54] *O you who believe, whoever of you apostatises from his religion*: three groups apostatised towards the end of the Prophet's time (may God bless him and grant him peace): the people of the false prophet al-ʿAnsī, who was slain by Fayrūz; the people of the false prophet Musaylima, who was slain by [Abū Bakr] al-Ṣiddīq; and the people of the false prophet Ṭulayḥa, who fled from Khālid [b. al-Walīd] and then converted to Islam; *then God will assuredly bring a people*—meaning Abū Bakr and his companions, or the Persians, or the Ashʿarīs—*whom He loves*: by giving them grace and honour; *and who love Him*: by obeying Him, as is explained in the verse, *Say: 'If you love God, follow me, and God will love you…'* [Q. 3:31]; *humble towards believers*: lowly with them despite their dignity; *stern towards disbelievers*: firm and ascendant over them; *struggling in the way of God, and fearing not the reproach of any reproacher*: because of their steadfast adherence to the faith. *That*—those qualities—*is God's bounty; He gives it to whom He will; and God is Embracing* with His bounty, *Knowing* of those who deserve it.

[5:55] *Your* ultimate *patron is God only, and His Messenger and the believers* in a secondary sense, which is why He did not say 'your patrons'; *who observe the prayer and pay zakāt as they bow down*: like ʿAlī (may God be pleased with him), who threw his ring to a beggar while he was praying. The verse does not allude to his imamate, however, as is obvious from the context which concerns not taking disbelievers as patrons, as well as the use of the plural. The verse is proof that a small amount of extraneous action is permitted during prayer, and that voluntary charity can be called *zakāt*.

[5:56] *Whoever affiliates with God and His Messenger and the believers*, by taking them as patrons, *then truly the party of God*, meaning them, *are the victors*: by decisive proof, always.

[5:57] *O you who believe, do not take as patrons those who take your religion in mockery, and as a game, from among those who were given the Book before you and* do not take *the disbelievers* as patrons either; *and fear God*: by refraining from taking them as patrons; *if you are believers*. Q. 5:55

[5:58] *And when you make the call to prayer, they take it*—the call or the prayer itself—*in mockery and as a game*: this is evidence for the lawfulness of the call to prayer. *That is because they are a folk who do not comprehend*: for comprehension ought to prevent one from mocking something that is intelligible and lawfully ordained.

[5:59] *Say: 'O People of the Book, do you spite us*—revile us—*for any other cause than that we believe in God, and what has been revealed to us, and what was revealed before, and that most of you are wicked folk?'*

[5:60] *Say: 'Shall I tell you of what is worse than that* reviled faith, *by way of reward from God?* He referred to it as *reward* ironically. *Those*—that is, the religion of those—*whom God cursed* because of their perversions, *and with whom He was wroth, and whom He transformed into apes* as He did to the violators of the Sabbath, *and swine* as He did to their masters, *and* the religion of those *who worshipped the false deity*—meaning the calf; it can also be read as 'the worshippers of the false deity', meaning their religion—*they are worse situated*, because they will be situated in the pit of Hell, *and further astray from the even way'*: that is, their situation is worse absolutely, not relatively, as has been covered before.

[5:61] *When they*—those accursed ones who are contemporary to you—*come to you, they say, 'We believe* in your religion'; *but they have entered* your homes clothed *in disbelief, and so they have departed* clothed *in it*: that is, they were not affected by what they heard. *And God knows very well what they were hiding*: meaning their disbelief.

[5:62] *And you see many of them vying in sin*, unlawful things, *and enmity*, injustice, *and their consuming of unlawful gain*: He singled this out for its vileness. *Evil*, by God,[1] *is that which they have been doing.*

[5:63] *Why*—the phrase *law lā* (why not) implies an exhortation when used to refer to the present, and a condemnation when used to refer to the past—*do the divines*, meaning their ascetics, *and the rabbis*, meaning their scholars, *not forbid them from uttering sin*, calumny, *and consuming unlawful gain? Evil*, by God, *is what they have been contriving*: by failing to forbid them. The word *ṣunᶜ* (to contrive) is more emphatic than *ᶜamal* (to do), because it means 'to do with great effort and care'. This is why He condemned their elites especially, and also because refraining from good is even worse than committing sin.

Q. 5:62

[5:64] *The Jews said*, when they became straitened as a consequence of their denial of the Prophet, *'God's hand is fettered'*: a euphemism for stinginess. *Fettered be their hands!* In other words, they are the stingy ones. Or it means, 'May their hands be truly fettered!' to reflect their words. Both ended up being their fates. *They are cursed for what they have said. Nay, but His hands are extended out wide* with perfect generosity; *He expends how He will*: whether broadly or narrowly. *And what has been revealed to you from your Lord*—the Qur'ān—*will surely increase many of them in insolence and disbelief*: whereupon the purpose of it being sent to them was to establish proof against them, and to make his message universal, and to honour him. *And We have cast between them*—between the factions of the Jews—*enmity and hatred until the Day of Resurrection. Every time they light the fires of war* with the Muslims, *God extinguishes them*: by causing enmity to break out among them. *And they hasten about the earth in corruption*: to spread corruption; *and God does not love corrupters.*

[5:65] *But had the People of the Book*, despite those crimes, *believed* in the Qur'ān *and feared* sin, *We would have absolved them of their* past *evil deeds*: this implies that faith without God-fearing is not enough, and there is a *ḥadīth* to support this; *and We would have admitted them to Gardens of Bliss.*

[5:66] *And had they observed the Torah and the Gospel* by acting in accordance with them rather than perverting them, *and what was revealed to them*

1 The word *bi's* (evil) is preceded by the particle *la*, implying an unspoken oath, hence the author's interpolation here and in similar instances.

from their Lord in the Books of the prophets, *they would surely have received nourishment from above them*—from the blessings of the sky—*and from beneath their feet*: fruits and crops. This signifies abundant providence, and it refers to the People of the Book who said, 'God's hand is fettered,' and whom God then straitened as punishment for this. However, there are no grounds to object that many righteous people also live in straitened circumstances, for wealth and poverty are not signs of honour or humiliation, as God says, *And as for humanity, whenever his Lord tests him and honours him and is gracious to him, he says, 'My Lord has honoured me.' But when he tests him and restricts his provision for him, he says, 'My Lord has humiliated me.' No, indeed!* [Q. 89:15–17]. *Some of them are a just community*: who neither go to excess nor fall short, such as the believers among them; *but many of them—evil is that which they do.*

[5:67] *O Messenger, make known* all of *that which has been revealed to you from your Lord*: even if the Jews object to it, and fear not. Or it could be that this referred only to those things that are related to the general welfare of humanity, and that certain divine secrets were excluded from it, as a *ḥadīth* suggests. *For if you do not* convey it all, *you will not have conveyed His Message*: like a person who leaves out one of the integral actions of his prayer. *God will protect you from people*: so fear not. In other words, He will guard your spirit. Hence the incident when his head (may God bless him and grant him peace) was wounded in battle does not contradict this, although in any case that occurred before this verse was revealed. *God will not guide the disbelieving folk* to succeed in their plot against you. Q. 5:67

[5:68] *Say: 'O People of the Book, you have no basis*—no worthy religion—*until you observe the Torah and the Gospel, and* all of *what was revealed to you from your Lord'*: aside from what has been abrogated, without any perversions or omissions. *And what has been revealed to you from your Lord will surely increase many of them in insolence and disbelief; so do not grieve for the disbelieving folk*: for they are not worth the trouble.

[5:69] *Truly, those who believe*, who make public their faith, *and those of Jewry, and the Sabaeans*, worshippers of angels, as was discussed before, *and the Christians—whoever believes* truly *in God and the Last Day and behaves righteously—no fear shall befall them* at the moment of ultimate calamity, *neither shall they grieve* for what they have lost in the world.

[5:70] *And We made a covenant with the Children of Israel, and We sent messengers to them*: to remind them of their covenant. *Every time a messenger came to them with what their souls did not desire, some* of the messengers *they denied, and some they slay*: this was explained earlier.

[5:71] *And they thought there would be no trial*, tribulation and punishment on account of this deed of theirs; *and so they were wilfully blind and deaf* to the truth when they worshipped the calf. *Then God relented to them*: accepted their repentance; *then they were wilfully blind and deaf* once more, *many of them; and God sees what they do*: and will requite them.

[5:72] *They certainly are disbelievers, those who say, 'Truly, God is the Messiah, son of Mary'*: Jesus son of Mary, as was explained before. *For the Messiah said, 'O Children of Israel, worship God, my Lord and your Lord*: that is, 'I am like you.' *Truly, he who associates anything with God* in his worship, *for him God has made the Garden forbidden, and his abode shall be the Fire* because of his disbelief. *And for evildoers there shall be no helpers.'*

[5:73] *They certainly are disbelievers, those who say, 'God is the third of three'*: meaning God, the Messiah and his mother. This means the Nestorians and Melkites among them, who preached the doctrine of the three hypostases, namely the Father, which is the Essence, and the Son, which is the Word, and the Holy Spirit, which is the Life. They hold
Q. 5:71 that together the three are one, just as the sun comprises the disc, the rays and the heat, and that God is one of the hypostases, namely that of the Father. *Yet there is no god but One God. If they do not desist from what they say, those of them who disbelieve shall suffer a painful chastisement.*

[5:74] *Will they not turn in repentance to God* from this doctrine, *and seek His forgiveness? God is Forgiving, Merciful*, and will accept repentance even from this enormous sin.

[5:75] *The Messiah, son of Mary, was only a messenger; messengers passed away before him*: and he was like them. *His mother was a truthful woman* who believed in the Words of her Lord; *they both used to eat food* out of necessity, which contradicts divinity. *Behold how We make the signs clear to them, then behold how they are turned away* from the truth.

[5:76] *Say: 'Do you worship besides God what cannot hurt* or protect you from hurt, *or profit you* or bring profit to you? One might have expected profit to come before hurt, but in such contexts it should be put first because it is of greater importance, since the reason they associated idols with God was to seek intercession for protection against harm. *God is the Hearer* of your words, *the Knower* of your beliefs.'

[5:77] *Say: 'O People of the Book, do not go to extremes*, do not go beyond the bounds, *in your religion,* when your religion is *other than that of truth, and do not follow the whims of a people who went astray formerly*, before Islam, *and have led many* people *astray, and strayed from the even way*: the way of Islam.'

[5:78] *Cursed were the disbelievers of the Children of Israel by the tongue of David*: in the Psalms, or when he prayed against them because of their violation of the Sabbath so that they were transformed into apes; *and by Jesus son of Mary*: in the Gospel, or when he prayed against them because of their disbelief after the table was sent down, so that they were transformed into apes and swine. *That* curse *was because of their disobedience and their transgression.*

[5:79] *They did not prevent one another any indecency that they committed* or desired to commit; *indeed*, by God, *evil was what they used to do.*

[5:80] *You see many of them*, the hypocrites, *affiliating with those who disbelieve*, the idolaters, out of hatred for you. *Evil is that which their souls have offered on their behalf, such that God is wroth with them and in the chastisement they shall abide.*

[5:81] *Yet had they believed in God and the Prophet*, Muḥammad (may God bless him and grant him peace), *and what has been revealed to him*—the Qur'ān—*they would not have affiliated with them*: with the idolaters; *but many of them are wicked folk*: outside the bounds of their religion.

[5:82] *You will truly find the most hostile of people to those who believe to be the Jews and the idolaters*: the Jews are more hostile, which is why He named them first. A *ḥadīth* says, 'If ever two Jews were alone with one Muslim, they were tempted to kill him.' *And you will truly find the nearest of them in love to those who believe to be those who say*—who claim—*'We are Christians'*: supporters of God's religion. *That* nearness *is because some of them are priests*: meaning scholars—the word *qissīs* (priest) is from *qass* meaning 'to follow', or *qiss* meaning 'Christian leader'; *and monks*—ascetic worshippers—*and because they are not disdainful* as the Jews are. This indicates that humility, selflessness and knowledge are praiseworthy traits, even in a disbeliever.

❁ Q. 5:78 ❁

[5:83] *And when they hear what has been revealed to the Messenger*, Muḥammad (may God bless him and grant him peace)—this refers to the delegation of the Negus—*you see their eyes overflow with tears*: this is a metaphor meant to impart emphasis; *because of what they recognise of the truth*: the Qur'ān. *They say, 'Our Lord, we believe* in this, *so inscribe us among the witnesses* to its truth.

[5:84] *'And why should we not believe in God and what has come to us of the truth*—the Qur'ān—*and* why should we not *hope that our Lord should admit us with the righteous folk?'*: the community of Muḥammad (may God bless him and grant him peace).

[5:85] *So God has rewarded them for what they have said*—namely their words, 'Our Lord, we believe...'—*by Gardens with rivers flowing from beneath them, abiding therein—that is the requital of those who are virtuous.*

[5:86] *But those who disbelieve and deny Our signs*—such as the disbelievers among the People of the Book—*they are the inhabitants of Hell-fire*.

[5:87] *O you who believe, do not forbid the good things*—the things that are pleasant and pleasing—*that God has made lawful for you, and do not transgress*: do not wrong yourselves by forbidding what is lawful, such as meat, fat and women. *God does not love transgressors*.

[5:88] *And eat of the lawful and good food which God has provided you*: ditto; *and fear God, in Whom you are believers*.

[5:89] *God will not take you to task for a slip in your oaths*: this means what the tongue utters without thought, such as, 'No, by God,' or 'Yes, by God,' as is described in an authentic *ḥadīth*. This was the opinion of Shāfiʿī (may God be pleased with him). *But He will take you to task for that to which you have pledged oaths* with a firm intention, should you violate them. *The expiation thereof*, the expiation of a broken vow that washes away its sin, *is the feeding of ten needy people*, meaning people who do not have enough Q. 5:86 to support themselves, *of the midmost food you feed your families* in your own land, with regard to type and quantity. Shāfiʿī considered this to be a *mudd* of food for each person, while the Ḥanafīs consider it to be a half *ṣāʿ*.[1] *Or the clothing of them* with something that can be accurately described as 'clothing', meaning a garment that covers the private parts; *or the setting free of a slave*: that is, a believing slave, by analogy to the ruling on the expiation for murder. The options here are presented as choices; the best is the third, and then the second. *And whoever does not find the means* to do any of them, *then* his expiation is *the fasting of three days*: Shāfiʿī said that they need not be consecutive. *That is the expiation of your oaths, if you have sworn* and then broken them; *but guard your oaths* by not swearing them in the first place, and by not breaking them if you do, unless it be a vow to abstain from something that the Sunna recommends, or to do something that the Sunna dislikes. *Thus*—by this elucidation—*God makes clear to you His signs, so that you might be thankful*: for His favours.

[5:90] *O you who believe, truly wine, and games of chance*, all forms of gambling, *and idols*, the stones before which they would slaughter their sacrifices to venerate them, *and divinatory arrows*—this was explained before, and here it means the use of them[2]—*are an abomination*: the word

1 A *ṣāʿ* is equal to four *mudd*; sources differ as to their exact values. See M. Ismail Marcinkowski, *Measures and Weights in the Islamic World: An English Translation of Walther Hinz's Handbook "Islamische Masse und Gewichte"*, Kuala Lumpur: International Institute of Islamic Thought and Civilisation (ISTAC) & International Islamic University Malaysia (IIUM), 2003.

2 See Q. 5:3.

rijs (abomination) means the same as *najas* (impure), except that *najas* generally refers to things that are repulsive by nature, whereas *rijs* refers to things that are repulsive to the intellect; it is also said to mean sin and malcontent; *of Satan's work*: because it leads to his ascendance. *Thus avoid it*—avoid such abomination—*so that you might prosper*: by avoiding it.

[5:91] *Satan desires only to precipitate enmity and hatred between you through wine and games of chance*: He singled these two out for repeat mention because they are the main topic at hand here, since these words are addressed to the believers; and He grouped them with the other things before to illustrate how severely they are forbidden; *and to bar you* by distracting you with them *from the remembrance of God and from prayer*: He singled out these two because of their importance. *So will you then desist*, now that you know about these corrupt things, or not*?*

[5:92] *And obey God and obey the Messenger, and beware* disobedience; *but if you turn away, then know that Our Messenger's duty is only to proclaim plainly*: and he has done so.

[5:93] *Those who believe and perform righteous deeds are not at fault*—guilty Q. 5:91
of sin—*in what they may have consumed, so long as they feared* unlawful things; *and believed and performed righteous deeds*: and continued to do so; *and then feared* what was forbidden afterwards, such as wine; *and believed*: continued to have faith; *and then feared*: continued to fear sin; *and were virtuous* in deed: 'Virtue means to worship God as though you see him; for if you see Him not, He sees you.' It is said that the repetition here refers to the past, present and future. *God loves the virtuous* who have such traits.

[5:94] *O you who believe, God will surely try you*, test you, *with some*, with a trivial amount of *game, which will be caught by your hands*, such as small animals and nestlings, *and your lances*, such as larger animals, *so that God may know*, may see, *who fears Him in the Unseen*: though they cannot see Him. *Whoever transgresses thereafter*—after this proclamation—*his shall be a painful chastisement.*

[5:95] *O you who believe, do not slay game while you are in the state of pilgrimage inviolability* (*ḥurum*): meaning in the consecrated state (*iḥrām*), or inside the Sanctuary (*ḥaram*), for an animal slaughtered in such a way is tantamount to carrion, by consensus, because it is forbidden to slaughter it due to a certain characteristic that it possesses, like an animal slaughtered by a Magian. It is permitted to kill those animals that are not eaten, because the meaning of 'hunting' is 'killing for food'; thus a *ḥadīth* states that there are five animals that may be slain whether in pilgrimage inviolability or outside it. The same applies by analogy to other harmful pests.

It is equally unlawful to assist in such hunting as it is to do it directly. *Whoever of you slays it wilfully*: the word 'wilfully' is a description of the usual situation, not a stipulation. This is because the verse was revealed about someone who did it deliberately, namely Abū al-Yusr, and so it is not meant to be exclusive. It is said that this verse affirms the rule for the one who does it deliberately, while the Sunna affirms that it applies also to the one who does it accidentally; *then the* obligatory *compensation shall be the equivalent of what he has slain* in terms of size and quality, according to Mālik and Shāfiʿī, *of cattle, to be judged* regarding the equivalency *by two just men among you*, O Muslims; and the judged animal should be *an offering to reach the* Sacred Precinct of the *Kaʿba* to be slaughtered and given away in charity there. *Or an expiation: food for the poor* consisting of the staple food of the land, which he must buy with the value of the compensation and then give a *mudd* measure to each poor person; *or the equivalent of that* feeding *in fasting*: such that he fasts one day for every *mudd*—the majority say that the word *or* here denotes a free choice; *so that he may taste the evil*
Q. 5:96 *consequence of his deed*. Ibn ʿAbbās said, 'Those things for which there is no expiation are weighty indeed.' *God has pardoned what is past*: before the prohibition; *but whoever offends again, God will take vengeance on him; God is Mighty*, Omnipotent, *Lord of Retribution* upon those who persist in sin.

[5:96] *Permitted to you is the game of the sea*: meaning that which lives solely in water; the Ḥanafīs say that it means fish only. This applies whether one is in pilgrimage inviolability or not. *And food from it*—meaning what you take from it to eat when it is dry and salty, or what washes up already dead—*is a provision for you and for the wayfarers; but forbidden to you is the hunting of game on the land*: or even assisting in it; this means hunting wild animals that live on land for the purpose of eating them; *so long as you remain in pilgrimage inviolability. And fear God, to whom you shall be gathered.*

[5:97] *God has appointed the Kaʿba*: it was named so because it is cubical; *the Sacred House as an institution*: something to preserve the affairs of the religion and the world by affording them with security and the like; *for people, and* He has appointed *the sacred month* as an institution for them through the *ḥajj* and the security from fighting, *and the offering* that is dedicated to the Kaʿba, *and the garlands*: the garlanded animals, as was explained before,[1] since they would guarantee their safety. *That* appointment *is so that you may know that God knows all that is in the heavens and in the earth, and that God has knowledge of all things*: for He ordained these edicts to prevent

1 See Q. 5:2.

harms before they occur, and to bring the benefits that result from them, as signs of the perfect knowledge of the Lawgiver.

[5:98] *Know that God is severe in punishment* to those who insist on violating His sacred things, *and that God is Forgiving, Merciful* to those who honour them and who repent.

[5:99] *The duty of the Messenger is only to convey*: and indeed he has conveyed. *And God knows what you reveal and what you hide*: whether belief or denial.

[5:100] *Say: 'The evil*, the base, such as unlawful things, *and the good*, the decent, such as lawful things, *are not equal, even though the abundance of the evil attracts you.' So fear God* regarding evil things, *O people of pith*—sound minds—*so that you might prosper.*

He then explains one type of evil by saying:

[5:101] *O you who believe, do not ask* Muḥammad (may God bless him and grant him peace) *about things which, if disclosed to you, would trouble you*: sadden you, such as when Ibn Ḥudhāfa asked, 'Who is my father?' and he replied, 'Ḥudhāfa,' while he had thought it was someone else. Or when someone asked him when the *ḥajj* was made obligatory, 'Does that mean every year?' Sometimes a question is necessary, such as asking about those things for which we have been made accountable, while other times it is recommended, such as asking about those things we have been encouraged to do. *Yet if you ask about them while the Qur'ān is being revealed, they will be disclosed to you. God has pardoned those things*: those previous questions of yours; *for God is Forgiving, Forbearing*: and does not hasten to punish. Q. 5:98

[5:102] *A people before you asked* their prophets *about them*—about such things—*and then they disbelieved in them*: in those things. He then explains another type of evil by saying:

[5:103] *God has not ordained anything such as a baḥīra, a sā'iba, a waṣīla or a ḥām*: a *baḥīra* was a she-camel that had given birth five times. If the fifth was male, they would eat it and then cut slits (*baḥar*) into her ears and forbid that she be ridden; if it was female, they would pierce the mother's nose for the rest of her life and forbid that she be ridden or milked. A *sā'iba* was a she-camel whose owner vowed to stop riding if his wish came true. A *waṣīla* was a female camel born in the seventh litter of its mother. If a male was born along with it, they would set the female loose for their gods and refrain from slaughtering the male, and would say that the female had brought (*waṣalat*) her brother to join her. If the seventh litter was a lone male, whether born alive or dead, they would feed it to the men. If it was a lone female, they would set it loose for their gods. A *ḥām* was a male camel who sired ten litters, after which they would never load its back again because its back was henceforth protected (*ḥumiya*). That is the most well-known explanation for the terms, though there are others. *But the disbelievers invent lies against God*: by declaring them forbidden; *and most of them do not understand*: and merely follow their leaders.

[5:104] *And when it is said to them, 'Come to* follow *what God has revealed and to* follow *the Messenger,' they say, 'What we have found our fathers following suffices us.' What*, is that what they think, *even if their fathers knew nothing and were not guided?* It is only right to follow those who are known to be folk of knowledge and guidance.

[5:105] *O you who believe, you are responsible for* the rectifying of *your own souls; he who is astray cannot hurt you, if you are rightly guided*: this applies as long as you have ascertained that your advice will not do them any good, as is stated in an authentic *ḥadīth*; for when he (may God bless him and grant him peace) was asked about this, that was the answer he gave. The meaning of *your own souls* is 'the people who share your religion'. *Unto*
Q. 5:104 *God you shall return, altogether, and He will inform you of what you used to do.*

[5:106] *O you who believe*—regarding what has been ordained for you—*let testimony between you, when death draws near to one of you, at the time of a bequest, be that of two men of justice among you*, among the Muslims, *or of two others from another folk*, such as the Christians, *if you are travelling in the land*: this implies that it is only permitted to dictate one's bequest to a disbeliever if one's death occurs during travel; *and the affliction of death befalls you.* And if you are uncertain, *Then you shall empanel them*—delay them—*after the prayer*: the afternoon prayer; *and if you are in doubt* about them, *they shall swear by God: 'We will not sell it*, the testimony—or it can be read as, 'We will not sell, by God'—*for any price*, any worldly advantage, *even if he*, the one for whom we are testifying, *be a near kinsman* of ours. What this means is, 'We will be truthful, even if it is to our detriment.' *Nor will we hide testimony to God* as He commands, *for then we would surely be among the sinful* if we concealed it.'

[5:107] *But if it be discovered that both of them have merited sin* by proffering false oaths, *then two others shall take their place*—the place of the witnesses by swearing their own oaths—*from among those who were deprived of their right*: if this is read in the passive voice, it means those who were sinned against, namely the heirs, *the two nearest in kin*; or if it is read in the active voice, then it means 'from the heirs above whom the first two had more right to testify and swear, because of their greater knowledge', meaning the other two. What it means is that two of the relatives of the heirs should take their place; *and they shall swear by God* to the treachery of the first two witnesses, and say, *'Our* sworn *testimony is truer than their testimony, and we have not transgressed*: we have not gone beyond the bounds of truth; *for then,* if we transgressed, *we would assuredly be among the evildoers'*: the reason for the mention of this specific number was that this was what actually happened in the incident about which this verse was revealed, because in fact it is valid to dictate one's bequest to a single person. The two deserving people about which the verse was revealed were ʿAmr b. al-ʿĀṣ al-Sahmī and al-Muṭṭalib b. Abī Rifāʿa al-Sahmī, and the deceased man was Budayl the freedman of ʿAmr b. al-ʿĀṣ, and the two doubtful witnesses were Tamīm al-Dārī and ʿAdī b. Zayd when they were still both Christians. The incident occurred during a journey to Syria. It is related that ʿUmar (may God be pleased with him) said that this verse is the most complex ruling in the whole of this *sūra*. The exegetes agree that it is extremely difficult to parse and break down, but we have explained how to unravel it.

It was related that once when they were still Christians, Tamīm and ʿAdī were travelling to Syria with Budayl, who was Muslim, when Budayl fell ill. He wrote down instructions regarding all the things he had with him, and put the note into his pack without telling them about it. Then he told them to take his pack to his family, and died. They looked through his things and found a silver bowl weighing 300 *mithqāl*,[1] engraved with gold, which they hid. Then when his family found the note, they asked them for the bowl, but they denied all knowledge of it. So a complaint was made about them to the Prophet (may God bless him and grant him peace) and the verse *O you who believe...* [Q. 5:106] was revealed. After the afternoon prayer, the Prophet called upon them to swear oaths beside the pulpit, and then let them go their way. Thereafter the bowl was found in their possession, and they said, 'We bought it from him, but we did not have any proof of this, so we were loathe to admit it.' Hence they took them back to the Prophet, and the verse *But if it be discovered* [Q. 5:107] was revealed, and so ʿAmr and al-Muṭṭalib swore oaths.

Q. 5:108

[5:108] *Thus*—by this ruling regarding the counter-oath—*it is likelier that they will bear the testimony in its true form*: in a way that conforms to reality; *or that they will be afraid that after their oaths, other oaths may be taken*: from the family of the deceased, exposing them. What this means is that the ruling makes two things more likely: either they will give the testimony truthfully, or at least refrain from giving it falsely. *Fear God and listen*

1 A measure equal to around four grams.

obediently. *God does not guide* to the path of the Garden *the wicked folk* who do not listen. And remember:

[5:109] *The day when God shall gather the messengers and say* reproachfully, *'What answer were you given?'* In other words, 'Were you accepted, or denied?' *They shall say*, confounded by the horrors of that day, *'We have no knowledge*: that is, we do not know the inner truth of their affairs, for which they will be judged. *You, only You, are the One Who best knows the Unseen'*: and You know what we know not.

[5:110] *When God said, 'O Jesus son of Mary, remember My favour to you and to your mother, when I strengthened you with the Holy Spirit*—meaning Gabriel, as was discussed before—*to speak to people* and call them to God *in the cradle* and an infant, *and in maturity*: meaning after he descends from the heavens, for he was still a young man when he was taken up; *and when I taught you the Book*, meaning writing, *and wisdom*, meaning knowledge and action in accordance with it, *and the Torah, and the Gospel; and how you*
Q. 5:109 *create*, mould, *out of clay the likeness of a bird by My permission*, My command,
and how you breathe into it, and it becomes a living, flying *bird by My permission; and you heal the blind and the leper by My permission, and you raise the dead* from their graves by returning them to life *by My permission*: as was explained; *and how I restrained the Children of Israel from* slaying *you when you brought them clear proofs*— prophetic miracles—*and the disbelievers among them said, "This is nothing but manifest sorcery."*

[5:111] *'And when I revealed to the disciples* through your tongue, *"Believe in Me and in My Messenger," they said, "We believe! Bear witness*, O Jesus, *that we have submitted."'* And remember:

[5:112] *When the disciples said, 'O Jesus son of Mary, is your Lord able*: that is, will He respond and answer your request; or it is akin to how you say, 'Can you come with me?' when you know full well that the other person is able to do so; a variant reading has, 'Are you able [to ask] your Lord?' [Is your Lord able] *to send down on us a table* laden with food *from the heaven?' He*, Jesus, *said, 'Fear God* and do not ask for such a sign, *if you are believers.'*

[5:113] *They said, 'We desire to eat of it*: and so we are not merely asking for a sign; *and that our hearts be reassured*: by an increase to our knowledge; *and that we may know* through eye-witnessing *that you have spoken truthfully to us* when you promised that God would aid us, *and that we may be among the witnesses thereof'*: of that table, and testify about it to those of the Children of Israel who did not witness it.

[5:114] *Jesus son of Mary, said, 'O God, our Lord, send down upon us a table from the heaven, that it shall be a celebration for us*—meaning a cause of celebration and joy—*for the first and the last of us, and a sign from You* of the perfection of Your power and my prophethood. And since it was sent down on Sunday, that day became a holy day for them. *And provide for us; You are the Best of Providers.'*

[5:115] *God said*, in response to them, *'Truly, I shall send it down to you; but whoever of you disbelieves afterward, I shall surely chastise him with a chastisement wherewith I chastise no other being from among all the worlds*: meaning the worlds of their time.*'* The soundest position is that the table was actually sent down. It is said that it descended between two clouds, a red table laden with grilled fish free of skin and bones, seasoned with salt at the head and vinegar at the tail, surrounded by all manner of vegetables except for leeks, and five pieces of bread with oil, honey, butter, cheese and jerked meat. They ate, and then asked for another sign, so he said, 'O fish, return to life by God's leave!' The fish began to quiver with life. Then he said, 'Be as you were,' and it became grilled again. Thereafter the table rose into the air. But they still did not believe, and so they were
transformed into apes and swine. It is said that none before them had ever Q. 5:115
been transformed into swine.

[5:116] *And when God said* to Jesus when he was taken up, or He will say it to him at the Resurrection, if the past tense here is taken as a way of evoking the proximity of that event, *'O Jesus son of Mary, did you say to people, "Take me and my mother as gods, besides God?"'* He specified *besides* (*dūn*) because worshipping Him along with others is the same as not worshipping Him at all. Or it could be that *dūn* is used here in the sense of 'below', since they worshipped them as an intermediary to Him. Thus it cannot be argued that they took them as gods, but not besides Him. This question is akin to how the infant daughter buried alive will be asked *for what sin she was slain* [Q. 81:9], as a rebuke of the guilty parties, or to mark them so that he would not intercede for them. *He said, 'Glory be to You!* Far be it that You should have any partner. *It is not mine to say what I have no right to* say. *If I had said it, You would have known it. You know what is in my self* even if I conceal it, *but I do not know what is within Your Self* if You conceal it—this is a parallelism, or *self* means 'essence' in the case of God, rather than the inherent substance that attaches to the body for the purpose of control [in the case of humanity]. *You are the One Who best knows the Unseen'*: so he denied it in five ways, the fifth being:

[5:117] *'I only said to them*, regarding the matter of Oneness, *that which You commanded me*: for a command can denote an obligation or a permission; *"Worship God, my Lord and your Lord." And I was a witness over them*—bearing witness to their states—*whilst I was amongst them; but when You took me*—when You raised me up to the heavens—*You were Yourself the Watcher over them*: observing their states; *and You Yourself are Witness*—Aware—*over all things.*

[5:118] *'If you chastise them, they are indeed Your servants* and under Your power; and the master may do as he will with his servants; *and if You forgive them* despite their disbelief, for that is not beyond Your power, *then You, only You, are the Mighty*—the Dominant—*the Wise* in rewarding and punishing.*'* The use of *if* here implies that it is possible for idolatry to be forgiven, and indeed this is not rationally impossible, though God warns elsewhere that it will not be.

[5:119] *God said* in answer to his declaration of innocence, *'This is the day*: meaning the Day of Resurrection, although it can also be read as 'God said on that day'; *those who were truthful* in this world, in both word and action by avoiding ostentation, *shall profit by their truthfulness*: such that their profit from it in this world will become as though it were nothing
Q. 5:118 because of its ephemerality. As for Satan's truthfulness when he will say, *Truly, God promised you a promise of truth*... [Q. 14:22], it will not profit him because of his deceit in this world, which is the abode of action. *Theirs will be Gardens with rivers flowing from beneath them, abiding therein forever. God is well-pleased with them, and they are well-pleased with Him*, which is the nature of their profit; *that is the great triumph.'*

[5:120] *To God belongs the kingdom of the heavens and of the earth, and all that is in them*: by creation and sovereignty; *and He has power over all things.* He used the term *that is* rather than 'who are', stressing the dominance of the non-rational beings therein, in order to indicate how all of them fall short of the level of lordship. But God knows best what is correct.

6
Cattle
SŪRAT AL-ANʿĀM

Revealed in Mecca

Having stated that the kingdom of the heavens and the earth and all that is in them belongs to Him, He then tells us that He alone is worthy of praise for His creation of them, saying:

In the Name of God, the Compassionate, the Merciful

[6:1] *Praise be to God Who created the heavens and the earth*: He said *heavens* in the plural because of their differing characters, with regards to both essence and influence, unlike the case for the earth; and He singled out these two for mention because they are the greatest of all tangible creations. *And He made darknesses and light*: He used the term *made*, which implies the sense of guarantee, meaning that something is attained through the power of another as though guaranteed by him, rather than the term 'creation', which implies the sense of ordainment, in order to stress how they are unable to subsist through their own power, contrary to the belief of the dualists. He said *darknesses* in the plural because of its many causes, such as night and eclipses, and because of the many agents that bear it—for every material thing has a shadow, and shadows are darkness; and because *nūr* (light) is a gerund, as is stated in the *Mufaṣṣal*;[1] and because they represent error, which is manifold, and guidance, which is one. *Then*—this denotes incredulity—*those who disbelieve ascribe equals to their Lord!*

[6:2] *It is He Who created you* in the beginning *from clay*, because the drop of fluid comes from nourishment, which comes from clay, or because Adam was created from it; *then He decreed a term*: meaning death. *And a term is stated with Him*: meaning knowledge of the Resurrection; *yet thereafter you doubt*.

1 Meaning *al-Mufaṣṣal fī ʿIlm al-ʿArabiyya,* a grammatical treatise by Zamakhsharī.

[6:3] *He is God*—the One Who deserves to be worshipped—*in the heavens and in the earth*: this refers to how the meaning implied by the Name of God, namely the Attributes of perfection, apply to Him throughout them; it is akin to saying, 'He is Ḥātim among Ṭayy,' to describe someone's generosity. It does not refer to the word, since it is a Name rather than an Attribute. Or it refers to how He then says, *He knows your secrets and your utterances*: He mentioned them both for the sake of the poetic contrast; *and He knows what you earn*: whether good or evil.

[6:4] *Not a verse of the verses of their Lord comes to them* showing His Oneness and the truth of His messengers, *but they turn away from it*: and decline to reflect on it.

[6:5] *They denied the truth*—the Qur'ān—*when it came to them, but there shall come to them the news of what they were mocking*: meaning the Qur'ān.

[6:6] *Have they not seen*, do they not know, *how many a generation* (*qarn*), meaning a community who live together over the course of a hundred years,[1] *We destroyed before them*? *We established them*: We gave them that which made them stable, such as life and wealth; *as We have not established you*. *How We unleashed the heaven*, meaning rain or clouds, *upon them in torrents*, heavy rain, *and made the rivers flow beneath them*: beneath their homes. *Then We destroyed them because of their sins* with such things as droughts and storms; *and We raised up after them another generation* to replace them; so let them reflect on this.

Q. 6:3

[6:7] *And had We revealed to you a Book* written *on parchment, and had they then touched it with their hands*—for touching confers a higher degree of knowledge than mere seeing—*the disbelievers would have said, 'This is nothing but manifest sorcery.'*

[6:8] *And they say, 'Why has an angel not been sent down to him?'*—meaning to Muḥammad in order to confirm his prophethood. *Yet had We sent down an angel* for them to see, which they too would have denied, *the matter would have been decreed*: and their doom would have been sealed, for it is God's way to annihilate those who demand a sign and then still do not believe after they are given it; *and then they would not be given any respite*.

[6:9] *And had We appointed him*—the one sent to Muḥammad—*an angel* to attest to his sincerity, *We would assuredly have made him a man*: that is, We would have given him the form of a man, because human beings, aside from messengers, cannot see angels in their true forms; our own Prophet (may God bless him and grant him peace) saw Gabriel in his true form

1 The word *qarn* can mean 'generation' or 'century'.

twice. *And* had We made him a man, *We would have assuredly confused for them what they are confusing*: and so they would not have known whether he was an angel or not, and they would deny this and belie him.

[6:10] *And messengers were indeed mocked before you*: so be patient just as they were; *but those who scoffed at them*—at the messengers—*were encompassed by* the evil consequences of *that which they mocked*.

[6:11] *Say* to them: *'Travel in the land*: for you are unlettered folk who have not kept the company of scholars—this was explained further in *Sūrat Āl ʿImrān*;[1] *and then behold the nature of the consequence for the deniers*: and reflect on it.' The difference between this verse and the aforementioned verse, which had *travel in the land and behold* [Q. 3:137], was that the previous verse referred to travelling specifically for the purpose of beholding, while in this verse *Travel* is a command of permission for travelling for such things as commerce, and then *behold* is a command of obligation, hence the word *then*, which marks the contrast between the two commands. Or it could be that the verse command is also an obligation, such as in, 'Perform ablutions and then pray,' in which case the word *then* would Q. 6:10
serve to mark the distinction between the two obligations.

[6:12] *Say: 'To whom belongs what is in the heavens and in the earth?'*—by creation and sovereignty. *Say: 'To God'*: for they will not deny this. *He has prescribed for Himself mercy*: He has chosen, in His grace, to adhere to mercy, which includes providing guidance to knowledge of Him, and delaying the consequences of disbelief. *He will surely gather you together on the Day of Resurrection* to requite you, *of which*—in which day—*there is no doubt. Those who have forfeited their own souls* by squandering their innate disposition, *they do not believe*.

[6:13] *And to Him belongs all that resides* (*sakan*)—meaning all that dwells—*in the night and the day*: that is, all that they contain, meaning at all times. He put *night* first because it was the first, and since it corresponds to His Words, *He it is Who made for you the night that you should rest therein, and the day to see* [Q. 10:67]. The verb *sakan* here can be understood in the sense of *suknā* (to reside) or *sukūn* (to rest); and He sufficed with mentioning one half of the contrasting pair. *And He is the Hearer, the Knower*: and nothing escapes His attention.

[6:14] *Say: 'Shall I take as a protector*—an object of worship—*other than God, the Originator of the heavens and the earth, while He is the One Who feeds and is not fed?'* In other words, He Who needs nothing but is needed by

1 See Q. 3:137.

all. He expressed this by referring to food, since it is our primary need. *Say: 'I have been commanded to be the first to submit*: for he was the leader of his community in submission; *and* I have been told, *"Do not be among the idolaters"'*: by seeking their approval.

[6:15] *Say: 'Truly, I fear, if I should rebel against my Lord, the chastisement of a dreadful day'*: which is what they have incurred.

[6:16] *He from whom it is averted*—He from whom God averts it—*on that day, He will have shown him mercy; and that* aversion *is the manifest triumph*.

[6:17] *And if God touches you with an affliction*: such as illness. It is said that this can also be understood as: 'If God causes you to touch an affliction.' The root meaning of 'touch' is for two bodies to come into contact. *Then none can remove it except Him; and if He touches you with good*—such as health—*then He has power over all things*: and nothing can repel His grace.

[6:18] *He is the Vanquisher*—the Overwhelmer and Dominator—*over*
His servants: in a manner that befits His majesty. The word *qahr* (to van-
quish) can mean 'to overwhelm' or 'to humiliate'; and here it means the
Q. 6:15 former, as it does in, *Truly, we shall vanquish them* [Q. 7:127]. An example
of the latter meaning is found in: *So as for the orphan, do not oppress* (*taqhar*)
[Q. 93:9]. *And He is the Wise* in His deeds, *the Aware* of your secrets.

[6:19] *Say: 'What thing*—what witness—*is greatest in testimony* of my prophethood*?' Say: 'God*: for there could be no other answer; He *is Witness between me and you*: do not take this to mean that it is permitted to call upon God by saying, 'O Thing,' for it is only right to call upon Him with expressions that imply praise and perfection. *And this Qur'ān has been revealed to me*, delivering proofs, *that I may warn you,* O people of Mecca, *and* warn *whomever it may reach*: whomever the Qur'ān reaches. *Do you truly bear witness that there are other gods with God?' Say: 'I do not bear witness* to that.*' Say: 'He is only One God, and I am innocent of what you associate* with Him.*'*

[6:20] *Those to whom We have given the Book recognise him* by means of the descriptions of him found in their Books, *as they recognise their own sons*. *Those* of the disbelievers *who have forfeited their own souls do not believe* in him.

[6:21] *And who does greater evil*—this was explained earlier[1]—*than he who invents a lie against God*, such as the disbelievers, *or denies His signs*, such as the Qur'ān and prophetic miracles. *Truly, the evildoers shall not prosper*: never mind those who are even more evil than they.

[6:22] *And* remember *on the day We shall gather them altogether*—the

1 See Q. 2:114.

worshippers and what they worshipped—*then We shall say* scornfully *to those who associated other gods with God, 'Where are those associates*—those gods—*of yours whom you were claiming* to be partners?'

[6:23] *Then their dissension*—their way of absolving themselves by their own claim, that is, the excuse which they offered to save themselves—*was only to say* on the Day of Resurrection, *'By God, our Lord, we were never idolaters'*: then their mouths will be sealed, and their limbs will testify against them.

[6:24] *See how they lie against themselves*: by denying their idolatry in the Hereafter; *and how that which they were forging*—claiming as divine—*has failed them*: with its absence.

[6:25] *And there are some of them who listen to you* when you recite the Qur'ān, *yet We have placed veils upon their hearts so that they do not understand it; and in their ears a heaviness*: a deafness which prevents them from receiving it. *And if they were to see every sign*—[every] prophetic miracle—*they would not believe in it, so that* their obstinacy reaches a level that *when they come to you to argue with you, the disbelievers say, 'This* Qur'ān *is nothing but the fables*—stories—*of the ancients*: meaning their false legends.' Q. 6:23

[6:26] *And they forbid it*—forbid the people from the Messenger—*and keep away from it; and it is only themselves they destroy* by this distancing, *though they do not perceive*: as though they were beasts.

[6:27] *If you could see when they are made to stand before the Fire* to behold its horrors, you would see something horrific indeed. *And they will say, 'Oh would that we might be returned* to the world, *then we would not deny the signs of our Lord, but would be among the believers!'*

[6:28] *Nay, that which they used to conceal before has now become evident to them*: meaning their vile deeds, and so they only wish for faith out of panic, not love; *and even if they were returned* to the world, *they would return to that which they are forbidden*: meaning disbelief, because this was ever their fate. *Truly, they are liars*: in what they promise about this wish.

[6:29] *And they say, 'There is nothing*—no life—*other than our present life; we shall not be resurrected.'*

[6:30] *If you could see when they are made to stand before their Lord* like a disobedient slave standing before his master. *He*, God, *will say, 'Is this* Resurrection *not the truth?' They will say, 'Yes Truly, by our Lord!' He will say, 'Then taste the chastisement because you disbelieved.'*

[6:31] *They have indeed lost, those who deny the encounter with God*, meaning the Resurrection and all that follows it, their denial persisting *until when the Hour comes upon them suddenly*, meaning its portent, death, *they say, 'Alas for us*—woe betide us—*for all that we neglected there* in the world*!' On their backs they shall be bearing their burdens*—their sins, represented in the most hideous forms—as We lead them to Hell. *Ah, evil is that which they bear!*

[6:32] *The life of this world is nothing but a game*: something that distracts you from what is good for you and leads you to what is of no benefit; *and a diversion*: something that turns the soul from gravity to levity—that is, it is as useless as they are. *Surely*, by God, *the abode of the Hereafter is better for those who fear*: because its joys are endless. It is also better for such people as the insane and children,[1] by implication. *What, do they not understand* that it is so*?*

[6:33] *Truly*—in such instances this term (*qad*) is meant only to impart emphasis[2]—*We know truly that what they say*, their denial, *grieves you; yet it is not that they deny you* in reality, *but that the evildoers knowingly reject the signs of God*: this is like saying to your slave, 'It was not you that they disgraced, but me.' Another example of such a turn of phrase is: *Truly, those who*
Q. 6:32 *pledge allegiance to you, in fact pledge allegiance to God* [Q. 48:10].

[6:34] *Messengers indeed have been denied before you; yet they endured patiently the denial and the persecution until Our victorious help came to them*: so be patient until it comes to you. *There is none to change the words of God*: meaning His promises, so be not hasty. As for His threats, they can be changed by His pardon. *And there has already come to you* some of the *tidings of the messengers*: and how they were patient.

[6:35] *And if their aversion* to you *is grievous*—difficult—*for you, then if you can, seek out a hole in the earth* to escape into, *or a ladder to heaven* to climb, *that* from either of them *you may bring them a sign* that compels them to believe. In other words, Our eternal decree cannot be changed, so be patient. *But had God willed, He would have gathered them together in guidance; so do not be among the ignorant*: by insisting on something that We did not will. The reason He spoke to Noah more gently than this, saying, *I admonish you, lest you be among the ignorant* [Q. 11:46], was that he had a plain excuse, since He had promised him that He would save his family, while our Prophet (may God bless him and grant him peace) knew that their faith was subject to God's will.

[6:36] *Only those who hear will answer* your call, not those whose hearing has been sealed. *As for the dead*—symbolising the disbelievers—*God will*

1 In other words, those who will enter Paradise even if they do not have the capacity to be God-fearing.

2 Sometimes *qad* can mean 'perhaps'.

resurrect them: and make them answer, so that finally they will know the truth, though it will no longer do them any good. *And then to Him they will be returned* for requital.

[6:37] *And they say, 'Why has a sign not been sent down to him from his Lord?'* [For instance,] such as an angel to bear witness for him. *Say: 'Truly, God has the power to send down a sign*—as they request—*but most of them do not know'* that if He did, it would harm them because they would not benefit from it, and then they would be destroyed after it, as is God's way. It cannot be argued that every prophet could have given this answer, and so would not have needed prophetic miracles, because this answer was only given after his prophethood had already been established by a prophetic miracle.

[6:38] *There is no animal on* any part of *the earth, nor any bird that flies with its wings*—the descriptions are meant to imply complete universality, or to dispel any notion of metaphor, since otherwise it might have been suggested that the word *animal* was not meant literally, just as it is a common figure of speech to say that a person in a hurry is 'flying'—*but they are* Q. 6:37
communities like to you: whose provisions, lifespans and fates are measured out; and He is well able to send them a sign through any of them. He said *communities* in the plural to indicate that every one of them is a community of its own. *We have neglected nothing in the Book*: in the Preserved Tablet, for it contains everything that occurs in the world. *Then to their Lord they shall be gathered* and requited, and even the hornless sheep will demand retribution from the horned sheep that butted it, as a *ḥadīth* describes. Ibn ʿAbbās (may God be pleased with him) related that the Hereafter of animals occurs when they die.

[6:39] *And those who deny Our signs are deaf*: unable to hear them receptively; *and dumb* to the truth, *in darkness*: the darkness of disbelief, ignorance and obstinacy. *He whom God wills* to send astray, *He sends astray*: causing him to die in a state of disbelief; *and whom He wills* to guide, *He sets him on a straight path*: so that he dies in a state of submission to Him.

[6:40] *Say*, O Muḥammad, *'Tell me* (*ara'aytakum*):[1] that is, show me, teach me and tell me—they [the Arabs] symbolised the request for information as a request for knowledge and sight, since they are of the same essential nature; *if God's chastisement comes upon you* before your death, *or the Hour comes upon you* along with all its horrors, *will ye call upon any other than God* to repel it, *if you be truthful* about how these idols are gods?'

1 Literally, 'Do you see yourselves?'

[6:41] *Nay, upon Him you will call*: and Him alone; *and He will remove that which you call upon Him* to remove, and the torment of the Hour, *if He wills, and you will forget what you associate with Him*: and will not call upon it at that time.

[6:42] *Truly, We sent* messengers *to communities before you*: and they belied them; *so We seized them with misery*: misfortunes such as droughts; *and hardship*: such as disease; *so that they might be humble*: and repent to God.

[6:43] *If only, when Our might came upon them, they had been humble*: that is, they were not humble, though they ought to have been. *But their hearts were hard*: and did not soften; *and Satan adorned for them what they were doing*: so that they persisted in it.

[6:44] *So, when they forgot that whereof they were reminded*—namely that misery and hardship, instead of taking admonition from it—*We opened to them the gates of all things* that they desired, to lead them on, *until, when they rejoiced in what they were given* and became pleased with their situation, *We seized them suddenly and lo! they were confounded*: despairing of all that is good.

Q. 6:41 [6:45] *So the last remnant of the people who did evil was cut off. Praise be to God, Lord of the Worlds*: He teaches us to praise Him for sparing us from their evil.

[6:46] *Say: 'Have you considered*—pray, tell—*if God were to seize your hearing and your sight*, rendering you deaf and blind, *and set a seal upon your hearts* so that you understood nothing, *who is the god other than God to give it back to you?' See how We dispense*—how We clarify and repeat—*the signs! Yet thereafter they are turning away*: rejecting them.

[6:47] *Say: 'Have you considered*—pray, tell—*if God's chastisement were to come upon you, suddenly or openly*, whether with portents to herald it or not, *would any be destroyed except the evildoing folk?' Destroyed* here means annihilated by the wrath of God, as the communities of old were, so it need not be objected that all people are ultimately destroyed [by death].

[6:48] *We do not send messengers except as bearers of glad tidings and as warners*: that is, We do not require signs from them once their religion has been clarified by prophetic miracles. *Whoever believes and makes amends* by rectifying their deeds, *no fear shall befall them* at the Great Calamity, *neither shall they grieve* for what they have lost in this world.

[6:49] *But those who deny Our signs, the chastisement shall afflict them because they were wicked*: when they belied him, one of their arguments was, 'If you are truthful, then prove it by showering us with riches and telling us about the future and what we shall eat then.' Therefore the verse was revealed:

[6:50] *Say: 'I do not say to you, "I possess the treasure houses of God* that I might shower you with riches"; *and I do not have knowledge of the Unseen* that I might tell you of the future. *And I do not say to you, "I am an angel* that I might be able to go without food." He did not say, 'And I do not say, "I have knowledge of the Unseen,"' because many people claim to have this knowledge; hence he denied it for himself and repudiated the claims of the others. *I only follow what is revealed to me* as the messengers who came before me did.' *Say: 'Is the blind person equal to the seeing person?* Is the errant person equal to the person who is guided? *Will you not then reflect* and so be guided*?'*

[6:51] *And warn therewith*—with the Qur'ān—*those who fear* the horror of the moment when *they shall be gathered to their Lord*: and do not deny it; for those who deny it are damned and will not benefit from this warning. *Apart from Him they have no protector* to watch over their affairs, *and no intercessor* to intercede for them if He does not permit it, *that they might be wary* of sin.

Q. 6:50

[6:52] *And do not drive away*—do not cast the poor believers from your company at the behest of the chiefs of Quraysh—*those who call upon their Lord at morning and evening*, meaning at all times, *desiring His countenance*: sincerely devoted to His Essence. *You are not accountable for them in anything*: the value of their faith has not been revealed to you, and it might be that their faith is greater in God's sight than the faith of those on whose behalf you are driving them away, hoping that they will believe; *nor* likewise *are they accountable for you* and your faith *in anything*: the two sentences are as one, and express the same sentiment as *no burdened soul shall bear the burden of another* [Q. 6:164]. What it means is: 'You shall not be taken to account for them, nor shall they be for you.' Thus it was not enough to say only, 'You are not accountable for them in anything.' So do not do so, *that you should drive them away and be of the evildoers.*

[6:53] *And even so*, by such tribulations, *We have tried*, tested, *some of them by others*, such as a high-born disbeliever by a lowly believer, *so that they may say* about the poor believers, *'Are these the ones whom God has favoured from among us?'* In other words, 'Had He favoured anyone, it ought to have been us.' *Is God not best aware of those who are thankful?* And He will grant them grace on account of their thankfulness.

[6:54] *And when those who believe in Our signs*—the poor folk whom you are forbidden to drive away—*come to you, say: 'Peace be upon you*: from yourself, or convey Our peace to them. *Your Lord has prescribed for Himself mercy*: that is, He has promised it. *Truly whoever of you does evil in ignorance*: without being mindful of its dire consequences—al-Ḥasan said that everyone who commits a sin is ignorant; *and repents thereafter and makes amends* by rectifying his deeds, *truly He is Forgiving* of him, *Merciful* to him.*'* The word *truly* (*innahū*) can also be read as 'that' (*annahū*), referring back to *mercy*.

[6:55] *And thus*, by this elucidation, *We distinguish the signs*, clarify the truth, *and that the way of the sinners may be become clear*: and the way of the believers become distinct from it. Or it is akin to how He says *garments that protect you from the heat* [Q. 16:81].[1]

[6:56] *Say: 'Truly, I have been forbidden to worship those whom you call upon*—whom you worship—*besides God.' Say: 'I shall not follow your whims*: this imparts emphasis to put a decisive end to their hopes, and to illustrate the root of their misguidance; *for then I would have surely gone astray* if I did so, *and I would not be of the rightly guided*: just as you are not of them.*'*

[6:57] *Say: 'I am upon a clear proof from my Lord, and you have denied it*: the proof, in the form of the Qur'ān. *I do not have that which you seek to hasten*: meaning the punishment, an allusion to their words, *Then rain down stones*
Q. 6:55 *upon us from the heaven*... [Q. 8:32]. *The judgement* of separation between us by means of punishment *is God's alone. He proclaims* (*yaquṣṣ*) *the truth*: He follows it, or He speaks it; it can also be read as *He decrees* (*yaqḍī*); *and He is the Best of Deciders*: judges.*'*

[6:58] *Say: 'If I did have what you seek to hasten*—the punishment—*the matter between you and me would have been decided* by its hastening; *and God knows best the evildoers*: and the right time for their chastisement.*'*

[6:59] *And with Him are the keys*—the treasuries—*of the Unseen*: He alone possesses knowledge of unseen things, or the five things listed at the end of *Luqmān*.[2] *None but He knows them. He knows what is on land and in the waters*: that is, everything; *and not a leaf falls, but He knows it*: because it falls at His will. *Not a grain in the shadows of the earth, nothing of wet or dry*: again, meaning everything; *but it is in a clear book*: the Preserved Tablet. The second *but* here means 'and', and this is also true of similar constrictions where one exception follows another.[3]

[6:60] *It is He Who takes you*—causes you to sleep—*at night*: by claiming

1 Without adding 'and the cold', since this goes without saying.

2 *Truly, God, with Him lies knowledge of the Hour, and He sends down the rain, and He knows what is in the wombs. And no soul knows what it will earn tomorrow, and no soul knows in what land it will die. Truly God is Knower, Aware* (Q. 31:34).

3 The author's concern here is to dispel the notion that there is a distinction between what is contained in the divine knowledge and what is written in the Preserved Tablet, as though the former does not encompass the latter.

your souls; *and He knows what you commit by day*: both *night* and *day* here refer to what is more usual, and are not exhaustive. *Then He raises you up*, wakes you, *therein*, in the day, *so that an appointed term may be accomplished*: meaning the decreed lifespan; *and afterward to Him is your return* with death. *Then He will inform you of what you used to do*: by requiting you for it.

[6:61] *He is the Vanquisher*—the Overpowerer—*over His servants*: in a manner of 'over-ness' (*fawqiyya*) that befits His majesty. *And He sends guardians over you* to guard your bodies, meaning the attendants;[1] or guardians of your deeds, meaning the noble recording angels. The wisdom of sending them is that if we know that our deeds are being recorded and will be shown to us for all to witness, this will deter us more than it would if our deeds were strictly between us and our Generous Lord, since we would rely on His kindness. *Until, when death approaches one of you, Our messengers take him*: meaning the angel of death and his assistants; *and they neglect not*: none of the aforementioned are remiss in their duties.

Q. 6:61

[6:62] *Then they*, meaning all God's servants, as implied by *one of you* [Q. 6:61], *are restored to God their Master* (*Mawlā*), the One Who oversees their affairs, *the True*, the Just. As for His Words *the disbelievers have no patron* (*mawlā*) [Q. 47:11], *mawlā* there is meant in the sense of 'helper', so there is no contradiction. *Surely His is the judgement* on that day, and no other's. *He is the swiftest of reckoners*: He will reckon us over the duration of half a single day of this world, as a *ḥadīth* affirms.

[6:63] *Say* in reproach: *'Who delivers you from the darkness*—the hardships—*of the land and the sea? You call upon Him openly and secretly,* saying, "By God, *if You deliver us from this* darkness, *we shall truly be among the thankful."'*

[6:64] *Say: 'God delivers you from that*—from the darkness—*and from every distress. Yet you associate others with Him*: and are not thankful.'

[6:65] *Say: 'He* alone *has the power to send forth upon you a chastisement from above you*: such as the chastisement of ʿĀd or the tribulation of evil rulers; *or from beneath your feet*: such as being swallowed up by the earth or the tribulation of evil servants; *or to confound you in parties*—split you into opposing factions—*and to make you taste the violence of one another*: by unleashing some of you against others through war, or the like.' *See how We dispense*—clarify and repeat—*the signs that perhaps they might understand.*

[6:66] *Your people have denied it*: the Qurʾān that the signs affirm. *Yet it is the truth. Say: 'I am not a guardian over you*: sent to you to ensure that you do not deny.

1 *For him are attendants, to his front and to his rear, guarding him through God's command* (Q. 13:11).

[6:67] *'Every tiding*—every decree of God—*has a conclusion*: a time to occur. *And you will come to know*: whether in this world, the Hereafter, or both.*'*

[6:68] *When you see those who engage in discourse about Our signs*—such as poking fun at them—*turn away from them* by leaving their company *until they discourse on some other topic. And if Satan should make you forget*—for he is the one who whispers these insinuations—*then do not sit, after the reminder, with the evildoing folk* such as them.

[6:69] *Those who fear are not accountable for them*—for that for which they are accountable—*in anything*: in their sin if they sit with them; *but it is the reminder* for which they are responsible, and to admonish them, *so that perhaps they will be wary* of such discourse. It is said that this verse was abrogated by the verse in *Sūrat al-Nisā'*.[1]

[6:70] *And forsake*—turn away from—*those who take their religion as a game and a diversion*: such as the worship of stones and the banning of *baḥā'ir*,[2] as well as those whose observance consists of wine-drinking,

Q. 6:67

music, dancing and the like; *and whom the life of this world has deluded. Remind thereby*, with the Qur'ān, *lest a soul*, any soul, *perish*, fall into perdition, *for what it has earned* of evil deeds. *It has no protector besides God and no intercessor* to ward off punishment from it; *and though it offer every compensation*—every ransom imaginable—*it shall not be accepted from it. Those are the ones who perish*—fall into chastisement—*by what they have earned; for them shall be a draught of boiling water* that scorches the insides, *and a painful chastisement, because they disbelieved.*

[6:71] *Say: 'Shall we call upon*, worship, *instead of God, that which neither profits us nor hurts us*, such as idols, *and so be turned back*, returned to idolatry, *after God has guided us?' Like one whom the devils have lured in the earth* away from the straight path into the wilderness, *bewildered*: lost from the path. *He has companions who call him to guidance*, to the straight path, saying, *'Come to us* and do not pay regard to them.*' Say: 'Truly, God's guidance*—His religion—*is guidance*: and all else is error; *and we have been commanded* with this *to submit* with sincere worship *to the Lord of the Worlds.*

[6:72] *'And to observe the prayer and fear Him. He it is to Whom you shall be gathered*: for requital.'

[6:73] *He it is Who created the heavens and the earth in truth*: in wisdom and not frivolity. *And* He created *the day* when *He says* to whatever He

1 Q. 4:140.
2 See Q. 5:103.

desires to exist, *'Be!' and it is*: this was explained earlier.[1] *His Words are the truth* which penetrates all beings; *and His is the kingdom on the day when the trumpet is blown*: Isrāfīl will blow it, and all the inhabitants of heaven and earth will hear it. He singled it out for mention here because on that day His sole sovereignty over it will be manifest. *Knower of the Unseen*: what is absent; *and the visible*: what is present. *He is the Wise* in His creation, *the Aware* of the inner realities of things.

[6:74] *And when Abraham said to his father Āzar*: this was his nickname, while his proper name was Terah; *'Do you take idols as gods? I see you and your people in manifest error.'*

[6:75] *And so* by this enlightenment *We showed Abraham the kingdom of the heavens and the earth*: that is, We showed him the signs of Our lordship over them, or their wonders, that he might meditate upon them; *and that he might be of those knowing with certainty.*

[6:76] *When night descended upon him*—covering him with darkness— *he saw a planet*: it was Venus or Jupiter; *and said*, arguing against his people, *'This is my Lord'*: he was speaking as one who treats his interlocutor's position fairly despite recognising its falsehood, before refuting it with sound logic. Thus he said this by way of argument and reasoning, as is made clear by the upcoming verse, *That is Our argument which We bestowed upon Abraham…* [Q. 6:83], and his Words, *O my people, surely I am innocent of what you associate* [Q. 6:78]. His people worshipped idols representing the planets. *But when it set*—when it vanished from view—*he said, 'I love not* to worship *those that set'*: for they are subject to change. He cited the setting of the planet rather than its rising because its evidentiary value was greater: as well as being a change, it was also a veiling. Q. 6:74

[6:77] *And when he saw the moon rising, he said, 'This is my Lord.' But when it set he said, 'Unless my Lord guides me, I shall truly become one of the folk who are astray'*: with this he was implicitly suggesting to his people that they were astray.

[6:78] *And when he saw the sun rising, he said, 'This is my Lord. This is greater'*: in size and in brilliance. *But when it set, he said, 'O my people, surely I am innocent of what you associate*: these physical bodies that are in need of a creator.

[6:79] *'Truly, I have turned my face*, sincerely devoted my religion, *to Him Who originated*, made without any previous model, *the heavens and the earth*; for I am *a ḥanīf*: one who inclines away from falsehood; *and I am not of the idolaters'*: that is, not one of you.

1 See Q. 2:117.

[6:80] *But his people disputed with him* about monotheism, and tried to instil fear of their gods in him. *He said, 'Do you dispute with me concerning* the Oneness of *God when He has guided me* to it*? I have no fear of what you associate with Him, unless my Lord wills something* evil to befall me from their direction. *My Lord encompasses all things through His knowledge. Will you not take heed*: and so renounce your idolatry*?*

[6:81] *'How should I fear what you have associated* when they are but inanimate objects, *and you fear not, that you have associated with God*—the One Who truly ought to be feared—*that for which He has not revealed to you any warrant*: any justification for associating it*?' Which of the two parties*—the monotheist or the idolater—*has more right to security, if you have any knowledge* of what ought to be feared*?*

[6:82] *Those who believe and have not confounded*, mixed, *their belief with evildoing*—meaning idolatry as a *ḥadīth* affirms, or mixing it with corrupt beliefs—*theirs is security; and they are rightly guided.*

Q. 6:80 [6:83] *That*, namely the dialogue about the rising and setting, *is Our argument which We bestowed upon*, inspired to, *Abraham against his people. We raise up in degrees whom We will. Truly, your Lord is Wise* in how He raises and lowers, *Knowing* of those who deserve it.

[6:84] *And* one example of how He raised his degrees is how *We bestowed upon him Isaac and Jacob*: He singled out Isaac rather than Ishmael, though he was the younger son, because he was born to a barren elderly woman and so the blessing of him was more obvious; *each one* of them *We guided. And Noah We guided before*: before Abraham—and the nobility of the father is shared by the son; *and of his seed*—the seed of Abraham, or some say of Noah given the mention of Jonah and Lot—*David and Solomon and Job and Joseph, and Moses and Aaron; and so We requite the virtuous.*

[6:85] *And Zachariah, and John, and Jesus*: for the daughter's son is also counted among a man's seed; *and Elias*: the grandson of Aaron, brother of Moses; *all were of the righteous*: the folk of perfect righteousness.

[6:86] *And Ishmael, and Elisha, and Jonah, and Lot*: the two sons of Haran the brother of Abraham, mentioned here by association and because he emigrated with him; *all We preferred above all the worlds*: with prophethood.

[6:87] *And* We preferred *of their fathers, and of their seed*, including the Master of the Worlds (may God bless him and grant him peace), *and of their brethren; and We chose them and We guided them to a straight path.*

[6:88] *That*—their path and their religion—*is God's guidance wherewith He guides whom He will of His servants; had they been idolaters*—despite their greatness—*all that they did would have been in vain*: because of their disbelief.

[6:89] *They are the ones to whom We gave the Book*—meaning the class of scripture—*judgement*: meaning wisdom, which is knowledge and action according to it; *and prophethood; so if these*, the people of Mecca, *disbelieve therein*, in prophethood or in all three, *then We have entrusted it*, the care of it, *to a people who do not disbelieve in it*: meaning the Companions and those who came after them, or the Persians.

[6:90] *They*, the prophets, *are the ones whom God has guided; so follow their guidance*: meaning that upon which they agreed regarding principles, or the matter of monotheism and ethics. He instructed him with this so that all of their virtues would be combined in him. It did not mean that he was supposed to worship according to their Law, except regarding those branching matters upon which they all agreed. Beyond this, it means following their guidance inasmuch as it is the path of the intellect and the Law. Thus there is no need to object that for doctrines it is required to derive proofs from the intellect and revelation, rather than blindly follow. *Say: 'I do not ask of you any wage for it*: for delivering the message; *it*—the Qur'ān—*is only a reminder to all the worlds.'* Q. 6:89

[6:91] *They*, the Jews or the idolaters, *measured not God with His true measure*: they did not know Him as He ought to be known; *when they said, 'God has not revealed anything*—any scripture—*to any mortal.' Say* to them: *'Who revealed the Book which Moses brought, a light and guidance for people? You put it*—this is addressed to the Jews, or to the idolaters since they also believed in that scripture, which is why they used to say, *If the Book had been revealed to us, we would have surely been more rightly guided than they are* [Q. 6:157]; *on parchments*—volume by volume—*which you disclose* in part, *but you hide much*: they wrote it on many pages to facilitate disclosing some parts while hiding others; *and you have been taught*—through the Qur'ān—*what you did not know, neither you nor your fathers'*: this evokes the verse, *Truly, this Qur'ān recounts to the Children of Israel* [*the means to resolve*] *most of that concerning which they differ* [Q. 27:76]. *Say: 'God* revealed it, and this is the only answer'; *then leave them to play in their discourse*: their falsehoods. Your only duty is to deliver the message.

[6:92] *And this* Qur'ān *is a blessed Book*—full of benefit—*We have revealed, confirming that which was before it*: the previous heavenly Books for the blessings; *and that you may warn* with it *the Mother of Towns*: the folk of Mecca, for the earth was rolled out from beneath it; *and those around it*: the people of the East and the West. *And those who believe in the Hereafter* with faith that is of value, unlike some of the People of the Book, *believe in it*—in the Qur'ān—*and they observe their prayers*: for fear of the Hereafter encourages one to reflect until one comes to believe in the Prophet and the Book and to observe the chief pillar of the religion.

[6:93] *And who*—no one—*does greater evil than he who invents lies against God* by inventing laws, *or who says, 'It is revealed to me,'* such as Musaylima, *when nothing has been revealed to him*: this is a description of a specific scenario of the aforementioned general principle; *or*, which is even more heinous, *he who says, 'I will reveal the like of what God has revealed'*: such as those who said, *If we wish we can speak the like of this* [Q. 8:31]. *If you could only see when the evildoers*, all of them, *are in the agonies of death and the angels extend their hands* to claim their spirits as though forcefully wresting a debt from them, saying reproachfully, *'Give up your souls!* A *ḥadīth* says, 'The spirits of the disbeliever will refuse to come out, so the angels will beat them until they do.' *Today*—the day of death—*you shall be requited with the chastisement of humiliation because you used to say about God other than the truth, and that you used to scorn His signs*: instead of believing in them.*'*

Q. 6:93

[6:94] *And now you have come to Us singly*—divided from all intercessors, family and property—*as We created you the first time; and you have left what We conferred on you*—the property with which We graced you—*behind your backs; and We do not see with you your intercessors whom you claimed to be associates* with God *amongst you; your connection has been severed*: this can also be read as 'what was between you has been severed'; *and that which you claimed* about them being associates and intercessors *has failed you*.

[6:95] *God is the Cleaver of the grain*: by causing crops to grow; *and the date-stone*: by causing trees to grow. *He brings forth the living*, such as trees and animals which grow and take nourishment, *from the dead*, such as seeds and drops of fluid, *and is the Bringer-forth*: this refers back to *Cleaver*, because *He brings forth* acts as an elucidation of *Cleaver*, and it would not have been as effective to say 'the Bringer-forth of the living' to achieve this purpose, which is why He changed the rhetorical style here, unlike other similar passages; *of the dead*, such as seeds and drops of fluid, *from the living*, such as plants and animals. *That* Doer *is God. How then are you deluded*: straying from monotheism*?*

[6:96] *Cleaver of the daybreak*: the pillar of dawn from the darkness of night, or the Cleaver of the darkness of daybreak, or the Creator of daybreak, meaning light; *and He has appointed the night for stillness*: a time of repose after the toil of day; it can also be read as 'the Appointer of the night', referring to how He is ever renewing this appointment; *and the sun and the moon for reckoning* of time according to their cycles. *That*—all of the aforementioned—*is the ordaining of the Mighty*, the Dominant, *the Knowing* of what He has ordained.

[6:97] *And He it is Who appointed*—created—*for you the stars* in addition to the sun and moon *that you may guide your course by them amid the darkness of* night in the *land and sea. We have distinguished*—elucidated—*the signs for a folk who have knowledge*: so that they will benefit from them.

[6:98] *And He it is Who produced you from a single soul*—Adam—*and so a dwelling-place* is yours, such as the womb, *and so a repository*, such as the loins. Know that the womb, the loins, the world, the grave, and the Gathering to the Garden and the Fire are all dwelling-places and repositories in a relative sense. *We have distinguished the signs for a folk who understand*: He used the term *fiqh*, which means 'subtle, contemplative understanding', because understanding that is derived from contemplation of the soul is subtler than understanding that is derived from contemplation of the stars on the horizon, because the latter is more obvious. Thus God says, *Assuredly the creation of the heavens and the earth is greater than the creation of people; but most people do not know* [Q. 40:57].

[6:99] *And He it is Who sent down water from* the edge of *the sky, and therewith*—by means of that water—*We bring forth plants of every kind*: every kind Q. 6:97
of plant, or provision for every kind of creature; *and therefrom*, from those plants, *We bring forth verdure*, greenery, *bringing forth from it*, from that verdure, *thick-clustered grain*: its parts clustered together, meaning ears of corn; *and* We bring forth *from the palm-tree—from its spathe*, its trunk—*bunches of dates, near to hand*: easy to pick because the trees are short. He singled out the near ones for mention because of their greater blessing, and mentioned the spathe as well as the tree because that is the part that provides food and sustenance, unlike the rest of the trunk. He mentioned plants first because of how the sustenance comes before the fruit. *And* We bring forth *gardens of grapes, and olives, and pomegranates, similar* in the appearance of their leaves, *but not alike* in their fruits; or both words apply to the fruit in the sense that there are different types, such as how there are large, white, sweet pomegranates and other kinds. *Look upon their fruits*—the fruits of each of them—*when they have borne fruit, and their ripening*: and behold in this evidence of His omnipotence. *Truly, in all that are signs* of His perfect omnipotence *for a folk who believe*: save for those who stubbornly resist.

[6:100] *Yet they ascribe to God as associates the jinn*: meaning the hidden (*mujtinna*) angels, or the demons, for they obey them as they ought to obey God; *even though He created them. And they falsely impute to Him sons*, such as Ezra and Christ, *and daughters*, such as the angels, *without any knowledge* or contemplation. *Glory be to Him*—transcendent be He—*and exalted be He above what they describe* about Him!

[6:101] *The Originator*—maker—*of the heavens and the earth*: this was explained earlier.[1] It means that He is the Creator of all bodies, and the reproductive faculty is in them alone. *How should He have a son, when He has no consort*: and children are produced by two equal partners; *and He created everything, and He has knowledge of everything?* He said *of everything* rather than simply 'of it' to make clear what the pronoun's antecedent is.

[6:102] *That then*—the One described as such—*is God, your Lord. There is no god but Him, the Creator of all things, so worship Him. And He is Guardian over all things*: so resign all your affairs to Him.

[6:103] *Vision cannot attain Him* in this world, because in the world it is only possible to see that which has a spatial direction, and God is the Creator of all direction. But when He manifests with His countenance, it will be possible to see Him, and this vision will attain Him, as is described in several authentic narrations. The change will be on the part of the beholder, not the Almighty. The negative statement does not apply universally to all times, nor all persons, because it is a particular negation, as if
Q. 6:101 we said, 'Not every vision can attain Him,' which could be understood to apply to specific individuals only. In any case, a negation does not imply an impossibility, and so the claim of the Muʿtazila in this regard is outlandishly false.[2] *But He attains* [*all*] *vision*: because He created it. Vision is singled out here because of the general context. *And He is the Subtle* Whom vision cannot attain, *the Aware* Who attains all vision.

[6:104] *Clear insights*: the verses of the Qur'ān—insight is to the heart as sight is to the eyes; *have come to you from your Lord; whoever perceives* and believes in them, *then it is for his own good; and whoever is blind* to them, *then it will be to his own hurt. And* [say:] *'I am not a keeper over you'*: 'I am but a messenger.'

[6:105] *And so*, by this elucidation, *We dispense the signs*, elucidating and repeating them, *and* We elucidate them *that they*, the idolaters, *may say, 'You have studied with someone'*: a Jew or a Persian; *and that We may make it*—the Qur'ān—*clear for a folk who have knowledge* of its content. As He says, *Thereby He leads many astray, and thereby He guides many* [Q. 2:26].

[6:106] *Follow what has been revealed to you from your Lord*: by acting in accordance with it. *There is no god but Him*: and so His command must be followed; *and turn away from the idolaters*: it is said that this was abrogated by the verses about warfare.

1 See Q. 2:117.
2 The Muʿtazila denied the possibility of the beatific vision, even in the Hereafter.

[6:107] *Had God willed, they would not have been idolaters*: but He has a wise purpose for sending them astray. *And We have not set you as a keeper over them* to guard their actions, *nor are you a guardian over them* to attend to their affairs.

[6:108] *Do not revile those whom they call upon*—worship—*besides God*: meaning their idols—this is one aspect of turning away from them; *lest they then revile God out of spite*, injustice, *without knowledge*: ignorantly. This indicates that it is forbidden to do something virtuous if it is likely to cause sin, unlike if the sin has already been committed. *Thus have We adorned for every* disbelieving *community their deeds; then to their Lord they shall return, and He will tell them what they used to do*: by requiting them for it.

[6:109] *They have sworn by God the most earnest oaths that if there came to them a sign* like the signs of Moses and Jesus, *they would believe in it. Say: 'Signs are only with God*: not with me. *But what will make you realise?'* In other words, they will not realise. *Truly, when they come*—those signs—*they will not believe*: and God knows this.

Q. 6:107

[6:110] *And We would confound their hearts* to the truth even if We produced everything that they demand, so that they would not understand it, *and their eyes* so that they would not behold it, *just as they did not believe in it the first time* when We sent them signs such as the cleaving of the moon and others; *and We shall leave them in their insolence*—their error—*wandering blindly* in confusion.

[6:111] *And if We had sent down the angels to them* to see with their own eyes, *and the dead had spoken with them* about the truth of the Qur'ān, *and We had gathered against them all things in droves, they would not have believed* even then, *unless God willed* to alter their natures. *But most of them are ignorant* to the fact that they would not believe even if they were given those signs, which is why they make such oaths.

[6:112] *And so*, just as We have appointed enemies for you, *We appointed to every prophet an enemy,* rebellious *devils of humankind and jinn who inspire*, suggest and insinuate, *fine speech*, embellished falsehoods, *to each other in delusion*: for the purpose of delusion. The rebellious jinn inspire rebellious people, and delude them; or some people delude others, and some jinn others. *Yet, had your Lord willed, they would never have done it*: engaged in that inspiration. *So leave them with what they fabricate* about you to belie you.

[6:113] *And that*—this refers back to *in delusion*—*the hearts of those who do not believe in the Hereafter may incline to it, and that they may be pleased with it, and that they may acquire what they are acquiring*: namely sin; each one of these leads to the other, for it is arranged beautifully.

[6:114] Say, O Muḥammad, *'Shall I seek other than God as a judge* between me and you, *when it is He Who revealed to you the Book*—the Qur'ān—*clearly explained*: so that you have no need for the verdict of any other?' *Those to whom We have given the Book*—their scholars—*know that it is revealed from your Lord in truth*: because of what is made clear in their Books; *so be not of the waverers* regarding their knowledge of it.

[6:115] *Perfected*, completed, *is the Word of your Lord*, the Qur'ān, *in truthfulness* regarding reports and promises, *and justice* regarding its edicts. *None can change His Words*: by corruption, abrogation or the like. *He is the Hearing* of your words, *the Knowing* of your thoughts, and so He will not overlook them.

[6:116] *If you obey most of those on earth*—namely the ignorant folk—*they will lead you astray from the way of God*: because the errant person enjoins nothing but error. *They follow only supposition* in their doctrines, supposing that their forefathers were rightly guided; *they are merely guessing* and lying.

Q. 6:114 [6:117] *Your Lord knows best those who stray from His way and He knows well the rightly guided.*

[6:118] *So eat from that over which God's Name has been invoked* at its slaughter, and no other name, *if you believe in His signs*: for faith means permitting only what He permits, and nothing more.

[6:119] *What is wrong with you*—what purpose have you—*that you do not eat from that over which God's Name has been invoked* and instead eat other things, *when He has detailed for you what He has forbidden*, when He said, *He has only forbidden you carrion...* [Q. 2:173] and so on, *except that* which is forbidden but *to which you are compelled? But truly many are led astray* by forbidding and permitting *by their whims without any knowledge* or proof. *Truly, your Lord knows the transgressors*: those who go outside the bounds of truth.

[6:120] *And forsake the outward aspect of sin*: meaning what is committed publicly; *and its inward aspect*: meaning what is committed secretly; or it means, respectively, what the limbs commit and what the heart commits. *Truly, those who earn sin shall be requited for what they used to perpetrate.*

[6:121] *And do not eat from that over which God's Name has not been invoked*: meaning that which has been consecrated to anything but God, given the context; *and indeed it*—that over which it has not been invoked—*is certainly wickedness*: that which has been consecrated to anything but God. This is a circumstantial clause, and the emphasis imparted by *indeed* and *certainly* serves to strenuously forestall any attempt they might make to deny the wickedness of this act. As for that over which neither the Name of God nor anything else has been invoked, it is lawful to eat according to Shāfiʿī, Mālik and Ibn ʿAbbās. There is also the *ḥadīth* in which the Prophet was asked about something over which the Name had not been invoked, and replied, 'Eat it, for God's Name is invoked in the heart of every believer.' Another *ḥadīth* says, 'The Muslim's slaughter is lawful, even if he did not invoke God's Name over it.' Consider also how the verse *He has detailed for you what He has forbidden* [Q. 6:119] refers back to the verse, *He has only forbidden you carrion*...[Q. 2:173]. *And truly the devils inspire*, whisper insinuations to, *their friends*, the disbelievers, *to dispute with you; and if you obey them* and their edicts about what is lawful and what is forbidden, *you are truly idolaters*.

[6:122] *Is he who was dead* in his ignorance and error, *and then We gave him life* through guidance, *and appointed for him a light*—the Qur'ān—*by which to walk among people*: guidance on how to deal with the villains among them, as men like ʿUmar, Ḥamza and ʿAmmār were guided; *as him whose likeness is* as a person *in darkness whence he cannot emerge*: such as Abū Jahl? *So*, just as faith has been adorned to the believers, *what the disbelievers have been doing has been adorned for them*. Q. 6:122

[6:123] *And thus*, just as We made the likes of Abū Jahl the greatest sinners of Mecca, *We have made in every city its sinners great ones, that they may plot therein* to send people astray; *but they plot only against themselves*—for the dire consequences will be theirs—*though they do not perceive* this.

[6:124] *And when a sign comes to them* to confirm the truth of Muḥammad (may God bless him and grant him peace), *they say, 'We will not believe, until we are given the like of what God's messengers were given'*: by revelation coming directly to them, as we shall see presently. *God knows best where to place His message*: regarding the word *aʿlam* (knows best) here, when the superlative form [such as this] is used without a definite article or in an *iḍāfa* construction[1] it can have the meaning of the simple active participle or adjective, such as in *that is easier for Him* [Q. 30:27], where *ahwan* (easier) means simply *hayyin* (easy). So here it means simply 'God knows where,' and there is no need to engage in the convoluted parsing some have done to suggest that the word *ḥayth* (where) here is a direct object of the superlative form *aʿlam*.[2] And God knows best. *Humiliation from God and a terrible chastisement shall smite those who have sinned for their plotting*: on the Day of Resurrection.

[6:125] *Whomever God desires to guide, He expands*—broadens—*his breast* and his heart *to Islam*: by making him receptive to monotheism; *and*

1 That is, an 'X of Y' construction, such as *aḥsan al-nās* (the best of people).

2 Which would render a translation along the lines of, 'God knows the right place to put His Message,' as is suggested in the *Tafsīr al-Jalālayn* and elsewhere.

whomever He desires to send astray, He makes his breast narrow and constricted: tightly closed so that the truth cannot enter it; *as though he were straining to ascend to heaven*: which is impossible for him to do. *So God casts ignominy*—torment—*over those who do not believe.*

[6:126] *And this*—Islam—*is the path of your Lord, a straight one*: without any deviation. *We have detailed the signs for a folk who remember* how to contemplate.

[6:127] *Theirs will be the abode of peace*: meaning the Garden—*peace* (*al-salām*) here means God, or security; *with their Lord; and He will be their Patron*—their Guardian—*because of what they used to do*: because of their deeds.

[6:128] *And* remember *the day when He shall gather them altogether*, saying, *'O assembly of jinn, you have garnered much of humankind'*: 'You have much deluded them, or you have mustered many of them to your cause, like a commander mustering his army.' *Then their friends*—those dutiful servants—*from among humankind will say* in response, *'Our Lord, we enjoyed*
Q. 6:126 *one another*: that is, we benefitted from each other: the men benefitted by attaining their desires, and the jinn benefitted by seeing their delusions accepted; *but now we have arrived at the term which You have appointed for us*: the Resurrection and Gathering.*'* *He*, God, *will say, 'The Fire is your lodging to abide therein'*—*except what God wills*: God knows what the exception might be, or it might refer to the sinful believers. *Truly, your Lord is Wise* in His acts, *Knowing* of your deeds.

[6:129] *So*, by this damning through enjoyment, *We let some of the evildoers have power over others*—loosing them upon one another or making them allies—*because of what they are wont to earn*: their sins.

[6:130] *'O assembly of jinn and humankind, did not messengers come to you from among you*: the soundest position on this matter is that the messengers were all humans, and the jinn were all followers, or there may have been messengers among the jinn as well; *to recount to you My signs and to warn you of the encounter of this day of yours?'* [The latter refers to] the Day of Resurrection. *They shall say* in reply, *'We bear witness against ourselves* that indeed they did warn us.*'* Then He says, *And the life of this world deluded them; and they bear witness against themselves that they were disbelievers*: this refers to a different occasion than the one in which they will say, *By God, our Lord, we were never idolaters* [Q. 6:23].

[6:131] *That* sending of messengers *is because your Lord would never destroy* the people of *the towns through*—on account of their—*injustice, while their inhabitants were heedless* and had not been warned by messengers.

[6:132] *All* those who speak then *shall have degrees according to what they have done. Your Lord is not heedless of what they do.*

[6:133] *Your Lord is Independent* of His creation, *the Lord of Mercy. If He will, He can remove you,* O sinners, if you sin further, *and leave whom He will* from among the obedient folk *to succeed after you, just as He produced you from the seed of another folk*: and then destroyed them.

[6:134] *Truly, that which you are promised will surely come to pass*: for it is inevitable; *and you cannot escape* from God.

[6:135] *Say: 'O my people, act according to your state*: remain in the state of disbelief in which you exist—this is a warning phrased as a command. *Truly, I am acting* according to my own state. *And assuredly you will know for whom is the ultimate abode*: the praiseworthy end for which this abode was created. *Surely the evildoers*—those who die in disbelief—*will not prosper.'*

[6:136] *They*, the Arab idolaters, *assign to God, of the tillage and the cattle which He multiplied*—created—*a portion*, and another portion for their idols, *saying, 'This is for God—so they claim*: the root meaning of *zaʿam* (to claim) is 'to issue a statement which is likely false'—*and this is for our associates'*: they would give the portion assigned to God to their guests, and the portion assigned to the idols to the ones who served the idols. If any produce dedicated to the idols fell out, they would put it back; but if it was ruined, they would take some from God's portion to replace it. Conversely, if any produce from God's share was ruined or fell into the share for the idols, they would leave it be, saying, 'God is Rich, while their servants are poor and needy.' Thus He said: *So that which is intended for their associates does not reach God, and that which is intended for God does reach their associates. Evil is that which they decree!*

Q. 6:132

[6:137] *And thus*, by such adornment, *those associates of theirs*—the devils for in truth they worship them, as we have seen—*have adorned for many of the idolaters the slaying of their children that they may destroy them and to confuse their religion for them*: for originally they followed the religion of Abraham, but then they abandoned it. *Had God willed, they would not have done it; so leave them and that which they fabricate* about God.

[6:138] *They say* of what they dedicate to their gods, *'These cattle and tillage are sacrosanct. No one is to eat of them except whom we will'*: namely the servants of the idols; *so they claim*: though God does not command it; *and cattle whose backs have been forbidden*: such as the *sā'iba* and so on;[1] *and cattle over which they do not invoke the Name of God* when slaughtering it, rather

1 See Q. 5:103.

invoking the names of their gods, *forging lies against Him. He will assuredly requite them for what they used to fabricate.*

[6:139] *And they say, 'That which is within the bellies of these cattle*—the unborn young of the *baḥīra* and the *sā'iba* if they are born alive—*is reserved for our males and forbidden to our spouses*: our women; *but if it be dead, then they all*—both the males and females—*may be partakers thereof.' He*, God, *will assuredly requite them for their describing* such falsehood. *Truly, He is Wise* in His acts, *Knowing* of our deeds.

[6:140] *They are losers who slay their children*—burying their infant daughters alive in fear that they will not be able to provide for them—*in folly without knowledge*, proof, *and yet have forbidden what God has provided them*, such as the *baḥīra, in calumny against God. Truly, they have gone astray, and are not guided* back to the truth after straying.

[6:141] *And He it is Who produces gardens*, vineyards, *trellised*, set upon supports or spread out like melons, *and untrellised*: left on the surface of the earth
Q. 6:139 or raised on stems like date palms; *and* He produces *palm trees, and crops diverse in flavour*: bearing fruits of differing tastes, colours and shapes; *and olives, and pomegranates, alike* in their plants and appearances, *and unalike* in their fruits or flavours—this was explained further earlier.[1] *Eat of the fruit thereof when it bears fruit*, even before it ripens, *and pay the due thereof*, meaning God's due, namely charity, *on the day of its harvest*: this was before *zakāt* was made obligatory, according to the majority. *And be not prodigal*: whether in giving charity or in eating, so that your portion will remain. *Truly, God does not love the prodigal.*

[6:142] *And* He produces *of the cattle some for burden*, those that carry cargo, *and some for light support*, those that are lain down for slaughter in their youth; *eat of that which God has provided you*—whether fruits, crops or cattle—*and do not follow the steps*, the pathways, *of Satan*: by inventing your own permissions and prohibitions. *Truly, he is a manifest foe to you.*

[6:143] *Eight pairs*—this refers back to *some for burden and some for light support* [Q. 6:143]; a pair means two things of the same kind that go together—*of sheep two*, the ram and the ewe, *and of goats two*, the buck and the doe. *Say*, O Muḥammad, *'Is it the two males* of each *He has forbidden, or the two females* of each, *or that which the wombs of the two females contain? Inform Me with knowledge*—with proof that they are forbidden—*if you speak truly* when you claim this.'

[6:144] *And of camels two, and of oxen two. Say: 'Is it the two males He has forbidden or the two females? Or what the wombs of the two females contain?* Why

1 See Q. 2:25.

do they forbid the males at times, and the females at others, and the offspring at others yet? *Or were you witnesses*—were you present—*when God charged you with this* prohibition? That is to say, you have neither rational nor tangible proof for it. *Then who does greater evil than he who invents a lie against God, that he may lead people astray without any knowledge*: without any proof? *Truly, God does not guide evildoing folk.'*

[6:145] *Say: 'I do not find, in what is revealed to me*, regarding the matter of those things which they used to permit, *anything forbidden to him who eats thereof except it be carrion or blood poured forth*: meaning spilled blood, not the blood that is retained in the liver or pancreas or what is intermixed with the flesh; *or the flesh of swine, for truly it*, swine, *is an abomination; or a wicked thing*: this was explained earlier,[1] and is qualified here as: *that has been hallowed to other than God. But whoever is constrained* to eat any of these, *neither coveting*, wronging his fellow constrained person, *nor transgressing*, indulging in more than what he needs, *then truly your Lord is Forgiving, Merciful* to him, and will not take him to task.' This verse does not contradict the prohibitions of other things that were issued later. Q. 6:145

[6:146] *And to those of Jewry, We forbade every beast with claws*: meaning every animal that does not have a cloven hoof, such as camels, ostriches or ducks. The word *ẓufur* (claws) can mean the footpads of a camel, or the claws of a predator. *And of oxen and sheep We forbade them the fat of them* all, *save what their backs carry*, meaning the fat that adheres to the back, *or* the fat that adheres to *their entrails*, meaning the innards, *or what* fat *is mingled with bone*, meaning the rump. *Thus*, by this prohibition and inconvenience, *We requited them for their insolence*: their evildoing—this is explained further in *Sūrat al-Nisā'*;[2] *and surely We are truthful* about this, such as how they said that Israel forbade them of his own accord, not due to any sin on their part.

[6:147] *So if they deny you, say: 'Your Lord is of the Lord of all-embracing mercy*: and so He shall let you be for the time being; *yet His might*—His punishment—*will never be driven back from the sinful folk* when it does descend, and you will not escape it.'

[6:148] *The idolaters will say*, by way of arguing that they are in the right, not by way of proffering an excuse, *'Had God willed* otherwise, *we would not have been idolaters, neither our fathers, nor would we have forbidden anything'*: and since He did not will otherwise, so they claimed, He must approve of this. They did not differentiate between the divine will and

1 See Q. 2:26.
2 See Q. 4:160.

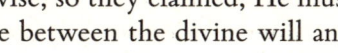

the divine command and approval, just like the Muʿtazila. The upshot is that they argued two things: that idolatry is by God's will, and that the claim of the Prophet was refuted by this. Therefore God castigated them for the second argument, saying: *Just so*, with this same specious reasoning, *those who were before them gave the lie* to the Messengers. If He had meant to castigate them for the first argument, He would have said 'lied' rather than *gave the lie*. Thus this verse is not proof in support of the Muʿtazilite position. Furthermore, had they meant these words as an excuse, the reply to it would have been in their favour. *Until they tasted Our might*: and realised that their religion was not pleasing to Us. *Say: 'Have you any knowledge*—any proof for your claim—*such that you can produce it for us*: show it to us? *You follow only supposition*: not knowledge; *you are merely guessing'*: and lying about God.

Q. 6:149

[6:149] *Say*, when it becomes clear that they have no arguments, *'To God belongs the conclusive argument* of utmost rectitude and clarity; *for had He willed, He could have guided all of you'*: but He willed to send some of you astray, for wise reasons.

[6:150] *Say: 'Come,* summon *your witnesses, those who can testify that God has forbidden this'*: since they are your exemplars, and are duty bound to come forth. *Then if they testify* in their obstinacy, *do not bear witness with them*: that is, do not yield to them, since that is what this would amount to. *And do not follow the whims of those who deny Our signs*, meaning the People of the Book, *and those who do not believe in the Hereafter*, meaning the idolaters, *and ascribe equals to their Lord*.

[6:151] *Say: 'Come, I will recite that which your Lord has made a sacred duty for you: that you associate nothing with Him; that you be dutiful to parents*: meaning that you do not offend them; *and that you do not slay your children because of poverty*: meaning the poverty in which you find yourselves presently; *We will provide for you and them*: this is addressed to those who are already poor, which is why He did not say 'fear of poverty' and why He said *for you* first; the verse in *al-Isrāʾ* is addressed to the wealthy, which is why He did mention fear and worded it the inverse way;[1] *and that you do not draw near any acts of lewdness*, meaning major sins, *whether it be manifest or concealed*, public or private, *and that you do not slay the life which God has made sacred* by any means, *except rightfully*: lawfully. *This is what He has charged you with*—charged you to preserve—*that perhaps you will understand*: and be rightly guided.*'*

1 *And do not slay your children, fearing penury; We shall provide for them and for you* (Q. 17:31).

[6:152] *And do not approach the property of the orphan save with that* approach *which is fairer*: namely that which is to his benefit. The same applies to the wealth of an adult, but He singled out the orphan child for mention because it is at greater risk of being usurped unlawfully because of his weakness, and also because of the greater enormity of that sin; *until he is of age*: that is, until he reaches adulthood, at which point you should hand it over to him. *And give full measure and full weight, in justice*: do not hold back anything. *We do not charge any soul beyond its capacity*: and anything beyond this is excused for it. *And if you speak* about anything, *then be just* with your words—that is, do not neglect to be fair even when you speak; the implication is that this is all the more true when it comes to action; *even if he*—the one for whom or against whom you speak—*should be a kinsman. And fulfil God's covenant*: and do not renege on it. *This is what He has ordained for you, that perhaps you will remember*: He stressed remembrance of these things in particular because they are subtle and require particular effort and recollection, unlike the first five which are so obvious that they Q. 6:152
require only basic mindfulness.

[6:153] *And that this is My straight path*—My religion—*so follow it*: the first word of the verse can be read as *wa-inna*, denoting a new sentence, or *wa-anna*, denoting causation, in reference to 'so follow it'. *And do not follow other ways, lest it separate you away*—cause you to deviate—*from His way*: the straight path. *This* following *is what He has ordained for you, that perhaps you will be wary* of error.*'*

[6:154] *Then*—this denotes the succession of statements [rather than chronology], referring back to 'He has ordained for you'—*We gave Moses the Book, complete* in favour *for him who does good* by acting in accordance with it, *and a detailing of all things* that are needed, *and as a guidance and a mercy, that perhaps they*, the Children of Israel, *might believe in the encounter with their Lord*: the Resurrection.

[6:155] *And this*—the Qur'ān—*is a blessed*, greatly beneficial, *Book which We have revealed; so follow it, and be wary* in contravening it, *that perhaps you might find mercy*: by following it.

[6:156] And We have revealed it, *Lest you should say, 'The Book was revealed only upon two parties before us*—the Jews and Christians—*and we truly have been unacquainted with their study'*: 'We did not understand it, for it was not in our language.'

[6:157] *Or lest you should say, 'If the Book had been revealed to us, we would have truly been more rightly guided than they are.' For now*, if indeed that were true, *a clear proof*, a manifest argument that makes the lawful and unlawful plain, *has come to you from your Lord, and a guidance and a mercy* to all who act in accordance with it. *And who does greater evil than he who denies God's signs* after recognising that they are real, *and turns away from them*: rejecting them or barring others from them? *We shall surely requite those who turn away from Our signs with dreadful chastisement for their aversion*: for how they rejected them or barred others from them.

[6:158] *Are they waiting for nothing less than that the angels should come to them* to claim their spirits, *or that your Lord should come* on the Day of Resurrection for the reckoning, coming forth in a way that befits His majesty, or that His command for punishment should come, *or that one of your Lord's signs*—the portents of the Hour—*should come? On the day that one of your Lord's signs comes*, such as the sun rising from the West, or the moment of death, *it shall not benefit a soul to believe*, nor to acquire any good deeds, *if it had not believed theretofore or earned in its* prior *belief some good*: what this implies is that on that day, the faith of the disbeliever will be of no avail, nor the virtue of the wicked person. This is better than interpreting it to mean that faith is contingent upon action, given the *ḥadīth* which states that anyone who says 'There is no god but God' sincerely will enter the Garden, as well as the fact that the context of this verse concerns those who deny God's signs and turn away from them. *Say: 'Wait* for any of those three. *We too are waiting* for them.'

Q. 6:158

[6:159] *Those who have sundered their religion*: by believing in part of it but not all, such as the People of the Book and the heretics among this community; *and have become differing parties*: sects with each following their own leader; *you have no concern with them at all*: you are not responsible for them and their sundering, or you are absolved of them. *Their case will go to God. Then He will inform them of what they used to do*: by means of the requital.

[6:160] *Whoever brings a good deed shall receive tenfold the like of it*: this is the least reward promised; *and whoever brings an evil deed shall only be requited the like of it*: and it will not be multiplied; *and they shall not be wronged*: whether by losing out on reward or receiving extra punishment.

[6:161] *Say: 'As for me, my Lord has guided me* with revelation *to a straight path, a right religion*—solid and upright: *the creed of Abraham* when he was *a ḥanīf*, one who inclined away from falsehood; *and he was not of the idolaters'*: as they claimed.

[6:162] *Say: 'My prayer and my rituals*—my sacrifices and the *ḥajj* and *ʿumra*, for the idolaters would sacrifice in the names of their idols, or it means my worship—*and my living*, my life, *and my dying*, my death—that is, all of my actions which are contained within them—*are all* sincerely *for God, the Lord of the Worlds.*

[6:163] *'No associate has He. And to this* path *I have been commanded, and I am the first of those who submit'*: as was discussed earlier.[1]

[6:164] *Say: 'Shall I seek any other than God for a lord, when He is the Lord of all things?' Every soul earns only against itself*: in terms of sin; *and no burdened soul shall bear the burden*—the sin—*of another*: that is, it cannot bear it voluntarily. This is a response to their words, *Follow our path and we will bear your sins* [Q. 29:12]. However, if the sin is attributable to the other soul, whether directly or by causality, then it does share in the burden of it, as He says, *And they shall certainly bear their own burdens, and other burdens along with their own* [Q. 29:13]; *That they may bear their burdens complete on the Day of Resurrection and also of the burdens of those whom they lead astray without any knowledge* [Q. 16:25]. Likewise, there are narrations about how the sins of the victims of oppression and creditors will be borne by their oppressors and debtors, and the like. *Then to your Lord shall you return* on the Day of
Resurrection, *and He will inform you of that over which you differed*: by requit- Q. 6:163
ing each one for their deeds.

[6:165] *And He it is Who has made you successors*—successors of the communities of old, or God's successors—*in the earth; and has raised some of you above others in degrees* of wealth and nobility, *so that He may try you*—test you—*in what He has given you*: whether wealth, renown or poverty, to see who will give thanks and who will have patience. *Truly, your Lord is swift in punishment* to the sinners, because what is to come is near; *and Truly, He is Forgiving, Merciful*: He described Himself as possessing abundant forgiveness, but described His punishment obliquely without attributing it directly to Himself, in order to indicate that He is intrinsically Forgiving but incidentally punishing, emphatic in the former and lenient in the latter.

1 See Q. 6:14.

7
The Heights
SŪRAT AL-AʿRĀF

Revealed in Mecca, except for the verses from *And question them…* [7:163] unto *And when We wrenched…* [7:171], or some say *…and turn away from the ignorant* [7:199]

In the Name of God, the Compassionate, the Merciful

[7:1] *Alif. Lām. Mīm. Ṣād*: this was explained earlier.[1]

[7:2] This is *A Book that is revealed to you; so let there be*, after its revelation, *no inhibition*, disquiet, *in your breast because of it*: that is, do not feel uneasy about conveying it because of your fear that it will be belied; *that you may warn* the disbelievers *thereby, and as a reminder*—a counsel—*for those who believe*.

[7:3] *Follow what has been revealed to you from your Lord* through the tongue of your Prophet, as Book and as Sunna, *and do not follow beside Him any patrons*: lest they lead you astray. *Little do you remember*: and take heed.

[7:4] *How many a city have We destroyed!* Many indeed did We will to destroy. *And Our might*—Our punishment—*came upon it at night* as they slept, like the folk of Lot, *or while they dozed at noon*: as they took their siesta (*qaylūla*), which means to rest at midday whether one sleeps or not, like the people of Shuʿayb. They are both times of repose, and so punishment dealt out during them is all the more severe.

[7:5] *And their only plea, when Our might came upon them, was to say, 'Truly, we were evildoers'*: that is, all they could do was to acknowledge the reality of the punishment.

[7:6] *Then indeed We shall question those to whom the message was sent*: about how they responded to the messengers; *and We shall question the*

1 See Q. 2:1.

messengers: about how they conveyed the message. His Words *The guilty will not be questioned about their sins* [Q. 28:78] mean that they will not be questioned for the purpose of attaining knowledge, or refer to another occasion.

[7:7] *And We shall narrate to them*, narrate to the messengers and nations all of their deeds, *with knowledge*, having knowledge of all of them; *for We were not absent* from them, such that they could be concealed from us.

[7:8] *The weighing* of deeds *on that day*—the day of questioning—*will be true*: just. Their records will be weighed upon a scale composed of two balances, so that justice is manifest and all arguments are silenced. The exact modality of this is known to God alone, but it is said that the deeds will take on forms fair and foul. *As for those whose scales are heavy* with good deeds—the word *scales* is given in the plural because of its multiple parts, due to how they play the role of the scales—*they are the successful*. A *ḥadīth* says, 'Evil deeds are light, even if there are many; and good deeds are heavy, even if there are few.'

Q. 7:7

[7:9] *And as for those whose scales are light* with evil deeds, *those are the ones who have lost their souls* by squandering their sound innate disposition, *because of how they mistreated Our signs* by denying them.

[7:10] *And We have given you power* to act freely *in the earth, and have appointed for you therein livelihoods*: means by which to live; *little thanks you show.*

[7:11] *And We created you*—meaning your father Adam—*then shaped you* by shaping him; or it can be read literally, as al-Ḥākim preferred, in which case the word *then* would be taken to denote the succession of statements [rather than chronology]; *then We said to the angels, 'Prostrate yourselves before Adam!' So they fell prostrate, all save Iblīs, he was not of those who make prostration*: this was explained earlier.[1]

[7:12] *He said, 'What prevented you from falling prostrate when I commanded you?' He said, 'I am better than him. You created me from fire, while him You created from clay'*: that is, 'The nobility of my constitution prevented me.' He was blind to how He had created Adam with His own hand and breathed His spirit into him. He [Satan] was the first to declare that good and evil can be determined rationally.[2]

[7:13] *Said He*, God through the tongue of an angel, *'Then go down from it*: from the Garden or the heavens; *it is not for you to show pride here, so go forth!* He specified *here* because pride is especially out of place in the realm

1 See Q. 2:34.

2 A jibe at the Muʿtazila and other schools who held this opinion, contrary to the Ashʿarī position that good and evil are determined by revelation.

of those who are brought near to God. It does not mean that there is some other place where pride is appropriate. *Truly, you are among the abased!'*

[7:14] *Said he, 'Reprieve me*—spare me from death—*until the day when they are resurrected'*: meaning all creation, or the abased ones.

[7:15] *Said He, 'Truly, You are of those reprieved'*: such as how the angels are reprieved until the first trumpet blast. It is said that this was not a favourable response to his request, but rather a simple elucidation of something that had already been destined. Others said that he was allowed this for the greater good of the world.

[7:16] *Said he, 'Now, because You have sent me astray*: that is, 'By Your sending me astray' or 'By Your misguidance of me'—he swore an oath by the act of God; *I shall surely sit in ambush for them* as highway robbers do for travellers, *on Your straight path*: the road of Islam.

[7:17] *'Then I shall come upon them from before them and from behind them and from their right and from their left*: he meant that he would do whatever he could to lead them astray. He did not say 'from above them' because that is the direction from which mercy descends, nor 'from beneath them' because approaching from that direction would only frighten them off. *And You will not find most of them thankful* to You by obeying You.*'* He said this based on his own opinion: *And indeed Iblīs proved true his opinion of them* [Q. 34:20].

Q. 7:14

[7:18] *Said He*, meaning God, *'Go forth from it, degraded*: degradation is the worst kind of condemnation; *and banished*: cast out. And by God, *As for those of them who follow you, I shall assuredly fill Hell with all of you'*: He said *all of you* because it applies to most.

[7:19] *And* We said, *'O Adam, dwell, you and your wife, in the Garden, and eat from whence you will, but do not come near this tree, lest you become evildoers'*: this was explained earlier.[1] He did not say 'easefully' this time because the previous mention of it was sufficient.

[7:20] *Then Satan whispered to them*: he casts his whisperings and discourse into the heart; the root meaning of *waswasa* (whisper) is a low voice, whinny or rustle; *that he might manifest*—make plain—*to them that which was hidden to them of their shameful parts*: there had been a light over them to cover them, but it disappeared when they ate from the tree. This indicates that it is blameworthy to expose one's private parts even to one's spouse. *And he said, 'Your Lord prohibited you from* eating from *this tree only lest you become angels* in terms of power and the lack of need for such things

1 See Q. 2:35.

as food. This is not proof that angels are superior to humans, because it was obvious even then that realities are not transformed. What they desired was to attain the innate perfection that angels possess; *or become immortals*: in the Garden.'

[7:21] *And he swore to both of them, 'Truly, I am a sincere advisor to you'*: to swear means to emphasise one's statement by invoking something that is generally revered, as if to say that one's words are just as true as the thing by which one is swearing.

[7:22] *Thus did he lead them on*—thus did he bring them down from their position, or tempt them to eat—*by delusion* from him; *and when they tasted of the tree*, meaning its fruit, *their shameful parts were manifested to them* when their coverings disappeared, *and they began to piece together onto themselves*—onto their private parts—*some of the leaves of the Garden. And their Lord called them, 'Did I not prohibit you from this tree*: this implies that an unqualified prohibition denotes unlawfulness; *and say to you, "Truly, Satan is a manifest enemy to you"?'* This refers to His Words, *Adam, truly this is an enemy of yours*...[Q. 20:117]. Q. 7:21

[7:23] *They said, 'Our Lord, we have wronged ourselves; and if You do not forgive us and have mercy on us, we shall surely be among the lost'*: these are [the Words] which *Thereafter Adam received from his Lord* [Q. 2:37], according to the soundest opinion on the matter.

[7:24] *Said He*, meaning God, *'Go down, each of you an enemy to the other*: that is, mutual enemies, as was discussed earlier.[1] *There will be for you on earth an abode*—a place of settlement—*and enjoyment for a while*: until an appointed time,' as was discussed earlier.

[7:25] *Said He, 'There you shall live, and there you shall die, and from there you shall be brought forth* for the Reckoning.'

[7:26] *O Children of Adam, We have sent down on you*, from heaven by means of such things as rain, *a garment to conceal your shameful parts*: so that you need not recourse to using leaves; *and feathers*: for the production of beautiful garments—the root meaning of *rīsh* (feathers) is beauty and wealth, from *tarayyasha* (to amass wealth); *and the garment of God-fearing*—meaning righteous deeds that protect one from punishment—*that is best*: for it covers one from the calamities of the Hereafter. *That* sending-down *is one of God's signs*—the proofs of His mercy—*that perhaps they will remember* and be admonished.

[7:27] *O Children of Adam, let not Satan tempt you* into going astray, *as*

1 See Q. 2:36.

he caused your parents to go forth from the Garden by his temptation, *stripping them of their garments*, since he was the cause of this, *to manifest to them their shameful parts*: for neither of them had seen the private parts of the other before that. *Truly, he sees you, he and his tribe*—his hosts—*from where you do not see them*: so beware an enemy who sees you though you do not see it. This does not preclude the possibility of their appearing to us in physical forms, for such occurrences are mass-transmitted and affirmed in authentic narrations. *We have made the devils friends*—beloved ones—*of those who do not believe*: because of the correspondence between them.

[7:28] *And when they commit any indecency*, such as how they would expose their private parts when circumambulating the Kaʿba, *they say, 'We found our fathers practising it, and God has enjoined it on us'*: for they claimed to be followers of the religion of Ishmael. *Say: 'God does not enjoin indecency*, as you claim. *Do you say concerning God that which you do not know*: such as claiming that He does enjoin it*?'*

Q. 7:28

[7:29] *Say: 'My Lord enjoins justice* upon me.*' And* He enjoins that you *set your faces* towards the *qibla in every place of worship*: at every time or place of prostration,[1] rather than delaying the prayer beyond its proper time until you get to your official place of worship, as the Jews would—this is how Ibn ʿAbbās interpreted this verse. *And call upon Him, devoting your religion*—your obedience—*to Him. As He brought you into being* at the first creation, *so you will return* when He calls you back for the requital. The similitude here is centred on the simple act of creation without modality.

[7:30] *A party He has guided* to faith, *while another party has deserved to go astray*: the second *party* here is in the *naṣb* grammatical state, marking it as the object of a verb, which can be interpolated as 'He has forsaken' or the like, as the context suggests. *They have taken devils as patrons instead of God*: and they follow them; *and think that they are guided.*

[7:31] *O Children of Adam, don your adornment*—garments to cover your private parts—*at every place of worship*: whether prayer or circumambulation; *and eat and drink, but do not be excessive* by straying to what is unlawful or wasteful. Ibn ʿAbbās (may God be pleased with him) said, 'Eat what you will, and wear what you will, as long as you do not stray into two traits: excess or pride.' Or it refers to declaring what is lawful to be forbidden, for during their *ḥajj* they would circumambulate naked and refrain from eating fat. *Truly, He does not love those who are excessive.*

1 The author explains the word *masjid* here to mean 'venue of prostration', whether physical or temporal.

[7:32] *Say: 'Who has forbidden the adornment of God which He has brought forth* from plants, animals and minerals *for His servants, and the good things*—the enjoyable things—*of provision?'* For you have forbidden His adornment in circumambulation, and His provision during the *ḥajj*. *Say: 'These* good things *are* created *for those who believed during the life of this world* primarily, and also for the disbelievers secondarily, *exclusively* for the believers *on the Day of Resurrection'*; or they are created exclusively for those who will enjoy them, as in this world. *Thus*, by this detailing, *We detail the signs for a folk who have knowledge.*

[7:33] *Say: 'My Lord forbids only indecencies*—meaning things that are grossly vile, such as major sins—*such of them as are apparent*, public, *and such as are hidden*, private, *and sin* in general aside from those specific kinds, *and wrongful transgression*: the word *wrongful* here is meant to impart emphasis, or *transgression* here means pride; *and that you associate with God that for which He never revealed any warrant*: any authority for its association; *and that you say*—invent—*concerning God that which you do not know.'*

Q. 7:32

[7:34] *Every community* that denies the messengers, such as the folk of Mecca, *has a term* for the descent of their punishment. *When their term comes they shall not delay it a single hour, nor shall they bring it forward*: the last clause is independent, since the conditional 'when' can only refer to the future.

[7:35] *O Children of Adam, if there should come to you*—this was explained earlier[1]—*messengers from among you, narrating to you My signs, then whoever fears* idolatry *and makes amends* by rectifying his deeds, *no fear shall befall them* at the Great Calamity, *neither shall they grieve* for what they have left behind in the world.

[7:36] *And those* among you *who deny Our signs and scorn them, those shall be the inhabitants of the Fire, therein they will abide.*

[7:37] *And who does greater evil than he who invents a lie against God* by saying things about Him of which he has no knowledge, *or denies His signs? Those—their portion of the Book shall reach them*—meaning that which is written for them concerning their lifespans, provisions and deeds—*until, when Our messengers come to them*, the Angel of Death and his aides, *to claim them*, to take their spirits, *they will say* reproachfully, *'Where is that upon which you used to call*—where are those gods whom you used to worship—*beside God?' They will say, 'They have gone astray from us*: they have left us, and we cannot benefit from them'; *and they will bear witness against themselves that they were disbelievers.* As for their claim, *By God, our Lord,*

1 See Q. 2:38.

we were never idolaters [Q. 6:23], it will be uttered after the Resurrection.

[7:38] *He will say*—God will say to them on the Day of Resurrection—*'Enter, among* the ranks of *communities of* the disbelieving *jinn and humankind who passed away before you, into the Fire.' Every time a community enters* that Fire, *it curses its sister-community*: those whose religion it followed and thus went astray by emulating; *until, when they have all followed one another there* and been gathered together there, *the last of them* to enter *shall say of the first of them*, addressing God, *'Our Lord, these led us astray*: they paved the way to error for us, and we followed their lead; *so give them a double*—a multiplied—*chastisement of the Fire.' He*, God, *will say, 'For each* of you *will be double* chastisement unto infinity; or the leaders will have double the punishment of a follower because of how they disbelieved and led astray, while the followers will have double the punishment of a leader because of how they disbelieved and blindly followed; or each will have double what the other beholds, for some punishment is outward, and some inward, and each of them will witness only what is outward; this is
Q. 7:38 supported by how He then says *but you do not know.'*

[7:39] *And the first of them shall say to the last of them*—that is, they will address them directly—*'You have no advantage over us*: they will base this on what God said to them—that is, 'We are equal in chastisement and misguidance'; *so taste the chastisement for what you used to earn.'*

[7:40] *Those who deny Our signs and scorn them, truly the gates of heaven shall not be opened for them*: for their spirits, or for their prayers and deeds, which will plummet to the depths of Sijjīn;[1] *nor shall they enter the Garden until the camel passes through the eye of the needle*: that is, it is impossible for them to enter it. *Thus*, with such a requital, *do We requite the sinners.*

[7:41] *Hell shall be their bed, and over them coverings. Thus do We requite the unjust*: He spoke of sin in connection with the deprivation of the Garden, and then injustice in connection with the entrance into the Fire, by way of implying that injustice is the worst kind of sin.

[7:42] *And those who believe and perform righteous deeds—We do not charge any soul beyond its scope*: this is a parenthetical clause, implying that it is no easy feat to reach this level—*those are the inhabitants of the Garden, therein they will abide.*

[7:43] *We shall strip away all rancour*—the enmity and envy that existed among them in this world—*that is in their breasts; and with rivers flowing from beneath them; and they will say* when they see Our favours, *'Praise be to God,*

1 See Q. 83:7.

Who guided us to this: gave us the grace to attain it; *for we would surely never have been guided if God had not guided us. The messengers of our Lord did surely bring the truth*: and this favour is ours thanks to their direction.' *And they will be called* after they enter the Garden, *'This is the Garden. You have inherited it* from the inhabitants of the Fire *for what you used to do*; or it has come into your possession without being earned by labour, like inheritance.'

[7:44] *And the inhabitants of the Garden will call to the inhabitants of the Fire* in reproach, *'We have found that which our Lord promised us* through the tongues of His messengers *to be true. Have you found that* chastisement *which your Lord promised to be true?' They will say: 'Yes!' And then a crier shall proclaim between them, 'God's curse is on the evildoers,* [7:45] *who bar* other people *from God's way*—His religion—*desiring it crooked*: by so calling it in order to dissuade others from following it, or by sowing doubt about it, or they pursue it crookedly, or desire a religion other than it; *disbelieving in the Hereafter.'*

[7:46] *And between them*—between the Garden and the Fire—*is a barrier*: preventing the affects of either from reaching the other. *And on the Heights* of the barrier, meaning the upper parts of it—and we believe in it, Q. 7:44
even though the Garden is in the Pedestal while the Fire is in the lowest depths—*are men* whose good and bad deeds are exactly equal, *who know each* of the inhabitants of the Garden and the Fire *by their mark*: their sign, such as the whitening or blackening of the face; *and they will call to the inhabitants of Paradise, 'Peace be upon you!' They have not entered it, although they aspire* to enter it. Ḥudhayfa is reported to have said, 'They will enter it in the end.'

[7:47] *And when their eyes are turned towards the inhabitants of the Garden, they will say*, invoking God's protection, *'Our Lord, do not assign us with the evildoing folk* therein.'

[7:48] *And those of the Heights will call to certain men*, the chiefs of the disbelievers, *whom they know by their mark, saying, 'Your masses* of wealth and helpers, *and your pride* towards the truth, *have not availed you*: protected you from the chastisement. Then they will turn their attention to the weak folk among the believers, and say to the disbelievers:

[7:49] *'Are these the ones of whom you swore that God would never grant them mercy?'* Then they will say to those weak ones, *'Enter the Garden. No fear shall come upon you, nor shall you grieve.'*

[7:50] *And the inhabitants of the Fire will call out to the inhabitants of the Garden, 'Pour on us some water, or some of that which God has provided you*: meaning food or drink besides water.' *They will say, 'God has forbidden both to the disbelievers*:

[7:51] *'Those who took their religion*—the true religion—*for a diversion and a game*: this was explained earlier,[1] or it means they took their customs as religion; *and whom the life of this world has deluded*: so that they forgot the Hereafter.*' Therefore today We have forgotten them*: We shall treat them as though We have forgotten them, abandoning them in the chastisement; *just as they forgot the encounter of this day of theirs* by denying it, *and because they used to deny Our signs.*

[7:52] *And indeed We have brought them a Book*—the Qur'ān—*which We have detailed*, explained its edicts, *with knowledge* from Us of what is detailed therein, and which is also *a guidance and a mercy for a folk who believe.*

[7:53] *Are they waiting for anything but its fulfilment*: for that which it heralds to come to pass, confirming the truth of it*? On the day when its fulfilment comes*, namely the Day of Resurrection, *those who were forgetful of it*, who declined to believe in it and act according to it, *before* that day *shall say, 'Truly, our Lord's messengers came with the truth*: and we belied them. *Have we then any intercessors, that they might intercede for us* today, *or might we*
Q. 7:51 *be returned* to the world *that we might act otherwise than we used to act?' Truly, they have lost their souls*: by spending their lives in disbelief; *and that which they used to invent has failed them*: for their gods have not availed them aught.

[7:54] *Truly, your Lord is God, Who created the heavens and the earth in* the span of *six days* in the reckoning of this world, for days did not yet exist then; or it means 'six measures of time', as in, *Whoever turns his back to them on that day…* [Q. 8:16]; He did it gradually in order to encourage deliberation, and so that the angels could witness it stage by stage and contemplate it; *then rose above the Throne* in a manner befitting His majesty without any 'how'; or it means 'presided'. The Throne is the body that surrounds all other bodies; some say it means the realm of divine sovereignty (*mulk*). *He cloaks the night with the day*, and vice versa, which He omitted because it is obvious, or because the wording implies both;[2] *each following the other in swift pursuit*: as though they are upon each other's heels without any space between them; *and* He created *the sun and the moon and the stars, made subservient by His command*: His decree of fate. *His is the creation* of the heavens mentioned here, *and the command* of this subservience. *Blessed*—sublime and magnificent—*be God, the Lord of the Worlds!*

[7:55] *Call upon your Lord humbly and quietly*: the soundest position is that raising the voice when supplicating is disliked. *Truly, He loves not*

1 See Q. 6:32.

2 In the Arabic there is no preposition equivalent to 'with', but rather 'day' and 'night' are both direct objects of the verb, and thus could be considered interchangeable.

the transgressors: those who go beyond the bounds of what they are commanded to do, such as requesting things that are not on their level, or supplicating for too long, as is stated in a *ḥadīth*, or such as raising the voice when supplicating.

[7:56] *And work not corruption in the land* by sinning *after it has been set right* by the legislation of edicts, or after it has been created in the soundest state; *and call upon Him in fear* of His punishment, *and in hope* of His reward. *Truly, the mercy of God*—His reward—*is near to the virtuous*: the obedient.

[7:57] *He it is Who sends the winds, unfolding*: this can be read as *bushran* (meaning 'bearing rain') or as *nushuran* (meaning 'spreading') or as *nasharan* (meaning 'mustering clouds'); *before*—ahead of—*His mercy*: meaning rain, for the easterly wind produces clouds, while the northerly wind gathers them, the southerly wind causes them to rain, and the westerly wind disperses them. *Until, when they bear heavy clouds*—when the winds bear clouds heavy with rain—*We lead it*: one such cloud; He switched from the third to first person to draw attention to how this is a sign of His perfect omnipotence and wisdom, as in similar passages; Q. 7:56 *to a dead land* where no benefit can be found, *and then We send down water thereon, and bring forth thereby*—by that water, or in that land—*fruits of every kind. Just so*, with this bringing forth and this revival, *We shall bring forth the dead* from their graves to life with water like semen, *so that you might remember* that the One Who can do the former can also do the latter.

[7:58] *As for the good land*, the fertile soil, *its vegetation comes forth by the leave*—by the will—*of its Lord*: swiftly and abundantly, like the believer who benefits from admonition. *As for the bad*—the poor soil, like the disbeliever who does not benefit from it—*it comes forth only miserably*: scantly and devoid of benefit. Both are by God's leave, and the purpose of the distinction between them is to teach us good manners. *Even so, We dispense*—explain and repeat—*the signs for a folk who are thankful* for His favours through contemplating them.

[7:59] *Indeed, We sent Noah*—the first prophet God sent after Enoch, when he was aged fifty or forty—*to his people. He said, 'O my people, worship God* alone*! You have no god other than Him. Truly, I fear for you the chastisement of an awful day*: the Resurrection.'

[7:60] *The council*—the nobles—*of his people said, 'Truly, We see you in manifest error*: for abandoning the religion of your forefathers.'

[7:61] *He said, 'O my people, there is no error in me*: not even the slightest amount of it; *but I am* rightly guided, for I am *a messenger from the Lord of the Worlds*.

[7:62] *'I convey to you the messages of my Lord, and I counsel you; for I know from God* through revelation *what you know not* concerning the Attributes of His subtle kindness and overwhelming power.

[7:63] *'Do you then* deny, and *marvel that a reminder*—a counsel—*from your Lord should come to you through* the tongue of *a man from among you, that he may warn you* of the dire consequence of sin, *and that you may fear* sin, *and that you might be shown mercy* by virtue of this fear*?'*

[7:64] *But they denied him, and so We delivered him* from the Flood *and those with him in the Ark*—eighty or ninety people in all—*and We drowned those who denied Our signs. Truly, they were a people blind*: their hearts were blind to understanding God's signs.

[7:65] *And* We sent *to* the people of *ʿĀd their brother*—their kinsmen, or one of them—*Hūd. He said, 'O my people, worship God! You have no god other than Him. Will you not fear* God*?'*

[7:66] *The council*, the nobles, *those of his people who disbelieved*—this
Q. 7:62 implies that some of them did believe—*said, 'Truly, we see you* to be mired *in folly, and we truly deem you to be*—we know you to be—*of the liars.'*

[7:67] *He said, 'O my people, there is no folly in me, but I am* of perfectly sound mind, for I am *a messenger from the Lord of the Worlds.*

[7:68] *'I convey to you the messages of my Lord, and I am your truthful advisor* regarding this message.

[7:69] *'Or do you then* deny, and *marvel that a reminder from your Lord should come to you through* the tongue of *a man from among you, that he may warn you? And remember* His favour, *when He made you vicegerents after the people of Noah*—upon earth, or in their former dwellings—*and increased your stature in extension*: in physical height, strength and wealth. *Remember then God's bounties, so that you might prosper* by their remembrance.*'*

[7:70] *They said, 'Have you come to us* intending *that we should worship God alone, and forsake what our fathers worshipped*: their idols*? Then bring upon us what you promise us*—meaning the implied chastisement—*if you are of the truthful.'*

[7:71] *He said, 'Already, terror*—chastisement—*and wrath from your Lord have fallen on you*: have become incumbent upon you. *Do you dispute with me concerning* meaningless *names which you have named* as gods, *you and your fathers, for which*—for these names or their worship—*God has not revealed any warrant? Then await* the chastisement. *Truly, I shall be with you waiting.'*

[7:72] *So We delivered him and those with him by a mercy from Us, and We cut the root of those who denied Our signs*: the phrase *qaṭʿ al-dābir* literally means 'to cut the thing that exists behind', meaning 'to annihilate from the root'.

[7:73] *And* We sent *to* the tribe of *Thamūd their brother*—their kinsman—*Ṣāliḥ. He said, 'O my people, worship God! You have no god other than Him. Truly, there has come to you a clear proof*—a prophetic miracle—*from your Lord* of my truthfulness: *this is the she-camel of God, a sign for you*: the attribution to God was meant as a mark of honour for the she-camel. It emerged from a rock before their eyes on the festival day when they asked for it as a sign that they might believe. *Leave her to graze throughout God's earth, and do not touch her with harm, lest you be seized by a painful chastisement* on a terrible day.

[7:74] *'And remember* His favour: *how He made you vicegerents after ʿĀd* in their dwellings, *and gave you habitations in the land, making castles in its plains* for summer residences, *and hewing its mountains into houses* for winter residences. *So remember God's bounties and do not be degenerate*—do not engage in excessive corruption—*in the earth, seeking corruption'*: this was explained earlier.[1]

[7:75] *Said the council*, the nobles, *of those of his people who were proud*—too proud to have faith—*to those who were oppressed*, their subjects, *such of them as believed, 'Are you aware that Ṣāliḥ has been sent from his Lord?'* They asked this mockingly. *They said, 'Truly, we believe in the message with which he has been sent'*: they said this instead of simply saying 'Yes' by way of implying that the answer ought to have been obvious. Q. 7:73

[7:76] *Said the ones who were proud, 'Truly, we are disbelievers of that which you believe!'*

[7:77] *So they hamstrung*—slaughtered—*the she-camel* with the consent of them all, *and flouted*—arrogantly disregarded—*the commandment of their Lord*: meaning his words, *Leave her to graze*... [Q. 7:73]; *and said, 'O Ṣāliḥ, bring upon us that which you promise us*—meaning his words *lest you be seized*... [Q. 7:73]—*if you are indeed a messenger.'*

[7:78] *So the Trembling seized them*: first the earthquake, and then the Cry, for He says, *And those who did evil were seized by the Cry* [Q. 11:67], so that their very hearts were torn apart within their breasts; *and they lay in their habitations*—their land—*lifeless*: motionless corpses.

[7:79] *So he turned his back on them and said*, after they had been destroyed, *'O my people, I conveyed to you the message of my Lord, and gave you sincere advice; but you do not love sincere advisors'*: this was akin to how our Prophet (may God bless him and grant him peace) spoke to the idolaters who had been slain at Badr; or he may have said it as a lament.

1 See Q. 2:60.

[7:80] *And* We sent *Lot, when he said to his people, 'Do you commit abomination*—this is an allusion to sodomy—*such as no one in all the worlds ever committed before you?* They were the first people ever to engage in it.

[7:81] *'Do you come lustfully to men*—this is an allusion to how the sexual impulse ought to be borne of a desire for procreation, not mere lust—*instead of women? Nay, you are a wanton folk*: and it is your wantonness that has incited you to do so.'

[7:82] *And the only response of his people was that they said, 'Expel them,* Lot and his followers, *from your city. Truly, they are folk who would be pure* of this act.'

[7:83] *So We delivered him and his family*—those who believed in him—*except his wife*, who was a disbeliever named Wāhila; *she was of those who stayed behind* in their homes, and so was destroyed.

[7:84] *And We rained upon them a rain* of stones. *So behold what was the end of the sinners*: and reflect upon it.

Q. 7:80

[7:85] *And* We sent *to* the folk of *Midian* son of Abraham *their brother*—their kinsman—*Shuʿayb. He said, 'O my people, worship God! You have no god other than Him. Truly, there has come to you a clear proof*—a prophetic miracle—*from your Lord*: its nature is not described in the Qur'ān. There are narrations about how the staff of Moses (may God grant him peace) fought the dragon, and how the sheep which he delivered to Shuʿayb all bore young with black heads and white bodies, as he had promised they would; but these ought to be counted as prophetic miracles of Moses to affirm his prophethood, because they occurred after the prophethood of Shuʿayb had already been established. *So give full measure and weight, and do not defraud people's goods*: do not withhold what is rightfully theirs—it is said that the custom of his people was to always weigh and measure unfairly; *and do not work corruption in the earth* by sinning *after it has been set right*: this was explained earlier.[1] *That* enjoined action *is better for you, if you are believers*: as for the disbeliever, there is no good in him.

[7:86] *'And do not sit in every path, threatening* those who come to Shuʿayb to follow him *and barring from God's way those who believe in Him, and desiring that it be crooked*: using it to stray from what is right, as was explained earlier. *And remember* His favour *when you were but few* in numbers and other matters, *and then He multiplied you* with wealth and offspring. *And behold what was the end of the agents of corruption*: and reflect on it.

[7:87] *'And if there is a party of you who believe in that with which I have*

1 See Q. 7:56.

been sent, and a party who do not believe, then be patient until God judges between us by chastising the disbelievers and succouring us. *He is the best of judges.'*

[7:88] *Said the council of those of his people who were disdainful, 'Surely we will expel you, O Shuʿayb, and those who believe with you, from our city, unless you return to our creed'*: that is, 'unless you convert to our creed'; or they were addressing the majority of the group, for Shuʿayb was never a follower of their creed. *He*, Shuʿayb, *said, 'What, even though we are averse?* Could we bear to do so, though we detest it?

[7:89] *'We would be forging a lie against God if we were to return*, or even consider returning, *to your creed, after God has delivered us from it. It is not* right *for us to return to it, unless God our Lord wills* for us to do so. *Our Lord embraces all things through His knowledge. In God we have put our trust* that He will aid us. *Our Lord, decide between us and our people*: send down upon each of us what we deserve; *for You are the best of deciders.'*

[7:90] *Said the council of those of his people who disbelieved, 'If you follow Shuʿayb, you shall truly be losers*: because you will lose out on your unjust profiteering.*'* Q. 7:88

[7:91] *So the Trembling*, the earthquake, *seized them, and they lay motionless in their habitations*, slain by all manner of chastisement—clouds that rained down brands of fire, a cry from the heavens, and a trembling of the earth.

[7:92] *Those who denied Shuʿayb—it was as if they had never dwelt there* in their homes. *Those who denied Shuʿayb, they were the losers*: contrary to what they claimed.

[7:93] *So he turned back on them*—as in the story of Ṣāliḥ—*and said, 'O my people, I conveyed to you the messages of my Lord and advised you sincerely, and you disbelieved; why, then, should I grieve for a disbelieving folk?'*

[7:94] *And We did not send a prophet to any city* whose folk then belied him, *but that We seized its people with misery*, hunger, *and hardship*, sickness, *so that they might be humble*: and desist from their prideful ways.

[7:95] *Then We gave them in place of evil*, tribulation and misfortune, *good*, security and comfort, *until they multiplied* in wealth and numbers, *and said, 'Hardship and happiness befell our fathers before* and we are like them.*' So We seized them suddenly, while they perceived not* that the chastisement was nigh.

[7:96] *Yet had the people of the towns* to whom messengers were sent *believed, and been fearful* of sin, *We would have truly opened upon them blessings from the heaven and the earth*: that is, from all directions; *but they denied* Our messengers, *and so We seized them on account of what they used to earn.*

[7:97] *Do the people of the towns feel secure from the coming of Our might*—Our chastisement—*upon them at night while they are sleeping?*

[7:98] *Or do the people of the towns feel secure from the coming of Our might upon them in the daytime*—in the hours of midmorning—*while they are playing?* That is the time when they are busy with their worldly affairs.

[7:99] *And so do they feel secure from God's plotting?* This is a figure of speech for how He takes the servant to task when he least expects it. *None feels secure from God's plotting but the folk who are losers*: who have lost their innate disposition.

[7:100] *Has it not been shown to those who inherit the land*—those who dwell in the homes of those who came before them—*after those who inhabited it* were destroyed, *that if We willed, We could smite them* with tribulation *for their sins*: just as We did to those who were before them; *and seal up their hearts so that they do not hear* the admonition with receptivity*?*

[7:101] *Those towns* aforementioned, *We relate to you some of their tidings. Their messengers brought them clear proofs*, patent prophetic miracles,
but they would not believe, when they brought them to them, *in what they
had denied before*: but rather clung to their disbelief. *Thus does God seal*
Q. 7:98 *up the hearts of the disbelievers*: both the inheritors and those from whom
they inherited.

[7:102] *And We did not find in most of them*—the communities of old—*any covenant*: any loyalty to the covenant between them of God or His messengers. *Nay, We found that most of them were truly wicked folk*: outside the bounds of obedience to Us.

[7:103] *Then We sent after them*, after those messengers, *Moses with Our signs*, his prophetic miracles, *to Pharaoh and his council*: the nobles of his people; for if they had submitted, the subjects would have followed them; *but they mistreated them*: mistreated those signs because of their disbelief. *So behold*, O Muḥammad,[1] *what was the end of those who work corruption.*

[7:104] *And Moses said, 'O Pharaoh, I am a messenger from the Lord of the World,* [7:105] *as one for whom it is right*, because of the message, *to say nothing but the truth about God*: and to attribute nothing but the truth to Him. *I have come to you with a clear proof*—a prophetic miracle—*from your Lord. So send forth with me the Children of Israel* that we might go to the Holy Land.*'* Pharaoh had burdened them with difficult labours.

[7:106] *Said he*, Pharaoh, *'If you have come with a sign, then produce it, if you are of those who speak the truth.'*

[7:107] *Then he cast down his staff and lo! it was a serpent*—a huge

1 The verb is a singular imperative, hence this interpretation.

snake—*manifest*: it is said that it was hairy, and when it opened its mouth its jaws stretched eighty cubits wide. It headed towards Pharaoh, who fled with his people, twenty-five thousand of whom died.

[7:108] *And he drew forth his hand* from his pocket and placing it inside, *and lo! it was white*—shining brighter than the sun—*for the beholders*: that is, it was not naturally that colour, since he was dark-skinned.

[7:109] *The council of Pharaoh's people said*, in accord with his own verdict as described in *al-Shuʿarāʾ*,[1] *'Truly, this man is a cunning sorcerer,* [7:110] *who would expel you* Egyptians *from your land* of Egypt. *So what do you command?'* What counsel can you offer as to how to deal with him?

[7:111] *They said*, after coming to an agreement, *'Put him and his brother off a while, and send into the towns* of Upper Egypt *summoners* to gather their sorcerers, [7:112] *to bring you every cunning sorcerer.'*

[7:113] *And the sorcerers*, after being summoned, *came to Pharaoh, saying, 'Truly, there will be a reward for us if we are the victors* over Moses.'

[7:114] *He said, 'Yes,* you shall be rewarded, *and truly you shall be of those brought near.'* Q. 7:108

[7:115] *They said*, certain of their victory, or out of professional courtesy, *'O Moses, either you cast* your staff first, *or we shall cast* our instruments of sorcery.'

[7:116] *He,* Moses, *said, 'Cast!'* [This was either] to show them courtesy or to humour them. *And when they cast, they put a spell upon the people's eyes*: they deceived their eyes with false illusions; *and overawed them*: striking them with fear. There were fifteen thousand of them in all, each one having a staff and a rope, which they turned into snakes. We discussed the nature of this sorcery in *Sūrat al-Baqara*;[2] *and produced a mighty sorcery.*

[7:117] *And We revealed to Moses* [*saying*], *'Cast your staff'*: and so he cast it. *And lo! it swallowed up the illusions they were creating.*

[7:118] *Thus did the truth come to pass*: thus was it established; *and that which they were doing was proved false.*

[7:119] *Thus were they*, Pharaoh and his people, *defeated there, becoming humiliated*: abased and overwhelmed.

[7:120] *And the sorcerers fell down in prostration*: this does not mean that they were compelled to prostrate against their will, for what it means is that the prophetic miracle of the prophet moved them to prostrate willingly.

1 See Q. 26:34–35.
2 See Q. 2:102.

[7:121] *They said, 'We believe in the Lord of the Worlds,* [7:122] *the Lord of Moses and Aaron'*: not the supposed lord of the Egyptians. Note that it is permitted for two prophets to exist at the same time, but not two imams [of the entire polity of the Muslims], because if the two imams were to engage in independent reasoning (*ijtihād*) on a particular matter and reach two different conclusions, this would lead to disunity.

[7:123] *Pharaoh said, 'Have you believed in him before I gave you leave? Truly, this is a plot you have plotted* with Moses *in the city* before you left it, *that you may expel its people*, the Egyptians, *from it* and claim Egypt for your own. *But you shall come to know* the dire consequence of this, which is:

[7:124] *'I shall assuredly have your hands and feet cut off on opposite sides*—the right hand and the left foot—*then I shall have every one of you crucified.'*

[7:125] *They said, 'Truly, to our Lord we shall be restored* in death, and so we do not fear your threat.

[7:126] *'You are vindictive towards us only because we have believed in the*
Q. 7:121 *signs of our Lord when they came to us.* Then they turned to God and said,
Our Lord, pour out onto us patience: that we might adhere to Your religion
with constancy; *and take us to You as men who have submitted.'*

[7:127] *Then the council of Pharaoh's people said*, to goad him, *'Will you leave Moses and his people to work corruption in the land* by calling them to worship other than you, *and flout you and your gods?'* This referred to the idols he had made for them to worship as a means of drawing nearer to him. The Torah indicates that he appointed chiefs over every tribe who were called their gods. *He*, Pharaoh, *said, 'We shall slaughter their sons and spare their women*: keep them alive to serve us, as we did with them already. *Truly, we shall vanquish them!'*

[7:128] *Moses said to his people* when they were downcast upon hearing Pharaoh's words, *'Seek help in God and be patient. Truly, the earth is God's and He bequeaths it to whom He will from among His servants. The sequel*—the good outcome—*belongs to those who are wary.'*

[7:129] *They*, his people, *said, 'We suffered harm* by this slaughtering of men and sparing of women *before you came to us* with the message, *and after you came to us.' He*, Moses, *said, 'Perhaps your Lord will destroy your enemy and make you successors in the land*—in their kingdom—*that He may observe how you shall act*: and whether you will be righteous or wicked.'

[7:130] *And We seized the people of Pharaoh with years of dearth*: famine and drought; *and* great *scarcity of fruits, so that they might remember*: and desist.

[7:131] *But whenever goodness*, such as wealth, *befell them, they said, 'This belongs to us'*: rather than [attributing it to] God's grace; *and if an evil thing*—

a tribulation—*smote them, they would augur ill of Moses and those with him*: He said *goodness* rather than 'a good thing', and used the word *when* rather than 'if', in order to allude to its frequency, and to refer to the essence of goodness itself, in contrast to evil. *Surely their ill augury is with God*—from God alone—*but most of them do not know*: the word *ṭā'ir* (ill augury) is a collective noun, literally meaning 'the hardship, happiness, benefit and harm that the birds (*ṭayr*) bring'.

[7:132] *And they said* to Moses, *'Whatever sign you bring us*, as you claim, *to cast a spell upon us*, to delude our eyes, *therewith, we will not believe in you'*: and so he prayed against them.

[7:133] *So We unleashed upon them the flood*: the heavy rains that covered their houses and trees alone, while all others were spared, for seven days; *and the locusts* which consumed their property, even the nails in their doors; *and the lice*: the word *qummal* here means adult gnats, infant locusts, mites or lice; *and the frogs* which filled their houses and pots so that they were unable to eat; *and the blood* into which their water was transformed, even if they drank from the same cups as the Muslims did. Q. 7:132 *Distinct signs; but they were too scornful* to believe, *and were a sinful folk.*

[7:134] *And when the terror fell upon them*—meaning all of these signs as well as the plague, which was the sixth—*they said, 'O Moses, pray to your Lord for our sake by* the right of *the covenant which He has made with you*: meaning prophethood and the answering of your prayer. *Truly,* by God, *if you remove from us the terror, we will surely believe in you and let the Children of Israel go with you.'*

[7:135] *But when We removed the terror from them to a term which they should reach*, whereupon they would be chastised by them once more, or the term of their deaths, *lo! they were already reneging*: they were swift to break their oath.

[7:136] *So We exacted*—We determined to exact—*retribution from them, and therefore We drowned them in the sea*—the word *yam* means 'deep sea'—*for they denied Our signs and were heedless of them.*

[7:137] *And We bequeathed upon the people*—the progeny of the people—*who were oppressed* because of the slaying of the prophets and such things, *the eastern parts of the land* of Syria *and the western parts thereof which We had blessed* with ample provision. *And the fair word of your Lord*—the promise of succour—*was fulfilled for the Children of Israel because they endured patiently* the hardships of the Egyptians; *and We destroyed utterly what Pharaoh and his people had been constructing, and what they had been planting*: meaning their gardens and orchards.

[7:138] *And We brought the Children of Israel across the sea*: and drowned their enemies; *and they came upon a people cleaving in devotion to idols they had*: they were the remnants of the Amalekites, whom Moses had been commanded to fight. *They said, 'O Moses, make for us a god*—an idol to worship—*just as they have gods.' He*, Moses, *said, 'Truly, you are an ignorant folk*: the way of ignorance is ever raising its head among you.

[7:139] *'Truly, as for these* worshippers, *their way will be destroyed, and what they have been doing*—meaning their religion—*is in vain.'*

[7:140] *He said, 'Shall I seek other than God as a god*—an object of worship—*for you, when He has favoured you above all the worlds?'*

[7:141] *And* remember *when We delivered you from the people of Pharaoh, who were inflicting upon you terrible chastisement, slaying your sons and sparing your women* for servitude; *and therein*, in that deliverance, *was a tremendous trial*, test, *from your Lord*: this was explained earlier.

[7:142] *And We appointed for Moses* the passing of *thirty nights*: the month
Q. 7:138 of Dhū al-Qaʿda, for the revelation of the Torah. He fasted the month and then cleaned his teeth with a stick on the last day, and the change in his breath brought on by fasting departed; *and completed them with ten* for Dhū al-Ḥijja, so that he would fast them and his breath would change again. *Thus was the time appointed by his Lord concluded as forty nights* in total. Or it could be that the revelation and communion took place in those ten. The reason for this last sentence is either to add emphasis, or to dispel the suggestion that the *ten* meant hours, or was included in the *thirty*. This is akin to His Words in *Sūrat Ḥā Mīm* [*Fuṣṣilat*]: *in four days* [Q. 41:10]. *And Moses said to his brother Aaron, 'Succeed me*—be my vicegerent—*among my people, and be righteous*: gently encourage them to be obedient; *and do not follow the way of the agents of corruption.'*

[7:143] *And when Moses came at Our appointed time* which We had decreed for him, namely the Day of ʿArafa, *and his Lord spoke with him*—and he desired to meet with Him—*he said, 'My Lord, show me* Yourself by making me able to see You, *that I may gaze upon You!'* This is proof that it is possible to see Him, since the prophets would never request something that is impossible, especially something that is tantamount to ignorance of God. Some argued that he only said this to refute those who said, *'Show us God openly'* [Q. 4:153]; but this is false because in that case he would have been obliged to declare their ignorance, rather than show such impudence. Note that vision is a trait closely bound to the organ of sight, not a power within it, as can be deduced with the least amount of contemplation; and therefore it is possible for God to make it capable of seeing Him.

This settles the dispute, since those who deny it only deny that He can be seen with this particular eye. It is always better to reconcile disputes. *Said He, 'You shall not see Me* in this world, because of the *ḥadīth* to that effect. This was discussed in *Sūrat al-Anʿām.*[1] *But behold the mountain*: and its immense stability. *If it remains in its place* upon beholding Me, *then you shall see Me'*: again, this implied that it was possible, since it was contingent upon the stability of the mountain, which was certainly possible. Even if we argued that it was impossible because it would amount to simultaneous motion and stillness, namely stability at the moment of perception, it would not harm our argument because it would not prove a general rule. *And when his Lord revealed Himself to the mountain*—when He showed it a tiny sliver of His light—*He levelled it to the ground* so that it was rendered flat, *and Moses fell down senseless*: unconscious. *And when he recovered his senses he said, 'Glory be to You!* I declare Your transcendence beyond all that does not befit You. *I repent to You* of making requests without permission, *and I am the first of the believers* of my people, or the first to believe that You cannot be seen in this world.*'* Q. 7:144

[7:144] *He said, 'O Moses, I have elected you*—chosen you—*from among the people*: from among the people of your time—Aaron neither partook in the divine communion nor was given a Law; *for My messages*—My revelation—*and My Speech* without an intermediary. *So take what I have given you*—the message—*and be of the thankful* for it.*'* He gave it to him on the Day of Sacrifice.

[7:145] *And We inscribed for him in the Tablets* of the Torah *about all things* pertaining to the religion which they required, *as an admonition and a detailing of all things*, whether edicts or other matters, saying, *'Take them*, the Tablets, *firmly*, with strength and resolve, *and enjoin your people*, recommend to them, *to adhere to the fairest of it*: meaning the best qualities described in it, such as forgiveness and patience; or it is akin to saying, 'Summer is hotter than winter.' *I shall show you the abode of the wicked folk* in Egypt, that you might reflect on it.

[7:146] *'I shall turn away from My signs*—prevent them from understanding the signs on the horizons and within themselves—*those who behave arrogantly in the earth without right*: unlike the justifiable pride of a believer towards a disbeliever; *and if they see every sign* sent down, *they do not believe in it* out of stubbornness; *and if they see the way of rectitude*—guidance—*they do not adopt it as a way; and if they see the way of error, they adopt it*

1 See Q. 6:103.

as a way. That is because they have denied Our signs, and were heedless of them: instead of contemplating them.

[7:147] *'Those who deny Our signs and the encounter*—the abode—*in the Hereafter: their deeds have failed. Shall they be requited anything but what they used to do?'*

[7:148] *And the people of Moses*, meaning the Samaritans, *after him*, after he went into the mountains, *made of their ornaments*, the jewellery they had borrowed from the Egyptians and then claimed as their own when they were destroyed, *a calf, a body* of flesh and blood, or a golden body, *which lowed*: it made the sound of a cow, or something like it, when the wind blew through it from the back to the front and came out of its mouth, as Ibn ʿAbbās related. Then the dust of the tracks of Gabriel's horse fell upon it and brought it to life. *Did they not see*, when they took it as a god, *that it spoke not to them, nor guided them to any way? Yet they took it as such, and were evildoers.*

Q. 7:147

[7:149] *And when the regret fell into their hands*: this is an allusion to the remorse a man feels that prompts him to bite his fingernails anxiously; *and they saw*—knew with certainty—*that they had gone astray, they said, 'Unless our Lord is merciful to us* by accepting our repentance, *and forgives us, surely we shall be among the losers.'*

[7:150] *And when Moses returned to his people, angry* with them *and bitterly grieved* because of what God had told him, as detailed in *Sūrat Ṭā Hā*,[1] *he said* to them, *'Evil is that which you have followed in my place*—by worshipping the calf—*after I had gone. Would you hasten on the command*—the promise—*of your Lord?'* This refers to the forty days, or to the promise of His wrath. Note that to hasten means to seek something before its time has come. It is blameworthy; and if it is ever praised in the context of good things, then what is meant is promptness, which means to do something at the very first moment of its proper time. *And he cast*, threw, *down the Tablets, and he seized his brother by the head*, the hair, *dragging him toward him*: because he thought he had done a poor job of preventing them. *He*, Aaron, *said*, to appease him, '*Son of my mother!* They were full-blood brothers, Aaron the elder by three years. *Truly, the people judged me weak, and they were close to killing me* when I tried to stop them. *Do not make my enemies gloat over my misfortune* by disgracing me, *and do not count me among the evildoing folk*: by punishing me.*'*

[7:151] *He said*, when he saw that Aaron was innocent, *'My Lord, for-*

1 See Q. 20:85.

give me for what I did with the Tablets, *and my brother* if he fell short, *and admit us into Your mercy, for You are the Most Merciful of the merciful.'* Then God said:

[7:152] *Truly, those who chose the calf* as a god, *wrath shall come upon them from their Lord*: by the command that they slay themselves; *and abasement in the life of this world*: such as their continued estrangement from their home, and the deprivations of their progeny. *Even so We requite those who invent lies*: such as how they said, *This is your God and the God of Moses* [Q. 20:88].

[7:153] *But those who commit evil deeds* such as idolatry and sin, *and repent thereafter and believe* with sincere faith, *truly your Lord thereafter*—after that repentance and sincerity—*is truly Forgiving, Merciful.*

[7:154] *And when the anger abated*, quieted and ceased, *from Moses, he took the Tablets, and in their copy*, their written copies, *there was guidance and mercy for all those who hold their Lord in awe*: those who fear Him.

[7:155] *And Moses chose of his people seventy men for Our appointed time*: to apologise for worshipping the calf; or to demand the beatific vision, for they said, 'Take some of us to witness how God speaks to you,' and then after they heard Him speaking to him they said, 'Show us God openly,' and so the thunderbolt seized them. *But when the Trembling*—the thunderbolt—*seized them* and caused them to die, *he said, 'My Lord, had You willed You would have destroyed them long before*: before this calamity, or 'Before we had seen what we have seen'; *and me too*: this indicates that he meant this in the sense of: 'If only You had done it.' *Will You destroy us for what the foolish ones among us have done*: by worshipping the calf or demanding the beatific vision? *It is but Your trial*—Your test, for You created the lowing of the calf, and allowed them to hear Your speech so that they desired to see You—*whereby You send astray whom You will, and guide whom You will. You are our Protector*: the One Who sees to our affairs; *so forgive us and have mercy on us, for You are the Best of all who show forgiveness*: You can exchange the bad deed for the good.

Q. 7:152

[7:156] *'And prescribe*, affirm, *for us in this world good*, health, *and in the Hereafter*: nearness to You. *We have turned to You*: we have come back to You.*' He said*—God said in response to this—*'My chastisement*—*I smite with it whom I will, and My mercy embraces all things* in this world, even inanimate objects; *and so I shall prescribe it*—affirm My mercy in the Hereafter—*for those who fear* sin *and pay zakāt*: He singled this out because it was especially difficult for them; *and those who believe in* all *Our signs.*

[7:157] *'Those who follow the Messenger* with respect to God, *the unlettered Prophet* with respect to us, who neither reads nor writes, unlike all the other messengers, *whom they will find inscribed* with his name and attributes *in their Torah and Gospel, enjoining them to decency and forbidding them indecency, making lawful for them the good things*, the pleasant things that were forbidden to them, *and making unlawful for them the vile things*, those things that sound nature finds repulsive, *and relieving them of their burden and the shackles that they used to bear*: the difficult responsibilities that were like shackles on their necks, such as the obligation of retribution for accidents as well as deliberate injuries, and the amputation of sinful limbs, and the cutting of any place touched by impure matter. *Then those who believe in him and honour him*, venerate him, *and help him, and follow the light*, the Qur'ān, *that has been revealed with him*—with his prophethood, meaning the Qur'ān, or with his following, meaning the Sunna—*they are the ones who will prosper*: and win salvation.'

[7:158] *Say: 'O people, I am the Messenger of God to you all, of Him to Whom belongs the kingdom of the heavens and the earth. There is no god but Him. He gives life and makes to die. Believe, then, in God and His Messenger, the unlet-*
Q. 7:158 *tered Prophet who believes in God and His Words*—all of His Books—*and follow him, so that you might be guided.'*

[7:159] *And among the people of Moses there is a community*—a group from the people of his time, such as Ibn Salām—*who guide* people *by the truth* to it, *and act justly according to it* in their verdicts.

[7:160] *And We divided them*—the children of Israel—*into twelve tribes, communities*: twelve tribes from the twelve sons of Jacob. *And We revealed to Moses, when his people asked him for water* in the wilderness, *'Strike the rock with your staff.'* So he struck it, *and there gushed forth from it twelve fountains; each people*—each tribe—*knew their drinking-place. And We made the clouds overshadow them* to protect them from the sun, *and We sent down to them manna and quails, saying, 'Eat of the good things We have provided for you'*: but they did not give thanks. *And they did not wrong Us* with their ingratitude, *but they wronged themselves.*

[7:161] *And* remember *when it was said to them, 'Dwell in this city,* Jerusalem, *and eat therein wherever you will, and say, "Exoneration"*: 'We seek forgiveness'; *and enter the gate, prostrating. We shall forgive you your transgressions. We shall give more* reward *to those who are virtuous'*: the independent clause indicates that this was a gift of pure grace.

[7:162] *But the evildoers among them substituted a saying other than that which had been said to them. So We sent down upon them terror*—a chastisement—*from the heaven for their evildoing*: these verses were explained earlier.[1]

1 See Q. 2:58–59.

[7:163] *And question them*, the Jews, by way of reproach, *about* the people of *the city that was by the sea*, meaning Elath by the Red Sea: *how they would transgress*—violate God's boundaries—*on the Sabbath; how their fish would come to them on the day of their Sabbath floating at the surface* of the water; *but on the day they did not observe the Sabbath*—this was their own Sabbath day, which was not Saturday—*they would not come to them* floating on the surface. *Thus were We trying them*: by making the fish appear on the day when it was forbidden to catch them, but not on the days when it was permitted; *for their wickedness*: their straying from obedience to God.

[7:164] *And when a community among them said* to another group of them who told them to refrain from this, *'Why do you preach to a folk whom God is about to destroy or chastise with a severe chastisement?'* [This was] because they will not pay any heed. *They*, the ones who were trying to preach to them, *said, 'As an exculpation before your Lord*: that is, we preach to them so that we are not taken to task for failing to do so; *and so that they might be wary* about fishing on the Sabbath.' So there were three groups: the guilty ones, the ones who preached to them, and the ones who remained silent. Q. 7:163

[7:165] *And when they forgot that whereof they had been reminded*—when they abandoned it as though they had forgotten—*We delivered those who forbade evil* because they had tried to prevent it, *and seized those who did wrong with a grievous chastisement for their wickedness*: the soundest opinion is that the silent party were also spared.

[7:166] *And when they disdained* to refrain from *that which was prohibited to them, We said to them* so that they heard a herald utter it, *'Be apes, despised!'* This was a command of creation, and they were transformed into apes through and through.

[7:167] *And lo! your Lord proclaimed that He would send against them*, the Jews, *until the Day of Resurrection, those who would inflict on them grievous torment* with all manner of degradations. *Truly, your Lord is swift in requital* to those who persist in sin when the time for their punishment comes—so this does not mean that He is not forbearing in the meantime; *and truly He is Forgiving, Merciful* to those who repent.

[7:168] *And We divided them into communities in the earth*: never to be united under one aim. *Some of them are righteous, and some of them are otherwise*: wide of the mark of righteousness. *And We tried them*, tested them, *with good things*, favours, *and evil things*, misfortunes, *so that they might revert* to obedience.

[7:169] *And there succeeded after them*, after these two factions, *a rabble*, an inferior replacement, *who inherited the Book*, the Torah, *choosing the transient things of this inferior life* as bribes for altering the laws of God, *and saying, 'It will be forgiven us.' Yet* the truth is that *if similar transient things were to come to them, they would take them*: that is, they hope for forgiveness despite persisting wilfully in their sin. *Has not the covenant of the Book been taken from them* in the Torah, *that they should not say about God anything but the truth? And they have studied what is in it*: and so they know of this covenant even as they abandon it. *And the abode of the Hereafter is better for those who are wary* of sin. *Do they not understand*, that they might desist*?*

[7:170] *And those who adhere* firmly *to the Book, and observe the prayer*—He singled out these two things because of their great importance—*Truly, We shall not let the wages of* such *reformers go to waste.*

[7:171] *And when We wrenched*—lifted—*the mountain above them, as if it were a canopy*: the word *ẓulla* (canopy) means anything that gives you shade; *and they thought that it was about to fall upon them*, [God said,] *'Take firmly*—earnestly—*what We have given you, and remember what is in it*—so that you do not forget it—*that you might be wary* of evil.*'*

[7:172] *And* remember *when your Lord took from the Children of Adam,*
Q. 7:170 *from their loins, their seed*: He brought out his seed, each from the loins of
the other, in the order of their procreation; *and made them testify*—each one of them—*against themselves*, saying, *'Am I not your Lord?'* The reason He brought us forth was to manifest the truth of this proclamation, and to reveal it to Adam and console him by showing him how great his progeny would be. Most exegetes hold that the meaning of this testimony is that it is a symbol of how He made them able to know Him and gave them the ability to attain this knowledge. This is similar to *He but says to it 'Be!' and it is* [Q. 2:117], and *He said to it and to the earth*...[Q. 41:11], because most people understand things better by means of concrete examples. *They said, 'Yea, indeed we testify* to this.*'* [They were made to affirm] *lest they should say on the Day of Resurrection, 'Truly, of this*—of the fact that You are our Lord—*we were unaware'*; or according to the second interpretation, 'We did not pay attention to the evidence.'

NOTE: It is said that the aforementioned majority opinion among the exegetes contradicts the *ḥadīth*s about this verse. The response given to this is that the truth is that God established two covenants with humanity. The first refers to those things to which the intellect can be guided by following the evidence that He has provided, leading to a situational (*ḥālī*) recognition of them; and this is what the verse describes in the opinion of the later imams. The second is the discursive (*maqālī*) recognition, which refers to those matters that can only be known through divine revelation. It was to this that the Prophet (may God bless him and grant him peace) referred when he said when asked about this verse, 'God created Adam and then laid His right hand onto his back and drew his progeny out of him, and said, "I created these people for the Garden, and they shall do the deeds of the inhabitants of the Garden." Then he laid His left hand on his back and drew his progeny out of him, and said, "I created these people for the Fire..."' and so on. This answer was an example of the 'method of the sage' (*uslūb al-ḥakīm*),[1] for he was asked about the situational covenant but replied about the discursive while also including the situational in the most subtle way possible. It is clear that the *ḥadīth* affirms the verse as well as adding some information about which the verse was silent. Thus it cannot be argued that He should not have made them forget the covenant, since this gave them an excuse. And God knows best.

[7:173] *Or lest you should say, 'It is merely that our fathers were idolaters before* our time, *and we were descendants of theirs*, so we emulated them. *Will You then destroy us*, chastise us, *for that which those who follow falsehood*, our fathers, *did?'* The influence of idolatry and blind tradition, when it is always possible to attain true knowledge, is not an excuse. Q. 7:173

[7:174] *Thus We detail the signs* for their manifold benefits, *and that they might revert* from falsehood.

[7:175] *And recite to them the tidings of him to whom We gave Our signs*: the books of heaven and the Supreme Name. This was Balaam, who was asked to pray against Moses, but refused. Then, when offered a bribe, he agreed to pray against him, and so Moses suffered in the wilderness. When he heard of this, he prayed against Balaam, whose faith[2] was wrested from him. *But he cast them off*: in his disbelief, he cast off those signs; *and Satan pursued him*: followed him to tempt him, or made him his follower; *and he became of the perverse*.

[7:176] *And had We willed, We would have raised him up* to the high ranks *thereby*: by means of those signs; *but he was disposed to the earth*: he inclined towards the comforts of the world; *and followed his whims* in preferring them to the Hereafter, and so We brought him low. *Therefore his likeness*—his situation in the depths of the world, whether you advise him or leave him be—*is as the likeness of a dog*: in the most base of its states, namely how it pants; *if you attack it* by rebuking it and shooing it, *it lolls its tongue out, and if you leave it* without rebuke, *it lolls its tongue out*. It is narrated that Balaam

1 Jurjānī defines this as 'answering the question that should have been asked, rather than the one that actually was.' See ʿAlī b. Muḥammad al-Jurjānī, *al-Taʿrīfāt*, Beirut: Dār al-Fikr, 1997, p 21, §119.

2 One manuscript has 'signs' (*āyāt*) in place of 'faith' (*īmān*).

ended up panting like a dog. *That is the likeness of those people who deny Our signs. So recount the tale* to the disbelievers, *that they might reflect.*

[7:177] *Evil as an example are the people who denied Our signs, and were wont to wrong themselves*: it was only themselves that they wronged.

[7:178] *He whom God guides, he is guided; and he whom He sends astray—truly they are the losers*: He referred to the former in the singular and the latter in the plural because guidance is one, while the paths of error are many.

[7:179] *And We have indeed urged*—destined—*unto Hell many of the jinn and humankind*; and this is their sign: *having hearts wherewith they do not understand* the truth, *and having eyes wherewith they do not perceive* and so reflect, *and having ears wherewith they do not hear* counsel. *These—they are like cattle* in how their sensibilities are confined to their desires; *nay, rather they are further astray*: because cattle do what they were created to do, naturally or by divine control. *These—they are the heedless* to the extremes of heedlessness.

[7:180] *And to God belong the Most Beautiful Names*: because they symbolise the most beautiful meanings. This applies to the words and to the
Q. 7:177 Attributes, which are countless; *so invoke Him*—name Him—*by them, and leave those who blaspheme*—corrupt—*His Names* by calling Him things for which they have no revealed warrant, or words whose meaning is unknown, or by using corrupted versions of His Names to refer to their idols, such as ʿUzzā, which is from *al-ʿAzīz* (the Mighty). *They will be requited for what they did*: the blasphemy in which they engaged.

[7:181] *And of those whom We created*—this wording alludes to how they are the minority—*there is a community who guide by the truth* and to it, *and act justly therewith.* A *ḥadīth* says, 'They are this community.' This is evidence for the validity of consensus (*ijmāʿ*), because it means that such a community will exist in every generation, as a *ḥadīth* says, 'My community will always contain a community who uphold God's command…' and so on.

[7:182] *And those who deny Our signs, We will draw them on by degrees*: leading them into perdition little by little; or it means simply, 'We will lead them into destruction,' as *darj* means both 'degree' and 'destruction'; *whence they do not know*: each time they sin further, they will be given another favour, for which they will fail to give thanks.

[7:183] *And I will respite them—Truly, My scheme*—My reprimand, *is strong*: severe. He called it a *scheme* because on the surface it seems to be a blessing when truly it is a curse.

[7:184] *Have they not considered*—striven to attain knowledge—*that there is no madness in their comrade*, Muḥammad (may God bless him and grant him peace)? *He is but a clear warner.*

[7:185] *And have they not reflected*, contemplated the signs of the Oneness, *upon the dominion*, the great kingdom, *of the heaven and of the earth* and their wonders, *and what things God has created, and that it may be that their term is already near*, so that they rush towards what will save them*? In what fact, then, after this*—after the Qur'ān—*will they believe*, if they do not believe in it?

[7:186] *Whomever God sends astray, he has no guide. And He leaves them in their insolence to wander on blindly.*

[7:187] *They ask you about the Hour*—the Resurrection—*when it shall come to pass. Say: 'The knowledge of it is only with my Lord. He alone shall reveal it at its proper time*: it will remain unknown to us until it arrives. *It weighs heavily*—tremendous and difficult to bear—*in the heavens and the earth*: upon their inhabitants, because of its horror. *It will not come on you save all of a sudden* when you are busy with your worldly affairs and commerce.*' They ask you as if you were preoccupied with it*: as if you were their fellow seeker of it, or as if you knew of it. *Say: 'Knowledge of it is only with God, but most people do not know* that it is known to Him alone.*'* Q. 7:185

[7:188] *Say: 'I have no power to bring benefit to myself* by any artifice, *or* to ward off *hurt*: this was explained earlier; *except as God wills* to give me power over them. *Had I knowledge of the Unseen, I would have acquired much good*: and I would always have been successful and profitable; *and adversity would not touch me*: and I never would have suffered losses or setbacks. *I am but a warner, and a bearer of glad tidings to a folk who believe'*: who were destined before time to believe, and it is they who will benefit.

[7:189] *He it is Who created you from a single soul*, Adam, *and made from him*—from his rib—*his spouse*, Eve, *that he might take rest in her*: that the soul might find tranquillity because of their correspondence and identity. *Then, when he covered her*, when he had sexual intercourse with her, *she bore a light burden*, a drop of fluid, *and moved to and fro with it*: bearing it until the time of its delivery without miscarrying it; *but when she became heavy* as the child grew larger, *they cried to God their Lord, 'If You give us one*, a child, *that is sound*, of sound and healthy body, *we truly shall be of the thankful* to You.*'*

[7:190] *But when He gave them a sound one, they ascribed to Him associates in that which He had given them*: such as by naming their child 'Servant of the Ploughman' by order of Satan, not knowing that Ploughman was Satan's name. Of course this is not truly idolatry, because names are not necessarily supposed to be literal; but He referred to it that way here in order to condemn it sternly, and because given names still bear the suggestion of their literal meanings. The verse can be read as 'associate' in the singular or 'associates' in the plural, because the one who attributes a single partner to God would have no problem with attributing more. *But exalted is God above what they associate*: whether openly or secretly.

[7:191] *Do they associate those who cannot create anything*—the idols—*but are themselves created?* He used the verb *yukhlaqūn* (created) with the rational plural form[1] in order to reflect their own beliefs.

[7:192] *And who are not able to give them*—their worshippers—*any help, nor can they help themselves* if any harm is done to them?

[7:193] *And if you call them to guidance, they will not follow you*: if you ask them for guidance, they will not answer you. *It will be the same for you whether you call them or remain silent.*

[7:194] *Truly, those on whom you call*—those whom you worship—*besides God are servants like you*: created slaves. *Call them then* for help or harm, *and let them answer you, if you are truthful* that they are gods.

[7:195] *Have they feet wherewith they walk, or have they hands wherewith they can grasp, or have they eyes wherewith they can see, or have they ears wherewith they give ear?* You are more perfect beings than they are. *Say: 'Call upon*
Q. 7:191 *your associates* in enmity towards me, *then scheme*—do your worst—*against me, and waste no time*: you need not give me respite, for you worry me not.

[7:196] *'Truly, my Protector is God Who reveals the Book*: the Qur'ān; *and He takes charge of the righteous*: and all the more so His messengers.

[7:197] *'And as for those on whom you call besides God, they have no power to help you, nor can they help themselves.'*

[7:198] *And if you call upon them to guidance*—to what is good for them—*they do not hear; and you see them gazing at you* because they were sculpted with eyes, noses and ears, *but they do not perceive* because they are lifeless objects.

[7:199] *Indulge with forgiveness*: one aspect of good character is to forgive those who wrong you, and give to those who withhold from you, and reconnect with those who forsake you; *and enjoin what is right*: meaning what the Law approves; *and turn away from the ignorant*: and do not indulge them.

[7:200] *And if any insinuation from Satan should provoke you*: meaning his whispered temptations to sin—the verb *nazagh* (provoke) literally means 'to spur', as a rider spurs his horse; *seek refuge in God. Truly, He is Hearing, Seeing.*

[7:201] *Truly, the God-fearing, when a visitation*—a temptation—*from Satan touches them, they remember* Our commands and prohibitions, *and then see clearly* where the pitfalls are, and avoid them.

1 As opposed to *tukhlaq*, for non-humans or non-rational objects.

[7:202] *And their brothers*, the brothers of the devils, meaning the disbelievers, *they lead them*—the devils lead them—*further into error, and do not stop short*: they do not cease to delude them.

[7:203] *And when you do not bring them a sign* from the Qur'ān which they request, *they say, 'Why have you not chosen one?'* meaning 'invented it yourself, like the rest of what you recite.' *Say: 'I follow only that which is revealed to me from my Lord. This* Qur'ān *is insight* for the heart *from your Lord, and a guidance and a mercy for a folk who believe'*: meaning, 'If you only had insight, it would be enough for you.'

[7:204] *And when the Qur'ān is recited, listen to it and pay heed, so that you might find mercy*: this was revealed about the command to cease conversation during prayer. It does not mean that the congregant is not required to recite for himself, because it is perfectly possible for listening silently to be required, and then for reciting to be required also. The imam is required to be silent when the congregants recite *Sūrat al-Fātiḥa* for themselves.

[7:205] *And remember your Lord within yourself* when you invoke and recite: that is, be audible to yourself alone; or this is a command to the congregant to recite silently after the imam finishes reciting; *humbly and fearfully, and more quietly than speaking out loud*—without yelling—*at morning and evening. And do not be among the heedless* of Our remembrance. Q. 7:202

[7:206] *Truly, those who are with your Lord*—the angels brought nigh—*are not too proud to worship Him; they glorify Him*—declaring His transcendence—*and to Him* alone *they prostrate* even though they are completely safe from damnation, which ought to encourage all creatures who are subject to divine judgement to do likewise.

8
Spoils of War
SŪRAT AL-ANFĀL

Revealed in Medina except, some say, for the verse, *O Prophet, God suffices you, and the believers who follow you* [Q. 8:64]

Having taught the Prophet to indulge with forgiveness, and to enjoin what is right, and to turn away from the ignorant folk, and the proper way to dispel the insinuations of devils and such matters, He then follows this with an account of those who debated with the Prophet ignorantly, and how he attempted to enjoin righteousness upon them, and how he forgave them. Thus He says:

In the Name of God, the Compassionate, the Merciful

[8:1] *They question you concerning* the ruling on *the spoils of war*: this was when the young men argued with the elders about the spoils of the Battle of Badr. *Say: 'The spoils of war belong to God* in terms of ruling, *and the Messenger* in terms of elucidating the ruling. *So fear God* lest you disobey Him, *and set things right between you* by reconciling; *and obey God and His Messenger, if you are* truly *believers.'*

[8:2] *The believers*—those with complete faith—*are only those who, when God is mentioned, their hearts tremble* with fear; *and when His verses are recited to them, they increase their faith*: because there is more for them to believe in; *and who rely upon their Lord*: and trust in Him.

NOTE: We noted the dispute about the true nature of faith earlier.[1] One consequence of this dispute is that it raised a further debate about whether or not it is possible for faith to increase and decrease. Those who say that action is part of faith agree that it can, while some of the Ashᶜarīs say that it cannot because faith is defined by certainty, which either exists

1 See Q. 2:3.

wholly or does not exist at all, in which case there is no faith. The soundest position is that it is possible for faith to increase and decrease, not in terms of action, but in terms of the increase and decrease of the object of faith, or in terms of the stability of the certainty, which is commensurate with the obviousness of the proofs of faith in the eye of the beholder.

[8:3] *Those who observe the prayers* consistently, *and who expend from that with which We have provided them* on righteous ends—[8:4] *those are the true believers* without doubt. He then evokes the three ranks which pertain to the heart, body and property, saying: *For them are ranks with their Lord* in the Garden, *and forgiveness, and generous provision* therein.

[8:5] *As* this ruling on the spoils was issued with the truth, though the people may have been averse to it, and likewise: *your Lord brought you forth from your home* in Medina to seize the caravan of Quraysh which was returning from Syria, and aided you against the idolaters at Badr, *with the truth*—with wisdom and rectitude—*though truly a party of the believers were averse* to going out. When the caravan of Quraysh returned from Syria, the Prophet went out to raid it and the idolaters came out to defend it. Q. 8:3 The Prophet (may God bless him and grant him peace) wanted to fight, so he left the caravan and promised that they would be victorious; but they said, 'Why did you not tell us that we would be fighting when we were readying to depart?' Then they met at Badr, and were victorious.

[8:6] *They dispute with you concerning the truth* of *jihād*, *after it had become clear* that they would be victorious by your foretelling, *as though they were being driven to death while they looked* upon its portents, for they were fewer in number and resources.

[8:7] *And* remember *when God promised you one of the two parties*—the caravan and the army of Mecca—*that it should be yours, and you longed that other than the armed one should be yours*: meaning the unarmed caravan; *but God willed that the truth be realised*—affirmed—*by His Words*: by His commands to fight them; *and to cut the root of the disbelievers.*

[8:8] *And* He did what He did *that He might cause the truth to be realised and annul falsehood, however much the sinners were averse*: this is not repetition, because the first referred to the disparity between the two desires, while the second elucidated the reason why He decreed that the Prophet choose the armed party, and then gave him victory.

[8:9] *When you sought help from your Lord*: this refers to the Prophet's prayer (may God bless him and grant him peace) when he saw that the enemy numbered a thousand while he and his Companions were only three hundred strong with just two horsemen; *and He answered you: 'I shall reinforce you with a thousand angels, rank upon rank'*: following one another, so that he sent one thousand, and then another two thousand, and another two.

[8:10] *And God appointed it*—that reinforcement—*only as glad tidings, and that your hearts might thereby be reassured. Victory comes only from God*: not the angels. *Truly, God is Mighty*, Omnipotent, *Wise* in His acts. And remember too:

[8:11] *[Remember] when He caused slumber to overcome you* at Badr, and also at Uḥud, *as security from Him*: because He had made you safe; *and sent down upon you water from the heaven to purify you thereby* from ritual impurity, *and to remove from you the evil of Satan*: his insinuations that if you were in the right, you would not be thirsty and ritually impure while the idolaters occupied the site of the wells; *and to strengthen your hearts* with trust in Him, *and to make firm your feet* for war *thereby*: by that strengthening, or that rain.

[8:12] *[Remember] when your Lord inspired the angels: 'I am with you* with
Q. 8:10 aid, *so make the believers stand firm*: by rallying them, or fighting their enemies. The soundest opinion is that they participated in the fighting. It is narrated that Gabriel descended among five hundred angels on the right flank where Abū Bakr al-Ṣiddīq was, and Michael descended among five hundred angels on the left flank where ʿAlī [b. Abī Ṭālib] al-Murtaḍā was, and they fought. *I shall cast terror into the hearts of the disbelievers. So smite above the necks*—on the throats or the heads—*and smite of them every finger!'* This was how they identified those whom the angels had slain.

[8:13] *That* smiting *was because they had contended with God and His Messenger: whoever contends with God and with His Messenger, surely God is severe in retribution* to them.

[8:14] *That* decree *is for you*, O disbelievers, *so taste it*: the chastisement—that is, most of it was still yet to come. *And [know] that for the disbelievers*—that is, for you—*is the chastisement of the Fire.*

[8:15] *O you who believe, when you encounter the disbelievers inching forward* in their multitudes, *do not turn your backs to them*: this was further clarified by the verse, *And urge on the believers* [Q. 4:84].

[8:16] *Whoever turns his back to them on that day*, the day of battle, *unless manoeuvring for battle*, such as making a false retreat to trick the enemy into pursuing, and then turning round and slaying them, *or joining another detachment* of the Muslims to enlist their help, *he has truly incurred the wrath of God, and his abode will be Hell—an evil journey's end!* The ruling of this verse applied only to Badr. The fact that the verses before and after it clearly refer to Badr in the past tense does not undermine this, because there is no reason they could not have been revealed after it. He then alludes to their pride at slaying the enemy at Badr:

[8:17] *You did not slay them, but God slew them*: as was described earlier; *and you threw not*, O Muḥammad, at their eyes *when you threw*: that is, when you went through the motions of throwing, because a single handful of pebbles thrown by a human hand could not have struck the eyes of so many soldiers; *but God threw* by making the pebbles smite them to vanquish them; *and that He might try*—favour—*the believers with a fair test*: a blessing from God. *Truly, God is Hearing* of their prayers, *Knowing* of their thoughts. The *Ḥadīth* scholars assert that the throwing of pebbles occurred only at Ḥunayn, while the exegetes hold that it occurred at both Badr and Ḥunayn.

[8:18] *That* decree *is for you: and* the fact is *that God weakens*, nullifies, *the plot*, the machinations, *of the disbelievers*.

[8:19] *If you had sought victory*, O idolaters, by saying, 'O God, give victory to the greater of the two sides,' and the like, *then victory has now come to you*: this is meant ironically. Q. 8:17 *And if you desist* from idolatry, *it will be better for you. But if you return* to fighting him, *We shall return* to aiding him, *and your host will not avail you in any way*—your group will not ward off any harm from you—*regardless of how numerous it may be. And God is with the believers* to aid them.

[8:20] *O you who believe, obey God and His Messenger, and do not turn away from Him*—this could mean either of them, or the Messenger, since to obey him is to obey God—*while you are listening* to the Qur'ān obediently.

[8:21] *And do not be as those who say, 'We hear,' and they hear not* obediently.

[8:22] *Truly, the worst of beasts*—all creatures that walk upon the earth—*in God's sight are those who are deaf* to the truth, *and dumb* to it, *those who do not understand* the truth.

[8:23] *For had God known of any good in them, He would have made them hear* with understanding; *and had He made them hear*, knowing that there was no good in them, *they would have turned away* without accepting it. Or this may refer to the hearing of Quṣayy b. Kilāb, whom they asked the Prophet to raise from the dead to prove his prophethood. *And they are averse*: it is their wont to turn away.

[8:24] *O you who believe, respond to God and the Messenger* with obedience *when He calls you*—the singular pronoun is used again for the same reason as before—*to that which will give you life*: through the knowledge or deeds that give life to the heart; *and know that God comes in between a person and his heart*: that is, his intentions by examining them; or it is a figure of speech to illustrate how close He is to him; *and that to Him you shall be gathered*: and He will requite you.

[8:25] *And be afraid of a trial*—a sin—*which*, if it afflicted you, its dire consequences *would certainly not fall exclusively upon the evildoers among you*: such as the emergence of heresy or negligence in the duty of enjoining what is right, as a *ḥadīth* describes. *And know that God is severe in retribution* to those who do not fear.

[8:26] *And remember*, O Emigrants, *when you were few and oppressed in the land*: in Mecca before the Emigration; *and feared lest men should snatch you away*: lest the disbelievers should accost you and torment you; *how He gave you refuge* in Medina, *and reinforced you with His help* against the enemy, *and provided you with the good things*—the spoils—*that you might be thankful* for My favours.

[8:27] *O you who believe, do not betray God and the Messenger*: as Abū
Q. 8:25 Lubāba did; *and* do not *betray your trusts* among one another, *while you are aware* of your treachery.

[8:28] *And know that your wealth and your children are a trial*—a test for you—*and that with God is a tremendous wage* which is better than both.

[8:29] *O you who believe, if you fear God, He will grant you a criterion*: guidance in your hearts by which you will be able to distinguish between truth and falsehood; *and absolve you of your evil deeds*: cover them; *and forgive you; and God is of tremendous bounty* in how He grants all this.

[8:30] *And* remember *when the disbelievers were plotting against you* in the council of Mecca *to confine you or slay you or expel you* from Mecca, so We commanded you to emigrate; *and they were plotting, and God was plotting* to redirect their plot against them; *and God is the best of those who plot*: the One Who knows it best.

[8:31] *And when Our verses were being recited to them, they said* obstinately—the person who said it was Naḍr b. al-Ḥārith—*'We have already heard! If we wish, we can speak the like of this—this is nothing but the fables of the ancients*: legends or tall tales.'

[8:32] *And when they* mockingly *said*—again, it was al-Naḍr who said it—*'O God, if this* Qur'ān *be indeed the truth from You, then rain down stones upon us from the heaven*: he specified that they come from the heaven because otherwise they might have fallen from the mountains, which would not have been as convincing; *or bring on us a painful chastisement.'*

[8:33] *But God was not about to chastise them while you were among them*: that is, residing in Mecca, so their chastisement at Badr is not a contradiction of this; or it refers to the chastisement of total annihilation; *nor was God about to chastise them while they sought forgiveness*: that is, while there were some among them who prayed for forgiveness, and were unable to emigrate from Mecca.

[8:34] *But what have they now, that God should not chastise them*—now that you have left along with the believers—*when they bar* the believers *from the Sacred Mosque*, such as in the year of Ḥudaybiya, *though they are not its guardians*: worthy of guarding it? *Its only guardians are those who are wary* of idolatry, *but most of them do not know* that they are not its true guardians.

[8:35] *And their prayer at the House was nothing but whistling and handclapping*: that is, they did those things instead of praying; *therefore taste now the chastisement*—at Badr or in general—*for your disbelief!*

[8:36] *The disbelievers expend their wealth in order to bar from God's way*: this refers to how they took loans to fund their preparations for the Battle of Uḥud. *They will expend it, and then it will be a source of anguish for them*: because their wealth will be gone, but they will not attain their desire. *Then they will be defeated* in the end, *and the disbelievers* who die in a state of Q. 8:34 disbelief *will be gathered into Hell.*

[8:37] *That God may distinguish*, separate, *the wicked*, the damned, *from the good*, the saved, *and place the wicked*, the factions of the damned, *one upon another*, crowded together, *and heap them up altogether and put them in Hell: those* wicked ones, *they are the losers.*

[8:38] *Say to the disbelievers that if they desist* from disbelief and enmity, *that which is past*—their sins—*will be forgiven them; but if they return* to disbelief and fighting, *the way of the ancients has already gone before*: which was that the army of God was triumphant, as at Badr.

[8:39] *And fight them until sedition*—idolatry—from them *is no more, and religion is all for God*: so that none but Him are worshipped. *If they desist* from disbelief, *then, Truly, God sees what they do*: and will requite them and you as well.

[8:40] *But if they turn away* and do not desist, *know that God is your Protector*: your Helper; *an excellent Protector, and an excellent Helper* is He.

[8:41] *And know that whatever spoils you have taken* by force from the disbelievers, such as at Badr, even if only something small, *the fifth of it is for God* for the blessings, *and for the Messenger*: which now should be distributed in the same way the Messenger used to distribute it (may God bless him and grant him peace); *and for the kinsmen*: meaning the Banū Hāshim and the Banū al-Muṭṭalib; *and the* poor Muslim *orphans*; *and the needy* who do not have enough to support themselves; *and the traveller*: and

the rest goes to the fighters. Obey this, *if you believe in God and* in *that which We sent down upon Our servant*, Muḥammad (may God bless him and grant him peace), meaning the signs and the victory *on the Day of Discrimination*, Badr, when truth was distinguished from falsehood, *the day the two armies met* (Muslim and disbeliever)—*and God has power over all things*: including granting victory to the few against the many—[8:42] *when you were on the nearer bank*, the one closer to Medina, *and they*, the disbelievers, *were on the yonder bank*, the one furthest from it, *and the cavalcade* coming from Syria *was below you* by the coast; *and had you* and the disbelievers *agreed to meet* in battle without having God's help, *you would have surely failed to keep the meeting*: because of your small number and their large number; *but* you met without any appointment *so that God might conclude a matter that was already done* in His knowledge, namely to aid His partisans, *that he who perished might perish*—that he who disbelieved might disbelieve—*after a clear proof*: namely the victory of the believers despite their small numbers,
Q. 8:43 whereafter there could be no further excuse for disbelieving; *and that he who survived*—he who believed—*might live after a clear proof. Truly, God is Hearing* of words, *Knowing* of intentions.

[8:43] [*Remember*] *when God showed them to you in your sleep as few* despite their large numbers, to hearten the believers. Dreams are either visions of the Prophet, visions of Satan, or jumbled confusions and thoughts. The disparity does not mean that the Prophet's dreams were not all true, because what that means is that they were all significant and never meaningless. Or it could be that *sleep* here means 'the location of sleep', meaning 'your eyes'. *And had He shown them to you as many, you would have faltered*—lost courage—*and quarrelled over the matter* of whether to fight them; *but God delivered* His partisans from quarrelling. *He knows that which is in the breasts.*

[8:44] *And when God made you see them when you met*, before the fighting had begun, *in your eyes as few*, so that you thought there were only between seventy and a hundred of them, though in fact there were a thousand, in order to strengthen your resolve; *and He made you seem as few in their eyes*: so that they would not prepare properly; but then after the fighting had begun, He made them see them as twice their numbers; *so that God might conclude a matter that was already done*: this was explained earlier. *And to God all things are returned.*

[8:45] *O you who believe, when you meet a host* of disbelievers in battle, *stand firm and remember God much* during the fighting, *that you may succeed*: and win victory.

[8:46] *And obey God and His Messenger, and do not quarrel with one another, lest you falter*—lose courage—*and your wind* fade, meaning your strength or your succour. *And be patient. Truly, God is with the patient*: to give them aid. As for debating with well-reasoned arguments to establish the truth, it is permitted and indeed obligatory, as long as its requirements are met, which include that it be done with the intention of establishing the truth, no matter from which side it comes.

[8:47] *And do not be like those who went forth from their dwellings in recklessness*—pride or transgression—*and to show off to men*: to be praised for their courage, such as Abū Jahl and the like when they headed out to Badr; *barring* people *from the way of God, while God encompasses what they do*: and will requite them for it.

[8:48] *And* remember *how Satan*, in the guise of Surāqa b. Mālik al-Kinānī, with a troop and a banner, *adorned their deeds*—their enmity towards the Messenger at Badr—*for them and said, 'Today no person shall overcome you* from the Banū Kināna, who fear you, *for I shall be your protector.' But when the two armies sighted each other*, when he was hand-in-hand Q. 8:46
with Ḥārith b. Hishām, *he turned his back in flight*: al-Ḥārith said to him, 'Where are you going?' But he pushed him away, *and said* to them, *'I am quit of you, for I see what you do not see*: meaning the angels. *I fear God*: lest He chastise me through them; *and God is severe in retribution'*: then the idolaters were routed.

[8:49] *When the Hypocrites and those in whose hearts is a sickness*—namely those who had embraced Islam in Mecca and then gone out with the Quraysh to Badr, and when they saw how few Muslims there were they apostatised—*said, 'Their religion has deluded them* that they would dare to challenge an army as large as ours.*' But whoever relies on God*, He will aid him; *for truly God is Mighty*, Overpowering, *Wise* in His acts. This is a response to them.

[8:50] *And if you could only see when the angels take the disbelievers* at Badr, you would have seen something terrible indeed, *beating their faces* when they advanced *and their backs* when they retreated, *and* saying, *'Taste the chastisement of the blazing Fire.*

[8:51] *'That* chastisement *is for what your hands have sent before you*: your sins—*and [know] that God is never unjust to His servants'*: this was explained in *Sūrat Āl ʿImrān*.[1]

[8:52] Their way is *like the way*—the custom—*of the people of Pharaoh*

1 See Q. 3:182.

and those disbelievers *before them*; and their custom was that *they disbelieved in God's signs and so God seized them* with chastisement *because of their sins. Truly, God is strong* and none can overcome Him, *severe in retribution.*

[8:53] *That* seizing *is because God would never change a grace that He had conferred on a people until they changed what was in themselves* to something worse than it, such as how Quraysh changed their kinship and good relations with the Prophet (may God bless him and grant him peace) and his Companions by trying to destroy them; *and God is Hearing, Knowing.* He then emphasises this by saying:

[8:54] *Like the way of the people of Pharaoh and those before them: they denied the signs of their Lord, so We destroyed them for their sins, and We drowned the people of Pharaoh* along with him; *and all*—the former and the latter alike—*were evildoers.*

[8:55] *Truly, the worst of beasts in God's sight are those who disbelieve*: and
who persist in their disbelief; *for they will not believe*: faith is not expected
from them; [8:56] *those of them with whom you have made a pact* not to assist
Q. 8:53 the idolaters, *and then break their pact every time*—such as Qurayẓa—*and they
are not fearful* of the dire consequence of such treachery.

[8:57] *So if you come upon them anywhere in the war, cause those* fighters *behind them to scatter by their means*—by their chastisement—*so that they might remember*: and take admonition.

[8:58] *And if you fear from any folk some treachery*—if it seems obvious that they mean to renege on the treaty—*then cast it back to them*, annul their treaty, *with fairness*: by informing them that the treaty is ended, lest you be accused of treachery yourself. *Truly, God does not love the treacherous.*

[8:59] *And do not let those who disbelieve suppose that they have gone ahead*: that they have escaped Us, such as those who fled on the day of Badr; it can also be read as, *Let no one suppose that those who disbelieve have gone ahead. Truly, they cannot escape* Us.

[8:60] *Make ready for them*—to fight them—*whatever force you can*: of those things that give one strength in war—a *ḥadīth* states that it means archers; *and of horses tethered* for God's cause, *that thereby you may dismay*, strike fear in, *the enemy of God and your enemy*, the disbelievers of Mecca, *and others*, other disbelievers, *besides them, whom you know not: God knows them. And whatever thing you expend in the way of God shall be repaid to you in full* with reward, *and you will not be wronged* by the squandering of your labours.

[8:61] *And if they incline to peace*, to a truce, *then incline to it*, to peace, *and rely on God* therein. *Truly, He is the Hearer, the Knower.*

[8:62] *And if they desire to trick you* with this offer of truce, *then God is sufficient for you*: He will suffice you and succour you. *He it is Who strengthened you with His help and with the believers,* [8:63] *and reconciled their hearts*: despite the animosity that was between them. *Had you expended all that is in the earth* to reconcile them, *you could not have reconciled their hearts*: because of this animosity, such as that which existed between the Aws and Khazraj; *but God reconciled their hearts. Truly, He is Mighty*, Overpowering, *Wise* in His acts.

[8:64] *O Prophet, God suffices you, and the believers who follow you.*

[8:65] *O Prophet, urge on the believers to fight* the disbelievers. *If there be twenty of you, steadfast, they will overcome two hundred*: this is a stipulation in the form of a command—that is, one man must be steadfast if he is to overcome ten. *If there be a hundred of you, they will overcome a thousand of those who disbelieve*: that is, the ruling for a few is the same as for a many, for otherwise it could be that ten would not overcome a hundred, while a hundred would overcome a thousand, and so on; *for they are a folk who do not understand*: they are ignorant of God, and fight only for the world, and so they will not be firm in times of strife. Q. 8:64

[8:66] *Now God has lightened the burden for you*: He has abrogated the former; *for He knows that there is* physical *weakness in you. So if there be a hundred of you, steadfast, they will overcome two hundred; and if there be a thousand of you, they will overcome two thousand by the leave of God. And God is with the steadfast*: to succour them. This is not undermined by the fact that there have been occasions when a hundred disbelievers got the better of a hundred or even two hundred of us; for God promises the Muslims this victory only on condition that we are steadfast, and that there is harmony among us all both outwardly and inwardly. Furthermore, it could well be that this verse referred exclusively to the Companions.

[8:67] *It is not* right *for any prophet to have prisoners* whom he does not execute *until he has made slaughter in the land*: and after this, he may choose between this and munificence, for the purpose is to humiliate the disbelievers. *You desire*—you would all prefer—*the transient things of this world* by accepting ransoms for them, *while God desires the Hereafter*: meaning its reward; *and God is Mighty*, Omnipotent, *Wise*: He knows what is best in every situation.

[8:68] *Had it not been for an ordinance from God which had preceded* in the Tablet, that the person who errs in his independent reasoning will not be punished, or the folk of Badr, *an awful chastisement would have afflicted you for what you took*: meaning the ransoms.

[8:69] *Now eat of what you have plundered*, including the ransoms, *as lawful and good, and fear God*: lest you disobey Him. *Truly, God is Forgiving* of what you did in the past; *Merciful*: in His mercy He has permitted you to take ransoms. This indicates that the prophets engage in independent reasoning, and can err therein, but God will not allow them to persist in the error.

[8:70] *O Prophet, say to those captives who are in your hands*, such as ʿAbbās and those who were captured alongside him [at Badr], *'If God knows of any good*—any faith or sincerity—*in your hearts, He will give you better than that which has been taken from you*—meaning the ransoms—*and will forgive you. Truly God is Forgiving, Merciful.'*

[8:71] *And if they*, the captives, *desire to betray you* by breaking the treaty, *they have betrayed God before* by going out to fight alongside the idolaters; *but He gave power* to you *over them* on the day of Badr, and if they go back then We shall too; *and God is Knower* of their treachery, *Wise* to their plans.

[8:72] *Truly, those who believed and emigrated and strove with their wealth and their lives in the way of God, and those who provided refuge* to the Emigrants
Q. 8:70 in their homes *and assisted* them—*those are allies of one another* with respect to inheritance, ahead of their kinsmen. This was subsequently abrogated when the laws of inheritance were revealed. *And those who believed but did not emigrate—you have no duty to make an alliance* (*walāya*) *with them*: this can be read as *walāya*, meaning a bond of kinship and assistance, or as *wilāya*, meaning a bond of authority—they will not inherit from you, nor share the spoils with you, *until they emigrate. But if they ask you for assistance in the matter of religion, then it is your duty to assist* them against the idolaters, *except against a folk between whom and you there is a covenant*: in which case you may not violate the treaty by assisting them; *and God sees what you do*: and will requite you for it.

[8:73] *And those who disbelieve are allies of one another* in terms of inheritance and assistance. *Unless you do this*, as you are commanded, *there will be sedition in the land and great corruption* in religion, because of the power of disbelief.

[8:74] *And those who believed and emigrated and strove for the way of God, and those who provided refuge and assisted—those are the true believers*: the folk of genuine faith; *and for them is forgiveness and a generous provision* in the Garden.

[8:75] *And those who believed afterwards*—after the first Emigration before Ḥudaybiya—*and emigrated* after it but before the conquest of Mecca, *and strove with you—they are of you; and those related by blood are nearer to one another* in terms of inheritance than they are to those outside the family, *according to the Book of God*: the Qurʾān. This abrogated the ruling of the previous verse. The citation of this verse to support the opinion that all blood relatives inherit is weak, because the verse itself stipulates that only what is found in the Qur'ān should be followed, and the Qur'ān affirms which specific members of the family may inherit. *Truly, God is Knower of all things*: including how inheritance is tied to the bond of Islam first, and the bond of kinship second. But God knows best what is right.

Q. 8:75

9
Repentance
SŪRAT AL-TAWBA

Revealed in Medina[1]

The correct view is that the Prophet (may God bless him and grant him peace) instructed that this *sūra* be placed after *Sūrat al-Anfāl* but without the *basmala* formula to begin it, and that he was instructed to do this by a revelation. This was stated by such great masters as Qāḍī Abū Bakr, the Imam,[2] and others. After proclaiming the alliance of the believers, God then followed this by commanding enmity with the idolaters, saying:

[9:1] This is *a declaration of immunity*—the annulment of inviolability—*from God and His Messenger to the idolaters with whom you made a pact*: that is, both are absolved of the pact which you made, so disregard it and make no further pacts.

[9:2] *Journey freely*, O idolaters, *in the land for four months* from the Day of Sacrifice in the year 9 until the 10th of Rabīᶜ al-Ākhar, *and know that you cannot escape God* no matter how much respite He gives you, *and that God will degrade*—humiliate—*the disbelievers* in both worlds.

[9:3] *A proclamation from God and His Messenger to people on the day of the Greater Pilgrimage*: the Day of Sacrifice, or ᶜArafa, or the days of the *ḥajj*. The Lesser Pilgrimage is the *ᶜumra*. The Prophet (may God bless him and grant him peace) gave this proclamation to Abū Bakr, who was the leader of the pilgrims, along with ᶜAlī to read it aloud to the pilgrims and said, 'Let no one speak for me but a man who is from me,' for it was the custom of the Arabs that no one would deal with pacts or their abolishment except for a man who was from them, as some narrations indicate.

1 One manuscript has 'revealed in Mecca, or Medina according to some.' All other manuscripts have 'revealed in Medina', and one adds that it was the last *sūra* to be revealed in Medina except for the final two verses.

2 Fakhr al-Dīn al-Rāzī.

NOTE: It has become commonplace to refer to the *ḥajj* as 'Greater' when the Day of ʿArafa happens to fall on a Friday. Perhaps this is because of the *ḥadīth* narrated by Razīn, 'Friday is the best of days, except for the Day of ʿArafa. If it falls on a Friday, it is better than seventy years wherein it does not.' In addition, the *ḥadīth*, 'When it falls on a Friday, God forgives all the people at the standing-place.' Furthermore, this distinction is because there is a special hour on Friday when prayers are answered, and because it involves emulation of the Prophet since the ʿArafa of the Farewell Pilgrimage fell on a Friday. One might take issue with the second *ḥadīth*, since there is another *ḥadīth* stating that this is the case for every *ḥajj* in general; but one could interpret the former *ḥadīth* to mean that they are forgiven without any intermediary, and the latter to mean that He gifts forgiveness to some on account of others. And God knows best.

That God is free from obligation to the idolaters, and so is His Messenger. So if you repent of idolatry, *it will be better for you; but if you turn away* from repentance, *then know that you cannot escape* the chastisement of *God. And give tidings to those who disbelieve of a painful chastisement,* [9:4] *excepting those of the idolaters with whom you have made a pact, and who have not cheated you in any way* with regard to the terms of the pact, *nor supported anyone* of your enemies *against you: fulfil your pact with them until the term* is fully reached. *Truly, God loves those who fear* reneging on their pact. Q. 9:5

[9:5] *Then, when the sacred months have passed*—which was the term for those who did not break the pact, while it was four months for the rest—*slay the idolaters* universally *wherever you find them,* whether on sacred ground or not, *and take them* prisoner, *and confine them*—imprison them—*and lie in wait for them at every place of ambush*: so that they cannot disperse through the land. *But if they repent* of idolatry, *and observe the prayer and pay zakāt, then leave their way free* after the months have passed. *God is Forgiving, Merciful* to those who repent.

[9:6] *And if any one of the idolaters,* after the months have passed, *seeks your protection*—asks for security from the slaughter—*then grant him protection so that he might hear the Words of God*: and reflect on them; *and afterward convey him to his place of security*: that is, he will be granted protection until he decides to return home, if he does not embrace Islam. *That* protection *is because they are a folk who have no knowledge* about what Islam is, so give them protection that they might learn.

[9:7] *How can the idolaters*—that is, they cannot—*have a pact with God and His Messenger, except for those with whom you made a pact at the Sacred Mosque?* This refers to Ḥudaybiya, and they are the ones for whom the exception was made before. *So long as they are true to you* by honouring the pact, *be true to them* by honouring it. *Truly, God loves those who fear*: as above.

[9:8] *How* could they have a pact, *when if they get the better of you, they do not respect any bond* of oath or kinship, *or treaty with regard to you? They please you with their words, while their hearts refuse* what they say, *and most of them are wicked folk*: renegades.

[9:9] *They have purchased*—exchanged—*with the signs of God a small price*: namely the pursuit of caprices; *and have barred* people *from His way*: His religion. *Truly, evil is that which they are wont to do.*

[9:10] *They respect neither bond*, oath, *nor treaty*, pact, *with regard to a believer; those, they are the transgressors* who go beyond the bounds of iniquity.

[9:11] *Yet if they repent and observe the prayer and pay zakāt, then they are your brothers in religion; and We detail*—elucidate and repeat—*the signs for a folk who have knowledge*: and reflect on them.

[9:12] *But if they break their oaths*—their treaties—*after their pact and*
Q. 9:8 *assail your religion, then fight the leaders of disbelief*: meaning them, for they are
its leaders. *Truly, they have no oaths*—no binding pacts—*so that they might desist*: the citation of this verse to prove that the oath of a disbeliever is void is obviously weak.

[9:13] *Will you not fight a people who broke their oaths*—meaning the people of Mecca, *and intended to expel the Messenger*—this was explained earlier[1]—*initiating* the fighting *against you first?* This means on the day of Badr, after others had escaped. *Are you afraid of* fighting *them? God is more worthy of your fear*—that you should fear Him by fighting them—*if you are believers*: for the believer fears nothing but Him.

[9:14] *Fight them! God will chastise them at your hands and degrade them*—humiliate them—*and give you victory against them; and He will heal the breasts of a folk who believe*: meaning those who had been harmed by them.

[9:15] *And He will remove the rage in their hearts*: at how they had been treated by them. *God relents to whomever He will*: such as Abū Sufyān and the like. *And God is Knowing* of all that will be, *Wise* in His acts.

[9:16] *Or did you suppose*, O believers, *that you would be left alone when God did not yet know*—when His knowledge was not yet manifest—*those of you who had struggled and had not taken, besides God and His Messenger and the believers, any intimate friend* to whom they divulged their secrets*? And God is aware of what you do.*

[9:17] *It is not* right *for the idolaters to attend*—to enter and sit inside—

1 See Q. 8:30.

God's places of worship, especially the Sacred Mosque, *bearing witness against themselves to disbelief*: such as how they would say while circumambulating, 'At Your service! You have no associate, save those associates who are Yours, whom You own along with all they own,' all the while professing to worship al-Lāt and ʿUzzā. *Those, their deeds have failed*: come to naught; *and in the Fire they shall abide*.

[9:18] *The only one to attend God's places of worship*—such as by building them, decorating them with carpets and lamps, worshipping in them and refraining from worldly talk in them—*is he who believes in God and the Last Day*: He did not mention the Messenger because faith in them is not complete without faith in him; *and observes the prayer and pays zakāt, and fears none but God alone. It may be that those will be among the rightly guided*: He said *it may be* in order to frustrate the disbelievers and instil fear in the believers.

[9:19] *Do you reckon the giving of water to pilgrims and the attendance of the Sacred Mosque*—that is, those who engage in them—*to be the same as he who believes in God and the Last Day and struggles in the way of God? They are not equal in God's sight*: but those who struggle are better; *and God guides not* Q. 9:18
the evildoing folk: the idolaters.

[9:20] *Those who believe, and have emigrated, and have struggled in the way of God with their possessions and their lives, are greater in degree*—rank—*with God* than those who have not done all of these; *and those, they are the triumphant* who will attain complete salvation.

[9:21] *Their Lord gives them glad tidings of mercy from Him and beatitude; and for them shall be Gardens wherein is enduring*—perpetual—*bliss*, [9:22] *abiding therein forever. Truly, with God is a tremendous reward* that would make every worldly delight seem utterly worthless.

[9:23] *O you who believe, do not take your fathers and brothers for your friends, if they prefer disbelief over belief; whoever of you takes them for friends, such are the evildoers*.

[9:24] *Say: 'If your fathers, and your sons, and your brothers, and your wives, and your clan*—your relatives—*and the possessions which you have acquired, and merchandise for which you fear there may be no sale, and dwellings which you love*—which you enjoy—*are dearer to you* by your choice, not by natural affection, for which you are not held accountable, *than God and His Messenger and struggling in His way, then wait until God brings about His command*: His chastisement. It is said that this means the conquest of Mecca. *And God does not guide the wicked folk'*: this is a severe judgement, and there are few who can evade it.

[9:25] *God has already helped you on many fields*: many occasions of war—the noun *mawṭin* (field) here refers to time rather than place; *and* He helped you *on the day of Ḥunayn* when you fought with the Hawāzin after the Conquest of Mecca—Ḥunayn is a valley between Mecca and Ṭā'if; *when your vast numbers were pleasing to you*: they numbered twelve thousand men, while the disbelievers were only four thousand strong, and so one of them said in exultation, 'We shall certainly not be defeated today by so few!' *But it*—your greater numbers—*availed you nothing* against the enemy, *and the earth for all its breadth*—despite its vastness—*was straitened for you*: so fearful were you; *and then you turned back, retreating*: and only ʿAbbās and Abū Sufyān b. al-Ḥārith remained with the Prophet (may God bless him and grant him peace); or some say that ten remained: Abū Bakr, ʿUmar, ʿAlī and ʿAbbās.

[9:26] *Then God sent down His Spirit of Peace*—His soothing mercy—*upon His Messenger and upon the believers*: and ʿAbbās rallied them at the behest of the Prophet (may God bless him and grant him peace), and they all turned around as one, crying, 'At your service! At your service!'
Q. 9:26 *And He sent down legions* of angels *you did not see*—though they heard voices from the heavens—*and chastised the disbelievers*: by slaughter and capture—some six thousand were captured. *Such is the requital of the disbelievers.*

[9:27] *Then afterwards God will relent to whom He will*: to those of them who embrace Islam. *And God is Forgiving, Merciful* to those who repent.

[9:28] *O you who believe, the idolaters are indeed unclean*: inwardly and religiously, or physically too; *so do not let them come near the Sacred Mosque*: that is, bar them from the Sacred Precinct—this implies that they are held accountable for the secondary matters of faith; *after this year of theirs*: the ninth year of the Emigration. *If you fear impoverishment* on account of losing out on their commerce, *God will surely enrich you from His bounty, if He will*: He compensated them with the *jizya* tribute and the wealth brought from the surrounding lands. *God is Knowing* of your situation, *Wise* in His acts.

[9:29] *Fight those who do not believe in God, nor in the Last Day*—with correct faith—*and who do not forbid what God and His Messenger have forbidden*, such as wine and usury, *nor do they hold to*—believe in—*the religion of truth* which abrogates all others, *from among of those who have been given the Book, until they pay the jizya by hand*: that is, from a position of wealth by sending it willingly, or by means of a conquering hand upon them; *being subdued*: humbled. It should also be taken from those who may be following a Book, such as the Magians, based on the practice of the Prophet (may God bless him and grant him peace), as Shāfiʿī affirmed.

[9:30] *The Jews say*—that is, some of them, while the others are silent—*'Ezra is the son of God'*: because he was raised from the dead, and dictated the Torah to the people after they had all forgotten it; *and the Christians say, 'The Messiah is the son of God.' That is the utterance of their mouths*—that is, it is a thoughtless and nonsensical claim, or a plain blasphemy—*imitating the utterances of those who disbelieved before*: their predecessors whom they emulate. *God assail them!* This is an expression of incredulity at the vileness of their claim. *How they are deviated*: errant from the truth.

[9:31] *They have taken their rabbis*, the Jewish clerics, *and their monks*, the Christian ascetics, *as lords beside God*: by obeying them instead of Him in matters of the lawful and forbidden, or as was discussed in *Sūrat al-Anʿām*; *and the Messiah, son of Mary*: by calling him God, or the Son of God; *when they were commanded* in their Books *only to worship One God*: God Himself. *There is no god except Him. Glory be to Him*—transcendent be He—*above what they associate.*

[9:32] *They desire to extinguish God's light*—His religion—*with their tongues*: by their denials, or He means to liken them to one who tries to extinguish a huge fire by blowing on it; *but God refuses but to perfect His light*—to manifest His religion and make His Word ascendant—*though the disbelievers be averse* to seeing it perfected. Q. 9:30

[9:33] *He it is Who has sent His Messenger with guidance*— prophetic miracles—*and the religion of truth, that He may manifest it*—make it triumphant—*over every religion* by abrogating them, *though the disbelievers be averse* to this.

[9:34] *O you who believe, many of the rabbis and monks truly consume*, usurp, *people's goods by false means*, by taking bribes to change their rulings, *and bar* people *from the way of God. And those who hoard up gold and silver*, such as those rabbis and monks—a 'hoard' (*kanz*) is money for which the *zakāt* is not paid, as a *ḥadīth* describes—*and do not expend it*, the hoarded wealth, or the silver and so *a priori* the gold, *in the way of God*—*give them tidings of a painful chastisement.*

[9:35] *On the day when it*, the hoarded wealth, *shall be heated in the fire of Hell, and therewith*, with the hoarded wealth, *their foreheads and their sides and their backs shall be branded*: burned. He singled out those areas because they contain the main body parts which constitute the fundamentals of the four directions, and because of how those people used to frown at beggars, turn away from them, and show their backs to them. The burning will cover their skin until it has reached every part, and they will be told, *'This is what you hoarded up for yourselves: so taste now* the consequence of *what you used to hoard!'* The verse is of general import.

[9:36] *Truly, the number*, the total, *of months with God*—that is, not invented by humans—*is twelve months in the Book of God*, the Tablet, affirmed *from the day that He created the heavens and the earth; four of them are sacred*: Rajab, Dhū al-Qaʿda, Dhū al-Ḥijja and Muḥarram. *That* sacredness *is the right religion*: the upright measure, contrary to the Arab custom of delaying the months. *So do not wrong yourselves* by sinning *during them*: for sins during them are all the more heinous—this is akin to *no lewdness, nor wickedness, or disputing in the ḥajj* [Q. 2:197]. The majority hold that the law forbidding the initiating of fighting during the sacred months was abrogated. *And fight the idolaters altogether*—during all the months—*even as they fight you altogether; and know that God is with those who fear Him.*

[9:37] *Postponement*, the custom of delaying the sacredness of a month until another month in order to allow fighting in the former and then abstaining from it in the latter, *is nothing but an excess of disbelief*, because it constitutes a compound act of disbelief, both permitting what is forbid-
Q. 9:36 den and forbidding what is permitted, *whereby those who disbelieve are led astray. One year they make it profane*, profaning one of the sacred months and fighting during it, and then making another month sacred in its place, *and hallow it another* by retaining its sacredness, *that they may make up the number which God has hallowed*: namely four months out of every year, no matter when they might fall. *Thus do they profane what God has hallowed. Their evil deeds have been adorned for them; and God does not guide the disbelieving folk*: according to His knowledge.

[9:38] *O you who believe, what is wrong with you that, when it is said to you*—it was the Prophet (may God bless him and grant him peace) who said it to them—*'Go forth in the way of God,'* such as at the Expedition of Tabūk, *you sink down heavily to the ground*: preferring to stay at home? *Are you so content with the life of this world, rather than with the* Garden of the *Hereafter? Yet the enjoyment of the life of this world is*, when compared *to the Hereafter, but little.*

[9:39] *If you do not go forth, He will chastise you with a painful chastisement* in both lives, *and He will substitute* you with *another folk other than you* who are obedient, *and you will not hurt Him at all* by refusing to go out, *for God has power over all things*: including replacing you.

[9:40] *If you do not help him*, the Prophet (may God bless him and grant him peace), then God will help him, for *God has already helped him, when the disbelievers drove him forth* from Mecca. The act is attributed to them because they were about to do it, or because they were the reason why it happened, when he was *the second of two*: namely he and Abū Bakr; *when the two were in the cave* in Mount Thawr, where they spent three days, *when he said to his companion* Abū Bakr, when the disbelievers who were searching for them were almost upon them, and he expressed his concern to Muḥammad (may God bless him and grant him peace), *'Do not despair! Truly, God is with us*: with His protection.*' Then God sent down His Spirit of Peace*, His security, *upon him*, upon Muḥammad or his companion, for he was despairing and so was in need of it, *and supported him with legions you did not see*: the angels who guarded him in the cave and elsewhere; *and He made the word of those who disbelieved*, meaning the call of idolatry, *the nethermost*, the vanquished, *and the Word of God*, monotheism, *was the uppermost*: the vanquisher. *And God is Mighty* in His decree, *Wise* in His ordain.

[9:41] *Go forth* to Tabūk, *light* of weapons or mounts, *and heavy* of weapons, or on foot, *and struggle in the way of God with your possessions and your lives. That* struggle *is better for you* than staying at home, *if only you knew*: if only you were people of knowledge, you would not stay at home. Then when this proved too difficult for them, He qualified it by revealing the verse, *As for the weak*...[Q. 9:91], and revealed about the Hypocrites who stayed at home: Q. 9:41

[9:42] *Had it*, the thing to which they were summoned, *been a near gain* of worldly profit, *and an easy journey, then they*, the Hypocrites, *would have followed you; but the distance was too great for them*: the word *shuqqa* (distance) means a distance which is traversed with difficulty (*mashaqqa*). *Still they will swear by God* upon your return, *'Had we been able*—physically or materially—*we would have gone forth with you,' destroying their souls* with this false oath. *God knows that truly they are liars.*

[9:43] *May God pardon you* for permitting them to stay behind*!* He pardoned him before elucidating the prohibition, which is the way of a loving person with the one he loves. *Why do you give them leave* to stay behind, instead of waiting *until it was clear to you which of them spoke the truth* regarding their excuses, *and you knew those who were lying* about this*?*

[9:44] *Those who believe in God and the Last Day do not ask leave of you* to stay behind—this is meant as a prohibition, like *no lewdness* [Q. 2:197]; *that they may struggle with their possessions and their lives; and God knows the pious*: and will reward them.

[9:45] *They alone ask leave of you who do not believe in God and the Last Day, and whose hearts are doubtful* about the faith, *so in their doubt they waver* in confusion.

[9:46] *If they had desired to go forth* with you, *they would have made some preparation for it*: such as readying provisions and mounts, since they had been provided with the funds to do so; *but* they loitered because *God was loathe to rouse them*: by prompting them to go out. According to this interpretation, there is no suggestion that He was leading them on into perdition. *So He slowed them down* and held them back from going out, *and it was said* to them, whether by Satan or by one of them, *'Stay back*—a command with the sense of a threat—*with those who stay back*: such as the women.*'*

[9:47] *Had they gone forth among you, they would only have caused you more trouble*: more sedition in addition to that which was sowed by the Hypocrites who did go out with you; *and would have hurried to and fro among you* spurring their mounts—this is a metaphor for spreading gossip; *seeking to stir up sedition between you*: thus He commanded them to go out so that they would have no excuse and their hypocrisy would be made manifest. *And among you there are some who would listen* obediently *to them; and God knows the evildoers*: and will requite them.

Q. 9:47

[9:48] *Truly, they sought to stir up sedition* by undermining your command *already before*: such as on the day of Uḥud when Ibn Ubayy and his companions turned around; *and machinated affairs*, cooked up plots, *against you until the truth*, the divine assistance, *came and God's command*, His religion, *prevailed, while they were yet averse.*

[9:49] *And there are some of them who say, 'Grant me leave* to stay at home—this refers to al-Jadd b. Qays—*and do not tempt me'*: with the 'daughters of the yellow folk' (*banāt al-aṣfar*), as the race of the Byzantines were known. *Surely they have fallen into temptation* by staying behind; *and truly Hell encompasses the disbelievers* even now, because the means which lead to it encompass them.

[9:50] *If good fortune befalls you*, such as victory or spoils, *it vexes them; but if an affliction befalls you*, such as at Uḥud, *they say, 'We took our precaution before* by staying behind,*' and they turn away, rejoicing* in what has befallen you.

[9:51] *Say: 'Nothing shall afflict us but that which God has written for us* in the Tablet. *He is our Protector*, Who takes care of our affairs; *and in God let the believers put their trust*: and in no other.*'*

[9:52] *Say: 'Are you waiting for anything for us but one of the two fair things*: victory or martyrdom*? We are waiting in your case too* for one of the two evil things: *for God to afflict you with a chastisement from Him* from Heaven, *or at our hands* by granting us leave to fight you. *So wait* for our outcome; *we too are waiting with you* for yours.*'*

[9:53] *Say* to those who request permission*: 'Expend willingly or unwillingly, it shall not be accepted from you. Truly, you are a wicked folk*: outside the religion.*'*

[9:54] *And nothing prevents their expenditure from being accepted from them, but that they have disbelieved in God and His Messenger, and that they do not come to prayer save as idlers, and that they do not expend without their being reluctant.*

[9:55] *So let not their wealth or their children impress you*: for they are only means of drawing them on into perdition. *God only desires to chastise them thereby in the life of this world*: by tiring them out with amassing it and keeping hold of it, and them losing it without having enjoyed it; *and that their souls should depart*—be wrested out of them—*while they are disbelievers*: this will be explained when we come to the verse, *And let not their wealth or their children impress you* [Q. 9:85] presently.

[9:56] *And they swear by God that they truly are of you; but they are not of you*: because of their hypocrisy; *they are a folk who are afraid* of both sides.

[9:57] *If they could find a shelter* such as a fortress, *or some caverns, or any place to enter, they would turn and bolt away to it*: rushing like galloping horses, fleeing from falling into your hands.

[9:58] *Some of them defame you concerning* the distribution of *the voluntary charity. If they are given a share of them, they are content; but if they are given none, then they are enraged*: and critical. Q. 9:55

[9:59] *If only they had been content with what God and His Messenger have given them* from the spoils and charity, *and had said, 'Sufficient for us is God. God will give us from His bounty, as will His Messenger*, from some other spoils or charity; *to God we are suppliants* that He enrich us.' In other words, it would have been better for them had they done this.

[9:60] *Charitable offerings*—the prescribed charitable donations—*are only for* distribution to *the poor*: meaning those who have no wealth or income to meet their needs, such as those whose caravans have been robbed; *and the needy*: meaning those who do have wealth or income but not enough to meet their needs, such as those who are unable to work because of disability; *and those who work with them*: meaning those who work to administer the alms such as collectors, distributors, guards, secretaries and accountants; *and those whose hearts are to be reconciled*: meaning those to whom some is given to encourage them to make good their conversions to Islam, or to encourage their peers to convert; *and towards* the freeing of *slaves*: by assisting them with their freedom contracts—the use of *towards* here indicates that the funds are directed on their behalf [rather than directly to them], while the repeated application of the initial preposition to each of the objects in the list serves to emphasise the necessity; *and the debtors*: meaning those who incurred debts for things which are not sinful, or incurred them for sinful things and then repented, and have no means of repaying them, or to bring about a reconciliation [between rival parties]; *and towards the way of God*: meaning warriors who have no other claim to public funds; *and the traveller*: meaning those who are abroad and cut off from their own property. There is prescribed for all of these *a duty imposed by God. And God is Knower* of Your deeds, *Wise* in what He commands.

NOTE: The apparent meaning of this verse is that charity is exclusively for these eight categories, and that it must be given to whichever category can be found, and that it should be equally apportioned among them. This was the view of Shāfiʿī; but it is related that ʿUmar, Ḥudhayfa, Ibn ʿAbbās and other Companions and Followers said that it is permitted to give them to a single category, and this was also the view of the three other imams[1] as well as some in our [Shāfiʿī] school. This is supported by the argument that the purpose of this verse must be to make clear that charity is restricted to these eight categories, like the *ḥadīth*, 'The caliphate is for Quraysh alone,' meaning for them and no other, not that
Q. 9:61 every individual who gives charity is duty bound to divide it among every individual member of the categories who are its valid recipients. This is obvious. However, the literal meaning of the verse does support Shāfiʿī, since the general rule with distribution is that the ruling applies to every individual. Nevertheless, the relevance of the verse to the opinion that it is obligatory to give it to three individuals from each category[2] is not obvious. And God knows best.

[9:61] *And of them are those who injure the Prophet* by saying things that ought not to be said about him, *and say* when rebuked for this, *'He is only an ear'*: meaning 'Who listens to everything that is said? And so if we deny it and swear to him, he will believe us.' They called him after the body part by way of exaggeration. *Say*: indeed he is *'an ear*—a listener— *to good for you*: and he accepts it, but not an ear to evil, as He made plain. *He believes in God, and believes in*, trusts and respects, *the believers* because he knows of their sincerity—the preposition *bi* is used for belief in God here, and *li* for belief in the believers, to indicate the difference between belief in the sense of 'faith' and belief in the sense of 'trust'; *and* he is *a mercy to those of you who believe*: to those who profess faith, for he does not uncover the hidden truth about them. *Those who injure God's Messenger, for them there is a painful chastisement.'*

[9:62] *They swear by God to you* to mollify you and offer excuses, *so*

1 Abū Ḥanīfa, Mālik and Aḥmad

2 This was an opinion related from Shāfiʿī.

that they might please you with their oaths, *but God and His Messenger are more deserving that they should please Him* with obedience—the singular pronoun is used here since the way to please either of them is one and the same—*if they are* truly *believers*.

[9:63] *Do they not know that whoever opposes God and His Messenger* by disbelieving, *for him shall be the fire of Hell to abide therein? That is the great abasement*: disgrace.

[9:64] *The Hypocrites are cautious*—fearful—*lest a sūra should be revealed about them*: the word *ʿalayhim* [literally 'to them'] here means 'about them', akin to God's Words *about Solomon's kingdom* [Q. 2:102], where *ʿalā mulk Sulaymān* [literally 'to the kingdom of Solomon'] means 'about it'. In other words, lest a *sūra* about them should be revealed to the believers, *informing them*—exposing to them—*what is in their hearts*: the disbelief they harbour. *Say*, as a warning*: 'Keep mocking! God will bring out*—lay bare—*that which you fear* to be revealed.*'*

[9:65] *And if you question them* about their mocking when they said on the way to Tabūk, 'This man means to conquer the palaces of Syria! Not Q. 9:63
a chance!'—*assuredly they will say, 'We were only chattering* as travellers do, *and jesting* to pass the time.*' Say* in rebuke: *'Was it God, and His signs, and His Messenger that you mocked?* for they are lying.

[9:66] *'Make no excuses* for it. *You have disbelieved*: your disbelief has been made manifest by this mockery; *after believing. If We forgive a party of you* because they repent, *We will chastise another party* of you *because they were sinners* who persisted in their hypocrisy.*'*

[9:67] *The hypocrites, both men and women, are of one another*: alike in disbelief like the various parts of a single object. He said *of one another* but used a different phrase when describing the believers later,[1] by way of rebutting them for swearing that *they truly are of you* [Q. 9:56]. *They enjoin indecency*, disbelief, *and forbid decency*, faith; *and they withhold their hands shut* to piety because of their stinginess. *They have forgotten God* by refusing to obey Him, *so He has forgotten them* by excluding them from His kindness. *Truly, the hypocrites, they are the wicked folk*: the folk of total disobedience.

[9:68] *God has promised the hypocrites, both men and women, and the* open *disbelievers the fire of Hell, abiding therein: it will suffice them* as a just requital, *and God has cursed them, and theirs will be a lasting*—perpetual—*chastisement*: so that they will never grow accustomed to it as some have claimed.

[9:69] You hypocrites are *like those before you who were far mightier than*

1 See Q. 9:71.

you, and more abundant in wealth and children. They enjoyed their share of the enjoyments of this world, *so enjoy your share too, just as those before you enjoyed their share*: this is not needless repetition, because the first was to lay the ground for the comparison and the rebuke, while the second was to deliver the comparison along with the context; *and you indulged* in your falsehoods *just as they indulged. Those, their deeds have become invalid in this world*: by not being accepted or repaid with a swift reward, such as goodly praise or love for them being instilled in people's hearts; *and in the Hereafter; and those, they indeed are the losers*: and you are just like them.

[9:70] *Has not the tidings of those before them reached them—the people of Noah* who were destroyed by the flood, *and ʿĀd* by the wind, *and Thamūd* by the cry, *and the people of Abraham* whose ruler and gods were destroyed by a swarm of insects, *and the dwellers of Midian* by the fire of darkness, *and the deviant* cities that fell down upon the people of Lot? *Their messengers brought them clear proofs*: patent prophetic miracles, but they denied them and so were taken to task. *God would never have wronged them*: it is not His
Q. 9:70 way to wrong people by punishing when there was no crime; *but they wronged themselves* by denying.

[9:71] *And the believers, both men and women, are allies of one another*: helpers of one another—the reason for the altered phrasing here was explained earlier; *they enjoin decency and forbid indecency, and observe the prayer and pay zakāt, and obey God and His Messenger. Those, God will have mercy on them*: the future tense is used here to impart emphasis. *Truly, God is Mighty*, Omnipotent, *Wise* in His acts.

[9:72] *God has promised the believers, both men and women, Gardens with rivers flowing from beneath them, abiding therein, and pleasant dwellings* pleasing to the soul *in the Gardens of Eden*: residences there, or the highest levels of it—the conjunction *and* is used here [even though both clauses describe the same thing] to indicate how the promise is offered to every individual, or to denote plurality in the sense of distribution, or to separate the differing descriptions; *and beatitude from God is greater* than all of them. *That is the supreme triumph.*

[9:73] *O Prophet, struggle against the disbelievers* with arms, *and the Hypocrites* with words, *and be harsh with them*: with ruthlessness; *for their abode will be Hell, an evil journey's end!*

[9:74] *They swear by God that they said nothing* to insult you; *but they did indeed say the word of disbelief* by denying you, *and did disbelieve after their submission. And they purposed that which they never attained*: which was to slay you on the way to Tabūk when ʿAmmār repelled them; *and they were only spiteful*—they only denied—*that God and His Messenger should have enriched them of His bounty*: the upshot of this is that his only sin against them was that God enriched them through his blessing. *So if they repent, it will be better for them*: and indeed it is related that the one who said this did repent; *but if they turn away* from repentance, *God will chastise them with a painful chastisement in this world and in the Hereafter, and they will have none on earth as protector or helper* to save them, never mind in the Hereafter.

[9:75] *And some of them have made a covenant with God*, namely Thaᶜlaba b. Ḥāṭib: *'If He gives us of His bounty, we will give voluntary charity and become of the righteous.'*

[9:76] *Yet when He gave them of His bounty* thanks to the prayer of the Prophet (may God bless him and grant him peace), when the livestock of the Medinans had dwindled, *they became miserly with it* by refusing to pay the *zakāt*, *and turned away* from obedience *in aversion*.

[9:77] *So He penalised them with hypocrisy in their hearts*, allowing it to take root there, *until the day they meet Him* upon death, *because they failed God in what they promised Him* about charity and righteousness, *and because they lied*. Then after this was revealed, they brought [Thaᶜlaba b. Ḥāṭib's] *zakāt* Q. 9:75
to the Prophet (may God bless him and grant him peace), but he would not accept it. Then later they took it to Abū Bakr and ᶜUmar [during their caliphates], but they too would not accept it, and he died during the rule of ᶜUthmān (may God be pleased with him).

[9:78] *Did they not know that God knows their secret* hypocrisy *and their confidential talks* wherein they insulted the faith, *and that God is the One Who best knows the Unseen?*

[9:79] *Those who find fault with the believers who offer charity voluntarily*, accusing those who gave in abundance of being ostentatious, such as Ibn ᶜAwf, and accusing those who gave a little because of their own poverty of giving it in order to be noticed so that they might receive it from others, *and* find fault with *those who find nothing but their endeavours*, whatever they might have, such as Abū ᶜAqīl al-Anṣārī who offered a *ṣāᶜ* of dates, *and deride them—God derides them*: He will requite them for their derision; *and theirs will be a painful chastisement*.

Then the following verse was revealed about Ibn Ubayy when he died:

[9:80] *Ask forgiveness for them, or do not ask forgiveness for them*: they are equally without benefit. *If you ask forgiveness for them seventy times*: that is, a great many times.

NOTE: It is commonplace to use seven, seventy, seven hundred and so on to symbolise large numbers because of how seven comprises most of the categories of number, such as the pair or the prime, which means a number other than one which cannot be divided into other [natural] numbers, and the composite, meaning that which can be divided into others. An example of a prime number is three, and a composite is [twenty]-five.[1] Then there are the prime and composite pair; the square, which is the result of multiplying a number by itself; the root, which is the number that is so multiplied, such as six; the number which is both of these, such as four; the perfect number, which is a number that is the sum of its divisors, such as six; the deficient number, which is a number that is greater than the sum of its divisors. It is also said that there is an abundant number, which is a number that is less than the sum of its divisors. Seven consists of four and three, which divided make twelve. Seventy is the limit of the limit, since the limit of units is the ten. Thus what is meant here is that He will never forgive them:

God will not forgive them. That hopelessness *is because they disbelieved in*
God and His Messenger: it is not due to stinginess on Our part, or laxity on
Q. 9:80 yours; *and God does not guide the wicked*, rebellious, disbelieving *folk* to sal-
vation. It is said that when this verse was revealed the Prophet (may God bless him and grant him peace) took the number literally and said, 'My Lord has permitted me, so I shall go beyond seventy.' Then He revealed, *It will be the same for them whether you ask forgiveness for them or do not ask forgiveness for them: God will never forgive them* [Q. 63:6], which abrogated this.

NOTE: Some have suggested that this was an example of the 'method of the sage'[2] on the part of the Prophet, a deliberate misreading of the situation similar to the account of how Qabaʿtharī reacted when [al-Ḥajjāj b. Yūsuf[3]] threatened him with the words, 'I shall have you carried off on a black horse,'[4] to which he replied, 'One such as the Emir may use either black or white horses for his burdens, as he pleases!' However, this interpretation is somewhat disrespectful [to the Prophet], because the method of the sage is a way of suggesting that one's own idea on the matter is the better way to proceed, which is not something that any prophet would suggest to the Almighty. In any case, the *ḥadīth*s about the incident refute this interpretation.

1 The text has here 'five', which is obviously an error, but similar passages in other works give 'twenty-five' as the example, which is likely what the author intended here.

2 See note on Q. 7:172.

3 The governor of Kufa for the Umayyad caliph ʿAbd al-Malik. See Abū Jaʿfar Muḥammad b. Jarīr al-Ṭabarī, *Tārīkh al-rusul wa'l-mulūk: dhayl al-mudhayyal*, trans. Ella Landau-Tasseron as *The History of al-Ṭabarī: An Annotated Translation, Volume XXXIX: Biographies of the Prophet's Companions and Their Successors*, New York: SUNY Press, 1988, p. 51.

4 A euphemism for imprisonment.

In that case, you might ask: how could the Prophet overlook the reality of the situation, given that he was the most eloquent of all the Arabs? The answer is that the verse affirmed that there would be no forgiveness, not that forgiveness ought not to be sought; and though his prayers for forgiveness might not have resulted in forgiveness being granted, they could well have had some other benefit, namely to show the extent of his mercy to those to whom he was sent, and to encourage us to be merciful to one another. Note how he said, 'If my Lord allows me, I shall go beyond seventy, as long as I am not forbidden to do so.' And God knows best.

[9:81] *Those who were left behind*—instead of going to Tabūk—*rejoiced at remaining behind the Messenger of God, and were averse to striving with their wealth and their lives in the way of God. And they said* to the believers, *'Do not go forth* to the Expedition of Tabūk *in the heat!' Say: 'The fire of Hell is hotter still*: and you have chosen it by disobeying.*' If only they understood* this, they would not have stayed behind.

[9:82] *But let them laugh a little* in the days of this world, *and weep much* in the Hereafter, *as a requital for what they used to earn*: their hypocrisy. Q. 9:81

[9:83] *So if God brings you back to a party of them*—of those who remained behind—*and they ask leave of you to go forth* to the Expedition of Tabūk, *say: 'You will never go forth with me, and you shall never fight with me against an enemy. You were content to stay behind the first time* at the Expedition of Tabūk, *so stay behind with those who stay behind*: the women and the like, or the sowers of corruption.*'*

[9:84] *And do not pray over* the funeral bier of *any one of them*, such as Ibn Ubayy, or do not supplicate for him, *when he dies, ever*: that is, when he dies as a disbeliever. This can be understood as 'when he dies forever', since his being raised to life only to be punished is tantamount to eternal death, or some say as 'never pray over him'.[1] *Nor stand over his grave* to visit it, or the like. *Truly, they disbelieved in God and His Messenger, and died while they were wicked folk.*

[9:85] *And let not their wealth and their children impress you; God desires only that He chastise them thereby in this world, and that their souls should depart while they are disbelievers*: this was explained earlier,[2] and is repeated here for emphasis; or it could be that it refers to other people this time. The word 'so' is not used here, unlike the previous verse, because in that verse it served to illustrate the link between their reluctance to expend

1 The placement of the word *abadan* (ever, forever) in the verse directly after *māt* (dies) is the cause of this ambiguity, which is difficult to reproduce in English.

2 See Q. 9:55.

and their impressive wealth, unlike the case for this verse. This verse has *and their children* rather than *or their children*, as in the previous verse, to dispel the possible implication that their children were more impressive than their wealth. The first verse has *to chastise*, while this verse has *that He chastise*, by way of indicating that God's actions have no external cause. The previous verse had *in the life of this world* while this verse has *in this world*, in order to indicate how the life of this world is of such inherent value to them that it goes without saying, and one need only speak of the world.

[9:86] *And when a sūra*—a part of the Qur'ān—*is revealed saying, 'Believe in God and strive with His Messenger,' the affluent among them ask leave of you, saying, 'Leave us to be with those who sit at home* with a valid excuse.'

[9:87] *They are content to be with those* women *who stay behind* in their houses, *and a seal has been set upon their hearts, so they do not understand* what is good for them.

[9:88] *But the Messenger and those who believe with him*—He linked
Q. 9:86 their faith with his faith—*strive with their wealth and their lives*: that is, if they stay behind, then others who are better than them will go to him. *For them are the good things* known only to God; *and those, they are the successful.*

[9:89] *God has prepared for them Gardens with rivers flowing from beneath them, abiding therein—that is the supreme triumph.*

[9:90] *And those Bedouins who had an excuse*—the word used here is *muʿadhdhirūn*, from the verb *ʿadhdhara*, meaning 'to fall short', or 'to proffer an excuse', 'to be excused', 'to prepare an excuse'—*came asking for leave* to stay behind, which he granted; *but those who lied to God and His Messenger* about their claims of faith *stayed behind* instead of coming to proffer their excuses. *A painful chastisement shall befall those of them who disbelieve.*

[9:91] *As for the weak*, such as the elderly, *and the sick, and those who find nothing to expend* on the struggle, *no blame*—no sin for staying behind—*falls upon them if they remain true to God and to His Messenger* through obedience in public and private. *There is no way*—no justification to invoke blame—*against those who are virtuous. And God is Forgiving* of their shortcomings, *Merciful* to them.

[9:92] *Nor against those who, when they came to you so that you might give them a mount*—this refers to seven poor men—*and you said to them, 'I cannot find anything to carry you,' turned back, their eyes flowing with tears*: this is an exaggeration for the sake of emphasis; *for sorrow that they could not find the means to expend* on the battle.

[9:93] *The way* of blame *is only against those who ask leave of you when they are rich, while they are content to be with those* women *who stay behind; and God has set a seal on their hearts*: so that they do not take admonition; *and so they do not know*: like madmen.

[9:94] *They will make excuses to you*, for staying behind, *when you return to them. Say: 'Do not make excuses. We will never believe you*, because *God has already told us* some *of your tidings. And God will see your work, as will His Messenger*: and whether you will repent or persist; *and then you will be returned to the Knower of the Unseen and the visible, and He will tell you what you used to do*: by requiting you for it.*'*

[9:95] *They will swear to you by God, when you turn back to them*: proffering their excuses for staying behind, *so that you may leave them be* without rebuking them. *So leave them be, for they are an abomination*: an impurity, and will not be cleansed of their hypocrisy; *and their abode shall be Hell, as requital for what they used to earn.*

[9:96] *They will swear to you so that you may be satisfied with them; but if you are satisfied with them* by believing them, *God will truly not be satisfied with the wicked folk*: meaning them, for He is not in the least confused about those Hypocrites. Ibn ʿAbbās related that there were eighty of them, and the Muslims were forbidden to sit or speak with them. Q. 9:93

[9:97] *The Bedouins are more intense in disbelief and hypocrisy* than the city dwellers because of their boorishness and how they spend no time with scholars—a *ḥadīth* says, 'The one who lives in the wilderness will dry up'; *and are more likely not to know the bounds of what God has revealed to His Messenger. And God is Knower* of their hearts, *Wise* in how He deals with them.

[9:98] *And of the Bedouins there is he who takes what he expends* in jihād *as a penalty*: a loss for which he expects no reward; *and awaits turns of fortune for you*: hopes that your fortunes will change, that he might be rid of you. *Theirs shall be the evil turn of fortune*: this is a term used to mean the dire consequences of time. *And God is Hearer* of their words, *Knower* of their thoughts.

[9:99] *And of the Bedouins there is he who believes in God and the Last Day, and takes what he expends as offerings to bring him nearer to God, and to the prayers*—supplications—*of the Messenger*: for he would supplicate for those who offered charity. *Surely these*—their donations—*will bring them nearer. God will admit them into His mercy*: the future tense here denotes emphasis. *Truly, God is Forgiving, Merciful.*

[9:100] *And the first to lead the way, of the Emigrants and the Helpers*, meaning those who prayed to the two *qiblas*,[1] or who fought at Badr, or who converted to Islam before the Emigration, or the Companions in general, *and those who follow them by being virtuous*, meaning faith and obedience until the Day of Resurrection, or those who invoke God's pleasure upon them and praise them, *God will be pleased with them, and they will be pleased with Him* on account of the favours of the two worlds which they will attain; *and He has prepared for them Gardens with rivers flowing beneath them*: it is said that the difference between this turn of phrase and other passages which have *from* [*beneath them*] is that the latter implies that the rivers spring forth from the Gardens; *abiding therein forever—that is the supreme triumph*.

[9:101] *And among those around you*, O folk of Medina, *of the Bedouins there are Hypocrites, and among the townspeople of Medina* there are people *who are obstinate*—persistent and wilful—*in hypocrisy. You do not know them* individually, O Muḥammad, *but We know them, and We shall chastise them twice*: with exposure in this world and the chastisement of the grave, or
Q. 9:101 simply time and again, meaning often; *and then they will be returned to a terrible chastisement* in Hell.

[9:102] *And others* among them *have confessed their sins*: and how they stayed behind from Tabūk without an excuse; *they have mixed a righteous deed*, such as regret and confession of sin, *with another that was bad*, such as how they stayed behind. In other words, they mixed the one deed with the other, or mixed them both together. *It may be that God will relent to them*: by accepting their repentance—He said *it may be* so that they would have hope without becoming complacent. *Truly, God is Forgiving, Merciful.*

[9:103] *Take of their wealth*—the wealth of those who stayed behind and then repented, such as Abū Lubāba and his party—*some charity to purify them* of their sins, *and to cleanse them*, cause their good deeds to grow, *thereby*: he took a third of their wealth and gave it to charity; *and pray for them*: supplicate for them. *Truly, your prayers are a comfort*—a mercy or tranquillity—*for them*: showing that their repentance has been accepted. *And God is Hearer* of your supplication, *Knower* of those for whom it is made.

[9:104] *Do they not know*—this is a rhetorical question meant to impart encouragement—*that God accepts repentance from His servants and takes*, accepts, *the voluntary charity*: which fall into His hand before they fall into hand of the beggar; *and that God is the Relenting and the Merciful?*

[9:105] *And say: 'Act* as you wish, O you who stayed behind, *for God will surely see your actions, as will His Messenger and the believers*: for God will show

1 Initially, it was Jerusalem, and then later Mecca.

[such actions] to them; *and you will be returned to the Knower of the Unseen and the visible, and He will tell you what you used to do*: by requiting you for it.'

[9:106] *And others* of those who stayed behind *are deferred to God's command*: to His verdict regarding them; *either He will chastise them, or relent to them*: this refers to the three men who stayed behind; *and God is Knower* of their state, *Wise* in what He does with them.

[9:107] *And* among them are *those who have chosen*—built—*a mosque by way of harm*: to harm the people of Qubā'; *and* to strengthen the cause of *disbelief; and to cause division among the believers*: by rivalling the Qubā' mosque; *and as an outpost for those who waged war against God and His Messenger before* at Badr. This refers to Abū ʿĀmir al-Rāhib, who after Badr went to Syria to ask the emperor to lend him some troops. In the meantime, they built the mosque for him on his orders to be ready for his return. *They will swear, 'We desired nothing but good* when we built it, such as for prayer'; *but God bears witness that they are truly liars* in their oath.

[9:108] *Never stand there* to pray in their mosque. He then ordered
that it be demolished, and the site remained in ruins. *A mosque which was* Q. 9:106
founded upon piety from the first day—from the moment of its incipience—*is worthier for you to stand therein*: this means the mosque of Qubā', as is related in a *ḥadīth* in Bukhārī. This is further supported by the general context of the account as well as a *ḥadīth* in Ibn Māja. Or it might mean the mosque of Medina, as is related in Muslim and elsewhere. The truth is that the narration of how it was revealed about the mosque of Qubā' does not contradict how the Prophet stated that it meant the mosque of Medina, because there is nothing to say that it had to refer exclusively to the people of Qubā'. *In it are men who love to purify themselves*: by washing themselves with both earth and water as the people of Qubā' did, as Ibn Māja and others narrated, or it means purify themselves from sin; *and God loves those who purify themselves*: outwardly and inwardly.

[9:109] *Is he who founded his building upon* the foundation of *fear of God and beatitude*—the seeking of His approval—*better, or he who founded his building upon the brink of a bank* of a river in Hell *that was crumbling*, ready to collapse, *so that it toppled with him*, with the building or the builder,[1] *into the fire of Hell?* It is authentically narrated that they saw smoke rise from it when they dug it up. *And God guides not the evildoing folk* to that which gives them salvation.

1 The ambiguity here is caused by the fact that the Arabic singular pronoun can mean either 'he' or 'it'.

[9:110] *The buildings which they have built will never cease to be a misgiving*—a cause of doubt and hypocrisy—*in their hearts*, for their envy only grew when it was demolished, *unless their hearts are cut to pieces* in the grave when they are no longer seats of consciousness; *and God is Knower* of their intentions, *Wise* in the command to demolish it.

[9:111] *Truly, God has purchased from the believers their lives and their possessions, so that theirs will be the Garden*: this is a metaphor for their reward. *They shall fight in the way of God and shall kill and be killed*: this is a separate clause to describe what that purchase involves. [*It is*] *a promise which is binding upon Him*, emphatically affirmed *in the Torah and the Gospel and the Qur'ān. And who*—no one—*fulfils his covenant better than God? Rejoice then in this bargain of yours which you have made, for that is the supreme triumph.*

[9:112] They are *those who repent, those who worship* with sincerity, *those who give praise* to God, *those who fast*—*sā'iḥūn* can mean 'those who fast' or 'those who seek knowledge'—*those who bow, those who prostrate themselves* in prayer, *those who enjoin decency and those who forbid indecency*: the word *and* here
Q. 9:110 is meant to link these two to what follows them as a single attribute—some say it is to mark the eighth item, since the list was completed with seven because the Arabs thought of seven as the ultimate number just as we think of it as ten, and eight to be a new beginning, but this is a baseless claim; *and those who maintain God's bounds*: His laws. *And give glad tidings to the believers.*

[9:113] *It is not* right *for the Prophet and those who believe to ask forgiveness for the idolaters*, such as Āmina or Abū Ṭālib, *even though they be kinsmen, after it has become clear to them that they are inhabitants of Hell-fire*: because of how they died in disbelief.

[9:114] *Abraham's prayer for the forgiveness of his father was only because of a promise he*, Abraham, *had made to him* if he submitted to God, when he said, *I shall ask forgiveness for you* [Q. 60:4]; *but when it became clear to him*—when he died in disbelief—*that he was an enemy of God, he declared himself innocent of him. Truly, Abraham was soft of heart*, humble and much given to sighing, *forbearing*, patient in enduring persecution.

[9:115] *And God would never send a people astray*—task them as He does with errant folk—*after He had guided them* to Islam, *until He had made clear to them that which they should be wary of*: that which they ought to avoid; and so He would not take them to task for asking forgiveness for the idolaters before that. *Truly, God is Knower of all things.*

[9:116] *Truly, to God belongs the kingdom of the heavens and of the earth. He gives life and He makes to die; and you do not have besides God any protector or helper*: so turn towards Him and away from them.

[9:117] *God has indeed relented to the Prophet and the Emigrants and the Helpers who followed him*: that is, He has absolved them of the link to sin, similar to His Words, *That God might forgive you* [Q. 48:2]; *in the hour*, the time, *of hardship* during the Expedition of Tabūk when it was very hot and uncomfortable, *after the hearts of a party of them had almost deviated; and then He relented to them*: this adds emphasis to what came before. *Truly, He is Gentle, Merciful to them.*

[9:118] *And* He relented *to the three who were left behind*—God delayed their verdict beyond the verdict of those who tied themselves to the pillars of the mosque and those who confessed their falsehoods—*when the earth was straitened for them, for all its breadth*: despite its vastness—this is a metaphor for their intense bewilderment; *and their souls were straitened for them* because of their anxiety, *until they thought*—came to know—*that there is no refuge from* the wrath of *God except in Him*: by humbly entreating Him. *Then He relented to them*—granted them the grace of repentance—*that they might repent. Truly, God is the Relenting, the Merciful* Who accepts repentance Q. 9:117
by His mercy.

[9:119] *O you who believe, fear God and be with those who are truthful* to their faith and their covenants.

[9:120] *It is not for the people of Medina and for the Bedouins around them to stay behind God's Messenger, and to prefer their lives to his life*: to hold their lives above his; rather, they should be with him in times of strife and hardship. *That* prohibition *is because neither thirst nor toil nor hunger afflicts them in the way of God, nor tread they any tread* in any place *that enrages the disbelievers, nor gain any gain from the enemy* by slaughter or otherwise, *but a righteous deed is therefore recorded for them*: detailing all of this, for which they earn a generous reward. *Truly, God does not leave the wage of the virtuous to go to waste.*

[9:121] *Nor expend they any sum* on God's cause, *small or great, nor do they cross any valley, but it*—the reward for it—*is recorded for them, that God may reward them the best* reward for the best *of what they used to do.*

[9:122] *It is not* apt *for the believers to go forth altogether* for an expedition; for they had begun to go out altogether because of their fear of what had been revealed about those who stayed behind. This applies to detachments, while the preceding passages applied to those who went out on expeditions alongside the Prophet (may God bless him and grant him peace). *Why should not a party*, a small group, *of every section*, every large group, *of them go forth so that they*, the ones who remain behind, *may become learned in religion and that they may warn their people* about the edicts that were revealed in their absence *when they return to them* from the expedition, *so that they may beware* them? This indicates that the reports of lone narrators (*khabar al-āḥād*) are valid proofs.[1]

[9:123] *O you who believe, fight those of the disbelievers who are near to you*: the nearest and then the next nearest; *and let them find harshness*—strength—*in you*: that is, fight them fiercely; *and know that God is with the pious*: to aid them.

[9:124] *And whenever a sūra is revealed, there are some of them*, the Hypocrites, *who say* to others among them, or to the weak believers mockingly, *'Which of you has this increased in faith?' As for those who believe, it has increased them in faith*, in belief, since now there is more to believe in, *and they rejoice* in its revelation.

[9:125] *But as for those in whose hearts is sickness*, hypocrisy, *it only adds abomination to their abomination*, disbelief to their disbelief, *and they die while they are disbelievers*.

Q. 9:123

[9:126] *Do they not see that they are tested* by droughts and the like, *every year once or twice*: that they might take heed? *Still they do not repent, nor do they remember*: and reflect.

[9:127] *And whenever a sūra is revealed, they look at one another* as if planning to flee, saying, *'Will anyone* of the Muslims *see you?'* If they see them, they get up to pray; but if not, they get up to leave. *Then they turn away* from the Prophet (may God bless him and grant him peace). *God turns their hearts away* from faith *because they are a folk who do not understand*: or reflect.

[9:128] *There has come to you a messenger from among yourselves for whom it is grievous*—troubling—*that you should suffer*: that anything should harm you, or that you should sin; *who is full of concern for you*: for your welfare; *to the believers full of pity*, compassion, *merciful* to them.

[9:129] *So if they turn away* from believing in you, *say: 'God suffices me. There is no god except Him. Upon Him* alone *I rely* and trust, *and He is the Lord of the Tremendous Throne* that encompasses all creation.'

1 There is a dispute about this among the jurists of the Four Schools and others.

10
Jonah
SŪRAT YŪNUS

Revealed in Mecca

In the Name of God, the Compassionate, the Merciful

[10:1] *Alif. Lām. Rā'*: this was explained earlier.[1] *These are the signs of the Wise Book*: meaning the Book which contains wisdom, or the Book which will not be abrogated by another.

[10:2] *Is it for the people* of Quraysh *a wonder that We have inspired a man from among them: 'Warn the* disbelieving *people and give glad tidings to those who believe that they have a* prior *standing of truth*—meaning a reward for what they have sent ahead—*with their Lord'?* When the Arabs wished to praise something, they would say that it was 'of truth'. This will be discussed further later. *The disbelievers say, 'Truly, this* Qur'ān, or this messenger,[2] *is manifest sorcery.'*

[10:3] *Truly, your Lord is God Who created the heavens and the earth in* the duration of *six days, and then rose above the Throne*: this was explained in *Sūrat al-Aʿrāf*.[3] *He directs the affair*: ordaining it entirely by His wisdom. *There can be no intercessor save after His permission. That*—the One so described—*is God, your Lord, so worship Him* alone. *Will you not remember*: and take admonition*?*

[10:4] *To Him is the return of all of you* upon death—*God's promise, in truth*: affirmed to Him and to all others. *Truly, He originates creation and then recreates it, that He may requite those who believe and perform righteous deeds justly*: the word *justly* could refer to His justice, or to theirs. *And those who*

1 See Q. 2:1.

2 Depending on whether it is read as *siḥr* (sorcery) or *sāḥir* (sorcerer), both of which are canonical.

3 See Q. 7:54.

disbelieve, for them will be a draught of boiling water so hot that a drop of it would boil an ocean, *and a painful chastisement because of how they disbelieved*: He switched the rhetorical style here in order to emphasise how this is entirely what they deserve. He singled out the first group for mention of justice, though He will be just to them all, in order to emphasise His greater concern for them.

[10:5] *He it is Who made the sun a radiance*: an object of radiance, which indicates that it is the means by which other things can be seen; *and the moon a light*: an object of light, which means that by which the luminous object itself can be seen.

NOTE: The word *ḍaw'* (radiance) is usually used to refer to outspreading rays, while *nūr* (light) is used to mean the light in the thing itself. This means that *ḍaw'* is a branch of *nūr*, but is nevertheless more significant because sight depends on it, while *nūr* only allows the source of the light to be seen. Thus He made the sun a lamp (*sirāj*), for it allows other things
Q. 10:5 to be seen, but made the moon a light (*nūr*) so that it could be seen and used for navigation.

And He determined it—meaning both of them, or the moon in particular because it is the one which has stations and the one by which the lunar months of the year are counted—*in stations so that you might know the number of the years and the reckoning* of months and days for your interactions. *God did not create that save* adorned *in truth. He details the signs for a folk who have knowledge*: and can benefit from it.

[10:6] *Truly, in the alternation of night and day*—in length and light and their opposites—*and what God has created in the heavens and the earth there are signs for a folk who fear* consequences, for it inspires them to contemplate.

[10:7] *Truly, those who do not expect to encounter Us* because they deny the Resurrection, *and are content with the life of this world* instead of the Hereafter, *and feel reassured in it*—at peace with it—*and those who are heedless of Our signs* both cosmological and scriptural, by refusing to contemplate them, [10:8] *their abode will be the Fire because of what they used to earn*: their sins.

[10:9] *Truly, those who believe and perform righteous deeds, their Lord will guide them through their faith* to that which leads to the Garden. *Rivers will flow from beneath them in the Gardens of Bliss.*

[10:10] *Their prayer therein*—their supplication for whatever they desire—*shall be, 'Glory be to You, O God!'* Thereupon whatever they desire will appear before them. *And their greeting* to one another *therein will be 'Peace'* for what they have there will be safe from ever fading. *And their final prayer* when they eat *will be, 'Praise be to God, Lord of the Worlds.'*

[10:11] *And if God should hasten for people evil* when they pray against themselves, such as when they said, *If this be indeed the truth from You, then rain down stones upon us from the heaven*... [Q. 8:32], *as they would hasten good* when they call for it, *their term would already have been concluded for them*: and He would have done away with them; but instead He gives them respite. *But We leave those who do not expect to encounter Us*—leading them on into perdition—*to wander blindly in their insolence*: utterly bewildered.

[10:12] *If misfortune should befall a man, he calls upon Us* to repel it, lying *on his side, or sitting or standing*: that is, no matter what his situation might be; *but when We have relieved him of his misfortune, he passes on* and continues just as he was before the misfortune came, *as if he had never called upon Us to* dispel *a misfortune that had befallen him. So*, just as both situations were adorned for him, *is adorned for the prodigal* disbelievers *that which they do.*

[10:13] *And indeed We have destroyed generations before you*, O people of Mecca, *when they did evil*: by denying their messengers; *and their messengers brought them clear proofs* of their sincerity, *but they would not believe*: that is, they did not even come close to believing. *So*, by such destruction, *shall We requite the sinful folk*: so beware of them. Q. 10:11

[10:14] *Then We made you* their *successors in the earth after them, that We might behold how you would behave*: and requite you for it.

[10:15] *And when Our clear verses are recited to them, those who do not expect to encounter Us* at the Resurrection *say, 'Bring a Qur'ān other than this* one which speaks of monotheism, *or change it* by removing from it those parts that we dislike.' *Say: 'It would not be* right *for me to change it of my own accord. I only follow that which is revealed to me. Truly, I fear, if I should disobey my Lord* by changing it, *the chastisement of a dreadful day*: the Resurrection.'

[10:16] *Say: 'If God had willed* that I not recite it, *I would not have recited it to you, nor would He have made it known to you* through me. This can also be read as *but* [*instead*] *He would have made it known to you*, meaning through someone else. *For I have already dwelt among you a lifetime*—forty years—*before this*: and I am unlettered and have never seen a teacher nor issued a sermon. *Will you not understand* that it is from God*?'*

[10:17] *And who does greater evil than he who invents a lie against God* by associating others with Him, *or denies His signs? Truly, the sinners shall not prosper* from their idolatry.

[10:18] *And they worship besides God that which can neither hurt them* if they leave it *nor profit them* if they worship it; *and they say, 'These* idols *are our intercessors with God* in this life and the next, if indeed there is a resurrection.' *Say: 'Would you tell God of what He does not know*, namely that He has a partner, though it does not exist *in the heavens or in the earth?'* For if God does not know of something, this means that it does not exist. The mention of the heavens and earth indicates that whether their associates were heavenly or earthly beings, they were nothing but weak creatures just like them. *Glory be to Him! And High be He exalted above what they associate!*

[10:19] *People* between Adam and Noah *were but one community*—surrendered to God—*but then they differed* because of idolatry. *And had it not been for a word that had already preceded from your Lord* that every community would have a fixed term, *it would have been decided between them* immediately *regarding that over which they differed*: by the destruction of the errant party.

[10:20] *And they*, the idolaters, *say, 'Why has a sign not been sent down on him*—on Muḥammad—*from his Lord* in the manner that we suggested*?' Say: 'The Unseen belongs only to God*: and perhaps He knows that to send it down would cause harm. *So wait. I am waiting with you* to see what God will do with you.*'*

Q. 10:19

[10:21] *And when We made people taste mercy*, such as comfort, *after adversity had afflicted them*, such as discomfort, *behold! they have some plot concerning* attacking *Our signs. Say: 'God is swifter at plotting* for He has already planned your downfall. *Truly, Our messengers*, the recording angels, *are writing down that which you are plotting*: for the requital.*'*

[10:22] *He it is Who conveys you*—allows you to travel—*across the land and the sea, until when you are in ships*: the word *until* here implies 'you travel until, when this occurs and the stormy winds blow, and the waves swell up, and it seems that ruin is nigh, and you call out, the fair wind comes', and so on; so everything that follows the word *when* is governed by it. Hence there is no need to object to the word *until* on the grounds that such a situation is the purpose of travelling. *And they sail with them*—note the switch in pronoun—*with a fair breeze, and they rejoice therein, there comes upon them*, the ships, *a stormy wind* of great strength *blows, and waves come on them from every side*—every direction—*and they think that they are overwhelmed*, doomed, *they call upon God, secure in their faith only to Him*, having abandoned idolatry, saying, *'If You deliver us from this* hardship, *we shall surely be of the thankful.'*

[10:23] *Yet when He has delivered them, behold that they despoil*—sow corruption—*in the earth wrongfully*: this qualification is to make their acts distinct from rightful despoilment, such as laying waste to the property of the disbelievers. *O people, your despoilment is only against yourselves*: for its dire consequences will befall you alone. This is but the *enjoyment of the life of this world*, which you may enjoy for a while, *but then to Us is your return, and We shall inform you of what you used to do* by requiting you for it.

[10:24] *The likeness of the life of this world* and how it will be over swiftly, and how you are deluded by it, *is only as water which We send down from the heaven, and the plants of the earth mingle with it*, draw it into themselves, *whereof people eat*, as with crops, *as do cattle*, as with grass, *until, when the earth has taken on its ornaments and has adorned itself* with all manner of plants, *and its inhabitants think that they are masters of it* and its resources, *Our command*—Our chastisement—*comes upon it by night or day, and We make it*—its crops—*as reaped corn* cast down upon the earth, *as though the previous day it had not flourished*: as though it had not been covered in crops only a moment before. *Thus do We detail the signs for a folk who contemplate.*

[10:25] *And God summons to the Abode of Peace*: this was explained earlier;[1] *and He guides whomever He wills to a straight path.*

[10:26] *For those who do good is the fairest reward*: the Garden; *and more*: the vision of God's countenance, as an authentic *ḥadīth* states. *Neither dust nor ignominy shall cover their faces. Those are the inhabitants of the Garden, therein they will abide.*

Q. 10:24

[10:27] *And for those who earn evil deeds shall be the requital of an evil deed by the like thereof; ignominy shall overcome them—they have no protector against* the chastisement of *God—as if their faces had been covered*, so blackened they shall be, *with strips of darkest night*: this can also be read as *with a dark strip of night. Those are the inhabitants of the Fire, therein they will abide.*

[10:28] *And* remember *the day when We shall gather them altogether, then We shall say to those who associated, 'In your place* remain, *you and your associates*: to be requited': this refers to a moment other than the one wherein God will not speak to them.[2] *Then We shall make a separation between them*: severing their connection; *and their associates will say, 'It was not us that you were worshipping.*

[10:29] *'God suffices as a witness between us and you, that indeed we were unaware of your worship*: for we were inanimate objects.'

[10:30] *There*, in that station, *every soul shall experience*, be informed of, *what it did before*: and whether its deeds were harmful or helpful; *and they*—their case—*shall be returned to God, their rightful Lord* (*Mawlā*): the One Who takes responsibility (*yatawallā*) for dealing with them, not their false associates; *and that to which they laid claim* as their god *shall fail them.*

[10:31] *Say: 'Who provides for you out of the heaven* with rain, *and the earth* with plants, *or Who possesses hearing and sight*, having created them,

1 See Q. 6:127.
2 See Q 2:174 and Q. 3:77.

and Who brings forth the living from the dead by means of the drop of fluid, *and brings forth the dead from the living, and Who directs the affair* of the world*?' They will say, 'God'*: because this is obvious. *Say: 'Will you not then fear* idolatry, given this admission*?'*

[10:32] *That*—the One so described—*then is God, your true Lord* Whose lordship is affirmed; *so what is there*—there is nothing—*after truth except error? How then are you turned away* from worshipping Him*?*

[10:33] *Thus*, just as His lordship is justified, *the Word*—the verdict—*of your Lord is justified concerning those who are wicked*: those who rebel and stray outside the bounds of what is good for them; it is justified *that they do not believe.*

[10:34] *Say: 'Is there of those whom you associate one that originates creation, then recreates it?'* He referred to the recreation in the same breath as the creation, though they denied it, because of how demonstrably true it is. *Say: 'God originates creation, then recreates it*: for they deny this. *How, then, are you deviated:* turned from the truth*?'*

Q. 10:32

[10:35] *Say: 'Is there of those whom you associate one that guides to the truth?' Say: 'God guides to the truth. Is One Who guides to the truth more deserving of being followed, or one who does not guide, unless he is guided?* This is true even of those they revere, such as Christ, so how could it not be true of a stone? Or it means 'carried': is the One Who guides humankind more worthy to be followed or the one who has to be carried from place to place with the help of men? *So what is wrong with you? How do you judge* by something that is obviously false*?'*

[10:36] *And most of them*—meaning all of them—*follow nothing but conjecture* based on false analogies, such as drawing an analogy between the Creator and His creation by means of an imagined partnership. *Truly, conjecture avails nothing against truth*: this indicates that it is necessary to know the fundamentals of doctrine firsthand, without blindly following the belief of another. *Truly, God is Knower of what they do*: and will requite them.

[10:37] *And this Qur'ān is not such as could ever be produced by anyone besides God; but it is a confirmation of what is before it*—the [previous] Book—*and a detailing of the Book*, the laws that are written and ordained, *wherein is no doubt*, sent down *from the Lord of the Worlds.*

[10:38] *Or do they say, 'He*, Muḥammad, *has invented it'? Say: 'Then bring a sūra like it* of your own invention, of comparable eloquence, *and call upon whom you can besides God* to help you, *if you are truthful* in your claim that he has invented it, on the basis that you are more learned about poetry and letters than he is.*'*

[10:39] *Nay, but they denied that which they did not comprehend with knowledge*: namely the things in the Qur'ān whose reality was unknown to them—for a man is a natural enemy to that of which he is ignorant; *and whereof the sequel has not yet come to them*: the final outcome of the promises it contains. What this means is that they preferred to deny it before they had contemplated it and come to recognise its truth. *So those who were before them denied* their messengers. *Behold, then, what was the consequence for the evildoers*: and expect the same for them.

[10:40] *And of them are some who will believe in it* later, *and some who would never believe in it. And your Lord knows very well the corrupters*: the detractors.

[10:41] *If they deny you*—if they persist in denying you—*then say: 'Unto me is my work, and to you your work*: that is, absolve yourself of them. *You are innocent of what I do* in obedience, *and I am innocent of what you do* in disobedience.*'* This was abrogated by the Sword [Verse].

[10:42] *And of them are some who listen to you* when you recite the Qur'ān, though they do not accept it. *But will you make the deaf to hear*— Q. 10:39
can you give them the power to hear?—*even though they do not understand* in addition to their deafness*?* This implies that the true meaning of listening to words lies in understanding what they mean.

[10:43] *And of them are some who look toward you*: and behold the proofs of your truthfulness. *But will you guide the blind, even though they do not see?* In other words, even if they lack insight as well as physical sight? These are justifications for absolving yourself of them.

[10:44] *Truly, God does not wrong people in any way*: by removing their senses or intelligence. This indicates that humans have the ability to acquire and choose, contrary to the doctrine of the fatalists. *But people wrong themselves*: by squandering their own souls.

[10:45] *And* remember *the day when He shall gather them, as if they had not tarried but an hour of the day* in the world or the grave because of the panic of the Resurrection, *recognising one another* as though they had only known each other for an hour before their acquaintance was cut short. *Indeed, those will have lost who denied the encounter with God* at the Resurrection, *for they were not guided* to the welfare of this trade.

[10:46] *And whether We show you something of that which We promise them*—meaning that chastisement—*or We take you* before that, *to Us they shall return* for Our chastisement, which is inevitable in any event. *And God, moreover, is Witness of what they do*: this alludes to the consequence of this witnessing, which is requital.

[10:47] *And for every community there is a messenger* who calls them to the truth; *and when their messenger comes, judgement is passed between them* with their prophets *justly* with the annihilation of those who deny him, and the salvation of those who follow him, *and they are not wronged* by their chastisement, so there is no going back.

[10:48] *And they say*—the idolaters say incredulously—*'When will this promise* of chastisement *come to pass, if you*, the Messenger and his followers, *are truthful?'*

[10:49] *Say: 'I have no power to hurt myself or to benefit, except as God might will* for me to possess, so how could I bring this promise forward for you? *For every community there is an appointed time* for their destruction. *When their time comes, they cannot delay it by a single hour, nor bring it forward'*: this was explained earlier.[1]

[10:50] *Say: 'Have you considered if His chastisement comes upon you at* the time of *slumber or at day*: that is, when you are oblivious because of sleep or because of work. He did not say 'night' because if chastisement comes
Q. 10:47 suddenly and without warning, it will be more impactful, and there will be no sleeping through it. *What is there of it*—of this chastisement—*that the sinners seek to hasten?* All of it is detestable.

[10:51] *'Is it then, when it has come to pass, that you will believe in it?'* You will be told, *'What, now* do you believe in it, *when you have been hastening it on* in mockery*?'*

[10:52] *Then will it be said to those who were evildoers, 'Taste the everlasting chastisement! Are you requited for anything but what you used to earn?'*

[10:53] *And they ask you to tell them, 'Is it true*: what you say about the Resurrection and the rest*?' Say: 'Aye, by my Lord! Truly, it is true*—confirmed—*and you cannot escape.'*

[10:54] *And if each soul that has done wrong* to another, or to itself by idolatry, *had all that is in the earth*—all of its treasures—*it would offer it as ransom* from the chastisement; *and they will feel remorse within them when they see the chastisement*: but they will conceal it within themselves fearing lest they be blamed further for expressing it, so awful will that moment be; *but it has been decided justly between them* and their prophets, *and they are not wronged* by their chastisement, so there is no going back.

[10:55] *Why, surely to God belongs all that is in the heavens and the earth*: and He has power over all. *Why, surely God's promise is true, but most of them do not know*: because of their heedlessness.

1 See Q. 7:34.

[10:56] *He gives life and makes to die, and to Him you shall be returned* upon death.

[10:57] *O people, there has come to you an admonition from your Lord*: to elucidate what actions are beautiful and what are ugly, which is the meaning of practical wisdom; *and a healing for what* doubt *is in the breasts*: which is the meaning of speculative wisdom; *and a guidance* to the truth; *and a mercy for those who believe*: by saving them from error. The repeated use of the word *and* here serves to indicate how the different attributes all describe different aspects of the same thing. This is akin to the poet's words, 'To the master, the liege, and the Son of al-Humām.'

[10:58] *Say: 'In the bounty of God*, such as Islam, *and in His mercy*, such as the Qur'ān—*in that let them rejoice*. He says *in that* to add emphasis and to indicate that it is in the coming of the Book endowed with all the aforementioned attributes that they ought to rejoice. *It*, such rejoicing, *is better than that* wealth *which they hoard.'*

Q. 10:56

[10:59] *Say: 'Have you considered what provision God has revealed for you* by heavenly means, *and how you have made some of it unlawful*, such as the *baḥā'ir*,[1] *and some lawful*, such as carrion?' *Say: 'Has God given you permission* to declare these laws, *or do you invent lies concerning God*: by attributing them to Him?' This is sufficient rebuke to those who issue legal opinions without due diligence, as many of the jurists of this age do.

[10:60] *And what do they expect, those who invent lies concerning God, on the Day of Resurrection?* Do they expect that they will not be requited for it? *Truly, God is Bountiful to people*: by giving them respite, and much else; *but most of them do not give thanks*: for His favours.

[10:61] *And you*, O Muḥammad, *are not occupied with any business*, any activity, *nor do you recite anything regarding it*, regarding this business, *from the Qur'ān, nor do you perform any action* with your community, *but We are witnesses over you when you are engaged therein. And not so much as the weight of an atom*, a tiny ant or speck of dust, *in the earth or in the heaven*, meaning anywhere in existence, *escapes your Lord*: He placed *the earth* first here because the discourse concerns the folk of the earth, unlike in *Sūrat Saba'*;[2] and He singled out *earth* and *heaven* for mention because a person's senses do not extend beyond them. *Nor what is less than that* amount *or greater, but it is in a clear Book*: meaning the Tablet.

[10:62] *Assuredly God's friends*—those who undertake to obey Him

1 See Q. 5:103.

2 Q. 34:3, where *heaven* is placed before *earth* in an otherwise identical passage.

and whom He undertakes to honour—*no fear shall befall them* at the Great Calamity, *neither shall they grieve* at the loss of anything hoped-for.

[10:63] *Those who believed, and who used to fear* sin.

[10:64] *Theirs are glad tidings in the life of this world*: such as true dreams which they have, and which others have about them, or which the angels see at the Calamity; *and in the Hereafter*: such as the Garden. *There is no changing the Words*—the promises—*of God. That* tiding *is the supreme triumph.*

[10:65] *And let not what they say*—their threats—*grieve you. Truly, power*—might and omnipotence—*belongs wholly to God*: and He will strengthen you. As for His Words *power belongs to God, and to His Messenger, and to the believers* [Q. 63:8], this means strength, the manifestation of faith, and victory over enemies. *He is the Hearer* of your words, *the Knower* of your intentions.

[10:66] *Assuredly, to God belongs all who are in the heavens and all who are*
in the earth: and so all power is His. He singled out intelligent beings here[1]
because all other beings are included *a priori. Those who call upon*—wor-
Q. 10:63 ship—*besides God are not following associates* in reality, but only things which
they call associates; *they are following nothing but conjecture* that they are gods,
and they are only telling lies.

[10:67] *He it is Who made for you the night that you should rest therein* from the toil of the day, *and the day, which provides sight* of the means of your livelihood. He mentioned the purpose of the night's creation, but only described the day, so that each of them would imply what the other stated outright; He did not say 'that you should see', to draw a distinction between the time itself and the cause of its creation. *Truly, in that are signs for a folk who are able to hear* with reflection.

[10:68] *They say, 'God has taken a son*: such as the angels.*' Glory be to Him!* He is transcendently beyond procreation. *He is Independent*: and procreation is only done out of need. *To Him belongs all that is in the heavens and all that is in the earth. You have no warrant*—proof—*for this. Do you say about God what you do not know?*

[10:69] *Say: 'Truly, those who invent lies concerning God shall not prosper* in this life or the next.*'*

[10:70] *Enjoyment* for a short while *in this world*, such as by their fabrications to hold onto their authority, *and then to Us is their return* upon death; *and then We shall make them taste terrible chastisement because of how they used to disbelieve.*

1 By the use of the word *who.*

[10:71] *And recite to them the story of Noah*: that they might take admonition. *He said to his people, 'O my people, if my sojourn*, my existence among you, *is too great*, too weighty and difficult, *for you, as is my reminder* to you *by the signs of God, then in God have I put my trust. So decide upon your course of action* resolutely *together with your associates, and then let not your decision* regarding me *be a secret between you*, but rather make it public, *and then carry it out against me* however you wish to deal with me, *and do not put it off*: I am not concerned with you, for I trust in God.

[10:72] *'But if you turn away* from my reminder, *then I have not asked you for any wage* that I might lose if you turn away; *my wage falls only on God, and I have been commanded to be of those who submit* to God's command.*'*

[10:73] *But they denied him*: and persisted in denying him; *so We saved him and those with him* from drowning *in the Ark, and made them successors* of the drowned ones, *and We drowned those who denied Our signs. Behold, then, how was the consequence for those who had been warned*: but who denied.

[10:74] *Then after him*—after Noah—*We sent messengers to their people, and they brought them clear proofs* in the form of prophetic miracles, *but it was not for them to believe*—it did not seem right for them to believe—*in that* truth *which they had denied before* the messengers were sent, for they had grown accustomed to denying the truth. *Thus do We seal the hearts of the transgressors* who go beyond the bounds of God. Q. 10:71

[10:75] *Then after them*—after those messengers—*We sent Moses and Aaron to Pharaoh and his council*, the nobles of his people, for the commoners were their followers, *with Our signs, but they were disdainful and were a sinful folk* accustomed to iniquity.

[10:76] *So when the truth came to them from Us* in the form of his prophetic miracles, *they said, 'Truly, this is manifest sorcery.'*

[10:77] *Moses said, 'Do you say so of the Truth when it has come to you?* This refers to what they said, that is, 'Do you call it sorcery?' Or it means 'to speak of' in the sense of 'to criticise'. *Is this sorcery? Now sorcerers do not prosper'*: these were not the words of Moses himself, unless he meant it as a rhetorical question.

[10:78] *They said, 'Have you come to us to divert us from what we found our fathers following*—meaning idol-worship—*and that you both might attain greatness in the land? We will not believe you two.'*

[10:79] *And Pharaoh said, 'Bring me every cunning sorcerer* to oppose him.*'*

[10:80] *And when the sorcerers came, Moses said to them, 'Cast your cast!'* This was because he was not in the least bit concerned about them.

[10:81] *Then, when they had cast, Moses said, 'What you have brought is but sorcery*: unlike what I have brought. *Truly, God will bring it to nothing*: and erase it. *Truly, God does not make right*—strong—*the work of those who do corruption*.

[10:82] *'And God will vindicate*, affirm, *the Truth by His Words*, His command, *however much the sinners be averse.'*

[10:83] *But none believed in Moses save a few of his people*: such as a few youths—*his people* could mean the people of Moses on his mother's side, or the people of Pharaoh on his father's side; *out of fear of Pharaoh and their council*: the nobles of his people. The use of the plural pronoun here refers to how he had many companions who carried out his orders; it is not a plural of majesty, since that is only used in direct speech, although some said it can be used in any context. *That he might persecute them; for truly Pharaoh was despotic*—tyrannical—*in the land, and truly he was of the prodigal*: in his arrogance.

[10:84] *And Moses said, 'O my people, if you have believed in God then put your trust in Him, if you have submitted*: surrendered to His command'; for
Q. 10:82 belief is a condition for its obligation, while submission is a condition for its attainment. So this is not a case of a ruling being dependent on two conditions, as if you said, 'If you go in there, you are divorced if you speak.' Rather, it is akin to saying, 'If you go in there, you are divorced if you are my wife.'

[10:85] *So they said, 'In God we have put our trust. Our Lord, do not make us a cause of beguilement for the evildoing folk*: by allowing them to dominate and oppress us on account of our religion, which will only delude them into thinking that they are in the right. This implies that if one trusts in God before calling on Him, He will surely answer.

[10:86] *'And deliver us by Your mercy from* the plot of *the disbelieving folk.'*

[10:87] *And We inspired Moses and his brother: 'Appoint*—take as residences—*houses for your people in Egypt and make your houses oratories*: places of prayer, for they would only pray in their temples, but feared Pharaoh; *and observe the prayer* therein; *and give glad tidings*, O Moses, *to the believers* that they will be helped': He used the dual first[1] because appointing is done by the leader, and then the plural[2] because devoting spaces to prayer was obligatory for every individual, and then the singular[3] because glad tidings are given by the bearer of the Law.

1 For *tabawwa'ā*, literally, 'appoint, both of you'.
2 For *ijʿalū*, literally 'make, all of you', and *aqīmū*, 'observe, all of you'.
3 For *bashshir*, 'give glad tidings'.

[10:88] *And Moses said, 'Our Lord, You have truly given Pharaoh and his council splendour*: meaning things that provide comfort and beauty; *and riches in the life of this world. Our Lord, that they may lead astray from Your way*: that is, You gradually led them on into perdition by giving them those things. *Our Lord, obliterate their riches*: take away their light and their splendour—and so their precious metals became base, and their silver coins became engraved stones; *and harden their hearts so that they do not believe*—heed the call—*until they see the painful chastisement'*: he prayed this because of the rage he felt for the sake of God's and His religion once he had lost hope that they would ever believe, in the same way as we invoke curses upon Satan. To be content with disbelief inasmuch as it is disbelief is itself an act of disbelief, and no individual is turned into a disbeliever as a punishment. It could also be read as a continuation of *that they may lead astray*. Some say that it means 'for they have not believed'.

[10:89] *He*, God, *said, 'Your prayer has been answered*: because Aaron
said 'amen' to his prayer. *So the two of you remain upright*: and continue to Q. 10:88
call to Me; *and do not follow the way of those who have no knowledge*: by asking
for haste.*'* It would be another forty years before the prayer was granted.

[10:90] *And We brought the Children of Israel across the sea*: upon the sea bed; *and Pharaoh pursued them together with his hosts, in insolence and transgression until, when drowning overtook him, he said, 'I believe that there is no god save Him in whom the Children of Israel believe, and I am of those who submit'*: so Gabriel filled his mouth with clay, lest his statement be accepted. Then God or Gabriel said:

[10:91] *'Now?* In your moment of despair, do you believe? *But their faith was of no benefit to them when they saw Our doom* [Q. 40:85]; *when hitherto you have disobeyed* for your entire life, *and been of those who do corruption*: and lead others astray*?*

[10:92] *'But this day We shall save you*: keep you from the pit of the sea and make you float on the surface—none of the drowned ones were ever seen again, except for Pharaoh; *in your body*: without any spirit, or in your armour, or 'We shall deliver it safely to land'—Ibn ʿAbbās (may God be pleased with him) said that he had a suit of gold armour by which he could be identified; *that you may be for those after you*—in the generations to come—*a sign*: an admonition. *But truly most people are heedless of Our signs:* and do not contemplate them.*'*

[10:93] *And We appointed for the Children of Israel an abode of truth*: meaning Syria or Egypt—note also what was said about *a standing of truth* [Q. 10:2]; *and We provided them with good things*: pleasant and delicious foods; *and they did not differ* about their religion *until the knowledge*—the Torah—*had come to them*: and so the cause of their unity became the cause of their dissent. *Truly, your Lord will judge between them on the Day of Resurrection concerning that wherein they used to differ*: by establishing the adherents of truth and punishing the adherents of falsehood.

[10:94] *So if you are in doubt concerning what We have revealed to you*: this was intended to spur him [the Prophet], or as a hypothetical, or to rebuke those who did doubt, such as when He said to Jesus, *O Jesus son of Mary, did you say to people, 'Take me and my mother as gods, besides God'?* [Q. 5:116]; *then question those who read the Book before you*: such as Ibn Salām, for they held him to be an authority. When this was revealed, the Prophet (may God bless him and grant him peace) said, 'I do not doubt, nor shall I ask.' *The truth from your Lord has surely come to you, so do not be of the waverers*: by stumbling from your certitude.

[10:95] *And do not be of those who deny God's signs, and so be of the losers.*

[10:96] *Truly, those against whom your Lord's Word*, His decree that they
Q. 10:94 die while in disbelief, *is justified*, confirmed, *will not believe* [10:97] *though every sign come to them, until they see the painful chastisement*: whereupon their belief will be of no use to them.

[10:98] *If only there had been*—this implies that were was not, though there should have been—*one town that believed*, whose people believed after witnessing the punishment firsthand, *and profited by its belief—except for the people of Jonah*: the folk of Nineveh in the region of Mosul; *when they believed* after witnessing it, and separated every animal from its young, and donned sackcloth garments and humbled themselves to God in repentance, *We removed from upon them the chastisement of degradation*, a black smoke that covered them, *in the life of this world, and We gave them comfort for a while* until they died.

[10:99] *And if your Lord willed, all who are in the earth would have believed together*: and been united in faith—this refutes the Qadariyya sect.[1] *Would you then compel people* to do what He wills not, *until they are believers?*

[10:100] *And it is not for any soul to believe save by the permission of God*: by His will; *and He causes abomination*—degradation—*to fall upon those who have no understanding* of God's proofs.

[10:101] *Say*: *'Behold*—contemplate on—*what is in the heavens and in the earth'*: His works. *But signs and warnings do not avail a folk who will not believe.*

1 The advocates of absolute free will.

[10:102] *What do they await, but the like of the days of those who passed away before them?* By doing what brings it on, they are essentially awaiting it expectantly. *Say: 'Then await. I shall truly be with you among the waiting.'*

[10:103] *Then We shall deliver Our messengers*: this refers to the past; *and the believers. Just so it is incumbent upon Us*—because of Our promise—*to deliver the believers.*

[10:104] *Say: 'O people, if you are in doubt about* the validity of *my religion, then I do not worship those whom you worship besides God; but I worship God, Who will take you to Him*: by claiming your spirits—He said this to instil fear in them so that they might desist from idolatry—*and I have been commanded to be of the believers* in God.

[10:105] *'And: Set your purpose for religion*—for uprightness therein—*as a ḥanīf*: one who inclines away from idolatry; *and do not be of the idolaters.*

[10:106] *'And do not call upon besides God that which can neither profit you* if you worship it *nor hurt you* if you abandon it; *for if you do, then you will surely be of the evildoers.* Q. 10:102

[10:107] *'And if God touches you with some harm, there is none who can remove it save Him; and if He desires good for you, there is none who can repel His bounty*: He mentioned desire in connection with good, and touching in connection with harm, though they might seem interchangeable, in order to imply that good is intrinsically desirable while harm is not. In the similar verse in *Sūrat al-Anʿām*,[1] He did not speak of desire because goodness belongs to Him and cannot be repelled; repelling only applies to things that will occur, while touching refers to things that have already occurred. Note also that He did not say 'there is none who can repel it save Him', because His desire cannot be repelled, and so instead He spoke of His bounty to imply that it is a gift, not something we have earned. *He strikes with it*—with good—*whomever He will of His servants. He is the Forgiving, the Merciful'*: so expose yourselves to His mercy by obeying Him.

[10:108] *Say: 'O people, the Truth*—the Qur'ān—*has come to you from your Lord. So whoever is guided* by it *is guided only for the sake of his own soul*: and for its good; *and whoever errs* by disbelieving in it *errs only against it*: and the consequence of his error will befall only himself. *And I am not a guardian over you*: responsible for your affair.'

1 *And if God touches you with an affliction, then none can remove it except Him; and if He touches you with good, then He has power over all things* (Q. 6:17).

Q. 10:109

[10:109] *And follow what is revealed to you*: for obeying and conveying; *and endure* their oppression *until God gives judgement* that you may struggle against them, or emigrate; *for He is the Best of Judges*: and His judgement never errs, for He knows all that is secret as well as all that is open. Glory be to Him!

11
Hūd
SŪRAT HŪD

Revealed in Mecca

After saying, *the Truth has come to you* [Q. 10:108], meaning the Qur'ān, and then saying, *Follow what is revealed to you* [Q. 10:109], He then follows this by describing it further, saying:

In the Name of God, the Compassionate, the Merciful

[11:1] *Alif. Lām. Rā'*. This is *a Book whose verses have been set clear*: arranged without any fissures in word or meaning, or whose verses will not be abrogated; or the *Book* here means the verses of this *sūra*, for none of them were ever abrogated; *then*, for the distinctions within the rulings, *detailed*: reiterated where needed; sent down *from One Wise* in the ordain of its edicts, *Informed* of how to reinforce its details.

[11:2] *To wit: 'Worship none but God. Truly, I am to you from Him*—from God—*a warner* to the sinners, *and a bearer of glad tidings* to the obedient.'

[11:3] *And: 'Ask forgiveness of your Lord* for sin, *then repent to Him*: return to Him with obedience; or the word *then* denotes the distinction between the two, or it means 'then they sought to draw nearer to Him by means of it'; or the former refers to prior sins, and the latter to future sins; *and He will give you fair enjoyment*: He will cause you to live in obedience and contentment or comfort, which means that this is not contradicted by how some committed sinners also enjoy life; *until a time appointed*: namely your death; *and He will give every person of merit*—good deeds—*his merit*: the reward for his merit in this life and the next. *But if you turn away, I fear for you the chastisement of an awful day*: the Resurrection.

[11:4] *'Unto God is your return, and He has power over all things*: including the power to punish those who turn away.'

[11:5] *Assuredly, they fold up their breasts*: conceal what is within them;

that they may hide from Him: from God in secret. *Why, surely the moment they cover themselves with their clothing* in their beds, *He knows what they keep hidden* in their hearts *and what they proclaim* with their mouths. *Truly, He knows what is in the breasts*: the hearts.

[11:6] *And there is not a creature walking*—He singled them out because they outnumber the birds—*in the earth but the sustenance thereof falls upon God*: those who dwell outside the earth have no need of sustenance. He described this as an obligation on His part in order to encourage us to trust in Him; or some say that *ʿalā* (fall upon) here means *min* (from), as it does in the verse *when they take measure from* (*ʿalā*) *people* [Q. 83:2]. *And He knows its habitation* in life *and its repository* in death; or see the similar passage in *Sūrat al-Anʿām*.[1] *All* of this, along with all its varying situations, *is in a manifest Book*, meaning the Tablet, for He knows all.

[11:7] *And He it is Who created the heavens and the earth in six days*: this was explained earlier;[2] *and His Throne was upon the water*: that is, a barrier between them had not been created—this is proof of the possibility of

Q. 11:6

the void (*khalāʾ*),[3] and that water was the first thing to be created after it; *that He might try you*—put you to the test—*as to which of you is best* (aḥsan) *in conduct*: through the heart and the limbs. The meaning of 'goodness' (*iḥsān*) in this context is sincerity. He used the superlative form, though the disbelievers were included in it, to encourage us to strive for the best of all that is good. In sum, what it means is 'to manifest your virtue to the most virtuous of you'. *And if you were to say, 'Truly, you shall be raised again after death,' those who disbelieve will say, 'This* Qurʾān which speaks of the Resurrection *is nothing but manifest sorcery.'*

[11:8] *And if we postpone the chastisement for them until* the coming of *some numbered moments*—a small amount of times or years—*they will surely say* mockingly, *'What is keeping it* from occurring*?'* Therefore God replies: *Assuredly on the day when it*—the chastisement—*comes to them, it shall not be averted from them, and that which they derided*—namely the chastisement—*shall surround them*.

[11:9] *And if We cause man to taste some mercy from Us* by granting him a blessing whose delight he experiences, *and then wrest it from him, truly he is despairing* and does not hope for any relief thereafter, *ungrateful* for his previous blessing.

1 See Q. 6:98.
2 See Q. 7:54.
3 The nothingness that preceded creation.

[11:10] *But if We cause him to taste prosperity after some misery that had befallen him, assuredly he will say, 'The ills*—the misfortunes—*have gone from me*: and nothing bad will ever befall me again.' The different verbs used here imply that prosperity is inherently desirable, while misery is not, which is an aspect of good etiquette with God. *Truly, he is exultant, boastful* to people about what he has received.

[11:11] *Save those who endure* misery *and perform righteous deeds* in gratitude; *theirs will be forgiveness* for their sins *and a great reward* in the Garden.

[11:12] *Perhaps*, because of how much you are forced to mix with them, *you might* think to *leave out* conveying *some of what is revealed to you*: namely those parts that condemn their gods and repudiate their religion, fearing that it will only cause their disbelief to increase further. This does not imply that this actually would have happened, since there could have been something to prevent it, such as his divinely-granted protection. *And your breast is straitened by it*: sometimes you feel uneasy about conveying it; fearing *that they might say, 'Why has a treasure not been sent down for him, or an angel not come with him?' You are but a warner*: your duty is only to warn; *and God is Guardian over all things*: so trust in Him. Q. 11:10

[11:13] *Or do they say*—as indeed they do—*'He has invented it?' Say: 'Then bring ten sūras the like thereof*—of equal eloquence—*invented*: for you are more learned in poetry and letters than me. When they proved incapable of this, He challenged them to produce a single *sūra*, as we saw.[1] Of course, the Qur'ān is not invented and cannot be harmed by imitations, but the challenge was issued according to the level of their own perspective on the matter. *And call* for help *upon whom you can beside God if you are truthful* about it being invented.'

[11:14] *And if they do not answer you* when you call upon them for help, O idolaters, *then know that it has been revealed only in God's knowledge*: adorned with that which is known only to God—that is, none know of how it was composed in the sublime heights of its level except for God, and so none but Him can achieve it; *and* know *that there is no god save Him*: for the powerlessness of your gods will be manifest. *Will you then submit?* Will you enter into submission when the proof has been established?

[11:15] *He who desires* by his virtue *the life of this world and its adornment* alone, *We shall repay them* the reward for *their deeds in it*: in the world by granting them comfort; *and therein they shall not be defrauded*: their reward shall not be lessened.

1 See Q. 2:23.

[11:16] *Those are they for whom there is nothing in the Hereafter but the Fire. What they contrive will have failed*: come to naught or been corrupted; *therein* because they will have lost the reward of the Hereafter; *and useless* in itself *is that which they used to do*: because it was not done properly.

[11:17] *Is he who relies on a clear proof from his Lord* which guides him to the truth, such as sound natural disposition and intellect—the predicate of this sentence is elided, but can be understood as 'Is such a person like them?' *It*—the proof—*is followed by a witness from Him*: of its veracity, which means the Qur'ān; *and before it*, before the Qur'ān, *was the Book of Moses*, the Torah, *as an example and a mercy* from God to them. *Those* who follow the proof *believe in it*, the Qur'ān, *but he who disbelieves in it of the partisans*, the factions of the disbelievers, *the Fire shall be his appointed place. So do not be in doubt concerning it*: concerning the appointed place, or the Qur'ān. *Truly, it is the Truth from your Lord, but most people do not believe* in it.

Q. 11:16

[11:18] *And who*—no one—*does greater wrong than he who invents a lie concerning God*, such as the idolater and the one who denies the Qur'ān*? Those shall be brought before their Lord* at the Resurrection, *and the witnesses*—the guardian angels, or their own body parts, or the community of Muḥammad (may God bless him and grant him peace)—*will say, 'These are they who lied concerning their Lord.' Assuredly, the curse of God is upon the evildoers.*

[11:19] *They who bar* people *from God's way*, His religion, *desiring it crooked*: perverted as they are—this was explained in *Sūrat al-Aʿrāf*;[1] *and in the Hereafter they are disbelievers.*

[11:20] *Such will not escape* from God *in the earth*: in this world, and their punishment is only delayed for a wise reason; *and beside God they have no allies* to protect them from His chastisement. *For them the chastisement will be double* because of how they strayed and led others astray, or because *they could not hear* the truth, *nor did they use to see*: their disdain for the truth reached such an extent that they were virtually unable to perceive it.

[11:21] *Such are they who have lost their souls*: their salvation, by exchanging it for the means of chastisement; *and that which they used to invent*—the gods and their intercession—*has failed them.*

[11:22] *Without doubt they will be the greatest losers in the Hereafter*: for none will lose more than they do.

[11:23] *Truly, those who believe and perform righteous deeds and humble themselves before their Lord*—content with Him and without any doubt in His lordship—*such will be the inhabitants of the Garden, therein they will abide.*

1 See Q. 7:45.

[11:24] *The likeness*, the description, *of the two parties*, disbeliever and believer, *is as the blind and the deaf, and the one who sees* and contemplates God's signs, *and the one who hears* the truth. *Are they equal in likeness? Will you not then reflect*: and distinguish between them?

[11:25] *And indeed We sent Noah to his people*: saying, *'I am for you a clear warner.*

[11:26] *'That you worship none but God. Truly, I fear for you the chastisement of a painful day'*: He described the day itself as *painful* by way of imparting emphasis.

[11:27] *The council*, the nobles, *of his people who disbelieved*—this was explained in *Sūrat al-Aʿrāf*[1]—*said, 'We see you but a mortal like us, and we see not that any follow you save the vilest among us*—only our lowliest people follow you—*through rash opinion*: following their instinctive thoughts without deliberating, or their surface thoughts without contemplating. *We do not see that you have any merit over us* at all; *nay, we deem you liars* regarding what you preach.*'* Q. 11:24

[11:28] *He said, 'O my people, have you considered*—tell me—*if I were upon a clear proof from my Lord* about my sincerity, *and He has given me mercy*—prophethood—*from Him, and it has been obscured from you*, if the proof were made difficult for you to see, *could we compel you to it*—to following its guidance—*while you were averse to it*: while you denied the proof?

[11:29] *'And O my people, I do not ask of you any wealth for this* in return for conveying it. *My wage falls only upon God. And I will not drive away those who believe*: so do not ask me to drive them away. *Truly, they shall meet their Lord*: and complain about the one who drove them away. *But I see you are a people who are ignorant* of their true ranks.

[11:30] *'And O my people, who would help me against God* by repelling His vengeance *if I drove them away* unjustly? *Will you not then reflect?*

[11:31] *'And I do not say to you, "I possess the treasure houses of God,"* that you might challenge my merit because of my poverty, *nor* do I say, *"I have knowledge of the Unseen,"* that you might deny me for such a far-fetched claim; *nor do I say, "I am an angel,"* such that you might object that I appear to you to be nothing but a man. *Nor do I say to those whom your eyes scorn*—those whom you belittle because of their poverty—*that God will not give them any good*, anything better than what He has given you. *God knows best what* perfection *is in their souls. Lo!* If I did say this, *then truly I would be of the evildoers.'*

1 See Q. 7:59 ff.

[11:32] *They said, 'O Noah, you have disputed with us, and disputed with us at length. Bring upon us that with which you threaten us*—the chastisement—*if you are of the truthful.'*

[11:33] *He said, 'Only God will bring it upon you, if He wills; and you cannot escape* His chastisement.

[11:34] *'And my counsel will not benefit you if I desire to counsel you when God desires to keep you astray*: this means: 'If God wishes to keep you astray, then if I wish to counsel you, it will not benefit you.' It is as if you said, 'You are divorced if you go into the house having spoken to Zayd'; so if she goes in and then speaks, she is not divorced, because the divorce was made contingent on her entering the house after speaking to Zayd, but she went in first and then spoke. *He is your Lord*—your Sovereign—*and to Him you will be returned*: for requital.'

[11:35] *Or do they say*—and indeed they do—*'He has invented it'?* In other words, they say that Noah has invented the things he conveys from
Q. 11:32 God. *Say: 'If I have invented it, then* the consequence of *my crime will be upon me; and I am innocent of what you commit*: by denying me.'

[11:36] *And it was revealed to Noah, 'None of your people will believe except he who has already believed. Do not be distressed*—do not grieve—*because of what they do*: by denying you.

[11:37] *'Build the Ark under Our eyes*: under Our protection as We watch over you; *and by Our inspiration* to you about how it should be built; *and do not address Me* with prayers *concerning those who have done evil. Truly, they shall be drowned* by the Flood.'

[11:38] *And as he was building the Ark, whenever a council of his people passed him, they scoffed at him*: by making comments like, 'He was a prophet, but now he is a carpenter!' *He said, 'Though you scoff at us, yet we shall scoff at you* when your chastisement comes, *even as you scoff* at us.

[11:39] *'And you shall know to whom will come a chastisement degrading him*: abasing him in this world; *and upon whom an enduring chastisement* in the Hereafter *will come down*: like a debt when it is due to be rendered.'

[11:40] So he continued to build it, *Until, when Our command came and the oven gushed forth* with water, which poured miraculously and wrathfully from that fiery place and rose up like a boiling pot, *We said, 'Load therein*, in the Ark, *of every kind a pair of two*, a male and female of every species of animal except for those that are born of dirt, such as insects and the like—the words *of two* are meant to add emphasis—*and* load *your family, save those against whom the Word has already gone forth* that they be destroyed, meaning his wife, his people and his son Kanʿān, *and* load *those who believe.' And none but a few believed with him*: they numbered twelve or eighty.

[11:41] *And he said*—Noah said to them—*'Embark therein! In the Name of God shall be its coursing*: this could mean the journey, the time or the place; *and its mooring*: that is, invoke the Name of God during both. *Truly, my Lord is Forgiving, Merciful*: and it is through His mercy that we are saved.*'*

[11:42] *And it sailed with them amid waves like mountains, and Noah called out to his son* Kanᶜān,[1] before it sailed away, *who was standing away* from the Ark, *'O my son, embark with us* on the Ark before it sets off, *and do not be with the disbelievers*: far from us*!'* What the verse means is 'Submit to God so that you deserve to embark with us, and do not remain in disbelief with them, lest you drown.' Thus it does not contradict Noah's words, *Your promise is the truth* [Q. 11:45]. God's answer that *he is not of your family* [Q. 11:46] means that the son fell short because he did not embark when he was told to. And God knows best.

Q. 11:41

[11:43] *He said, 'I shall take refuge in a mountain that will protect me from the water.' Said he, 'There is no protector today from God's command*—chastisement—*except whomever He has mercy upon'*: that is, the Merciful One, or the place of those on whom He has mercy, meaning the Ark; or *ᶜāṣim* (protector) here may mean 'one granted protection'. *And the waves came between them*—between Noah and his son—*and he was among the drowned.*

[11:44] *And* after the Flood had climaxed, *it was said, 'O earth, swallow your waters* that burst forth from you; *and O heaven, abate* from raining*'*: this was a command of creative power. *And the waters subsided, and the affair was accomplished, and it settled upon Jūdī*: a huge mountain in Mosul. It is narrated that when they disembarked from the Ark, they built a town which today is known as al-Thamānīn (The Eighty) in the region of Mosul or Syria. *And it was said, 'Away with the evildoing folk!'*

[11:45] *And Noah called out to his Lord*, that is, he intended to call out to him—in *Sūrat Maryam*,[2] the call means the call itself [rather than the intention], which is why there is no 'and'—*and said, 'My Lord, truly my son is of my family, and truly Your promise is the truth* that You would save them, which was implied when You commanded me to take them on the Ark. So why did You not save him? *And You are the Most Just of Judges.'*

[11:46] *He said: 'O Noah, truly he is not of your family*: for the bond of allegiance is severed between the Muslim and the disbeliever. *Truly, it is*

1 Not to be confused with the Biblical Canaan, grandson of Noah. Some sources give his name as Yam.

2 See Q. 19:3–4.

not a righteous deed: that is, he was not righteous, or this question is not righteous. *Do not ask of Me that whereof you have no knowledge* of the truth about it. He called it a question because of how he evoked His promise of salvation in connection with his son. *I admonish you*—forbid you—*lest you be among the ignorant'*: He called his question *ignorant* because his love for his son caused him to overlook how He had exempted *those against whom the Word has already gone forth* [Q. 11:40].

[11:47] *He said, 'My Lord, I seek refuge in You that I should ask of You* ever again *that whereof I have no knowledge. Unless You forgive me and have mercy on me, I shall be among the losers* whose deeds are squandered.*'*

[11:48] *It was said* after the Ark had settled upon Jūdī, *'O Noah, go down* from the Ark *in peace*, security, *from Us and blessings*, perfect boons, *upon you and upon some communities* that will arise *from those* believers *with you* until the Day of Resurrection, *and communities* from those who are with you *to whom We shall give enjoyment* in this world, *and then a painful chastisement will befall them:* namely the disbelievers.*'*

Q. 11:47

[11:49] *Those* stories *are of the tidings of the Unseen, which We inspire in you*, O Muḥammad. *You yourself did not know it, nor did your people before this. So be patient* like Noah. *Truly, the sequel*—the good end—*is for those who are wary* of disobedience.

[11:50] *And to ʿĀd* We sent *their brother Hūd. He said, 'O my people, worship God* alone*! You have no god other than He. You do but invent* associates for Him.

[11:51] *'O my people, I do not ask of you any wage for it*: for conveying the message. *My wage falls only upon Him Who originated me*: created me. *Will you not understand*: and recognise truth from falsehood*?*

[11:52] *'And, O my people, ask forgiveness of your Lord*: for what has passed; *then turn to Him repentant*: return to obedience of Him; *He will release the sky upon you in abundance, and He will add strength to your strength* with wealth, children and power. Al-Ḥasan (may God have mercy on him) is reported to have said, 'The one who abundantly prays for forgiveness will be granted abundant offspring.' *And do not turn away as sinners*: persisting in your sin.*'*

[11:53] *They said* obstinately, *'O Hūd, you have not brought us any clear proof* of your sincerity. He did not need a prophetic miracle because he was following the Law of a previous prophet, and only utilised rational arguments to preach to them. However, some say that his prophetic miracle was the taming of a ferocious wind. *And we are not going to forsake* the worship of *our gods because of your words, and we are not believers in you.*

[11:54] *'We say nothing, save that one of our gods has possessed you in some evil way'*: with madness because of how he reviled them. *He said, 'Truly, I call God to bear witness* over me, *and you bear witness also, that I am innocent of what you associate* [11:55] *beside Him*: that is, with Him. *So plot against me* with your full force and all your gods, *altogether, then give me no respite*: this was another of his prophetic miracles.

[11:56] *'Truly, I have put my trust in God, my Lord and your Lord; there is no creature but He takes it by the forelock*: this is a representation of His power over them and how He can do with them as He will. There is an element of wordplay here, as the phrase contains the name of the man who uttered it, a device known as *muʿammā*.[1] *Truly, my Lord is on a straight path*: the path of justice, and so He will requite each person according to their deeds; or He guides to a straight path.

[11:57] *'And if you turn away*, then I will not be blamed for it; *still I have conveyed to you that wherewith I was sent to you*: and my sole duty is to convey; *and my Lord will set in place of you a folk other than you* after you are gone. *You cannot injure Him in the least* by turning away. *Truly, My Lord is Preserver over all things*: and your deeds are not hidden from Him.'

Q. 11:54

[11:58] *And when Our command came to pass* that ʿĀd be destroyed, *We delivered Hūd and those who believed with him* from the chastisement of this world, which was a terrible wind that went into their noses and came out of their backs, cutting them to shreds, *by a mercy from Us*: not by means of their deeds; *and We delivered them from a harsh chastisement*: the chastisement of the Hereafter.

[11:59] *And that was* the tribe of *ʿĀd. They knowingly denied the signs of their Lord and disobeyed His messengers*: He used the plural because to disobey one messenger is to disobey them all; *and they followed the command of every rebellious tyrant*: meaning their chiefs.

[11:60] *And a curse was made to follow them in this world*: they were cursed upon the tongue of every prophet who came after them; *and on the Day of Resurrection. 'Assuredly ʿĀd disbelieved in their Lord. Lo! away with ʿĀd, the people of Hūd!'* This was after their destruction, to record how they deserved it. This means the First ʿĀd; He distinguished them from the ʿĀd of Iram, who were the Second ʿĀd, and alluded to the reason why they deserved their ruin.

[11:61] *And* We sent *to* the tribe of *Thamūd their brother*—their kinsman—

1 When the initial of *dābba* (creature) followed by *huwa* (He) are combined they spell 'Hūd.' *Muʿammā* is a kind of riddle where a person's name is woven artfully into a sentence or verse of poetry.

Ṣāliḥ. He said, 'O my people, worship God! You have no god other than He. He it is Who produced you from the earth, and has given you to live therein: given you the ability to thrive—this indicates that God wants the earth to thrive, not be neglected; or it means 'He has made your lives long,' for some of them lived to the age of a thousand. *So ask forgiveness of Him* for what has passed, *then turn to Him repentant*: and return to obeying Him. *Truly, my Lord is Near* with mercy, *Responsive* to those who call on Him.'

[11:62] *They said, 'O Ṣāliḥ, you had been one of promise*—one known for his wisdom and rectitude—*among us before this. Do you forbid us to worship what our fathers worshipped? Truly, we are in grave doubt concerning that to which you are calling us*: the forsaking of our idols.'

[11:63] *He said, 'O my people, have you considered*—tell me—*if I am upon a clear proof from my Lord, and He has given me from Him mercy*—prophethood—*who will help me against God*, protect me from His chastisement, *if I disobey Him* by not conveying it? *You would only be adding to my loss* by
Q. 11:62 attempting to recruit me to your cause, causing me to lose out on my good deeds, or to draw you into loss.

[11:64] *'And, O my people, this is the she-camel of God, a sign for you*: this was explained in *Sūrat al-Aʿrāf*.[1] *Leave her to eat in God's earth and do not cause her any harm, lest you be seized by a near*—immediate—*chastisement*.'

[11:65] *But they hamstrung her, and he said*—Ṣāliḥ said to them—*'Enjoy yourselves in your dwellings for three days* following the hamstringing: Wednesday, Thursday and Friday, and then you will be destroyed. *That is a promise that will not be belied*: that is undeniable.'

[11:66] *So, when Our command came* that they be destroyed, *We delivered Ṣāliḥ and those who believed with him by a mercy from Us*: not by means of their obedience; *and* We delivered them *from the ignominy of that day*: the day when they were destroyed by the Cry. *Truly, your Lord is the Strong*, the Powerful, *the Mighty*, the Omnipotent.

[11:67] *And those who did evil were seized by the Cry* along with an earthquake that rendered their hearts, as we saw before, *so that they ended up lying motionless*—dead—*in their habitations* [11:68] *as if they had never dwelt there. 'Assuredly Thamūd disbelieved in their Lord. Lo! away with Thamūd!'* The word 'Thamūd' is sometimes treated grammatically as though it were a masculine name, since they were named after their forefather, and other times as a feminine name, as the name of the tribe.

[11:69] *And indeed Our messengers*, twelve angels, *came to Abraham with*

1 See Q. 7:73.

glad tidings of a son, intimate friendship with God, and the salvation of Lot. *They said* in greeting, *'Peace!' He said, 'Peace!'* to return their greeting, *and did not delay to bring a roasted calf*: the word *ḥanīdh* means 'roasted on hot stones' or 'dripping with fat'.

[11:70] *And when he,* Abraham, *saw their hands not reaching to it, he was suspicious of them, and conceived a fear of them*: because only a foul guest does not eat. *They said, 'Fear not. Lo! we have been sent to the people of Lot* to chastise them.*'*

[11:71] *And his wife,* his cousin Sara, *standing by* to serve them, *laughed* in joy at the salvation of Lot, or at how she had begun to menstruate again, signalling that she could bear child. *And so We gave her*, through their mouths, *the glad tiding of Isaac, and, after Isaac, of Jacob*: the tidings were either of their names, like John, or just of their births, and then their names were given later but were mentioned here to lend clarity to the account.

[11:72] *She said, 'Woe to me! Shall I bear a child when I am an old woman,* Q. 11:70
and this my husband is an old man? She was ninety or ninety-nine, and he was one hundred and twenty. *Truly, this is a strange thing.'*

[11:73] *They said, 'Are you astonished by God's command*: by His power*? The mercy of God and His blessings be upon you, people of the House!* This was a prayer or a reminder—that is, 'It is not strange at all that such as you should be honoured this way.' *Truly, He is Praised, Glorious*: abundantly Good.*'*

[11:74] *And when the awe departed from Abraham and the glad tiding came to him, he began to plead with Us*—with Our messengers—*concerning* the salvation of *the people of Lot.*

[11:75] *Truly, Abraham was forbearing, imploring*: much given to lamenting for sins and for his fellow humans; *penitent*: ever returning to God. So the angels said:

[11:76] *'O Abraham, desist from this* pleading. *Truly, your Lord's command*—His chastisement—*has gone forth; and truly there will come upon them a chastisement which cannot be repelled* by any intercession.*'*

[11:77] *And when Our messengers came to Lot,* after leaving the village of Abraham, *he was distressed*—saddened—*by them, and the reach of his arm was straitened*: this is a figure of speech denoting incapacity, just as a broad reach of arm symbolises power, because the long-armed person can reach what the short-armed person cannot. The messengers appeared in the form of exceedingly handsome young men, and so he feared that his people would harbour evil intentions towards them; *and he said, 'This is a terrible day'.*

Then his wife told the people about his guests:

[11:78] *And his people came to him, rushing towards him* to engage in their abominations with them; *for they had long been committing evils*: abominations, which had become their norm. This is why they were bold enough to rush there openly. So he closed the door on his guests and stood behind the door to ward them off. *He said, 'O my people, here are my daughters*: marry them and leave my guests alone; for they had previously asked for their hands, but he had rejected them because of their foulness. *They are purer for you* than it would be to marry men, or in the sense that even carrion is purer than stolen food. *So fear God, and do not degrade*—scandalise—*me on account of my guests*: for to degrade his guests would also be to degrade him. *Is there not among you any decent man* who recognises the truth?'

[11:79] *They said, 'You know full well that we have no right to*—need for—*your daughters; and you know well what we desire*: namely the men.'

[11:80] *He said* when they persisted, *'Would that I had strength to resist you, or could resort to some strong support* on which I could rely to repel you!'

[11:81] *They*, the guests, *said, 'O Lot, truly we are messengers of your Lord.*
Q. 11:78 *They shall not reach you* to harm you by harming us, *so travel with your family during a part of the night, and let none of you turn round* to remain behind; or let none of you turn to look behind him at his belongings, lest he fall behind; *except for your wife*: do not take her with you. *Truly, she shall be smitten by that which smites them*: meaning the chastisement. *Truly, their tryst*—the appointed time for their chastisement—*is the morning*: so hurry. *Is the morning not nigh?'* So he went out with his two daughters at dawn, and was given the ability to traverse the earth quickly[1] in order to escape.

[11:82] *And when Our command* that they be chastised *came to pass, We made their uppermost*—the highest parts of their dwellings—*the nethermost*: Gabriel placed his wing beneath them and lifted them up until the inhabitants of Heaven could hear the barking of the dogs, and then turned them over. Four million people dwelled in the city. *And We rained upon them*, when it was levelled, *stones of baked clay* (*sijjīl*): the word was originally *singil*, meaning stone and clay, and then it was Arabicised; or it could be the name for the lowest heaven, just as *Sijjīn* is the name of the lowest earth; *one after another*: in succession, or each one falling atop the other.

[11:83] *Marked*—engraved with the names of those who would be slain by them—*in the presence of your Lord*: in His treasuries; *and it*—this scourge—*is not far from the evildoers* of this community, as a *ḥadīth* describes.

1 Literally 'the earth was rolled up for him like a rug', a common Arabic idiom for the miracle of instant transportation.

[11:84] *And to Midian* We sent *their brother*, one of their highborn folk, *Shuʿayb. He said, 'O my people, worship God!* They were idol-worshippers accustomed to crooked dealings. *You have no god other than He. And diminish not the measure or the weight. I see you in prosperity*: you are comfortable, so why must you resort to fraud? *And I fear for you the chastisement of a besetting day*: from which no one can escape—the use of the word to describe the day itself is figurative.

[11:85] *'O my people, give full measure and weight in justice*: he stated this plainly after prohibiting the inverse in order to make clear that weighing and measuring must be exactly fair, and that even giving too much is not allowed; *and do not defraud people in respect of their goods, and do not be degenerate*—excessively corrupt—*in the land* by engaging in banditry, all the while *working corruption* in your religion too; this was explained in *Sūrat al-Baqara.*[1]

[11:86] *'The remainder from God*—meaning that lawful part which He retains after the weighing and measuring has been done in full—*is better for you* than defrauding, *if you are believers*: for there is no good in the lawful Q. 11:84
unless one believes; *and I am not a guardian over you*: but only an advisor.'

[11:87] *They said* sarcastically, *'O Shuʿayb, does your prayer command you* with the responsibility *that we should leave what our fathers worshipped, or to* no longer *do as we will with our goods*: by engaging in fraud and trimming silver off coins*? You are truly the forbearing, the rightly guided!'* They said this to mock him.

[11:88] *He said, 'O my people, have you considered that I might be following a proof*—sound argument and insight—*from my Lord, and that He has provided me* without any effort on my part *with fair*—lawful—*sustenance from Him?* Does it seem likely that I would go against Him? *And I do not desire to be inconsistent with you in what I forbid you* by engaging in it myself to compete with you. *I desire only to set things right so far as I am able*: which is why I advise you. *My success* in doing what is right *is only through God*: by His help. *In Him I trust, and to Him I turn*: to Him I shall return after death.

[11:89] *'And, O my people, let not the breach with me*—your enmity towards me—*make you deserve that there befall you the like of what befell the people of Noah*, who were drowned, *or the people of Hūd*, who were destroyed by a wind, *or the people of Ṣāliḥ*, who were destroyed by a cry; *and the people of Lot are not far away from you*: it was not so long ago that they were destroyed, nor did they live far from you, so reflect on this.

1 See Q. 2:11 ff.

[11:90] *'And ask forgiveness of your Lord* for what has passed, *then repent to Him*: return to obeying Him. *Truly, my Lord is Merciful* to those who repent, *Loving*: full of love for them.'

[11:91] *They said* mockingly, *'O Shuʿayb, we do not understand much of what you say. Truly, we see you are weak among us*: for you are blind and have no servants; *and were it not for your clan* and their might, for they follow our religion—the word *rahṭ* (clan) literally means a group of between three and ten men—*we would have stoned you*: killed you by pelting you with stones; *for you are not powerful over us*: such that your power could prevent you from being stoned.'

[11:92] *He said, 'O my people, is my clan more venerable in your sight than God? And do you put Him behind you, neglected*: like something that has been cast behind one's back*? Truly, my Lord encompasses what you do*: and He will requite you for it.

Q. 11:90

[11:93] *'And, O my people, act according to your station*: the situation in which you find yourselves, such as idolatry; *I too am acting* according to my own station. *You will soon know upon whom will come the chastisement that will abase him*—expose him—*and who is a liar. And sit in watch*: awaiting that which I describe; *I too will be with you watching*: and waiting.'

[11:94] *And when Our command*—chastisement—*came, We delivered Shuʿayb and those who believed with him by a mercy from Us*: not by virtue of their own deeds; *and the Cry seized those who were evildoers*: Gabriel cried out at them, and they were destroyed; *and they ended up lying motionless*—dead—*in their habitations* [11:95] *as if they had never dwelt there: 'Lo! away with Midian* into destruction, *just as Thamūd was done away with'*: for they were also destroyed by the Cry, though their cry came from below them while the cry of these came from above them along with trembling and darkness.

[11:96] *And indeed We sent Moses with Our signs*, his prophetic miracles, *and a clear warrant*, a plain proof, [11:97] *to Pharaoh and his council; but they followed Pharaoh's command* to belie Moses; *and Pharaoh's command was not rightly guided*: it did not point to the truth.

[11:98] *He will go before his people on the Day of Resurrection, and he will lead them*, as though leading them to water, *to the Fire—an evil waterhole for those who are watered there*: for a waterhole is meant to cool down, but the Fire is the opposite of this.

[11:99] *And a curse was made to follow them in this world, as well as on the Day of Resurrection—evil is the assistance offered* to them, for it is nothing but a curse.

[11:100] *That* tiding *is of the tidings of the* destroyed *towns, which We relate to you*, O Muḥammad. *Some of them are standing* in ruins, such as their walls, *and some have been cut down* so that not a trace remains of them.

[11:101] *And We did not wrong them* by destroying them, *but they wronged themselves*: and so deserved it. *Their gods did not avail*—defend—*them in any way* from any of His chastisement, *those upon whom they called besides God, when the command of your Lord came* that they be chastised; *and they*, their gods, *did not increase them in anything but ruin*: destruction.

[11:102] *Such is the seizing of your Lord when He seizes* the people of *the towns while they are doing wrong*: which is why He seizes them. *Truly, His seizing is painful, severe*: and there is no hope of escaping it.

[11:103] *There is truly in that*, in their destruction, *a sign*, an admonition, *for him who fears the chastisement of the Hereafter. That*—the Last Day—*is a day to which people will be gathered, and that is a day* when all creatures are *witnessed*.

[11:104] *And We do not defer it*—the Day—*but to a term reckoned*: an established time. Q. 11:100

[11:105] *The day it comes*—or the day He comes—*no soul shall speak except by His permission*: this is in one station, while in another *they will not speak* [Q. 77:35]. So the division here[1] does not contradict the one described in *Sūrat al-Aʿrāf*.[2] *Some of them will be damned*: deserving of the Fire; *some joyous*: deserving of the Garden.

[11:106] *As for those who are damned, they will be in the Fire* on that day; *their lot therein will be wailing*: meaning the sound of breath being expelled, or a sound in the throat, or the first part of a donkey's bray; *and sighing*: meaning the sound of heavy breathing, or a sound in the chest, or the final part of its bray; [11:107] *abiding therein for as long as the heavens and the earth endure*: meaning the heavens and earth of the Hereafter, consisting of that which is above them and that which is below them; for their existence is known from a *ḥadīth*, and their perpetuity can be deduced from the perpetuity of the Garden and the Fire; or He simply meant this as a symbol of perpetuity, as was the custom of the Arabs; *except what your Lord may will* to exempt from this perpetuity, for the sinners will not remain in the Fire forever, or because of how they will come out of the Fire and into the Freeze (*Zamharīr*), and other such matters. Or God knows best what He meant by this exception. Some say it refers only to the part about

1 Into damned and joyous.

2 Therein a third category is described, namely the people on the Heights.

wailing and sighing, others that it is analogous to if you said, 'By God, I will beat you unless I change my mind,' when in reality you had already resolved to do it. *Truly, your Lord is Doer of what He desires*: and there can be no objections to Him.

[11:108] *And as for those who are made joyful, they shall be in the Garden, abiding therein for as long as the heavens and the earth endure, except what your Lord may will*: this refers to the duration of their connection to the Presence of Holiness, or the duration of the punishment of the sinners, which is supported by how He then says *an endless bounty*. Or the word *except* in both instances could mean 'apart from', as in, 'I owe him a thousand, apart from the other two thousand.' In other words, this is the duration of their abiding, apart from what your Lord wills. Or it means the duration of their standing for the Reckoning. Or *what* in both instances could mean 'whom', in which case the second would imply causality and both would imply accountability. In any case, the exception is not one that He would actually implement, but is only meant to show that if He had not wished
Q. 11:108 to keep them there in perpetuity, He would not have done it.

[11:109] *So do not be in doubt concerning what these* idolaters *worship*, and how it is nothing but disbelief that will lead them to the same fate that befell their ancestors. *They worship only as their fathers worshipped before*: and so they will meet the same end; *and We shall truly pay them their whole due* of requital, *undiminished*: this adds emphasis.

[11:110] *And We indeed gave Moses the Book, but differences arose concerning it*: some believed in it while others denied it, such as these people deny the Qur'ān. *And were it not for a word that went forth from your Lord* that they be given respite until the Resurrection, *the case would have been decided between them*: and their requital would have been dealt out already; *and truly they are in grave doubt concerning it*: your Book.

[11:111] *And truly to each*—to every believer and disbeliever, by God—*your Lord will pay for his deeds in full*: by requiting them. *Truly, He is Aware of what they do.*

[11:112] *So remain upright as you have been commanded*—without any laxity or excess—*and [along with] he who repents* from disbelief and embraces faith *with you; and do not transgress*: do not go beyond the bounds of what you are commanded. *Truly, He sees what you do*: this refers to the obligation of following sacred texts (*nuṣūṣ*) without being diverted from them by such things as analogy (*qiyās*) and juristic discretion (*istiḥsān*).

[11:113] *And do not incline* even slightly *toward the evildoers*—such as by wearing their garments or speaking highly of them—*lest the Fire touch you* on account of it. *And you have, besides God, no protectors* to save you from His chastisement; *and then you will not be helped*: God will not help you because of the stain of your inclination towards them.

[11:114] *And observe the prayer at the ends of the day*: dawn, midday and afternoon; *and in some* hours *of the night* shortly following the day, meaning sunset and evening; there is a difference of opinion about the exact designation of the prayers meant here. *Truly, good deeds*, all of them, *annul misdeeds. That* Qur'ān *is a remembrance*—an admonition—*for the mindful*: those who are willing to be admonished.

[11:115] *And be patient* in obedience, *for truly God does not waste the wage of those who are virtuous*.

[11:116] *If only*—this expresses incredulity and condemnation—*there had been among the generations before you men possessing a remnant* of goodness, *forbidding corruption in the earth, except* only *a few of those whom We delivered from among them* ever did forbid it. *But those who did wrong* by failing to
forbid it *followed the comfort they were given*: their blessings, meaning [the
fulfilment of] their desires to the expense of all else; *and were sinners*: Q. 11:114
and so they were annihilated. Some say it means that they followed their footsteps and their dwellings which were destroyed.

[11:117] *Yet your Lord would never destroy the towns because of injustice*—idolatry—*while their inhabitants were righteous* to one another by following [in obedience], because He is ever tolerant when it comes to His own rights, and puts the rights of His servants before His own when they clash. Some say it means that He would never destroy the towns unjustly.

[11:118] *Had your Lord willed, He would have made people one community* in submission to Him, *but they continue to differ* about all manner of corrupt beliefs, [11:119] *except those on whom your Lord has mercy*: who are united on the truth; *and it was for this* differing *that He created them*: the word *li* (for) here denotes consequence or enabling, as in, *He it is Who made for you the night that* (*li*) *you should rest therein* [Q. 10:67]; or it could mean 'on', as in *and he had laid him down on* (*li*) *his forehead* [Q. 37:103]. Or the word *this* could refer to *mercy*, and the pronoun to *those on whom*. *And the Word*—decree—*of your Lord has been fulfilled: 'I will surely fill Hell with* rebellious *jinn and people together'*: that is, from both races, not only one of them.

[11:120] *And all that*—every tiding—*We relate to you of the accounts of the messengers* is *so that We might strengthen your heart*: by increasing your certainty. *And in these* tidings *there has come to you the truth, and an admonition and a reminder to the believers*.

[11:121] *And say to those who do not believe: 'Act according to your ability*: your situation of aloofness; *we too are acting* according to ours.

[11:122] *'And wait* to see what our fates will be; *we are also waiting* for your comeuppance.'

[11:123] *And to God belongs the Unseen of the heavens and the earth*: nothing therein escapes His notice; *and to Him all matters are returned. So worship Him, and rely on Him; and your Lord is not heedless of what they do*: and will requite everyone as they deserve. Glory be to Him! And God knows best.

Q. 11:121

12
Joseph
SŪRAT YŪSUF

Revealed in Mecca

After saying, *And all that We relate to you*... [Q. 11:120], he then follows this with the best of narratives, saying:

In the Name of God, the Compassionate, the Merciful

[12:1] *Alif. Lām. Rā'. These*—the verses in this *sūra*—*are the verses of the manifest Book*, whose miraculous nature is evident.

[12:2] *We have revealed it*—the Book—*as an Arabic Qur'ān*: meaning a collection or something that is recited, in your own language: *so that you might understand*.

[12:3] *We will relate to you the best of narratives*: in terms of eloquence. Or the best of tales in terms of wisdom and anecdote; this most likely means that it is the best of its particular subject, not that it is better than every other narrative, even the story of the Beloved of God (may God bless him and grant him peace). Or it means, 'We will explicate it in the best way'; *in that We have revealed*, through Our revelation, *to you this Qur'ān, though prior to it you were of the heedless* of these narratives.

[12:4] Remember *when Joseph said to his father* Jacob, describing his dream (*ru'yā*), which means the imprinting of an image projected from the horizon of imagination onto the common sense. A dream is true when the soul becomes connected, the moment it is freed from the task of directing the body, to the realm of dominion (*malakūt*), wherein it envisages a concept which is then interpreted by the imagination in a form that corresponds to it and is conveyed to the common sense, which beholds it. If the correspondence is very direct, the vision will require no interpretation, but otherwise it will require it. *'O my father, I saw eleven spheres and the sun and the moon*: instead of saying thirteen, he said eleven and then added the details of the other two; *I saw them prostrating themselves before me'*: he used the rational plural *hum*[1] because prostration is usually something that only rational beings do.

[12:5] *He said, 'O my son*—he used the diminutive form[2] to express compassion—*do not relate your vision to your brothers, lest they plot against you some plot*: to ruin you out of envy, if they realise what the dream means, which is prophethood and dominion over them. *Truly, Satan is to humanity a manifest foe.*

[12:6] *'Thus*, by this dream, *will your Lord prefer you*: choose you for prophethood and kingship; *and teach you the interpretation of narratives*: meaning dreams, because true dreams are narrated by angels, and false dreams by Satan; or it means the interpretations of the Books; *and perfect His grace upon you and upon the House of Jacob*: meaning his sons—he interpreted the light of the spheres as symbolising their prophethood; *as He perfected it formerly on your fathers*, the grandfather and great-grandfather, *Abraham and Isaac. Truly, your Lord is Knower* of the deserving, *Wise* in His bestowal.'

Q. 12:5
[12:7] *Truly, in* the story of *Joseph and his brethren*, his half-brothers, *are signs for those who inquire*: and seek information.

[12:8] *When they said, 'Surely Joseph and his brother*, his full-brother, *are dearer to our father than we are, though we be a hardy band*: a group of strong men who accompany him, which makes us more deserving. *Truly, our father is in plain aberration* because he is being unfair: the divine protection afforded to the prophets does not necessarily preclude such things.

[12:9] *'Kill Joseph or cast him away into some* faraway *land so that your father might be solely concerned with you* instead of him, *and that thereafter*—after slaying him—*you might be a righteous folk*: by repenting of it.'

[12:10] *One of them*, Judah, *said, 'Do not kill Joseph, but cast him into the bottom of a well so that some caravan*—a group of travellers—*might pick him up; if you are to do anything*, then my advice is to do this.

[12:11] *They said, 'O father, what is wrong with you that you do not trust us*—that you fear us—*with Joseph? We are truly his well-wishers*: and we are concerned for him.

[12:12] *'Send him forth with us* out into the desert *tomorrow to frolic*—to have fun—*and play*: by engaging in racing and the like, which is similar to play. *Truly, we shall take good care of him.'*

[12:13] *He*, Jacob, *said, 'Truly, it grieves me that you should go with him*

1 As opposed to *hā*, denoting non-humans or inanimate objects.

2 *Bunayy*, literally 'my little son'.

because I cannot bear to be parted from him, *and I fear lest the wolf devour him*—they lived in a wolf-infested land—*while you are heedless of him* because of your sport.*'*

[12:14] *They said, 'Truly*, by God, *if the wolf were to devour him, when we are a band* of strong men, *then truly we should be losers*: fools.*'* They did not comment on Jacob's first reason not to send the boy, because it was the very thing that had enraged them. Consequently, he sent him with them.

[12:15] *So when they went off with him*—the main clause is elided here, but is implied by: *and agreed to put him*, drop him, *into the bottom of the well*: this was in Jerusalem, or some other place. *And We revealed to him* in the well, though he was still a young boy, like Jesus and John, *'Truly*, by God, *you shall inform them*, your brothers, *of this affair of theirs*: of what they have done—this was a glad tiding that he would eventually triumph over them; *when they are unaware* that you are Joseph, because of your high status then.*'*

[12:16] *And they came to their father in the evening, weeping.*

[12:17] *They said, 'O father, we went competing* in games of archery and
wrestling, *and left Joseph by our things*—our clothes—*and the wolf ate him. But* Q. 12:14
you would never believe us about this, *even though we speak the truth* because of how ill you think of us.*'*

[12:18] *And they came with false blood on his shirt. He said: 'Nay*, the wolf did not eat him, *but your souls have beguiled you into something* terrible. *Yet comely patience* is better. This means patience wherein one does not complain to any created being. *And God is the One Whose succour is sought for* bearing *that which you describe* about his death.*'*

[12:19] *And there came a caravan* travelling from Midian to Egypt, *and they sent their water-drawer*—the one who fetches water for the others—*and he let down his bucket* into the well, and Joseph grasped the rope and pulled himself out. *He said* when he saw him, *'Good news!* In other words, 'Come forward, good news, for this is your moment.' Or he was calling out to his companion named Bushrā (good news). *This is a young boy'*: he was seventeen years old at the time. *And they hid him*—the water-drawers hid him from the others so they would not have to share him with them—*as merchandise* to sell. Or it means that his brothers pretended that he was not their brother, and sold him to them. *But God knew well what they were doing.*

[12:20] *Then they*, the water-drawers or the brothers, *sold him for a very low price*: a price that is fraudulent or unfair; *a handful of dirhams*: it was twenty; *for they*, the sellers, *set small store by him*: they had no interest in Joseph, and only sold him because they feared he would be taken from them otherwise.

[12:21] *And he of Egypt who purchased him*, Potiphar the vizier, *said to his wife* Zuleikha, *'Give him an honourable place. Maybe he will be useful to us, or we may adopt him as a son'*: since he was infertile. *Thus We established Joseph in the land* of Egypt for good reasons, *and that We might teach him the interpretation of narratives*: dreams. *God's way ever prevails*: and nothing can repel what He wills; *but most people do not know* that all things are in His grasp.

[12:22] *And when he came of age*: when he reached the height of his powers, which is the age between thirty and forty. This was also explained in *Sūrat al-Anʿām*;[1] and in the story of Moses it is further qualified by *and was mature* [Q. 28:14], which means reaching the age of forty, since it was after this that his prophetic mission began. *We gave him judgement*: prophethood; *and knowledge* of religion and interpretation. *Thus do We reward the virtuous.*

[12:23] *And she in whose house he was*, [namely] Zuleikha, *attempted to seduce him*: that is, she made advances towards him, or it is a euphemism for trickery; *and she closed the doors*: all seven of them, and beckoned him.
Q. 12:21 *And she said, 'Come!' He*, Joseph, *said, 'God forbid!* I seek refuge with Him. *Truly, he is my lord, who has given me an honourable place*: so how could I disobey Him? Or he could have been referring to his master in the house. *Truly, evildoers* who are ungrateful for their blessings *never prosper.'*

[12:24] *And certainly she desired him*—desired to lie with him—*and he desired her too* in the natural sense for which a person is not held accountable; he did not intend to act on this desire; *had it not been that he saw the proof of his Lord*: namely the ugliness of adultery, or Gabriel, or Jacob biting his fingers and beating his chest, so that all of the passion left his body as though it flowed out of his finger, as Ibn ʿAbbās (may God be pleased with him) related. *So it was that We might ward off from him evil*, treachery, *and lewdness*, adultery. *Truly, he was of Our devoted servants*: We made him devoted solely to Our worship.

[12:25] *And they raced to the door*: Joseph to flee and Zuleikha to stop him; *and she tore his shirt from behind* when she pulled on it, *whereupon they encountered her master*—her husband—*at the door. She said*, implying that she had been the one fleeing from him, *'What is to be the requital of him who intends evil*—adultery—*with your folk, but that he should be imprisoned, or suffer a painful chastisement?'*

[12:26] *He*, Joseph, *said, 'It was she who attempted to seduce me.' And a witness of her own folk testified*: it was an infant still in the cradle, one of four

1 See Q. 6:152.

people in history who spoke in their infancy. He said, *'If his shirt has been torn from the front, then she speaks the truth, and he is of the liars*: because he must have pursued her and she tore it trying to push him off, or the like.

[12:27] *'But if his shirt has been torn from behind, then she has lied, and he is of the truthful*: because she must have followed him and pulled his shirt.'

[12:28] *So when he saw that his shirt was torn from behind, he said, 'Truly, this*—meaning her question, *What is to be the requital...*, and so on—*is of the guile of you women. Truly, your guile is great*: implying that such acts are commonplace among them. Then he said:

[12:29] *'O Joseph, ignore this*: keep it secret; *and you*, Zuleikha, *ask forgiveness for your sin: Truly, you have been of the erring'*: he was not a jealous man. In addition, the author of *al-Baḥr*[1] said in it that the very soil of Egypt produces this disposition in its folk, which is why lions do not dwell there; and if one did go there, it would not linger for long.

[12:30] *And some of the women in the city*, Miṣr,[2] *said, 'The vizier's wife has been seducing her boy*: her slave. *He has smitten her heart with love*: the verb *shaghafa* (smite) means 'to enter beneath the skin'. *Truly, we see her to be in plain aberration.'* Q. 12:27

[12:31] *And when she heard of their machinations*: their secret backbiting was akin to machinating; *she sent for them and prepared for them a banquet*: the word *muttaka'* (banquet) means something to recline on, or carpets to sit on, or food to be cut with knives. *She then gave each one of them a knife* to cut for themselves *and said after they had taken them, 'Come out*, O Joseph, *before them!' And when they saw him, they were in awe of him*: they were astounded at his beauty and how his face shone upon the walls, or it means that they were so excited they began to menstruate;[3] *and they* were so bedazzled that they *cut their hands and exclaimed, 'God be praised* for His omnipotence*! This is no human being; this is but a noble angel!'* [They said this because] such was his beauty; for it is natural to think of angels as the height of beauty just as devils are the height of ugliness.

[12:32] *She said, 'This is he on whose account you blamed me. Indeed, I did attempt to seduce him, but he withheld himself*: since her excuse had been made plain, she confessed. *Yet if he does not do what I bid him, he shall truly be imprisoned, and shall surely be of those brought low*: those abased.' Then, when the women told him to obey his mistress:

1 *Al-Baḥr al-muḥīt*, the exegesis of Abū Ḥayyān al-Andalusī (d. 1334).

2 Miṣr, the name for the whole of Egypt, generally designates Cairo when used to refer to a city; in this context, it likely means Heliopolis.

3 The verb *akbara* (to be awed) can also mean 'to menstruate'.

[12:33] *He said, 'My Lord, prison is dearer*—more preferable—*to me than that to which they are urging me*: namely to obey her. *And if You do not fend off their wiles from me, then I shall tend towards them*: because they also wanted to seduce him; *and become of the ignorant*: by committing indecencies.*'*

[12:34] *So his Lord answered him*: answered his implicit prayer; *and He fended off their wiles from him*: by granting him protection. *Truly, He is the Hearer* of prayers, *the Knower* of situations.

[12:35] *Then it seemed to them*, to the vizier and his companions, *after they had seen the signs* proving his innocence, *that they should imprison him for a while* so that the people would think that he was the guilty one, not his wife; and so they imprisoned him.

[12:36] *And there entered the prison with him two youths*, the king's cup-bearer and baker; their crime was attempting to poison the king. *One of them*, the cup-bearer, *said, 'I dreamed that I was pressing wine*: grapes.*' The other*, the baker, *said, 'I dreamed that I was carrying on my head bread whereof the birds were eating. Tell us its interpretation, for truly we see you as being among
Q. 12:33
the virtuous.'*

[12:37] *He said: 'The food with which you are provided shall not come to you before I tell you the interpretation thereof*—of your dreams, or the interpretation of the food that will come to you—*before it comes to you*: that is, he would describe something he had not yet seen, like the prophetic miracle of Jesus, *I will inform you too of what things you will eat* [Q. 3:49]. The root meaning of *ta'wīl* (interpretation) is to speak about something in the past—that is, to explain what it was and how it was. By saying this, he wanted to invite them to submit to God, and therefore he said: *This* knowledge *is from that which my Lord has taught me*: not from soothsaying or the like. *Truly, I have forsaken the creed of a folk who do not believe in God and who moreover are disbelievers in the Hereafter*: meaning the people of Egypt. By *forsaken* he meant 'rejected', not 'converted from', and the same applies to other similar passages.

[12:38] *'And I follow the creed of my fathers, Abraham and Isaac and Jacob. It never was* right *for us to associate anything with God. That* monotheism *is from God's bounty to us* through revelation, *and to people* through sending us to them to guide them; *but most people do not give thanks* for this, but ignore it.

[12:39] *'O my two fellow-prisoners! Are several lords better, or God, the One, the Almighty*: the Omnipotent to Whom none can be equal*?*

[12:40] *'That which you worship apart from Him are but names* without realities *that you have named, you and your fathers. God has not revealed any warrant*—proof—*regarding them*: and their worship. *Judgement* concerning worship *belongs only to God. He has commanded that you worship none but Him*: in other words, that you proclaim His Oneness. *That is the upright*—straight—*religion, but most people do not know*: and so they engage in idolatry.

[12:41] *'O fellow-prisoners! As for one of you*, the cup-bearer, *he* will be released after three days, and *will serve his lord wine to drink* having returned to his position; *and as for the other*, the baker, *he* will be released after three, and *will be crucified so that the birds will eat from his head*. They said, 'We do not believe you.' So he said: *Decided* already *is the matter regarding which you sought opinion.'*

[12:42] *Then he*, Joseph, *said to the one whom he deemed* with certainty—given how he had called it *decided*—*would be saved of the two*, meaning the cup-bearer, *'Mention me to your lord*: the supreme king Rayyān b. al-Walīd, so that he releases me from the vizier. *But Satan caused him*, the cup-bearer, *to forget to mention* him *before his master*: or caused Joseph to forget to mention God, so the cup-bearer went to the wrong person; *so he stayed in prison for some years*: the word *biḍʿ* (some) means 'three to nine'—in this case it Q. 12:41 was seven years.

[12:43] *And the* supreme *king said, 'I saw* in a dream *seven fat cows* emerging from a dry river and *being devoured by seven lean*—very thin—*ones, and seven green ears of corn*: their grains tightly bunched, *and* seven *others dry*, which wrapped around the green ones until they dominated them—this part was omitted since the description of the cows already suggested it. *O courtiers*, nobles, *advise me about my vision*: interpret it; *if you can interpret visions'*: dream interpretation means transferring the imaginal image into the psychological concept that it represents.

[12:44] *They said, 'A jumble of dreams!* The root meaning of *ḍighth* (jumble) is 'a mixture of things' or 'the result of mixing plants', used figuratively here to represent a false dream. The plural *aḍghāth* is used to emphasise its falsehood. *And we are not knowledgeable in the interpretation of dreams.'*

[12:45] *And he of the two who was released*, the cup-bearer, *remembering* about Joseph *at last*—a long time later—*said, 'I will inform you of its interpretation, so send me forth* to the man who knows how to interpret.' So he sent him, and he went to him and said:

[12:46] *'Joseph, O truthful one*—one who always tells the truth—*give us your opinion of seven fat cows devoured by seven lean ones, and seven green ears of corn and others dry, that I may return to the people*, the king and his folk, *that they might know* its interpretation.'

[12:47] *He said, 'You shall sow seven years consecutively*: consistently as you always do—this was the interpretation of the seven fat cows and green ears; *but that which you reap, leave it in the ear* so that it does not spoil, *except for a little which you eat* that year. This was sound advice.

[12:48] *'Then after that*—after those seven years—*shall come seven hard years which shall devour*, in which shall be consumed, *what you set aside for them* because of the famine, *all except a little which you have preserved* to use for sowing; this was the interpretation of the seven lean cows and dry ears.

[12:49] *'Then after that there shall come a year in which the people will be granted relief* from the famine, or rain, *and in which they will press* things such as grapes and olives, or in which they will prosper, or be given rain.' This was a tiding of the Unseen, and so perhaps he learned it by revelation. Then the cup-bearer returned with the interpretation.

[12:50] *And the king said, 'Bring him to me* from the jail.' *And when the messenger came to him* from the king, *he said, 'Return to your lord and ask him, "What of the women who cut their hands?"* This was in order that the king would know that he was innocent. However, he did not mention
Q. 12:48
Zuleikha by name out of respect. This shows that it is desirable to strive to make sure false accusations are disproven. *Truly, my Lord has knowledge of their guile'*: when they told him to obey his mistress.

[12:51] *He*, the king, *said, 'What was your business, women, when you solicited Joseph?'* Did you find any evil in him? *'God forbid!' they said. 'We know of no evil in him'*: then when they went to Zuleikha to bid her to confirm this, *the vizier's wife said, 'Now the truth is out*: she confessed, fearing that they would bear witness against her. *It was I who attempted to seduce him and he is truly of the truthful* regarding what he said about me.' So he went back and told Joseph, who said:

[12:52] *'That*—the sending back of the messenger first—*was so that he*, the vizier, *may know that I did not betray him in his absence, and that truly God does not guide the guile of the treacherous*. Then Gabriel said to him, 'Not even when you too were tempted?' So he said:

[12:53] *'Yet I do not exculpate my own soul. Truly, the soul* by its nature *is ever inciting* its owner *to evil, except that my Lord has mercy*: that is, 'except the soul on which He has mercy', or 'except that the mercy of my Lord prevented me'. *Truly, my Lord is Forgiving, Merciful*: and He will pardon her desire.'

[12:54] *And the king said, 'Bring him to me, that I may use him for myself*: and no other.' *And when he had spoken with him* after they had brought him, *he said, 'Truly, you are, on this day, in our presence, established* in a lofty station, *and honest*: trusted.'

[12:55] *He said, 'Place me in charge of the storehouses of the land* of Egypt. *I am truly a skilled custodian*: for I know how best to manage them.*'* This shows that it is permitted to request a position of authority, and to claim to be qualified for it, and for a Muslim to accept an appointment from a disbeliever if this is the only way to ensure justice. The fact that he requested it does not undermine the perfect asceticism of the prophets, for he did it to ensure that God's legal boundaries (*ḥudūd*) were upheld, since he knew that only he could do this.

[12:56] *Thus We established Joseph in the land* of Egypt, for the king donned his crown and deposed the vizier and put Joseph in his place; then the vizier died, and Joseph married his wife and found that she was a virgin; *that he may settle in it wherever he wished*: that is, he had full authority over all of it. *We confer Our mercy on whomever We will; and We do not waste the wage of the virtuous*: whether sooner or later.

[12:57] *Yet the wage of the Hereafter is better, for those who believe and are God-fearing*: such as Joseph, for his afterlife would be even better than his first life.

Q. 12:55

[12:58] *And Joseph's brothers*, except for Benjamin, *came* forty years later in a year of famine, to buy food from him. *And they went in to him, and he recognised them, but they did not recognise him.*

[12:59] *And when he had equipped them with their provision*: the root meaning of *jihāz* (provision) is what is prepared for a journey or a bride's wedding party—that is, he filled their packs generously. What happened was that when they arrived he said, 'Perhaps you are spies.' They said, 'God forbid! We are the sons of a righteous prophet. There were twelve of us, but the youngest died and his brother remained with his father in his place.' *He said, 'Bring me a brother of yours from your father*, if you are telling the truth. *Do you not see that I give full measure, and that I am the best of hosts* to my guests*?*

[12:60] *'But if you do not bring him to me, there will be no measure for you with me*: I shall not give you food ever again; *and you will not come near me*: or enter my land.*'*

[12:61] *They said, 'We will try* some scheme *to tempt his father away from him* by imploring him over and over. *That we will surely do.'*

[12:62] *And he*, Joseph, *said to his young men*, his servants who did the measuring, *'Place their merchandise*—the payment for their food, which was silver—*in their saddlebags so that they may recognise it* and see that it was returned to them *when they return to their folk, and so come back* when they notice this.*'* So they left Simeon with him as guarantor, and headed off with the food.

[12:63] *So when they returned to their father, they said, 'O father, the measure will be denied us* hereafter if we do not take our brother there, *so send forth our brother with us, that we may obtain the measure*: for otherwise we shall have nothing. *Truly, we will guard him well.'*

[12:64] *He said, 'Should I trust you with him like I trusted you with his brother* Joseph *before?* For you said the same about him. *Yet God is best at guarding*: so rely on Him; *and He is the Most Merciful of merciful ones*: and I ask Him to have mercy on me by guarding him.'

[12:65] *And when they opened their belongings, they found that their merchandise had been returned to them. They said, 'O father, what should we desire?* What more kindness can we ask than this? *Here is our merchandise returned to us*: so we shall use it again; *and we shall get provisions for our family*: and take food to them; *and guard our brother*: from any harm; *and we shall add an extra camel's load* of food, because he would give a load to every person. *That* which we brought this time *will be an easy measure*: a trifle compared
Q. 12:63 to the next one.'

[12:66] *He,* Jacob, *said, 'I will not send him with you until you give me a pledge* that I can trust *in the Name of God*—a pledge affirmed by the invocation of His Name—*that assuredly you will bring him back to me* no matter what, *unless you are besieged* on all sides and so cannot.' *And when they gave him their pledge, he,* Jacob, *said, 'God shall be Guardian over what we say*: He is aware of our pledge.'

[12:67] *And he said, 'O my sons, do not enter* the city *by one gate, but enter by separate gates* to avoid the evil eye. He did not advise this the first time because they were unknown then, or did not have Benjamin with them. *Yet I cannot avail you*—defend you—*against God in regards to anything* that He might ordain for you. *Judgement belongs only to God. On Him I rely, and on Him let all the trusting rely.'*

[12:68] *And when they entered in the manner which their father had bidden them,* through separate gates, *it did not avail them anything against* the ordain of *God* to do so, for indeed they were afflicted by being accused of theft and having their brother taken. *It was but a need*—a worry—*in Jacob's soul which he satisfied*: namely to ward off the evil eye. *And truly he was possessed of knowledge, because We had taught him* by revelation, which is why he said, *Yet I cannot avail you...*; *but most people do not know* that caution alone is not enough.

[12:69] *And when they went in to Joseph, he took his* full-blooded *brother into his arms*: for he accommodated the people in tables of two, and sat him down with him at his own table and embraced him; *saying, 'Truly, it is me, your brother, therefore do not despair*—grieve—*at what they used to do* to us.'

[12:70] *And when he had equipped them with their provision, he put the drinking-cup into the saddlebag of his brother*, Benjamin. It was the drinking-cup (*siqāya*) of the king, made of gold or gems, and was used to measure out food. The words *siqāya, suwā*^{c} *and ṣā*^{c} all mean a cup that is used for both drinking and measuring. *Then a crier shouted, 'O cameleers, you are surely thieves!'* There is no need to object that this seems to imply that he commanded them to issue a false charge, since they could have called out without his permission. Or one could argue that it was a lawful stratagem employed for the purpose of securing a lawful right. Or it could be that he was referring to how they had stolen Joseph from his father.

[12:71] *They*, the brothers of Joseph, *said, coming towards them*, the people who were looking for the cup, *'What is it that you are missing?'*

[12:72] *They said, 'We are missing the king's goblet. He who brings it shall have a camel's load* of food, *and I will guarantee that'*: this indicates the lawfulness of finder's fees, and the guarantee of payment before labour.

Q. 12:70

[12:73] *They said* incredulously, *'By God, you know very well* based on our righteous deeds, such as muzzling our animals so they do not eat any excess, or returning the goods that were placed in our packs, *that we did not come to work corruption in the land, and we are certainly not thieves.'*

[12:74] *They*, the criers, *said, 'So what shall be his*, the thief's, *requital if you prove to have been liars* about your innocence*?'*

[12:75] *They said, 'The requital shall be he in whose saddlebag it is found*: in other words, that he be enslaved; *he* alone *shall be the requital for it*: as was affirmed in the Law of Jacob. They repeated this to reaffirm the ruling, namely that the taking of the thief would be the requital, and nothing else. It is as if one said, 'Zayd has the right to be fed and clothed. That is his right, and nothing more.' *Thus do we requite those who do evil* by stealing.*'*

[12:76] *And so he*, the crier, *began with their sacks before his* full-blooded *brother's sack* in order to lift the suspicion, *and then he pulled it out of his brother's sack. Thus did We contrive for Joseph; he could not have taken his brother*—it would not have been valid to enslave the thief—*according to the king's law*, since their punishment for thieves was to beat them and seize from them an item of equal value to what they stole, *unless God willed* that he be enslaved according to the religion of Jacob, after his brothers stated that the punishment would be enslavement. *We raise by degrees whom We will* with knowledge, such as Joseph; *and above everyone endowed with knowledge is one who knows*: this has been cited in support of the opinion that God's knowledge is not extrinsic [to His being];[1] the rebuttal of this is that *everyone endowed with knowledge* refers to created beings, while *one who knows* refers to the One Who possesses infinite knowledge, namely God.

[12:77] *They said, 'If he*, Benjamin, *is stealing,* then it is no surprise, for *a brother of his stole before*: meaning Joseph.*'* They were referring to the story of how, when he was a child, his aunt was very fond of him and wanted to keep him to herself. So she took the belt of Abraham which she had inherited, tied it beneath his clothes, and then cried out that her belt had been stolen. Upon searching Joseph and finding her belt on him, she announced that he was guilty of theft and so she would take him as her slave, according to their religion. Others said that it refers to how he stole the idol of his mother's father and broke it, or to how he took a goat or chicken from the house and gave it to a beggar. *But Joseph kept it*—his distaste at hearing this—*secret in his soul and did not disclose it to them. He said*
Q. 12:77 to himself, *'You are a worse case!* You are worse thieves for how you stole your own brother and did him a terrible injustice. *And God knows very well what you are describing* about your brother.*'*

[12:78] *They said, 'O vizier*, meaning the sultan of Egypt, *truly he has a father, aged and great*: in years or stature, who loves him dearly. *Take one of us in his place. Truly, we see that you are among the virtuous*: you have been kind to us, so please continue to do so.*'*

[12:79] *He said, 'God forbid that we should take anyone save him with whom we found our property!* He did not say 'save him who stole', so as to avoid being untruthful; *for then we would truly be evildoers* if we took any other.*'*

[12:80] *So when they despaired of* getting any other response from *him, they withdrew to confer privately. The most senior of them* in age, Reuben, or in wisdom, Judah, or in leadership, Simeon, *said, 'Are you not aware that your father has taken a solemn pledge from you by God, and formerly you failed regarding Joseph? I will never leave this land* of Egypt *until my father permits me* to return, *or God judges for me* by freeing my brother; *and He is the best of judges*: for He judges only according to truth.

[12:81] *'Go back to your father and say, "O our father, your son has stolen; and we testified only regarding what we knew*: for the cup was taken from his pack; *we could not have guarded against the Unseen*: whether he stole the cup or it was planted there.

1 This is because it seems to draw a distinction between the one who is endowed with knowledge (*dhū ʿilm*) and the one who simply knows (*al-ʿalīm*, a Name of God).

[12:82] *'And ask the city in which we were*, the people of Egypt, about the story, *and the caravan with which we approached. Truly,* by God, *we speak the truth."'*

[12:83] So when they told him this, *he said, 'Nay, but your souls have beguiled you into something* terrible. *Yet comely patience* is better. *It may be that God will bring them all*, Joseph and his brothers, *to me. Truly, He is the Knower* of my state, *the Wise* in His acts.'

[12:84] *And he turned away from them* in disdain *and said, 'Alas, my grief for Joseph!'* [In other words,] 'Come forth, my sorrow, for now is your time.' *And his eyes turned white with grief*: this is a euphemism for his copious weeping; *such that he was filled with suppressed rage* towards his children, but he kept it to himself. He did not say, 'Truly, we belong to God, and truly to Him we shall return,' because that formula was gifted to our community alone, as a *ḥadīth* states, 'No community was given "Truly, we belong to God, and truly to Him we shall return" except for the community of Muḥammad (may God bless him and grant him peace). Consider Jacob
when, in the midst of his suffering, he said not this but only, "Alas, my Q. 12:82
grief!"' He spoke of Joseph in particular and not his brothers, although their misfortune was more recent, because his original loss was the beginning of all the others and the worst of them all. This was especially so given that he was confident that they were both alive but could not say the same for Joseph.

[12:85] *They*, his sons, *said, 'By God, you will never cease remembering Joseph until you are consumed* on the brink of ruin, *or you are of those who perish!'*

[12:86] *He said, 'I complain of my anguish*—my inconsolable woe—*and grief only to God*: so leave me alone to complain. *And I know from God what you do not know*: namely that he was alive, for an angel had told him this, as well as Joseph's dream about the spheres prostrating to him.

[12:87] *'O my sons, go* to Egypt *and enquire about Joseph and his brother, and do not despair of God's Spirit*: His mercy. *Truly, none despairs of the Spirit of God save the disbelieving folk'*: the believer always hopes for His mercy. So they returned to Egypt.

[12:88] *And so when they entered upon him*, the vizier, *they said, 'O vizier, misfortune*—famine—*has befallen us and our family; and we have come with poor merchandise* which no one will buy—there is a difference of opinion about what exactly it was. *Fill up for us the measure and be charitable to us*: by returning our brother. *Truly, God requites the charitable.'*

[12:89] So when he saw their powerlessness, *he said* out of compassion and hope that they would repent, *'Do you realise* the heinousness of *what you did to Joseph and his brother* when you separated them and humiliated him, *while you were ignorant* of what a terrible thing this was for the boy?' And tears began to fall from his eyes.

[12:90] *They said, 'Is it really you, Joseph?'* They recognised him because he removed his crown, revealing the white birthmark on his brow which he shared with Jacob and Sara. *He said, 'I am Joseph, and this is my brother. God has shown favour to us*: by reuniting us. *Truly, if one fears* God *and endures* His trials, *God surely does not waste the wage of those who are virtuous'*: such as he.

[12:91] *They said, 'By God! Indeed, God has preferred you*—chosen you—*over us* for knowledge, patience and kingship; *and truly we have been erring.'*

[12:92] *He said, 'There shall be no reproach on you this day*: nor any other. *God will forgive you, and He is the Most Merciful of the merciful*: He forgives sins both great and small.

Q. 12:90

[12:93] *'Go with this shirt of mine and lay it on my father's face, and he will recover his sight*: it was woven in the Garden and placed upon Abraham when he was cast into the fire. Any sick person upon whom it was laid was cured. Jacob placed it over Joseph for protection. *And bring me all your folk*: your women and children.'

[12:94] *And as the caravan set forth* from Egypt to Jacob, *their father said, 'Truly I sense the scent of Joseph*: he was still eighty days' journey away; *if only you did not think me doting*: you would believe me.' The term *fanad* (dotage) means the corruption of the intellect that occurs in old age. It is used only for men.

[12:95] *They said, 'By God, you are certainly in your misguidance of old*: your old love for him.'

[12:96] *Then, when the bearer of glad tidings came*, Judah with the shirt, *he laid it on his face, and he regained his sight. He said, 'Did I not say to you that I knew from God*—by His teaching—*what you knew not?'*

[12:97] *They said, 'O our father, ask forgiveness for us* of our Lord *for our sins. Truly, we have been errant.'*

[12:98] *He said, 'I shall ask forgiveness for you of my Lord*: he delayed until the hours before dawn, or early on Friday, or until Joseph had pardoned them. *Truly, He is the Forgiving, the Merciful.'*

[12:99] *And when they went in to Joseph* when he received them along with four thousand Egyptian dignitaries, *he took his parents*, his father and mother or aunt, *into his arms, and said, 'Enter into Egypt, if God will, in safety* from any harm.' He said 'God willing', though they had already entered, to underscore *in safety*. Then he sat down upon his throne.

[12:100] *And he raised his parents upon the throne, and they*, his parents and brothers, *fell down prostrating before him*: to express their humility, for this was permitted in their religion. *Then he said, 'O father, this is the interpretation of my vision of old*: the sun and moon were his parents, and the eleven spheres were his brothers. *My Lord has made it true*: this was forty or eighty years after the dream, or forty-five according to some. *And He has been gracious to me, for He brought me out of the prison*: he did not mention the well because of how he had said, *There shall be no reproach* [Q. 12:92]; *and has brought you from the desert*—for they were nomadic herders—*after Satan had incited ill feeling between me and my brethren. Truly, my Lord is Subtle in* ordaining *what He will. Truly, He is the Knower* of what is best, *the Wise* in His acts. Jacob then remained with him for another twenty-four years before he died and was taken back to Syria. Joseph lived on another twenty-three years. Then he began to yearn for the eternal kingdom and said:

[12:101] *'My Lord, You have given me* some *sovereignty* in Egypt, *and You have taught me the interpretation of narratives. Originator of the heavens and the earth! You are my Protector*—my Helper—*in this world and the Hereafter. Take* Q. 12:100
me to You in submission: he prayed for this in order to express his servitude and to teach his community—it was a desire to die in submission, not a desire to die; *and join me to the righteous* of my forefathers.' Then he died a week later, aged 120. They quarrelled about where to bury him before agreeing to place him in a marble coffin and bury him at the upper part of the Nile, so that his blessing would be shared by all. This they did, but then Moses (may God grant him peace) later moved him to the burial place of his forefathers.

[12:102] *That*—the story of Joseph—*is of the tidings of the Unseen which We reveal to you*, O Muḥammad; *for you were not with them*, Joseph's brothers, *when they agreed upon their plan and schemed*: but this came to you only through revelation, as He said elsewhere, *You yourself did not know it*...[Q. 11:49].

[12:103] *Yet most people, however eager you might be* that they believe, *will not believe*: for they are destined to be damned.

[12:104] *Nor do you ask them any wage for it*: for delivering the revelation; *it is but a reminder*—an admonition—*to all the worlds*.

[12:105] *And how many a sign*—a proof of His Oneness and beautiful Attributes—*is there in the heavens and the earth which they pass by*, seeing them, *but disregard* without reflecting on them.

[12:106] *And most of them do not believe in God*, even when they do acknowledge Him as Creator of all, *without ascribing partners*: this refers to the belief of the idolaters, or to those who believe in causality. It is said that it means such things as when a person says, 'Were it not for God and So-and-so, I would have died.'

[12:107] *Do they deem themselves secure from the coming upon them of a pall*—a punishment that whelms them—*of God's chastisement* in this world, *or the coming of the Hour upon them suddenly, while they are unaware*: and unprepared*?*

[12:108] *Say: 'This* call *is my way: I call to God, being upon sure knowledge*: a clear proof; *I and whoever follows me*: for they all call to God. *Glory be to God!* Transcendent be He beyond association! *And I am not of the idolaters.'*

[12:109] *And We did not send before you save men*—a rejoinder to their words, *He would have sent down angels* [Q. 23:24]—*inspired by revelation* like you *from among the people of the towns*: for they are more intelligent than the people of the wilderness (*ahl al-badw*). This indicates that there were no female prophets. *Have they not travelled in the land and seen the nature of the consequence for those who were before them* who denied, and be admonished by it*? Surely the abode*—the life—*of the Hereafter is better for those who are wary*
Q. 12:107 of idolatry. *Will you not understand?* Will you not use your intelligence and recognise this?

[12:110] But those communities persisted in their denial, *until when the messengers despaired* that they would ever believe, or that help would ever come, *and thought that they had been deceived*: that is, the people thought that the messengers had lied; or if it is read as *kudhdhibū* (denied),[1] it means that the messengers were sure that they had been denied; or the former reading could also be understood as meaning that the messengers thought that they had been deceived about the promise of victory; *Our help came to them; and whomever We wished, We delivered*: namely those who followed the messengers. *And Our wrath*—chastisement—*cannot be averted from the sinful folk.*

[12:111] *In their stories*—the stories of the prophets and their people, or Joseph and his brothers—*is truly a lesson for people of pith*: [those with] sound minds. *It*—the Qur'ān—*is not a fabricated discourse, but a confirmation of what was before it* from the [previous] Book, *and a detailing of everything* pertaining to religion, whether directly or indirectly, *and a guidance, and a mercy for a folk who believe* in it. And God knows best.

1 Rather than *kudhibū* (been deceived); both readings are canonical.

13
The Thunder
SŪRAT AL-RAʿD

Revealed in Medina, or some say in Mecca except for the final verse

Having said, *It is not a fabricated discourse*... [Q. 12:111], He then affirms that it is the truth, saying:

In the Name of God, the Compassionate, the Merciful

[13:1] *Alif. Lām. Mīm. Rā'*: this was explained earlier.[1] *Those are the verses*—this is a *sūra* of verses—*of the Book*: the Qur'ān; *and that which has been revealed to you from your Lord*, whether directly or indirectly, thus including such things as analogy and consensus, *is the truth*: or it means that it is endowed with the attribute of truthfulness, not falsehood; *but most people do not believe*: because of their ignorance.

[13:2] *God is He Who raised up the heavens without supports that you can see*: that is, as you can see, it has no supports; *then rose above the Throne*: this was explained before;[2] *and disposed the sun and the moon*: bent them to His will; *each one moving, until* the arrival of *an appointed time* for its movement to be ceased. *He directs the command*: He issues commands over His dominion of creation, destruction and the like. *He details the signs* of the Qur'ān[3] *so that you might be certain of the encounter with your Lord* by analogy to the first creation.

[13:3] *And He it is Who spread out the earth and set therein firm mountains and rivers; and of every fruit He has made in it two kinds*: two types such as sweet and sour, black and white, beneficial and harmful. *He covers the night with the day*: He makes the sky dark after making it light. *Truly, in that are signs*

1 See Q. 2:1.
2 See Q. 7:54.
3 The word *āya* means both 'verse' and 'sign'.

for a folk who contemplate on how their existence with particular characteristics and not others implies the existence of a Maker.

[13:4] *And on the earth are tracts*—various areas such as soil, salt pan and so on—*neighbouring each other*: directly connected; *and gardens*—orchards—*of vines and sown fields; and date palms sharing one root*: having two trunks or being intertwined; *and date palms otherwise, watered by the same water*: sometimes multiple kinds from the same source; *and We make some of them to excel others in flavour*: in the taste and other qualities of their fruits. *Truly, in that are signs for a folk who comprehend*: who employ their intellects to contemplate them. He said *understand* here, and *reflect* in the previous verse, because realisation [of His existence] is more easily attained by observing the variety of fruits.

[13:5] *And if you wonder* at how they deny the Resurrection, *then surely wondrous is their saying, 'When we have become dust, shall we truly then be* gathered *in a new creation?'* For the One Who is able to create all of this is certainly all the more able to recreate it. *Those are the ones who disbelieve in* Q. 13:4 *their Lord*: the folk of total disbelief. *Fetters shall be around their necks* with which they will be dragged into Hell; *and they shall be the inhabitants of the Fire, therein they will abide.*

[13:6] *And they would have you hasten on the evil*—chastisement—*rather than the good*: forgiveness, by way of mocking your warning; *yet there have truly occurred before them exemplary punishments* dealt out to the likes of them. The word *mathula* (exemplary punishment) means 'punishment' in the sense that it is the contrast (*mathal*) of forgiveness; a related word is *mithāl*, meaning 'like-for-like retribution'. *Truly, your Lord is forgiving to people despite their evildoing*: this indicates that it is possible for Him to pardon even before repentance, since the repentant man does not persist in his evildoing; *and truly your Lord is severe in retribution* to whomever He will.

[13:7] *And those who disbelieve say, 'Why has not some sign been sent down upon him from his Lord* according to our whim!' *You are only a warner*: not an attendant to their whims; *and for every people there is a guide*: a prophet, so you are not unique in this respect.

[13:8] *God knows what every female bears*: that is, its true nature and attributes; *and what the wombs reduce, and what they increase*: such as the foetus and the duration of its gestation, or the number of foetuses. Shāfiʿī said that there is no limit to how many foetuses there can be, and that the maximum duration of gestation is four years; Mālik said five years, and the Ḥanafīs say two. *And everything with Him is according to a measure* decreed by wisdom which it does not exceed, for He knows its quantity.

[13:9] *The Knower of the Unseen*, that which evades the senses, *and the visible*, that which is perceptible to them; *the Great, the High Exalted* above that which does not befit His perfection.

[13:10] *Equal* in His knowledge *is he among you who speaks secretly, and he who does so openly, and he who lurks* concealed *in the night, and he who goes forth* openly *by day*.

[13:11] *For him*—the pronoun refers to *he among you* from the previous verse—*are successive attendants*: angels who replace one another, meaning other angels aside from the Noble Scribes, or angels who constantly monitor his deeds and write them down; *to his front and to his rear, guarding him through God's command*: from His wrath, or by His command.[1] *Truly, God does not alter the state of a people*, whether it is blessed or wretched, *until they alter the state of their souls*, whether good or evil. *And if God wills misfortune for a people there is none that can repel it; and they have no protector apart from Him* to protect them from it.

[13:12] *He it is Who shows you the lightning, inspiring fear* of its harm *and hope* for rain; *and He produces the clouds that are heavy* with water. Q. 13:9

[13:13] *And the Thunder*—an angel with a whip of fire with which it beats the clouds—*proclaims His praise*, saying, 'Glory be to God, and praise be to Him!' *and so too the angels in awe of Him*: in awe of God, or in awe of the Thunder. *He unleashes thunderbolts*: fire that descends from the clouds; *and smites with them whom He will*: burning them; *yet* all the while *they dispute about* the Attributes of *God*—such as a disbeliever who said, 'What is your Lord made of, gold or silver?'—*though He is great in might*: the word *miḥāl* (might) here could mean 'power' (*ḥawl*) or 'strategy' (*mumāḥala*).

[13:14] *His is the call of truth*: it is His right to be worshipped; or it means the answered supplication, so that He answers those who call upon Him; *and those upon whom they call apart from Him*—their idols—*do not answer them anything, save as* the answer of *one who stretches forth his hands towards water* and calls upon it *that it may reach his mouth* by floating there from the well, *but it would never reach it*: for water is inanimate and is unaware of him; or it means one who scoops up water into his outstretched hand so that it slips through his fingers before it can reach his mouth; *and the call of the disbelievers*—their worship of their idols—*goes only astray*: for it is wasted and useless.

[13:15] *And to God prostrate* truly *whoever is in the heavens and the earth, willingly* like the believers, *or unwillingly* like the disbelievers in times of

1 Depending on whether *min amr* is understood as 'from the matter' or 'by the command'.

distress, or in how they are forced to yield to whatever events He wills to send their way; *and their shadows* in how they are projected, or in how they grow and shrink *in the mornings and the evenings*: that is, at all times. He singled out morning and evening for mention because the shrinking of the shadow is more obvious then as they are not times when shade is sought.

[13:16] *Say: 'Who is the Lord of the heavens and the earth?' Say: 'God'*: for they acknowledge Him. *Say*, compelling them based on their own acknowledgement: *'Then,* despite admitting this, *have you taken beside Him protectors who have no power to benefit or harm themselves*: never mind you*?' Say: 'Are the blind one*, a god who is unaware of you, *and the seer*, a God Who watched over you, *equal? Or are the darkness* of disbelief *and the light* of faith *equal? Or have they*—indeed they have—*set up for God associates who have created the like of His creation, so that creation seems alike to them?'* Does their creation seem alike to His, so that they could claim, 'They have created just as He has, so they deserve to be worshipped just as He does'? *Say:*
Q. 13:16 *'God is the Creator of all things*, so what is it that you worship? *And He is the One*, the Sole Divinity, *the Subjugator*, the Dominator of all.*'*

[13:17] *He sends down water from* the edge of *the sky, whereat the valleys*—the large rivers—*flow according to their measure* wherein God knows there is benefit, *so that the flood carries a scum that swells* on its surface; *and from that which they smelt in the fire*, the precious metals of the earth, *desiring ornaments* for women *or wares* such as vessels, there rises *a scum the like of it*: like the scum on water in terms of it being dirty, the worst part of it. *Thus God illustrates truth and falsehood* with parables. *As for the scum, it passes away as dross* when the water carries it away, *while that which is of use to people*—the pure part of them both—*lingers in the earth* to be of benefit. *Thus God strikes similitudes* to make things clear.

[13:18] *For those who respond to their Lord* when He calls them to repent, *there shall be the goodly reward* of the Garden. *And those who do not respond to Him* when He calls them, *if they possessed all that is in the earth*—the entire world—*and therewith the like of it, they would offer it to redeem themselves therewith* from His chastisement. *For such there shall be an awful reckoning*: for they shall be reckoned in full with none of their sins forgiven; *and their abode shall be Hell, an evil resting place.*

[13:19] *Is he who knows that what is revealed to you from your Lord is the truth*, and so responds to it, like Ḥamza (may God be pleased with him), *like him who is blind* of heart, like Abū Jahl*? But only people of pith remember.*

[13:20] *Such as fulfil God's covenant* which they made when they said, *Yea* [Q. 7:172], *and do not break the pact* in any way whatsoever.

[13:21] *And such as cement what God has commanded should be cemented,* such as family ties, *and fear their Lord* and His warnings, *and dread an awful reckoning*.

[13:22] *And such as are ever patient* in resisting their desires. He uses the perfect tense for the verbs here, unlike those in the preceding verses; when this is done in the Qurʾān, it alludes to how these actions take precedence over all other accountabilities. Such people are patient whilst *desiring their Lord's countenance*: seeking only to please Him and not to show off; *and maintain the prayer and expend of that which We have provided them, secretly and openly, and repel evil with good*: in order to efface it, or in order to receive good in return. *Theirs shall be*—they shall deserve—*the sequel of the Abode*; and that abode is:

[13:23] *Gardens of Eden* wherein to reside, *which they shall enter along with those who were righteous from among their fathers and their spouses and their descendants*: by association, even if they did not reach their level. The reference to righteousness indicates that kinship alone is not sufficient, and that Q. 13:21
ranks can be raised by intercession; *and the angels shall enter upon them from every gate* to their dwellings, bearing with them gifts from God and saying:

[13:24] *'Peace be upon you!* This reward is *for your patience'* in keeping obedient. *How excellent is the sequel of the Abode*: the Gardens of Eden!

[13:25] *And those who break God's covenant after pledging it, and sever what God has commanded should be cemented, and work corruption in the earth, theirs shall be the curse, and theirs shall be the awful abode*: Hell.

[13:26] *God expands provision for whom He will, and straitens it*: it is not done according to faith and disbelief, as they may suppose. *And they*, the idolaters of Mecca, *rejoice in the life of this world* and what has been granted to them therein, *yet the life of this world in* comparison to *the Hereafter is but enjoyment*: a short-lived pleasure like the meal a traveller takes with him on his journey.

[13:27] *And those who disbelieve say, 'Why has some sign not been sent down upon him from his Lord* in the way we desire*?' Say: 'Truly, God sends astray whomever He will*: just as He has sent you astray, regardless of how many signs might be sent down; *and He guides to Him*—to His religion—*those who turn in repentance*: and forsake their rebelliousness.'

[13:28] *Those who believe and whose hearts are reassured*—made tranquil and comforted—*by God's remembrance*; or it means the reassurance you feel when your brother swears to you about something of which you were uncertain. *Why, surely by God's remembrance are hearts reassured* from worry.

[13:29] *Those who believe and perform righteous deeds—theirs shall be goodness*: felicity. The word *ṭūbā* (goodness) is the gerund of the verb *ṭāba* (to be good), or the feminine form of *aṭyāb* (better, best). Ṭūbā is also the name of the tree in the Garden; *and a fair resort*: abode.

[13:30] *Thus*, just as We sent the messengers before you, *We have sent you to a community before whom other communities have passed away, that you may recite to them that which We have revealed to you; yet they disbelieve in the Compassionate. And when it is said to them, 'Prostrate yourselves before the Compassionate,' they say, 'And what is the Compassionate? Should we prostrate ourselves to whatever you bid us?' And it increases their aversion* [Q. 25:60]. *Say: 'He*, the Compassionate, *is my Lord; there is no god save Him. In Him I trust and to Him is my recourse*: my return.*'* When they asked him to make the mountains of Mecca move, and cause springs to gush forth, and raise the dead, He revealed:

[13:31] *And if there were a Qur'ān whereby the mountains were set in motion* from their places, *or the earth were cleft, or the dead were spoken to* so that they heard or responded, it would have been this Qur'ān; or they still would
Q. 13:30
not have believed. *Nay, but the affair* of guidance or misguidance *belongs entirely to God.*

Then when the Companions yearned that their demands would be granted, hoping that it would cause them to believe, He revealed: *Have they not realised, those who believe, that had God willed, He could have guided all people? And the disbelievers continue to be struck by devastation because of what they wrought*—their evil deeds—*or you alight near their home* that they might be admonished, *until God's promise comes to pass*: meaning death, or the Resurrection, or victory. *Truly, God does not break His promise.*

[13:32] *Messengers were certainly mocked before you, but I gave respite to those who disbelieved; then I seized them* with chastisement; *and how was My retribution!*

[13:33] *Is He*, God, Whose acts these are, *Who stands over every soul* observing *what it has earned* and requiting it—the predicate of this sentence is elided, but can be inferred as: Do they really not acknowledge His Oneness? *Yet they ascribe to God associates. Say: 'Name them!* Describe them, and see if they deserve this attribution, or invoke their names. This implies that they have no true names at all, never mind any identities. *Or will you inform Him of something*—namely associates—*which He does not know in the earth?* For if He does not know something, then it does not exist. *Or is it merely a manner of speaking?'* Do you call them 'associates' without meaning anything sensible by it, such as one who calls darkness light? One could also argue that this is a kind of *ilzām*[1] along the lines of: Are you telling me about something that is hidden and not known to Him, or something that is open and known to Him? If they say the former, they have argued themselves into a corner. If they say the latter, he should demand that they name them, whereupon they will realise that truly He has no equal or partner. *Nay, but their scheming*—their misrepresentation of this—*has been adorned for those who disbelieve, and they have been barred from the way* of truth; *and whomever God sends astray, for him there is no guide.*

[13:34] *For them there is chastisement in the life of this world* by being slain or the like; *and the chastisement of the Hereafter* for them *is more grievous; and they have no defender from God*: from His chastisement or His mercy.

[13:35] *The likeness of the Garden which has been promised to the God-fearing* is as follows: *with rivers flowing from beneath it; its food*—its fruits and victuals—*is everlasting, and its shade* is too. *That is the reward of those who were God-fearing. Yet the requital of the disbelievers is the Fire!*

[13:36] *And those to whom We have given the Book*—the believers among them—*rejoice in that which has been revealed to you* because it accords with Q. 13:34
their Books; *and among the factions*, the disbelievers among them, *are those who reject some of it* because it contradicts their religion. *Say* to them: *'I have been commanded only to worship God, and not to associate with Him*: and their rejection of some of it amounts to a refusal to worship Him. *To Him I call, and to Him shall be my return.'*

[13:37] *And so*, just as We revealed it to the messengers in their own languages, *We have revealed it*, the Qurʾān, *as a judgement*, an arbiter of wisdom, *in Arabic. And if you should follow their whims* by concealing what they dislike *after what has come to you of knowledge* of the truth of it, *you shall have no protector* to help you *against God and no defender* from His chastisement. Let this be a warning to all errant scholars!

[13:38] *And indeed We sent messengers before you, and We assigned to them wives and seed*: so why should they say, 'If he were a prophet, then prophethood would have kept him from marrying'? *And it was not* right *for any messenger that he should bring a sign* that was requested from him, *save by God's leave. For every term*—time—*there is a Book*: a ruling [of Law] ordained for His servants for their best interests.

[13:39] *God effaces*—abrogates—*whatever He will, and fixes*: maintains, whatever He will. *And with Him is the Mother of the Book*: which does not

1 Literally 'force', a technique of theological debate where one forces one's interlocutor to admit the absurdity of their position by drawing out their argument to its logical conclusion.

change, namely the Tablet, or God's own knowledge. This is supported by how Ibn ʿAbbās said, 'The Book is two: a book which He effaces as He wishes, and a book which never changes, which is the knowledge of God Almighty, and certain fate.' The majority, including Ibn ʿAbbās, held that salvation, damnation and lifespans cannot be changed, though outward appearances suggest otherwise.

[13:40] *And whether We show you a part of that* chastisement *which We promise them, or We take you to Us* before that, *it is for you only to convey*: and nothing more; *and it is for Us to do the reckoning*: so do not ask for their chastisement and reckoning to be hastened.

[13:41] *Or is it that they have not seen how We visit*—turn Our purpose towards—*the land* of the disbelievers, *diminishing it at its outlying regions* as the Muslims conquer them and add them to their own abode? This is what was promised by *whether We show you* in the previous verse. *And God judges; there is none that can repel His judgement; and He is swift at reckoning*: and will reckon them soon.

Q. 13:40

[13:42] *And indeed those that were before them plotted* against their prophets, just as these do; *but to God belongs all plotting*: and any plot is nothing compared to His own plotting. *He knows what every soul will earn* after He requites it. *The disbeliever shall assuredly know for whom shall be the sequel of the Abode*: the blessed end.

[13:43] *And those who disbelieve say, 'You have not been sent!' Say: 'God suffices as a witness between me and you, and he who possesses knowledge of the* heavenly *Book'*: for they recognise him, such as Ibn Salām, Salmān and others. And God knows best what is right.

14
Abraham
SŪRAT IBRĀHĪM

Revealed in Mecca

In the Name of God, the Compassionate, the Merciful

[14:1] *Alif. Lām. Rā'.* This is *a Book We have revealed to you that you may bring forth people*, by calling them to its content, *from darkness*, error, *into light*, guidance, *by the leave*, grace, *of their Lord,* and bring them *to the path of the Mighty*, the Dominant, *the Praised*, the One Who deserves praise. The invocation of these two Attributes in particular indicates that the one who travels this path will not be humiliated, and the one who asks of Him will not be disappointed.

[14:2] *God to Whom belongs all that is in the heavens and all that is in the earth. And woe to the disbelievers from a terrible chastisement.*

[14:3] They are *those who prefer the life of this world over the Hereafter, and bar* people *from God's way*—religion—*and seek to make it crooked*: so that they can pervert it; *they are far astray* from the truth.

[14:4] *And We have not sent any messenger except with the tongue*, language, *of his people*, the people to whom he belongs, *that he might make clear to them* what they have been commanded, so that they understand it and interpret it for others. *God then sends astray whomever He will*: after this is made clear; *and guides whomever He will*: by following it; *and He is the Mighty* Who imposes His will, *the Wise* in what He does.

[14:5] *And indeed We sent Moses with Our signs. 'Bring forth your people out of darkness*, error, *into light*, guidance, *and remind them of the Days of God'*: meaning the events which He sends to communities, whether favours or misfortunes; or it means the events He had sent their way in particular, such as the cleaving of the sea. *Truly, in that* reminder *are signs for every person enduring* of His tribulations, *thankful* for His favours.

[14:6] *And* remember *when Moses said to his people, 'Remember God's grace to you when He delivered you from the folk of Pharaoh, who were inflicting upon you an evil*—terrible—*chastisement, and were slaughtering your sons*: the *and* implies that the chastisement was something other than the slaughter, such as enslavement and the like, unlike the similar passages in *al-Baqara* and *al-Aʿrāf*[1] where the slaughter and slaying is the explanation of what the chastisement was; *and sparing your women; and in that was a tremendous trial from your Lord*: this was explained earlier.[2]

[14:7] *'And when your Lord proclaimed, "If you are thankful* by obeying Me, *then assuredly I shall give you more* of My favour; *but if you are thankless* towards My favour, *My chastisement is truly severe* to those who are thankless."'

[14:8] *And Moses said, 'If you are thankless, you and all who are on earth*, then the harm of your ingratitude will befall you alone, *then truly God is Independent* of all the worlds, *Praised*: inherently deserving of praise, even when He is not praised.'

Q. 14:6

[14:9] *Has there not come to you the tidings of those who were before you—the people of Noah, and ʿĀd and Thamūd, and those after them*: the other communities who denied? *None knows them save God* because of how numerous they are. *Their messengers brought them clear signs*—obvious prophetic miracles—*but they thrust their hands into their mouths*: their own mouths, or the mouths of the messengers. This is a metaphor for how they refused to heed them, or silenced them, or how they bit their nails in rage. *And said, 'Truly, we disbelieve in that wherewith you* claim to *have been sent, and truly we are in grave doubt concerning that to which you call us'*: this was explained earlier.

[14:10] *Their messengers said, 'Can there be doubt concerning* how worship is due only to *God, the Originator of the heavens and the earth? He calls you* to worship Him *so that He might forgive you* some *of your sins*: meaning those that are between you and Him, but not any injustices you may be doing to others. The reason He says *of* when addressing the disbelievers, but not the believers, is to indicate that some of their sins are still undecided so that they do not rely on faith alone, since the forgiveness that is offered them is conditional upon their faith, while the forgiveness that is offered the believers is conditional upon obedience and abstinence from sin, and so it includes injustices. Ibn al-Ḥājib said that the concept of the forgiveness of all sin could be specific to this community, in which case there would be no issue here. *And defer you to an appointed term* rather than punish you immediately.'

1 See Q. 2:49 and Q. 7:141 respectively.
2 See Q. 2:49.

They said, 'You are but mortals like us, desiring to bar us from that which our fathers used to worship. So bring us a clear warrant: proof of your superiority to us.'

[14:11] *Their messengers said to them, 'We are but mortals like you* in both species and image, *but God is gracious to whomever He will of His servants*: just as He has graced us with prophethood. This implies that prophethood is a pure gift from God. *And it is not for us*, we are not able, *to bring you any warrant save by the leave*, the will, *of God; and in God let believers put their trust*: and we shall trust in Him to help us bear your opposition and persecution.

[14:12] *'And why*—what excuse do we have—*should we not put our trust in God when He has guided us our ways*: the paths of guidance? *And we shall surely endure the hurt you do us. And in God let the trusting put their trust*: let them be constant in their reliance, to which their faith gives rise.' The first exhortation of trust referred to attaining it, the second to being constant in it.

[14:13] *And those who disbelieved said to their messengers, 'We will assuredly expel you from our land, or you will surely return*—convert—*to our creed.' Then their Lord inspired them*, their messengers, *'We shall surely destroy the evildoers.*

[14:14] *'And We shall surely make you dwell in the land*—their land—*after* Q. 14:11
them. That warning *is for whoever fears standing before Me* at the Resurrection,
and fears My threat: My warning.'

[14:15] *And they sought victory*: they asked the messengers for victory over their enemies; *and every rebellious tyrant*—every proud opponent of the truth—*was brought to nothing*: and defeated.

[14:16] *Beyond him*—awaiting him—*is Hell* into which he will be thrown; *and he will be given to drink of festering fluid*: liquid that flows from the skins of the inhabitants of the Fire composed of pus and blood, or from the loins of the adulterers.

[14:17] *He sips it*: he is forced to drink it; *but can scarcely swallow it; and* the cause of *death comes to him from every side* of his body, *yet he cannot die* to find relief; *and still beyond him*—awaiting him after that chastisement—*there is a harsh chastisement* besides this. In other words, there is no end to the methods of his torment.

[14:18] *The likeness*—description—*of those who disbelieve in their Lord* shall now be recited to you: *their deeds*—their good deeds such as freeing slaves and keeping family ties—*are as ashes over which the wind blows hard on a tempestuous day*: so they will not benefit from their deeds, just as not a speck of those ashes remains; *they will have no power* at the Resurrection *over anything that they have earned. That*—the fact that they are astray while imagining themselves to be rightly guided—*is extreme error*: distant from the truth.

[14:19] *Have you not seen*, O Muḥammad, *that God created the heavens and the earth in truth*: in the way that was right to create them? *If He will, He can do away with you all*—cause you all to cease to exist—*and bring about a new creation*: for the One Who was able to create it is certainly able to do that.

[14:20] *And that for God is surely no great*—difficult—*matter.*

[14:21] *And they sally forth* out of their graves—the perfect tense is used here[1] to evoke the certainty of the event—*to God altogether; then the weak* followers *say to those who were arrogant*—their leaders who disdained to worship God—*'Truly, we were your followers* in religion. *Will you then avail us*—defend us—*against the chastisement of God in any way?' They*, the leaders, *say* in apology, *'If God had guided us* to the path of salvation, *we would have guided you* to it; but the path to it was closed to us. *It is the same for us whether we rage or patiently endure*: it will make no difference either way; *we do not have any asylum*: anywhere to flee, and so your rage will be of no use.'

[14:22] *And Satan says, when the issue has been decided* and all have gone
Q. 14:19 to their abodes, whether the Garden or the Fire, addressing the damned, *'Truly, God promised you a promise of truth* which you denied, namely the Resurrection and the rest, *while I promised you and then failed you*: for my promise did not come true; *yet over you I had no warrant*—authority—*except that I called you and you answered me.* He referred to his call as a *warrant* figuratively, which is why he said *except. So do not blame me, but blame yourselves* for obeying me and disobeying Him. *I cannot heed your cry* for help, *nor can you heed mine. Truly, I disbelieve* today *in how you idolised me*—how you set me up as an associate with God by obeying me—*before. Truly, for the evildoers there shall be a painful chastisement.'* Here end Satan's words.

[14:23] *And those who believed and performed righteous deeds, they are admitted to Gardens with rivers flowing from beneath them, abiding therein by the leave of their Lord*: it will be the angels who admit them. *Their greeting therein* from the angels: *'Peace!'*

[14:24] *Have you not seen how God has struck*—established—*a similitude? A goodly word*—a proclamation of monotheism or the like—*is as a goodly tree*: the date palm; *its root set firm* in the ground, which is the heart of the believer; *and its shoots*—his righteous deeds—*are in heaven*: for that is where the goodly word ascends.

[14:25] *It gives its produce*, its fruit, which is God's reward in this life and

1 *Barazū*, literally 'they sallied'.

the next, *every season*, perpetually, *by the leave of its Lord*: by His will. *And God strikes similitudes for people, so that they might remember*: for they convey a deeper understanding.

[14:26] *And the similitude of a bad word*—idolatry—*is as a bad tree* like the colocynth, *uprooted from upon the earth* because of how shallow its roots grow, *having no stability*: like disbelief, which has neither root nor branch.

[14:27] *God confirms those who believe with a firm word*—faith in their hearts like a goodly tree—*in the life of this world, and in the Hereafter* He inspires them in their graves with the answers to Munkar and Nakīr;[1] *and God sends astray the evildoers*: and does not inspire them with their answers; *and God does what He will*: whether affirming or sending astray.

[14:28] *Have you not seen those*, the disbelievers of Quraysh such as the Banū al-Mughīra and Banū Umayya clans, *who exchanged God's grace*, that is, gratitude for His grace such as Muḥammad and his teachings, *for ingratitude*, so that it was taken from them and they suffered drought and were captured and slain, *and who caused their people*, their followers, *to take up residence in the Abode of Ruin?* Q. 14:26

[14:29] *Hell, to which they shall be exposed*: admitted; *an evil place to settle!*

[14:30] *And they have set up rivals*—equals—*with God, that they might lead* people *astray from His way*: His religion. The word *that* here denotes consequence. *Say: 'Enjoy* your worldly lives, *for truly your journey's end shall be to the Fire!'*

[14:31] *Tell My servants who believe that they are to observe the prayer*: that is, tell them to do so; *and expend of that which We have provided them, secretly and openly*: it is better to be open with obligatory spending, and secretive with recommended spending; *before a day comes wherein there will be neither bargaining*, such that they could purchase what they lack, *nor befriending*: natural affection; but the love of the righteous who pray and pay *zakāt* will benefit them.

[14:32] *God it is Who created the heavens and the earth, and He sends down water from* the edge of *the sky, and with it He brings forth fruits as sustenance for you. And He has disposed for you the ships, that they may run upon the sea at His commandment*, by His will, *and He has disposed for you*, for your benefit, *the rivers*.

[14:33] *And He has disposed for you the sun and the moon, constant*: always moving for our benefit without any volition on their part, as though they are at our disposal; *and He has disposed for you the night* for your rest *and the day* for your livelihoods.

1 The interrogating angels.

[14:34] *And He has given you* some *of all that you could ask of Him*: for that which exists of every type of thing is only part of what God is able to give, but He has given that amount which is best. This refers to the present request: that is, He does not wait for you to ask out of need. *And if you were to enumerate the grace of God, you could never number it*: you could not even count it, never mind give ample thanks for it. This indicates that when a singular noun is used in an *iḍāfa* construction,[1] it is exhaustive. *Truly, humanity does wrong* by failing to give thanks, *ungrateful*: much given to ingratitude.

[14:35] *And* remember *when Abraham said, 'My Lord, make this land*, Mecca, *secure and turn me and my sons* from my loins *away from serving idols*: He included himself in this prayer to express fear, or with the intention of joining him and his sons together so that the prayer would be answered for them all by his blessing.

Q. 14:34

[14:36] *'My Lord, truly they*, the idols—he referred to the instrument as though it were the cause, such as when one says 'a cutting sword'—*have led many people astray. So whoever follows me* religiously *truly belongs with me; and whoever disobeys me, truly You are Forgiving, Merciful*: You are able to forgive him. This indicates that it is possible for every sin to be forgiven, even idolatry, although this is not what has been promised.

[14:37] *'Our Lord, truly I have made some of my seed*, Ishmael, *to dwell in a valley where there is no sown land* because of the lack of water there—this was a prayer that water be granted; *by Your Sacred House* which You have forbidden be taken lightly, *our Lord, that they may observe the prayer* at it. *So make some hearts*—the word *af'ida* can be the plural of *wafd* (delegation) or *fu'ād* (heart)—*from among the people yearn towards them*: had he said 'the hearts of people', all of humankind would have rushed there together. *And provide them with fruits, that they might be thankful* for Your grace.

[14:38] *'Our Lord, You know what we hide and what we proclaim*: and our prayer is but an expression of worship and servitude to You. *And nothing* whatsoever *is hidden from God in the earth or in the heaven*: for it is all equally His.

[14:39] *'Praise be to God Who has given me, despite old age, Ishmael* at the age of ninety-nine, *and Isaac* at the age of one hundred and twenty. This indicates that he made the prayer after the House was built, and that the prayer and the praise were uttered on two separate occasions, because the prayer was made in Ishmael's infancy, before Isaac was born. *Truly, my Lord is the Hearer* and answerer *of supplication*.

1 As in 'the grace of God'.

[14:40] *'My Lord, make me an establisher*—a constant observer—*of the prayer, and* make *of my seed* the same. He said *of* because he knew that some of them would be disbelievers, whether because God had told him or because that is simply the way with people. *Our Lord! And accept my supplication*: all of it, or my worship.

[14:41] *'Our Lord, forgive me and my parents*: his mother was a believer, and he hoped that his father would submit; *and the believers on the day when the reckoning shall come to pass'*: literally 'when the reckoning stands', a euphemism for its firmness.

[14:42] *And do not suppose*, because of how He gives the evildoers respite, *that God is heedless of what the evildoers do*: He said this to strengthen the conviction of the Prophet (may God bless him and grant him peace); or He meant, 'Do not suppose He will leave them be forever.' *He but gives them respite*—delays their requital—*until a day when eyes shall stare wide open* in terror, [14:43] *as they come hastening* to the Gathering *with their heads turned upwards* to the sky, *their gaze returning not to them*—staring constantly without ever blinking—*and their hearts as air*: emptied of understanding, Q. 14:40
or agitated like wind.

[14:44] *And warn people of the day when chastisement will come upon them, and those who did evil*—idolatry—*will say, 'Our Lord, give us respite* and send us back to the world *for a brief while, that we might respond to Your call and follow the messengers'*: so the angels will say to them: *But did you not swear before that for you there would be no passing?*

[14:45] *And you dwelt in the dwelling-places of those who wronged themselves* with disbelief, *and it became clear to you how We dealt with them, and We struck*—clarified—*similitudes for you* for their states and how you were like them, but you did not reflect.

[14:46] *And they plotted their plot* to undermine the truth, *but their plotting is* written *with God*, and He will requite them, *even if their plotting was such*—so terrible—*that mountains should be moved*: whether literally, or signifying the firm religion.

[14:47] *So do not suppose that God will fail His promise to His messengers* to help them. *Truly, God is Mighty*, Omnipotent, *Lord of Retribution* for His allies.

[14:48] *The day when the earth will be changed to other than the earth*: so that it is made of silver; *and the heavens* will be changed to other than the heavens, so that they are made of gold. This was ʿAlī's opinion (may God be pleased with him), while Muslim narrated that humankind will be upon the Bridge on that day.[1] Some said that it will be the same earth, but its attributes will be changed. Others said that it will become a piece of white bread that the believer will find in front of him, and pick up and eat. *And they shall come forth* from their graves *to God, the One, the Almighty*: the Overwhelmer Who cannot be overwhelmed.

[14:49] *And you shall see the sinners on that day coupled* with their cohorts in deed and doctrine, or their devils, *in chains* because of how they were united in error.

[14:50] *Their shirts of pitch*: the viscous black resin produced by the juniper plant, which is used to treat camels suffering from scabies as it is strong enough to burn their skin; *and their faces are engulfed by the Fire.*

[14:51] *That*—this refers back to *And they shall come forth* [Q. 14:48]—*God may requite every soul for what it has earned. Truly, God is swift at reckoning*: because one account does not distract Him from another.

[14:52] *This* Qur'ān *is a proclamation*—a holistic admonition—revealed
for people that they might be admonished, *and so that they may be warned*
Q. 14:49 *thereby, and that they may know that He is One God*: by reflecting on the signs;
and that people of pith—sound minds—*may remember*: and so be dissuaded
from evil.

1 Above Hell.

15
Ḥijr
SŪRAT AL-ḤIJR

Revealed in Mecca

Having said, *This is a proclamation...* [Q. 14:52], and so on, He then states that this is what is written in the Preserved Tablet, saying:

In the Name of God, the Compassionate, the Merciful

[15:1] *Alif. Lām. Rā'. These*—the verses of this *sūra—are the verses of the Book*, the Tablet in which all things are recorded, *and of a manifest Qur'ān* that clarifies righteousness from error. He put *the Book* first here as an allusion to the perspective of objective existence, while in *Sūrat al-Naml* He said *the signs of the Qur'ān and a Manifest Book* [Q. 27:1], alluding to the perspective of the order in which we learn of them.

[15:2] *Perhaps*—in this context it means 'most definitely', with the term being used figuratively to imply its opposite by way of imparting emphasis—*those who disbelieve will wish that they had submitted*: when they meet with the [believing] sinners in Hell, they will say to them, 'Islam does not seem to have done you any good!' But then God will become enraged with them, and take all the sinners out of Hell.

[15:3] *Leave them to eat and to enjoy* in their world, *and to be diverted by hope* instead of preparing for the Hereafter; *for they will come to know* the evil of their conduct. This was abrogated by the permission to fight them.

[15:4] *And We did not destroy any town, but that it had a known decree*: a time ordained for its destruction.

[15:5] *No community can outstrip its term, nor can they delay it*: this was explained earlier.[1]

[15:6] *And they say* mockingly, *'O you, to whom the Remembrance*, the Qur'ān, *has been revealed, lo! you are truly mad!*

1 See Q. 7:34.

[15:7] *'Why do you not bring us the angels* to confirm you, *if you are of the truthful?'* So God replied on his behalf:

[15:8] *The angels do not descend save with the truth*: for a wise purpose, and there is no wise purpose for it now, because then you would be annihilated; yet it is destined that some of your descendants will be believers. *And then they would not be reprieved*: given respite.

[15:9] *Truly, it is We Who have revealed the Remembrance, and truly We will preserve it* from alteration, and so We have made it a prophetic miracle.

[15:10] *And indeed We sent before you* messengers *to former factions.*

[15:11] *And never did a messenger come to them but that they mocked him*: just as your people do.

[15:12] *Thus*, by placing such mockery in the hearts of these, *We cause it to find its way into the hearts of the sinners.*

[15:13] *They do not believe in him*, the messenger, *even though the example* of God regarding *of the men of old*—the destruction of the deniers—*has already gone before.*

Q. 15:7 [15:14] *And even if We were to open for them a gate from the heaven, and they were to continue ascending through it* and so behold the angels all through the day, [15:15] *they would say* stubbornly, *'It is merely that our eyes have been dazzled*: blocked by sorcery. *Nay, we are a folk bewitched!'* In other words, 'Muḥammad has bewitched our minds!' For this is what they said about other prophetic miracles.

[15:16] *And indeed We have placed*—created—*in the heaven constellations*: twelve of them with different shapes and properties, though in reality the heaven is one; *and We have adorned it* with stars *for beholders.*

[15:17] *And We have guarded it from every outcast devil*, so that he cannot spy on them, [15:18] *except the one who listens by stealth*: approaching them secretly; *but he is pursued by a clear flame*: a powerful tongue of fire that is visible to the beholders. It is related that this flame was sent on the occasion of the Prophet's birth (may God bless him and grant him peace), but that does not mean it could not also have been sent before him for various other reasons. It is also related that they were barred from three [of the heavens] upon the birth of Jesus, and from the rest upon the birth of Muḥammad (may God bless him and grant him peace).

[15:19] *And the earth We have stretched it forth*—spread it out—*and cast therein firm mountains, and caused to grow therein*—in the earth—*every kind of balanced thing*: apportioned with wisdom.

[15:20] *And We have made for you therein livelihood*: the means to live; *and* We have made for you *those for whom you could not provide*: such as your dependents and those you imagine you provide for.

[15:21] *And there is not a thing but that the stores thereof are with Us*: this is a metaphor for the totality of His power—He likens His power to do anything to stores wherein all things are kept, ready to be taken out whenever the time is right; *and We do not send it down except in a known measure*: as Our wisdom dictates.

[15:22] *And We send the winds as fertilisers* (*lawāqiḥ*): carrying water in the clouds, which We cause to run through the clouds until they swell up like the udders of a mother camel (*liqḥa*); or it refers to the *mulāqiḥ*, the one who cross-pollinates trees; *and send down out of the heaven water so that We give it to you to drink; for you are not the storers thereof*: of the rain, but rather it is in Our stores.

[15:23] *Truly, it is We Who give life and bring death, and We are the heirs* Who will remain after all creation is gone.

[15:24] *And well do We know the predecessors among you* all the way back to Adam, *and well do We know the successors*: those who will come until the end of the world.

[15:25] *And it is truly your Lord Who will gather them* for the requital. Q. 15:21
Truly, He is the Wise in His acts, the *Knower* of all.

[15:26] *And We created man*, Adam, *out of sounding clay*, dry clay that clinks when it is tapped, or wet clay, *of malleable mud*: the word *masnūn* means malleable, poured or viscous.

[15:27] *And the jānn*, the father of the jinn, or Iblīs, or the devils, *We created beforehand*—before Adam—*out of the scorching fire*: the extremely hot fire, or a smokeless fire which to our fire is like ice to water, or stone to dust.

[15:28] *And* remember *when your Lord said to the angels, 'Truly, I am going to create a mortal out of a sounding clay from a malleable mud.*

[15:29] *'So when I have proportioned him*, balanced his creation, *and breathed of My spirit in him*—the attribution of the spirit to God here denotes honour, and the breathing symbolises the attainment of the necessary means of life within him—*fall down in prostration before him!'*

[15:30] *And so the angels prostrated, all of them together*: the expression imparts emphasis, or means that they all did it together as one; [15:31] *except Iblīs, who refused to be among those prostrating*: this was explained earlier.[1]

[15:32] *He said, 'O Iblīs, what is wrong with you*—what is your purpose—*that you are not among those prostrating?'*

1 See Q. 2:34.

[15:33] *Said he, 'I was not about*—it would not be right for me—*to prostrate myself before a mortal whom You have created out of sounding clay from malleable mud.'*

[15:34] *Said He* when Iblīs displayed his pride, *'Then be gone from hence*: from your station, as was explained earlier;[1] *for you are truly accursed*: those banished from goodness.

[15:35] *'And truly the* perpetual *curse shall rest upon you until the Day of Judgement'*: He set this limit because it corresponds to the duration of the world of accountability. As for His Words, *And then a crier shall proclaim between them*... [Q. 7:44], and so on, this refers to something else, and this one will be forgotten then, because it is the furthest limit that people imagine.

[15:36] *Said he, 'My Lord, reprieve me*—delay my fate—*until the day when they shall be resurrected'*: by this he meant that he wished not to die.

[15:37] *Said He, 'Then truly you are of those reprieved,* [15:38] *until the*
Q. 15:33 *day of the known time* for your fate,' namely the blowing of the Trumpet,
whereupon he will die for forty years.

[15:39] *Said he, 'My Lord,* I swear that *because You have led me astray*—this was explained earlier[2]—*I shall adorn* sin *for them in the earth*, the world, *and I shall lead them astray, all of them,* [15:40] *except those servants of Yours who are sincerely devoted*: those whom You have made devoted to Your obedience.'

[15:41] *He said, 'This*—their escape from you—*is a straight path* that does not deviate, whose maintenance is incumbent *upon Me.* Or: 'This sincerity is a path that leads to Me without deviating.' We saw before that these words were delivered through an intermediary such as an angel or the like.

[15:42] *'Truly, over My servants*—all of them—*you shall have no warrant, except those who follow you from among the errant'*: this confirmed what he had said. The two exceptions are the inverse of each other,[3] which means that in the second one the exception must be from the minority, since otherwise they would be contradictory, unless it is taken as a 'severed exception'.[4]

[15:43] *And truly Hell shall be their tryst*—the tryst of the errant—*all of them.*

1 See Q. 7:13.

2 See Q. 7:16.

3 In other words, in the first statement the sincerely devoted are the ones excepted, while in the second it is the errant.

4 *Ishithnāʾ munqaṭiʿ*, where what is excepted is wholly different to the term from which it is excepted.

[15:44] *It has seven gates* for the seven levels of Hell: *Jahannam* (Gehenna), then *Laẓā* (Blaze), then *Ḥuṭama* (Crushing Fire), then *Saʿīr* (Raging Fire), then *Saqar* (Scorching Fire), then *Jaḥīm* (Hell-fire), then *Hāwiya* (Abyss). Each level has its own gate; the wisdom behind its confinement is the confinement of the things which lead to perdition through reliance on sensory things, passion and irascibility. *To each* level is a gate, and to each *gate belongs an appointed portion of them*: of his followers. The sinful monotheists go on the top, then the Jews, then the Christians, then the Sabaeans, then the Magians, then the idolaters, then the hypocrites.

[15:45] *Truly, the God-fearing shall be amidst Gardens and springs*. It will be said to them:

[15:46] *'Enter them in peace*: at peace, or greeted with peace; *secure* from loss.'

[15:47] *And We remove whatever rancour*—worldly envy or jealousy for the different levels of the Garden—*may be in their breasts. As brethren* in affection, *upon couches facing one another*: the couches turned so that they will not see each other's backs.

[15:48] *No toil will touch them therein, nor will they be expelled from thence.* Q. 15:44

[15:49] *Tell My servants that truly I am the Forgiving, the Merciful.*

[15:50] *And that My chastisement is the painful chastisement*: He did not say, 'I am the Chastiser,' because His mercy has precedence. By mentioning forgiveness, He indicated that by 'God-fearing' He did not mean only those who avoid sinning at all.

[15:51] *And tell them of the guests of Abraham,* [15:52] *when they went in to him, and said,* 'We greet you with *Peace!' He,* Abraham, *said,* returning their greeting, *'Truly, we are afraid of you'*: this was explained in *Sūrat Hūd.*[1]

[15:53] *They said, 'Do not be afraid. Truly, we give you glad tidings of a knowledgeable boy*: Isaac.'

[15:54] *He said, 'Do you give me glad tidings* of a son, *when old age has befallen me?* This cannot be. *So of what do you give me glad tidings?'* [This is as if he was saying] 'for such a tiding may as well not exist at all'.

[15:55] *They said, 'We give you glad tidings in truth*: not of the impossible; *so do not be of the despairing.'*

[15:56] *He,* Abraham, *said, 'And who*—no one—*despairs of the mercy of his Lord, save those who are astray?'* In other words, 'I did not mean to express despair, but only ordinary astonishment.'

[15:57] *He said, 'So what is your business*, the purpose for which you have been sent, *O you who have been sent?'* He knew that they had not been

1 See Q. 11:69 ff.

sent only to deliver that glad tiding, since one messenger would have been sufficient for that task, as with Jesus and John, and because they had only mentioned it to assuage his fear.

[15:58] *They said, 'We have been sent to a sinful folk*: the people of Lot, [15:59] *except the family of Lot. Truly, we shall save them, all of them,* [15:60] *except his wife—We have decreed that she truly should be of those who will remain behind* with the disbelievers to be destroyed along with them.'

[15:61] *And when those who had been sent came to the family of Lot,* [15:62] *he said, 'Truly, you are strangers*: I am wary of you, lest you mean me evil.'

[15:63] *They said,* 'We have not come bearing evil. *Nay, we have come to you because of that which they*, your companions, *used to doubt*: meaning the chastisement.

[15:64] *'And we have brought you the truth*: the certain news of their chastisement; *and truly we speak truthfully.*

[15:65] *'So travel with your family in a portion of the night and follow their*
Q. 15:58 *rear*: go behind them; *and let none of you turn round* behind him when he
hears the Cry; *and go whither you are commanded,* namely Syria.'

[15:66] *And We conveyed to him the matter*, which was *that those folk were to be eradicated by morning.*

[15:67] *And then came the people of the city*, Sodom, the city of Lot, *rejoicing* in his guests and desiring them. The story was told in *Sūrat Hūd* in chronological order, while here it is placed after the mention of how the angels said *we have come to you*... [Q. 15:63], even though it occurred before it, because the first account is meant as an elucidation of how the patient are given help, while the second pertains to the sins of the communities.

[15:68] *He*, Lot, *said, 'Truly, these are my guests, so do not disgrace me* by disgracing them.

[15:69] *'And fear God, and do not humiliate me.'*

[15:70] *They said, 'Have we not forbidden you from* telling *anyone?'*

[15:71] *He said, 'These here are my daughters*: marry them, *if you must be doing anything* to slake your lust': this was explained earlier.[1]

[15:72] *By your life*, O Muḥammad, do I swear: *in their drunkenness they were bewildered*: the imperfect verb is used here[2] to evoke the reality of their bewilderment; or it could be a parenthetical description of the Quraysh.

[15:73] *Then the Cry* of ruin from Gabriel *seized them at sunrise*: the word *mushriqīn* means 'as they were reaching the time of the sun's rising',

1 See Q. 11:78.
2 *Yaʿmahūn*, literally 'they are bewildered'.

and the related gerund *ishrāq* means 'the brightness of sunrise', suggesting that the Cry lasted from the beginning of dawn until that time.

[15:74] *And We made their topmost part*—the highest dwellings of the town—*their nethermost, and We rained on them stones of baked clay*: this was explained earlier.[1]

[15:75] *Truly, in that there are signs for those who take note*: those who are given to reflection.

[15:76] *And truly it*, that town, *is on a road that remains still*: and you travel on it and see it.

[15:77] *There is truly a sign in that for believers.*

[15:78] *And certainly the folk of the Wood*, a tree near Midian, *were evildoers*: this means the people of Shuʿayb. God destroyed the folk of the Wood with the Shadow, and the folk of Midian with the Cry.

[15:79] *So We exacted retribution from them*: as was just explained. *And certainly both of them*, Sodom and the Wood, *are upon an open road* upon which you travel.

Q. 15:74

[15:80] *And indeed the dwellers in Ḥijr*—a valley between Medina and Syria—*denied those who had been sent*: this means Thamūd, who denied Ṣāliḥ, which was tantamount to denying all the messengers, as was noted earlier.

[15:81] *And We brought them Our signs*—such as the she-camel—*but they were averse*: and did not reflect on them and realise their truth.

[15:82] *And they used to hew out dwellings from the mountains, feeling secure* from God's chastisement, thinking that it would be repelled.

[15:83] *But the Cry seized them in the morning.*

[15:84] *And so that which they used to count as gain*—their homes and the rest—*did not avail them*: or protect them from the chastisement.

[15:85] *We did not create the heavens and the earth and all that is between them save* as a creation adorned *with the truth*: which is why evil things never last long. *And truly the Hour shall come*: whereupon We shall exact retribution from the deniers. *So be forgiving*: turn away from them; *with gracious forgiveness*: without conflict. This was abrogated by the permission to fight them.

[15:86] *Truly, your Lord, He is the Creator* of all things, *the Knowing* of all situations.

[15:87] *And indeed We have given you seven of the oft-repeated* verses of *Sūrat al-Fātiḥa*—*mathānī* (oft-repeated) is from *tathniya* (to repeat) or *thanā'* (to praise), as we discussed in [the commentary of *Sūrat*] *al-Fātiḥa*; *and the Glorious Qur'ān*: the whole here being mentioned after the part.

1 See Q. 11:82.

[15:88] *Do not extend your glance*—do not look with desire—*toward that which We have given different groups of them*, the disbelievers, *to enjoy*: for the Qur'ān is sufficient for you; *and do not grieve for them* if they do not believe; *and lower your wing*—be humble—*to the believers*: this is a euphemism for sound leadership and compassion, based on a bird lowering its wing to its chick and hugging it to itself.

[15:89] *And say: 'Truly, I am the clear warner* heralding His torment.'

[15:90] *Even* such chastisement *as We sent down on those who made division*: this may mean the twelve men who dispersed around the entrances to Mecca during the *ḥajj* season to dissuade the people from joining Muḥammad (may God bless him and grant him peace), and then met their demises at Badr. This interpretation is debatable, however, since this *sūra* was revealed in Mecca. A better interpretation is that *those who made the division* (*muqtasimīn*) means those who swore to one another (*mutaqāsimīn*) to assassinate Ṣāliḥ, and those who opposed the prophets. Their identity is further clarified by the next verse:

Q. 15:88

[15:91] *Those who have reduced the Qur'ān to parts*: pieces of soothsaying, sorcery or the like. And God Almighty knows best.

[15:92] *By your Lord, We shall question them all.*

[15:93] *About what they used to do*: including this division. As for His Words *on that day no man will be questioned about his sin* [Q. 55:39], they refer to another occasion and to questioning for the purpose of obtaining information, while the questioning meant here is for the purpose of rebuke.

[15:94] *So proclaim* aloud *what you have been commanded*—the laws—*and turn away from the idolaters.*

[15:95] *Truly, We have sufficed you against the mockers*: this means five people who used to abuse the Prophet (may God bless him and grant him peace), and who were swiftly destroyed.

[15:96] *Those who set up besides God another god—soon they will know* the dire consequence of this.

[15:97] *And indeed We know that your breast is oft straitened by what they say*: their attacks against your religion.

[15:98] *So glorify the praise of your Lord*: say, 'Glory be to God, and praise be to Him!' In other words, declare His transcendence above what they say, and praise Him for what He has given you. *And be of those who prostrate themselves* in prayer.

[15:99] *And worship your Lord* constantly *until certainty comes to you*: death, which is the certain fate of all. And God knows best what is right, and to Him is the return and the final rest.

16
The Bee
SŪRAT AL-NAḤL

Revealed in Mecca

After telling him not to let his heart be straitened by thoughts of the hastening of God's succour and His promised chastisement, He then said:

In the Name of God, the Compassionate, the Merciful

[16:1] *God's commandment*—His promise about the Resurrection and the rest—*has come*: it will certainly come to pass; *so do not seek to hasten it*, O idolaters, for it is inevitable. *Glory be to Him and exalted be He above* the association of *what they associate!*

[16:2] *He sends down the angels*, meaning Gabriel specifically, *with the Spirit*, revelation that gives life to hearts, *from His command*, by His decree, *to whomever He will of His servants*, telling them: *Warn* and know *that there is no God save Me: so fear Me.*

[16:3] *He created the heavens and the earth with the truth*: wisdom. *Exalted be He above* the association of *what they associate!*

[16:4] *He created man from a drop of fluid, yet behold!* When he becomes independent, *he is disputatious* with his Lord, *openly.*

[16:5] *And the cattle, He created them for you. In them there is warmth*: the means of keeping warm and protecting from the cold; *as well as other uses*: such as farming and the like; *and of them you eat*: the order in which these items are arranged implies that eating game and birds is essentially a luxury, as well as preserving the prose-rhyme scheme of the terminating word of each verse (*murāʿāt al-fāṣila*).[1]

[16:6] *And for you there is in them beauty*—splendour—*when you bring them* home *to rest, and when you drive them forth to pasture*: He mentioned

1 *Ta'kulūn* (you eat) maintains the *ūn/īn* rhyme scheme which has so far been established in the *sūra*.

resting first because the splendour of them is more evident when their bellies are full and their udders swollen with milk.

[16:7] *And they bear your burdens to a land which you could not reach* without cattle *save with great trouble to yourselves*: never mind the added toil of transporting your burdens there on your own backs. *Truly, your Lord is Gentle, Merciful*: and in His mercy He created them for you.

[16:8] *And horses and mules and asses, that you may ride them*: the word *that* implies facilitation, as in His Words, *He it is Who made for you the night that you should rest therein* [Q. 10:67]; *and for adornment*: He switched the rhetorical style[1] here to evoke the vastness of their benefits. *And He creates what you do not know*.

NOTE: This verse has been cited as evidence for the position that eating horseflesh is forbidden, on the grounds that He did not mention eating them when listing their benefits, but did mention something else that is of lesser significance. This is faulty reasoning, however, because most of their benefits are a matter of custom, except for eating them, which is not
Q. 16:7 true in the case of cattle. Mentioning only the most common benefits for the sake of brevity is the usual way of the Qur'ān. Furthermore, there are authentic *ḥadīth*s, in the two *Ṣaḥīḥ* collections, stating that horseflesh is lawful. Note also that the verse was revealed in Mecca, while domesticated donkey meat was not prohibited until the year of Khaybar.

[16:9] *And upon God is the direction*—the elucidation of the straight path from within the class—*of the way, and some of them*, some ways, *are deviant*: divergence from the truth. *And had He willed, He would have guided you all* to the direction of the way.

[16:10] *He it is Who sends down water from the heaven, whence you have drink*: since it gives rise to springs; *and whence are trees*: it is said that this means every kind of plant; *whereat you let your animals graze*: He put this before olives and the rest because of how it then becomes animal-based nourishment, which is the noblest of all forms of nourishment.

[16:11] *With it*, water, *He makes the crops grow for you, and olives and date palms and vines and* some *of all kinds of fruit*: for the entire range of them can only be found in the Garden. *Truly, in that there is a sign* of the totality of His power *for folk who contemplate*.

[16:12] *And He disposed for you*—prepared for your benefit—*the night and the day, and the sun and the moon; and the stars* too give you benefit when they *are disposed*, or they are disposed in many ways, or many kinds of

1 In other words, rather than saying 'and that you might derive adornment'.

disposal; *by His command*: His ordain. *Truly, in that there are signs for a folk who comprehend*.

[16:13] *And* He has disposed for you *what He has created for you in the earth*—of animate and inanimate things—*diverse in hue*: form. *Truly, in that there is a sign for folk who reflect* on the variety of its natures and forms despite the unity of its substance, which could only be done by a being that is wise and knowing. He said *a sign* in the singular here so that it would correspond to *what He has created*, although it applies to a great many things. The same applies to the first,[1] because deriving proof of God's power from the sending-down of water is one thing. Then He used the plural in the second[2] because it describes several things that are signs of His power. He also referred to understanding for that one, and contemplation for the first, because the signs of the celestial bodies are obvious.

[16:14] *And He it is Who disposed the sea, that you may eat from it fresh meat*: fish. He singled it out for mention because it is the freshest kind of meat. Mālik cited this as evidence that if someone vows that he will not eat meat Q. 16:13
but then eats fish, he had broken his oaths. The rebuttal of this is that oaths are based on convention, and generally the word 'meat' is not understood to include fish. It is like if a man vowed not to ride on the back of a beast, but then rode on the back of a disbeliever; he would not break his vow by doing so, even though God does speak of the disbelievers in those terms. *And* [that you may] *bring forth from it ornaments*—pearls and coral—*which you wear*: which your women wear for you. *And you see the ships ploughing therein*: cutting through the water, or churning it up, or bearing heavy burdens upon it; *and that you may seek of His bounty*: His vast provision when you sail upon it for trade; *and that you might be thankful* for His favour.

[16:15] *And He cast into the earth firm mountains, lest it should shake with you, and* He made therein *rivers and ways*—roads—*that you might be guided* to your destinations.

[16:16] *And landmarks* for travellers to use to navigate, such as mountains and hills; *and by the star*—by its class—*they are guided* on land and sea.

[16:17] *Is He then Who creates as he who does not create*: such as your associates*?* One might expect this to be worded the opposite way round, but He worded it this way to show the heinousness of how they liken Him to a powerless created being. *Will you not then reflect*: and recognise how corrupt this belief is*?*

1 See Q. 16:11.
2 See Q. 16:12.

[16:18] *And if you were to count God's grace you could never reckon it*: so how could you possibly give thanks for it? *Truly, God is Forgiving, Merciful*: and will not take you to task for your shortcomings in giving thanks for it.

[16:19] *And God knows what you keep secret and what you disclose.*

[16:20] *And those* gods *whom you invoke*—worship—*besides God do not create anything, but are themselves created.*

[16:21] *They are dead, not living*: He said the latter to dispel the suggestion that this is only a figure of speech, or that they will ever come to life like a drop of semen does; *and they are not aware when they shall be raised*: while God is alive, and knows all that is Unseen.

[16:22] *Your God is One God*: and this is the only conclusion to which the evidence points. *But those who do not believe in the Hereafter, their hearts are in denial*: and they do not contemplate the evidence; *and they are* too *arrogant* to follow the messengers.

[16:23] *Without doubt God knows what they keep secret and what they disclose*: and will requite them. *Truly, He does not love the arrogant* of any kind,
Q. 16:18 and certainly not them. This was revealed about Naḍr b. al-Ḥārith.

[16:24] *And when it is said to them*—the *ḥajj* pilgrims who passed by used to ask them—*'What is it that your Lord has revealed* to Muḥammad*?' they say* that what he claims to have been revealed is but *'Fables of the ancients*: not revelation from God.'

[16:25] *That*—the consequence of which is that—*they will bear their burdens complete on the Day of Resurrection and also* some *of the burdens of those whom they lead astray without any knowledge*: that is, those who were ignorant to the fact that it was misguidance. This qualification indicates that it is essential to research and seek to differentiate between the truthful and the deceitful, and then follow the example of the truthful. *How evil is the burden they bear*: namely their deeds*!*

[16:26] *Those before them had plotted* to destroy the edifice of God's religion; *then* the command of *God came at their edifice from* the direction of *the foundations* upon which they had built it, *and so the roof collapsed upon them from above them, and the chastisement came upon them whence they were not aware*: this is a metaphor for their destruction, or refers to the tower of Nimrod and how it collapsed upon them. Ibn ʿAbbās (may God be pleased with him) is reported to have said that when Nimrod built the tower to ascend to the heavens, he made it five thousand cubits high, but then the wind blew the top into the sea and the rest collapsed upon them as they stood beneath it.

[16:27] *Then on the Day of Resurrection He will disgrace them* with the

Fire, *and He will say* in reproach, *'Where are those associates of Mine concerning whom*—for whose cause—*you used to make breaches*: conflicts with the believers*?' Those who were given knowledge*—the ones who tried to call them to guidance—*will say* disdainfully, *'Truly, disgrace on this day, and misfortune*—punishment—*are for the disbelievers.*

[16:28] *'Those whom the angels take while they are wronging themselves.' Then they will offer submission*: surrendering to the angels of chastisement and saying: *'We were not doing any evil*: disbelief.' So the angels will say: *'Nay*: truly you were. *Truly, God is Knower of what you used to do*: and will requite you.'

[16:29] *So enter the gates of Hell*—each type to its appropriate gate—*abiding therein! Evil undoubtedly is the lodging of the arrogant*: those who were too proud to worship Him, for they are Hell-bound.

[16:30] *And it is said*—the ones who said it were the *ḥajj* pilgrims—*to those who fear, 'What has your Lord revealed?' They will say,* 'He has revealed *Good! For those who were virtuous in this world, there will be virtue*: a goodly life; *and undoubtedly the abode of the Hereafter is better* for them. *And truly excellent is the abode of the God-fearing.* ❁ Q. 16:28 ❁

[16:31] *'Gardens of Eden which they will enter, with rivers flowing from beneath them, wherein they shall have whatever they wish*: desire. *Thus does God reward the fearful.*

[16:32] *'Those whom the angels take away while they are goodly*: pure from injustice, or joyous; *They*, the angels, *will say, 'Peace be on you!* No ill will ever befall you again. *Enter the Garden*—when you are resurrected, or immediately, as an authentic *ḥadīth* indicates—*because of what you used to do.'*

[16:33] *Do they await anything*—the disbelievers await nothing else—*but that the angels should come to them* to seize their spirits, *or that there should come your Lord's command?* This is in reference to the Resurrection, or annihilating chastisement. *Such*—the very same denial—*did those before them. And God did not wrong them* by chastising them, *but* only requited them for how *they used to wrong themselves* with their deeds, by which they earned that requital.

[16:34] *So that the evils*—the dire consequences—*of what they did smote them, and there besieged*—surrounded—*them that which they used to mock.*

[16:35] *And the idolaters say* mockingly, for they did not believe in the evil of their deeds, *'Had God willed* for us not to worship anything but Him, *we would not have worshipped anything besides Him*—*neither we, nor our fathers*—*nor would we have deemed anything sacred besides Him*: such as the *baḥā'ir.'*[1] *So did those before them*: this was explained in *Sūrat al-Anʿām.*[2] *Yet are messengers charged with anything save plain conveyance*: to offer them guidance*?*

[16:36] *And We sent forth among every community a messenger: 'Worship God and shun false deities*: idols.*' Then among them were some whom God guided* to faith, *and among them were some who deserved to be in error*: had He not given them grace? *So travel,* O Quraysh, *in the land and observe the nature of the consequence of those who denied,* who came before you.

[16:37] *Though you are eager,* O Muḥammad, *for them to be guided,* it will not do any good, *for God does not guide he whom He has sent astray*: whom He wills to go astray; *and they will have no helpers* to save them.

[16:38] *And they swear by God their most earnest oaths that God will not resurrect the dead. Nay*: He will undoubtedly raise them; *it is a promise upon Him* to keep, *in truth; but most people do not know* that they will be raised along with them.

Q. 16:36

[16:39] *That He may make clear to them,* to those whom He raises, *that wherein they differ,* namely the truth, *and that the disbelievers may know that they were liars* when they vowed that God would not raise the dead. He then clarifies the obviousness of its possibility by saying:

[16:40] *All that We say to a thing, when We will it* to come into existence, *is to say to it 'Be!'*—'Exist!'—*and it is*: it exists without any need for material or time. So what about that which is already composed of matter?

[16:41] *And those who emigrated for God's cause after they had been wronged* by persecution and other things, *We shall truly lodge them in this world in a goodly lodging*: by giving them power in the land and making them rule over God's servants; *and the reward of the Hereafter is surely greater* than this, *did they but know?* If the disbelievers knew, they would join them.

[16:42] *Those who endure* persecution *and put their trust in their Lord.*

[16:43] *And We did not send before you anything other than men to whom We revealed*: so why should they claim that God is too great to send a mortal as His messenger? This implies that He never sent a woman or an angel to convey revelation. *So ask the followers of the Remembrance*—the two Books—*if you do not know*: this indicates that it is obligatory to consult learned folk when one does not know something.

[16:44] We sent them *with clear signs*—patent prophetic miracles—*and the Scriptures*: the Books; *and We have revealed to you the Remembrance*, the

1 See Q. 4:119 and Q. 5:103.
2 See Q. 6:148.

Qur'ān, *that you may make clear to people what has been revealed to them* therein through your message, *and that perhaps they might reflect* on it and be guided.

[16:45] *Do those who have schemed evil*—by attempting to dissuade the Companions from faith—*feel secure that God will not cause the earth to swallow them*: like as happened to Korah; *or that the chastisement will not come upon them whence they are not aware*: from a direction where they do not expect it, such as how they were slain at Badr*?*

[16:46] *Or that He will not seize them in their going to and fro*: while they are going about their livelihoods; *whereupon they will not be able to escape* from God*?*

[16:47] *Or that He will not seize them with a gradual wasting*: by subtracting from them little by little until they are annihilated*? Truly, your Lord is Gentle, Merciful*: for He will not punish you immediately.

[16:48] *Or have they not observed that which God has created of things, how their shadows incline to the right* of the sun when it is in the East at the first part of the day, *and to the left* of it when it is in the West at the end of the day;[1] or right and left may represent simply the sides of every object, a figure of speech based on the right and left hands of the human being; *prostrating to God*—yielding to His will—*and how they are subject*: dominated by His power*?* Q. 16:45

[16:49] *And to God prostrates*—yields—*whatever is in the heavens and whatever is on the earth of living creatures*: the word *dābba* (creature) is from *dabīb*, meaning 'physical motion', and so it covers both races [men and jinn] as well as all unintelligent animals; *as do the angels*: those who say that angels are incorporeal beings have cited this as proof for their opinion,[2] but the rebuttal of this is that He only singled them out for special mention in order to honour them; *and they are not arrogant*: not too proud to worship Him.

[16:50] *They fear their Lord* lest He send down upon them chastisement *from above them*: or they fear their Lord Who is above them by His dominant power; *and they do what they are commanded* to do.

[16:51] *And God has said, 'Do not choose two gods, paired*: the word *paired* is added to show that the root of the prohibition is this duality, or to

1 The author notes here that the word 'shadow' can be read as *ẓilāl* in the plural or *ẓill* in the singular, and that the pronoun connected to it is in the singular (literally 'its shadow'), and that 'left' is *shama'il* in the plural form, and explains that this is because of the word 'that' *mā*, which is strictly singular even though in this context it describes a plural. I elected to move his parenthetical observation of this to a footnote to retain the clarity of the commentary.

2 Since if they had bodies they would already have been included in the term *dābba*.

imply that duality undermines divinity, which He affirms by saying, *There is only One God*: for the purpose is to affirm His Oneness, or to indicate that monotheism is an integral aspect of divinity, and that God is the One God. *So be in awe of Me*: and no other.'

[16:52] *And to Him belongs whatever is in the heavens and the earth. And to Him belongs the religion*—the obedience—*that endures*: that is constant, for He alone deserves worship. *Will you then fear any other than God?*

[16:53] *Whatever grace you have, it is from God. Then when misfortune befalls you, to Him you cry for help*: raising your voices in supplication.

[16:54] *Then when He has rid you of the misfortune, behold, a group of you attribute partners to their Lord,* [16:55] *that they may deny that* grace *which We have given* them: the word *that* here denotes consequence, or a warning. *So enjoy, for soon you shall know* the consequence.

[16:56] *And they assign, to what they do not know*—meaning their gods, for they are inanimate objects—*a portion of that which We have provided them*,
Q. 16:52 saying, as we saw before: *'This is for God,' so they claim*... [Q. 6:136]. *By God, you will assuredly be questioned* reproachfully *about what you used to fabricate* by associating them.

[16:57] *And they*, the tribes of Kināna and Khuzāʿa, *assign to God daughters*: meaning the angels, though they themselves disdain daughters. *Glory be to Him* beyond such a thing*! And to them* will be the best of *what they desire*: meaning sons. Or it means, 'And they assign to themselves sons.' The mention of 'themselves' is not required because they are not the direct objects of the verb 'to assign', similar to such passages as *shake the trunk of the palm tree towards you* [Q. 19:25], and *draw your arm to you* [Q. 28:32].

[16:58] *And when one of them is given the tidings of a girl, his face becomes darkened*: a euphemism for intense disappointment; *and he chokes inwardly*: filled with rage at his wife.

[16:59] *He hides from people out of distress at the tidings given to him*, saying to himself: *shall he retain it in humiliation, or bury it*—conceal it—*in the dust? Why, surely wretched is what they judge*: by attributing this to God Almighty.

[16:60] *For those who do not believe in the Hereafter there is an evil description*: a deficient attribute; *and the loftiest description belongs to God*: for He is transcendentally Sublime beyond all deficiency. *And He is the Mighty, the Wise*: the sole Possessor of perfect wisdom and power.

[16:61] *And if God were to take people to task for their evildoing, He would not leave upon it*—upon the face of the earth—*any living being*: because of their evil. The attribution of wrongdoing to them is by reference to the majority, and does not include the prophets. It is not far-fetched that innocent people might be destroyed alongside evildoers because of their evil, and indeed this befell many communities of old. Or it means 'any evil living being'. Or it means that had He destroyed the forefathers because of their disbelief, their descendants would never have lived at all. *But He gives them respite until an appointed term*: the time of their death, to allow them to procreate; *and when their term comes, they will not defer by a single hour nor advance*: this was explained earlier.[1]

[16:62] *Still, they assign to God what they dislike* for themselves, such as daughters and associates in leadership. *And their tongues relate the lie that theirs will be the best reward*: meaning the Garden, for they said: *even if I am returned to my Lord, I will truly have the best with Him* [Q. 41:50]. *Assuredly, theirs shall be the Fire and they shall be abandoned*—cast—*therein.*

[16:63] *By God! Indeed, We sent to communities before you, but Satan adorned for them their deeds*: and they persisted in them. *So he is their patron*—helper—*today* in this world, but on the Day of Resurrection they will have no helper; *and for them there will be a painful chastisement* in the Hereafter. Q. 16:62

[16:64] *And We have not revealed to you the Book, except that you may make clear to them*, to the people, *that wherein they differ* and guide them to the truth, *and as a guidance and as a mercy for a folk who believe.*

[16:65] *And God sends down water from the heaven and therewith revives the earth after its death*: this was explained earlier.[2] *Truly, in that there is a sign for a folk who are able to hear*: and reflect.

[16:66] *And truly for you there is in cattle a lesson* for contemplation. *We give you to drink of that which is in their bellies*: the masculine singular pronoun is used here[3] because the word *anʿām* (cattle) is a collective noun, while the similar passage in *Sūrat al-Mu'minūn*[4] uses the feminine plural pronoun[5] because the meaning is plural—that is, the noun which refers to type can be viewed to be acting as a plural; *from between the waste matter* in the bowels *and the blood, pure milk* free from the colour of blood and the stench of waste matter, *palatable*—easy to swallow—*to drinkers*: the *between* here is figurative, because they say that the filth matter from the stomach is then digested by the liver a second time, whereupon four admixtures occur, one of which is water-based, after which the brain directs what is left over to the kidneys, gallbladder and spleen, and then the rest is

1 See Q. 7:31.
2 See Q. 2:164.
3 *Buṭūnihi*, literally 'its bellies'.
4 Q. 23:21.
5 *Buṭūnihā*, 'their bellies'.

distributed across the body according to its needs. In the female, it is further mixed according to its nutritive value because of its greater coolness and moisture, so that what is left over is directed first to the womb for the foetus; then, after it is born, some or all of that amount is directed to the udders and becomes white because of its proximity to the animal's fatty white meat, thereby becoming milk. *So blessed be God, the best of creators!* [Q. 23:14].

[16:67] *And* some *of the fruits of date palms and vines from which*—from that part of them, or from their class, as was discussed before—*you draw an intoxicant*: wine—this was revealed before it had been forbidden; *and goodly provision*: such as date-syrup, or some say that *intoxicant* refers to what is drunk and *provision* to what is eaten. *Truly, in that there is a sign for a folk who comprehend*: who use their intelligence to contemplate it.

[16:68] *And your Lord revealed to the bee* by inspiration—the feminine imperative is used here to denote the plural, or it is the Hejaz dialect;[1]
Q. 16:67 *'Choose among the hills habitations* that human architects would be unable to build without the use of instruments and precise measurements, *and* habitations *among the trees, and among the trellises which they raise* for them.

[16:69] *'Then eat from every fruit* which you desire, *and follow the ways of your Lord* which He inspires to you for making honey or grazing, which are *made easy*: facilitated for you'; or this refers to the bees themselves, in which case it means 'made subservient to His command'. This is why the queen bee divides the labour among the other bees, so that some of them produce wax, others honey, and others construct the habitations, and others bring water and pour it into the hive. Glory be to Him *Who gave to everything its own nature, and then guided* [Q. 20:55]. *There comes forth from their bellies a drink*: this supports the opinion that honey is bee bile; those who say that honey is composed of particles that the bee gathers with its mouth and stores inside it would have to interpret *bellies* here to mean 'mouths'; *of diverse hues*—white and other colours—*wherein is a* tremendous *cure for humankind* for those with phlegmatic constitutions, whether by itself or when mixed with other things; or the indefinite article is meant to imply that it is one of many. *Truly, in that there is a sign for a folk who contemplate* on God's handiwork.

[16:70] *And God has created you, and then He takes you* [*in death*]*; and there are some among you who are relegated to the most abject* final *stage of life*: infirmity and dementia. It is related that the one who recites the Qur'ān

1 The word *naḥl* (bee) is usually masculine.

regularly will not be relegated to this; some say that it specifically refers to the disbeliever, which is supported by the end of *Sūrat al-Tīn*.[1] *So that he knows nothing after having knowledge*: and becomes like a child in terms of mental faculties. This implies that the different spans of life are nothing but the ordain of the All-Powerful, All-Wise One. *God is Knowing* of His handiwork, *Able* to do as He wills.

[16:71] *And God has favoured some of you above others in provision* for a wise reason. *Now those who have been favoured* in provision *would not hand over their provision to those whom their right hands possess*: they would not give their provision to their slaves; *so that they*, the slaves and freedmen, *became equal in respect thereof*: of provision. *Is it then the grace of God that they deny*: by denying such proofs after He has graciously clarified them?

[16:72] *And God made for you mates from your own selves*—your own kind—*and made for you, from your mates, sons*: He did not mention daughters because they disdained them, and He was enumerating His favours to them; *and grandchildren*: the word *ḥafada* can mean 'grandchildren', Q. 16:71
'daughters' or 'handmaiden' because of the promptness of their service, since *ḥāfid* means 'one who serves promptly'. *And He provided you with the good things*: the things that are enjoyable. *Is it then in falsehood*—idols—*that they believe, and in the grace of God that they disbelieve*: by attributing them to others than Him?

[16:73] *And they worship besides God that which has no power to give them any provision from the heavens and the earth, nor do they have the capacity* to possess it. He used the singular and then the plural to express both the word and the meaning.

[16:74] *So do not strike*—make—*any similitude for God* to compare Him to them, for making a similitude is to compare one state to another; or it means, 'Do not make any similitudes for Him at all.' *Truly, God knows* the falsehood of your similitudes, or how to make them properly, *and you do not know* it; or, according to the second interpretation, it is an allusion to how the Names of God can only be known by revelation. Then He strikes a similitude for the one who worships other than Him, and another for Himself, saying:

[16:75] *God strikes a similitude: A slave who is a chattel*, owned by another, *having no power over anything*, no autonomy, unlike one who has been allowed certain freedoms; this represents the idols, or some say the disbeliever who is incapable of doing anything good; *and one on whom We have*

1 Q. 95:4–6.

bestowed a fair provision from Us, such that he spends thereof secretly and openly: this represents God Himself, or some say the believer, who is like a free man who chooses to devote himself to God. *Are they equal* in kind, slaves and freemen*? Praise*—all praise—*belongs to God* alone. *But most of them do not know* this, and so they worship other than Him.

[16:76] *And God strikes a similitude: Two men, one of whom is dumb* from birth, *having no power over anything*, any labour, *and who is a liability*, a burden, *to his master*: this implies that he is a slave; *wherever he*, his master, *directs him, he does not bring any good*: this represents the idols, or the disbelievers. *Is he equal to one who* is able to speak and is rightly guided, and who *enjoins justice and follows a path that is straight?* Wherever he heads, he arrives there. This represents God Himself, or the believers.

[16:77] *And to God belongs the Unseen*—knowledge of what is Unseen—*of the heavens and the earth. And the matter of* the rising of *the Hour is but* as swift and easy *as the twinkling of an eye*: as quick as switching one's gaze from upwards to downwards, as they say of it; and then He says, for His
Q. 16:76
own part, *or* indeed *it is even nearer*: even swifter. Thus there is no need to object that the word *or* suggests uncertainty, and the word 'nay' changing one's mind, both of which are impossible for God. The same applies to other similar passages, such as *a hundred thousand or more* [Q. 37:147], and *or even yet harder* [Q. 2:74]. In other words, such ought to be your view on the matter. *Truly, God has power over all things*: including their resurrection.

[16:78] *And God brought you forth from the bellies of your mothers while you did not know anything, and He made*, created, *for you hearing and sight and hearts*, the instruments for attaining knowledge both particular and universal, *that perhaps you might give thanks*: by utilising them to attain knowledge, which He explicates further by saying:

[16:79] *Have they not observed the birds, made subservient*—facilitated for flight by the wings that were created for them—*in the air of heaven? Nothing holds them* in those heights *except God*: for their weight, without anything to suspend it or support it, ought to make them fall. *Truly, in that* creation, subservience, and upholding *there are signs for a folk who believe.*

[16:80] *And it is God Who has made for you your homes as a place of rest*: a place in which you can take your repose; *and He has made for you out of the skins of cattle* and the hair upon them *homes*, which was how most of the Arabs lived, *which you find light on the day of your migration and on the day of your halting*: when travelling and when halting or settling; *and of their wool* for sheep, *and their fur* for camels, *and their hair* for goats, *furniture* for your homes, such as rugs, *and wares* for commerce, *for a while*: a limited time.

[16:81] *And it is God Who has made for you, from what He created*, of trees and the like, things under which you can find *shade; and He has made for you, in the mountains, places of refuge*: places to hide in, such as caves. *And He has made for you garments that protect you from the heat*: He did not mention the other extreme [cold] because heat was more relevant to the Arabs; *and garments* for war, such as armour, *that protect you from your violence*: your warfare such as stabbing and the like. *So*, by such creation, *He perfects His favour to you* by creating what you need, *so that you might* reflect upon it and *submit* to His decree.

[16:82] *But if they turn away* from submission, then you are not to blame, for *your duty is only to convey plainly*.

[16:83] *They recognise God's grace* and how it is from Him, *and then deny it* by associating others with Him; *and most of them are ungrateful*: while the minority among them are those who do not know that it is from Him to begin with.

[16:84] *And* remember *the day We shall raise up from every community a witness*: their messenger who was witness over them; *then the disbelievers will not be given permission* to apologise, *nor will they be asked to make amends*: they will not be asked to seek God's approval, for it will not be a day of labour. Q. 16:81

[16:85] *And when those who did wrong behold the chastisement* in Hell, *it shall not be lightened for them, nor will they be granted any respite.*

[16:86] *And when those who associated behold their associates, they will say* in rage at their gods and their worldly lives, *'Our Lord, these are our associates whom we used to invoke*—worship—*besides You.' But they will fling to them the saying*: that is, they will say to them, *'You are truly liars* for truly you only worshipped your own desires*!'*

[16:87] *And they*, the disbelievers, *will offer submission to God on that day* and surrender to His decree, *and that which they used to invent*—namely the help of their gods—*will fail them.*

[16:88] *Those who disbelieve and bar* people *from the way of God*—His religion—*We shall add chastisement to their chastisement* which they earned by their disbelief, namely scorpions with fangs as long as palm trees, *because of the corruption they used to cause*: because of how they strayed and led others astray.

[16:89] *And* remember *the day We shall raise up from every community a witness against them from among themselves*, namely their prophet, *and We shall bring you*, O Muḥammad, *as a witness against these*: your community. *And We have revealed to you the Book as a clarification*—a thorough elucidation—*of all things* they need for religion, *and as a guidance and a mercy* for all, which is only denied to those who ignore it, *and glad tidings to those who submit* alone. This verse serves as an explication of how the Qur'ān is a clarification of details or general principles, by reference to the Sunna or analogy.

[16:90] *Truly, God enjoins justice*: temperance in doctrine, such as monotheism rather than atheism or idolatry; and in action, such as worship rather than indolence or monasticism; and in ethics, such as generosity rather than stinginess or extravagance; *and virtue* in action, or kindness to all creation; *and giving to kinsfolk*: keeping family ties; *and He forbids lewdness*, meaning vile sins, such as adultery, *and abomination* according to the Law, *and aggression*: injustice, which He singled out because of its importance. Or the first means excess in pursuing the appetitive faculty, the second the indulgence of the irascible faculty, and the third engaging in the oppression of other people, which is the dictate of the estimative faculty; for there is no evil in the soul except through the mediation of one of these three. *He admonishes you so that you might remember*: and be alert.

[16:91] *And fulfil God's covenant*—the pledge of Islam, or any covenant
Q. 16:90 in general—*when you make a covenant, and do not break oaths after pledging them* and invoking God's Name on them, *and having made God surety*—witness—*over you*: by swearing by Him. *Truly, God knows what you do* when you break them.

[16:92] *And do not*—by breaking them—*be like her who undoes her yarn after having made it strong*: breaking it after spinning it neatly, or some say while she is in the middle of spinning it; *into fibres*: unravelled bits of thread—she was a madwoman of Mecca named, it is said, Rīṭa bint Saʿd al-Qurashiyya, who used to spin all day and then unravel it; *by making your oaths a deceit*—false and treacherous—*between you*: the word *dakhal* (deceit) is from the verb *yadhkhul* (to enter), in the sense of introducing something to a place it has no reason to be; *because one group*—community—*is more numerous than another*: when they made a treaty with a tribe but then found another tribe that was stronger, they would ally with the stronger and betray the weaker one. *God only tries*—tests—*you thereby*: by commanding you to honour your oaths, or by the other group being more numerous, in order to see whether you will be true or not. *And certainly He will make clear to you on the Day of Resurrection that wherein you used to differ* in this world, by requiting you.

[16:93] *For if God had willed, He could have made you one community* sharing a single religion, *but He leads astray whom He will and guides whom He will* for a wise reason; *and you will surely be questioned about what you used to do*: for requital.

[16:94] *And do not make your oaths a deceit*—a plot—*between you* in any circumstance, *lest a foot should slip*—lest your feet should slip from the path of Islam—*after being steady* upon it—He said *foot* in the singular to imply that not even a single foot should slip, never mind several; *and lest you should taste evil*—chastisement in this world—*forasmuch as you barred* others *from the way of God*: for those who violated the pledge and apostatised, implicitly encouraged others to do the same; *and lest there be a tremendous chastisement for you* in the Hereafter.

[16:95] *And do not sell*—exchange—*God's* entire *covenant for a small price*: a worldly advantage. *For truly what is with God*—His reward—*is better for you* than that, *if you should know.*

[16:96] *That which is with you*—your worldly advantages—*will come to an end; but that which is with God remains* forever. *And He shall surely pay those who were patient* in obedience to Him *their reward according to the best of*—with a reward that is better than—*that which they used to do*: or more hopeful, such as the reward for obligatory things; or it means simply 'good'. Q. 16:94

[16:97] *Whoever acts righteously, whether male or female, and is a believer, him We shall revive with a goodly life*: with lawful provision, or contentment, or the Garden. *And We shall surely pay them*—deliver to them—*their reward according to the best of what they used to do*: this was explained above.

[16:98] *And when you* are about to *recite the Qur'ān, seek refuge in God from* the whispered insinuations of *Satan the accursed*: this command is on the level of recommendation [rather than obligation], as is evidenced by the fact that the formula is not repeated for each cycle of prayer [wherein the Qur'ān is recited]. In other words, recite the formula, 'I seek refuge in God from Satan the accursed.' The Messenger of God (may God bless him and grant him peace) related this formula from Gabriel, from the Pen, from the Tablet—that is, a pen copied it from the Tablet, and Gabriel brought it down to the lowest heaven; for the Supreme Pen has a higher level than the Tablet.

[16:99] *Truly, he has no power*—authority—*over those who believe and put their trust in their Lord.*

[16:100] *His power is only over those who choose him as their patron*: by obeying him; *and those who ascribe partners to Him*: to God.

[16:101] *And when We exchange a verse in place of a verse* by abrogation; *and God knows best what He reveals*: and what is right to reveal; *they say, 'You are just a fabricator* about God.*' Nay, most of them do not know* the art of lawmaking.

[16:102] *Say: 'The Holy Spirit*, Gabriel, *has revealed it from your Lord with truth*—wisdom—*to strengthen those who believe*: in their faith, for they know that there are good reasons for abrogation; *and as guidance and glad tidings for those who have submitted.'*

[16:103] *And indeed We know that they say, 'It is only a human that is teaching him*, meaning Jabr al-Rūmī, the slave of ʿĀmir b. al-Ḥaḍramī.*' The tongue*, language, *of him to whom they refer,* the one they believe teaches him, *is foreign, while this* Qur'ān *is a clear Arabic tongue* of clarity and eloquence.

[16:104] *Truly, those who do not believe in God's signs*—His knowledge—*God does not guide them*: which is why they utter such things; *and there is a painful chastisement for them* in the Hereafter.

[16:105] *Falsehood is only invented by those who do not believe in God's signs, and it is they who are the liars* in truth. The repetition is for emphasis, and serves as a rebuttal to how they said, 'You are only a fabricator.'

[16:106] *Whoever disbelieves in God after having believed—except for him who is compelled* to utter words of disbelief *while his heart is at rest in faith*:
Q. 16:102 the main clause of *whoever* is elided here, but explained by what follows: *but he who opens up his breast*—his soul—*to disbelief, upon such shall be wrath from God, and there is a great chastisement for them.*

[16:107] *That* disbelief, or that wrath, *is because they have preferred*—chosen—*the life of this world to the Hereafter, and because God does not guide the disbelieving folk*: according to His knowledge.

[16:108] *They are the ones for whom God has set a seal on their hearts and their hearing and their sight*: so that they cannot understand, hear or see the truth; *and it is they who are* truly *heedless.*

[16:109] *Assuredly in the Hereafter they are the ones who will be the losers*: for they will have squandered their innate disposition.

[16:110] *Then truly your Lord, for those who emigrated*: that is, He is for them and not against them; or its predicate is elided but elucidated by the predicate of the second *truly*; *after they were persecuted*: tortured to force them to recant, such as ʿAmmār; *and then struggled and were patient* in adversity for God's sake; *Truly, your Lord after that*—after those three things—*is Forgiving* of their sins, *Merciful* to them.

[16:111] *The day when every soul will come pleading for itself*: for its own essence and its salvation—the first *soul* here[1] represents the entirety of the essence and the person; *and every soul will be repaid* the reward of *what it has done, and they will not be wronged* in their payment.

1 The word *nafs* means both 'soul' and 'self'.

[16:112] *And God strikes a similitude: A town*—this represents those who are granted favours but are ungrateful for them, and so He sends misfortune their way—*which was secure*, such as Mecca, *peaceful*—its inhabitants not threatened by fear—*its provision coming to it plenteously from every place*: from all around. *But it rejected God's graces* by refusing to obey Him, *and so God made it taste the garb of hunger*: they were beset with a seven-year drought after the Prophet (may God bless him and grant him peace) prayed against them; *and fear* of the strength of the Muslim forces—'tasting' here is a metaphor for their experience of that harm, and the *garb* symbolises how they were enveloped by the hunger and fear that God made them *taste*, as it were—*because of what they used to do*.

[16:113] *And indeed there came to them a messenger from among them*—from their own kinsfolk—*but they denied him, and so the* aforementioned *chastisement seized them while they were evildoers*.

[16:114] *So eat of the lawful and good food which God has provided you, and be thankful for God's grace, if it is Him that you worship*: obey.

Q. 16:112

[16:115] *He has forbidden you*—that is, for now—*only carrion, blood, the flesh of swine, and that which has been hallowed to other than God*: the other forbidden things were not made forbidden until later, by the Sunna. *Yet whoever is compelled, neither craving nor transgressing, then truly God is Forgiving, Merciful*: this was explained earlier.[1]

[16:116] *And do not say, concerning that which your own tongues qualify, falsehood*; that is, do not say, *'This is lawful, and this is unlawful'* by inventing laws about the young in the wombs of certain animals, and so on, because then your tongues would be describing falsehood—this is an exaggerated description of their untruthfulness, as though the reality of falsehood were unknown, but could be qualified and defined by their words; *that you may*—the word 'that' here denotes consequence—*invent lies against God. Truly, those who invent lies against God will not prosper*: they will not find salvation.

[16:117] *A brief enjoyment* in the world, *and* in the Hereafter *for them there will be a painful chastisement*.

[16:118] *And to those of Jewry, We forbade that which We have related to you already*: in *Sūrat al-Anʿām*; *and We did not wrong them*: by straitening them with prohibitions; *but it was they who wronged themselves*: and so they deserved it. This was explained earlier.[2]

1 See Q. 2:173.
2 See Q. 6:146.

[16:119] *Then truly your Lord—to those who did evil out of ignorance, and then repented after that and made amends*: corrected themselves—*Truly, your Lord after that*—after their repentance—*is Forgiving* of their sins, *Merciful* to them.

[16:120] *Truly, Abraham was a community*: one who was followed, venerated and emulated by people, or one whose virtues were so manifold he was a community in himself; *obedient to God, a ḥanīf*: one who inclined away from falsehood; *and he was not of the idolaters*: despite what Quraysh claimed.

[16:121] *Grateful for His graces*: even a small amount of them, so what of a large amount?[1] *He chose him* for prophethood, *and guided him to a straight path* for calling to Him.

[16:122] *And We gave him in this world good*: such as the prophethood of his sons and how he was made beloved to humankind; *and in the Hereafter he will truly be among the righteous*: the folk of perfect righteousness and a model of righteousness.

Q. 16:119 [16:123] *Then We revealed to you: 'Follow the creed of Abraham* in matters of rites and creed, as well as most branching matters; *for he was a ḥanīf*: the reason it is permitted for a superior to follow his inferior is that he was the first of them to speak the truth and act in accordance with it;[2] *and he was not of the idolaters*: despite what Quraysh claimed.*'*

[16:124] *The Sabbath*—meaning the obligation of venerating it—*was only prescribed for those who differed concerning it*: meaning the Jews, for they were commanded to venerate Friday, according to the creed of Abraham, but then most of them said that they would rather venerate the Sabbath because that was the day God finished with the creation. A small band of them obeyed, but then when they were commanded to venerate the Sabbath, only that small band obeyed. *And truly your Lord will judge between them on the Day of Resurrection, concerning that wherein they used to differ*: by requiting them.

[16:125] *Call to the way of your Lord*—His religion—*with wisdom*: clarifying proofs of the truth, or the Qurʾān; *and fair exhortation*: placid words, or the admonitions of the Qurʾān; *and dispute with them by way of that which is best*: namely gentleness. The first is for the spiritual elite among the community, the second for the masses, and the third for the opponents.

1 The word *anʿum*, used in this verse, is the 'small plural' (*jamʿ al-qilla*) of *niʿma* (grace), suggesting a small number.

2 In the source text this comment is found in the similar verse Q. 16:120 above. It clearly belongs here and was likely misplaced there, whether by the author or a copyist.

Truly, your Lord knows best those who stray from His way and He knows best those who are guided: and so your only duty is to convey the message. This was before the command to fight was issued.

[16:126] *And if you retaliate, retaliate with the like of what you have been made to suffer*: for that is an aspect of wisdom and fair exhortation; *and yet if you endure patiently* and forgive, *surely that* patience *is better for the patient* than retribution.

[16:127] *So be patient* in adversity, O Muḥammad; *and your patience is only through God*: by His grace. *And do not grieve for them*—for the disbelievers, or for the believers because of what has been done to them—*nor be in distress because of that which they scheme.*

[16:128] *Truly, God*, by His help, *is with those who fear* sin, *and those who are virtuous* in their deeds along with you. And God knows best what is right, and to Him is the return.

Q. 16:126

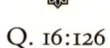

17
The Night Journey
SŪRAT AL-ISRĀ'[1]

Revealed in Mecca, except some say for His Words, *And truly they were about to beguile you*... [Q. 17:73] and the following eight verses

After saying, *God is with those who fear*... [Q. 16:128], He then expounds on the nearness of the master of the God-fearing and righteous, saying:

In the Name of God, the Compassionate, the Merciful

[17:1] *Glory be to Him*: that is, may He be declared transcendent, holy and distant from evil in Essence, Attributes, acts, Names and decrees. The root meaning of the verb *sabbaḥa* (to glorify) is 'to swim far', and *qaddasa* (to declare holy) means 'to travel far upon the earth'. The expression means to declare the subject's transcendence beyond flaws, as though one were saying, 'How distant is the One Who possesses this power from all flaws.' For this reason, it can only be used for God. [*Glory be to Him*] *Who carried His servant by night*: the verb *asrā* already means 'to carry at night', but He added the Words *by night* (*laylan*), with the indefinite noun, to indicate that it was only a small part of the night; *from the Sacred Mosque* in the Ḥijr, bodily and in a waking state after the prophetic mission began, though before that he had experienced it in a dream, just as he dreamed of the Conquest of Mecca in the year 6, before it came to pass in the year 8; *to the Farthest Mosque*, Jerusalem, for at that time there was no other mosque beyond it—usually it would take thirty days to reach it; *the environs of which We have blessed* with both religious and worldly blessings, and then from there to the Lote Tree of the Uttermost End, as is described in authentic *ḥadīth*s. The reason He took him there first was so that he could

1 Some manuscripts give the alternative name for the *sūra*, *Banī Isrā'īl* (The Children of Israel).

tell the people about its appearance, in order that they would believe the rest of his account, and also because it is the meeting-place for the spirits of the prophets and the gathering-place of all humankind, and so both they and he would receive its blessings. The reason He said *the environs of which* was that the trees and rivers[1] were only in its environs, or because by saying that its environs were blessed; He was implicitly saying that it was also itself blessed, while this would not be true had He said simply 'which We have blessed'. *That We might show him some of Our signs*: the wonders of the heavens and the earth. He said (may God bless him and grant him peace), 'I saw my Lord, the Exalted and Glorious,' as al-Ḥākim narrated. *Truly, He is the Hearing* of what the believers and deniers say, *the Seeing* of them, and will requite them.

[17:2] *And We gave Moses the Book, and made it a guidance for the Children of Israel, that they should not choose beside Me any guardian* to whom to resign their affairs.

[17:3] *The descendants of those whom We carried with Noah. Truly, he was a grateful servant* who was ever praising, so follow his example. Q. 17:2

[17:4] *And We decreed*—revealed—*to the Children of Israel in the Book*, the Torah: *'You shall truly work corruption in the land*, Syria, through sin, *twice*: firstly the slaying of Zachariah or Isaiah, and secondly the imprisonment of Jeremiah, or the slaying of Zachariah and John; *and you shall truly become great tyrants*: proud or unjust folk.*'*

[17:5] *So when the time for* the punishment of *the first of the two came, We roused against you servants of Ours*, Nebuchadnezzar the ruler of Babylon and his army, *of great might*—strength—*who ransacked habitations* in pursuit of you, slaying and capturing; *and it was a promise fulfilled*: because it was decreed fate.

[17:6] *Then We gave you back the turn*—power and domination—*over them*: a hundred years later when Daniel was allowed to defeat the army of Nebuchadnezzar, or when David defeated Goliath; *and We aided you with wealth and children* until you returned to your previous strength, *and made you greater in number*: the word *nafīr* (number) is the plural of *nafar* (group of men), or means the one who goes out (*yanfur*) with you from your people.

[17:7] *If you are virtuous* through obedience, *you are being virtuous for your own souls; and if you do evil* by being corrupt, *it is for them*: to their detriment. He said *for* in order to achieve rhetorical balance (*izdiwāj*), or similar to *they*

1 In other words, the nature of the blessing.

fall down on their faces [Q. 17:109], or *on his forehead* [Q. 37:103].[1] *So when the time for* the punishment for *the other* time *came,* We sent them forth *that they might discountenance you*: humiliate you with slaying and capturing, or that they might disgrace your leaders; *and that they might enter the Temple*—the Farthest Mosque—*just as they entered it the first time*: and destroyed it; *and that they might destroy all that they conquered*: that which they ruled, or for as long as they ruled it; *utterly*: He sent against them Ju'dhar, who was a Persian king, or Nebuchadnezzar, and they did the same to them as the first had.

[17:8] *It may be that your Lord*, O Children of Israel, *will have mercy upon you*: by returning your power to you; *but if you revert* to sin, *We too will revert* to punishment. And indeed they did revert by denying Muḥammad (may God bless him and grant him peace), and so he was unleashed upon them to deliver slaughter and other punishments. *And We have made Hell a dungeon*—a prison or a pit—*for the disbelievers.*

Q. 17:8

[17:9] *Truly, this Qurʾān guides to that* path *which is straightest*: the soundest of all paths; *and gives glad tidings to the believers who perform righteous deeds that there is a great reward for them.*

[17:10] *And that those who do not believe in the Hereafter, We have prepared for them a painful chastisement.*

[17:11] *And man prays* to God *for ill* for himself and his family when he is angry, or prays for things he imagines are good when in fact they are evil, *as*—in the same way that—*he prays for good. And humankind is ever hasty*: by praying recklessly without considering his situation.

[17:12] *And We made the night and the day two signs* of Our power. *Then We effaced the sign of the night*: this refers to how the moon becomes overcast, or shrinks in brightness until it is completely invisible; *and We made the sign of the day sight-giving*, luminous or plain, *that you may seek* therein *bounty*, the means of your livelihoods, *from your Lord, and that you may know* by means of them both, or by the sign of the night, *the number of years and the reckoning*: this is not repetition, because number is the subject of reckoning. *And everything* you need *We have detailed very distinctly*: made plain without any ambiguity.

[17:13] *And We have attached every person's omen*—his deeds or his fate—*upon his neck*: like a halter that cannot be removed; *and We shall bring forth for him, on the Day of Resurrection, a book which he will find wide open*. And it will be said to him:

1 In both cases, the particle *li* (usually 'for') clearly bears the meaning 'on', and the author is suggesting that the same is true of *lahā* (for them) here.

[17:14] *'Read your book! This day your soul suffices as your own reckoner'*: this refers to another occasion than the one in which He will reckon them personally, about which He says, *And We suffice as reckoners* [Q. 21:47].

[17:15] *Whoever is guided is guided only for his own soul; and whoever goes astray goes astray only to its detriment*: the benefit and harm of it go no further than his own self. *No burdened soul shall bear the burden of another*: this was explained in *Sūrat al-Anʿām*.[1] *And We never chastise until We have sent a messenger* who is then denied; and those who grow up in a place where they never hear of a messenger are excused.

[17:16] *And when We desire to destroy a town, We command*—with a command of fate—*its affluent ones*: the ones who enjoy iniquity; or it means, 'We multiply them,' or 'We make them rulers,' or 'We command them to obey'; this does not negate the fact that *God does not enjoin indecency* [Q. 7:28]. According to the first interpretation, the reason they are singled out for mention is that they are the first to fall into madness and iniquity, while the rest only follow their example. *But they fall into wickedness therein, and so the*
Word—the decree of chastisement—*is justified concerning it, and We destroy it* Q. 17:14
utterly: annihilate it. The ruling on those who stay silent instead of dissuading them was discussed in connection with His Words, *And be afraid of a trial which would certainly not fall exclusively upon the evildoers among you* [Q. 8:25].

[17:17] *How many generations We have destroyed since Noah!* He was the first one to be denied. *And your Lord suffices as One Informed and Beholder of the sins of His servants*: Informed of the inward, and Beholder of the outward.

[17:18] *Whoever desires* by his obedience *the hasty world*: the life of this world alone, such as the hypocrites—it does not mean that those who are not ascetic in this world will inevitably go to Hell; *We hasten for him therein whatever We wish, for whom We please* to hasten it. *Then We appoint for him Hell, to which he will be exposed, condemned*—debased—*and rejected*: cast out.

[17:19] *And whoever desires*, prefers, *the Hereafter* to the world *and strives for it with the necessary effort*, as it ought to be striven for, *being a believer*—*for such* who combine all three, *their effort will find favour* and be rewarded.

[17:20] *Each We supply* with such things as provisions and health, *to these* who desire the world *and to those* who desire the Hereafter, *from your Lord's bounty* in this world. *And your Lord's bounty is not confined*: not denied to all in this world. This refers to the decree of provision, not the amounts of possessions.

1 See Q. 6:52.

[17:21] *See how We have given preference to some of them over others*: in wealth, health and such matters. *And truly the Hereafter is greater in degrees and greater in preferment*: so be more greatly concerned with it.

[17:22] *Do not set up*—this is directed to the singular,[1] but refers to the entire community—*another god besides God, or you will sit*—become—*blamed* by humankind, *forsaken* by God. This implies that the monotheist is praiseworthy and supported.

[17:23] *And your Lord has decreed*—commanded definitively—*that you worship none save Him, and* that you maintain *kindness to parents. If they should reach old age with you*—He said *with you* because that is the most usual situation and so the universality of it is more apparent—*one of them or both, then do not say to them, 'Fie'*: a simple expression of discontent—that is, do not say even this, never mind anything more. Thus the Prophet (may God bless him and grant him peace) forbade Ḥudhayfa from slaying his father in battle, though he was in the ranks of the idolaters. *Nor repulse them*—chide them—*but speak to them gracious* and beautiful *words*.

Q. 17:21

[17:24] *And lower to them the wing of humility*: be humble with them and hug them to you as a bird hugs its chick with its wing; *the wing of humility* means 'your humble wing'; *out of* overflowing *mercy* for them, *and say: 'My Lord, have mercy on them, just as they* had mercy on me when they *reared me when I was little.'*

[17:25] *Your Lord knows best what is in your souls*: and whether you aspire to be dutiful. *If you are righteous*, if you aspire to righteousness, *then truly to those who are penitent*, those who repent or return to His obedience, *He is Forgiving* and does not overlook them.

[17:26] *And give the kinsman his due* of kinship and duty, *and the needy and the traveller too; and do not squander recklessly*: the word *tabdhīr* (to squander) means to dispense money on things that the Law does not warrant. The difference between it and *isrāf* (extravagance) is that *isrāf* means to spend too much, while *tabdhīr* means to spend on the wrong things. In this context, both meanings are intended.

[17:27] *Truly, squanderers are the brothers*—kindred spirits or followers—*of devils*: evil folk; *and the Devil was ever ungrateful to his Lord*: much given to ingratitude, so do not follow him.

[17:28] *But if you must overlook them*, meaning the aforementioned deserving ones, *seeking mercy from your Lord*, awaiting provision from Him,

1 *Lā tajʿal* (do not set up), with the singular masculine imperative, as though spoken to a single person.

which you expect will come to you so you can give it to them, *then speak to them gentle words*: such as praying for them or making promises to them.

[17:29] *And do not keep your hand chained to your neck*: a metaphor for total stinginess; *nor open it completely*: by squandering; *or you will sit*—become—*blameworthy*: because of your miserliness for the former; *and denuded*: broke and regretful for the latter. The exception to this is the one who truly relies on God, as the context implies.

[17:30] *Truly, your Lord expands provision for whomever He will and He straitens* it for whomever He will. *Truly, He is ever Aware and Seer of His servants*: He knows their secrets and their public lives, and whether they are deserving or not.

[17:31] *And do not slay your children, fearing penury*: poverty. This was explained in *Sūrat al-Anʿām*.[1] *We shall provide for them and for you. Slaying them* for any reason *is truly a great sin*.

[17:32] *And do not come near fornication*: He said *near* in order to include the precursors to it. *It is truly an indecency and an evil way.* Q. 17:29

[17:33] *And do not slay the soul that God has made inviolable*—forbidden to kill—*except with due cause*: which is one of three things, as a *ḥadīth* describes.[2] This refers to a deliberate act of killing, and so it does not include killing done in self-defence, since the intent behind this is defence, not killing for its own sake. *Whoever is slain wrongfully* without having done anything to deserve it, *We have certainly given his heir a warrant*: a rightful claim against the killer, whether to demand his death, take blood money, or pardon him. *But let him*, the heir, *not commit excess in the matter of the killing*: by doing something that it is not permitted as retribution; *for he is truly supported*: God supported him when He commanded that he be helped; or the victim is supported by the retribution carried out on his killer, and by heavenly reward.

[17:34] *And do not come near an orphan's property*—never mind utilise it—*except in the fairest manner until he comes of age*: this was explained in *Sūrat al-Anʿām*.[3] *And fulfil the covenant*: whatever covenant it may be. *Truly, the covenant will be enquired into*: and punishment will be dealt if it is broken.

[17:35] *And give full measure when you measure* without any trickery—this implies that the seller is the one who should do the measuring; *and weigh with a right*—fair—*balance*: *that is better and fairer in return*: consequence.

1 See Q. 6:151.

2 Adultery, murder and treason, as narrated by Bukhārī, Muslim, et al.

3 See Q. 6:152.

[17:36] *And do not pursue*—follow, such as blind conformity or guesswork—*that of which you have no knowledge*: meaning a justified belief based on certainty or confidence. It does not mean that it is forbidden to follow one's confident intuition. *Truly, the hearing and the sight and the heart—of each of these* body parts *it will be asked*: asked about itself and how it was used.

[17:37] *And do not walk in the earth exultantly*: proudly. *Truly, you will not rend the earth* with your heavy footsteps, *nor attain the mountains in height* by puffing yourself up, lifting your head and stretching your neck, so why should you be proud? This is meant ironically.

[17:38] *All of that*—everything from *Do not set up another god* [Q. 17:22], a total of twenty-five qualities enjoined and forbidden—*is evil*: it can also be recited as *the evil of it is*;[1] *in the sight of your Lord, hateful*: detested and displeasing, even though it is His will.

[17:39] *This* set of decrees *is of the wisdom*—the knowledge of truth for its own sake, and of goodness that it might be acted upon—*which your Lord has revealed to you. And do not set up*—again, this is addressed to the whole
Q. 17:36 community—*with God any other god, or you will be cast into Hell, blamed* by God and creation, *abandoned*: cast out.

[17:40] *Has your Lord then preferred you*—singled you out, O you who claim that He has taken daughters for Himself—*with sons and chosen for Himself females*, daughters, *from among the angels? Truly, you are speaking a monstrous word!*

[17:41] *And truly We have dispensed*—clarified and repeated this concept—*in this Qur'ān, so that they may remember*: and be admonished; *but it only increases them in aversion* to the truth.

[17:42] *Say*: *'If there were with Him gods, as they say, then they would have sought some path against the Lord of the Throne'*: by vying with Him as kings do, or by obeying Him because of their knowledge of His power.

[17:43] *Glory be to Him*—transcendent be He—*and exalted be He above what they say, greatly!* He described the exaltation as 'great' by way of affirming His utter transcendence.

[17:44] *The seven heavens and the earth*—the reason for *earth* in the singular was discussed earlier[2]—*and all that is therein proclaim His praise. And there is not a thing, but proclaims His praise*: saying, 'Glory be to God, and praise be to Him!' However, only the perfected ones, such as the Prophet and some of the Companions, could hear it. The majority of the early

1 Depending on whether it is read as *kāna sayyi'atan* (is evil), or *kāna sayyi'uhu* (the evil of it is...).
2 See Q. 6:1.

Muslims said that this is meant literally, while some said that it most likely means that glorification can be uttered in spirit as well as in word, given How He attributes it to those things that can be imagined to speak as well as those that cannot. The later scholars said that everything glorifies in the 'language of state' (*lisān al-ḥāl*), in the sense that they all point towards the existence of a sole Creator. *But you do not understand their glorification*, O idolaters. *Truly, He is Forbearing* and so does not punish you immediately, *Forgiving* to those who repent.

[17:45] *And when you recite the Qur'ān*—any amount at all, or three well-known verses from *al-Naḥl*, *al-Kahf* and *al-Jāthiya*[1]—*We place between you and those who do not believe in the Hereafter a hidden barrier*: so that they cannot see you, concealed from the senses. After this verse was revealed, his tormentors would pass right by him without seeing him when he recited.

[17:46] *And We place upon their hearts veils*—coverings of aversion—*lest they should understand it, and in their ears a deafness*: to prevent them from listening to it. *And when you mention your Lord alone in the Qur'ān* without mentioning their gods, *they turn their backs in aversion*: shrinking from monotheism.

Q. 17:45

[17:47] *We know best how they listen* to you, namely with derision or denial, *when they listen to you, and when they are in secret counsel*, secretly discussing their disbelief, *when the evildoers*, meaning them, *say, 'You are only following a man bewitched*: sent mad by a spell.'

[17:48] *Look how they strike similitudes for you*: likening you to a bewitched man, a madman, and so on; *and they go astray* from the truth, *and cannot find a way* to undermine it.

[17:49] *And they say*, arguing for your insanity, *'What, when* after death *we are bones and fragments, shall we really be raised up in a new creation*: as you claim?'

[17:50] *Say*, whether as a command of derision or compulsion: *'Be you* as hard as *stones or iron*.

[17:51] *'Or some creation yet greater in your breasts'*: all the more difficult to revive, yet He will revive you all the same, by His power. *They will then say, 'Who shall bring us back* when we are stones or iron?' *Say: 'He Who originated*—created—*you the first time'*: for that was more difficult still. *Then they will shake their heads at you* in denial, *and they will say, 'When will it be?' Say: 'Maybe it is near!'* For that which will certainly come to pass is always near. And remember:

1 Q. 16:108, Q. 18:57 and Q. 45:23. See Rāzī's commentary on this verse.

[17:52] *'The day He calls you* from your graves, *you will respond* to His call, or you will be raised up, *with His praise*: by his command, or uttering praise of Him, though it will be of no use to you but only to the believers; *and you will think*—such is the horror—*that you have remained* in the world, or in the isthmus between life and death, *only a little.'*

[17:53] *And tell My* faithful *servants to speak*, when they converse, *that which is finer*: rather than being coarse, such as saying to the disbelievers, 'You are the inhabitants of the Fire!' *For Satan truly incites ill feeling between them, and Satan is truly humanity's manifest enemy.*

[17:54] *Your Lord knows you best. If He wishes, He will have mercy on you*: by saving you from the persecution of the disbelievers; *or if He wishes, He will chastise you*: by giving them power over you. *And We did not send you to be a guardian over them*: a trustee of their affairs.

[17:55] *And your Lord knows best all who are in the heavens and the earth*: and chooses whom He wills for what He wills, so do not find it far-fetched
Q. 17:52 that the orphan of Abū Ṭālib was chosen. *And indeed We have preferred some of the prophets above others*: with personal virtues alone, such as Muḥammad (may God bless him and grant him peace), as He indicates by saying: *and We gave David the Psalms*, wherein is written, *The land shall be inherited by My righteous servants* [Q. 21:105], meaning the community of Muḥammad (may God bless him and grant him peace). The prohibition of preferring one prophet to another should be taken to refer to the level of pure favouritism; for, in fact, Muḥammad is the superior, and then Abraham, and then Moses (may God's blessings and peace be upon them all).

[17:56] *Say: 'Call* for relief *on those whom you assumed* to be divine *besides Him*: such as Jesus or the angels; *yet they have no power to relieve you of misfortune* in any way; *nor to transfer'*: to replace it, for relieving misfortune means to replace it with well-being. Thus there is no need to object that the part about transferring is stating the obvious, since the one who does not have the power to relieve it certainly does not have the power to transfer it elsewhere.

[17:57] *Those whom they call seek a means to their Lord,* seeking *which of them is nearer* than them to Him, namely the means of obedience, so what of any other? *And they hope for His mercy and fear His chastisement*: so why should they deserve to be called 'gods'? *Truly, your Lord's chastisement is* truly *a thing to be greatly feared.*

[17:58] *There is not a town but We shall destroy it before the Day of Resurrection* with death, *or chastise it with terrible chastisement* if it does last until the Day of Resurrection. The first refers to the towns of the believers, the second to the towns of the disbelievers, as was narrated from some of the early Muslims. *That was inscribed* before time began *in the Book*, the Tablet.

[17:59] *Nothing prevented Us from sending*—this is a figure of speech for how He elected not to send messengers bearing *the signs* that were suggested to them, such as transforming Mount Ṣafā into gold, *except that the ancients denied them*: that is, they denied such signs, not that one in particular. Furthermore, your people are just like them in nature, so if We were to send the sign, they would be annihilated when they denied it for that very reason. Yet some of their descendants are destined to be believers. *And We gave Thamūd the she-camel* when they requested a sign, *visible*: apparent; *but they wronged it*: disbelieved in it, so We punished them without delay. *And We do not send* messengers bearing *signs*—Qur'ānic verse and prophetic miracles—*except to inspire fear* of Our chastisement.

[17:60] *And* remember *when We said to you, 'Truly, your Lord encompasses people'*: hence they are under His power, so instil fear in them and do not fear them. *And We did not appoint the vision that We showed you* at
the Ascension and in the waking world, *except as a test for people*: for many Q. 17:59
people apostatised by denying it, while others only increased in faith; *and* We only appointed *the cursed tree*—the harmful tree, or the tree banished from the place of mercy, or the reviled tree, namely the Zaqqūm tree—*in the Qur'ān* as a test for the people, some of whom said, 'How could a fresh tree grow in a fire whose fuel is people and stones?' *And We instil fear in them, but it only increases them in gross insolence.*

[17:61] *And* remember *when We said to the angels, 'Prostrate yourselves before Adam,' and so they prostrated themselves, except Iblīs*: this was explained earlier.[1] *He said, 'Shall I prostrate myself before one whom You have created from clay?'*

[17:62] *Said he*, Iblīs, *'Do You see*—tell me—*this one whom You have honoured above me?* By God, *truly if You defer me*—delay my death—*to the Day of Resurrection, I shall surely eradicate his seed* by tempting them, *save a few'*: he knew how easy this would be because of how the angels had said, *What, will You appoint therein one who will do corruption therein*...[Q. 2:30], or from how He had instilled desire and irascibility into their natures.

[17:63] *Said He*: *'Begone*: the meaning of this was explained earlier.[2] *Whoever of them follows you—truly, Hell shall be your requital*: you along with them, which is *a requital that is ample*: total.

1 See Q. 2:34.
2 See Q. 2:36 ff.

[17:64] *'And tempt whomever of them you can with your voice*: by calling to such things as wealth and every other motive for sin; *and rally against them*, cry out to stir against them *your cavalry and your infantry*: your harbingers of sin on horseback and on foot. In other words, 'Do whatever you can against them.' The command was a threat, or a decree of fate. *And share with them in wealth*: by amassing it by unlawful means, and spending it on unlawful things; *and children*: by encouraging them to engage in adultery and other vile matters, and leading them astray, and the like; *and make* false *promises to them:* such as how they may rely on the nobility of their forebears.' *And Satan promises them nothing but delusion*: meaning the adornment of error so that it seems like truth.

[17:65] *'Truly, as for My* faithful *servants, you shall have no warrant*—authority—*over them.' And your Lord suffices as a guardian* for them.

[17:66] *Your Lord is He Who drives for you the ships upon the sea that you may seek of His bounty*: whether provision or otherwise. *Truly, He is ever Merciful towards you*: and in His mercy He has subdued them to your power.

Q. 17:64

[17:67] *And when distress*—fear of drowning—*befalls you at sea, those whom you invoke are no longer present* in your minds, *except Him. But when He delivers you* from drowning *to land, you turn away* from Him; *for humanity is ever* by nature *ungrateful* for His favours.

[17:68] And once you are safely home from sea, *Do you feel secure that He will not cause a side of the earth to swallow you up*: that is, for it to collapse as you stand upon it, for the sea and land are equally under His power; *or unleash upon you a squall of pebbles*: a rain of stones or a wind carrying pebbles*? Then you will not find for yourselves any guardian* to save you.

[17:69] *Or do you feel secure that He will not return you to it*—to the sea—*a second time and unleash upon you a shattering gale* that breaks everything it blows upon, *and drown you for your ungratefulness? And then you will not find for yourselves any redresser for this against Us*: any petitioner to call upon us for aid or protection.

[17:70] *And indeed We have honoured the Children of Adam* with a beautiful form, intellect, speech and so on, *and carried them over land* on beasts *and sea* on ships, *and provided them with good things*: enjoyable things; *and We have preferred them above many of those whom We created with a marked preferment*: the exception to this is the archangels. Yet the fact that the human species in general is not superior to them [the angels] does not mean that some humans cannot be superior to them, just as some women are superior to some men despite the general superiority of men over women.

NOTE: There is a dispute among the Sunnis about the superiority of the angels. Ibn ʿAbbās held the angels superior, while the companions of Abū Ḥanīfa and many Shāfiʿīs and Ashʿarīs held that human messengers are absolutely superior, and then angelic messengers are superior to other humans and angels, followed by the angels in general, and then humanity in general. It is also said that perfected human beings are superior. Imam Rāzī said that the cherubim are absolutely superior, then human messengers, then perfected humans, then the angels in general are superior to humanity in general. Ghazālī seems to have implied the same in several of his writings.

[17:71] And remember: *The day when We shall summon all men with their leader*: the word *imām* here means their leader, or the book of their deeds. Some say that it is the plural of *umm* (mother),[1] and is meant as an honour for Jesus and others and to avoid the degradation of children born out of wedlock, but this is a groundless interpretation. *And whoever is given his book*—the record of his deeds—*in his right hand, those will read their book* gladly, *and they will not be wronged*: their reward will not be decreased by so
much as *a single date-thread*: that is, not at all. This implies that those who Q. 17:71
are given their book in the left hand will not read it out of shame, woe and blindness, as is indicated by what follows:

[17:72] *And whoever has been in this* world *blind* of heart, not seeing his guidance, *will be blind in the Hereafter*: unable to see the path to salvation; or he will be even blinder still, losing his insight as well—this is why Abū ʿAmr did not recite the word *aʿmā* (blind) here with *imāla*,[2] to suggest the meaning *blinder* rather than simply *blind*; *and* [*even*] *further astray from the way* than he was in this world because of losing the instrument, the aptitude and the disposition.

[17:73] *And Truly,* because of their efforts, *they were about to beguile you*: draw you into temptation—this means Thaqīf and Quraysh; *away from that which We revealed to you*—from the edicts—*so that you might invent against Us something else; and then*, had you followed them, *they would have taken you as a friend.*

[17:74] *And had We not made you firm, certainly you might* almost *have inclined to them a little*: but We protected you from approaching such a thing.

1 In which case the translation would be 'when We call all people by their mothers'.

2 *Imāla* means to pronounce the letter *alif* as though it were somewhere between an *alif* and a *yā'*, sounding as an a>e shift, somewhat like the vowel in the English word 'may'. In the canonical recitation described by Abū ʿAmr, the first occurrence of *aʿmā* in the verse has *imāla*, while the second does not, suggesting that it is supposed to be the superlative form, spelled identically but pronounced slightly differently.

[17:75] *Then*, had you approached it, *We would have surely made you taste a double* chastisement *in life*: the chastisement of this world; *and a double upon death*: the chastisement of the Hereafter—that is, double what anyone else would have received therein, for the corruption of the best is worst. *Then you would not have found for yourself any helper against Us* to protect you from Our punishment. When this was revealed, the Prophet said, 'O God, do not leave me to my own devices for the blink of an eye!'

[17:76] *And truly they*, the disbelievers, *were about to provoke you*—intimidate you—*out of the land* of the Arabs, for the Jews said, 'Go to Syria, for that is the land of the prophets'; *to expel you from it, but then*, had you left, *they would not have remained after you except a little* while from God.

[17:77] That is *the way in the case of those whom We have sent from among Our messengers before you*: namely that every community whose prophet left them was destroyed. *And you will not find any change*—alteration—*in Our way*.

[17:78] *Observe the prayer from the sun's decline* when it passes the
Q. 17:75 zenith—the root meaning of the word *dulūk* (decline) is 'movement', and the same is true of all words composed of the letters *dāl* and *lām*, such as *dalaḥ* (to float), *dalaja* (to transfer), *dalaʿa* (to hang down) and *dalafa* (to stroll); *until the dark of night*: this covers the midday, afternoon, sunset and evening prayers, and indicates that the time for the latter continues until the twilight disappears; *and the recital of dawn*: meaning the dawn prayer by reference to the name of the integral action of it. This does not mean that it is obligatory to recite in it, since it could be interpreted as a recommendation only. *Truly, the dawn recital is ever witnessed*: by the angels of night and day.

[17:79] *And for a part of the night, keep vigil* (*tahajjud*): that is, go without sleep (*hujūd*); or pray *therewith*—with the Qur'ān—*as a supererogatory devotion for you*: an extra obligation for you alone, and not your community. *It may be that your Lord will raise you to a praiseworthy station*: meaning the station of general intercession, whereupon all from the first to the last will praise you.

[17:80] *And say: 'My Lord, make me enter with a veritable entrance*: an entrance that is pleasing to You; *and bring me out with a veritable departure*: a departure that is pleasing to You. *And grant me from Yourself a favourable authority*: a proof or strength for me against those who oppose me.'

[17:81] *And say* in exultation: *'The Truth*, Islam, *has come and falsehood*, disbelief, *has vanished away. Truly, falsehood is ever bound to vanish.'*

[17:82] *And We reveal of the Qur'ān that which is a cure* for ailments of religion and body, *and a mercy for believers* through which they attain knowledge and wisdom, *though it only increases the evildoers in loss*: because of their disbelief in it.

[17:83] *And when We are gracious to* the species of *man, he is disregardful* of gratitude *and turns aside*: turns his back to the Giver of grace, or is proud; *but when an ill befalls him*—such as sickness or poverty—*he is in despair* of Us. As for His Words *but when ill befalls him, he makes prolonged supplications* [Q. 41:51], they refer to another kind of people.

[17:84] *Say: 'Everyone acts according to his character*: his way that reflects his nature, whether common nature or religion; *and your Lord knows best who is better guided to the way*: and will reward them.'

[17:85] *And they*, Quraysh at the instigation of the Jews, *question you concerning* the nature of *the Spirit* which gives life to the body. *Say: 'The Spirit is of the command of my Lord*: something whose knowledge He has reserved for Himself. Or it means that it exists and is created by His command without matter, akin to how the question, *What is the Lord of the Worlds?* [Q. 26:23] was answered with: *The Lord of the heavens and the*
Q. 17:83
earth...[Q. 26:24]. *And of knowledge you have not been given*—all of you—*except a little*: which you attain through your senses, though perhaps the majority of things that exist cannot be perceived by the senses.'

[17:86] *And if We willed We could take away what We have revealed to you*: by erasing the Qur'ān from your pages and your hearts. *Then you would not find on your behalf for that matter*, for the return of it, *anyone to trust*, to rely upon, *against Us*, [17:87] *save only a mercy from your Lord*: which perhaps would return it to you. *Truly, His favour to you is ever great*: including how He sent it down and preserved it.

[17:88] *Say: 'Should humankind and jinn come together to produce the like of this Qur'ān*, in terms of eloquence or otherwise, *they could not produce the like thereof*, for they have not the power to do it, *even if they backed one another with assistance.'*

[17:89] *And indeed We have dispensed*—repeated and elucidated—*for people in this Qur'ān every similitude*: every meaning like a similitude in ingenuity and beauty; *but most people insist on disbelieving* out of stubbornness, though they cannot produce the like of it.

[17:90] *And they say, 'We will not believe you until you make gush forth for us from the ground* of Mecca *a spring* that never ceases to flow.

[17:91] *'Or until you have a garden*—orchard—*of date palms and vines, and cause streams to gush forth therein, abundantly.*

[17:92] *'Or until you cause the heaven to fall upon us, as you assert, in pieces*:

by this they were referring to His Words, *We can make the earth swallow them or let fall on them fragments from the heaven*...[Q. 34:9]; *or bring God and the angels in front* of us in plain view.

[17:93] *'Or until you have a house adorned with gold, or ascend into the heaven* by a ladder; *and we will not believe because of your ascension* alone, *until you bring down to us*, one by one, *a book* with each person's name to confirm you, *that we may read it.' Say: 'Glory be to my Lord!* This is an expression of incredulity at their demands. *Am I*—I am not—*anything but a human, a messenger?'* The messenger can only produce things with God's permission.

[17:94] *And nothing prevented people from believing when guidance came to them*—meaning the miraculous Qur'ān—*but that they said, 'Has God sent a human as a messenger?'* In other words, their only reason to doubt is that a human being was sent.

[17:95] *Say: 'Had there been in the earth angels, walking* as you walk, *secure*—residing there—*We would have sent down to them from the heaven an*
Q. 17:93 *angel as messenger'*: because they would have been able to receive from him because of their affinity, unlike humans.

[17:96] *Say: 'God suffices as a witness* to my sincerity *between me and you. Truly, He is Aware, Seer of His servants.'*

[17:97] *And he whom God guides is rightly guided, and he whom He sends astray—you will not find for them any guardians besides Him* to guide them. *And We shall assemble them on the Day of Resurrection* walking or being dragged *on their faces* to Fire, *blind* to anything that would give joy to their eyes, *dumb* to any excuses, *and deaf* to anything that would please them to hear. *Their abode shall be Hell—whenever it abates*, whenever its blaze dies down after consuming their bodies, *We shall intensify for them the blaze* by replacing their flesh and skin.

[17:98] *That* chastisement *is their requital because they disbelieved in* all of *Our signs, and said, 'What, when we are bones and fragments* of dust, *shall we really be raised in a new creation?'* They will be punished by being repeatedly recreated after being annihilated, because of how they denied the return.

[17:99] *Have they not seen*—do they not know—*that God, Who created the heavens and the earth, has the power to create the like of them*: both the first time and at the return*? He has appointed for them*—for their return—*a term whereof is no doubt; yet the evildoers insist on disbelief*: denial, even after the proofs are established.

[17:100] *Say: 'If you possessed the treasuries of my Lord's mercy*—grace—*you would surely withhold* stingily *for fear of spending*: lest they be exhausted, and so it would not benefit you to have springs gushing forth, and so on; *and humanity is ever miserly*: stingy by nature.'

[17:101] *And indeed We gave Moses nine manifest signs*: the famine, the dearth of fruits, the flood, the locusts, the lice, the frogs, the blood, the hand, and the staff. When two Jews asked the Messenger of Allah (may God bless him and grant him peace) about the signs, he replied, 'They were the prohibitions of idolatry, stealing, adultery, murder, sorcery, usury, accusing innocent people of crimes so that they are executed, accusing innocent women of adultery, and fleeing battle.' Then he said, 'And then one for you Jews alone: not to violate the Sabbath.' In that case, the meaning of *signs* here is universal edicts for all religions. However, some say that actually they may have been asking about the Ten Commandments, but then the narrator Ibn Salām (may God be pleased with him) confused this with the nine signs. *So*, O Muḥammad, *ask the Children of Israel* about them to establish your sincerity to the idolaters. *When he came to them, Pharaoh said to him, 'O Moses, I truly think that you are bewitched*: driven mad by sorcery.' Q. 17:101

[17:102] *He said, 'You know well* by the proofs *that none revealed these except the Lord of the heavens and the earth, as elucidations*: admonitions, so why should you oppose me? It can also be read as *Truly, I know*, in which case the meaning is obvious. *And I truly think*, that is, 'I know'—he said *I think* to echo Pharaoh's own words back at him—*that you, O Pharaoh, are doomed'*: the word *mathbūr* (doomed) literally means 'diverted'—that is, diverted from anything good.

[17:103] *So he*, Pharaoh, *desired to scare them*, Moses and his people, *from the land* of Egypt; *so We drowned him and those with him, altogether.*

[17:104] *And after him*—after he had been drowned—*We said to the Children of Israel, 'Dwell in the land* of Egypt; *but when the promise of* the abode of *the Hereafter comes to pass, We shall bring you in mixed company* to the standing place.' The word *lafīf* (mixed company) means a collection of different tribes gathered together.

[17:105] *With the truth have We revealed it*, the Qur'ān, *and with the truth has it been revealed*: that is, 'What We revealed was only revealed with the truth'; *and We have not sent you except as a bearer of glad tidings* to the obedient *and a warner* to the sinners.

[17:106] *And into a Qur'ān We have divided it*—'We revealed it piecemeal over thirteen years'—*that you may recite it to people at intervals*: gradually, to make it easier to memorise; *and We revealed it by gradual revelation*: according to the unfolding of events.

[17:107] *Say: 'Believe in it, or do not believe*: for that will not raise up the

Qur'ān, nor put it down. *Truly, those who were given knowledge before it*—before the Qur'ān was revealed, meaning the believers among the People of the Book—*when it*, the Qur'ān, *is recited to them, fall down in prostration on their faces*: to give thanks for the fulfilment of His promise.

[17:108] *'And they say, "Glory be to our Lord!* Far be it that He would ever break a promise! *Truly, Our Lord's promise*, in His Books of how He would reveal it, *was bound to be fulfilled."*

[17:109] *'And they fall down on their faces, weeping* because of how moved they are by its exhortations—the first mentioning of falling described the beginning of the prostration, while this one describes how they weep passionately; *and* hearing *it increases them in humility'*.

[17:110] *Say* to them when they say, 'Do you forbid us from calling to multiple gods, while you call God the Compassionate?' *'Invoke* in worship *God, or invoke the Compassionate. Whichever you invoke* of them, it is good, for *to Him*, the One to Whom they both refer, *belong the Most*
Q. 17:108 *Beautiful Names:* and they are two of those Names.*' And do not be loud in your prayer*: by reciting or supplicating loud enough that the idolaters can hear it, lest they insult your God; *nor be silent therein*: so that your companions behind you cannot hear it; *but seek between that a way*: a middle way between loud and silent.

[17:111] *And say: 'Praise be to God, Who has neither taken a son*, as the Jews and idolaters claim, *nor has He any partner in sovereignty*, divinity, as the Christians and idolaters claim, *nor has He any ally*, helper, *out of weakness*, as the Christians and Magians claim.*' And magnify Him* above all that does not befit Him, *with* perfect *magnifications*. And God knows best.

18
The Cave
SŪRAT AL-KAHF

Revealed in Mecca, except for the verse, *And restrain yourself*... [Q. 18:28]

In the Name of God, the Compassionate, the Merciful

[18:1] *Praise be to God, Who has revealed to His servant the Book*: the Qur'ān. He linked the praise to it in order to indicate that its revelation was one of the greatest of His graces. *And has not allowed for him*, His servant, *any crookedness*: any divergence from the truth.

[18:2] [*He has made it*] *upright*—adherent to what he has been commanded to do—*to warn* the disbelievers *of severe chastisement from Him, and to bring to the believers who perform righteous deeds the glad tidings that theirs will be a fair reward,* [18:3] *wherein*—in that reward—*they will abide forever.*

[18:4] *And to warn*—He repeated this because of the enormity of the sin—*those who say, 'God has taken a son'*: He singled them out for mention because of the heinousness of their disbelief.

[18:5] *They do not have of this any knowledge*: because it is impossible—they only follow what their fathers believed; *nor did their fathers* who said it in the first place. *Dreadful is the word*, this claim, *that comes out of their mouths*: this implies that such a word should never even be described by an impulse of the heart, never mind a spoken word. The words do not really 'come out' of their mouths to be borne on the air, but rather they are modalities by which the voice is shaped, and so this is a figure of speech. *They speak nothing but lies*.

[18:6] *Yet it may be that you will consume*—kill—*yourself in their wake* if they turn away from belief, *if they should not believe in this discourse*, the Qur'ān, *out of grief*: intense sorrow.

He then explains this prohibition by saying:

[18:7] *Truly, We have made all that is on the earth*—all of the property therein—*as an adornment for it, that We may try*—test—*them* [*to see*] *which of them is best in conduct*: namely which of them is least attached to those adornments.

[18:8] *And truly We shall turn all that is therein into barren shreds*: dry earth from which nothing can grow.

Now when Quraysh found the story of the Companions of the Cave far-fetched and asked the Prophet (may God bless him and grant him peace) to test him about it, God revealed:

[18:9] *Or did you think*, O humankind, *that the Companions of the Cave* and how they lived on in sleep for a long time, *and al-Raqīm*, the mountain on which their cave was situated, or the tablet by the mouth wherein their lineages were recorded; or they were three men who went into a cave to escape the rain, but then a boulder fell in front of the mouth, and so each of them interceded to God by invoking one of his good deeds, and they were let out, as a well-known *ḥadīth* describes; *were a marvel from among Our signs?*

Q. 18:7

[18:10] *When the youths*, the seven young men, *took refuge in the Cave*: the dispute concerning the matter was either among themselves, as is described later by, *One of them said, 'How long have you tarried?'* [Q. 18:19] and so on, or among the folk of their town when they fled from Decius when he tried to force idolatry upon them. *They said, 'Our Lord, give us mercy from Yourself* to conceal us from them, *and remedy for us our affair*—our present emergency—*through rectitude*: guidance.'

[18:11] *So We smote about their ears* a veil to prevent hearing—that is, 'We put them into a deep sleep,' from the expression 'to smite his hand', meaning to prevent him from acting; *in the Cave for several years*.

[18:12] *Then We roused them*—woke them up—*that We might know*, witness, *which of the two parties* who disputed the length of their stay *was better*, more accurate, *in calculating the term they had tarried*: that is, how much time they had spent in the Cave.

[18:13] *We relate to you their story with truth. Truly, they were youths who believed in their Lord, and We increased them in guidance*: with stability.

[18:14] *And We strengthened their hearts* with fortitude in times of peril, *when they stood up* in front of Decius when he threatened them for forsaking the idols, *and said, 'Our Lord is the Lord of the heavens and the earth. We will not call on any god besides Him, for then*, if we did call on any but Him, *we should certainly have uttered an outrage*: a heinous blasphemy.

[18:15] *'These, our people, have taken gods besides Him. Why do they not bring some clear warrant regarding them*: any justification for worshipping them*? And who does greater wrong than he who invents a lie against God* by associating partners with Him*?'*

[18:16] *'And*—one of them said to another—*when you withdraw from them and from that which they worship except God*, for they worshipped idols as well as God, *then take refuge in the Cave. Your Lord will reveal for you something of His mercy* in both worlds, *and prepare for you in your affair some comfort*: for your benefit, such as food and the like.*'* So they went into the Cave and fell asleep, and their prayer was answered.

[18:17] *And you might have seen*, had you seen them, *the sun, when it rose, inclining away from their Cave towards the right*—to the right of the Cave—*and when it set, go past them on the left*: so that its rays never fell upon them, lest they be burnt; the Cave faced South, towards the constellation of the Plough; *while they were in a cavern therein*: a large area inside the Cave so that they could feel the breeze. *That was one of God's signs. Whomever God guides, he indeed is rightly guided; and whomever He leads astray, you will not find for him a guiding friend.*

[18:18] *And you would have supposed them awake* because of how the Q. 18:16
breeze kept their eyes open, *though they were asleep. And We caused them to turn over to the right and to the left*: back and forth as they slept, to protect their bodies from the ground; *and their dog lay stretching its forelegs*—asleep too—*on the threshold* of the Cave. It was a hunting dog belonging to one of them. They tried to send it away, but it said, 'I love the beloved ones of God. Sleep, and I shall guard you.' *If you had observed them, you would have turned away from them in flight, and you would have been filled with awe of them*: this was a fear that God struck into people so that they would not go in to them. When Muʿāwiya invaded Anatolia, he ordered that the Cave be opened to behold them, but Ibn ʿAbbās forbade him and cited this verse. So he sent a group to scout ahead; and when they went inside the Cave a wind blew on them and burned them up.[1]

[18:19] *And so it was that We roused them, that they might question one another* about how long they had been there, so that their certainty would grow. The word *that* here denotes consequence and causality. *One of them said, 'How many* days *have you tarried* asleep*?' They said, 'We have tarried a day, or part of a day'*: for that is usually how long one sleeps, or because they went into the Cave at dawn and woke up at sunset. But then, when they became less sure of this as they saw how long their fingernails and the like

1 Qūnawī's commentary on Bayḍāwī, likely the author's source for this account, notes that some manuscripts have *akhrajat-hum* (drove them out) rather than *aḥraqat-hum* (burned them up) here.

had grown: *They said, 'Your Lord knows best how long you have tarried. Now send one of you with this silver coin of yours to the city* from which you came, which is now called Tarsus but in those days was called Ephesus, *and let him see which* of the people of the town *has the purest*—most lawful—*food, and bring you a supply thereof*: this indicates that it is the way of those who trust in God to take provisions. *Let him be careful* in his dealings, and be discreet, *and not* do anything to *make anyone aware of you.*

[18:20] *'Truly, if they*, the people of the town, *should come to know of you, they will stone you* to death, *or make you return*—convert—*to their creed; and then you will never prosper* if you disbelieve.*'*

[18:21] *And so it was*—by that resurrection—*that We disclosed them* to the people of the town, *that they*, the townsfolk, *might know that God's promise* of the Resurrection *is true*: just as it was true for that long sleep; *and that in the Hour there can be no doubt. Behold,* We disclosed them as *they were disputing among themselves their affair*: the matter of their religion and whether the Resurrection is in spirit only or in body too. *They said, 'Build over them a building. Their Lord knows them best.' Those who prevailed regarding their affair*— their king and the believers among them—*said, 'We will set up over them a place of worship*: and pray in it.*'* Then, when the one they had sent with the silver coin from the rule of Decius went in, they accused him of having discovered treasure. He said, 'But I was just here in this town yesterday afternoon!' They were incredulous at this, and the Christian king had him detained. But some people who knew of the history [of the Sleepers] believed him. Then the king and the local people went to them and spoke to them about what had happened, and the young men bade the king farewell, and died. The king buried them and built a place of worship over them.

Q. 18:20

[18:22] *They*, the Jews of your time, *will say* that they were *'Three; their dog the fourth of them'*: and that the dog was not originally theirs, but belonged to a shepherd who followed them on the road; *and they*, the Christians, *will say, 'Five; their dog the sixth of them'*—*guessing at random*: trying to hit an unseen target. *And they*, the Muslims, *will say, 'Seven; and* they will say *their dog the eighth of them'*: as though they stated it twice because of their knowledge of it.[1] It is implied that this opinion is the approved one, since the first two were described as random guesses. It is not the 'and of eight' (*wāw al-thamāniya*).[2] The most common opinion is that it is

1 The issue at hand is the presence of the word *and* this time, unlike in the first two statements.

2 The *wāw al-thamāniya* describes the customary use in Arabic of the word 'and' when reaching the eighth member of a list.

the kind of 'and' that occurs in a sentence to introduce a description of an indefinite noun, or to introduce the state of a definite noun. Other explanations have been given for it besides these. Their names were Yamlīkhā, Makthalīnā, Marnūsh, Barnūsh, Shādhanūsh and Kafashṭayṭūsh, who were the king's right and left hand men, and their shepherd and their dog Qiṭmīr. *Say: 'My Lord knows best their number, and none knows them except a few'*: Ibn ʿAbbās said, 'I am one of those few. They were seven.' ʿAlī (may God be pleased with him) is reported to have said the same. *So do not contend concerning them, except in an outward manner*: without delving deeply into it, and tell them about this, and do not leave them ignorant; *and do not question about them* and their story *any of them*: whether rhetorically or to seek further information.

[18:23] *And never say regarding something* you mean to do, *'I will do that tomorrow*: or in the future in general,*'* [18:24] *unless* you qualify *that God will*: such as by saying, 'God willing.' When they asked him about it, he said, 'I shall tell you tomorrow,' without qualifying this, and hence the revelation was delayed for fifteen days, and so they belied him. The word *unless* refers back to *never say*, not to *I will do*, since otherwise it would not make sense. *And remember* the will of *your Lord if you forget* to say so and then remember later. When this was revealed, he (may God bless him and grant him peace) said, 'God willing.' Ibn ʿAbbās cited this as evidence that the one who swears an oath may subsequently qualify it, even a year later; but the majority disagreed with this, because it would obviously lead to abuse. Ibn Khuzayma interpreted it to apply only to vows about performing regular prophetic (*sunna*) actions. It was also narrated from Ibn ʿAbbās that qualifying an oath after as long as a year is something that would be allowed only for the Prophet (may God bless him and grant him peace). *And say: 'Perhaps my Lord will guide me to something closer than this*—the tale of the Companions of the Cave—*by way of guidance* that proves my prophethood.*'* And indeed He did guide him. It is also said that this means: 'Remember your Lord when you forget something and then remember it; and if you do not remember it, then say, "Perhaps my Lord..." and so on.'

Q. 18:23

[18:25] *And they tarried in their Cave*—from when they lay down until they were roused—*three hundred years* by the solar calendar of the Jews, *and some added nine* for lunar years, since the solar year is 365 days and a little more, while the lunar year is 354 days and a little more, such that every hundred years there is a three year difference between them.

[18:26] *Say*, when they argue with you about this number: *'God is more knowledgeable of how long they tarried. To Him belongs the* knowledge of *the Unseen of the heavens and the earth. How well He sees! How well He hears!* How wondrous are His hearing and sight, such that His perception is beyond all other perception! *They*, the inhabitants of the heavens and the earth, *have no guardian besides Him* to tend to their affairs, *and He makes none* of them *to share in His rule.'*

[18:27] *And recite that which has been revealed to you of the Book of your Lord. There is none who can change His Words* besides Him, or none who can change His rule; so it does not contradict, *And when We exchange a verse...* [Q. 16:101]. *And you will not find, besides Him, any refuge*: no matter how you search.

[18:28] *And restrain yourself along with those who call upon their Lord at morning and evening*: that is, at all times; *desiring His countenance*: His approval—this means the impoverished Companions, for the nobles of Quraysh demanded that he host a special meeting for them where others were excluded; *and do not let your eyes overlook them* by turning to the wealthy
Q. 18:27 folk, such as ʿUtayba and his companions, *desiring the glitter of the life of this world. And do not obey*—by banishing them—*him whose heart We have made oblivious to Our remembrance, and who follows his own whim, and whose conduct is prodigality*: extravagance.

[18:29] *And say: 'The truth is from your Lord*: not your desire; *so whoever will, let him believe; and whoever will, let him disbelieve'*: this is a warning worded as a command. It does not mean that we are independent, for our will is not really 'will'. *Truly, We have prepared for the evildoers*, the disbelievers, *a Fire, and they will be surrounded by its pavilion*: a metaphor for the smoke and flames that surround it. *If they cry out for relief* from their thirst, *they will be succoured with water like molten copper*—the word *muhl* means molten copper or hot oil—*which scalds faces* when they go to drink it. *What an evil drink* is that molten copper, *and how ill a resting-place* is that fire*!* This foreshadows the contrasting *fair resting-place* [Q. 18:31] that will be mentioned presently.

[18:30] *Truly, those who believe and perform righteous deeds—Truly, We do not leave the reward of those who do good deeds*—such as them—*to go to waste.*

[18:31] *Those, for them there shall be Gardens of Eden, with rivers flowing from beneath them; therein they shall be adorned with bracelets of gold*: such as the kings of Persia wear in this world; *and they shall wear green garments of silk and brocade*: that is, fine silk and heavy silk, the combination of which symbolises everything that the soul could desire; *reclining*, lying or sitting cross-legged, *therein*, in the Gardens, *on couches*: beds in chambers decorated for brides. *How excellent a reward* is this, *and how fair a resting-place!*

[18:32] *And strike for them*, for the disbeliever and the believer, *a similitude: two men*, brothers, a believer named Yahūdhā and an disbeliever named Quṭrūs, who both inherited some money; one of them bought some date palms and other worldly goods, while the other donated it to good causes. *To one of them*, the disbeliever, *We assigned two gardens*—orchards—*of vines, and surrounded them with date palms, and set between them*—between the vines and the palms—*crops*.

[18:33] *Each of the two gardens yielded its produce without stinting anything thereof*: without falling short in its yield. *And We caused a stream to gush forth therein*.

[18:34] *And he*, the owner, *had fruits*: abundant wealth aside from the two gardens. *So he said to his companion*, the believer, *as he conversed with him* boastfully, *'I have more wealth than you, and am stronger in respect of men*: retinue and family.*'*

[18:35] *And he entered his garden* with the other's hand in his. He said *garden* in the singular because what is meant here is the favour that was given to him, by way of implying that he would not be given any other garden besides it, such as the Garden that is promised to the righteous, or because the two gardens were connected, as one was inside the other. [*And he entered his garden*] *having wronged himself* with his disbelief and pride. *He said, 'I do not think that this* garden *will ever perish*: cease to exist, so delusional and confident was he. Without doubt, the wealthy folk of our time are just like him, and only their fear of the sword of the Law prevents them from saying the same.

Q. 18:32

[18:36] *'Moreover, I do not think that the Hour* of the Resurrection *will ever come; and even if I were returned to my Lord*, for the sake of argument, *I would surely find better than this*—than my garden—*as a resort*: because He only gave it to me because I deserved it.*'*

[18:37] *His companion*, the believer, *said to him as he conversed with him, 'Do you disbelieve in Him Who created you of dust*—the origin of your matter or the matter of your origin—*then of a drop of fluid, then fashioned you a man?*

[18:38] *'But lo*, as for me, *He is God, my Lord, and I do not ascribe any partner to my Lord*, unlike you.

[18:39] *'And if only, when you entered your garden, you had said, "What God has willed* shall be. *There is no power except in God"*: to acknowledge your own powerlessness. *If you see me as less than you in wealth and children*, [18:40] *then perchance my Lord will give me something better than your garden, and unleash upon it*, your garden, *bolts from the heaven so that it becomes a bare plain*: so that the garden becomes empty and smooth.

[18:41] *'Or its water will sink down* into the earth, *so that you have no means of acquiring it.'*

[18:42] *And his fruit was beset*—destroyed—*and so he began to wring his hands* in woe *because of what he had spent on it, as they*, the trees, *lay fallen on their trellises*, their supports on the ground, *saying* in his grief at their loss, *'O, I wish I had not ascribed any partner to my Lord*: in order that He would not destroy my garden*!'*

[18:43] *But there was no party to help him, besides God, nor could he help himself.*

[18:44] *There*—at the station of the descent of His chastisement—*all protection belongs to God*: *walāya* (protection) can also be read as *wilāya* (sovereignty); *the True*: this can also be read as 'all true protection belongs to God.' *He is better at rewarding* those who obey Him, *and best in consequence* for them.

Q. 18:41

[18:45] *And strike for them a similitude for* the beauty of *the life of this world*—in its splendour and short-lived glory—*as water which We send down out from the heaven, and the vegetation of the earth mingles with it*: and draws it into itself; *and then it becomes chaff*—dry and broken—*scattered by the winds. And God is Omnipotent*, Powerful, *over all things.*

[18:46] *Wealth and children are an adornment of the life of this world*: and they quickly pass away. *But the enduring righteous things*: righteous deeds whose effect endures, such as the phrases 'glory be to God', 'praise be to God', 'there is no god but God', and 'God is Greatest', and the canonical prayers, the *ḥajj*, fasting Ramaḍān, and goodly words, all of which have been offered as interpretations for this; *are better with your Lord for reward, and better for hope*: because the one who does them will attain that which he hopes for.

[18:47] *And* remember *the day when the mountains shall be set in motion* in the air after they are uprooted, *and you will see the earth exposed*: flattened without any hills or dips, and all the buried dead and treasures within it laid bare. *And We shall have gathered them*: the use of the past tense verb here indicates that the gathering will be before the mountains are set in motion, so they can witness it; *and We will not leave out anyone of them.*

[18:48] *And they shall be presented before your Lord in ranks*: lined up like an army being presented to the ruler for judgement; and they will be told: *'You have come to Us just as We created you the first time*: naked and without possessions, or alive. *Nay*—this word shifts the focus from one issue to another—*you claimed that We would not appoint for you a tryst* for the Resurrection.*'*

[18:49] *And the Book*—the record of deeds—*shall be set in place* in the hands, or in the balance. *And you will see the sinners apprehensive*—fearful—*of what is in it, and they will say, 'O woe to us!* O, our destruction, come forth and exult! *What is it with this Book, that it leaves out neither small nor great* of our deeds, *but has counted it?'* This does not contradict, *If you avoid the grave sins that are forbidden you, We will absolve you of your evil deeds* [Q. 4:31], because the fact that they are counted does not mean that they are not absolved. *And they shall find all that they did present* in the records. *And your Lord does not wrong anyone*: by recording against them anything that they did not do.

[18:50] *And* remember *when We said to the angels, 'Prostrate before Adam,' and so they prostrated, except Iblīs. He was of the jinn*: this was explained earlier.[1] It implies that angels cannot sin, and the only reason he sinned was that he was a jinn; however, Ibn ʿAbbās is reported to have said that he was one of the most noble of angels, the Keepers of the Gardens. *And he transgressed against*—refused to obey—*his Lord's command*: by declining to prostrate. *Will you*, O Children of Adam, *then* Q. 18:49
take him and his offspring: his children, or some say it is a metaphor for his followers; some say that devils procreate just as humans do, while others say that Satan places his tail into his anus and then lays eggs, each of which contains several devils; *for your patrons instead of Me* by obeying them and disobeying Me, *though they are an enemy to you? How evil for the evildoers is that substitute!* In other words, how evil is the substitution of Iblīs and his progeny for God!

[18:51] *I did not make them*, the devils, *a witness to the creation of the heavens and the earth, nor to their own creation*: by allowing some of them to witness the creation of others. *Nor do I take misleaders* such as them *as supporters*: helpers; for sharing the creative act implies sharing divinity.

[18:52] *And on the day when He will say, 'Call those partners of Mine, as you used to claim* as My partners, to help you'; *they will call them, but they will not respond to their call, and We shall set between them a gulf of doom* which they will share, namely the Fire, or a gulf between them to prevent them from connecting.

[18:53] *And the sinners will behold the Fire and realise that they are about to fall into it*: their plummet into it will last as long as forty years, to heighten their despair. *And they will find no means of avoiding it*.

[18:54] *And indeed We have dispensed*—elucidated repeatedly—*in this*

1 See Q. 2:34.

Qur'ān, the Book, *for people* an example *of every kind of similitude*: that they might be admonished. *But humanity is most disputatious* on behalf of falsehood, except for those who are divinely protected.

[18:55] *And nothing prevented people*, Quraysh, *from believing when the guidance*, the Messenger and the Qur'ān, *came to them, and from asking forgiveness of their Lord, except* the expectation *that there should come upon them the precedent of the ancients*, meaning their chastisement, *or that the chastisement* of the Hereafter *should come upon them before their very eyes*: the word *qubulan* here means 'before their eyes', or 'in manifold forms'.

[18:56] *And We do not send messengers except as bearers of glad tidings* for the believers *and as warners* for the disbelievers. *But those who disbelieve dispute with falsehood*, such as by saying, 'Has God sent a human messenger?' *that they may refute therewith*, with falsehood, *the truth*, the Qur'ān. *And they have taken My signs*—the Qur'ān—*and that whereof they have been warned derisively*: mockingly.

Q. 18:55 [18:57] *And who does greater wrong than he who has been reminded of the signs of his Lord, yet turns away from them* instead of reflecting on them, *and forgets what* sins *his hands have sent ahead? Truly, on their hearts We have cast veils*, coverings, *lest they should understand it*, the Qur'ān, *and in their ears a deafness*: an inability to hear the truth with receptivity; *and though you call them to guidance, they will not be guided then, ever*: whether truly or by way of blindly following.

[18:58] *And your Lord is the Forgiver*, the One of vast forgiveness, *Full of Mercy. Were He to take them to task for what they have earned, He would have hastened for them the chastisement; but they have a tryst from which they will not find any escape*: any refuge from Him at that tryst.

[18:59] *And those towns* around Mecca, such as ʿĀd, *We destroyed them*, their inhabitants, *when they did evil, and We appointed for* the time of *their destruction a tryst*: so take admonition from this.

[18:60] *And when Moses said to his lad*, Joshua son of Nun, son of Ephraim, son of Joseph (may the blessings and peace of God be upon him), *'I will not give up until I have reached the juncture of the two seas*: the place where the seas of Persia and Anatolia meet, for his meeting with Khiḍr. *The two seas* have been interpreted to symbolise those two figures, since Moses was a sea of outward knowledge, Khiḍr of inward knowledge. *Though I march on for an age'*: a long spell, or a year. The story behind this was that after the destruction of the Egyptians, someone asked Moses, 'Is there anyone more knowledgeable than you?' to which he replied, 'No.' Then God revealed to him, 'Nay, there is Our servant Khiḍr. He is at the juncture of the two seas.' Khiḍr lived in the time of Dhū al-Qarnayn the Greater, the one who met Abraham, built the dam and travelled the world, not Dhū al-Qarnayn the Lesser of Greece who searched for the Water of Life but did not find it.[1]

[18:61] *So* Moses and his lad went on, and *when they reached a juncture between the two* seas, Moses lay down to rest by a rock and the grilled fish fell out of their pack and into the sea. It is said that the fish was salted, but when a drop of water fell onto it after Joshua used it for ablutions, the fish came to life. So *they forgot their fish*: Moses forgot to search for it, or Joshua forgot to speak of how he had seen it come to life; *and so it made its way into the sea, burrowing* through it as though it were a hole, the water freezing around its path instead of flowing into it. The verse switches the order of events; but it is not curious that he forgot about this Qur'ānic miracle (*al-muʿjiza al-Qurʾāniyya*), since he was used to witnessing such astounding feats and they had become unremarkable to him.

[18:62] *And when they had made the traverse* beyond the rock and trav- Q. 18:61
elled through the night and next morning until noon, *he said to his lad* Joshua, *'Bring us our breakfast. We have certainly encountered on this journey of ours much fatigue* after traversing it.' This was the only occasion Moses had ever been tired by travel, as his words here indicate.

[18:63] *He said, 'Do you see* what has befallen me? *When we sheltered at the rock, truly I forgot* to tell the story of *the fish; and none but Satan made me forget to mention it; and it*, the fish, *made its way into the sea in an amazing manner'*: as was just described.

[18:64] *Said he*, Moses, *'That is what we have been seeking!'* The forgetting of the fish was a portent of the goal. *So they turned back, retracing their footsteps.*

[18:65] *So* by the rock *they found one of Our servants*, Khiḍr, lying on a cloak on the ground—his real name was Balyā b. Malkān; *to whom We had given mercy from Us*: prophethood or sainthood, the latter being more likely—he still lives unto this day; *and We had taught him knowledge from Us*: knowledge of Unseen matters that can only be attained through Our grace.

[18:66] *Moses said to him, 'May I follow you*—keep your company—on condition *that you teach me of what you have been taught of guidance?'* It is necessary that the messenger know more than those to whom he is sent about the fundamentals and branches of his religion [but not necessarily other things],

1 Alexander the Great.

so it was not a shortcoming on the part of Moses to ask this, even if Khiḍr was not a prophet. So Khiḍr said, 'Is not the Torah enough knowledge for you?' to which Moses replied, 'My Lord has commanded me thus.'

[18:67] *Said he*, Khiḍr, *'Truly, you will not be able to bear with me* when you see me do something that seems to contravene your Law.

[18:68] *'And how can you bear with that* the inner realities *whereof you have never been informed?'* In other words, 'things of which you have no information and which seem to be unlawful'.

[18:69] *He said, 'You will find me, God willing, patient* with you, *and I will not disobey you in any matter'*: he did not say 'God willing' again about disobeying, and so went on to disobey.

[18:70] *He said, 'If you follow me then do not question me concerning anything* of which you may disapprove *until I make mention of it to you* of my own accord, to explain it.*'*

[18:71] *So they set off* searching for a ship, with Joshua in tow, *until, when they embarked on the ship, he made a hole in it* by taking an axe to two
Q. 18:67 of its boards. It is said that the water did not actually leak into it. *Said he*, Moses, *'Did you make a hole in it to drown its people? You have certainly done a dreadful thing.'*

[18:72] *He said, 'Did I not say that you would not be able to bear with me?'*

[18:73] *He*, Moses, *said, 'Do not take me to task on account of that which I forgot* about your counsel, *and do not exhaust me*—burden me—*in this affair of mine with difficulty*: by taking me to task for forgetting.*'*

[18:74] *So they set off* after disembarking the ship, *until they met a boy*, a young lad named Jaysūr playing with the other boys, *and he slew him* by decapitating him. The verb *qatal* (slew) is preceded by the particle *fa-*, which indicates immediacy and lack of delay, unlike the case for what happened with the ship. *He said, 'Have you slain a* seemingly *pure soul*: Abū ʿAmr said that *zākiya* (innocent) means one that has committed no sin, while *zakiyya* (pure) means one that sinned and was then forgiven—some leading exegetes said that he may have preferred the latter reading[1] for this reason, since it refers to a child;[2] *not in retaliation for another soul? Truly, you have committed an evil thing'*: He said *dreadful* [Q. 18:71] for the first, meaning a great evil, because killing several people is worse than killing one. It is related that when Khiḍr heard this objection, he became enraged and

1 Abū ʿAmr and others preferred to recite *zākiya* here.

2 The author follows this with the rejoinder: *wa yuraddu ʿalayhi mā marra ikhtiyār al-MLK* [?], which is incomprehensible to me. The editor ʿAbd Allāh al-Shabrāwī notes an alternative from one of the other source manuscripts, but it is no less baffling.

pulled off the boy's left shoulder and ripped the flesh from it, and there written upon the shoulder-blade was 'a disbeliever who will never believe in God'.

[18:75] *He said, 'Did I not say to you that you would never be able to bear with me?* You are now twice condemned, for you have broken your oath twice.*'*

[18:76] *He said, 'If I ask you* disapprovingly *about anything after this, then do not keep me in your company, for you have accepted enough excuses from me* for repeatedly disobeying you.*'*

[18:77] *So they set off, until, when they came to the folk of a town*, Antioch, *they asked its folk for food*: a *ḥadīth* states that they walked around the gatherings there asking them for something to eat. This shows how trifling the world is in God's eyes. *But they refused to extend them any hospitality. They then found in it a wall* standing one hundred cubits tall, *about to collapse*: literally 'wanting to collapse', a metaphor for how nigh its collapse was; *so he straightened it* by rubbing his hand over it, according to Ibn ʿAbbās. *He said, 'Had you wished, you could have taken a wage for it*: for we are hungry.*'*

Q. 18:75

[18:78] *Said he, 'This* question *is the parting between me and you*: the reason he parted with him for this one in particular, and not the first two, was that this time he was motivated by the desire of his own belly, while the first two were motivated by his strong piety. *I will inform you the interpretation of that over which you were not able to maintain patience.*

[18:79] *'As for the ship, it belonged to poor people*: whether monetarily poor, or unable to protect themselves from injustice—if it was the former, then this suggests that a person can be 'poor' even if he has possessions, if those possessions are not sufficient for him; *who earned a living on the sea; and I wanted to make it defective, for behind them was a king seizing every ship* in good condition *by force*: he worded this backwards, for one would have expected him to mention the king first and then say how he wanted to make it defective, in order to justify this desire.

[18:80] *'And as for the boy, his parents were believers and We feared lest he should overwhelm*—overburden—*them with insolence and disbelief*: lest they follow him in his disbelief because of their love for him. A *ḥadīth* states that the boy was marked for disbelief; we noted the story about his shoulder-blade earlier.

[18:81] *'So we desired that their Lord should give them in exchange* for him *one better than him in purity*, innocence from sin, *and closer to mercy*: dutifulness to his parents. Later they were blessed with a daughter who went on to marry a prophet, and she gave birth to a prophet by whom God guided a community.

[18:82] *'And as for the wall, it belonged to two orphan boys in the city*, named Aṣram and Ṣuraym, *and beneath it there was a treasure belonging to them*: tablets of gold inscribed with counsels. *Their father had been a righteous man*: a weaver or smith named Kāshiḥ—he was their forefather from seven generations back; *and your Lord desired that they should come of age*, adulthood and sound reason, *and extract their treasure*, which would have been lost had the wall fallen, *as a mercy from your Lord. And I did not do it of my own accord*: but by God's command, whether by revelation or inspiration. *This is the interpretation of that over which you could not maintain patience'*. Among the lessons of the story are: we should not be proud of our knowledge, nor rush to condemn things we do not like; we should always seek to learn more, and be humble with our teachers; we should alert a sinner to his sin, so that we can ascertain whether or not it is truly wrong, and then pardon him and separate from him if he persists.

Q. 18:82 Note that he attributed the first act to himself[1] because he did it directly, and the second to the two of them[2] because the exchange was done by the boy's destruction and then God's creation of his replacement, and then the third to God alone,[3] because he played no part in their coming of age. Also, the first act was inherently evil, the third good, and the second mixed. Note also that the gnostic in his beginnings sees himself and his deeds, and then sees himself and his Creator, and finally sees nothing but the Creator.

[18:83] *And they question you concerning Dhū al-Qarnayn*: the soundest view is that he was Alexander the Greek, who circled the House with Abraham and whose advisor was Khiḍr. He was called Dhū al-Qarnayn (He of the Two Horns) because he wore a helmet with brass horns, or because he travelled from one 'horn', namely side, of the world to the other. Some say he was the Greek who lived three hundred years before Christ, and whose advisor was Aristotle. *Say: 'I shall recite to you a mention of him*: Dhū al-Qarnayn.'

[18:84] *Truly, We empowered him throughout the land*: by allowing him to do as pleased therein; *and We gave him to everything* he desires *a way* to reach it, whether through knowledge, power or instruments.

[18:85] *And he followed a way* towards the West, [18:86] *until, when he reached the setting of the sun, he found it setting in a muddy spring*: this means

1 By saying *I wanted* (Q. 18:79).
2 God and Khiḍr, by saying *We feared* (Q. 18:80).
3 By saying *your Lord desired* (Q. 18:82).

that it appeared so, not that it was actually so, for the sun is in the fourth heaven and is 160 times larger than the earth. This is why He said *he found it setting* rather than 'it was setting'. The word *ḥami'a* (muddy) means 'composed of black mud', not to be confused with *ḥāmiya*, meaning 'hot'. *And he found by it*—by the spring—*a folk* of disbelievers. *We said* to him through revelation, or through the prophet of his time, or by inspiration, *'O Dhū al-Qarnayn, either chastise* by slaying and the like, *or treat them kindly* by guiding them.*'* So he chose to be kind:

[18:87] *He said, 'As for him who does wrong* by insisting on disbelief, *we shall chastise him* by slaying him. *Then he shall be returned to his Lord, and He shall chastise him with an awful chastisement* the like of which he will never have experienced.

[18:88] *'But as for him who believes and acts righteously, he shall have the fairest reward*: meaning the Garden. It can also be read as 'he shall have, as reward, that which is fairest.' *And we shall speak to him mildly in our command*: we shall enjoin upon them action that is not difficult to do.*'*

Q. 18:87

[18:89] *Then he followed a way* towards the East, [18:90] *until, when he reached the rising of the sun*—the first inhabited place over which it rose—*he found it rising on a people*, the Zanj,[1] *for whom We had not provided against it*, the sun, *any cover*: meaning clothing, or shade from buildings, trees and the like. What this means is that in the summer the sun was always up for them, above the horizon. This was beyond Berbera[2] from the direction of Bulgaria; the sun would circle around in the summer above the ground, but without ever falling as low as their heads.

[18:91] *So* was Dhū al-Qarnayn given sovereignty over all that, *and We encompassed whatever pertained to him in knowledge* regarding the many means at his disposal.

[18:92] *Then he followed a way* between East and West, [18:93] *until, when he reached between the two barriers*, the mountains of Armenia and Azerbaijan between which the barrier was built, *he found on this side of them a folk that could scarcely comprehend speech* because of their low intelligence.

[18:94] *They said, 'O Dhū al-Qarnayn, truly Gog and Magog*—two tribes from the descendants of Japheth, or Gog was from the Turks, and Magog from the mountains—*are causing corruption in the land*: our land. *So shall we pay you a tribute on condition that you build between us and them a barrier* to keep them away from us*?'*

1 The people of south-east Africa.
2 In present-day Somalia.

[18:95] *He said, 'That wherewith my Lord has empowered me*—my wealth and sovereignty—*is better* than any tribute you could offer me; *so help me with strength*: instruments of assistance; *and I will build between you and them a rampart*: a secure boundary even larger than a regular barrier.

[18:96] *'Bring me ingots of iron!'* In other words, 'Pass them to me!' It does not contradict how he refused their tribute. *Until, when he had levelled*, filled, *between the two flanks*, the two sides of the mountains by having coal and firewood piled up between the iron ingots, *he said* to the workers, *'Blow!' Until when he had made it* as hot as *a fire, he said, 'Bring me molten copper to pour over it* to strengthen it.'

[18:97] *And so they were not able to scale it* because of how smooth it was, *nor could they pierce it* because of how strong it was.

[18:98] *Said he, 'This* barrier *is a mercy from my Lord* to His servants. *But when the* time for the *promise of my Lord comes to pass* that they come out, or when the Hereafter is nigh, *He will level it* into flat ground, *for my Lord's promise is always true.'* Here ends the story of Dhū al-Qarnayn.

Q. 18:95 [18:99] *And on that day, We shall let some of them*—some of Gog and Magog—*surge against others*: like the waves of the sea, so numerous will they be; *and the Trumpet*—the Horn, as was discussed earlier[1]—*shall be blown and We shall gather them altogether* for the requital.

[18:100] *And on that day We shall present Hell to the disbelievers, plain to view.*

[18:101] *Those whose eyes were masked*, covered, *from* beholding *My remembrance*—from reflecting on My signs—*and who could not hear* My Words because of their deafness to the truth.

[18:102] *Do the disbelievers reckon that they can take My servants as patrons beside Me* without enraging Me? *Truly, We have prepared Hell for the disbelievers as hospitality*: meaning that which is prepared for the guest when he first arrives, so how shall the rest of their stay be?

[18:103] *Say: 'Shall We inform you who will be the greatest losers in* all *their* different manner of *deeds?* They shall be:

[18:104] *'Those whose effort goes astray*—to naught—*in the life of this world, while they reckon that they are doing good work* because of their self-satisfaction and ignorance.

[18:105] *'Those are they who disbelieve in the signs of their Lord and the encounter with Him.' So their deeds have failed*: come to naught because of their disbelief; *and on the Day of Resurrection We shall not assign any weight*—value—*to them*. Or it means, 'We shall not weigh their deeds at all, for they

1 See Q. 6:73.

will have come to naught.' As for His Words, *And as for those whose scales are light*... [Q. 7:9], they refer to the sinners [rather than the disbelievers].

[18:106] *That is their requital—Hell—because they disbelieved and took My signs and My messengers in mockery* instead of reflecting on them.

[18:107] *Truly, those who believe and perform righteous deeds—theirs will be the gardens of Firdaws*, the highest Garden, *as hospitality*: this was explained above.

[18:108] *Abiding therein, with no desire to be removed from them.*

[18:109] *Say: 'If the* waters of the *sea were ink for* writing *the Words of my Lord*—meaning His wisdoms—*the sea would be spent*, for it is finite, *before the Words of my Lord were spent*, for they are infinite, *even if We brought the like of it*, the like of the entire sea, *as replenishment.'*

[18:110] *Say: 'I am only a human being like you. It has been revealed to me that your God is only One God*: I am only special because of the revelation. *So whoever hopes to encounter his Lord*—whoever desires a pleasant meeting with Him—*let him do righteous work* in accordance with the Law, *and not associate with the worship of his Lord anyone'*: whether by ostentation or seek- Q. 18:106
ing reward, such as the one who likes his worship to be seen. This is what is called 'hidden idolatry' (*shirk khafī*), as a *ḥadīth* describes.

APPENDIX
PERSONS CITED IN THE TEXT[1]
(Excluding prophets and the like)

ᶜABBĀS B. ᶜABD AL-MUṬṬALIB (d. 32 [653]). The Companion and uncle of the Prophet. He converted to Islam shortly before or after the Battle of Badr, but remained in Mecca living covertly as a Muslim rather than emigrating to Medina. The Abbasid dynasty was founded by his descendants.

ABŪ ᶜALĪ (d. 377 [987]). A Persian grammarian.

ABŪ ᶜĀMIR AL-RĀHIB (d. 9-10 [631]). An early opponent of Islam, said to have been the one who instigated the construction of the Masjid al-Ḍirār, the Hypocrites' mosque. (Osman, 'Pre-Islamic Arab Converts', 73.)

ABŪ ᶜAMR (d. 154 [770-1]). A Qur'ān reciter and grammarian of Basra.

ABŪ ᶜAQĪL AL-ANṢĀRĪ. A Companion of the Prophet and narrator of *ḥadīth*.

ABŪ BAKR B. AL-ᶜARABĪ (d. 543 [1148]). An Andalusian jurist and theologian, not to be confused with the philosopher and Sufi Ibn ᶜArabī.

ABŪ BAKR AL-ṢIDDĪQ (d. 13 [634]). A businessman of Mecca who personally accompanied the Prophet on his emigration to Medina. Abū Bakr became the Prophet's closest advisor, and after his death became the first caliph. He is recorded as having narrated 142 *ḥadīths*. (*Disciplining*, 210; Ṣiddīqī, *Ḥadīth Literature*, 17.)

ABŪ AL-DAḤDĀḤ. A Companion of the Prophet.

ABŪ DĀ'ŪD AL-SIJISTĀNĪ (d. 275 [889]). A major *ḥadīth* scholar, compiler of one of the six canonical collections of Sunni Islam.

ABŪ DHARR (d. 32 [652-3]). A Companion of the Prophet and one of the earliest converts to Islam.

ABŪ ḤANĪFA (d. 150 [767]). A jurist of Kufa, and eponymous founder of the Ḥanafī school, one of the four major schools of Sunni jurisprudence.

1 Any references to *Disciplining* and *Remembrance* refer to the notes, often slightly amended, from T. J. Winter in Ghazālī, *On Disciplining the Soul* and Ghazālī, *On Remembrance of Death*, respectively. The abbreviated references can be located in the Bibliography according to the author and book title.

ABŪ HURAYRA (d. 58 [677]). A Companion of the Prophet and prolific *ḥadīth* narrator, who is recorded to have conveyed 5,374 *ḥadīths*. (Ṣiddīqī, *Ḥadīth Literature*, 18.)

ABŪ JAHL (d. 2 [624]). One of the leaders of Quraysh who rejected the Prophet's early mission in Mecca. He would remain a staunch opponent of Islam, eventually being killed at the Battle of Badr.

ABŪ LAHAB (d. 2 [624]). One of the leading opponents of Islam in Mecca, condemned in *Sūrat Tabbat* (Q. 111). (Guillaume, *Life,* 310.)

ABŪ LUBĀBA. A member of the Aws tribe who converted to Islam, but later passed information to the Qurayẓa tribe during the siege of Qurayẓa. Wracked with guilt about this, he tied himself to a pillar in the Medina mosque and vowed he would not leave until God forgave him this treachery. (Lings, *Muhammad*, 230.)

ABŪ SUFYĀN B. ḤARB (d. 32-3 [653]). The elder of Quraysh who led the Meccans in Battle at Uḥud and the Trench, but then converted to Islam after the Conquest of Mecca.

ABŪ SUFYĀN B. AL-ḤĀRITH (d. 32-3 [653]). A cousin and Companion of the Prophet.

ABŪ ṬĀLIB (d. 619 CE). The uncle of the Prophet and father of ʿAlī b. Abī Ṭālib. His well-respected nobility in Mecca allowed him to afford the Prophet a measure of protection from Quraysh's persecution in the early years of Islam.

ABŪ AL-YUSR (d. 55 [675]). A Companion of the Prophet, said to have been the last surviving veteran of the Battle of Badr.

ABŪ ZAYD SAʿĪD AL-ANṢĀRĪ (d. 215 CE). A major Arab linguist of Basra.

ʿADĪ B. ZAYD (d. 587 CE). A pre-Islamic Christian Arab.

AḤMAD B. ḤANBAL (d. 241 [855]). A jurist of Baghdad, and eponymous founder of the Ḥanbalī school, one of the four major schools of Sunni jurisprudence.

ʿĀʾISHA BINT ABĪ BAKR (d. 58 [678]). The third and most beloved wife of the Prophet. During his final illness he asked his other wives for leave to stay in her house, where he died. After his death, she was involved in the revolt of Ṭalḥa and al-Zubayr against the Caliph ʿAlī, following which she lived quietly at Medina until she died. Her narration of *ḥadīth* was extensive, with only three other Companions narrating more than her 2,210 narrations. She was also famed for her expertise in Islamic law and medicine, in addition to being well-versed in Arab history and in poetry. (*Disciplining*, 212; Ṣiddīqī, *Ḥadīth Literature*, 17–18 and 21.)

AKHNAS B. SHURAYQ. He was an eloquent Hypocrite who would feign faithfulness to Islam before the Prophet but then belie the message upon his departure. (Shafi, *Maʿariful Qurʾan*, I. 512) ᶜALĪ B. ABĪ ṬĀLIB AL-MURTAḌĀ (d. 40 [661]). The cousin and son-in-law of the Prophet, having married his daughter Fāṭima. He lived a life of austerity and piety. Upon the death of ᶜUthmān (d. 35/656) he accepted, with some reluctance, the office of Caliph, which he held for five years disturbed by several rebellions, including that of Muᶜāwiya, the governor of Syria. He was assassinated at Kufa by a member of the extreme Khārijī sect, which repudiated him for having agreed to negotiate with Muᶜāwiya. Only ten Companions narrated more than his 536 *ḥadīth*. (*Disciplining*, 213; Ṣiddīqī, *Ḥadīth Literature*, 18.)

ᶜAMALĪQ B. LĀWADH B. SĀM. The Arabic name of Amalek, the founder of the Amalekite nation.

ĀMINA (d. c 575 CE). The mother of the Prophet.

ᶜĀMIR B. AL-ḤAḌRAMĪ (d. 2-3 [624]). A pagan of Quraysh slain at the Battle of Badr.

ᶜAMMĀR B. YĀSIR (d. 37 [657]). A Companion and one of the earliest Muslims. His mother Sumayya was the first martyr of Islam. He narrated sixty-two *ḥadīth*. (Ghazālī, *Condemnation of Pride*, 156 (note by Rustom); Ṣiddīqī, *Ḥadīth Literature*, 17.)

ᶜAMR B. AL-ᶜĀṢ AL-SAHMĪ (d. 42 [664]). A Companion of the Prophet, and military leader and governor under Abū Bakr.

ᶜAMR B. AL-JAMŪḤ AL-ANṢĀRĪ (d. 3-4 [625]). A Companion of the Prophet, slain at the Battle of Uḥud.

ANAS B. MĀLIK (d. 91-3 [709–712]). A Companion of the Prophet, whom he served from the age of ten until the Prophet passed away. He is the third most prolific narrator of *ḥadīth* amongst the Companions, with 2,286 traditions. (*Disciplining*, 213; Ṣiddīqī, *Ḥadīth Literature*, 18 and 20–1.)

ᶜANSĪ (d. 10-11 [632]). A false prophet of Yemen who ruled over the country for a time until defeated by Fayrūz al-Daylamī.

ᶜĀSHIR. The author's brief mention of Jesus raising the daughter of ᶜĀshir to life may refer to the biblical account of the raising of the daughter of Jairus (Mark 5:21–43).

AṢMAᶜĪ (d. 212-3 [828]). A leading grammarian of the Basran school.

AṢRAM. Said to be the name of one of the orphan boys in the account in *Sūrat al-Kahf* (Q. 18:81).

ᶜATTĀB B. ASĪD (d. 23 [644]). A Companion of the Prophet, who appointed him governor of Mecca after its conquest.

BALAAM. The *tafsīr* tradition asserts that he was a spiritually-enlightened person who lived at the time of Moses. It is narrated that his supplications were answered, and that he knew God's Greatest Name. He was either forced or bribed to try and supplicate against Moses, whereby he forsook the faith.

BARNŪSH. Said to be the name of one of the Sleepers in the Cave.

BAYHAQĪ (d. 458 [1066]). A major *ḥadīth* scholar of Nishapur.

BENJAMIN. The Prophet Joseph's younger brother, as named in the Bible. According to Q. 12:69, Joseph revealed his true identity to Benjamin when the latter was imprisoned on the pretext of a plot to steal, which was simply a ruse by Joseph. (Kaltner & Mirza, *The Bible and the Qur'an*, 101–2.)

BILĀL B. RABĀḤ (d. 17-21 [639-43]). A Companion of the Prophet and the first muezzin of Islam.

BUDAYL THE FREEDMAN OF ʿAMR B. AL-ʿĀṢ. A Companion of the Prophet.

BUKHĀRĪ, Muḥammad b. Ismāʿīl (d. 256 [870]). A major *ḥadīth* scholar of Khorasan. His *Ṣaḥīḥ* is one of the six canonical collections of Sunni Islam, and universally held to be the greatest and most authentic of them.

BUSHRĀ. Possibly one of the group who found Joseph in the well (see Q. 12:19), although this is unlikely.

DĀRIMĪ (d. 255 [869]). A major *ḥadīth* scholar of Samarkand.

DAWĀNĪ, Jalāl al-Dīn al-Kāzarūnī (d. 907-8 [1502]). A renowned theologian and jurist of Safavid Persia.

DECIUS (d. 251 CE). From a military background, he was a senior senator before becoming Roman Emperor. His short reign came to an end when he was killed after launching an attack on the Goths. (Potter, ed., *Companion to the Roman Empire*, 25, 156 and 219.)

DHŪ AL-QARNAYN THE GREATER. The author identifies this figure as the Dhū al-Qarnayn meant in *Sūrat al-Kahf*; it may mean the Himyarite king Ṣaʿb, said to have travelled the world and met with al-Khiḍr.

DHŪ AL-QARNAYN THE LESSER. The author identifies this figure as Alexander the Great.

ḌUBĀʿA. A Companion of the Prophet.

EPHRAIM. See the entry for Zuleikha.

FĀṬIMA (d. 11 [632]). The youngest of the daughters of the Prophet, who once told her, 'God is angry when you are angry, and glad when you are glad.' In the year 2/623-4 she married ʿAlī b. Abī Ṭālib in the union which was to produce al-Ḥasan and al-Ḥusayn. Her piety made her greatly revered by later generations. (*Disciplining*, 215.)

FAYRŪZ AL-DAYLAMĪ (d. 23-35 [644–56]). A Persian Muslim commander who defeated the false prophet ʿAnsī.

FINḤĀṢ B. ʿĀZŪRĀʾ. A Medinan Jewish leader.

AL-GHAZĀLĪ, ĀBŪ ḤAMID (d. 504-5 [1111]). The great Persian polymath, known as *Ḥujjat al-Islām*, 'the Proof of Islam.' In his magnum opus, *The Revival of Religious Sciences* (*Iḥyāʾ ʿulūm al-dīn*), he sought to revitalise the Islamic faith and practice by bridging the gap between jurisprudence, theology and mysticism, and reconnecting the faithful to the heart of the religion.

AL-ḤĀKIM AL-NĪSĀBŪRĪ (d. 497-8 [1014]). A major *ḥadīth* scholar of Khorasan.

ḤAMZA B. ʿABD AL-MUṬṬALIB (d. 3-4 [625]). The Companion and uncle of the Prophet, martyred at the Battle of Uḥud, after which the Prophet gave him the title, 'Master of Martyrs.'

HANNAH. Some exegetes identify Hannah as the mother of Mary, who vowed before her birth to dedicate her child to the Temple (see Q. 3:35).

HARAN. The brother of Abraham.

ḤĀRITH B. HISHĀM (d. 18 [639]). A Companion of the Prophet who fought against the Muslims at Badr and Uḥud but converted at the Conquest of Mecca.

ḤĀRITH B. SUWAYD. A Companion of the Prophet, who apostatised for a time and then returned to the fold.

AL-ḤASAN B. ʿALĪ B. ABĪ ṬĀLIB (d. 49 [669]). The grandson of the Prophet, son of ʿAlī and Fāṭima, dearly beloved to the Prophet and revered by Sunnis and Shi'ites alike.

AL-ḤASAN AL-BAṢRĪ (d. 110 [728]). Perhaps the best known personality among the second generation of Muslims, he was born in Medina and took part in the conquest of eastern Iran. He then moved to Basra, where his sanctity and eloquence attracted great numbers to his circle. He was also a judge and an authority on *ḥadīth*. His tomb at Basra remains an important centre for devout visits. (*Disciplining*, 215.)

ḤĀTIM AL-ṬĀʾĪ. A pre-Islamic Arab famed for his generosity.

ḤUDHAYFA B. AL-YAMĀN (d. 36 [657]). A Companion and close confidant of the Prophet.

AL-ḤUSAYN B. ʿALĪ B. ABĪ ṬĀLIB (d. 61 [680]). A grandson of the Prophet, who, although he acquiesced in the Caliphate of Muʿāwiya, refused to recognise his son al-Yazīd upon his accession in 60/680. Against the advice of Ibn ʿAbbās and ʿAbd Allāh b. ʿUmar, al-Ḥusayn marched with a handful of supporters to Kufa, where he believed that he could muster support. The Kufans, however, intimidated by al-Yazīd's governor, met him in battle at nearby Karbala, where he was slain. (*Remembrance*, 293–4)

IBN ᶜABBĀS (d. 68 [687–8]). A cousin and close Companion of the Prophet respected for his piety, and commonly acknowledged as the greatest scholar of the first generation of Muslims, the fifth most prolific narrator of *ḥadīth* amongst the Companions (with 1,660 traditions) and the founder of the science of Qur'ānic exegesis. (*Disciplining*, 216; Ṣiddīqī, *Ḥadīth Literature*, 18.)

IBN AL-AᶜRĀBĪ (d. 230-1 [845]). A leading grammarian of the Kufan school.

IBN AL-ḤĀJIB (d. 646-7 [1249]). An Egyptian jurist and linguist.

IBN ᶜAWF (d. 33-4 [654]). A Companion of the Prophet, one of the ten to whom he promised Paradise.

IBN ḤUDHĀFA. A Companion of the Prophet.

IBN KHUZAYMA (d. 310-11 [923]). A major *ḥadīth* scholar of Nishapur.

IBN MĀJA (d. 274-5 [887]). A major *ḥadīth* scholar, compiler of one of the six canonical collections of Sunni Islam.

IBN MĀLIK (d. 672-3 [1274]). An Andalusian grammarian.

IBN MASᶜŪD, ᶜAbd Allāh al-Hudhalī (d. 32-3 [652-3]). Of Bedouin origin, Ibn Masᶜūd is said to have been either the third or the sixth convert to Islam. He became one of the most erudite Companions. He was particularly well versed in the recitation and interpretation of the Qur'ān, and was an expert in matters of Law. His narration of 848 *ḥadīth* places him eighth on the list of Companion narrators. (*Disciplining*, 216; Ṣiddīqī, *Ḥadīth Literature*, 18.)

IBN AL-MUSAYYAB, Saᶜīd (d. 96-7 [715]). A major genealogist and legal expert of Medina, held by some to have been the most erudite of the second Muslim generation. He refused to marry his devout and learned daughter to the Caliph al-Walīd b. ᶜAbd al-Malik, for which he was flogged. (*Disciplining*, 220.)

IBN SALĀM, ᶜAbd Allāh (d. 42-3 [663]). A Jewish convert to Islam.

IBN UBAYY (d. 9-10 [631]). The chief of the Khazraj in Medina, known as the 'leader of the hypocrites.' (Lings, *Muhammad*, 322.)

IBN ᶜUMAR (d. 73 [693–4]). The son of ᶜUmar the second Caliph and a Companion of the Prophet. The second most prolific narrator of *ḥadīth* amongst the Companions, with 2,630 traditions, despite it being narrated that he was very cautious about transmitting. (*Disciplining*, 217; Ṣiddīqī, *Ḥadīth Literature*, 18 and 20.)

IBN AL-ZUBAYR (d. 72-3 [692]). A Companion of the Prophet who laid claim to the Caliphate in Mecca and was recognised by much of the Hejaz, in opposition to the Umayyads.

JABR AL-RŪMĪ. A Christian slave of ᶜĀmir b. al-Ḥaḍramī.

JADD B. QAYS. A chief of the Banū Salama tribe of Medina.

JAPHETH. One of the sons of Noah.

JAYSŪR. Said to be the name of the boy whom Khiḍr slew (Q. 18:74).

JU'DHAR. Apparently, a king of Persia or Babel (the name may be corrupted).

KAᶜB B. AL-ASHRAF (d. 2-3 [624]). A Jewish leader and poet of Medina, and a major opponent of the Prophet.

KAFASHṬAYṬŪSH. Said to be the name of one of the Sleepers in the Cave.

KANᶜĀN. The author identifies him as the son of Noah, but may be confusing him with Canaan son of Ham son of Noah.

KĀSHIḤ. Said to be the name of the father of the orphan boys of *Sūrat al-Kahf* (Q. 18:82).

KHĀLID B. SINĀN. A monotheistic sage of Arabia said to have lived a generation before the Year of the Elephant (around 570 CE), and considered a prophet by some.

KHĀLID B. AL-WALĪD (d. 21 [642]). The great Arab military commander who first fought against the Muslims, and then joined them and became a Companion.

KHIḌR, identified by the author as BALYĀ B. MALKĀN. The enigmatic figure encountered by Moses, as portrayed in *Sūrat al-Kahf*. He is held in Islamic tradition to be a saintly traveller who, having drunk from the water of life, will not die until the end of time. Until then, he wanders the world seeking people worthy of sharing his wisdom.

KISĀ'Ī (d.189 [805]). The founder of the Kufan school of grammar.

KORAH. He is named three times in the Qur'ān, and in two of them he is mentioned alongside Pharaoh and Haman as enemies of Moses. He mistreated people, sought to divide them and attributed his vast wealth to his own ability. His worldly end occurred with him being swallowed up by the earth. (Kaltner & Mirza, *The Bible and the Qur'an*, 105.)

LAZARUS. The man miraculously raised to life by Jesus, as told in John 11:1–44.

MAKTHALĪNĀ. Said to be the name of one of the Sleepers in the Cave.

MĀLIK B. ANAS (d. 179 [795]). The great jurist of Medina, eponymous founder of the Mālikī school, one of the four major schools of Sunni jurisprudence.

MARNŪSH. Said to be the name of one of the Sleepers in the Cave.

MEDAN. One of the sons of Abraham.

MIDIAN. One of the sons of Abraham.

MIQYAS B. ṢUBĀBA (d. 7-8 [629]). A Meccan who pretended to be Muslim in order to exact revenge on a Muslim who had accidentally killed his brother. (Guillaume, *Life,* 551 n. 1)

MISṬAḤ B. UTHĀTHA. A Companion of the Prophet who was involved in spreading the Calumny against ᶜĀ'isha.

MUᶜĀDH B. JABAL (d. 18 [639–40]). An early convert to Islam, he became well versed in *fiqh* in a short space of time. He was the Prophet's governor of the Yemen, and died in Syria. He narrated 157 *ḥadīth*. (*Remembrance*, 301; Ṣiddīqī, *Ḥadīth Literature*, 18.)

MUᶜĀWIYA B. ABĪ SUFYĀN (*regn.* 40-60 [661-80]). A Companion of the Prophet and first Caliph of the Umayyad dynasty.

MUJĀHID B. JABR (d. 104 [722-3]). A second-generation scholar and exegete.

MUṢᶜAB B. RAYYĀN. Said to be the name of the Egyptian Pharaoh in the time of Moses.

MUSAYLIMA (d. 10-11 [632]). The false prophet of Yamāma, where he was defeated by Khālid b. al-Walīd during the rule of Abū Bakr.

MUSLIM B. AL-ḤAJJĀJ (d. 261 [875]). The great *ḥadīth* scholar of Nishapur. His *Ṣaḥīḥ* is one of the six canonical collections of Sunni Islam, held to be second only to that of Bukhārī.

AL-MUṬṬALIB B. ABĪ RIFĀᶜA (or Wadāᶜa) AL-SAHMĪ. A Companion of the Prophet, who accepted Islam on the day of the Conquest of Mecca. He later passed away in Medina, where he resided. (Laknawī, on narrators in *Muwatta of Imam Muhammad*, 541.)

NAḌR B. AL-ḤĀRITH (d. 2-3 [624]). A pagan Arab satirist and early opponent of Islam.

NASĀ'Ī, Aḥmad b. Shuᶜayb (d. 915). A major *ḥadīth* scholar, compiler of one of the six canonical collections of Sunni Islam.

NEBUCHADNEZZAR (d. 562 BC). The Neo-Babylonian king.

NEGUS (d. 9-10 [631]). The Christian ruler of Abyssinia who gave shelter to Muslim emigrants in the early years of Islam.

NIMROD. In the genre of 'Stories of the Prophets', he is presented as a local ruler who had declared divinity and refused to accept Prophet Abraham's message of monotheism. His death is brought about during his attempt to fight God. (Kaltner & Mirza, *The Bible and the Qur'an*, 14.)

NUᶜAYM B. MASᶜŪD. A Companion of the Prophet and notable tribal leader.

Before his conversion, he was sent as an envoy to Medina by Abū Sufyān to exaggerate the numbers of the Meccan forces in order to strike fear into the Muslims (see the commentary above for Q. 3:173 and Q. 3:175). During the Battle of the Trench (5/626-7), he secretly came to the Prophet declaring his Islam; yet he maintained his faith in secrecy and then proceeded to work discord amongst the disbelieving forces, which led to them abandoning their assault on Medina and the Muslims. (Nadwi, *Prophet of Mercy*, 227–8.)

NUN. The father of the Biblical Joshua.

PHARAOH. The ruler of Egypt mentioned almost seventy-five times in the Qur'ān, mostly in relation to Moses and the latter's liberation of the Israelites from Pharaoh's tyrannical rule.

POTIPHAR. The Egyptian vizier who purchased Joseph as a slave.

QABAᶜTHARĪ. A Basran famed for his eloquence.

QUṢAYY B. KILĀB (d. 480 CE). A pre-Islamic king of Mecca.

QUSS B. SĀᶜIDA. A pre-Islamic Christian Arab famed for his eloquence.

QUṬRŪS. Said to be the name of one of the brothers mentioned in Q. 18:32.

RAYYĀN B. AL-WALĪD. Said to be the name of the Egyptian Pharaoh in the time of Joseph.

RĀZĪ, Fakhr al-Dīn, also cited as 'THE IMAM' (d. 420 [1209]). The Persian polymath, author of one of the most esteemed works of Qur'ānic exegesis in the Sunni tradition.

RAZĪN (d. 534-5 [1140]). An Andalusian *ḥadīth* compiler.

REUBEN. One of the brothers of Joseph.

RĪṬA BINT SAᶜD AL-QURASHIYYA. An eccentric woman of Mecca during the time of the Prophet.

SAKKĀKĪ (d. 626 [1229]). A Persian linguist.

SALMĀN AL-FĀRISĪ (d. 36 [656]). A Persian convert to Islam and Companion of the Prophet, greatly revered by Sunnis and by Shiᶜīs.

SHĀDHANŪSH. Said to be the name of one of the Sleepers in the Cave.

SHĀFIᶜĪ, Muḥammad d. Idrīs (d. 204 [820]). The great jurist from Gaza, eponymous founder of the Shāfiᶜī school, one of the four major schools of Sunni jurisprudence.

SĪBAWAYH (d. 175-6 [792]). The great master of the Basran school of grammar.

SUDDĪ (d. 127 [745]). The scholar and narrator of Kufa.

ṢUHAYB AL-RŪMĪ (d. 38 [658-9]). An Arab captured and enslaved by the Byzantines in his youth, who subsequently escaped and made for Mecca, where he converted to Islam. Quraysh held him captive and tortured him, but he managed to escape once more and emigrated to Medina.

SURĀQA B. MĀLIK AL-KINĀNĪ (d. 24-5 [645]). An early opponent of Islam who later became a Muslim and Companion of the Prophet.

ṢURAYM. Said to be the name of the other orphan boy in Q. 18:82.

TAMĪM AL-DĀRĪ (d. 40-41 [661]). A Christian convert to Islam and Companion of the Prophet.

ṬAYĀLISĪ (d. 204-5 [820]). A *ḥadīth* scholar of Iraq.

TERAH. The real name of Āzar, Abraham's father referred to at Q. 6:74.

THAʿLABA B. ḤĀṬIB. A Companion of the Prophet. The account given by the author regarding his fate is disputed, and most consider him a Companion in good standing and a veteran of Badr.

TIRMIDHĪ (d. 278-9 [892]). A major *ḥadīth* scholar of Khorasan, compiler of one of the six canonical collections of Sunni Islam. (Ṣiddīqī, *Ḥadīth Literature*, 38.)

ṬULAYḤA (d. 21 [642]). A false prophet of the Khuzayma tribe who was defeated by Khālid b. al-Walīd and later became Muslim.

ʿUMAR B. AL-KHAṬṬĀB (d. 23 [644]). One of the closest Companions of the Prophet, and the second Caliph after Abū Bakr. At first a fierce opponent of Islam, he later converted and became the religion's most ardent defender. He is recorded to have narrated 537 *ḥadīth*s, making him the tenth most prolific narrator from the Companions. (*Remembrance*, 293–4; Ṣiddīqī, *Ḥadīth Literature*, 18.)

ʿUTAYBA B. ABĪ LAHAB. Son of Abū Lahab, the Prophet's major rival in Mecca. He married the Prophet's daughter Umm Kulthūm in Mecca before the advent of his prophethood, but divorced her at his father's behest when the Prophet began to preach publicly. Unlike his brothers, he never converted to Islam, and is said to have been devoured by a lion in Syria.

ʿUTHMĀN B. ABĪ ṬALḤA. He was carrying the standard of the idolaters' army at the Battle of Uḥud, whereupon he was killed by Ḥamza b. ʿAbd al-Muṭṭalib. (Guillaume, *Life*, 377.)

ʿUTHMĀN B. ʿAFFĀN (*regn.* 23-35 [644-56]). A wealthy merchant who became a Muslim before the Emigration. He became known as 'Dhū al-Nūrayn'—'the man of the two lights'— because he married two of the Prophet's daughters: firstly Ruqayya, and then, after her death, Umm Kulthūm. He became Caliph after ʿUmar. During the latter years of his Caliphate, he was accused of nepotism, a charge which brought about his murder by a group of dissidents from Egypt, who besieged his house, it is said, for forty-nine days, and then stormed it and stabbed him to death while he was reading the Qur'ān. He is recorded to have narrated 146 *ḥadīths*. (*Remembrance*, 313–4; Ṣiddīqī, *Ḥadīth Literature*, 17.)

ʿUTHMĀN B. ṬALḤA. He converted to Islam upon the Conquest of Mecca. Prior to his conversion, he had responsibility for the keys of the Kaʿba; and the Prophet thereafter confirmed that he and his descendants would continue to be custodians of the keys. (Nadwi, *Prophet of Mercy*, 138 n. 1 and 294; Lings, *Muhammad*, 300.)

WĀBIṢA. A Companion of the Prophet.

WĀHILA. Said to be the name of the wife of Lot.

YAHŪDHĀ. Said to be the name of the other brother mentioned in Q. 18:32.

YAMLĪKHĀ. Said to be the name of one of the Sleepers in the Cave.

ZAJJĀJ (d. 310-11 [923]). An exegete and grammarian of Baghdad.

ZAMAKHSHARĪ (d. 538 [1143]). A major Persian exegete and theologian.

ZAYD B. ASLAM. A narrator of the second generation of Muslims.

ZULEIKHA. The wife of Potiphar who, though not mentioned by name in the Qur'ān, is said to have tried to seduce Joseph.

BIBLIOGRAPHY

Aṣfahānī, al-Rāghib al-, *al-Tafsīr*, Medina: Umm al-Qurā University Press, 1422 AH.

Brockelmann, C., *Geschichte der arabischen Litteratur*, 2nd ed., Leiden, 1943–1949; *Supplement*, Leiden, 1937–1942.

Guillaume, A., *The Life of Muhammad: A Translation of Ibn Isḥāq's Sīrat Rasūl Allāh*, Oxford: Oxford University Press, 1955.

Ghazālī, Abū Ḥāmid al-, *On Condemnation of Pride and Self-Admiration* (Book XXIX of *The Revival of the Religious Sciences*), translated by Mohammed Rustom, Cambridge: Islamic Texts Society, 2018.

——, *On Disciplining the Soul & On Breaking the Two Desires* (Books XXII & XXIII of *The Revival of the Religious Sciences*), translated by T. J. Winter, Cambridge: Islamic Texts Society, 1995, repr. 1997.

——, *The Remembrance of Death and the Afterlife* (Book XL of *The Revival of the Religious Sciences*), translated by T. J. Winter, Cambridge: Islamic Texts Society, 1989.

Jurjānī, ʿAlī b. Muḥammad al-, *al-Taʿrīfāt*, Beirut: Dār al-Fikr, 1997.

Kaltner, John and Younus Y. Mirza, *The Bible and the Qur'an: Biblical Figures in the Islamic Tradition*, London and New York: Bloomsbury, 2018.

Kāzarūnī, Nūr al-Dīn Aḥmad al-, *al-Ṣirāṭ al-mustaqīm*, ed. ʿAbd Allāh al-Shabrāwī, Cairo: Dār al-Risāla, 2017.

Lings, Martin, *Muhammad: His Life Based on the Earliest Sources*, Cambridge: Islamic Texts Society, 1983.

Marcinkowski, M. Ismail, *Measures and Weights in the Islamic World: An English Translation of Walther Hinz's Handbook "Islamische Masse und Gewichte"*, Kuala Lumpur: International Institute of Islamic Thought and Civilisation (ISTAC) & International Islamic University Malaysia (IIUM), 2003.

Makkī, Muḥammad al-, *Tuḥfat al-laṭā'if*, Beirut: Dār al-Kutub al-ʿIlmiyya, 1971.

Nadwi, Abul Hasan Ali, *Nabiyy-i Raḥmat*, trans. Mohiuddin Ahmad as *Prophet of Mercy*, London: Turath Publishing, 2014.

Nasr, Seyyed Hossein et al., eds, *The Study Quran: A New Translation and Commentary* (*SQ*), San Francisco: HarperOne, 2015.

Naysābūrī, Maḥmūd b. Abī al-Ḥasan al-, *Ījāz al-bayān ʿan maʿānī al-Qur'ān*, Riyadh: Maktabat al-Tawba, 1997.

Osman, Ghada, 'Pre-Islamic Arab Converts to Christianity in Mecca and Medina: An Investigation into the Arabic Sources', *The Muslim World*, vol. 95, January 2005, pp. 67–80.

Potter, David S., ed., *Companion to the Roman Empire*, Oxford: Blackwell, 2006.

Qūnawī, Ismaʿīl b. Muḥammad al-, *Ḥāshiyat al-Qūnawī ʿalā Tafsīr al-Bayḍāwī*, Beirut: Dār al-Kutub al-ʿIlmiyya, 2001.

Shafi, Muhammad, *Ma'ariful Qur'an: A Comprehensive Commentary on the Holy Quran*, trans. Muḥammad Shamīm et al., Karachi: Maktaba-Darul-Uloom Karachi, 1998–2004.

Shaybani, Muhammad ibn al-Hasan ash-, *The Muwatta of Imam Muhammad*, trans. Mohammed Abdurrahman et al., London: Turath Publishing, 2004.

Ṣiddīqī, Muḥammad Zubayr, *Ḥadīth Literature: Its Origins, Development & Special Features*, ed. Abdal Hakim Murad, Cambridge: Islamic Texts Society, 1993.

Suyūṭī, Jalāl al-Dīn al- & Jalāl al-Dīn al-Maḥallī, *Tafsīr al-Jalālayn*, Cairo: Dār al-Ḥadīth, n.d.

Ṭabarī, Abū Jaʿfar Muḥammad b. Jarīr al-, *Tārīkh al-rusul wa'l-mulūk: dhayl al-mudhayyal*, trans. Ella Landau-Tasseron as *The History of al-Ṭabarī: An Annotated Translation, Volume XXXIX: Biographies of the Prophet's Companions and Their Successors*, New York: SUNY Press, 1988.

Thomas, David & Alex Mallett, *Christian-Muslim Relations: A Biographical History*, Boston: Brill, 2013.

Zādah, Muḥyī al-Dīn Shaykh, *al-Ḥāshiya ʿalā Tafsīr al-Bayḍāwī*, Istanbul: Maktabat al-Ḥaqīqa, n.d.

INDEX

Aaron, 77, 161, 172, 206, 238, 240, 241, 242–3, 297, 299
abasement, 30, 111, 125, 243, 275
ᶜAbbās, 262, 268
the Abbasids, 56
Abel, 173–4
ablution, 195, 407; dry ablution, 68, 138, 168; *ḥadīth*, 138, 167, 168; The Table (Sūrat al-Mā'ida, Q. 5), 138, 167–9; see also purity
Abraham, 388, 407, 410; Abraham (Sūrat Ibrāhīm, Q. 14), 350–1; angels/guests visiting Abraham, 312–13, 357–8; The Bee (Sūrat al-Naḥl, Q. 16), 378; belt of, 332; Cattle (Sūrat al-Anᶜām, Q. 6), 205–206, 215, 220; The Cow (Sūrat al-Baqara, Q. 2), 43, 44–7, 79–80; creed of Abraham, 45, 46, 108, 154, 220, 326, 378; The Family of ᶜImrān (Sūrat Āl ᶜImrān Q. 3), 104, 108; as God's close friend, 154; *ḥadīth*, 16; as *ḥanīf*, 46, 104, 108, 154, 205, 220, 378; House of Abraham, 140; Hūd (Sūrat Hūd, Q. 11), 312–14, 357; intercession by, 313; Joseph (Sūrat Yūsuf, Q.12), 332, 334; Kaᶜba, 44, 108, 410; lawful food, 108; prayer, 284, 350–1; prophethood, 378; religion of Abraham, 104, 215; scriptures of Abraham, 58; shirt of, 334; sons of, 45, 313, 350, 357, 378; witnessing a revival, 81
Abraham (Sūrat Ibrāhīm, Q. 14): Abraham, 350–1; astray, 347, 349, 350; chastisement, 346, 347, 351; disbelievers, 347; forgiveness, 346; Garden, 348; guidance, 345, 347, 348; Ḥijr (Sūrat al-Ḥijr, Q. 15), 357–8; idolatry, 350, 351; as Meccan *sūra*, 44, 345; messengers, 345, 346–7, 351; Moses, 345–6; path, 345, 348; prayer, 349, 350–1; Prophet Muḥammad, 348, 349, 351; Qur'ān, 345, 352; Resurrection, 347, 348; Satan, 348; worship, 346–7, 351; *zakāt*, 349
abrogation (*naskh*), 40, 212, 343; Qur'ān: abrogated verses, 40, 57, 58, 60, 67, 88, 92, 109, 131, 136, 165, 176, 177, 204, 210, 262–3, 278, 293, 303, 353, 359, 375–6
abstinence, 27
Abū ᶜAlī, 167
Abū ᶜĀmir al-Rāhib, 283
Abū ᶜAmr, 391, 408
Abū ᶜAqīl al-Anṣārī, 277
Abū Bakr b. al-ᶜArabī, 264
Abū Bakr al-Ṣiddīq, 7, 56, 69, 84, 122, 178, 264, 277; Battle of

Badr, 254; Battle of Ḥunayn, 268; cave in Mount Thawr, 271; emigration from Mecca, 270–1
Abū al-Daḥdāḥ, 68
Abū Dā'ūd al-Sijistānī, 70
Abū Dharr, 55
Abū Ḥanīfa, 7, 42, 44, 48, 62, 69, 72, 75, 86, 114, 136, 167, 391
Abū Ḥayyān al-Andalusī: *Al-Baḥr al-muḥīt*, 325
Abū Hurayra, 148
Abū Jahl, 213, 259, 340
Abū Lahab, 15
Abū Lubāba, 256, 282
Abū Sufyān b. Ḥarb, 121, 266
Abū Sufyān b. al-Ḥārith, 268
Abū Ṭālib, 284, 388
Abū al-Yusr, 186
Abū Zayd Saᶜīd al-Anṣārī, 168
accountability, 72–3, 318, 356, 383; Cattle (Sūrat al-Anᶜām, Q. 6), 201, 204, 221, 383
action, 374; faith and, 13, 252–3; six stages of impulse that lead to, 74
ᶜĀd, 203, 232, 233, 276, 310, 311, 346, 406; First/Second ᶜĀd, 311
Adam, 63, 97, 127, 355; The Cow (Sūrat al-Baqara, Q. 2), 22, 23–5, 225; creation of, 102, 193, 223, 247, 355; expelled from the Garden, 25; The Family of ᶜImrān (Sūrat Āl ᶜImrān Q. 3), 102; forbidden tree in the Garden, 25, 224–5; The Heights (Sūrat al-Aᶜrāf, Q. 7), 25, 223, 224–5, 246; Ḥijr (Sūrat al-Ḥijr, Q. 15), 355–6; knowledge, 23–4; prophethood, 25; Satan and, 24, 223–5, 355–6, 389, 405
ᶜ*adhāb*, see chastisement
ᶜAdī b. Zayd, 189
adultery, 324, 374, 390; punishment for, 95, 131, 134, 175; stoning, 95, 131, 134, 170, 175, 176; Women (Sūrat al-Nisā', Q. 4), 131, 132, 134, 135; see also lewdness
age of ignorance, 51, 55, 63–4, 70–1, 85, 110, 118, 132, 133, 178
ᶜĀ'isha bint Abī Bakr, 69, 79, 88, 92, 112, 150, 160
Akhnas b. Shurayq, 64–5
ᶜAlī b. Abī Ṭālib, 84, 103, 133, 156, 264, 351, 401; *basmala*, 7–8; Battle of Badr, 254; Battle of Ḥunayn, 268; on retaliation, 56; *zakāt*, 179
the Alids, 56
the Amalekites, 27, 77, 240
ᶜAmalīq b. Lāwadh b. Sām, 27
Āmina, 284
ᶜĀmir b. al-Ḥaḍramī, 376
ᶜAmmār b. Yāsir, 65, 104, 213, 276, 376
ᶜAmr b. al-ᶜĀṣ al-Sahmī, 189
ᶜAmr b. al-Jamūḥ al-Anṣārī, 66
analogy (*qiyās*), 318, 337, 374
Anas b. Mālik, 7
angels, 22–3, 87, 230, 333; Abraham and, 312–13, 357–8; angel of death, 131, 149, 160, 203, 227; angelic messengers, 391; angels of chastisement, 365; archangels, 390; Battle of Badr, 113, 149, 253–4, 259; Battle of Ḥunayn, 268; cherubim, 391; disbelievers and, 208; divinity of, 162, 296, 388; dreams and, 322; earthly angels, 23; Garden,

341, 405; gnosis, 8, 23; guardian angels, 306; Hārūt and Mārūt, 39; heavenly angels, 23; as incorporeal substances, 23, 367; Isrāfīl, 205; Keepers of the Gardens, 405; knowledge of, 23–4; Michael, 24, 37, 254; Munkar and Nakīr, 349; Noble Scribes, 339; the ones-brought-near, 23, 251; perfection of, 23, 225; prayers and, 392; Prophet Muḥammad and, 271; prostration to Adam, 24, 223, 355, 389, 405; prostration to God, 367; Qur'ān, revelation of, 14; recording angels, 203; reinforced by God with a thousand angels, 113, 253–4; scribe-angels, 14; superiority of, 162, 390–1; testimony by, 94; see also Gabriel

angels, mention in Sūras: The Bee (Sūrat al-Naḥl, Q. 16), 361, 365, 367, 368; Cattle (Sūrat al-Anᶜām, Q. 6), 194–5, 199, 208, 211, 220; The Cave (Sūrat al-Kahf, Q. 18), 405; The Cow (Sūrat al-Baqara, Q. 2), 22–3, 42, 87; Ḥijr (Sūrat al-Ḥijr, Q. 15), 354, 355, 356, 358; The Night Journey (Sūrat al-Isrā', Q. 17), 388, 389, 390, 394; The Thunder (Sūrat al-Raᶜd, Q. 13), 338, 341

animals, 199, 367; apes, 31, 139, 179, 183, 191, 245; bats, 100; bees, 370; birds, 81, 120, 360, 361, 372; camels, 29, 82, 94, 108, 165, 187–8, 216–17, 228, 352, 355, 372; carrion, 54, 165, 185, 212, 213, 217, 295, 314, 377; cattle, 94, 153, 164–5, 215–16, 361–2, 369–70, 372; cow, sacrifice of, 31–2; dogs, 399, 400; fish, 186, 245, 363; game, 165, 166, 185, 186, 361; golden calf, 28–9, 36; Hereafter, 199; horses, 94; hunting, 165, 166–7, 185–6; scorpions, 373; she-camel, 233, 312, 359, 389; slaughter of, 165, 166; snakes, 25; swine, 31, 54, 139, 165, 179, 183, 191, 217, 377; wolves, 323

al-ᶜAnsī, 178

anthropomorphism, 91

Antichrist, 160

apostasy, 15, 47, 107, 110, 148, 152, 157, 178, 375, 389; Battle of Badr, 259

ᶜaql, see intellect

Arabic language, 12; Hejaz dialect, 370; Qur'ān and, 4, 12, 91, 321, 343, 376; *tafsīr* and, 4; *ta'wīl* and, 3

arbitration, 141–2; between husband and wife, 136

Aristotle, 410

arrogance, 35, 298, 348, 364, 365, 367; see also pride

ᶜarsh, see Throne

asceticism, 329, 383

Ashᶜarī school, 22, 25, 69, 178, 252–3, 391

al-ᶜĀshir, 100–101

ᶜĀshūrā', 57

Aṣmaᶜī, 128

Aṣram and Ṣuraym, 410

association (of any partner with God), 139, 153, 182, 191, 336;

The Bee (Sūrat al-Naḥl, Q. 16), 361, 363, 365, 368, 369, 373; Cattle (Sūrat al-Anᶜām, Q. 6), 197, 203, 205, 208, 209, 215, 218, 221; The Cave (Sūrat al-Kahf, Q. 18), 398–9, 405, 413; The Heights (Sūrat al-Aᶜrāf, Q. 7), 227, 249–50; Ḥijr (Sūrat al-Ḥijr, Q. 15), 360; jinn, 209; Jonah (Sūrat Yūnus, Q. 10), 289–90, 291, 296; The Night Journey (Sūrat al-Isrā', Q. 17), 384, 386, 388, 396; The Thunder (Sūrat al-Raᶜd, Q. 13), 342–3

astray: Abraham (Sūrat Ibrāhīm, Q. 14), 347, 349, 350; The Bee (Sūrat al-Naḥl, Q. 16), 366, 373; The Beginning of the Book (Sūrat al-Fātiḥa, Q. 1), 1, 10; Cattle (Sūrat al-Anᶜām, Q. 6), 199, 202, 204, 205, 211, 212, 213–14, 218; The Cow (Sūrat al-Baqara, Q. 2), 21, 41; The Heights (Sūrat al-Aᶜrāf, Q. 7), 222, 225–6, 228, 248, 249; Hūd (Sūrat Hūd, Q. 11), 306, 308; Repentance (Sūrat al-Tawba, Q. 9), 284; Satan, 225–6, 390

atheism, 15, 374

ᶜAttāb b. Asīd, 143

awe (of God), 9, 26, 243, 339, 368, 399

the Aws, 110, 261

Balaam, 247–8

Banū Asad, 112

Banū Ḥāritha, 112

Banū Hāshim, 147, 257

Banū Kināna, 259

Banū al-Mughīra, 349

Banū al-Muṭṭalib, 257

Banū al-Naḍīr, 35, 178

Banū al-Najjār, 148

Banū Umayya, 349

basmala, 264; The Beginning of the Book (Sūrat al-Fātiḥa, Q. 1), 7–8, 9; *ḥadīth*, 7

Baṭn al-Nakhl, 150

Battle of Badr, 76, 146, 147, 233, 266, 282, 360, 367; angels, 113, 253–4, 259; angels of death at, 149; apostasy at, 259; The Family of ᶜImrān (Sūrat Āl ᶜImrān Q. 3), 93–4, 113, 115, 119, 120; Gabriel, 254; martyrdom, 50–1; pebbles thrown at the enemy, 254, 256–7; prisoners of war, 262; Prophet Muḥammad, 258, 259; spoils of war, 252, 257; Spoils of War (Sūrat al-Anfāl, Q. 8), 253–5, 257, 258–9, 260, 262; victory at, 93–4, 113, 253, 257, 258

Battle of Ḥunayn, 255, 268

Battle of Khaybar, 134, 362

Battle of Uḥud, 144, 254, 272; defeat at, 115, 117; The Family of ᶜImrān (Sūrat Āl ᶜImrān Q. 3), 112, 113, 115, 116–18, 119–21; spoils of war, 116, 117, 118; Spoils of War (Sūrat al-Anfāl, Q. 8), 254, 257

Bayhaqī, 7–8

Bedouins, 280–2, 285

The Bee (Sūrat al-Naḥl, Q. 16), 387; Abraham, 378; angels, 361, 365, 367, 368; association, 361, 363, 365, 368, 369, 373; astray, 366,

373; the bee, 370; chastisement, 364, 369, 373, 376; covenant, 374–5; creation, 361–2, 372–3; creation, process of, 363, 366; disbelief, 376; disbelievers, 365, 368–9, 373; Emigration, 366, 376; Gabriel, 361, 375, 376; Garden, 362, 365, 369, 375; God's Oneness, 364, 367–8; Hell, 365, 373; Hereafter, 364, 368, 369, 376; idolatry, 364, 365–6, 371–2, 374; injustice, 374; justice, 374; lawful food, 362, 363, 370, 377; messengers, 364, 366–7, 373, 377; Prophet Muḥammad, 366–7, 373, 375, 379; provision, 362, 363, 371; Qur'ān, 373–4, 375–6, 378; the Quraysh, 366, 378; repentance, 378; Resurrection, 361, 364–5, 366; retaliation, 379; reward, 375; Satan, 369, 375; worship, 368, 374

begging, 82; refraining from, 63, 84

The Beginning of the Book (Sūrat al-Fātiḥa, Q. 1), 251, 359; *Allāh*, 7; 'amen', 10; astray, 1, 10; *basmala*, 7–8, 9; *bism Allāh*, 6–7; blessing, 6–7; Companions of the Prophet, 1; Day of Judgement, 1, 9; Divine Attributes, 9; Divine Names, 6–7, 9; family of the Prophet, 1; *fātiḥa* (beginning), 5; guidance, 10; *ḥadīth*, 6; Mother of the Book, 6, 11; names of the *sūra*, 5–6; nearness to God, 1; path, 1, 10; place of revelation of, 6; praise, 7, 8–9; Prophet Muḥammad, 1; prophets, 1, 10; worship, 9, 10; wrath, 1, 9, 10

believers: believer/disbeliever comparison, 307; Cattle (Sūrat al-Anᶜām, Q. 6), 201, 202, 213; The Cave (Sūrat al-Kahf, Q. 18), 402–403, 406, 413; The Cow (Sūrat al-Baqara, Q. 2), 65; faith in the hearts, 348, 349; The Family of ᶜImrān (Sūrat Āl ᶜImrān Q. 3), 96, 102, 119, 122; Gardens, 276, 280, 282, 284, 288, 402–403, 411, 413; goodness/felicity, 341–2; Hell, 125; People of the Book, 111; Repentance (Sūrat al-Tawba, Q. 9), 267, 276, 282, 284; Spoils of War (Sūrat al-Anfāl, Q. 8), 252; The Thunder (Sūrat al-Raᶜd, Q. 13), 339

Bilāl b. Rabāḥ, 65

blessing: The Beginning of the Book (Sūrat al-Fātiḥa, Q. 1), 6–7; blessing of existence, 144

bliss, 94, 120

body (human body): after death, 51; birthmarks, 334; face, 95, 110, 139, 229, 291, 352, 368; hands, 367, 391; resurrection of, 20; virtuous habits, 43

the Bridge, 352

Budayl, 189

al-Bukhārī, Muḥammad b. Ismāᶜīl, 283

the Byzantines, 272

Cain, 173–4

Caleb, 172

calendar, 401; see also months of the year

calumny, 132, 152, 159, 176, 328, 395
Cattle (Sūrat al-Anʿām, Q. 6), 18, 301, 304, 324, 385; Abraham, 205–206, 215, 220; accountability, 201, 204, 221, 383; angels, 194–5, 199, 208, 211, 220; association, 197, 203, 205, 208, 209, 215, 218, 221; astray, 199, 202, 204, 205, 211, 212, 213–14, 218; believers, 201, 202, 213; cattle, 215–17; chastisement, 200, 203, 213; creation, process of, 193, 204–205; disbelievers, 156–7, 194, 196–9, 200, 203, 211, 213; guidance, 213, 218; idolatry, 197, 199–200, 202, 204, 205–206, 207, 210–11, 215, 217–18, 366; Islam, 213–14; Jews, 207, 217, 219, 377; jinn, 209, 211, 214; lawful/unlawful food, 212–13, 217, 377; messengers, 195, 200, 201, 214, 218; monotheism, 206, 207, 208, 213; People of the Book, 207, 218, 219; praise to God, 193, 196, 200; Prophet Muḥammad, 194, 196, 198, 201, 202, 210, 212, 213; prophets, 206–207, 211; provision, 216, 218; punishment, 202, 204, 221; Qur'ān, 194, 201, 202, 203, 207, 210, 212, 219; Resurrection, 197, 214, 219; Satan, 204; sin, 201–202, 212, 218, 221; straight path, 199, 206, 214, 219, 220; submission, 199; 'there is no god except God', 210, 220; travelling, 195; trials, 200, 201, 221; *zakāt*, 216
causality, 221, 318, 336, 399
The Cave (Sūrat al-Kahf, Q. 18), 387; angels, 405; association, 398–9, 405, 413; believers, 402–403, 406, 413; chastisement, 404; Companions of the Cave/the Sleepers, 398–401; Dhū al-Qarnayn the Greater, 407, 410–12; disbelievers, 397, 403, 406, 412–13; Gardens, 402, 411, 413; Hell/Fire, 405; idolatry, 398, 413; Joshua, 406–408; Khiḍr, 30, 406–410; messengers, 406, 413; Moses, 406–407; prayer, 399; Prophet Muḥammad, 401, 406, 413; provision, 400; Qur'ān, 397, 406; Resurrection, 400, 403, 404; Satan, 24, 405; wealth, 402, 403, 404
celestial bodies, 124, 363; moon, 60, 205, 208, 230, 288, 337, 349, 362, 382; moon, cleaving of, 211; planets, 205; stars, 31, 209, 230, 354, 362, 363, 399; sun, 205, 208, 230, 288, 337, 349, 362, 367, 392, 399, 410
certainty, 319, 399; faith and, 252–3; meaning, 14
charity, see *zakāt*
chastisement (*ʿadhāb*): Abraham (Sūrat Ibrāhīm, Q. 14), 346, 347, 351; angels of chastisement, 365; The Bee (Sūrat al-Naḥl, Q. 16), 364, 369, 373, 376; Cattle (Sūrat al-Anʿām, Q. 6), 200, 203, 213; The Cave (Sūrat al-Kahf, Q. 18), 404; chastisement of the Hereafter, 44, 311, 317, 343, 392, 406; The Cow (Sūrat al-Baqara,

Q. 2), 15, 20, 52, 53, 54, 83, 346; The Family of ʿImrān (Sūrat Āl ʿImrān Q. 3), 93, 96, 102, 113, 121, 122–3; The Heights (Sūrat al-Aʿrāf, Q. 7), 228, 230, 232, 235, 346; Ḥijr (Sūrat al-Ḥijr, Q. 15), 357, 358, 359, 360; Hūd (Sūrat Hūd, Q. 11), 304, 306, 308, 311, 312, 314, 316–17, 319, 320; Jews, 36, 381; Jonah (Sūrat Yūnus, Q. 10), 293, 294, 296; meaning, 15; The Night Journey (Sūrat al-Isrā', Q. 17), 383, 388, 392, 394; Repentance (Sūrat al-Tawba, Q. 9), 265; Spoils of War (Sūrat al-Anfāl, Q. 8), 256–7, 259–60; The Thunder (Sūrat al-Raʿd, Q. 13), 338, 342, 343, 344; Women (Sūrat al-Nisā', Q. 4), 127, 140, 146; see also punishment

children, 273, 279–80, 404; financial provision from the father, 72; slaying of, 216, 218, 385; suckling, 72–3; as trial, 256; see also orphans

Children of Israel, 26; branching peoples of, 106–107; see also Jews

Christians, 396; astray, 10; baptism, 46; covenant, 170; The Cow (Sūrat al-Baqara, Q. 2), 30–1, 42, 43, 46–7, 49, 78; as disbelievers, 177, 182; Jacobites, 170, 171; Jesus and, 30–1, 42, 103, 104, 106, 162; praiseworthy traits, 183; sects of, 78, 170; The Table (Sūrat al-Mā'ida, Q. 5), 170–1, 181, 182, 183, 188; Trinity, 103, 162, 182; see also Gospel; Jesus; People of the Book

communities, 199, 200, 290, 346, 353, 374; community of Muḥammad, 88, 101, 183, 306, 333, 342, 373, 388; 'for every community there is a messenger', 294, 366, 373; to every community there is a Law, a path, and a way, 177; *ḥadīth*, 248; sister-community, 228

Companions of the Cave/the Sleepers, 398–401; dog of, 399, 400; names of, 401

Companions of the Prophet, 140, 145, 207, 260, 282, 342, 367, 386, 402; The Beginning of the Book (Sūrat al-Fātiḥa, Q. 1), 1; The Cow (Sūrat al-Baqara, Q. 2), 16, 87; exegesis by, 3, 22, 25; The Family of ʿImrān (Sūrat Āl ʿImrān Q. 3), 96; 'We hear and obey', 87, 169

compassion (*raḥma*), 72–3, 286, 322, 333–4, 360; the Compassionate, 7, 9, 83, 114, 342, 396; Divine Attribute, 7, 9, 33

concealment: by Jews, 47, 51, 54, 95, 104, 124, 170, 175; as sin of the heart, 87

consensus (*ijmāʿ*), 130, 153, 337; as valid legal proof, 47, 111, 248

contemplation, 91, 124–5, 164, 209, 363, 369

corruption (*fasād*), 279, 334, 341, 373; corruption of the best is worst, 392; corruption in religion, 262,

315; The Cow (Sūrat al-Baqara, Q. 2), 16, 21, 30, 51, 55, 64–5, 315; The Heights (Sūrat al-Aʿrāf, Q. 7), 231, 233, 234, 236, 238, 240; meaning, 16
covenant, 340; The Bee (Sūrat al-Naḥl, Q. 16), 374–5; break of, 341, 385; Christians, 170; The Cow (Sūrat al-Baqara, Q. 2), 21, 26, 44; discursive/situational covenant, 246–7; The Heights (Sūrat al-Aʿrāf, Q. 7), 236, 246–7; Jews, 31, 34–5, 37, 105, 124, 159, 169–70; The Table (Sūrat al-Māʾida, Q. 5), 164, 169–70, 181; The Thunder (Sūrat al-Raʿd, Q. 13), 340, 341; types of, 164
The Cow (Sūrat al-Baqara, Q. 2): Abraham, 43, 44–7, 79–80; Adam, 22, 23–5, 225; angels, 22–3, 42, 87; astray, 21, 41; *Āyat al-Kursī* (Q. 2:255), 5, 78–9; believers, 65; certainty, 14; chastisement, 15, 20, 52, 53, 54, 83, 346; Christians, 30–1, 42, 43, 46–7, 49, 78; Companions of the Prophet, 16, 87; corruption, 16, 21, 30, 51, 55, 64–5, 315; covenant, 21, 26, 44; cow, sacrifice of, 31–2; creation, process of, 19, 22, 246; disbelievers, 15–18, 20, 21, 37, 53–4, 65, 78, 79; divorce, 69–71, 72, 74–5; faith, 13, 55, 59, 79, 82, 87; fasting, 27, 57, 58; fighting, 60–1, 66–7; God-fearing, 12–13, 31; gratitude, 50, 54; guidance, 14, 21, 43; *ḥajj*, 43, 45, 51, 58, 60–4, 82; Hell, 53, 54; Hereafter, 12, 53, 54, 64, 65; human perfections, 55; hypocrisy, 15, 16, 17, 33, 64; idolatry, 15, 19, 52, 61, 67; inheritance and testaments, 56–7, 73, 75; intercession, 27, 79; Jews, 26, 27–37, 42–3, 46–7, 50, 51, 54, 65, 76–8; Kaʿba, 44–5, 48, 49, 50; lawful/unlawful food, 53, 54, 212, 213; lying, 16, 33; messengers, 78; Moses, 27–32, 35, 41, 46, 76, 78; nearness to/of God, 58–9, 120; obedience, 50, 53; patience, 27, 50, 51; People of the Book, 15, 41, 46–7, 49, 54–5; Pharaoh, 27–8, 30; piety, 55, 60, 63; prayer, 26, 27, 50, 55, 59, 64, 75; Prophet Muḥammad, 19, 26, 39–41, 45, 49, 50, 51, 65, 78, 79, 87; prophets, 46, 55, 66; provision, 13, 20, 29–30, 44, 63, 75; punishment, 19–20; purification, 46; *qibla*, 24, 42, 44, 47–50, 54–5, 75; Qurʾān, 14, 18, 19, 35, 40, 46, 50; Ramaḍān, 57–9; remembrance, 50, 63, 75; repentance, 25, 28; Resurrection, 20, 22, 27, 33, 37, 53, 80, 87, 121; retaliation, 55–6, 61; return to God, 51, 65; reward, 25, 27, 46, 51, 68, 82, 83, 85, 91, 94; Satan, 24–5, 53, 65, 79, 83; senses, seal on, 15, 18, 53–4; sexual intercourse, 59, 68, 69, 74; Solomon, 37, 275; sorcery, 37–9, 237; speech, 14; spending, 66, 67, 81–4;

submission, 45, 65, 75; Torah, 26, 28, 31, 33–7, 41, 47, 49, 51, 56, 58, 77, 81; trials, 51; wickedness, 21, 37, 63; women, 69–74; *zakāt*, 26, 34, 55, 78, 82–4, 85
creation: The Bee (Sūrat al-Naḥl, Q. 16), 361–2, 372–3; changing God's creation, 153–4; Divine ownership of, 41, 42, 79, 87, 114, 124, 155–6, 171, 192, 195, 368; God's favour through, 372–3; good hidden within, 8; kindness to all creation, 374; praise of God by, 386–7; signs in, 8–9, 52, 124, 288, 296, 335, 337–8, 362–3, 369, 372, 381; thriving of, 312
creation, process of, 124, 230, 287, 337, 354; Adam, creation of, 102, 193, 223, 247, 355; 'Be!' as command of creation, 42, 98, 102, 162, 205, 246, 366; The Bee (Sūrat al-Naḥl, Q. 16), 363, 366; Cattle (Sūrat al-Anʿām, Q. 6), 193, 204–205; The Cow (Sūrat al-Baqara, Q. 2), 19, 22, 246; 'the creation of the heavens and the earth is greater than the creation of people', 209; the Creator, 335, 340, 387; the Creator of all direction, 210; first creation, 226, 337; 'God created Adam and then laid His right hand onto his back…', 247; Hūd (Sūrat Hūd, Q. 11), 304; humankind, creation of, 91, 127, 193, 209, 223, 226, 249, 361, 387; jinn, creation of, 355; Jonah (Sūrat Yūnus, Q. 10), 287, 292; the Originator, 42, 195, 210, 335; plants, creation of, 209; The Thunder (Sūrat al-Raʿd, Q. 13), 337; void and water, 304
creed: creed of Abraham, 45, 46, 108, 154, 220, 326, 378; Islamic creed, 87; *milla*, 43, 45
the Cry, 29, 233, 276, 312, 316, 358–9
curse, 183, 311; *bahla*, 103; God's curse, 103, 135, 140, 229, 275; *laʿn*, 51; permission to, 107; upon Satan, 299, 356

Daniel, 381
Dārimī, 70
David, 77–8, 140, 161, 183, 206, 381, 388
al-Dawānī, Jalāl al-Dīn al-Kāzarūnī, 103
Dāwardān, Iraq, 76
Day of Judgement, 1, 9, 356
day of questioning, 223
Day of Resurrection, 39, 44, 51, 68, 108, 122, 192, 197, 213, 214, 220, 221, 228, 230, 282, 310, 369, 388–9
death: angel of death, 131, 149, 160, 203, 227; burying the dead, 114; as decreed by God, 116, 193, 231, 355; disbelievers, 208; dying/killing distinction, 116, 118, 120; dying as Muslims, 109, 138; dying in the Sacred Precincts, 108; dying in state of disbelief, 20, 52, 67, 107, 132, 161, 279, 284, 300; dying in submission, 335; human body after death,

51; mourning period, 75; people of Dāwardān, 76; restoring life to the dead, 32–3, 80–1, 96, 100–101, 190, 208, 231; as trial, 51; see also inheritance and testaments; killing
debts, 273; contracting a debt, 86–7; repayment of, 85, 105, 114; Sunna, 86, 87; 'a trust', 87
deception, 16, 38
Decius, 398, 400
desire (*irāda*), 301, 324, 328, 341, 360; meaning, 21
deviation (*jawr*), 92, 135, 214
Dhāt al-Riqāᶜ, 151
dhikr, see remembrance
Dhū al-Qarnayn the Greater, 407, 410–12
Dhū al-Qarnayn the Lesser of Greece (Alexander the Great), 407
dīn, see religion
disbelief, 21, 299, 376, 387; as absence of affirmation, 13; as absence of faith, 15; dying in state of disbelief, 20, 52, 67, 107, 132, 161, 279, 284, 300; meaning, 15; middle way between disbelief and faith, 158; sorcery and, 39; types of, 15
disbelievers: Abraham (Sūrat Ibrāhīm, Q. 14), 347; angels and, 208; astray, 10; The Bee (Sūrat al-Naḥl, Q. 16), 365, 368–9, 373; believer/disbeliever comparison, 307; Cattle (Sūrat al-Anᶜām, Q. 6), 156–7, 194, 196–9, 200, 203, 211, 213; The Cave (Sūrat al-Kahf, Q. 18), 397, 403, 406, 412–13; Christians, 177, 182; conversion to Islam, 136; The Cow (Sūrat al-Baqara, Q. 2), 15–18, 20, 21, 37, 53–4, 65, 78, 79; death of, 208; The Family of ᶜImrān (Sūrat Āl ᶜImrān Q. 3), 93, 95, 102, 107, 111–12, 118, 121–2, 126; fighting against, 151, 260, 261, 266, 268, 270, 271, 276, 286, 353, 359; forgiveness of, 277–9, 359; *ḥadīth*, 208; The Heights (Sūrat al-Aᶜrāf, Q. 7), 229–30, 251; Hell, 54, 114, 338, 353, 382; Hereafter, 53, 107; Ḥijr (Sūrat al-Ḥijr, Q. 15), 353–4, 358, 359–60; hypocrisy, 15, 112; Jews, 35–7, 101, 156; The Night Journey (Sūrat al-Isrā', Q. 17), 382, 388; as patrons, 96, 179, 329; People of the Book, 111, 184; repentance, 107; spending, 112; Spoils of War (Sūrat al-Anfāl, Q. 8), 254, 256, 260–1; The Table (Sūrat al-Mā'ida, Q. 5), 171, 175, 176, 179–80, 184; The Thunder (Sūrat al-Raᶜd, Q. 13), 338, 339–40, 341, 342, 344; usury, 114; wealth of, 126; Women (Sūrat al-Nisā', Q. 4), 156–7, 158, 161–2; *zakāt*, 78, 84, 107
disdain, 162–3, 183; disdain for the truth, 306
disobedience, 131, 275, 293; Jews, 30, 36; to messengers, 311
dispensations, 64, 138
divination, 67, 184

Divine Attributes, 82, 91, 92, 123, 248, 335, 380, 387; The Beginning of the Book (Sūrat al-Fātiḥa, Q. 1), 9; eternal nature of, 14; letters of the alphabet and, 11
Divine Attributes, list of: compassion, 7, 9, 33; divinity, 9; eternality, 91; forgiveness, 139, 153, 221, 334, 346, 378; freedom of volition, 8; goodness, 301; holiness, 380; independency, 82, 83, 155, 215, 296, 346; justice, 122–3, 311, 319; knowledge, 14, 23–4, 69, 78, 79, 96, 111, 124, 140, 161, 194, 202–203, 331–2, 339, 344, 385; lordship, 8, 9, 292, 306; majesty, 196, 203, 220, 230; mastery, 9; mercy, 7, 9, 25, 89, 107, 195, 201–202, 225, 262, 285, 295, 300, 328, 330, 333, 357, 378, 390; omnipotence, 52, 209, 231, 296; perfection, 7, 8, 97, 194; power, 78, 91, 95, 98–9, 124, 192, 296, 311, 355, 362–3, 368, 380, 387, 390; speech, 14; transcendence, 21, 23, 42, 78, 162, 209, 251, 336, 360, 380, 386; wisdom, 24, 43, 155, 231, 287, 368, 371, 413; see also God's Oneness
Divine Names, 380; The Beginning of the Book (Sūrat al-Fātiḥa, Q. 1), 6–7, 9; *bism Allāh*, 6–7; invoking God's Name, 166–7, 212–13, 215, 330, 374; letters of the alphabet and, 11; the Most Beautiful Names, 248, 396
Divine Names, list of: the All-Hearing, 69; the All-Wise, 42–3; *Allāh*, 7; the Avenger, 45; the Aware, 196, 205, 210; the Bringer-forth, 208; the Cleaver, 208; the Compassionate, 7, 9, 83, 114, 342, 396; the Creator, 335, 340, 387; the Creator of all direction, 210; the Dominant, 113, 208, 345; the Eternal, 90, 171; the Eternal Sustainer, 78–9; the Giver, 82; the Guardian, 330; the Hearer, 97, 182, 326, 350; the Hearing, 45, 212, 381, 386; the Helper, 104, 112, 117, 139, 335; the Holy, 35; the Knower, 24, 136, 332n1, 335; the Knower of the Unseen, 122–3, 339; the Living, 78, 90; the Lord, 106; Lord of all Worlds, 8; the Maker, 8, 28, 338; the Master, 9; Master of the Day of Judgement, 9; the Merciful, 7, 9, 25, 28, 45, 47, 51, 285; the Mighty, 95, 192, 208; the Most Merciful of the merciful, 334; the One, 340; the One Who best knows the Unseen, 123; the Originator, 42, 195, 210, 335; the Overwhelmer, 196, 352; the Patron of Favour, 89; the Powerful, 18; the Praised, 345, 346; the Protector, 79; the Proud, 82; the Relenting, 25, 28, 45, 51, 285; the Subjugator, 340; the Sublime, 79; the Supreme Name, 38, 90, 247; the Vanquisher, 196, 203; the Wise, 24, 91, 95, 113, 192, 335

divorce, 69, 70; annulment (*khulʿ*), 71; The Cow (Sūrat al-Baqara, Q. 2), 69–71, 72, 74–5; third pronouncement of, 70–1; 'with kindness'/'with honour', 70–1, 74–5; Women (Sūrat al-Nisā', Q. 4), 132, 155
doubt, 19, 81, 90, 102
dream (*ru'yā*), 258; angels and, 322; interpretation of, 321, 322, 326, 327–8, 335; Joseph (Sūrat Yūsuf, Q.12), 321–2, 326, 327–8, 333, 335; Prophet Muḥammad, 258, 380; Satan and, 258, 322; true dreams, 296, 321–2
Ḍubāʿa, 61

Egypt, 30, 143, 237, 238, 241, 298, 299, 395; Joseph (Sūrat Yūsuf, Q.12), 323–4, 325, 326, 329, 332, 333–5; Miṣr, 325; see also Pharaoh
Elias, 206
Elisha, 206
Emigration/the Emigrants, 6, 47, 125, 143, 149, 267, 268, 282, 302; Abū Bakr al-Ṣiddīq, 270–1; The Bee (Sūrat al-Naḥl; Q. 16), 366, 376; first Emigration, 262; importance of, 149; Prophet Muḥammad, 270–1; Spoils of War (Sūrat al-Anfāl, Q. 8), 256, 262
enmity: enmity with idolaters, 264; friendship between enemies, 96; Satan as enemy of humankind, 53, 224, 225, 226, 356, 388, 390
Enoch, 231
envy, 173, 322, 357; Jews, 36, 102, 105; People of the Book, 40, 49, 66, 95
error, 2, 88; difference between *sayyi'a* (evil) and *khaṭī'a* (error), 34; ignorance and, 79
ethics, 207, 374
Eve, 63, 127, 224, 249
evil, 187, 386; difference between *sayyi'a* (evil) and *khaṭī'a* (error), 34; evil deeds, 223; evil soul, 37; good and evil can be determined rationally, 223; good within, 9; *sharr*, 30; source of, 144; types of, 187; uttering evil out loud, 158
evil eye, 330
evildoers, 78, 368–9; being denied guidance, 10; reward for, 291
exegesis (*tafsīr*), 2; by Companions of the Prophet, 3, 22, 25; *ḥadīth* and, 3–4; known through transmission, 3; meaning of, 3; by Moses, 28; reason and, 4; seeking refuge with God before doing exegesis, 4; sources of, 4; subject of the art of, 4; *tafsīr/ta'wīl* distinction, 3–4
Expedition of Tabūk, 270, 271–2, 275, 276, 279, 282, 284
Ezekiel, 76
Ezra, 42, 80–1, 103, 104, 171, 209, 269

faculties, 21, 22, 27, 374
fairness, 219, 260, 385
faith (*īmān*): action and, 13, 252–3; affirmation and, 13, 75, 106, 107; certainty and, 252–3; The Cow (Sūrat al-Baqara, Q. 2),

13, 55, 59, 79, 82, 87; faith in the hearts, 348, 349; faith/religion distinction, 107; faith/submission distinction, 107; faith without God-fearing is not enough, 180; *ḥadīth*, 13; increase/decrease of, 252–3; meaning, 13; middle way between disbelief and faith, 158; miserliness and, 137; Spoils of War (Sūrat al-Anfāl, Q. 8), 252–3, 260
falsehood, 59–60, 119, 377, 406; differentiating truth from falsehood, 16, 28, 91, 256, 258; falsifying the Scriptures, 104, 105–106, 124, 126, 139, 175, 180, 244; *ḥanīf*: one who inclines away from falsehood, 205, 220, 378
family: family ties, 341, 347, 374; large family, 128
The Family of ʿImrān (Sūrat Āl ʿImrān, Q. 3): Abraham, 104, 108; Adam, 102; Battle of Badr, 93–4, 113, 115, 119, 120; Battle of Uḥud, 112, 113, 115, 116–18, 119–21; believers, 96, 102, 119, 122; chastisement, 93, 96, 102, 113, 121, 122–3; disbelievers, 93, 95, 102, 107, 111–12, 118, 121–2, 126; Family of ʿImrān, 97; Garden, 94, 98, 114, 115; God-fearing, 13, 109, 115, 117, 126; God's Oneness, 101, 104, 124; Gospel, 91, 100, 101, 104; Hannah, mother of Mary, 97–8; Hell/Fire, 96, 114, 125; human body after death, 51; intercession, 100, 125; Islam, 104, 107, 109–10, 116, 117; Jesus, 98, 99–103; Jews, 27, 93, 95–6, 100–101, 102, 104–105, 109, 124; John, 98; lust, 94; Mary, mother of Jesus, 97–8, 99–100, 102, 103; obedience, 97, 99, 107, 119, 125, 126; patience, 117, 118, 124, 126; People of the Book, 103–107, 109, 111, 126; piety, 107–108, 110; prayer, 99, 103, 105, 111; Prophet Muḥammad, 92–3, 95, 96, 99, 104–107, 109, 111, 116, 117–18, 123, 125; Qur'ān, 90–3, 105, 107, 109, 111, 119, 125, 126; religion, 95, 102, 104, 106, 109; remembrance, 99, 124, 126; Resurrection, 92, 120, 121, 125; Satan, 98; submission, 95, 107; 'there is no god except God', 90, 91, 94–5, 103; Torah, 91, 95, 99, 100, 101, 104, 105–106, 108, 124; travelling, 115, 195; trials, 124, 126; worship, 91, 101, 103; Zachariah, 98–9
famine, 51, 238, 328, 329, 333, 395
Farewell Pilgrimage, 166, 265
fasād, see corruption
fasting, 240, 284; The Cow (Sūrat al-Baqara, Q. 2), 27, 57, 58; as expiation, 184, 186; Ramaḍān, 57, 58, 404; redemption by feeding a poor person, 57; Sunna, 59; while travelling, 57, 58
Fāṭima, 103
favouring, 10; gifted/acquired favour, 10; worldly/other-worldly favour, 10

Fayrūz al-Daylamī, 178
fighting (*jihād*), 60, 65, 126, 142–3, 210; against disbelievers, 151, 260, 261, 266, 268, 270, 271, 276, 286, 353, 359; against idolaters, 67; armours, 151, 299, 373; The Cow (Sūrat al-Baqara, Q. 2), 60–1, 66–7; drowsiness during, 118; Jews, 76–7; praying during war (prayer of peril), 150–1, 169; prisoners of war, 261, 262; ransoms, 261–2; Repentance (Sūrat al-Tawba, Q. 9), 67, 266, 268, 270, 271–2, 276, 279–81, 285, 286; spending in, 61, 281; staying behind instead of going out to war, 149, 270, 271–2, 279–81, 285; Sword Verse, 67, 265, 293; Women (Sūrat al-Nisāʾ, Q. 4), 142–4, 146, 147, 148–9, 150–1; see also Battle of Badr; Battle of Uḥud; spoils of war
Finḥāṣ b. ʿĀzūrāʾ, 105, 122
fiqh, 4, 209
fisq, see wickedness
Followers, 274
food and drinks: The Bee (Sūrat al-Naḥl, Q. 16), 362, 363, 370, 377; camel, 108; carrion, 54, 165, 185, 212, 213, 217, 295, 314, 377; Cattle (Sūrat al-Anʿām, Q. 6), 212–13, 217, 377; The Cow (Sūrat al-Baqara, Q. 2), 53, 54, 212, 213; excess of, 53, 226; fish, 363; forbidden food, 53, 54, 108, 165–6, 176, 184, 212, 217, 362, 377; *ḥadīth*, 362; horseflesh, 362; invoking God's Name on, 166–7, 212–13, 215; lawful food, 53, 54, 108, 164–5, 166–7, 184, 212–13, 362, 363, 370, 377; luxuries in, 361; milk, 108, 362, 369–70; Sunna, 377; swine, 108, 165, 217, 377; The Table (Sūrat al-Māʾida, Q. 5), 164–7, 176, 184, 185–6; wine, 67, 138, 184, 185, 204, 370
the forbidden, 165–6, 184–5; forbidden food and drinks, 53, 54, 108, 165–6, 176, 184, 212, 217, 362, 377; forbidden marriages, 132–3; reasons for being forbidden, 160
forgiveness, 252; as aspect of good character, 250; conditional upon obedience and abstinence from sin, 346; of disbelievers, 277–9, 359; Divine Attribute, 139, 153, 221, 334, 346, 378; of idolaters, 284, 350; praying for, 115, 119, 257, 277–9, 284, 310, 334; Prophet Muḥammad, 252
free will, 144–5, 146, 293, 402
the Freeze (*Zamharīr*), 317
friendship: Abraham as God's close friend, 154; between believers and disbelievers, 112, 156–7, 318–19; between believers and Hypocrites, 281; between believers and People of the Book, 178; between enemies, 96; God's friends, 295–6; *khulla* (close friendship), 154

Gabriel (*Jibrīl*), 24, 37, 242, 299, 314, 316, 358; Battle of Badr, 254; The Bee (Sūrat al-Naḥl,

Q. 16), 361, 375, 376; 'I seek refuge with God from Satan the accursed', 375; Jesus and, 35, 190; Joseph (Sūrat Yūsuf, Q.12), 324, 328; Mary and, 99–100, 162; Prophet Muḥammad and, 195–5; Qur'ān, revelation of, 14, 376; Torah and, 31; Zachariah and, 98
gambling, 67, 184
games of chance, 184–5
Garden(s), 40, 94, 114, 141, 192, 296; Abraham (Sūrat Ibrāhīm, Q. 14), 348; Adam, expelled from the Garden/fall, 25; ᶜAdn (Eden), 20, 341; angels, 341, 405; barrier between the Garden and the Fire, 229; The Bee (Sūrat al-Naḥl, Q. 16), 362, 365, 369, 375; believers, 276, 280, 282, 284, 288, 402–403, 411, 413; The Cave (Sūrat al-Kahf, Q. 18), 402, 411, 413; Dār al-Khuld (the Abode of Eternity), 20; Dār al-Salām (the Abode of Peace), 20, 121, 214, 291; divine mercy and admission into, 110; The Family of ᶜImrān (Sūrat Āl ᶜImrān Q. 3), 94, 98, 114, 115; Firdaws (Paradise), 20, 413; forbidden tree, 25, 224–5; *ḥadīth*, 20, 50, 247, 365; The Heights (Sūrat al-Aᶜrāf, Q. 7), 223–5, 228–30; Ḥijr (Sūrat al-Ḥijr, Q. 15), 357; Hūd (Sūrat Hūd, Q. 11), 317, 318; ᶜIlliyyūn (the High Dwellings), 20; inhabitants of, 229–30, 247, 291, 306, 318, 341, 357; Jannat al-Ma'wā (the Garden of Refuge), 20; levels of, 357; martyrs, 120, 121; Naᶜīm (Bliss), 20; prayer in, 288; Presence of Holiness, 318; Satan, expulsion from the Garden, 223–4; testimony and entering the Garden, 220; The Thunder (Sūrat al-Raᶜd, Q. 13), 340, 341–2, 343; Ṭūbā, 342
Gathering, 146, 209, 214, 293, 351, 381, 404
al-Ghazālī, Abū Ḥāmid, 391
God: divine command, 31, 98, 217–18; Divine Essence, 7, 40, 84, 191, 201, 380; divine will, 8, 32, 42, 135, 170, 198, 217–18, 231, 311, 318, 388; 'God willing', 401, 408; God's love, 52–3; life of, 22; as origin of everything, 144; vision of, 210, 240–1, 291; see also Divine Attributes; Divine Names; God's Oneness
God-fearing (*taqwā*), 12, 357; The Cow (Sūrat al-Baqara, Q. 2), 12–13, 31; faith without God-fearing is not enough, 180; The Family of ᶜImrān (Sūrat Āl ᶜImrān Q. 3), 13, 109, 115, 117, 126; *ḥadīth*, 109; The Heights (Sūrat al-Aᶜrāf, Q. 7), 13, 250; levels of, 12–13
God's Oneness, 194, 249, 327, 335, 342; affirmation of, 52; The Bee (Sūrat al-Naḥl, Q. 16), 364, 367–8; The Family of ᶜImrān (Sūrat Āl ᶜImrān Q. 3), 101, 104, 124; the One, 340; The Table (Sūrat al-Mā'ida, Q. 5), 191–2
Gog and Magog, 411–12

Goliath, 76, 77–8, 381
good, 187, 386; calling people to good, 110; good deeds, 223; *khayr*, 30; refraining from good is worse than committing sin, 180; relative good, 30; reward for good deeds, 291, 303; source of, 144
Gospel, 26; The Family of ʿImrān (Sūrat Āl ʿImrān Q. 3), 91, 100, 101, 104; revelation of, 58; The Table (Sūrat al-Māʾida, Q. 5), 170, 177, 180, 181, 183, 190; see also Christians
gossip, 38, 272
grace, 53, 125, 144, 394; guidance and, 10; kindness to a sinner is grace, 123
gratitude, 8, 305; The Cow (Sūrat al-Baqara, Q. 2), 50, 54; see also thankfulness
Great Calamity, 26, 200, 227, 296
greeting, 146, 148, 288, 341, 357, 365
guidance, 145, 213; Abraham (Sūrat Ibrāhīm, Q. 14), 345, 347, 348; The Beginning of the Book (Sūrat al-Fātiḥa, Q. 1), 10; Cattle (Sūrat al-Anʿām, Q. 6), 213, 218; The Cow (Sūrat al-Baqara, Q. 2), 14, 21, 43; The Heights (Sūrat al-Aʿrāf, Q. 7), 248, 251; The Table (Sūrat al-Māʾida, Q. 5), 188; The Thunder (Sūrat al-Raʿd, Q. 13), 342, 343; types of, 10

ḥadīth: ablution, 138, 167, 168; Abraham, 16; ʿAlī b. Abī Ṭālib, 56; authentic *ḥadīth* (*ṣaḥīḥ*), 2; *basmala*, 7; Bedouins, 281; The Beginning of the Book (Sūrat al-Fātiḥa, Q. 1), 6; 'Beloved to me, of your world, are women and perfume; and… prayer', 109; community, 248; disbelievers, 208; dispensations, 64; exegesis and, 3–4; faith, 13; Gardens, 20, 50, 247, 365; 'God created Adam and then laid His right hand onto his back…', 247; God-fearing, 109; *ḥajj*, 61, 265; hypocrisy, 157–8; idolatry, 413; inheritance, 57, 131; intercession, 27, 146; interpretation, 92–3; lawful food, 362; marriage, 133; miserliness, 137; mosques, 283; Night Journey, 380; oaths, 184; piety, 110; prayer, 75; Qurʾān, 14, 92–3; retaliation, 176; Sacred Precincts, 108; *Ṣaḥīḥ* collections, 7, 61, 69–70, 362; sound *ḥadīth* (*ḥasan*), 2; testimony, 220, 246–7; 'Truly, we belong to God, and truly to Him we shall return', 333; 'Virtue means to worship God as though you see him…', 185; women, 69–70, 134
ḥajj (Greater Pilgrimage), 165, 186, 220, 360, 364, 404; The Cow (Sūrat al-Baqara, Q. 2), 43, 45, 51, 58, 60–4, 82; Day of ʿArafa/of Sacrifice, 62, 63, 166, 240, 241, 264–5; as duty, 61, 63, 109, 187; *ḥadīth*, 61, 265; ʿĪd, 64; ritual sacrifice, 61–2, 64; see also pilgrimage
al-Ḥajjāj b. Yūsuf, 278

al-Ḥākim al-Nīsābūrī, 3, 223, 381
ḥamd, see praise
Ḥamrā' al-Asad, 121
Ḥamza b. ᶜAbd al-Muṭṭalib, 213, 340
Ḥanafī school, 61, 69, 109, 138, 149–50, 157, 174, 184, 186, 338
Ḥanbalī school, 138
ḥanīf, 330; Abraham as, 46, 104, 108, 154, 205, 220, 378; as one who inclines away from falsehood, 205, 220, 378
Hannah, mother of Mary, 97
ḥaqīqa, see Reality
Haran, 206
Ḥārith b. Hishām, 259
Ḥārith b. Suwayd, 107
al-Ḥasan b. ᶜAlī, 103
al-Ḥasan al-Baṣrī, 24, 134, 202, 310
hastiness, 114
Ḥātim al-Ṭā'ī, 194
the Hawāzin, 268
health and illness, 383–4; infirmity and dementia, 370–1; Qur'ān as cure for ailments of religion and body, 392–3
heart, 304; blindness of, 391; distractions of, 12; expansion of, 213; faith as conviction in the heart, 13; hardening of, 33, 200; inner heart, 12; intuition, 386; seal on, 15, 280, 297, 376; universalities and, 8; veils on, 387
The Heights (Sūrat al-Aᶜrāf, Q. 7), 11, 21, 306; Adam, 25, 223, 224–5, 246; angels, 251; association, 227, 249–50; astray, 222, 225–6, 228, 248, 249; chastisement, 228, 230, 232, 235, 346; corruption, 231, 233, 234, 236, 238, 240; covenant, 236, 246–7; disbelievers, 229–30, 251; Garden, 223–5, 228–30; garments, 225, 226; God-fearing, 13, 250; guidance, 248, 251; the Heights, 229; Hell/Fire, 228, 229–30, 248; Hereafter, 123, 229; idolatry, 227–8, 232, 243, 247, 249–50; indecency, 226, 227, 383; Jews, 236–43, 244–6; messengers, 222–3, 227, 229, 231–5, 236; Moses, 236–43, 244, 247; Noah, 231–2; prayer, 226, 230–1, 246, 251; Prophet Muḥammad, 222, 233, 236, 243–4, 248; punishment, 222, 227, 228; *qibla*, 226; Qur'ān, 222, 230, 244, 250, 251; religion, 229, 230; Resurrection, 249; Satan, 223–6; scales, 223, 413; she-camel, 233, 312; testimony, 164, 246–7; Torah, 238, 240, 241, 242–3, 244, 245–6; *zakāt*, 243
Hell/Fire, 114, 125, 157; barrier between the Garden and the Fire, 229; The Bee (Sūrat al-Naḥl, Q. 16), 365, 373; believers, 125; The Cave (Sūrat al-Kahf, Q. 18), 405; The Cow (Sūrat al-Baqara, Q. 2), 53, 54; disbelievers, 54, 114, 338, 353, 382; exit from, 53, 96, 175, 317; The Family of ᶜImrān (Sūrat Āl ᶜImrān Q. 3), 96, 114, 125; gates of, 357, 365; The Heights (Sūrat al-Aᶜrāf, Q. 7), 228, 229–30, 248; Ḥijr (Sūrat al-Ḥijr, Q. 15),

353, 356–7; Hūd (Sūrat Hūd, Q. 11), 306, 317–18; hypocrites, 157, 275, 281; inhabitants of, 229–30, 247, 338, 357, 388; jinn, 248; levels of, 357; The Night Journey (Sūrat al-Isrāʾ, Q. 17), 382, 383; Satan, 224; The Thunder (Sūrat al-Raᶜd, Q. 13), 340; Women (Sūrat al-Nisāʾ, Q. 4), 129, 157
the Helpers, 281–2, 285
Hereafter: animals, 199; The Bee (Sūrat al-Naḥl, Q. 16), 364, 368, 369, 376; chastisement of the Hereafter, 44, 311, 317, 343, 392, 406; The Cow (Sūrat al-Baqara, Q. 2), 12, 53, 54, 64, 65; denial of, 368; disbelievers, 53, 107; The Heights (Sūrat al-Aᶜrāf, Q. 7), 123, 229; Hūd (Sūrat Hūd, Q. 11), 317–18; The Night Journey (Sūrat al-Isrāʾ, Q. 17), 383
heresy, 15, 16, 92, 110, 256
Ḥijr (Sūrat al-Ḥijr, Q. 15): Abraham, 357–8; Adam, 355–6; angels, 354, 355, 356, 358; association, 360; chastisement, 357, 358, 359, 360; disbelievers, 353–4, 358, 359–60; Gardens, 357; God-fearing, 357; Hell, 353, 356–7; Ḥijr, 359; Lot, 358–9; as Meccan *sūra*, 353, 360; messengers, 354, 359; Qurʾān, 353, 359–60; Satan, 355–6
ḥilm, see mindfulness
holiness, 61; Divine Attribute, 380; the Holy, 35; holy rites, 45, 63; Presence of Holiness, 318; *qaddasa* (to declare holy: 'to travel far upon the earth'), 380
Holy Spirit (*rūḥ al-qudus*), 35, 78, 182, 190, 376
hospitality, 114, 126, 409. 412, 413
the Hour, 33, 197, 199–200, 220, 249, 336, 359, 372, 400, 403
houses/homes, 372; entering from the rear, 60; as places of prayer, 298
Hūd, 232, 310–11, 311n1, 315
Hūd (Sūrat Hūd, Q. 11): Abraham, 312–14, 357; astray, 306, 308; believer/disbeliever comparison, 307; chastisement, 304, 306, 308, 311, 312, 314, 316–17, 319, 320; creation, process of, 304; Garden, 317, 318; Hell/Fire, 306, 317–18; Hereafter, 317–18; Hūd, 310–11, 315; idolatry, 305, 306, 312, 315, 316, 318, 319; intercession, 313; Lot, 313, 314, 315, 358; messengers, 311, 313, 319; Moses, 316, 318; Noah, 307–10, 315; obedience, 303, 312, 316, 319; patience, 310; prayer, 319; Prophet Muḥammad, 310; Qurʾān, 303, 304, 305, 306, 319; Resurrection, 304; Ṣāliḥ, 312, 315; Shuᶜayb, 315–16; Torah, 306; trust in God, 304, 305; virtue, 304, 305; worship, 303
Ḥudaybiya Treaty, 60, 61, 257, 262, 265–6
Ḥudhayfa b. al-Yamān, 104, 229, 274, 384
humankind, 23; human perfections, 55; individual fate, 382; life of, 22; man as an abstract of the divine presence, 8; man as an

abstract of the world, 8; man as a cosmos himself, 8; record of deeds, 391, 404; as a single body, 174; stages of life, 370–1; as superior to angels, 27
humility, 81, 125, 396; as praiseworthy trait, 183; in prayer, 44; prostration and, 29, 159, 335; wing of humility, 384
al-Ḥusayn b. ʿAlī, 103
hypocrisy/hypocrites: as absence of conviction, 13; The Cow (Sūrat al-Baqara, Q. 2), 15, 16, 17, 33, 64; disbelievers, 15, 112; *ḥadīth*, 157–8; Hell, 157, 275, 281; Hypocrites, 33, 116, 118, 120, 121, 141–2, 144, 146–7, 157, 175, 259, 271–2, 275–6, 281, 282, 286; repentance, 158; Repentance (Sūrat al-Tawba, Q. 9), 271–3, 275–6, 277, 279, 281, 282, 286; as sickness, 16

Iblīs, see Satan
Ibn ʿAbbās, 7, 11, 22, 24, 47, 61, 83, 93, 114, 124, 129–30, 132, 141, 173, 174, 186, 199, 213, 226, 242, 274, 281, 299, 324, 344, 364, 391, 399, 401, 405, 409
Ibn al-Aʿrābī, 128
Ibn ʿAwf, 277
Ibn al-Ḥājib, 346
Ibn Ḥanbal, Aḥmad, 48
Ibn Ḥudhāfa, 187
Ibn Khuzayma, 401
Ibn Māja, 70, 283
Ibn Mālik, 167
Ibn Masʿūd, ʿAbd Allāh al-Hudhalī, 118, 152
Ibn al-Musayyab, Saʿīd, 75
Ibn Salām, ʿAbd Allāh, 95, 105, 111, 126, 139, 170, 244, 300, 344, 395
Ibn Ubayy, 120, 146, 272, 277, 279
Ibn ʿUmar, 7, 42, 70
Ibn al-Zubayr, 7
idolatry/idolaters, 41, 42, 153; Abraham (Sūrat Ibrāhīm, Q. 14), 350, 351; The Bee (Sūrat al-Naḥl, Q. 16), 364, 365–6, 371–2, 374; Cattle (Sūrat al-Anʿām, Q. 6), 197, 199–200, 202, 204, 205–206, 207, 210–11, 215, 217–18, 366; The Cave (Sūrat al-Kahf, Q. 18), 398, 413; The Cow (Sūrat al-Baqara, Q. 2), 15, 19, 52, 61, 67; enmity with, 264; fighting against, 67; forgiveness of, 284, 350; *ḥadīth*, 413; The Heights (Sūrat al-Aʿrāf, Q. 7), 227–8, 232, 243, 247, 249–50; 'hidden idolatry' (*shirk khafī*), 413; Hūd (Sūrat Hūd, Q. 11), 305, 306, 312, 315, 316, 318, 319; Isāf and Nāʾila, 51; Jews, 28, 108, 140, 240, 242; Jews and the golden calf, 28–9, 36, 156, 159, 179, 182, 242–3; al-Jibt and al-Ṭāghūt, 140; Jonah (Sūrat Yūnus, Q. 10), 289, 290, 292, 294, 301; Joseph (Sūrat Yūsuf, Q.12), 336; al-Lāt and ʿUzzā, 267; marrying idolaters, 68; places of worship and, 266–7; protection of idolaters, 265; repentance, 243, 265; Repentance (Sūrat al-Tawba, Q. 9), 42, 265–7, 268, 284; sacrifice to idols, 165–6, 184, 377; Spoils of War (Sūrat al-Anfāl, Q. 8), 255, 257; The Table (Sūrat al-Māʾida, Q. 5),

165–6, 184, 175; The Thunder (Sūrat al-Raᶜd, Q. 13), 339
ijmāᶜ, see consensus
īmān, see faith
indecency, 27, 115, 226, 275; The Heights (Sūrat al-Aᶜrāf, Q. 7), 226, 227, 383; Satan's command to, 53, 390
ingratitude, 29, 137, 244, 346, 349, 350, 384, 390
inheritance and testaments, 262; The Cow (Sūrat al-Baqara, Q. 2), 56–7, 73, 75; *ḥadīth*, 57, 131; indirect heirs, 163; injustice with, 131; Spoils of War (Sūrat al-Anfāl, Q. 8), 262–3; The Table (Sūrat al-Mā'ida, Q. 5), 188–9; while travelling, 188–9; women, 129, 154; Women (Sūrat al-Nisā', Q. 4), 129–31, 136, 154, 163
injustice (*ẓulm*), 122–3, 135, 259, 346, 374; against our own soul, 135; inheritance, 131; as the worst kind of sin, 228
innate disposition, 79, 195, 223, 236, 376
insight, 53, 80, 94, 210, 293, 315, 391; Qur'ān, 210, 251
intellect (*ᶜaql*), 136, 138, 164; corruption of intellect at old age, 334; meaning, 26–7; sound intellect, 83, 93, 145, 306
intercession, 287; by Abraham, 313; The Cow (Sūrat al-Baqara, Q. 2), 27, 79; The Family of ᶜImrān (Sūrat Āl ᶜImrān Q. 3), 100, 125; *ḥadīth*, 27, 146; Hūd (Sūrat Hūd, Q. 11), 313; ranks can be raised by, 341; reward for, 146; station of general intercession, 392; The Thunder (Sūrat al-Raᶜd, Q. 13), 341; Women (Sūrat al-Nisā', Q. 4), 146
interpretation (*ta'wīl*), 322, 360; Arabic language and, 3; as based on personal opinion, 3–4; *ḥadīth*, 92–3; meaning of, 3, 326; *tafsīr/ta'wīl* distinction, 3–4
inward aspect, 4; God, Informed of the inward, 383; of harmony, 261; Khiḍr as sea of inward knowledge, 406; of punishment, 228; of sin, 212
inzāl, see revelation
irāda, see desire
Isaac, 45, 46, 106, 161, 206, 313, 322, 326, 350, 357
Isaiah, 381
Ishmael, 30, 44–5, 46, 106, 161, 173, 206, 226, 350
Islam, 107, 109, 166, 182, 295, 353, 374, 375; Cattle (Sūrat al-Anᶜām, Q. 6), 213–14; conversion from Islam to other religions, 104, 116, 117, 400; conversion to, 136, 273, 282; The Family of ᶜImrān (Sūrat Āl ᶜImrān Q. 3), 104, 107, 109–10, 116, 117; Islamic creed, 87; meaning of, 13
islām, see submission
istiḥsān, see juristic discretion

Jabr al-Rūmī, 376
Jabriyya sect, 144–5
Jacob, 46, 106, 108, 206, 313;

children of, 26, 46, 161, 244, 322; Joseph (Sūrat Yūsuf, Q.12), 321–3, 324, 326, 330, 333, 334, 335; Judaism, 45; Law of Jacob, 331
al-Jadd b. Qays, 272
jawr, see deviation
Jaysūr, 408–409
Jeremiah, 381
Jerusalem, 29, 244; Christians in, 41; Farthest Mosque, 380, 382; *qibla*, 47, 49, 105
Jesus (ʿĪsā), 35, 99, 139, 206, 292, 391; birth of, 354; Christians and, 30–1, 42, 103, 104, 106, 162; conception of, 91, 99, 100, 162; crucifixion and death, 159–60; disciples of (*Ḥawariyyūn*), 101, 190; divinity of, 171, 182, 191, 269, 300, 388; The Family of ʿImrān (Sūrat Āl ʿImrān Q. 3), 98, 99–103; Gabriel and, 35, 190; Holy Spirit (*rūḥ al-qudus*) and, 35, 78, 190; Jews and, 36, 100–101, 102, 156, 159, 162, 183; Jonah (Sūrat Yūnus, Q. 10), 300; knowledge, 100, 101, 190; as messenger, 100, 162; the Messiah, 99, 104, 159, 162, 171, 182, 269; miracles, 78, 81, 100–101, 190; Night of Ordainment (*laylat al-qadr*), 101–102; Prophet Muḥammad and, 170, 171; prophethood, 99, 100, 102, 106, 191; raised up by God, 101–102, 159, 160, 190, 191; as 'son of God', 159, 162, 182, 209, 269; speech, 100; The Table (Sūrat al-Mā'ida, Q. 5), 171, 177, 190–2; untouched by Satan, 98; Women (Sūrat al-Nisā', Q. 4), 159–60, 162; see also Christians
Jews, 25; the Ark, 77; chastisement, 36, 381; concealment by, 47, 51, 54, 95, 104, 124, 170, 175; covenant, 31, 34–5, 37, 105, 124, 159, 169–70; as disbelievers, 35–7, 101, 156; disobedience, 30, 36; envy, 36, 102, 105; fighting, 76–7; golden calf, 28–9, 36, 156, 159, 179, 182, 242–3; Hebrew, 40; Holy Land, 172; idolatry, 28, 108, 140, 240, 242; ingratitude, 29, 244; Jesus and, 36, 100–101, 102, 156, 159, 162, 183; Judah, 31, 76; manna and quails, 29, 30, 244; prayer, 26, 34; Prophet Muḥammad and, 35, 36, 37, 40, 104–106, 180, 382; Qur'ān and, 36; remembrance, 50; Sabbath, 31, 159, 179, 183, 245, 378, 395; sexual intercourse, 68; transformed into apes and swine, 31, 139, 179, 183, 191, 245; transgression by, 30, 31, 179, 183, 245; tribes, 30, 169, 244; wrath against, 10, 29, 30, 242, 243; see also Children of Israel; Judaism; People of the Book; Torah
Jews: mention in Sūras: Cattle (Sūrat al-Anʿām, Q. 6), 207, 217, 219, 377; The Cow (Sūrat al-Baqara, Q. 2), 26, 27–37, 42–3, 46–7, 50, 51, 54, 65, 76–8; The Family of ʿImrān (Sūrat Āl ʿImrān Q. 3), 27, 93, 95–6, 100–101, 102, 104–105, 109, 124;

The Heights (Sūrat al-Aʿrāf, Q. 7), 236–43, 244–6; Jonah (Sūrat Yūnus, Q. 10), 299–300; The Night Journey (Sūrat al-Isrā', Q. 17), 381, 382, 395, 396; Repentance (Sūrat al-Tawba, Q. 9), 269; The Table (Sūrat al-Mā'ida, Q. 5), 169–71, 175–6, 179–80, 183; Women (Sūrat al-Nisā', Q. 4), 139, 156, 159–60

jihād, see fighting; struggle

jinn, 23, 248, 367; Cattle (Sūrat al-Anʿām, Q. 6), 209, 211, 214; creation of, 355; rebellious jinn, 4, 211, 319; Satan and, 24, 355, 405; seeking refuge from, 4

Job, 161, 206

John, 30, 35, 98, 206, 313, 381

Jonah, 161, 206, 300

Jonah (Sūrat Yūnus, Q. 10): association, 289–90, 291, 296; chastisement, 293, 294, 296; creation, process of, 287, 292; idolatry, 289, 290, 292, 294, 301; Jesus, 300; Jews, 299–300; Jonah, 300; messengers, 289, 293, 294, 297; Moses, 297–9; Noah, 297; obedience, 302; Prophet Muḥammad, 289, 290, 300; Qur'ān, 289, 292–3, 295, 301; Resurrection, 288, 293; reward for good deeds and evildoers, 291

Joseph, 206; beauty of, 325; burial place of, 335; casting into the well, 323, 335; death of, 335; dreams, 321–2, 326, 327–8, 333, 335; imprisonment, 326–7; Joseph (Sūrat Yūsuf, Q.12), 321–35, 336; married to Zuleikha, 329; prophethood and kingship, 322, 324, 334; scent of, 334; shirt of, 325, 334; sold at low price, 323

Joseph (Sūrat Yūsuf, Q.12): Abraham, 332, 334; association, 326; Benjamin, 322, 329, 330–2; desire, 324, 328; dreams, 321–2, 326, 327–8, 333, 335; Egypt, 323–4, 325, 326, 329, 332, 333–5; envy, 322; Gabriel, 324, 328; goblet, 331; idolatry, 336; Jacob, 321–3, 324, 326, 330, 333, 334, 335; Joseph, 321–35, 336; Joseph's half-brothers, 322–3, 329–35, 336; Joseph's parents, 334–5; king's cup-bearer and baker, 326–7, 328; knowledge, 331–2; patience, 323, 333, 334; Potiphar the vizier, 324, 326, 327, 328, 329; prayer, 326, 335; Prophet Muḥammad, 335; Qur'ān, 321, 336; Rayyān b. al-Walīd, Pharaoh, 327–8; Satan, 327, 335; submission, 335; worship, 326–7; Zuleikha, 324–6, 328, 329; see also Joseph

Joseph's half-brothers, 322–3, 329–32; Judah, 322, 332, 334; Reuben, 332; Simeon, 329, 332

Joshua, 29, 76–7, 172, 406–408

Judaism, 45, 104, 105; see also Jews

Ju'dhar, 382

juristic discretion (*istiḥsān*), 318

justice, 155, 287–8, 315, 374; Divine Attribute, 122–3, 311, 319

Kaᶜb b. al-Ashraf, 141
Kaᶜba, 2, 166, 186; Abraham and, 44, 108, 410; circumambulation, 51, 226–7, 410; The Cow (Sūrat al-Baqara, Q. 2), 44–5, 48, 49, 50; custodianship of, 141, 257; as place of prayer, 44; praying obligatory prayers inside the Kaᶜba, 48–9; as *qibla*, 48, 49, 50, 105; stone, 108; see also pilgrimage
Kanᶜān, 308–10
Karrāmiyya school, 32
Kāshiḥ, 410
al-Kāzarūnī, Nūr al-Dīn Aḥmad b. Muḥammad, 1, 2
Khālid b. Sinān, 171
Khālid b. al-Walīd, 178
khalīfa, see vicegerent
the Khawārij, 13, 110
the Khazraj, 110, 261
Khiḍr (Balyā b. Malkān), 80, 406–10; knowledge of Unseen matters, 407
killing, 346; between believers, 147, 148; Cain and Abel, 173–4; of children, 216, 218, 385; of disbelievers, 174; dying/killing distinction, 116, 118, 120; exceptions to the prohibition of, 385; of messengers, 35, 123, 181, 381; of prophets, 30, 36, 95, 116, 122, 239; punishment for, 174; in self-defence, 385; Sunna, 186
Kināna and Khuzāᶜa tribes, 368
kindness, 136–7, 411; to all creation, 374; divorce 'with kindness', 70–1, 74–5; kindness to a sinner is grace, 123; to parents, 136, 218, 384; towards women, 132
al-Kisā'ī, 128
knowledge, 164, 372; Adam's knowledge, 23–4; angels' knowledge, 23–4; Divine Attribute, 14, 23–4, 69, 78, 79, 96, 111, 124, 140, 161, 194, 202–203, 331–2, 339, 344, 385; Jesus' knowledge, 100, 101, 190; Joseph (Sūrat Yūsuf, Q.12), 331–2; the Knower, 24, 136, 332n1, 335; obligation to consult the learned, 366
Korah, 367

languages, 23; Hebrew, 40; messengers and, 345; see also Arabic language
Law (Divine Law, *sharīᶜa*), 45, 107, 126, 164; God-fearing, 12; legal edicts (*al-aḥkām al-sharᶜiyya*), 4; pilgrimage, 51; practical laws, 177
the lawful, 166, 184; lawful food and drinks, 53, 54, 108, 164–5, 166–7, 184, 212–13, 362, 363, 370, 377
laylat al-qadr, see Night of Ordainment
Lazarus, 100
letters (of the alphabet), 11–12; *Alif*, 11, 90, 222, 287, 303, 321, 337, 345, 353; *ᶜAyn*, 11; *Dāl*, 392; Divine Attributes and, 11; Divine Names and, 11; *Hā*, 11; *Kāf*, 11; *Lām*, 11, 90, 222, 287, 303, 321, 337, 345, 353, 392; *Mīm*, 11, 90, 222, 337;

Nūn, 11; *Qāf*, 11; *Rā*, 11, 287, 303, 321, 345, 353; *Ṣād*, 11, 222; *Sīn*, 11; single, duals, triplets, quadruplets, quintuplets combinations, 12; speech and, 11; *Ṭā*, 11; *Yā*, 11

lewdness, 27, 63, 218, 270, 271, 374; see also adultery

Lot, 206, 222, 234, 276; Ḥijr (Sūrat al-Ḥijr, Q. 15), 358–9; Hūd (Sūrat Hūd, Q. 11), 313, 314, 315, 358

love (*maḥabba*): God's love, 52–3; *khulla* (close friendship), 154; love for God, 52, 55, 97; meaning, 52, 97

lust (*shahwa*), 94

lying, 397; The Cow (Sūrat al-Baqara, Q. 2), 16, 33; meaning, 16

Magians, 31, 268, 357, 396

maḥabba, see love

Mālik b. Anas, 7, 42, 48, 56, 70, 87, 134, 167, 186, 213, 338, 363; on pilgrimage, 61, 62–3, 109

Mālikī school, 138

marriage: debarring a marriage, 72; forbidden marriages, 132–3; *ḥadīth*, 133; marrying idolaters, 68; marrying more than one woman, 128, 155; marrying women from People of the Book, 68, 167; marrying women previously married to men's own fathers, 132; slaves, 133, 134; waiting period, 74; widows, 127; Women (Sūrat al-Nisā', Q. 4), 127–8, 132–4, 155

martyrs/martyrdom, 50–1, 115, 116, 120–1, 142, 272

Mary, mother of Jesus, 159, 182, 191; The Family of ʿImrān (Sūrat Āl ʿImrān Q. 3), 97–8, 99–100, 102, 103; Gabriel and, 99–100, 162; untouched by Satan, 98

materialism, 15

meaning: 'allegorical' (*mu'awwal*), 92; 'ambivalent' (*mujmal*), 92; 'explicit' (*naṣṣ*), 92; 'literal' (*ẓāhir*), 92

Mecca, 41; Conquest of, 60, 143, 262, 267, 268, 380; first temple, 108; Qur'ān: Meccan chapters/verses, 6, 19, 44, 193, 222, 252, 287, 303, 321, 337, 345, 353, 360, 361, 362, 380, 397

Medan, 45

Medina, 282; Qur'ān: Medinan chapters/verses; 6, 11, 19, 48, 90, 127, 164, 222, 252, 264, 337, 380

mercy: Divine Attribute, 7, 9, 25, 89, 107, 195, 201–202, 225, 262, 285, 295, 300, 328, 330, 333, 357, 378, 390; divine mercy and admission into the Garden, 110; the Merciful, 7, 9, 25, 28, 45, 47, 51, 285; the Most Merciful of the merciful, 334

messengers, 87, 161; Abraham (Sūrat Ibrāhīm, Q. 14), 345, 346–7, 351; angelic messengers, 391; The Bee (Sūrat al-Naḥl, Q. 16), 364, 366–7, 373, 377; Cattle (Sūrat al-Anʿām, Q. 6), 195, 200, 201, 214, 218; The Cave (Sūrat al-Kahf, Q. 18), 406, 413; The Cow (Sūrat al-Baqara,

Q. 2), 78; death of, 116; denial of, 123, 181, 198, 227, 289, 293, 294, 311, 336, 346, 354, 359, 364, 377, 383, 389, 413; disobedience to, 311; 'for every community there is a messenger', 294, 366, 373; guidance and, 10; The Heights (Sūrat al-Aʿrāf, Q. 7), 222–3, 227, 229, 231–5, 236; Ḥijr (Sūrat al-Ḥijr, Q. 15), 354, 359; Hūd (Sūrat Hūd, Q. 11), 311, 313, 319; Jonah (Sūrat Yūnus, Q. 10), 289, 293, 294, 297; messengerhood (*risāla*), 78, 97; The Night Journey (Sūrat al-Isrā', Q. 17), 381, 383, 389; sending of, 21, 214; signs given by God to, 81; slaying of, 35, 123, 181, 381; The Thunder (Sūrat al-Raʿd, Q. 13), 342, 343

'method of the sage' (*uslūb al-ḥakīm*), 247, 278

Midian, 45, 234

Minā, 64, 108

mindfulness (*ḥilm*), 16, 219, 319

Miqyas b. Ṣubāba, 148

miracles: Jesus, 78, 81, 100–101, 190; Moses, 29–30, 36, 236–7, 244, 297–8, 395; portent (*irhāṣ*), 38, 407; prophetic miracle (*muʿjiza*), 35, 36, 38–9, 78, 98, 123, 152, 159, 174, 190, 196, 197, 199, 200, 233, 234, 236–7, 269, 276, 297, 310, 311, 316, 326, 346, 354, 366, 389; Qur'ānic miracle (*al-muʿjiza al-Qur'āniyya*), 407; saintly miracle (*karāma*), 38, 39, 98, 99

miserliness, 122, 137, 140, 277, 385, 395

Misṭaḥ b. Uthātha, 69

monasticism, 374

monotheism, 271, 289, 326, 348, 368, 374, 384, 387; Cattle (Sūrat al-Anʿām, Q. 6), 206, 207, 208, 213

months of the year, 288; Dhū al-Ḥijja, 58, 62, 240, 270; Dhū al-Qaʿda, 57–8, 62, 240, 270; *ḥajj* and, 62–3; Jumādā months, 58, 66–7; Muḥarram, 58, 270; Rabīʿ months, 57, 58, 264; Rajab, 58, 66, 270; sacred months, 265, 270; Ṣafar, 58; Shaʿbān, 58; Shawwāl, 57, 62; *ʿumra*, 63; see also Ramaḍān

Moses, 76, 97, 206, 207, 219; Abraham (Sūrat Ibrāhīm, Q. 14), 345–6; The Cave (Sūrat al-Kahf, Q. 18), 406–407; The Cow (Sūrat al-Baqara, Q. 2), 27–32, 35, 41, 46, 76, 78; fasting, 240; The Heights (Sūrat al-Aʿrāf, Q. 7), 236–43, 244, 247; Hūd (Sūrat Hūd, Q. 11), 316, 318; Jonah (Sūrat Yūnus, Q. 10), 297–9; Joseph and, 335; miracles and signs, 29–30, 36, 236–7, 244, 297–8, 395; The Night Journey (Sūrat al-Isrā', Q. 17), 381, 388, 395; Pharaoh (Muṣʿab b. Rayyān), 27–8, 30, 236–9, 240, 297–9, 316; prayer of, 299; prophethood, 234, 239; as sea of outward knowledge, 406; spoken to by God, 78, 161; staff of, 77, 234, 236–7, 244, 395; The Table (Sūrat al-Mā'ida, Q. 5), 171–2; Ten Commandments, 395; Torah/Tablets and, 28, 35,

238, 240, 241, 242–3, 318, 408; vision of God, 240–1
mosques, 138; Aqṣā Mosque, 42; Farthest Mosque (Jerusalem), 380, 382; *ḥadīth*, 283; Qubā' mosque, 283; Sacred Mosque, 42, 44, 48, 49–50, 267, 380; see also *qibla*
Mother of the Book, 6, 91, 343–4
Muʿādh b. Jabal, 104
Muʿāwiya b. Abī Sufyān, 120, 399
Mujāhid b. Jabr, 113, 131
Musaylima, 178, 208
Muslim b. al-Ḥajjāj, 102
Muʿtazila school, 13, 17, 19, 38, 106, 175, 218; on the divine will, 32; on intercession, 27, 125; on Resurrection, 120; on sins, 21, 27, 114
al-Muṭṭalib b. Abī Rifāʿa al-Sahmī, 189

Naḍr b. al-Ḥārith, 256, 364
nafs, see soul
Najrān delegation, 103
names, 23–4, 249, 342; see also Divine Names
al-Nasā'ī, Aḥmad b. Shuʿayb, 70
natural disposition, 153, 154, 166, 306
nearness to/of God, 1, 2, 281, 303; angels, 23, 251; The Cow (Sūrat al-Baqara, Q. 2), 58–9, 120; those brought near, 1, 224, 237
Nebuchadnezzar, 80, 381, 382
Negus, 126, 183
Night Journey, 78, 380–1, 389
The Night Journey (Sūrat al-Isrā', Q. 17), 24; angels, 388, 389, 390, 394; association, 384, 386, 388, 396; Banī Isrā'īl (The Children of Israel), 380n1; chastisement, 383, 388, 392, 394; disbelief, 387; disbelievers, 382, 388; from the Sacred Mosque to the Farthest Mosque, 380; glorification of God, 380, 386–7; Hell, 382, 383; Hereafter, 383; Jews, 381, 382, 395, 396; Lote Tree, 380–1; messengers, 381, 383, 389; Moses, 381, 388, 395; obedience, 381, 383; prayer, 382, 385, 392, 396; Prophet Muḥammad, 380–1, 382, 386, 388, 392; provision, 383–4, 385, 390; punishment, 381, 382; Qur'ān, 382, 392–6; Qur'ānic recitation, 387; Resurrection, 387–8; Satan, 388, 389–90; spending, 384
Night of Ordainment (*laylat al-qadr*), 58, 59, 101–102
Nimrod, 79–80, 81, 364
Noah, 57, 65, 97, 161, 177, 198, 206, 231–2, 290, 346, 381, 383; Ark, 232, 297, 308–309, 310; Flood, 232, 276, 297, 308, 309, 315; Hūd (Sūrat Hūd, Q. 11), 307–10, 315; Jūdī, Mosul, 309, 310; prophethood, 307
Nuʿaym b. Masʿūd, 121
nubuwwa, see prophethood
numbers, 277–8, 284
Nun, 406

oaths, 69, 184; breaking of, 239, 266, 363, 374; expiation of a broken vow, 184; false oaths, 60, 188–9,

375; 'God willing', 401; *ḥadīth*, 184
obedience, 2, 302; Companions of the Prophet, 87, 169; The Cow (Sūrat al-Baqara, Q. 2), 50, 53; The Family of ᶜImrān (Sūrat Āl ᶜImrān Q. 3), 97, 99, 107, 119, 125, 126; Hūd (Sūrat Hūd, Q. 11), 303, 312, 316, 319; The Night Journey (Sūrat al-Isrā', Q. 17), 381, 383; obedience to Prophet Muḥammad, 26, 142, 145, 252, 255; Spoils of War (Sūrat al-Anfāl, Q. 8), 252, 255, 258; Women (Sūrat al-Nisā', Q. 4), 142, 144, 145
orphans, 34, 136, 257; property of, 67, 127–9, 154, 219, 385; spending on provision for, 55, 66
outward/manifest aspect, 4, 344; God, Beholder of the outward, 383; of harmony, 261; Moses as sea of outward knowledge, 406; of punishment, 228; of sin, 212

Paradise: Firdaws, 20; maidens of Paradise, 64; see also Garden(s)
pardon, 114, 119, 170, 176; divine pardon, 198, 271, 328; divine pardon before repentance, 338
parents, 66, 409; inheritance and testaments, 56–7, 129–30, 136, 163; kindness to, 34, 136, 218, 384
path: Abraham (Sūrat Ibrāhīm, Q. 14), 345, 348; The Beginning of the Book (Sūrat al-Fātiḥa, Q. 1), 1, 10; Cattle (Sūrat al-Anᶜām, Q. 6), 199, 206, 214, 219, 220; sincerity as path, 356; straight path, 1, 10, 199, 206, 214, 219, 220, 311, 362, 378; *ṭarīqa*, 126
patience, 117, 118, 124, 221, 341, 379; The Cow (Sūrat al-Baqara, Q. 2), 27, 50, 51; The Family of ᶜImrān (Sūrat Āl ᶜImrān Q. 3), 117, 118, 124, 126; Hūd (Sūrat Hūd, Q. 11), 310; Joseph (Sūrat Yūsuf, Q.12), 323, 333, 334; meaning, 27
Pedestal, 24, 37, 79, 114, 229
Pen, 375; Supreme Pen, 8, 375
People of the Book, 15, 160, 396; as believers, 111; Cattle (Sūrat al-Anᶜām, Q. 6), 207, 218, 219; The Cow (Sūrat al-Baqara, Q. 2), 15, 41, 46–7, 49, 54–5; as disbelievers, 111, 184; envy, 40, 49, 66, 95; The Family of ᶜImrān (Sūrat Āl ᶜImrān Q. 3), 103–107, 109, 111, 126; marrying women from, 68, 167; prayer, 111; *qibla*, 49; The Table (Sūrat al-Mā'ida, Q. 5), 170–1, 178, 180–4; Women (Sūrat al-Nisā', Q. 4), 158–60, 162; wrath against, 111; see also Christians; Jews
people of truth, 110
Pharaoh, 4; The Cow (Sūrat al-Baqara, Q. 2), 27–8, 30; drowning of people of Pharaoh, 28, 239–40, 260, 299, 395; famine, drought and plagues suffered by the people of, 238–9; Muṣᶜab b. Rayyān,

Pharaoh in the time of Moses, 27–8, 30, 236–9, 240, 297–9, 316, 395; Rayyān b. al-Walīd, Pharaoh in the time of Joseph, 27, 327; way of the people of, 93, 259–60
piety: The Cow (Sūrat al-Baqara, Q. 2), 55, 60, 63; The Family of ʿImrān (Sūrat Āl ʿImrān Q. 3), 107–108, 110
pilgrimage, 51; circumambulation, 51, 226–7, 410; combining *ḥajj* and *ʿumra*, 62; consecrated state (*iḥrām*), 60, 62, 63, 165, 185–6; Farewell Pilgrimage, 166, 265; *labbayk*, 82; months of the year for, 62–3; provision for, 63, 109, 227; remembrance, 63, 64; Sacred Waymark, 63; Ṣafā and Marwa, 51; *ʿumra* (Lesser Pilgrimage), 51, 61–3, 165, 220, 264; see also *ḥajj*
plants and vegetation, 216, 231, 291, 362; colocynth, 349; creation of, 209; date palms, 82, 216, 338, 348–9, 362, 370, 393, 403; forbidden tree in the Garden, 25, 224–5; fruits, 337, 338, 343, 362, 370; juniper, 352; Ṭūbā, 342; vines, 82, 338, 370, 393, 403; Zaqqūm tree, 389
Pledge of Riḍwān, 169
poetry, 14, 292, 305; *muʿammā*, 311
Potiphar the vizier, 324, 326, 327, 328, 329
poverty, 83, 181, 218, 385, 409; the poor, 84; Satan and, 83
praise, 140, 155, 288, 360, 372, 396, 404; The Beginning of the Book (Sūrat al-Fātiḥa, Q. 1), 7, 8–9; Cattle (Sūrat al-Anʿām, Q. 6), 193, 196, 200; creation, praise of God by, 386–7; glorification of God, 380, 386–7, 404; God's praise of Himself, 8; *ḥamd*, 8; meaning of, 8; the Praised, 345, 346
prayer, 253; Abraham, 284, 350–1; afternoon prayer (*ʿaṣr*), 75, 169, 319, 392; angels and, 392; bowing, 26; call to, 179; canonical prayers, 26, 75, 404; challenge prayer (*mubāhala*), 103; congregational prayer, 26, 99; conversation during, 251; dawn prayer (*ṣubḥ*), 75, 105, 319, 392; distractions, 138, 185; drowsiness during, 118; evening prayer, 111, 392; forgiveness, praying for, 115, 119, 257, 277–9, 284, 310, 334; Garden, prayer in, 288; God's answer to, 59, 89, 98, 143, 146, 253–4, 265, 326, 339, 350, 399; *ḥadīth*, 75; Jewish prayer, 26, 34; Kaʿba, obligatory prayers inside, 48–9; middle prayer, 75, 319, 392; middle way between loud and silent, 396; Moses, 299; night prayer, 111; obligation of, 75; People of the Book, 111; places of, 44, 48; Prophet Muḥammad, 150–1, 277–9, 281, 377; prostration, 44, 98, 226, 360; requirements for, 138; Satan and, 118; Sunna, 44, 149–50; sunset prayer, 392; supplication, 63, 75, 98, 282, 288, 339, 350, 368; supplication,

raising the voice during, 230–1, 396; traveller's prayer, 42, 149–50; war, praying while in (prayer of peril), 150–1, 169; see also *qibla*; worship
prayer, mention in Sūras: Abraham (Sūrat Ibrāhīm, Q. 14), 349, 350–1; The Cave (Sūrat al-Kahf, Q. 18), 399; The Cow (Sūrat al-Baqara, Q. 2), 26, 27, 50, 55, 59, 64, 75; The Family of ᶜImrān (Sūrat Āl ᶜImrān Q. 3), 99, 103, 105, 111; The Heights (Sūrat al-Aᶜrāf, Q. 7), 226, 230–1, 246, 251; Hūd (Sūrat Hūd, Q. 11), 319; Joseph (Sūrat Yūsuf, Q.12), 326, 335; The Night Journey (Sūrat al-Isrā', Q. 17), 382, 385, 392, 396; Repentance (Sūrat al-Tawba, Q. 9), 277–9, 281, 282; The Table (Sūrat al-Mā'ida, Q. 5), 167, 169, 179, 185; Women (Sūrat al-Nisā', Q. 4), 138, 149–51
pride, 162, 175, 259, 386, 403; definition, 24; Satan, 24, 223–4; see also arrogance
Prophet Muḥammad: angels and, 271; Ascension/Night Journey, 78, 380–1, 389; Battle of Badr, 258, 259; birth of, 354; causing harm to, 274, 360; cave in Mount Thawr, 271; denial of, by disbelievers, 198, 213, 276, 293, 354, 382, 387, 389; dreams, 258, 380; duty to convey the message, 181, 187, 343, 344, 379; emigration from Mecca, 270–1; faith in, 267; family of, 1, 103; following the Prophet, 26, 95, 170, 243–4; forgiveness, 252; Gabriel and, 194–5; Jesus and, 170, 171; Jews and, 35, 36, 37, 40, 104–106, 180, 382; obedience to, 26, 142, 145, 252, 255; prayer, 150–1, 277–9, 281, 377; prophethood, 104, 140, 161, 194, 196, 198, 343, 401; Qur'ān, revelation of, 4, 14, 19, 85, 91, 181, 196, 222, 335, 337, 373–4, 395, 397, 413; Qur'ānic recitation, 7, 197; spoken to by God, 78; Torah and, 26, 34; the Trusted Chosen One, 1; the unlettered Prophet, 243, 289
Prophet Muḥammad, mention in Sūras: Abraham (Sūrat Ibrāhīm, Q. 14), 348, 349, 351; The Bee (Sūrat al-Naḥl, Q. 16), 366–7, 373, 375, 379; The Beginning of the Book (Sūrat al-Fātiḥa, Q. 1), 1; Cattle (Sūrat al-Anᶜām, Q. 6), 194, 196, 198, 201, 202, 210, 212, 213; The Cave (Sūrat al-Kahf, Q. 18), 401, 406, 413; The Cow (Sūrat al-Baqara, Q. 2), 19, 26, 39–41, 45, 49, 50, 51, 65, 78, 79, 87; The Family of ᶜImrān (Sūrat Āl ᶜImrān Q. 3), 92–3, 95, 96, 99, 104–107, 109, 111, 116, 117–18, 123, 125; The Heights (Sūrat al-Aᶜrāf, Q. 7), 222, 233, 236, 243–4, 248; Hūd (Sūrat Hūd, Q. 11), 310; Jonah (Sūrat Yūnus, Q. 10), 289, 290, 300; Joseph (Sūrat Yūsuf, Q.12), 335; The Night Journey (Sūrat al-Isrā', Q. 17), 380–1,

382, 386, 388, 392; Repentance (Sūrat al-Tawba, Q. 9), 264, 267, 274, 276, 277–9, 282; Spoils of War (Sūrat al-Anfāl, Q. 8), 253, 254, 255, 262; The Table (Sūrat al-Māʾida, Q. 5), 170, 171, 180, 181, 187; Women (Sūrat al-Nisāʾ, Q. 4), 137, 141, 145, 161, 162, 163
prophethood (*nubuwwa*), 46, 96, 140, 152, 199, 206, 207, 312; Abraham, 378; Adam, 25; as gift from God, 347; Moses, 234, 239; Noah, 307; Prophet Muḥammad, 104, 140, 161, 194, 196, 198, 343, 401; Shuʿayb, 234
prophets, 137; allies among prophets, 104; asceticism, 329; The Beginning of the Book (Sūrat al-Fātiḥa, Q. 1), 1, 10; Cattle (Sūrat al-Anʿām, Q. 6), 206–207, 211; The Cow (Sūrat al-Baqara, Q. 2), 46, 55, 66; enemies of, 211; female prophets, 336, 366; God's covenant with, 106; independent reasoning, 262; preferring one prophet to another, 388; prophetic miracle (*muʿjiza*), 35, 36, 38–9, 78, 98, 123, 152, 159, 174, 190, 196, 197, 199, 200, 233, 234, 236–7, 269, 276, 297, 310, 311, 316, 326, 346, 354, 366, 389; protected from major sins, 44; slaying of, 30, 36, 95, 116, 122, 239; The Table (Sūrat al-Māʾida, Q. 5), 171–2, 187
prostration (*sajda*), 322, 335, 339–40, 342, 367, 396; of angels to Adam, 24, 223, 355, 389, 405; humility and, 29, 159, 335; meaning, 24; in prayer, 44, 98, 226, 360
provision, 13, 341, 354; The Bee (Sūrat al-Naḥl, Q. 16), 362, 363, 371; Cattle (Sūrat al-Anʿām, Q. 6), 216, 218; The Cave (Sūrat al-Kahf, Q. 18), 400; The Cow (Sūrat al-Baqara, Q. 2), 13, 20, 29–30, 44, 63, 75; for divorced women, 75; Mary, mother of Jesus, 98; The Night Journey (Sūrat al-Isrāʾ, Q. 17), 383–4, 385, 390; pilgrimage, 63, 109, 227; for widows, 75
Psalms, 161, 183, 388
punishment, 93, 158; for adultery, 95, 131, 134, 175; Cattle (Sūrat al-Anʿām, Q. 6), 202, 204, 221; The Cow (Sūrat al-Baqara, Q. 2), 19–20; exemplary punishment, 31, 175, 338; The Heights (Sūrat al-Aʿrāf, Q. 7), 222, 227, 228; legal punishment (*ḥadd*), 135; for murder, 174; The Night Journey (Sūrat al-Isrāʾ, Q. 17), 381, 382; The Table (Sūrat al-Māʾida, Q. 5), 174, 175; for theft, 174, 175, 331; see also chastisement
purification, 10, 28, 46; *zakāt* as means of purification, 282
purity, 47, 140, 169, 409; periods of purity, 69–70; ritual impurity, 59, 138, 167, 169, 254; see also ablution

Qabaʿtharī, 278

Qadariyya sect, 144–5, 300
qibla (prayer direction), 47, 282; change of, 47–8, 49; Christians, 49, 55; The Cow (Sūrat al-Baqara, Q. 2), 24, 42, 44, 47–50, 54–5, 75; The Heights (Sūrat al-Aʿrāf, Q. 7), 226; Jews, 49, 55; Kaʿba, 48, 49, 50, 105; Mecca, 47, 108; the Rock, Jerusalem, 47, 49, 105; Sacred Mosque, 48, 49–50
qiyās, see analogy
Qur'ān, 4; ambiguous verses, 91–2, 93; Arabic language, 4, 12, 91, 321, 343, 376; *āya*, definition of, 5; as a clarification, 373–4; clear verses, 91, 92; closing *sūra*, 9; as cure for ailments of religion and body, 392–3; denial of, 202, 203, 256, 287, 293, 306, 318, 364, 374; *fāṣila*, 5, 361; as God's rope, 109; as God's Speech, 14; *ḥadīth*, 14, 92–3; insight, 210, 251; letters of the alphabet and, 11–12; 'passage' (*ṭā'ifa*), 5; preservation of, 176; as Remembrance, 353, 354, 366–7; *sūra*, definition of, 5; thematic links between chapters, 2, 9, 11, 12, 90, 127, 164, 193, 222, 303, 321, 337, 353, 361, 380
Qur'ān, mention in Sūras: Abraham (Sūrat Ibrāhīm, Q. 14), 345, 352; The Bee (Sūrat al-Naḥl, Q. 16), 373–4, 375–6, 378; The Beginning of the Book (Sūrat al-Fātiḥa, Q. 1), 1; Cattle (Sūrat al-Anʿām, Q. 6), 194, 201, 202, 203, 207, 210, 212, 219; The Cave (Sūrat al-Kahf, Q. 18), 397, 406; The Cow (Sūrat al-Baqara, Q. 2), 14, 18, 19, 35, 40, 46, 50; The Family of ʿImrān (Sūrat Āl ʿImrān Q. 3), 90–3, 105, 107, 109, 111, 119, 125, 126; The Heights (Sūrat al-Aʿrāf, Q. 7), 222, 230, 244, 250, 251; Ḥijr (Sūrat al-Ḥijr, Q. 15), 353, 359–60; Hūd (Sūrat Hūd, Q. 11), 303, 304, 305, 306, 319; Jonah (Sūrat Yūnus, Q. 10), 289, 292–3, 295, 301; Joseph (Sūrat Yūsuf, Q.12), 321, 336; The Night Journey (Sūrat al-Isrā', Q. 17), 382, 392–6; Repentance (Sūrat al-Tawba, Q. 9), 40, 280; Spoils of War (Sūrat al-Anfāl, Q. 8), 255, 262–3; The Table (Sūrat al-Mā'ida, Q. 5), 170, 176, 177, 183; The Thunder (Sūrat al-Raʿd, Q. 13), 337, 342, 343; Women (Sūrat al-Nisā', Q. 4), 139–40, 141, 144, 145, 151, 152, 156, 161, 163
Qur'ān, revelation of, 91, 305, 395, 397; abrogated verses, 40, 57, 58, 60, 67, 88, 92, 109, 131, 136, 165, 176, 177, 204, 210, 262–3, 278, 293, 303, 353, 359, 375–6; angels, 14; Gabriel, 14, 376; last verse to be revealed, 85; Meccan chapters/verses, 6, 19, 44, 193, 222, 252, 287, 303, 321, 337, 345, 353, 360, 361, 362, 380, 397; Medinan chapters/verses; 6, 11, 19, 48, 90, 127, 164, 222, 252, 264, 337, 380; Night of Ordainment (*laylat al-qadr*), 58,

59; Prophet Muḥammad, 4, 14, 19, 85, 91, 181, 196, 222, 335, 337, 373–4, 395, 397, 413
Qur'ānic exegesis, see exegesis; interpretation
Qur'ānic recitation, 2, 6, 251, 293, 321, 387; Abū Bakr al-Ṣiddīq, 7; benefits of, 370–1; *al-Fātiḥa*, 10; mass-transmission of, 9; Prophet Muḥammad, 7, 197; seeking refuge with God before Qur'ānic recitation, 4, 375; ᶜUmar b. al-Khaṭṭāb, 7
the Quraysh, 52, 63, 140, 169, 201, 274, 287, 349, 358, 391, 393, 402, 406; The Bee (Sūrat al-Naḥl, Q. 16), 366, 378; Spoils of War (Sūrat al-Anfāl, Q. 8), 253, 259, 260
Qurayẓa, 35, 175, 178, 260
Quṣayy b. Kilāb, 255
Quss b. Sāᶜida, 145

rage, 112, 266, 299, 333, 346, 348, 373; restrain of, 114
raḥma, see compassion
Ramaḍān, 57–9; fasting, 57, 58, 404; at night, 59
al-Rāzī, Fakhr al-Dīn ('the Imam'), 38, 264, 391
Razīn, 265
Reality (*ḥaqīqa*), 126
reasoning, 14, 48, 205, 218; debating with well-reasoned arguments, 259; faulty reasoning, 362; independent reasoning, 53, 238, 262; prophets, 262
reckoning, 344, 351, 382; 'God charges no soul save to its capacity', 87–8; the Reckoning, 220, 225, 318; reckoning of unspoken thoughts, 87, 88
reconciliation (*ṣalāḥ*), 16, 136, 155, 273–4
reliance, 13, 33, 63, 347
religion (*dīn*), 45; corruption in, 262, 315; faith/religion distinction, 107; The Family of ᶜImrān (Sūrat Āl ᶜImrān Q. 3), 95, 102, 104, 106, 109; fundamentals of religions, 104, 292; The Heights (Sūrat al-Aᶜrāf, Q. 7), 229, 230; The Table (Sūrat al-Mā'ida, Q. 5), 166, 177; taken as game and diversion, 204, 230; 'There is no compulsion in religion', 79; see also Islam
remembrance (*dhikr*), 251, 341; as better than other activities, 63; The Cow (Sūrat al-Baqara, Q. 2), 50, 63, 75; The Family of ᶜImrān (Sūrat Āl ᶜImrān Q. 3), 99, 124, 126; as farthest aim of worship, 63; pilgrimage and, 63, 64; Qur'ān as, 353, 354, 366–7
repentance (*tawba*): The Bee (Sūrat al-Naḥl, Q. 16), 378; The Cow (Sūrat al-Baqara, Q. 2), 25, 28; disbelievers, 107; heretics, 16; hypocrites, 158; idolaters, 243, 265; meaning, 25; Repentance (Sūrat al-Tawba, Q. 9), 17, 265, 275, 277, 282, 284; The Table (Sūrat al-Mā'ida, Q. 5), 175; The Thunder (Sūrat al-Raᶜd, Q. 13), 338, 340; turning away from, 17, 265, 277; Women (Sūrat al-Nisā', Q. 4), 131–2, 135, 152

Repentance (Sūrat al-Tawba, Q. 9), 44; astray, 284; believers, 267, 276, 282, 284; chastisement, 265; divine relenting, 45, 266, 268, 282, 285; Expedition of Tabūk, 270, 271–2, 275, 276, 279, 282, 284; fighting, 67, 266, 268, 270, 271–2, 276, 279–81, 285, 286; forgiveness of disbelievers and idolaters, 277–9, 284; hoarded wealth, 269; hypocrisy, 271–3, 275–6, 277, 279, 281, 282, 286; idolatry, 42, 265–7, 268, 284; Jews, 269; prayer, 277–9, 281, 282; Prophet Muḥammad, 264, 267, 274, 276, 277–9, 282; Qur'ān, 40, 280; repentance, 17, 265, 275, 277, 282, 284; repentance, turning away from, 17, 265, 277; struggle, 267; Sword Verse, 67, 265, 293; wealth and children, 273, 279–80; worship, 266–7, 268; *zakāt*, 273–4, 277, 281, 282

Resurrection, 92, 120, 121, 125; Abraham (Sūrat Ibrāhīm, Q. 14), 347, 348; The Bee (Sūrat al-Naḥl, Q. 16), 361, 364–5, 366; belief in, 87; Cattle (Sūrat al-Anᶜām, Q. 6), 197, 214, 219; The Cave (Sūrat al-Kahf, Q. 18), 400, 403, 404; The Cow (Sūrat al-Baqara, Q. 2), 20, 22, 27, 33, 37, 53, 80, 87, 121; Day of Resurrection, 39, 44, 51, 68, 108, 122, 192, 197, 213, 214, 220, 221, 228, 230, 282, 310, 369, 387–9; denial of, 37, 288, 293, 338, 348, 366; The Family of ᶜImrān (Sūrat Āl ᶜImrān Q. 3), 92, 120, 121, 125; The Heights (Sūrat al-Aᶜrāf, Q. 7), 249; Hūd (Sūrat Hūd, Q. 11), 304; Jonah (Sūrat Yūnus, Q. 10), 288, 293; The Night Journey (Sūrat al-Isrā', Q. 17), 387–8; resurrection of bodies, 20; The Thunder (Sūrat al-Raᶜd, Q. 13), 338, 342

retaliation, 174, 379, 385; blood money, 56, 147–8, 176, 385; The Cow (Sūrat al-Baqara, Q. 2), 55–6, 61; *ḥadīth*, 176; The Table (Sūrat al-Mā'ida, Q. 5), 56, 174, 176

return to God, 102, 111, 199, 203, 226, 303, 315, 320; The Cow (Sūrat al-Baqara, Q. 2), 51, 65; 'Truly, we belong to God, and truly to Him we shall return', 333

revelation (*inzāl*), 14, 99, 161; Scriptures, 13–14, 26; Torah, 58, 176, 240, 241; see also Qur'ān, revelation of

reward, 125, 375; The Cow (Sūrat al-Baqara, Q. 2), 25, 27, 46, 51, 68, 82, 83, 85, 91, 94; for evildoers, 291; for good deeds, 291, 303; for intercession, 146

rhetoric, 56, 101, 208, 288, 362, 381; rhetorical device, 41–2, 117; rhetorical question, 75, 95, 282, 297

righteous deeds, 169, 185, 225, 331, 348, 404; Garden, 154; performance in gratitude, 305; performance without ostentation, 20, 31

righteousness, 2, 94, 165, 252, 353, 384; claiming righteousness, 47; Garden and, 341, 413; perfect righteousness, 45, 100, 206, 378
Rīṭa bint Saᶜd al-Qurashiyya, 374
ru'yā, see dream

Sabaeans, 30, 181, 357
Sacred Precinct, 42, 60, 61, 62, 63, 123, 186; bar from, 268; dying in, 108; as place of prayer, 44, 48; visit to, 109
Ṣafā and Marwa, 51
sajda, see prostration
Sakkākī, 32
ṣalāḥ, see reconciliation
Ṣāliḥ, 233, 235, 312, 315, 359, 360
Salmān al-Fārisī, 344
Sara, 313–14, 334
Satan: Adam and, 24, 223–5, 355–6, 389, 405; astray, 225–6, 390; commanding to evil and indecency, 53, 390; curse upon, 299, 356; dreams and, 258, 322; as enemy of humankind, 53, 224, 225, 226, 356, 388, 390; expulsion from the Garden, 223–4; Hell, 224; 'I seek refuge with God from Satan the accursed', 4, 375; Iblīs, 24, 223; Jesus and Mary as untouched by Satan, 98; jinn/father of jinn, 24, 355, 405; Ploughman (name of Satan), 249; poverty and, 83; power of, 375; pride, 24, 223–4; *shāṭa*: 'to be false', 4; *shaṭana*: 'to be distant', 4; *Shayṭān*, 4; *shayṭana* (devilry), 4; temptation, 226, 250, 390; whisperings, 4, 25, 83, 204, 224, 375
Satan, mention in Sūras: Abraham (Sūrat Ibrāhīm, Q. 14), 348; The Bee (Sūrat al-Naḥl, Q. 16), 369, 375; Cattle (Sūrat al-Anᶜām, Q. 6), 204; The Cave (Sūrat al-Kahf, Q. 18), 24, 405; The Cow (Sūrat al-Baqara, Q. 2), 24–5, 53, 65, 79, 83; The Family of ᶜImrān (Sūrat Āl ᶜImrān Q. 3), 98; The Heights (Sūrat al-Aᶜrāf, Q. 7), 223–6; Ḥijr (Sūrat al-Ḥijr, Q. 15), 355–6; Joseph (Sūrat Yūsuf, Q.12), 327, 335; The Night Journey (Sūrat al-Isrā', Q. 17), 388, 389–90; Spoils of War (Sūrat al-Anfāl, Q. 8), 254; The Table (Sūrat al-Mā'ida, Q. 5), 185, 192; Women (Sūrat al-Nisā', Q. 4), 145, 147, 153–4
Saul, 76, 77–8
scales, 223, 413
Scriptures, 21, 58, 66, 87, 123, 207, 212, 219, 366; belief in, 14; falsifying the Scriptures, 104, 105–106, 124, 126, 139, 175, 180, 244; obligation of following sacred texts, 318; revelation, 13–14, 26; see also Gospel; Psalms; Qur'ān; Torah
seeking refuge in God, 4, 125, 375
senses, 15, 295; seal of, 15, 18, 53–4, 197, 199, 376
sexual intercourse, 234; The Cow (Sūrat al-Baqara, Q. 2), 59, 68, 69, 74; menstruating women, 68; Women (Sūrat al-Nisā', Q. 4), 132–3, 138

al-Shāfiʿī, Muḥammad b. Idrīs, 48, 56, 67, 75, 128, 174, 184, 186, 213, 268, 274, 338; on divorce, 72, 74; on pilgrimage, 61, 62, 109; on prayer, 75, 138
Shāfiʿī school, 7, 42, 48, 56, 61, 274, 391
shahāda, see testimony
shahwa, see lust
sharīʿa, see Law
Shayba, 141
Shayṭān, see Satan
Shuʿayb, 222, 234–5, 315–16, 359
Sībawayh, 130
ṣiddīqūn, see the truthful
siḥr, see sorcery
similitude/likeness, 17, 21, 226, 340, 348–9, 371–2, 393
sins: Cain, 174; covering of sins by God, 89; deliberate sins, 88; erasure of, 135; God-fearing and, 12; grave sins (*kabā'ir*), 135; ignorance and, 201–202; kindness to a sinner is grace, 123; major sins, 13, 21, 27, 38, 44, 125, 218, 227; public/secret sins, 212, 227; Spoils of War (Sūrat al-Anfāl, Q. 8), 256
slaves, 137, 172, 371–2; freeing of, 55, 184, 273, 347; marriage, 133, 134; sale of a Muslim slave to a non-Muslim owner, 157
Sodom, 358, 359
Solomon (*Sulaymān*), 37, 140, 161, 206, 275
sorcery (*siḥr*), 37, 237, 297–8, 354, 360, 395; The Cow (Sūrat al-Baqara, Q. 2), 37–9, 237; as disbelief, 37–8; Hārūt and Mārūt, 39; as major sin, 38; types of, 38
soul (*nafs*), 376; balance of, 16; contraction of, 20–1; evil soul, 37; struggle against, 4; virtuous soul, 38
speech, 14; ambiguous speech, 91–2; clear speech, 91; letters of the alphabet and, 11, 14; Speech of God, 14
spending: The Cow (Sūrat al-Baqara, Q. 2), 66, 67, 81–4; disbelievers, 112; The Night Journey (Sūrat al-Isrā', Q. 17), 384; obligatory spending/recommended spending, 349; Spoils of War (Sūrat al-Anfāl, Q. 8), 260; Women (Sūrat al-Nisā', Q. 4), 136–7; see also *zakāt*
spoils of war, 143, 272, 273; Battle of Badr, 252, 257; Battle of Uḥud, 116, 117, 118; Spoils of War (Sūrat al-Anfāl, Q. 8), 252, 256, 257–8
Spoils of War (Sūrat al-Anfāl, Q. 8): Battle of Badr, 253–5, 257, 258–9, 260, 262; Battle of Uḥud, 254, 257; believers, 252; chastisement, 256–7, 259–60; disbelievers, 254, 256, 260–1; Emigration, 256, 257, 262; faith, 252–3, 260; fighting against disbelievers, 260, 261; idolatry, 255, 257; inheritance, 262–3; obedience, 252, 255, 258; prayer, 253; pride, 259; prisoners of war, 261, 262; Prophet Muḥammad, 253, 254, 255, 262; Qur'ān, 255,

262–3; the Quraysh, 253, 259, 260; ransoms, 261–2; Satan, 254; sin, 256; spending, 260; spoils of war, 252, 256, 257–8; steadfastness, 261; trials, 256
stinginess, 82, 83, 140, 275, 278, 374, 385, 395
struggle (*jihād*), 267; against the soul, 4; Greater Struggle (*al-jihād al-akbar*), 50
submission (*islām*), 298; Cattle (Sūrat al-Anʿām, Q. 6), 199; The Cow (Sūrat al-Baqara, Q. 2), 45, 65, 75; dying in submission, 335; faith/submission distinction, 107; The Family of ʿImrān (Sūrat Āl ʿImrān Q. 3), 95, 107
Suddī, 121
Sufism: triad of *sharīʿa*, *ṭarīqa*, *ḥaqīqa*: 126
Ṣuhayb al-Rūmī, 65
Sunna, 40, 50, 119, 141, 152, 164, 184, 222, 244, 374; ablution, 168; blood money, 147–8; debts, 86, 87; divorced women, 69; fasting, 59; forbidden food, 377; killing, 186; marriage, 134; pilgrimage, 51; prayer, 44, 149–50; punishment, 175; *tafsīr* and, 4
Sunnis, 145, 390–1
Surāqa b. Mālik al-Kinānī, 259
Syria, 189, 239, 253, 258, 275, 283, 299, 309, 335, 358, 359, 381, 392

The Table (Sūrat al-Māʾida, Q. 5): ablution, 138, 167–9; apostasy, 178; Cain and Abel, 173–4; Christians, 170–1, 181, 182, 183, 188; covenant, 164, 169–70, 181; disbelievers, 171, 175, 176, 179–80, 184; *dūn* (besides), 103, 191; God's Oneness, 191–2; Gospel, 170, 177, 180, 181, 183, 190; guidance, 188; idolatry, 165–6, 184, 175; inheritance and testaments, 188–9; Islam, 166, 182; Jesus, 171, 177, 190–2; Jews, 169–71, 175–6, 179–80, 183; Kaʿba, 186; Law, 177; lawful/unlawful food, 164–7, 176, 184, 185–6; marriage, 167; Moses, 171–2; People of the Book, 170–1, 178, 180–4; prayer, 167, 169, 179, 185; Prophet Muḥammad, 170, 171, 180, 181, 187; prophets, 171–2, 187; punishment, 174, 175; Qurʾān, 170, 176, 177, 183; religion, 166, 177; repentance, 175; retaliation, 56, 174, 176; Satan, 185, 192; the table, 190–1; Torah, 170, 176, 177, 180, 181, 190; *zakāt*, 179
Tablet, 6, 261, 270, 295, 304, 344, 375, 389; humankind and, 8; Preserved Tablet, 172, 199, 202, 353; provision, 13; Qurʾān, revelation of, 14
tafsīr, see exegesis
Tamīm al-Dārī, 189
taqwā, see God-fearing
tawba, see repentance
taʾwīl, see interpretation
taxes: land tax (*kharāj*), 103; poll-tax (*jizya*), 111, 176, 268
Ṭayālisī, 102
temptation, 226, 250, 390, 391
Terah (Āzar), 205, 284, 351
testimony (*shahāda*): by angels, 94; entering the Garden and, 220;

ḥadīth, 220, 246–7; The Heights (Sūrat al-Aʿrāf, Q. 7), 164, 246–7; 'there is no god except God', 52, 78, 90, 91, 94–5, 103, 220, 404
Thaʿlaba b. Ḥāṭib, 277
Thamūd, 311–12, 316, 346, 359, 389
thankfulness, 113, 201, 221, 346, 364, 377; see also gratitude
Thaqīf, 391
Throne (*ʿarsh*), 114, 120, 230, 287, 304, 337
The Thunder (Sūrat al-Raʿd, Q. 13): angels, 338, 341; association, 342–3; believers, 339; chastisement, 338, 342, 343, 344; covenant, 340, 341; creation, process of, 337; desire, 341; disbelievers, 338, 339–40, 341, 342, 344; Garden, 340, 341–2, 343; guidance, 342, 343; Hell, 340; idolatry, 339; intercession, 341; messengers, 342, 343; patience, 341; Qur'ān, 337, 342, 343; remembrance, 341; repentance, 338, 340; Resurrection, 338, 342; Thunder, 339; worship, 343
Tirmidhī, 61, 70
Ṭīṭānūs the Jew, 159
Torah, 300, 306, 381, 408; The Cow (Sūrat al-Baqara, Q. 2), 26, 28, 31, 33–7, 41, 47, 49, 51, 56, 58, 77, 81; The Family of ʿImrān (Sūrat Āl ʿImrān Q. 3), 91, 95, 99, 100, 101, 104, 105–106, 108, 124; Gabriel and, 31; The Heights (Sūrat al-Aʿrāf, Q. 7), 238, 240, 241, 242–3, 244, 245–6; Moses and, 28, 35, 238, 240, 241, 242–3, 318, 408; Prophet Muḥammad and, 26, 34; revelation of, 58, 176, 240, 241; The Table (Sūrat al-Mā'ida, Q. 5), 170, 176, 177, 180, 181, 190; Women (Sūrat al-Nisā', Q. 4), 139, 140, 158, 159, 160; see also Jews
transgression, 34, 95, 135, 227; Jews, 30, 31, 179, 183, 245
travelling, 290, 363; Cattle (Sūrat al-Anʿām, Q. 6), 195; The Family of ʿImrān (Sūrat Āl ʿImrān Q. 3), 115, 195; fasting while, 57, 58; inheritance and testaments while, 188–9; *qaddasa* (to declare holy: 'to travel far upon the earth'), 380; traveller's prayer, 42, 149–50
trials, 181, 256; Cattle (Sūrat al-Anʿām, Q. 6), 200, 201, 221; The Cow (Sūrat al-Baqara, Q. 2), 51; The Family of ʿImrān (Sūrat Āl ʿImrān Q. 3), 124, 126
Trumpet, 22, 205, 224, 356, 412
trust in God, 304, 305, 347, 400
the truthful (*ṣiddīqūn*), 142, 232, 308, 325, 328; discerning between the truthful and the deceitful, 364
ṭughyān, see wantonness
Ṭulayḥa, 178
Ṭuʿma b. Ubayriq, 151–3
Two Sanctuaries, 6, 9

ʿUmar b. al-Khaṭṭāb, 7, 56, 67, 160, 189, 213, 277; arbitration, 141–2; *basmala*, 7; Battle of Ḥunayn, 268; charity, 274; the Distinguisher of Truth (*al-Fārūq*), 141; prayer, 150

the Unseen, 145, 166, 201, 290, 307, 310, 320, 335, 364; Khiḍr's knowledge of Unseen matters, 407; Knower of the Unseen, 122–3, 202, 205, 372, 401–402; the One Who best knows the Unseen, 123
unveiling, 3, 10, 94
uslūb al-ḥakīm, see 'method of the sage'
uṣūl, 92, 153
usury, 84–5, 114, 160
ᶜUtayba b. Abī Lahab, 402
ᶜUthmān b. Abī Ṭalḥa, 141
ᶜUthmān b. ᶜAffān, 81–2, 277
ᶜUthmān b. Ṭalḥa, 141

vicegerent (*khalīfa*), 23, 24, 232, 240
vigil, 59, 392
virtue, 304, 305, 374, 388; 'Virtue means to worship God as though you see him…', 185; virtuous habits, 43; virtuous soul, 38; virtuous traits, 43–4

Wābiṣa, 55
Wāhila, 234
Waᶜīdiyya sects, 93
wantonness (*ṭughyān*), 135, 234
warfare, see fighting
warning, 15, 70, 83, 215, 402; stern warning (*waᶜīd*), 135
wealth, 126, 144, 181, 273, 279–80, 390, 402, 404; hoarded wealth, 269; as trial, 256; wealthy folk, 402, 403
wickedness (*fisq*), 166, 212, 292; The Cow (Sūrat al-Baqara, Q. 2), 21, 37, 63
wisdom: Divine Attribute, 24, 43, 155, 231, 287, 368, 371, 413; practical/speculative wisdom, 295; the Wise, 24, 91, 95, 113, 192, 335
witnessing: bearing witness, 94, 101, 137, 156, 161, 191–2, 196; martyrs, 121
women, 390; adultery, 131, 132, 134, 167; arbitration between husband and wife, 136; calumny against, 132, 395; The Cow (Sūrat al-Baqara, Q. 2), 69–74; daughters, 129, 132–3, 216, 314, 358, 368, 369, 371, 386; divorced women, 69–70, 72, 74, 75; dowries, 70, 71, 74, 128, 132, 134, 154, 167; evil wife, 64; forswearing their women, 69; *ḥadīth*, 69–70, 134; honourable advances towards, 73–4; inheritance, 129, 154; inheriting women, 132; kindness towards, 132; maidens of Paradise, 64; marriage, 114; men as responsible for women, 136; menstruating women, 68, 69; ornaments, 340, 363; pregnancy, 70, 73, 338; righteous wife, 64; waiting period, 69–74, 157; widows, 127
Women (Sūrat al-Nisā', Q. 4): adultery, 131, 132, 134, 135; arbitration and reconciliation, 136, 141–2, 155; chastisement, 127, 140, 146; disbelievers, 156–7, 158, 161–2; disobedience, 131; divorce, 132, 155; fighting, 142–4, 146, 147, 148–9, 150–1;

Gardens, 141; guidance, 145; Hell, 129, 157; inheritance, 129–31, 136, 154, 163; intercession, 146; Jesus, 159–60, 162; Jews, 139, 156, 159–60; justice, 155; marriage, 127–8, 132–4, 155; messengers, 161; obedience, 142, 144, 145; orphans, property of, 127–9, 154; People of the Book, 158–60, 162; prayer, 138, 149–51; Prophet Muḥammad, 137, 141, 145, 161, 162, 163; Qur'ān, 139–40, 141, 144, 145, 151, 152, 156, 161, 163; repentance, 131–2, 135, 152; Satan, 145, 147, 153–4; sexual intercourse, 132–3, 138; spending, 136–7; Torah, 139, 140, 158, 159, 160; see also women

world (this world), 64, 123–4, 192, 198, 279–80, 341, 383, 391, 412; adornment and beauty, 402, 404; chastisement of this world, 39, 88, 102, 171, 174, 178, 279, 282, 311, 375, 392; lowest level of bliss, 94; man as an abstract of the world, 8; reward of, 116, 156

worship: Abraham (Sūrat Ibrāhīm, Q. 14), 346–7, 351; The Bee (Sūrat al-Naḥl, Q. 16), 368, 374; The Beginning of the Book (Sūrat al-Fātiḥa, Q. 1), 9, 10; The Cow (Sūrat al-Baqara, Q. 2), 19; divinity, 9; The Family of ʿImrān (Sūrat Āl ʿImrān Q. 3), 91, 101, 103; houses as places of prayer, 298; Hūd (Sūrat Hūd, Q. 11), 303; Joseph (Sūrat Yūsuf, Q.12), 326–7; places of, 41–2, 266–7, 268; Repentance (Sūrat al-Tawba, Q. 9), 266–7, 268; The Thunder (Sūrat al-Raʿd, Q. 13), 343; see also prayer

wrath (God's wrath), 94, 105, 200, 254, 339, 376; against Jews, 10, 29, 30, 242, 243; against People of the Book, 111; The Beginning of the Book (Sūrat al-Fātiḥa, Q. 1), 1, 9, 10; refuge from, 285

Yahūdhā and Quṭrūs, 403–404

Zachariah, 35, 98–9, 206, 381

al-Zajjāj, 130

zakāt (charity), 173; Abraham (Sūrat Ibrāhīm, Q. 14), 349; Cattle (Sūrat al-Anʿām, Q. 6), 216; The Cow (Sūrat al-Baqara, Q. 2), 26, 34, 55, 78, 82–4, 85; disbelievers and, 78, 84, 107; distribution of, 273–4; giving charity secretly/publicly, 83, 84; The Heights (Sūrat al-Aʿrāf, Q. 7), 243; as means of purification, 282; obligatory charity, 83, 216; Repentance (Sūrat al-Tawba, Q. 9), 273–4, 277, 281, 282; voluntary charity, 82, 83, 84, 85, 179, 273, 277, 282; see also spending

Zamakhsharī, 7

Zamharīr, see the Freeze

Zayd b. Aslam, 128

Zuleikha, 324–6, 328, 329

ẓulm, see injustice